BASIC PRINCIPLES OF AMERICAN GOVERNMENT

SECOND EDITION

WILLIAM R. SANFORD PH.D.
CARL R. GREEN PH.D.

Dedicated to serving

AMSCO

our nation's youth

When ordering this book, please specify:
either **R 552 H** or BASIC PRINCIPLES OF AMERICAN
GOVERNMENT, SECOND EDITION, HARDBOUND EDITION

AMSCO SCHOOL PUBLICATIONS, INC.
315 Hudson Street/New York, N.Y. 10013

Acknowledgments for Quotes

Page 60
From MIRACLE AT PHILADELPHIA: THE STORY OF THE CONSTITUTIONAL CON-
VENTION, MAY TO SEPTEMBER 1787 by Catherine Drinker Bowen. Copyright © 1966
by Catherine Drinker Bowen. By permission of Little, Brown and Company. (excerpts
from pages 234, 236–237, 240, 241)

Pages 240–242
Reprinted from THIRTEEN DAYS, A Memoir of the Cuban Missile Crisis, by Robert F.
Kennedy. By permission of W.W. Norton & Company, Inc. Copyright © 1971, 1969 by
W.W. Norton & Company, Inc. Copyright © 1968 by McCall Corporation. (excerpts from
pages 23, 101, 110–111, 127)

Page 495
From THE THIRD WAVE by Alvin Toffler. Copyright © 1980 by Alvin Toffler. By
permission of William Morrow & Company. (excerpts from pages 83–84, 434)

ISBN 0-87720-876-X

A note from the authors

British Prime Minister William Gladstone once hailed the Constitution of the United States as "the most wonderful work ever struck off at a given time by the brain and purpose of man." *Basic Principles of American Government* is a book about the system of government established by that Constitution. Just as important, it is about the ways in which that system has changed over the years to meet today's needs.

Common sense warns us that new drivers need to be trained before they are turned loose on the highways. Otherwise, everyone would be at risk while inexperienced teenagers learned to drive safely and to obey traffic laws. For much the same reason, the states require that high school students take a course in American government. After all, high school seniors will soon be voting in local, state, and national elections.

As authors and teachers, we believe that young people who understand the inner workings of our government are more likely to make good decisions when they vote. Before you can do so you need to understand the *how* and *why* of the nation's political system. *Basic Principles of American Government*, therefore, emphasizes *how* government works, in all its marvelous and sometimes frustrating complexity. It also pays careful attention to *why* government works the way it does—efficiently at times and haltingly at others. A careful reading of the text will help you understand the structure and role of all the major components of government. At the same time, you will learn how each local, state, and national governing body relates to the others.

Like the nation itself, *Basic Principles of American Government* has been changing. In the course of preparing this new edition, the authors took a fresh look at each chapter, simplifying and clarifying concepts, deleting material no longer relevant, and adding appropriate new information.

The revision has also given the authors a chance to catch up with the most recent changes in our system of government. At home, new departments have been added to the President's Cabinet. The population has grown, and the balance of political power has shifted. Budget deficits, trade imbalances, and other economic headaches have become part of the national vocabulary. Overseas, the Cold War has come to a close, but new conflicts have arisen to test our political leaders.

No matter what the challenge, the Constitution has weathered every storm. After 200 years, our guideline for democratic government still works well. Its flexibility allows for growth and change even as it sets strict limits on the powers of the three branches of the federal government. *Basic Principles of American Government* reflects this emphasis by spelling out the importance of checks and balances, the separation of powers, and the division of responsibilities between the federal government and the states.

The theme of *Basic Principles of American Government* can be stated in a single word: involvement. Even if we don't run for office we must stay informed about public events and government actions on all levels, and we must vote. Those of us who choose careers in government must serve the public with skill and devotion. Finally, all of us must monitor the behavior of our elected officials once we have given the reins of government into their hands. Democracy can endure only as long as *We the People* are willing to make the sacrifices that self government demands.

WILLIAM R. SANFORD
CARL R. GREEN

CONTENTS

LEARNING SKILLS

FYI (For Your Information)
FEATURES

Introduction
Student government—
opportunities available!

In spring, young Americans turn to thoughts of . . . student government. You don't agree? It must be so. Look around your school. Colorful election posters compete for attention everywhere you turn. Assemblies echo to the sound of political speeches. If your school has developed a tradition of lively campaigning, enthusiasm builds day by day as candidates rally their forces. When election day arrives, the would-be politicians wait impatiently outside the activities office while election officials count the ballots.

▲ Being active in student government helps you learn how government works.

1

Then, as suddenly as it began, the event is over. The big game, the dances, and unfinished term papers compete for your attention. The victorious candidates take their oath of office, gather at their appointed meeting place, and start work. When the next term begins, nothing much is heard from the new student council. After a while, you and your friends get together at lunch and complain all over again about the do-nothings you elected.

Perhaps your school doesn't fit this pattern. Somewhere, the law of averages tells you, a school must exist whose students are satisfied with their elected officials and with the rules that govern their school life. For most students, however, the following complaints will sound familiar:

"What happened to all those promises Bob and Donna made during the campaign? I haven't heard a word about an open campus or a better break for girls' sports since they took office."

"I give up! When we tried to vote for a student union, Mr. Kelly stood up and told us the motion was out of order. That's what happens every time we try to do something important."

"Student government? Do we have one? Nobody ever tells us what goes on in those meetings they hold every week."

"Just once I'd like to see someone elected to student council who didn't win strictly on the basis of popularity. How can you respect people like Sally Rah-Rah and Ted Superstar? I want to see some real changes made on this campus!"

"Did you see the figures from the last election? Less than 20 percent of the kids bothered to vote. So how can they say that the student council represents all of us?"

"I ran for office because I thought the job was important. Do you know what we debated at the last meeting? First, we voted to send flowers for Mrs. Gomez's funeral. Then we argued for half an hour about the theme for the fall dance. We never did discuss the plan for improving assemblies."

If these complaints related only to student government, they might not matter too much. But millions of Americans express similar complaints about the workings of their national, state, and local governments. Some of this unhappiness is based on real weaknesses in the way our system of government works. Other complaints have developed because many people don't understand the complicated machine called government.

Each of the criticisms just voiced about student government could be an excuse for "dropping out" of politics. On the other hand, these six complaints can be turned into ways of working for change, both in school and in the larger world outside. Let's take a closer look at the opportunities offered by student government that are suggested by the complaints themselves.

FOLLOWING THROUGH ON PROMISES

Politicians, whether they're running for student body president or President of the United States, make campaign promises to the voters. There's nothing wrong with that. Most of the people who run for office truly believe in the promises they make. Once in office, however, many of them seem to operate on the assumption that voters have short memories. They act as though they'll never be called on to deliver what they promised in the heat of a campaign.

Even the most dedicated officeholders soon learn that their power to bring about change is limited. All—from school government officials to federal government officials—face similar restraints on what they can do in office. Lack of money, unexpected political developments, and legal restrictions combine to reduce their power to deliver on their promises. *Here is your first opportunity.* Keep a list of what the candidates promised. When you're unhappy with what they actually accomplish, write and ask them why they haven't produced better results. Better yet, ask the officeholder in person. Politicians really do listen to the public. If they don't, they'll soon be out of work.

OVERCOMING LIMITS ON POWER

Just as student representatives often find their wishes blocked by the faculty adviser, Congress finds its actions subject to veto by the President. A state or national government has fewer limits on its power than the restrictions that control a student council, but the principle is the same.

The line of authority in your school begins with the state education code. Local policies and regulations are usually written by an elected school board. The board hires school administrators and teachers to whom they delegate the authority to run the schools. A few of these powers are further delegated to the student government, most often in the form of a constitution.

Your second opportunity begins with a requirement: Find out where the power lies, and then communicate your wishes. If a project

■ Speaking out in student council meetings is one way to make your ideas about issues known. What else can you do to influence government at any level? How should you present your ideas and arguments when you do speak out?

requires authority that the student council doesn't possess, the officers must find out who has the power and how to reach them. School boards often react favorably when a student council asks for a chance to explain its ideas. If you also line up some parent support, the project has an even better chance of being approved.

OPENING LINES OF COMMUNICATION

When you have an opportunity, ask some older people how their senator or representative voted on a recent national issue. If they're like most Americans, they won't know. In the same way, you probably don't know what your student council decided at its last meeting. Both situations revolve around the problem of communication. Politicians make speeches,

■ Keeping up with the news is a basic responsibility of a well-informed citizen. Student newspapers can include information about issues at any level of government.

send out newsletters, and hope the media will cover their activities. In most cases, only the most sensational news makes it into the newspaper or finds a slot on the evening newscast.

Can communications be improved? Yes, *that's your third opportunity.* Keep up on campus affairs by reading the daily bulletin and the school newspaper. If the editors aren't covering student council news, write and remind them that the newspaper's job is to keep everyone informed. It also helps to know the people who are running the student council. Catch the officers at lunch and tell them what you want them to do. You can also ask your government teacher to set aside some time to discuss current issues. Once you've started, you don't have to stop with campus politics. When you have a question about state and national issues, call the field offices of your elected representatives. They're listed in the phone book.

SELECTING SUITABLE CANDIDATES

An old political proverb says, "You can't beat somebody with nobody." Political managers know that people tend to vote for names and faces they recognize even though that often means movie stars, military heroes, or relatives of popular public officials. Is your student government overloaded with athletes, cheerleaders, and the socially "in" group?

If so, *you've found your fourth opportunity.* You can shake up campus politics with a relatively small investment of time and energy. First, pick someone to run for office who has good ideas and who can honestly do the job. Find others who agree with your point of view. Next, learn what steps are needed to register your candidate. You may have to file petitions, go through a grade check, and so on. When you've done all that, get ready for the campaign.

OVERCOMING VOTER APATHY

Unless your student government was elected by ballots cast by captive voters in each classroom, it's likely that only one in five students bothered to vote. A quick check of any recent election in your community will probably reveal a similarly low turnout. What's wrong? The low figures may represent a general distrust of politics and politicians. More often, it represents apathy—a loss of voter interest and involvement in public affairs.

Your fifth opportunity, then, centers on the problem of overcoming apathy. A colorful, active campaign will go a long way toward getting people involved. Ask the school administration to schedule an assembly where candidates can present their ideas. Plaster the campus with punchy campaign posters that spell out your candidate's goals. Once you've gotten started, shift into high gear. Organize a get-out-the-vote drive. Round up some ninth and tenth graders and put them to work. The younger students are often ignored in school elections, but their votes count, too! None of this will be easy. Overcoming apathy at any level also frustrates professional politicians.

DON'T GIVE UP

Have you ever watched a political body at work? Far from being high drama, the passage of laws is often tedious, wordy, and dull. The people involved express their opinions at great length. The legislators, from the local city council to the U.S. Congress, seem to spend far too much time on minor details. Spectators get bored and leave. Important decisions are made in front of empty seats.

The fact that so few speak up at meetings provides *your sixth opportunity*. Student councils, school boards, and city councils appreciate input. Begin by asking for a place on the agenda—or just show up and ask for a chance to speak. Take some time before the meeting to organize what you have to say. Keep it brief

■ The act of voting makes you a participant in government. By exercising this right, you help determine the quality of the representatives who create the laws.

■ The high school student at the right sits on the school board in San Juan Capistrano, California. She can directly influence the regulations that affect her school.

and logical. Go easy on emotional arguments. If you don't get action, come back to ask questions and state your views again and again. Don't worry about sounding like a "broken record." If your ideas have merit, you'll wear down the opposition.

MAKING THE MOST OF OPPORTUNITIES

This book hopes to enroll you as a participant in the political process. Change, growth, and social justice can be found within the American system. After you understand how and why our local, state, and national governments work as they do, you'll be ready to vote, attend meetings, and debate the issues. You might even think about running for public office yourself.

Your own student government is a good place to begin. Once you look into it, you may find that the student council works better—and accomplishes more—than most people think. If it doesn't, you can try to change it. This book stresses one vital point: Democratic government cannot endure without an informed electorate that cares enough to get out and work at the hard task of governing this great country. Whatever your political philosophy or party, there's room for you.

Get involved!

Unit One

The Principles Behind American Government

1 Basic theories of government

▲ *Mayflower* passengers signing the Mayflower Compact, November 1620

On November 10, 1620, a small sailing ship named the *Mayflower* reached the coast of North America after a long, rough journey from England. The gray, rainy morning revealed a silent and desolate shoreline. The *Mayflower* was far north of the tree-covered mid-Atlantic coastline that had been its original destination.

After 66 days at sea, the British colonists laughed and wept and gave thanks to God. The storms that had cracked one of the ship's main timbers were still fresh in their minds. The captain sailed the *Mayflower* along the coast, looking for a safe place to drop anchor. On November 11, the ship rounded the headland now known as Cape Cod and entered a wide, pleasant bay. The passengers were delighted to see great oaks, junipers, and pines. The woods were alive with birds.

Some of the colonists wanted to go ashore immediately. Others argued that the ship should sail southward. The sailors had their own

8

ideas. They wanted to put everyone ashore so that they could begin their return voyage.

A decision had to be made, but cooperation didn't come easily to the *Mayflower's* passengers. One group, now known as the Pilgrims, was made up of people who were fleeing from religious persecution. A second group was composed mostly of poor people who hoped to build a better life in the New World. The third group consisted of servants and hired workers. The individuals in each group feared that the others would keep them from fulfilling the dreams that had drawn them to the New World.

It was clear that the new colony would fail if the conflict wasn't settled. Everyone was on edge, and violence was in the air. Finally, the leaders decided to draw up a written agreement that would guarantee fair treatment for all three groups.

The idea of a written agreement about rights came naturally to these English colonists. They already had 400 years of written limits on government behind them. The document the Pilgrims drafted became known as the *Mayflower Compact*. Only a single page long, the Compact began by confirming their loyalty to King James I of England. Next, the colonists agreed to set up a government that would provide for public order. They further committed themselves to the task of passing just and equal laws for the good of all. Finally, the signers promised to obey the laws passed by the government they planned to create.

The leading Pilgrims were the first to sign. After a long pause, the poor immigrants and the servants stepped forward and signed. By now, they were confident that their rights would be protected by the Compact. In all, 41 men signed the Compact. None of the women signed, for women did not have full legal rights in the 1600s. As the next item of business, the colonists elected John Carver as their first governor. Only then did they dispatch an expedition to find firewood and fresh water.

By agreeing to treat everyone fairly and to elect their own leaders, the colonists took a long step toward creating a fair and equitable system of government. As the Mayflower Compact says, their goal was to provide for "ye generall good of ye Colonie." As you'll learn in this chapter, there are many ways to organize a government. The questions to be discussed are:

1. How have governments evolved over the centuries?

2. What is meant by the concept of "nation"?

3. Where is power held in the three basic systems of government?

4. How do governments differ in the ways they make decisions?

5. How do governments differ in the economic systems they choose?

1. How have governments evolved over the centuries?

Anthropologists are scientists who study people and their cultures, past and present. They report that even the most primitive tribes of the past possessed some system of organizing and regulating their social and economic relationships. If people are to live together, they must find ways to resolve the conflicts that always seem to occur. Thus, *government* probably began with the first human societies.

A primitive society, by definition, is one that has not progressed to "civilization" (an advanced stage of social development). Most primitive peoples led simple, communal lives of hunting and gathering. All members of the group shared the meat from the hunt and the produce from the fields. The people often wandered from place to place, seeking food for themselves and grazing for their animals. People at this level of development seldom had a written language.

Tribes developed as an extension of the family or clan. No formal body of laws existed in a tribe. The members obeyed tribal customs and taboos. Failure to do so, they believed, was certain to bring down the wrath of the gods on everyone. In time, the success of tribal life led to a more formal system of government.

Tribal governments usually developed out of the *extended family*. The extended family is a group made up of several generations linked by birth and marriage. An older, wiser, or stronger man or woman usually acted as the leader. Members of an extended family rarely questioned the decisions of the patriarch or matriarch. When several extended families lived in the same village, the leaders were usually advised by a tribal council. The council settled disputes, upheld tribal customs, and supervised religious ceremonies.

THE FIRST CIVILIZATIONS

About 10,000 years ago, wandering tribes began to settle in the great valleys of the Nile, Tigris-Euphrates, Indus, and Yellow rivers. (The Nile is in present-day Egypt; the Tigris-Euphrates is in Iraq; the Indus is in Pakistan; and the Yellow is in China.) The peoples who settled these river valleys built the first great civilizations. The rich soil grew so much food that they could stay in one place. Better farming methods created a food surplus, and some people were able to leave the land. These former farmers became full-time builders, artists, crafts workers, and priests.

A settled life, a food surplus, and a growing population did not do away with all problems. Less civilized tribes often raided the new settlements. They burned houses, carried off livestock, and took captives to use as slaves. In order to protect themselves, the farming peoples selected war leaders and taxed themselves to pay for their own defense. In time, the war leaders and landowners took on the role of an upper class known as the nobility. The nobles selected their own kings and queens and demanded absolute obedience from the lower classes.

THE CITY-STATE

As civilization developed, the *city-state* emerged as the basic unit of government. A city-state was a city that was also a small, independent country. It consisted of a city or town and the nearby farmland and villages. Most of the city-state's inhabitants were farmers, who supported the nobility with their labor. A small middle class performed skilled labor or managed business enterprises. At the top of the social order were nobles and priests, who administered the city's political, economic, and religious affairs. The upper class enjoyed whatever luxuries were available. The heavily taxed farmers and workers, by contrast, were usually poorly fed and housed.

In time, strong city-states extended their power over larger areas. The city-states of Egypt's Nile Valley unified under a god-king who was called the pharaoh. Rulers who combined military and religious authority were able to keep large populations under control. Whenever the power of the pharaoh weakened, the great nobles rebelled against the central government.

■ Egyptian pharaoh Ramses II leading troops into battle. Why did the artist make the figure of the pharaoh so much larger than the other figures?

In other river valleys, many city-states kept their independence. Without the stability that comes from national unity, these city-states had to fight constant wars with neighboring cities and with marauding peoples. The nomadic tribes envied the rich land and plentiful food supplies of the prosperous cities. All too often, they rode out of their forest and desert strongholds to ravage the countryside. Only the strongest cities were able to fight off the savage attacks.

EARLY EMPIRES

Civilization continued to advance despite these frequent wars. About 1700 B.C., King Hammurabi of Babylonia told his officials to carve the nation's laws in stone. By setting up a law code where everyone could see it, Hammurabi took a major step toward providing equal justice for all. In addition, new technologies gave people more control over their environment. Improved writing systems made it possible to keep written records. Better metals made tools and weapons more efficient.

Over thousands of years, other city-states followed Egypt in building great empires. After the Babylonians and Assyrians rose and fell in the Middle East, the Persians emerged as a great people. Persian rulers conquered an empire that stretched from the Mediterranean to the Indus River. Capable emperors maintained law and order, collected taxes, and carried on international trade. Even these mighty god-kings could not prevent conflict with other ambitious rulers. Wars were fought for land, trade, and natural resources.

The great empires didn't last. Many of the god-kings lost touch with their subjects. They gave themselves over to lives of pleasure, and their governments became corrupt and inefficient. For each empire that fell, another civilization gradually emerged to take its place.

GREEK AND ROMAN CONTRIBUTIONS

Western civilization, from which Americans borrow much of their world view, began with the Greeks and the Romans. These two cultures made important advances in government, art, science, and philosophy. Perhaps their most important contribution was to give human beings a new sense of personal worth. Earlier cultures believed that anyone who pried into the secrets of nature was risking the wrath of the gods. The Greeks and Romans, however, excelled in the scientific study of nature. Religion was important to them, but they didn't see it as the only reason for existence. Life was to be enjoyed, and government's role was to provide a secure world in which to enjoy it.

Greece invents democracy. The Greeks were the first to break with the Asian tradition

FYI* . . .
King Hammurabi's Code of Laws: An Eye for an Eye

Hammurabi ruled the kingdom of Babylonia almost 4,000 years ago. Archeologists unearthed his code of laws from the ruins of the city of Susa early in this century. The code was carved in beautiful cuneiform writing on a pillar of black stone. Although the code was popular with the Babylonians, many of its 282 laws seem harsh by modern standards. They stressed personal responsibility, the sacredness of oaths, and the need for written evidence. Here are a few typical laws from the Code of Hammurabi:

1. If a freeman destroys the eye of another freeman, his own eye shall be destroyed.

2. Money for which no receipt has been given is not to be included in accounts.

3. A man who slanders a woman will be lashed and one-half of his beard will be cut off.

4. A husband may divorce a childless wife by refunding her dowry and bridal price.

5. Those who lease land and do not cultivate it must pay the same rent as that paid by farmers who cultivate their fields properly.

6. If an innkeeper hears people hatching a conspiracy and does not arrest them, the innkeeper will be put to death.

*FYI means *For Your Information*. Each FYI feature contains interesting background material related to the nearby text.

of totalitarian rule. A handful of Greek city-states gradually exchanged their totalitarian systems for democratic governments.

Many of today's democratic practices began in ancient Athens during the fifth century B.C. Athenian men discussed public issues and passed laws as members of the Assembly. They elected officials by secret ballot and served on public committees and juries. Each man joined the army or navy as a matter of civic duty. Historians estimate that a third of all Athenian men took time out from their jobs and business activities each year to serve their city. This example of direct democracy has never been equalled.

The early Greek democracies had their faults. The Greeks kept slaves, and the men refused to let women take part in public affairs. In addition, some Greeks didn't agree that democracy was wise or just. Plato, one of history's great philosophers, believed that Athenian democracy permitted too much freedom. In *The Republic*, Plato described a perfect government as one in which a few wise men ruled for the benefit of all. A city that allowed everyone to vote, Plato claimed, would eventually elect tyrants as rulers.

The city-states of the Greek peninsula were never perfect examples of peaceful progress. Unable to unify, they wasted their resources in almost constant wars. Weakened by the struggle, the Greek city-states fell to the Macedonians. These conquerors were soon followed by the Romans.

Romans value citizenship. At its peak, the Roman empire stretched from the British

FYI . . .
Views on Democracy

Pericles of Athens was an ideal spokesperson for Greek democratic ideals. Speaking at a public funeral in 431 B.C., Pericles said, "Our form of government is called a democracy because it is placed in the hands, not of the few, but of the many. All, moreover, have equal rights under the laws that have to do with disputes between individuals. But in public esteem, each is honored in proportion to his renown in his particular field, his ability being fully as important as his social standing." More than 2,000 years later, a famous British prime minister added his own conclusion to Pericles' speech. Sir Winston Churchill said, "No one pretends that democracy is perfect or all-wise. Indeed, it has been said that democracy is the worst form of government except for all of the other forms which have been tried from time to time."

Pericles   Churchill

Isles to the Persian Gulf. Its long history can be divided into two periods—the Republic (509 to 27 B.C.), and the Empire (27 B.C. to A.D. 476) During the first five centuries, Rome changed from a monarchy to a limited representative democracy. True power remained in the hands of an upper class known as the patricians. The patricians controlled Rome's lawmaking body, the Senate. The lower classes had their own less powerful representatives.

The second half of Roman history saw democracy give way to a system controlled by all-powerful emperors. Supported by the Roman armies, the empire gave the Mediterranean world a long period of prosperity and peace. In its final centuries, however, Roman strength declined. Civil wars and corruption brought slow decay. Rome's final downfall came at the hands of invading barbarians from Asia and northern Europe.

The two periods of Roman history combined to make two great contributions to Western concepts of government: a code of just laws and the concept of citizenship.

1. *Codified laws.* About 450 B.C., Roman citizens demanded that the city's laws be written out for all to see and read. The result was the Laws of the Twelve Tables, which were divided into two parts. Public law governed the workings of the Roman state. Private law, by contrast, concerned the interests and behavior of individual citizens. According to the Romans, the test of any law was "what a person of common sense and good faith would know to be right." The law applied equally to each citizen anywhere in the empire. Roman law still provides the foundation for the legal codes of many European and Latin American countries.

2. *Citizenship.* Roman citizenship was one of the most prized possessions in the ancient world. Roman citizens were free subjects of the empire. They were entitled to vote, hold office, and enjoy the benefits of Roman justice. The empire's power and prestige were so great that non-Romans willingly placed themselves under Roman rule in order to gain citizenship. Citizens who lived in distant parts of the empire had the same privileges as those who lived in the city of Rome itself.

THE GROWTH OF FEUDALISM

Civilization declined for several hundred years after the collapse of the Roman Empire. Invaders reduced Europe to a tangle of isolated castles, small city-states, and frightened people. Only the Roman Catholic Church preserved learning, culture, and memories of a more settled way of life. The Church became Europe's dominant force, a kind of super government in its own right. This power was seldom challenged before the Protestant Reformation of the 1500s.

Gradually, a rough political and economic system called *feudalism* grew out of the chaos. Nomadic tribes accepted Christianity and settled down on the territory they had conquered. Victorious nobles handed out tracts of land called *fiefs* to loyal followers. In return, these *vassals* agreed to fight for their lord when called upon. Monarchy emerged as the most common form of government. Kings and queens held power, however, only as long as the great landowning nobles supported them.

The fiefs were isolated from the few remaining cities and from each other. Each one became a small, self-sufficient agricultural community called a *manor*. Peasant farmers (the *serfs*) did most of the hard work on the manor. The serfs exchanged their freedom and their labor for the use of the land and the protection of the lord's armored knights.

RETURN TO A CENTRAL GOVERNMENT

After the 1200s, life began to quicken in the almost forgotten cities of Europe. City-states such as Florence, Venice, and Genoa revived and grew in power. This new era began when nobles joined the Crusades and went off to recapture the Holy Land from the Muslims. The crusaders were unable to maintain a permanent foothold in the Holy Land, but they brought new ideas and trade goods back to Europe.

The static feudal society began to stir as a rebirth in the arts and sciences took place. Trade increased and an emerging middle class

■ A scene from feudal times. Note the manor house, the serfs in the fields, and the nobility on horseback. What type of political and economic system is represented?

of merchants and crafts workers gained a greater voice in the government of their cities. New coins replaced the direct exchange of goods as a means of paying debts and taxes. At the same time, the nature of warfare was also changing. Guns and cannon replaced the knight as master of the battlefield. The scene was set for the rise of the nation-state.

2. What is meant by the concept of "nation"?

The world today is divided into more than 160 nations. Whether a *nation* is large or small,

rich or poor, its people tend to identify with their land and its customs. This feeling of "belonging" gives people a sense of nationality. Because they're proud of their country and what it stands for, citizens are willing to obey the laws, pay taxes, serve in the military, and make other sacrifices for the common good.

Each nation has its own system of government. Political scientists, whose job it is to study how governments operate, often refer to a government as the *state*. If you see a phrase such as "the power of the state," you'll know that the reference is to a system of government. In other cases, the word "state" can also refer to a self-governing subdivision of a national government. The United States, indeed, is made up of 50 such states.

REQUIREMENTS OF NATIONHOOD

How does a society become a nation? It must meet four requirements:

1. *Clearly defined boundaries.* A nation has recognized borders. The territory enclosed by those borders doesn't have to be any particular size. Andorra, high in the Pyrenees mountains between France and Spain, covers only 179 square miles. By contrast, Canada spreads across almost four million square miles.

2. *Population.* A nation cannot exist without people who identify with and support its government and national goals. Again, size doesn't matter. The western Pacific island nation of Nauru has only 8,000 inhabitants. India, on the other hand, counts its population in the hundreds of millions.

3. *Sovereignty.* A nation possesses *sovereignty* when its people govern themselves, free of outside interference. A nation writes its own laws, carries on trade and political relations with other countries, and makes its own decisions.

4. *Government.* Every independent nation chooses a system of government that meets its own needs. Like the colonists on the *Mayflower*, people know that they need a government to make and enforce laws. They also want their government to insure their personal security and possessions.

WHAT DO MODERN GOVERNMENTS HAVE IN COMMON?

Modern governments share a number of practices. In part, these similarities can be traced back to Europe's rise to world dominance beginning in the 1500s. During the next 300 years, feudalism disappeared and more advanced systems of government took its place. Great Britain, for example, slowly evolved from a strong monarchy into a parliamentary democracy. At the same time, the European nations were colonizing large parts of Asia, Africa, and the Americas. When the colonies became independent, they often adopted governmental systems similar to those of their former rulers.

Each nation has its own story to tell about how its system of government developed. Some countries threw off colonial rule only to fall under the iron grip of home-grown dictators. In others, the form of the government changed many times over the years. In this century, Spain saw its ancient monarchy give way to a republic, which in turn was overthrown by Francisco Franco's Fascist dictatorship. After Franco died in 1975, Spain restored its monarchy—but handed political power to a parliamentary democracy. This type of change is still going on. After living under Communist dictatorships for over 40 years, the people of Czechoslovakia, East Germany, Hungary, Poland, and Romania threw out their rulers in 1989–1990 and installed governments more responsive to the people.

GOVERNMENT BODIES

Whatever its system of government, every nation has developed a lawmaking body, an executive branch and bureaucracy, and a court system.

Lawmaking body. In any governmental system, even a totalitarian one, a lawmaking body provides a useful link between the ruler and the people. In England, for example, early Parliaments served only as advisory bodies to the monarchs. Later, Parliaments gained power through their ability to raise taxes. This "power of the purse" gave lawmakers the tool they needed to wring concessions from the monarch.

Executive branch and bureaucracy. A government's executive branch administers the nation's day-to-day business. As governments increased in size, rulers found that they needed more people to conduct the public business. As a result, they hired *bureaucrats* to collect taxes, keep records, and run public services. These government employees take care of the hundreds of jobs that must be done in even the simplest form of government.

Court system. The rough justice of the feudal age slowly gave way to organized legal

■ The American constitutional system of government leads naturally to a peaceful exchange of power after a presidential election. Here, outgoing President Dwight Eisenhower (left center), a Republican, shakes hands with John Kennedy, a Democrat, moments after Kennedy was sworn in as President in January 1961. What principle does this action illustrate?

systems. Wise monarchs adopted uniform law codes and appointed judges to administer them. The courts helped protect the people's rights and provided society with a measure of stability. The law tended to remain constant, even when rulers died and their successors held differing views. Equal justice for all became a fact as well as a goal.

CONSTITUTIONALISM

In modern Europe, limits on the power of totalitarian government began when King John signed the Magna Carta in 1215. For the first time in English history, a monarch agreed to accept the principle that "the law is greater than the king." The idea of writing down the formal limits on government in a *constitution* became a common practice. A written constitution, however, does not guarantee that a government will respect the rights of its people. Many dictators have ruled under constitutions containing guarantees of civil rights that were never enforced. In other cases, developing countries have treated constitutions as goals to work toward, rather than as iron-clad laws restricting the authority of their leaders.

3. Where is power held in the three basic systems of government?

No two governments are exactly alike. As a result, political scientists have worked out a method of classifying them. Governments are labeled according to (1) the location of power, (2) the way political decisions are made, and (3) the way economic decisions are made. In

Where Power Is Located in Three Systems of Government

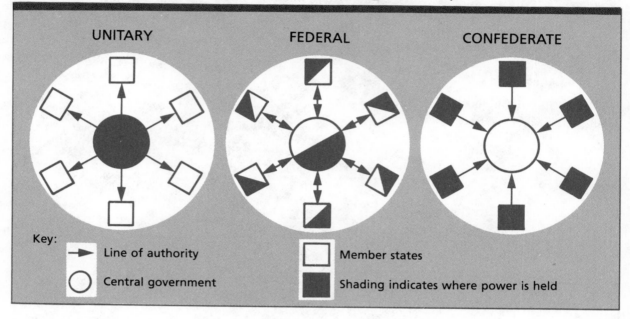

UNITARY   FEDERAL   CONFEDERATE

Key:

→ Line of authority

◯ Central government

☐ Member states

■ Shading indicates where power is held

this section, you'll learn to classify governments according to *where* the power is located.

UNITARY GOVERNMENT

A unitary system concentrates power in the central government. Small nations often use this system because it is simple and efficient, but it also works well for larger countries. In a unitary government, local governing bodies generally exist only to carry out the wishes of the central government.

France provides a good example of a unitary system. Most of the power is held in the hands of the government in the capital city of Paris. What happens if a mayor of a community in the Loire Valley wants to repair the city hall? The project must be approved by a bureaucrat (government official) in the capital.

Unitary governments need not be less democratic than other types. Safeguards that keep the national government from abusing its power are often written into the nation's constitution. In other cases, the people's rights are protected by traditions built up over the centuries.

FEDERAL GOVERNMENT

A federal government divides power between a central government and its member states. Each regional subdivision or state has its own governing body. A supreme law of the land, called a constitution, defines the duties, rights, and privileges of each level of government. In particular, the constitution spells out the way power is shared among national, state, and local governments. The power to change or amend the constitution usually rests with the people or their elected representatives. As you can see, this is a good description of the government of the United States.

CONFEDERATE GOVERNMENT

A confederate government (or confederation) is the opposite of a unitary government. In a confederation, local and state governments safeguard their authority by setting up a weak central government. In 1781, this country adopted a confederate system of government under the Articles of Confederation. The system worked poorly because the government lacked the power to collect taxes and enforce its laws. Within a few years, the nation's leaders replaced the confederation with a federal system of government.

Let's review for a moment

Do you sometimes get the feeling that humanity isn't doing a very good job of governing itself? Maybe it's because organized governments are only about 5,000 years old. That's when the first civilizations arose in Asian and Middle Eastern river valleys. The city-states that developed there formed loosely structured nations ruled by god-kings. These powerful rulers found that government was a useful device for keeping order, collecting taxes, carrying on trade, and fighting wars.

It was in Greece and Rome that governments first accepted the concept of *democracy*—rule by the people. The collapse of these great cultures left Europe in a state of unrest. The Roman Catholic Church became the strongest ruling force in Europe. Feudalism, the political and economic system of the time, worked against the development of a strong central government. After the Crusades, commerce and city life revived. Nations took shape as strong rulers emerged to lead their peoples.

What is a *nation*? It's an independent political unit that has recognized boundaries, national *sovereignty*, and an organized system of government. Every *government* has lawmaking bodies, an executive branch, a court system, and a bureaucracy to conduct the nation's business. Most nations have written *constitutions* that define their philosophy, establish a specific form of government, and guarantee individual rights.

Governments can be classified according to the way power is distributed. In a *unitary* system, power is concentrated in a central government. A *confederate* government, by contrast, operates with a weak central government and strong member states. A *federal* government balances the power between the central government and the states.

4. How do governments differ in the ways they make decisions?

In the give-and-take of daily living, most families work out a decision-making process. In one family, a dominant parent may make all the major decisions. In another, each family member may have a voice in deciding important questions. Whatever the system, these families have done exactly what nations must do. In order to exist, a nation must give some person or group the power to make decisions.

When classified on the basis of decision making, every nation's government falls into one of two categories. Like the family in which one parent makes all the decisions, *totalitarian* systems place total power in the hands of a single individual (or a small, elite group). By contrast, a *democratic* system gives its citizens an important role in making decisions.

TOTALITARIAN GOVERNMENTS

The rulers of a totalitarian nation possess almost unlimited power. No outside force, whether a constitution, free elections, or public opinion, can change their decisions. Modern totalitarian systems can be identified by four characteristics:

1. The totalitarian government usually comes to power by overthrowing the previous government.

2. The totalitarian government uses force to control or eliminate all opposition.

3. The totalitarian government controls the nation's schools, news media, and other systems of communication. A vast propaganda machine constantly "sells" the government's programs to the people.

4. The rulers form an elite, privileged class.

Totalitarian governments divide into three basic types:

1. *Monarchy.* As tribes grew in size during prehistoric times, tribal members accepted the leadership of a strong warrior, hunter, or priest. Over the years, these leaders and their children claimed their power by

Who Makes the Decisions?

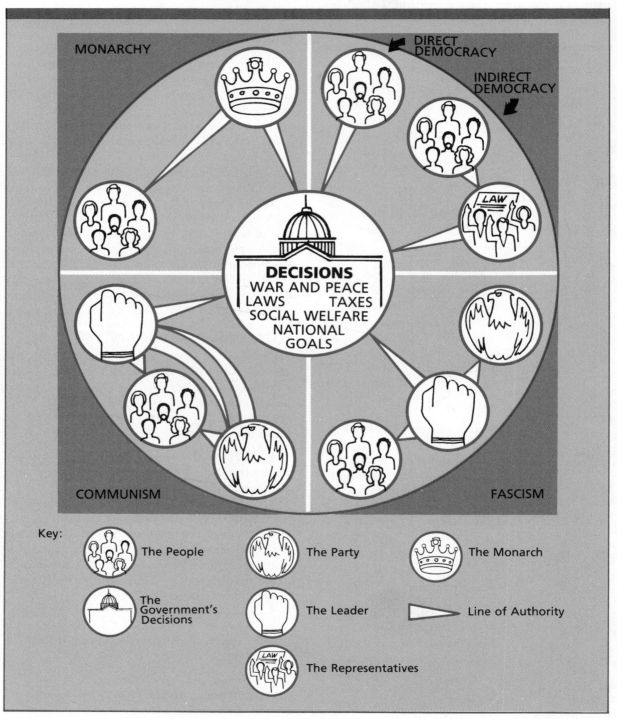

right of birth. Anyone who argued with the system was told that the gods wanted it that way.

The word *monarchy* means "rule by one person." Until this century, most monarchs held life-or-death power over their subjects. Some of them misused their power and led their countries into disastrous wars. Others treated their subjects with great cruelty. A few rulers, such as Queen Elizabeth I of England and Czar Peter the Great of Russia, provided intelligent economic, political, and military leadership.

Monarchy was the dominant form of government for thousands of years. In today's world, the system has fallen out of favor. The kings and queens who once claimed to rule by divine right (God's will) have largely passed from the scene. All but a few of the remaining monarchs have been reduced to the status of figureheads. They serve as symbols of their countries and have little real power.

2. *Oligarchy.* Most high school students know that their school is run by a handful of people—the school board, the superintendent, and the principal. Political scientists use the word *oligarchy* to describe systems of this type. An oligarchy is any government—whether of a school, a city, or a nation—in which the decisions are made by a small, select group of people.

In the past, oligarchies tended to put limits on admission to the ruling body. The members usually rejected challenges from those who wanted to share their power. The city of Venice in the 1400s and 1500s, where wealthy property owners ruled the city, is an example of an oligarchy. By contrast, membership in today's oligarchies usually isn't hereditary. The positions must be earned. The voters of your community elected the members of your school board. Unlike Venice, your school's ruling oligarchy is open to anyone who can win a seat on the school board.

3. *Dictatorship.* A *dictatorship* is a system of government in which one person, party, or class holds absolute power. Unlike a monarch, the dictator does not take on the robes and titles of royalty. The practice of dictator-

ship goes back to ancient Rome. That city's laws allowed for one-person rule during military emergencies. After the danger was over, the dictator returned his power to the people's representatives.

Modern dictators rule on a more permanent basis. Once they take over a government, they concentrate power in their own hands. Dic-

■ A huge portrait of Mao Zedong, Communist ruler of China from 1949 to 1976, hanging over a street in a city in China. Why would a dictator want such large pictures of himself in public places?

tators surround themselves with followers who obey them, even if the orders lead to torture and murder. They place the welfare of the state over the rights of the individual. If elections are permitted, the voting serves only as a public relations event. The people must approve the dictator's candidates and decisions.

Most dictators use violent means to gain power. They often begin by raising a military force that is strong enough to defeat the existing government in a revolution or civil war. Once they take office, few dictators resign or retire. Because no orderly system of picking a new ruler exists, another period of violence often follows a dictator's death.

DEMOCRATIC GOVERNMENT

A *democracy* is a government that places decision-making powers in the hands of the people. Typically, a democracy has free elections, limits on governmental power, competing political parties, and safeguards for individual freedoms. In addition, most modern democracies try to provide some degree of social and economic equality to go with political equality. Because they allow citizens to have a say in making decisions, democracies often seem to move slowly in comparison with dictatorships.

A democracy can be classified as either direct or indirect.

Direct democracy. When government units are small enough, they can practice *direct democracy*. In this form of government, all citizens are encouraged to take part in making decisions. In New England, for example, many townships hold meetings during which voters can approve or reject laws, taxes, and other items of town business. Direct democracy is also practiced in many cities and states in which citizens have the right to petition for new laws and then vote on them. Similarly, recall elections allow voters to remove officeholders who aren't doing their jobs properly.

Indirect democracy. In an *indirect democracy*, the people elect representatives to make political decisions for them. If the voters

don't think their representatives are working in their best interests, they may remove the representatives from office at the next election. The form of indirect democracy practiced by the United States is called a *republic* or a *representative democracy*.

Indirect democracies have developed two forms of leadership—presidential and parliamentary.

Presidential leadership. A single elected official holds executive authority in a system of presidential leadership. The people select their presidents in free elections for definite terms in office. Constitutions often limit the president to one or two terms (one six-year term in Mexico, two four-year terms in the United States). Most presidential systems draw a clear line between the role of the president and the role of the legislative branch of government. The legislators write the laws; the president carries them out.

Parliamentary leadership. In a *parliamentary system*, the political party that wins control of the nation's lawmaking body also takes over the executive branch. The leader of the majority party serves as the prime minister (the parliamentary system's equivalent of a president). When a parliament has more than one lawmaking body, the prime minister presides over the larger, popularly elected house. The prime minister performs administrative duties similar to those of the U.S. President and is also exposed to the daily pressures of legislative debate. If the majority party loses a vote on a major issue, the prime minister must resign and call new national elections.

5. How do governments differ in the economic systems they choose?

Many decisions that a government makes involve money—how to get it and what to spend it on. Anything that government does, from planning space labs to hiring office workers, costs something. Contrary to popular opinion, a government cannot print new money when-

■ Then Prime Minister Margaret Thatcher of Great Britain leaving the official residence in London. Mrs. Thatcher was the leader of the Conservative party, the majority party in Parliament.

ever it runs short. Such "printing-press money" causes inflation and quickly becomes worthless.

Financial support for government spending can be obtained in five ways. A government can (1) borrow money at home or abroad, (2) collect taxes from its people, (3) go into business for itself by making products and providing services, (4) expand the economy by the development of new resources, or (5) take resources from its weaker neighbors.

Most governments confine themselves to the first three options. Whatever method they choose, some basic questions must be answered: Who should be allowed to own property? Should business be allowed to operate freely, or should it be restricted? How should the nation's resources be distributed among its citizens? Each of the four main economic systems—capitalism, socialism, communism, and fascism—answers these questions differently.

CAPITALISM

Throughout its history, the United States has lived under the capitalist economic system. Thanks to the energy of the American people and the rich resources of the land, this system has created one of the world's highest standards of living. *Capitalism* is composed of four broad principles:

1. *Free enterprise.* People have the right to choose the way they make their living. They can work for someone else, or they can open their own businesses. Workers, from ditch-

FYI . . .
Contrasting Systems of Government

	United States	People's Republic of China	Great Britain	Mexico
Form of government	Presidential leadership. Federal system. Constitution is basic law of the land. Two-party system.	Dictatorship of the proletariat. Constitution has little meaning. Single party rule.	Parliamentary leadership. Unitary system. Monarchy reduced to ceremonial status. Multiple parties.	Presidential leadership. Constitution serves as goal for the nation. Single party dominates elections.
Economic system	Capitalism—government regulation of business and industry reduced in 1980s.	Communism—government owns the means of production and makes all economic decisions.	Mixed capitalism and socialism—government controls some basic industries, such as health care and mining.	Regulated capitalism—government's goal is to develop industrial independence.
Personal freedom	Guaranteed by the Constitution.	Limited rights. All citizens subject to Communist party control.	Common law and carefully observed tradition guarantee basic freedoms.	Guaranteed by the Constitution, but police authority sometimes overrides personal rights.
Status of the individual	Emphasis on worth of individual. High standard of living. Well-developed social welfare system.	Individual exists to serve the state. Rising living standards often sacrificed in favor of industry and armaments. Well-developed social welfare system.	Emphasis on worth of individual. Depressed economy in north contrasts strongly with prosperous south. Well-developed social welfare system.	Individual rights sometimes sacrificed for rapid economic development. High rate of population growth hinders needed improvement in living standards.

diggers to brain surgeons, expect the government to interfere as little as possible in the way they perform their jobs.

2. *Private ownership of the means of production.* The individual citizen, business, or corporation has the right to own and manage anything that produces a legal product or service. People can own their own homes, farms, factories, or businesses. They also can put their money to work in stocks, bonds, or other investments.

3. *The profit motive.* In a capitalist

How Do Economic Systems Differ?

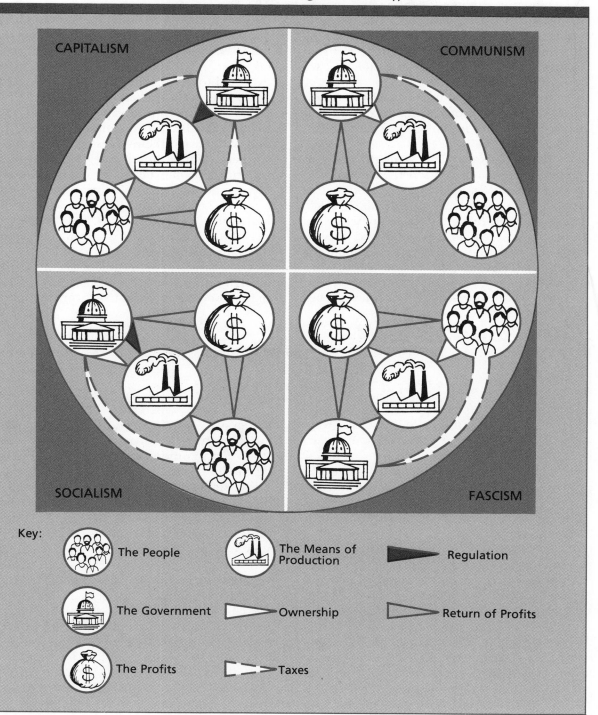

system, people are free to enjoy the fruits of their labor or savings. Profit is the money that's left after they pay the costs of doing business. It is their reward for taking risks. As economist Adam Smith wrote, "It is not from the kindness of the butcher or baker that we expect our dinner, but from their regard for their own interest." In other words, the capitalists' desire for profits helps to ensure efficiency and quality in the production of goods and services.

4. Competition. The struggle between competing companies to sell their goods and services results in lower prices and better products. If a town has only one taxi service, for example, the fares tend to go up, while the service goes down. If a second taxi service starts up, both companies must compete for customers. Prices go down and service improves.

Until this century, American capitalists op-
erated their businesses with few restrictions. The theory of *laissez-faire capitalism* stated that companies and individuals should be left alone to succeed or fail according to their abilities. *Laissez-faire* is French for "Let people do what they choose." The government was expected to keep a hands-off attitude, as long as no laws were broken.

Laissez-faire capitalism was widely practiced in the 1800s. Big companies used their power to enrich themselves at the expense of workers, competitors, and consumers. The American people began to demand government regulation so as to prevent the worst abuses. They were shocked by stock swindles, high prices, unhealthy foods, and shoddy products. Little by little, the government began to regulate business and industry.

The change to government regulation has been dramatic. In the 1700s, government's main economic role was to guarantee property

Learning Skills

Understanding Graphics

From time to time as you read this textbook, you'll find pages on which some space has been boxed off and filled with graphics. If you're a typical student, you may be tempted to ignore these boxes. If you do, you will be missing a good bet. Graphics can present information quickly and almost painlessly.

Let's use the illustration on page 18 as a starting point. In order to make the graphics easy to read, artists use some shorthand that everyone is expected to understand. Look at the visual. The title's clear enough, isn't it? You can see at a glance that this graphic is going to explain three basic systems of government in terms of where the power is held.

Now, look at the graphic itself. It's a combination of words, arrows, circles, and boxes. The first graphic represents a uni-
tary system of government. The circle stands for the central government and the boxes stand for the member states. What about the arrows? In graphic shorthand, an arrow stands for a line of authority or the direction of movement in a system. In this case, the arrows tell you that the central government controls the member states in a unitary system. The shading gives you a further clue. The solid color signifies authority in this graphic; white represents a lack of authority. What does the combination of color and white represent in the second graphic? Right! It must mean a balanced division of authority, since it's neither all color nor all white.

Are you ready to test yourself? Answer these questions based on your "reading" of two of the visuals found in this chapter:

rights. In the 1800s, government began the first steps toward regulating the activities of American corporations. Today, the U.S. system can be best described as a *mixed economy*. Private enterprise must cope with many government regulations, but it also benefits from a substantial amount of government support.

SOCIALISM

Socialism is an economic theory that calls for public ownership of the means of production. In practice, this means that government owns the nation's transportation, communication, energy, banking, health care, and all other important industries and services. Socialists say that government ownership is necessary because capitalism allows wealth and political power to be concentrated in the hands of a few. They believe that socialism leads to lower prices, better goods, and a rise in living standards. In addition, Socialists claim that their

system provides a more equal distribution of wealth. Critics of socialism argue that the lack of a profit motive kills initiative. Socialism, the critics add, discourages society's most capable workers by giving everyone the same benefits.

Most modern Socialists are willing to accept a democratic form of government. Sweden's Socialist government, for example, has gradually transferred the ownership of major industries to public hands without disrupting democratic traditions. Except for restrictions on private enterprise and property rights, most Socialist governments also protect personal freedoms.

COMMUNISM

Modern *communism* is a radical form of socialism. The basic theory comes from a book called *Das Kapital*, the work of a German economist named Karl Marx. Early Commu-

1. *Go back to the illustration on page 18.* Which form of government would you expect to find in a Fascist country? Why? Which graphic best represents the United Nations? the United States? Why? Now, draw a similar graphic that represents the lines of authority at your school. You'll have to design symbols to represent the school board, the superintendent, the school administrators, the teachers, and the students.

2. *See the illustration on page 20.* The graphic has more symbols because decision making is a complex process. Can you find the symbol for The People? The Party? The Leader? Once you study each symbol for a moment, it will be easy to recognize. Now, look at the sections that illustrate Monarchy and Fascism. Both are totalitarian. How are they different? The

graphic will tell you at a glance. Great Britain still has a monarch, but is that nation a monarchy in the sense of decision making? It helps to remember that Great Britain has elected representatives who sit in a lawmaking body called Parliament. There's no place for a Parliament in a monarchy, according to the graphic. Therefore, the answer to the question is "no." The United States is a democracy, of course, but is it a direct democracy or an indirect democracy? What about your state government? Or your local city government?

If you pick up a copy of any newsmagazine, you'll find many examples of modern graphics on which to practice. Once you puzzle out the shorthand, you'll find that graphics can be both interesting and instructive.

nists adopted the slogan, "From each according to his abilities, to each according to his needs." Communism attempts to reach this "classless state" by limiting private ownership of property to personal possessions. Along with a belief in public ownership of the means of production, Communists believe in a one-party, totalitarian political system. Individual freedoms must sometimes be denied, so the theory says, because it will take time to replace the old social classes with a society dedicated to communism.

In 1848, Marx attacked the worst excesses of laissez-faire capitalism in *The Communist Manifesto*. Marx's views were later modified by Lenin (real name: Vladimir I. Ulyanov), a leader of the revolution that brought communism to Russia in 1917. Marxist-Leninist theory can be summed up in five basic beliefs:

1. *Economic view of history.* Communist thinkers describe history as a struggle between the "haves" and the "have-nots." They claim that the proletariat (the workers) in an industrial society will always be exploited by the bourgeoisie (the property owners). That situation will continue, Communists argue, until Communist-led revolutions overthrow the bourgeoisie.

2. *Labor theory of value.* Marx said that the value of any product or service is determined by the materials and labor needed to produce it. The value of a glass vase, the theory teaches, is equal to the cost of the raw material (the glass), plus the costs of production (machines, electricity, and so on), plus the value of the labor (wages paid to the workers). Any surplus value (what the capitalists call profit) should belong to the workers, without whose labor the vase could not have been made.

This theory sounds logical, but it leaves out the important role played by the factory owners. After all, the factory wouldn't exist if the owners hadn't risked their capital to build it. The management skills of the owners are also important to the success of the enterprise.

3. *Dedication to revolution.* Communists believe that the bourgeoisie use government as a tool for oppressing the proletariat. They argue that any attempt to change a

capitalistic system by peaceful means is doomed to failure. All non-Communist governments, they conclude, must be overthrown by revolution if communism is to succeed.

4. *Dictatorship of the proletariat.* The true Communist state will be run by its workers. Communists call this system the dictatorship of the proletariat. In practice, an elite group of Communist party officials occupy the key party and government positions. In time, the theory promises, the state will "wither away" because it will no longer be needed. Despite this promise and despite the Soviet Union's current reform movement, the nation's Communist government has not yet withered away.

5. *Atheism.* Communist leaders demand complete dedication to the Communist state. As atheists, they deny the existence of God and try to destroy traditional religious beliefs. The theory says that religion's promise of a paradise after death is meant to distract people's attention from poor living conditions here on earth.

Karl Marx probably wouldn't recognize communism as it's now practiced in the Soviet Union, China, and other countries. Even though present-day Communist leaders allow their people only limited freedoms, they have been forced to borrow capitalistic methods in order to improve their sluggish economies. Communism's inability to provide its people with a high standard of living has become more and more evident as the century enters its final decade.

FASCISM

Fascism also leads to an all-powerful totalitarian state. Fascism can be summed up in two basic principles. First, the leadership principle states that the people owe total allegiance to the ruler, the ruler's deputies, and the ruler's political party. Second, the principle of state socialism puts every aspect of national life under state control. Those who oppose a Fascist dictator are labeled enemies of the people.

A Fascist country often looks prosperous to the casual visitor. The economy seems well

■ The signs list many of the problems that have become public recently in the Soviet Union. President Mikhail Gorbachev is the central figure on the wall. The word Gorbachev is shouting is the universal distress call. Why does Gorbachev need help? What policies of the Communist government may have contributed to the problems the Soviet Union is now facing?

managed, the people seem happy, and the streets are free of beggars. A look under the surface of a Fascist state, however, reveals a darker reality. Elections may take place from time to time, but the results are always determined in advance. If the state allows private enterprise, businesses operate under strict supervision. The Fascist rulers abolish personal freedoms and make all economic decisions.

During the 1930s, Fascist governments came to power in Italy, Germany, and Spain. As Italy's Fascist dictator, Benito Mussolini set up a series of "corporations" to control each specific area of the country's economic life. Those who protested Mussolini's decisions were crushed by his Fascist police. From factory owners to the most humble workers, Italians learned to obey the dictator's orders. Since the collapse of fascism in World War II, no major country has adopted a Fascist form of government.

Reviewing
what you've learned

1. Some 5,000 years ago, city-states formed nations that were ruled by god-kings. The governments of these early nations served to collect taxes, keep order, carry on trade, and fight wars. The first Western civilizations were born in Greece and Rome. The Greek city-states contributed the concept of *democracy;* Rome gave us codified laws and the idea of citizenship.

2. After the fall of Rome, western Europe entered a period of unrest. Only the Church kept classical civilization alive. Daily life was governed by the mutual obligations of a political and economic system known as feudalism. After the Crusades, city life and commerce revived. Nations took shape.

3. A modern *nation* has well-defined boundaries, sovereignty, and an independent system of *government*. Its people possess a sense of national identity. Many types of governments exist, but all possess lawmaking bodies, an executive branch, a court system, and a bureaucracy to perform everyday tasks.

4. Governments may be classified according to where the power is held. A *unitary* system gives the balance of power to the central governing body, and a *confederate* system allows its member states a high degree of independence. A *federal* system tries to balance power between the central government and its member states. Most governments have written *constitutions* that define the nation's philosophy, establish the form of government, and spell out individual rights.

4. Another way of classifying governments is to look at the process of making decisions. A *totalitarian* state, whether it is a *monarchy, oligarchy,* or *dictatorship* puts all power in the hands of one person or one elite group. By contrast, the people rule themselves in a democracy. *Direct democracies* allow the citizens to make their own decisions. In *indirect democracies,* the people elect representatives to govern them.

5. A nation's economic philosophy also influences the form its government will take. *Capitalism* creates a high standard of living by emphasizing private initiative, profitmaking, and competition. *Socialism* calls for public ownership of the means of production. Most Socialists are willing to accept gradual, democratic change toward this goal.

6. *Communism* is a form of socialism that demands revolutionary change so that the government can take control of the economy. Communists believe that a true Communist state can be built only by a dictatorship of the workers (the proletariat). In practice, this always turns out to be a dictatorship of the Communist party.

7. *Fascism* shares many of communism's totalitarian methods. These include a strong police force, strict government control of all economic and political life, and a single-party state. State socialism allows private enterprise, as long as it is closely supervised by the government.

Review questions and activities

TERMS YOU SHOULD KNOW

bureaucrat	democracy	government
capitalism	dictatorship	indirect democracy
communism	direct democracy	laissez-faire
confederate government	fascism	monarchy
constitution	federal government	nation

oligarchy	socialism	totalitarian
parliamentary	sovereignty	system
system	state	unitary system

REVIEW QUESTIONS

Select the response that best completes each statement or question.

1. In order for a nation to exist, which of the following must be true? (*a*) All the people must speak the same language. (*b*) A single religion must unify the country. (*c*) A strong central government must exercise total power over all local governments. (*d*) At least a million people must live within the borders of the country. (*e*) The country must be free to exercise sovereignty in handling its relations with other nations.

2. The *maximum* amount of personal freedom would be found under a (*a*) Fascist government. (*b*) Communist government. (*c*) Socialist government. (*d*) representative democracy. (*e*) direct democracy.

3. Which statement is *least* likely to be true of a totalitarian state? (*a*) The government maintains strict control over newspapers, radio, and television. (*b*) School administration and curriculum are left in the hands of local school committees. (*c*) Secret police arrest and imprison suspects without warrant or trial. (*d*) The government came to power via revolution or *coup d'etat*. (*e*) All governmental power is held by a single political party.

4. The type of democracy practiced by the national government of the United States is properly called (*a*) direct democracy. (*b*) parliamentary democracy. (*c*) state socialism. (*d*) representative democracy. (*e*) unitary confederation.

5. Which national leader would be forced to call a new election after losing a vote on a major issue in the legislature? (*a*) a military dictator. (*b*) a traditional monarch. (*c*) a president. (*d*) the Communist party's first secretary. (*e*) a prime minister.

6. The chief difference between modern capitalism and laissez-faire capitalism is that (*a*) modern capitalism has abolished private ownership. (*b*) government now regulates business to a considerable degree. (*c*) competition has been removed from business activities. (*d*) laissez-faire capitalism produced better, cheaper products. (*e*) industry has been completely deregulated.

7. Which is *not* basic to Marxist-Leninist theory? (*a*) economic view of history. (*b*) labor theory of value. (*c*) dictatorship of the proletariat. (*d*) opposition to religion. (*e*) all of these are Marxist-Leninist beliefs.

8. One of the most important concepts to come out of the civilizations of Greece and Rome was that (*a*) warfare should not be part of national life. (*b*) religion has no place in society. (*c*) humans are important and the universe is knowable. (*d*) totalitarian governments never work. (*e*) men and women should share equally in national life.

9. The best place to look for a bureaucrat would be in (*a*) a government agency such as the Treasury Department. (*b*) a parliamentary form of government. (*c*) a Communist dictatorship. (*d*) a Socialist government. (*e*) all of these, because bureaucrats are necessary in every form of government.

10. Modern Western democracy began when England's King John signed the (*a*) Bill of Rights. (*b*) Magna Carta. (*c*) Declaration of Independence. (*d*) Petition of Right. (*e*) bill giving full legislative powers to Parliament.

CONCEPT DEVELOPMENT

1. Contrast the office of the President of the United States with that of the Prime Minister of Great Britain in terms of (a) election to office, (b) executive powers, and (c) party responsibilities.

2. Patriotism has come into favor with many people in today's world. Is there anything wrong with loving one's country? Explain what is good and bad about patriotism and nationalism.

3. Why is a totalitarian government often considered to be more efficient than a democratic one? What freedoms do a people give up when they accept totalitarian rule?

4. The British poet Shelley once wrote, "We are all Greeks." Shelley meant, of course, that Western civilization owes a great debt to classical Greece. What contributions did those marvelously talented people make to our modern way of life?

5. What barriers do you see to increased cooperation among nations in today's world? Are there any factors that will contribute to better relations in the future?

HANDS-ON ACTIVITIES

1. How well do government and business get along in your community? One way to find out is to ask one or more local merchants to speak to your class. Assign them the topic "How Government Influences My Business." Ask the speakers to discuss taxation, government regulations, and other aspects of the free-enterprise system in today's business world.

2. Find four volunteers to work with you in preparing a roundtable "summit meeting" for the class. Each person will represent a different nation: the United States, the Soviet Union, Great Britain, Sweden, and Mexico. Each of these countries has a different form of government. Have the speakers prepare answers to questions such as the following: "How are elections run in your country? Does your economic system work for the good of all the people? Who really makes decisions in your country?" If the speakers have done enough research, they'll be able to speak with authority and answer questions accurately.

3. Pick three nations that have contrasting political systems. Prepare a poster on each one. Illustrate (a) the decision-making process, (b) the economic system, and (c) the degree of personal freedom found there.

4. Write a paper with the thesis "Modern communism has failed to fulfill its promise." Be sure to comment on the Communists' idea of a "classless society" in which each person works "according to his abilities" and receives "according to his needs." Is there a difference between theory and reality in the Communist world?

5. Read one or two of the many books written about the Fascist governments of Benito Mussolini (Italy) and Adolf Hitler (Germany). Examine the conditions that existed in Europe at that time, and trace the steps by which the two dictators came to power. When you're finished with your reading, write a brief essay on whether or not such a party could come to power in the United States. State the reasons that led you to your conclusion.

2 Free people in a free land: Building the American system of government

▲ Andros trying to stop a Connecticut legislator from blowing out the candle.

The time was Halloween evening, 1687. The new royal governor of the Dominion of New England rode into Hartford, Connecticut, at the head of a column of English redcoats. Sir Edmund Andros had been sent to collect the colony's charter. Andros was prepared to use force if the colonists resisted. Once Connecticut's charter was safely in his pocket, Andros planned to govern the colony according to the wishes of his king, England's James II.

King James was weary of the troublesome New England colonies and their representative assemblies. The colonists refused to abide by the Acts of Trade and Navigation. Taxes arrived late, if they came at all. To solve the problem, the king ordered Andros to consolidate the New England colonies (Massachusetts, Rhode Island, New Hampshire, and Connecticut) into one dominion. He was told to make sure they obeyed the king's laws.

Connecticut refused to join the new dominion. Andros blamed the colony's lack of cooperation on its liberal charter. Granted in 1662 by Charles II, the document gave Connecticut a high degree of self-government. As soon as he arrived in Hartford, Andros demanded that the colony's leaders surrender the charter.

During the evening of November 1, Andros met with the colony's assembly at the courthouse. In the king's name, Andros formally joined Connecticut to the Dominion of New England. The charter was then carried into the chamber in its leather-covered box. Governor Treat spoke out against the surrender of the charter. Finally, just as Andros reached for the box, the colonists snuffed out every candle in the room. By the time the candles were relighted, the charter had disappeared. Andros stormed out of the courthouse, angry and frustrated.

What happened when the candles went out? Lieutenant John Wadsworth, a member of the state militia, grabbed the charter and ran from the courthouse. He climbed a nearby oak, wrapped the charter in his cloak, and hid it in a hollow of the tree. The Charter Oak, as the tree came to be called, stood for another 169 years. People treasured it as a symbol of their resistance to tyranny until a storm toppled the old tree in 1856. Mourners draped flags over the stump as though the Charter Oak were a fallen hero.

■ The Charter Oak, the symbol of Connecticut's resistance to the king's tyranny.

England's Glorious Revolution drove James from the throne in 1688. When they heard the news, the people of Boston grabbed Andros and put him in jail. The Dominion of New England collapsed. William and Mary, the new monarchs, restored the hidden charter "in full force." From that time until 1818, the charter served as the basic state law of Connecticut.

As this story suggests, Americans were governing themselves long before they wrote the Constitution in 1787. The long period of colonial rule gave the colonists time to experiment with many different forms of government. During this period, the colonists fought for personal freedoms and self-government. This chapter will examine the following important questions:

1. **What different types of government did the colonies have?**

2. **What institutions existed within each colonial government?**

3. **What was the relationship between the monarch and the colonies?**

4. **What British legislative acts led to the Revolution?**

5. **What early efforts were made to unify the American colonies?**

6. **What did the First Continental Congress accomplish?**

7. **How did the Second Continental Congress govern the nation during the Revolution?**

8. **What were the strengths and weaknesses of the Articles of Confederation?**

9. **What events led the new nation to write the Constitution?**

10. **How was the Constitution ratified?**

1. What different types of government did the colonies have?

Late in the 1500s, Queen Elizabeth I gave Sir Walter Raleigh her permission to found a colony in America. The purpose of the expedition was clear. England wanted to invest in colonies so as to increase trade and find new sources of gold and silver.

The dominant economic theory of the 1500s lay behind this plan. Known as *mercantilism*, the theory stated that European nations prospered when their treasuries were full of precious metals and when they exported more goods than they imported. Colonies were needed to supply inexpensive food, timber, furs, and other raw materials to the home country. After the raw materials were turned into finished goods such as tools and clothing, the colonists were expected to buy the goods at high prices. In order to control trade with its colonies, the home country discouraged colonial industry and prohibited colonial trade with other nations.

England's first attempt at colonization in North America failed. Raleigh's Roanoke colony collapsed without ever finding treasures similar to those that had enriched the Spanish in Mexico and Peru. Despite their disappointment, England's leaders didn't give up. They blamed the failure of the first colony on its location (a barren island off the coast of North Carolina). Further expeditions were planned, and colonists were recruited. In 1607, the Virginia Company of London sponsored what became the first permanent English settlement in North America. The colony was located on a peninsula in Virginia's James River.

CHARTER COLONIES

The settlers who founded Jamestown carried with them a royal grant from King James I. This made them a *charter colony* with the right to colonize, set up a government, and trade with England. In 1619 the colonists started their own legislature, known as the House of Burgesses. The term "burgess" meant a delegate from a borough, roughly equal to a county. Thus, the Jamestown settlers were practicing self-government a year before the Pilgrims sailed to Massachusetts.

By 1732, the British had established a string of 13 colonies along the Atlantic coast. All colonies, charter and otherwise, were ruled by a governor and a two-house legislature. Governors of the charter colonies were either elected by popular vote or selected by the founding company. The upper legislative body, made up of the colony's leading citizens, was known as the *council*. The governors often

■ An early meeting of the House of Burgesses. Why is the creation of this legislative body important in the development of self-government in the United States?

Types of Colonial Governments

	CHARTER	ROYAL	PROPRIETARY
AUTHORIZATION	Royal grant to founding group	Directly under control of monarch	Owned by a single person who had received a royal grant of land
ADMINISTERED BY	Governor, usually elected, sometimes appointed by founders	Governor, appointed by monarch	Governor, appointed by proprietor
LAWMAKING BODIES	Council and Assembly, both elected	Council, appointed by governor; Assembly, elected	Council, appointed by proprietor; Assembly, elected

turned to the council for advice. The lower house, called the *assembly,* seated representatives from each town and city in the colony. Citizens of the charter colonies usually elected both houses by popular vote.

During colonial times, the term "popular vote" didn't mean what it does today. Only white adult males were allowed to vote. Generally voters had to own a certain amount of property and belong to a particular religious group. Women, blacks, and Indians could not vote. In some of the colonies, Catholics, Jews, and the poor were also denied voting rights.

Political and economic troubles caused most of the charter colonies to fail. One reason was that many activities of self-government, such as the printing of paper money, were forbidden. By the mid-1700s, only Connecticut and Rhode Island survived as charter colonies.

ROYAL COLONIES

Royal colonies (also known as crown colonies) remained under the direct control of the British monarchy. Each royal colony was ruled by a governor, council, and assembly. The governor and members of the council were appointed. The king picked the royal governors to be his personal agents in the New World. Their main task was to collect revenues for shipment back to Great Britain.

The governor appointed the members of the council from the upper classes. The assembly was popularly elected. All laws passed by the legislature of a crown colony were subject to review by the king and his ministers. As a result, colonial laws that violated mercantile theory were rejected. By the 1770s, Massachusetts, New Hampshire, New York, New Jersey, Virginia, North Carolina, South Carolina, and Georgia were all royal colonies.

PROPRIETARY COLONIES

Raleigh's ill-fated Roanoke colony was a *proprietary colony*—a colony owned by a single person. A powerful Quaker family, the Penns, at one time owned Pennsylvania and Delaware. The king gave Maryland to Lord Baltimore in the same way a medieval lord handed out manors to his nobles. As happened with the charter colonies, some proprietary colonies failed and were taken over by the crown. At the time of the Declaration of Independence in 1776, only Maryland, Delaware, and Pennsylvania remained in private hands.

In a proprietary colony, the governor and council were chosen by the proprietor. The people elected the members of the lower house. This led to many battles because the governor was loyal to the proprietor and the assembly was loyal to the people. The assembly's strength lay in its power to tax and to provide the money needed to run the colony. Assembly leaders used this power to force the proprietor to approve legislation that favored the colonists.

2. What institutions existed within each colonial government?

British colonists brought with them many traditions relating to government. Soon after the first towns were laid out, local and county governments were established. The governments administered county business, enforced the law, and managed the local courts. Most colonists still thought of themselves as British subjects, with all the rights and privileges enjoyed by their relatives in Britain. As colonists, however, they were no longer represented in Parliament.

Each colony's political institutions included (1) a government limited by a charter or constitution, (2) a governor, (3) the governor's council, (4) a popularly elected assembly, and (5) courts and local governments.

GOVERNMENT LIMITED BY AGREEMENTS

The Mayflower Compact made the first colonial statement about the rights of the governed. The Pilgrims drew up this simple plan for self-rule shortly after they arrived off the coast of Massachusetts in 1620. In the Compact, the colonists pledged obedience to their government and empowered it to make laws for the good of the entire colony.

The Mayflower Compact, along with other early constitutions, expressed a belief in limited government. Even in proprietary and royal colonies, colonial constitutions set restrictions on the power of the king and proprietor. This continued a tradition begun by the Magna Carta in 1215.

COLONIAL GOVERNOR

In each colony, the power to enforce the laws was given to a governor. In a self-governing colony, the governor's main duties were to administer the laws passed by the assembly and to oversee preparations for the defense of the colony in case of attack. In a proprietary colony, the governor's main job was to promote the interests of the owner.

Royal governors were charged by the crown with a long list of duties. They were instructed to (1) send back detailed reports, (2) make a profit for the crown, (3) maintain defense forces against nearby French or Spanish colonies, and (4) keep the legislatures and courts loyal to the crown. These instructions often led to a running conflict between a royal governor and the people of a colony. While the governor was concentrating on making the colony profitable for the crown, the colonists were concentrating on making a living from their farms and businesses.

The royal governors often earned incomes well above the local level. Although they were not nobles in the European sense, they modeled their life-styles after the courts of Europe. This did not endear the governors to the colonists, whose simple lives lacked most luxuries.

COUNCIL

A colonial council served as one of the two houses of the colonial legislature. The colony's leading political and business figures served on the council. Only in the charter colonies were the council members elected. In the others, they were appointed by the king or by the proprietor.

Acts of the assembly required the approval of the council before the governor could sign them into law. Because the council often failed to give this approval, many major problems went unsolved. The council was also called on to give advice to the governor on matters of trade, defense, and politics.

Learning Skills

Using a Textbook

Do you know how to use this textbook? Most students answer: "Sure I do. You open to the assigned pages and start reading. What's the big deal?"

If that's what you do when you start a new chapter, it's like trying to play basketball with one hand. You can do it, but you can't do it very well. Experts in learning psychology say that you can improve your use of this and other textbooks by following five simple steps.

Step 1: *Survey.* Before you plunge in, skim through the chapter to see what you're going to be learning. Look at pictures and charts, headings, and summaries. A few minutes invested at this point will help you make sense out of what you read later. Surveying the chapter is like checking the route before you start on a trip.

Step 2: *Query.* After the survey, take a moment to ask, "What am I trying to learn when I read this section?" This text helps to answer the question by phrasing the section headings in question form. Once you have the question in mind, read the section to find the answer. The material will make more sense.

Step 3: *Read.* Now it's time to read the material. This is where many people fall apart. If you don't read with understanding and concentration, you're wasting your time. Do you often find that you have to go back and reread paragraphs two or three times? That's a sign that you're not concentrating. If necessary, start by reading only a single paragraph, but read it well. When you've done that, take a short break. Then try another paragraph. In time, you'll work your way up to entire sections and chapters.

Step 4: *Recite.* Many students make a big mistake when they finish reading an assignment. They close their books, congratulate themselves, and go on to something else. If you want to retain what you've learned, stop for another couple of minutes to think back over what you've just read. Summarize the main ideas. Quiz yourself on names and dates and events. If you can't answer your own questions, go back and reread the parts that are giving you trouble. If you pass your own test, you can slam the book shut with a clear conscience.

Step 5: *Review.* You've probably noticed a sad fact about learning. Material you knew two weeks ago isn't there today when you need it. That's why good learners review important material from time to time. The night before a test is an obvious time, but it's better to review regularly. Use the chapter summaries, vocabulary lists, and review questions to help with your reviews.

This step-by-step method, known as SQ3R, won't turn you into a genius, but it will help you make the most of your study time. Think of it this way: Increased study efficiency pays off in higher grades and more free time. Why not give it a try?

ASSEMBLY

The members of the assembly were elected by popular vote in every colony except Georgia, where they were appointed. Only the assembly had the power to raise the money needed to pay for the costs of administering the colony. Even today, all money bills for the U.S. government must begin in the modern equivalent of the colonial assemblies—the House of Representatives. The colonists paid local taxes in addition to the taxes levied by the British Parliament. The assemblies also had responsibility for (1) raising local defense forces, (2) maintaining law and order, (3) regulating trade, (4) writing laws governing land ownership, and (5) dealing with Indian problems.

ENGLISH COMMON LAW

The colonies based their systems of local government and their courts on English *common law*. Developed over the centuries, common law is a body of written and unwritten rights and legal practices. One carefully safeguarded right was the right to a jury trial. In addition, the colonists prized their rights of free speech and the holding of elections. They did not think they were doing anything unusual. These new Americans believed that they were exercising the rights that belonged to all British citizens.

3. What was the relationship between the monarch and the colonies?

No colony was ever completely regulated by the British crown. Three factors dominated the relationship: salutary neglect, lack of communication, and a growing anger on the part of the monarch.

SALUTARY NEGLECT

For well over a hundred years, the British government followed a policy known as *salutary* (beneficial) *neglect*. Laws controlling colonial trade were written but not enforced.

The reasons for this are easy to see. During the 1600s and early 1700s, Great Britain faced constant turmoil at home and conflict overseas. Four wars with France, a civil war, plague and fire in London, and a struggle between the crown and Parliament all claimed the island nation's attention. As a result, the colonists were left to develop in their own way. Colonial shippers ignored both the letter and the spirit of British trade laws. In addition, Americans learned to take responsibility for their own economic and military security.

LACK OF COMMUNICATION

A great sea lay between Great Britain and America. Communication was slow and unreliable. Cut off from current news, the British monarchs had no real feeling for what was happening in the New World. They didn't realize that the colonists were developing new ideas regarding government and their relationship to the home country.

GROWING ROYAL ANGER

The monarch may have been unaware of the colonists' new attitudes, but one fact could not be ignored. The colonies were not fulfilling their original purpose. Contrary to mercantile theory, the budget for colonial administration and defense exceeded the income generated by the colonies. Indeed, the costs of collecting taxes often exceeded the amount of money collected. In the 1760s, King George III and his advisers began to look for ways to end the period of neglect. From their viewpoint, the colonies were simply not paying their own way.

4. What British legislative acts led to the Revolution?

A long series of wars between Great Britain and France ended in 1763. These wars had been fought in North America as well as in Europe. Anxious to profit from the victory, Parliament began work on plans designed to put the colonies on a paying basis. Instead, within a dozen years, these acts of Parliament brought the colonists to the point of revolt.

THE PROCLAMATION OF 1763

British policymakers saw the Appalachian Mountains as a natural barrier between the American colonies and Indian territory. Government officials believed that war could be prevented if they could keep the colonists separated from the Indians. In addition, by limiting the colonists to the Atlantic seaboard, the policymakers could reserve the Ohio Valley for London-based land speculators.

Parliament closed the western lands to further settlement by issuing the Proclamation of 1763. The move hit the colonists hard. For one thing, the proclamation guaranteed that the colonies' own land speculators would lose their investments in the West. In addition, it angered many Americans who didn't like being told that they couldn't move westward.

SUGAR ACT OF 1764

The Molasses Act of 1733, which put a high tax on non-British sugar and molasses, had never been strictly enforced. The Sugar Act of 1764 reduced the tax, but Britain was determined to enforce it. The act had the double purpose of raising revenue and ending trade with French colonies in the West Indies.

A Typical Triangular Trade Route

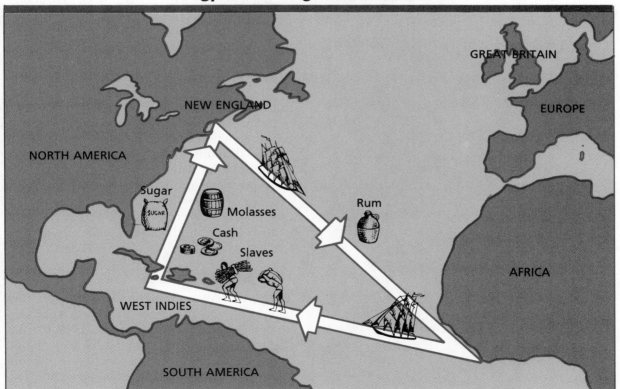

■ American colonists made large profits from their three-cornered trade with Africa and the West Indies. Without these profits, the colonists could not have afforded to buy the manufactured items they were required to import from Great Britain.

The colonies resisted the Sugar Act by smuggling foreign sugar and molasses. Without cheap sugar and molasses, the important triangular trade would have become less profitable (see the map on page 41). One leg of the trade began in New England, where molasses was turned into rum. Shippers traded the rum in Africa for slaves. Then the slaves were sold in the West Indies for more sugar and molasses and a cash profit. Without the profits from the rum-slaves-molasses exchange, the colonists couldn't afford to buy as many factory-made goods from Great Britain as they wanted.

STAMP ACT OF 1765

The Stamp Act placed taxes on colonial newspapers, licenses, legal documents, playing cards, and other printed material. In order to show that the tax had been paid, the items had to have a stamp placed on them or be printed on stamped paper. Great Britain needed the tax money to pay the costs of defending the colonies from Indian attacks. The colonists resisted the hated tax by refusing to buy the stamps and stamped paper. As resistance spread, they started street riots that frightened stamp distributors into resigning their jobs. Colonial leaders led a boycott of British goods. They also set up Committees of Correspondence to keep all the colonies up to date on what was happening. These committees, and others like them, proved their worth over the decade that followed.

The committees circulated pamphlets that attacked the Stamp Act. The writers pointed out that Americans were not represented in Parliament and concluded that British lawmakers didn't have the right to levy any taxes on the colonies. The slogan "No taxation without representation" became a colonial rallying cry. Alarmed over losses caused by the boycott on trade, British merchants urged Parliament to do away with the Stamp Act. The lawmakers reacted by repealing the act in 1766.

TOWNSHEND ACTS OF 1767

The British government needed to find another way to pay off the heavy debts it had run up during the wars with France. In 1767, Parliament passed the Townshend Acts, which tried to raise additional revenues by taxing colonial imports of glass, paper, paint, lead, and tea. The king appointed new officials to enforce the duties and specified that the royal governors would be paid from this source. Colonial leaders realized that they would no longer be able to use their control of the governors'

■ *Top:* Two examples of the stamps required by the Stamp Act of 1765.
■ *Bottom:* A Boston crowd protested the Stamp Act by burning paper sent from England to make stamps.

salaries as a weapon to influence policies. They organized another boycott of British goods that led to the repeal of every duty except the tax on tea. Parliament insisted on keeping that single tax as a token of its authority.

OTHER ACTS

Almost every move the British government made between 1763 and 1776 outraged the colonists. The Quartering Act, for example, forced townspeople to house British troops in their homes. *Writs of assistance*, or general search warrants, further infringed on colonial liberties. The writs allowed law officers to enter any home, building, or ship in search of smuggled goods.

In December 1773, a group of colonists threw a cargo of tea into Boston harbor as a protest against the unpopular tax. The British Parliament retaliated in 1774 by closing Boston harbor under the Boston Port Act. British forces were ordered to keep the port closed until the city paid for the tea.

The Boston Port Act, as well as other acts of Parliament designed to punish Massachusetts, were known in the colonies as the Intolerable Acts. The colonists became certain that the king's government would not stop trying to collect more taxes from the American colonies. By 1775, many conservative Americans had joined their liberal friends in thinking about independence. Not long afterward, the first shots of the Revolution were fired at Lexington and Concord.

5. What early efforts were made to unify the American colonies?

Despite their common dislike of British rule, the colonies were slow to coordinate their resistance to the Intolerable Acts. Over the years of colonial history, a few smaller colonies did merge with larger ones. New Haven Colony, for example, became part of Connecticut, and Plymouth Colony was absorbed by Massachusetts. More often, differences in attitudes, life-styles, and economic conditions, plus a lack of communication, isolated one colony from another. In London, colonial agents competed with one another in their efforts to protect the interests of individual colonies. As a result, Georgians believed they had more in common with Great Britain than with the people of Massachusetts.

Attempts at union did surface from time to time. Two major efforts were the Albany Plan of Union of 1754 and the Stamp Act Congress of 1765.

ALBANY PLAN OF UNION

In 1754, the threat of attack by the French and their Indian allies hung over the northeastern colonies. The danger was magnified because the colonies had never cooperated in military matters. Virginia, for example, had refused to send troops to help repel an attack on Pennsylvania. To solve this problem, the British government called representatives of seven colonies to a meeting in Albany, New York. Benjamin Franklin proposed the Albany Plan under which the colonies would unite in defense of any member faced with raids or invasion. The delegates agreed to a plan that provided for a grand council with powers to

■ This famous segmented serpent, designed by Benjamin Franklin in 1754, called on the colonies to unite. To the British, the symbol stood for "a snake in the grass." To Americans, it suggested strength and unity of purpose. The snake symbol appeared once more on the "Don't Tread on Me" flag.

THE PRINCIPLES BEHIND AMERICAN GOVERNMENT

levy troops, negotiate treaties, declare war, and administer the western lands.

The brave beginning signaled by the Albany Plan died as soon as the delegates returned home. No colonial assembly could be convinced that it should approve the plan. The British government also opposed it, but that was a minor problem. Most of the colonial assemblies refused to yield any part of their power to act independently.

STAMP ACT CONGRESS

Opposition to the stamp tax led to a more successful effort at cooperation. Delegates from nine colonies met in New York City in 1765 to petition the king for repeal of the hated act. The delegates pointed out that every sheet of every newspaper would have to be stamped. The tax would be a costly nuisance, they claimed.

The Stamp Act Congress inspired action in all 13 colonies. Angry colonists marched to the docks to prevent the unloading of the tax stamps. The boycott of British goods was enforced in the streets by groups of young Americans called the "Sons of Liberty." The resistance led to the repeal of the act and showed the colonists the advantages of acting together.

OTHER UNIFIED ACTIONS

Unified action became more common. The Sons of Liberty remained in existence after the Stamp Act was repealed. Its members organized violent street protests against British laws. The Committees of Correspondence, set up to resist the stamp tax, also remained active. Committees in each colony reported to the other colonies what they were doing to resist British oppression. Nonimportation Agreements in the colonies called for all Americans to boycott British products. In addition to striking against the mercantile theory, the agreements encouraged the manufacture of American-made products.

By 1774, the colonies had begun to replace their individual self-interest with cooperative efforts. That new unity led to the organization of the First Continental Congress.

Let's review for a moment

Many of the conflicts between Great Britain and its American colonies can be traced back to an economic theory called *mercantilism*. Briefly stated, this theory holds that colonies exist to enrich the home country by creating a favorable balance of trade.

Various experiments led to the creation of three types of colonies in America—*charter*, *proprietary*, and *royal*. The British monarchy and Great Britain's two-house system of parliamentary government served as a model for the colonial governments. The chief executive was the governor, who was elected in charter colonies, appointed in others. An upper house, called the *council*, advised the governor. Its well-to-do members were appointed in royal and proprietary colonies and elected in charter colonies. The council held veto power over legislation passed by the *assembly*. This lower house was elected by the colonists. Its members held the purse strings and led the fight against oppressive British taxes.

Until 1763, the British were busy with wars and other troubles. During that period of *salutary neglect*, the colonies enjoyed the freedom of self-government. Despite attempts to tax them, the colonies were a burden on the British treasury. Something had to be done to bring in more money.

After 1763, Parliament passed a series of laws designed to increase tax revenues and limit westward expansion. The laws were also meant to tighten the crown's control over the restless colonies. After their first attempts to cooperate with one another failed, the colonies began to work together. A successful boycott of British goods led to the repeal of the hated Stamp Act. Committees of Correspondence kept colonial leaders informed as to the progress of their resistance. The Sons of Liberty held violent protests in the streets. The colonies were now ready to demand a changed relationship with Great Britain.

6. What did the First Continental Congress accomplish?

The colonists reacted angrily to the British reprisals that followed the Boston Tea Party (1773). A number of colonial governments called for a meeting of all the colonies to discuss the Intolerable Acts. Delegates from 12 colonies (Georgia was not represented) met in Philadelphia on September 5, 1774.

DISCUSSIONS AND DECLARATION

The meetings of the First Continental Congress lasted nearly two months. Men whose names would one day be famous joined the debates, including George Washington, Patrick Henry, Samuel Adams, and John Adams. The talks centered on the conflict with Britain. Despite the radical speeches of Henry and the Adamses, most delegates were anxious to find a peaceful solution to their problems.

The First Continental Congress drafted a petition to the king that explained the feelings of the colonists. Many delegates hoped that this *Declaration of Rights and Grievances* would become the basis of a peaceful relationship between the colonies and the home country. The petition stated the delegates' position clearly and firmly: "The inhabitants of the English colonies in North America . . . are entitled to life, liberty, and property, and they have never ceded to any sovereign power whatever, a right to dispose of either without their consent." To reinforce this hope, the Congress planned a boycott of all trade with Great Britain. The boycott was meant to last until the Intolerable Acts were repealed.

IMPORTANCE OF THE CONGRESS

The delegates to the First Continental Congress did not try to act as a national government. Instead, the Congress proved that the colonies could forget their differences and work together. The delegates voted to meet again in May of 1775 if the British government didn't make a positive response to their petition.

In 1774, very few Americans were thinking

■ Patrick Henry in the First Continental Congress. His stirring words, "Give me Liberty or give me death!" furthered the move toward independence.

about independence. Throughout Massachusetts, however, armed militia known as "Minutemen" stepped up their training. Determined to protect their rights as British citizens, they stockpiled guns and ammunition. The Minutemen were ready for action if the British army tried to march into nearby towns from its bases around Boston.

7. How did the Second Continental Congress govern the nation during the Revolution?

When the Second Continental Congress met in Philadelphia on May 10, 1775, neither the British nor the Americans were in a mood for compromise. On April 19, the first shots had been fired at Lexington and Concord in Massachusetts. The battle started when a British force marched out from Boston to capture colonial war supplies. The Congress responded by organizing a "continental" army under the command of George Washington. The delegates agreed that the war in Massachusetts concerned them all. The creation of the new army, made up of units from several of the colonies, enforced that belief.

The delegates to the Second Continental Congress were experienced lawmakers. Many had attended the First Continental Congress. Among the new members were John Hancock of Massachusetts and Benjamin Franklin of Pennsylvania. Hancock was elected president. The Second Continental Congress served as the colonies' government for six years, from 1775 to 1781. No constitution spelled out its powers. No elections gave popular approval to its delegates. Even so, the Congress solved most of the problems that arose during the Revolution.

THE DECLARATION OF INDEPENDENCE

The war was a year old when Richard Henry Lee of Virginia proposed that Congress issue a *Declaration of Independence*. A five-member committee, led by Thomas Jefferson, worked on the early drafts. After a lengthy debate, the delegates approved the basic document but asked for several changes. Two days later, on July 4, 1776, the Declaration of Independence was formally adopted.

The Declaration contains three major sections. The introduction explains why it was necessary to declare independence. A middle section lists the wrongs suffered by the colonies at the hands of the king. Finally, the third section announces the creation of a new government.

Jefferson used the Declaration to spell out four important ideas about government: (1) All people are created equal, and they have certain basic rights. (2) The purpose of government is to safeguard these rights. (3) The right of a government to rule comes from the people. (4) The people have the right to change their government. (The full text of the Declaration of Independence is reprinted in the Appendix at the end of this book.)

The Declaration received a positive response from the American people. The stirring words raised morale at a time when Washington was losing battles in and around New York City. For many, the quarrel with Britain had seemed little more than a squabble over economic issues. Now it turned into a struggle for basic principles of freedom and human dignity.

FOREIGN RELATIONS

In foreign affairs, Congress spoke for all 13 of the new states. Aided by Ben Franklin's inspired diplomacy, Congress signed an alliance with France in 1778. Without French money and military forces, the Americans might have lost the War for Independence. Congress also negotiated agreements with the Netherlands. Like France, the Netherlands supported the new nation by declaring war on Great Britain.

DOMESTIC AFFAIRS

The weaknesses of the Second Continental Congress were most apparent in domestic affairs. To start with, the new states were jealous of one another. The country didn't have a chief executive to lead it, and it lacked a national court system. More importantly, Congress didn't have an effective system for collecting taxes. With bills to pay and with the treasury empty, Congress ordered the printing of over $200 million in paper money. Known as "continentals," the bills were backed only by the new republic's shaky credit. The phrase "not worth a continental" soon was being used to describe anything worthless.

DESIGNING A NEW GOVERNMENT

Congress couldn't cope with the new nation's political and economic problems. Members of Congress began to talk about the need for a strong central government. They realized that the nation would lose the war if the states didn't learn to cooperate. A committee first

■ Benjamin Franklin (right center) charmed the French into sending money, ships, and supplies to aid America during the Revolution. Franklin's diplomatic skills served his country well. Why is support from allies so important to a nation during a crisis?

proposed a new government in 1776, but the delegates turned it down. The debate dragged on for over a year.

Finally, in 1777, Congress approved a plan for union called the *Articles of Confederation.* The Articles required the approval of all 13 states before it could go into effect. Eleven states ratified within a year, but Delaware delayed until 1779 and Maryland until 1781.

8. What were the strengths and weaknesses of the Articles of Confederation?

At first, the Articles of Confederation seemed capable of giving the infant republic a working government. The states agreed to a number of cooperative measures. These included (1) the creation of a national legislative body scheduled to meet annually and authorized to con-

duct the nation's business; (2) one vote per state to be cast as instructed by the various state legislatures; and (3) proclamation of a league of friendship among the states. The government was empowered to provide for the common defense, safeguard individual liberties, and maintain the general welfare. As the name "confederation" suggests, however, the states didn't give up very much of their independence.

STRENGTHS OF THE ARTICLES

The Articles of Confederation helped the new nation survive a difficult time. Under the Articles, the states accomplished a great deal.

1. The new government showed that the states were willing to cooperate in the conduct of the war. This was the most important achievement of the Articles.

2. By forming a loose union, the states became less open to takeover by stronger European nations.

FYI...
Not Everyone Agreed: Differing Views on the American Revolution

Pro-British views

"They must all be subordinate. In all laws relating to trade and navigation especially, this is the mother country, they are the children; they must obey, and we prescribe."
—William Pitt, Earl of Chatham, 1770

"Johnny, you will be hanged, your estate will be forfeited and confiscated, you will leave your excellent wife a widow, and your charming children orphans, beggars and infamous."
—John Adams, reporting what John Dickinson's mother said when she warned him not to join the Revolution, 1775

"Better one tyrant three thousand miles away than three thousand tyrants not a mile away."
—Mather Byles, Boston minister, 1776

"When Jove resolved to send a curse,
And all the woes of life rehearse,
Not plague, not famine, but much worse—
He cursed us with a Congress."
—Tory poem poking fun at the Second Continental Congress, 1776

"Every means of distressing America must meet with my concurrence, as it tends to bring them to feel the necessity of returning to their duty. . . . Nothing but force can bring them to reason."
—George III, 1776

Pro-American views

"If I were an American, as I am an Englishman, while a foreign troop was landed in my country, I never would lay down my arms,—never—never—never!"
—William Pitt, Earl of Chatham, 1777

"You may spread fire, sword, and desolation, but that will not be government. . . . No people can ever be made to submit to a form of government they say they will not receive."
—Duke of Richmond, in a speech to the House of Lords, 1775

"Ye that dare oppose not only the tyranny but the tyrant stand forth! Freedom hath been hunted round the globe. O receive the fugitive, and prepare in time an asylum for mankind."
—Thomas Paine, American propagandist, 1776

"The time is now at hand which must probably determine whether Americans are to be freemen or slaves."
—George Washington, Order of the Day, 1776

"All eyes are open, or opening to the rights of men. The general spread of the light of science [reveals] that the mass of mankind was not born with saddles on their backs."
—Thomas Jefferson, 1776

3. The Confederation helped Americans think of themselves as citizens of a nation. People remained loyal to their states but took pride in their national government, too.

4. The Confederation dealt wisely with the vast new territories acquired in 1783. These were the lands that lay between the Appalachian Mountains and the Mississippi River.

The Land Ordinance of 1785 set up a system for surveying the lands, establishing townships, and holding public land sales. A second act, the Northwest Ordinance of 1787, encouraged settlement and provided a way for new states to join the union as equals with the original 13. The principles of the Northwest Ordinance far outlived the Articles of Confederation. Alaska and Hawaii were admitted to the Union under those same rules over 150 years later.

WEAKNESSES OF THE ARTICLES

The Articles of Confederation created the strongest government that the states would accept at that time. Right from the start, however, the system had some fatal weaknesses.

1. No solution was found for the financial problems that plagued the Continental Congress. The government had to operate without the power to tax. Financial support came from the states, which were often slow to meet the central government's requests. Continental currency remained almost valueless. The states printed equally worthless money of their own.

2. Because the government couldn't regulate interstate commerce, the states were free to set up tariff barriers to one another's goods. The revenues helped pay state bills, but business suffered.

3. The central government was given only limited military authority. Most Revolutionary soldiers were paid and controlled by their state legislatures.

4. No provision was made for a chief executive or for a national bureaucracy. Congressional committees tried hard, but they couldn't manage the nation's affairs without executive leadership or the help of full-time employees.

5. The government of the Confederation lacked police authority. It could not punish anyone. Moreover, without a national court system, nothing could be done to resolve conflicts between the states.

6. Each state was given one vote regardless of size or population. As a result, jealousies and rivalries among states were magnified.

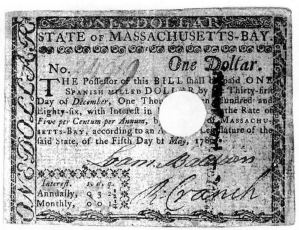

■ A one-dollar note issued by the State of Massachusetts. Under the Articles of Confederation, the government could not issue a uniform national currency.

7. Amendments to the Articles of Confederation required a "yes" vote by all 13 states. Even badly needed changes were almost impossible to achieve.

With luck, hard work, good leadership, and the help of European allies, the American colonies won their war for independence. Great Britain recognized the new nation in the Treaty of Paris, which officially ended the Revolutionary War in 1783. Freed from foreign rule, the Americans looked forward to becoming a strong, prosperous, and respected nation. However, the weaknesses of a central government dominated by 13 jealous states held the country back. The new United States needed a more effective way of governing itself.

9. What events led the new nation to write the Constitution?

As the victorious Americans faced the challenges of nationhood, the shortcomings of the Articles of Confederation became even more obvious. One major problem was finding a way to regulate interstate commerce. State

■ Massachusetts farmers fleeing from the state militia during Shays's Rebellion in 1786. The revolt caused people to wonder whether the central government could act quickly to put down such an action. Why is it important for a government to be able to maintain law and order?

delegates met in Virginia in 1785 and Maryland in 1786, but the meetings made little progress. The best the delegates could do was to schedule a third attempt for Philadelphia in 1787.

In the summer of 1786, Shays's Rebellion broke out. A group of debt-ridden Massachusetts farmers, led by Daniel Shays, marched on a courthouse and arsenal in Springfield. The farmers demanded lower taxes and an end to the collection of debts. The state militia put down the rebellion, but the warning was clear. The new nation might not survive if its government couldn't solve the problems raised by the rebels.

The *Constitutional Convention* gathered in Philadelphia on May 25, 1787. The convention, called to revise the Articles of Confederation, got off to a slow start. Rhode Island wasn't represented because its legislature opposed the creation of a strong central government.

New Hampshire's delegation was short of funds and didn't arrive until late July.

When the convention did begin, the 55 delegates included many of the new nation's leaders. Men such as George Washington, James Madison, Benjamin Franklin, and Alexander Hamilton later became known as the Framers of the Constitution. The convention pledged itself to secrecy in order to free itself of outside pressures. Thanks to Madison, who kept a daily journal, later generations have been able to follow the day-to-day work of the convention. The delegates began by electing Washington as president and then agreed that each state would have one vote and that a simple majority would carry any proposal.

DECISION TO CREATE A NEW GOVERNMENT

The Framers quickly decided not to patch up the Articles of Confederation. Instead, they agreed to create a new, strong federal government. In late May, Edmund Randolph of Virginia offered a proposal (largely written by Madison) known as the *Virginia Plan*. The plan called for a strong central government composed of three branches. There would be a legislative branch (to make the laws), an executive branch (to administer the laws), and a judicial branch (to interpret the laws and to administer the court system).

The convention's first real controversy arose over the issue of representation in the federal legislature. The Virginia Plan called for a *bicameral* (two-house) *legislature*. The number of representatives a state sent to each house would be based on (1) the state's population or (2) the amount of money the state donated to the national treasury. The smaller states objected, fearing that the larger states would dominate the legislature. (The terms "small state" and "large state" describe a state's population, not its size.)

New Jersey soon countered with a proposal for a *unicameral* (one-house) *legislature*. Every state would have equal representation in the single house. The New Jersey Plan was similar to the Articles of Confederation, which allowed the small states an equal voice with the large states. The issues of slavery and the regulation of interstate commerce caused additional controversy.

MAJOR COMPROMISES

Working through the heat of the Philadelphia summer, the convention reached three major compromises:

■ George Washington presides over a debate as the Constitutional Convention gets under way. In the weeks that followed, the delegates reached compromises that created a strong and flexible system of government. Why is the willingness to compromise differences so important in a governing body?

1. *Bicameral legislature.* The *Connecticut Compromise* solved the problem of representation in the federal legislature. All states would be equally represented in the Senate, and each state's population would determine its representation in the House. This compromise satisfied the smaller states, whose interests would be safeguarded by their equal representation in the Senate. At the same time, the larger states felt protected by their greater representation in the House.

2. *Slavery.* The compromise on slavery prohibited interference with the slave trade until 1808. In counting a state's population for representation in the House, each slave counted as three-fifths of a person.* The delegates believed that the southern states would not support the new constitution unless they agreed to this compromise.

3. *Interstate commerce.* The southern states feared that the North would promote its own textile industry by cutting off their cotton trade with Great Britain. The two sides worked out a compromise that allowed the government to regulate interstate commerce but forbade taxing exports.

OTHER DECISIONS

Even after the Connecticut Compromise was worked out, Article I took up much of the Convention's time. This lengthy section of the Constitution describes the powers and limitations of Congress.

Long arguments also took place over Article II, which spells out the system of electing the President (the head of the executive branch). Some of the Framers argued that if the President were elected by Congress, the legislative branch would dominate the executive. At this time, there was little support by the Framers for the direct popular election of the President. Most of the delegates believed that the people as a whole lacked the knowledge to make informed choices. Further, the Framers believed that direct election would favor the more populous states. Eventually, the convention reached a compromise. It placed the election of the President in the hands of an Electoral College. Defining how the members of the Electoral College should be chosen was left up to the states.

On September 17, 1787, the Framers signed the product of their labors—the Constitution of the United States of America. (The full text is reprinted in the Appendix at the back of this book.) Working without salaries or expense accounts, the delegates had given their best. Benjamin Franklin spoke for the nation when he said, "It therefore astonishes me, Sir, to find this system approaching so near to perfection as it does."

10. How was the Constitution ratified?

The ceremony of signing the Constitution was a dramatic event, but there was more to do. The process of *ratification* came next. Article VII stated that the Constitution would not go into effect until it was approved by two-thirds of the states (nine of thirteen).

STRUGGLE FOR RATIFICATION

The debate over ratification divided the nation into two political factions. Those who favored the new government were called *Federalists*. Those who opposed the Constitution were known as *Anti-Federalists*. Some famous names dotted the list of Anti-Federalists, including Patrick Henry, Richard Henry Lee, John Hancock, and Samuel Adams.

The Anti-Federalists' main argument against the Constitution was that it gave too much power to the central government. They complained that traditional personal liberties weren't protected. Patrick Henry spoke for those who feared the loss of freedom. He said, "I look upon that paper as the most fatal plan that could possibly be conceived to enslave a free people." Farmers who needed easy credit also opposed the new government. The farmers reasoned that interest rates would be driven

---

* This provision, so foreign to the modern-day belief in racial equality, was nullified by the Thirteenth Amendment in 1865.

FYI . . .

The Road to Union: A summary of key political events leading to the creation of our country

Year	Event	Significance
1600's	Colonial experiments with various forms of self-government	Self-government became an accepted part of American life.
1643	New England Confederation	Indian threat led to a brief period of colonial cooperation.
1754	Albany Plan	Not acceptable to the colonies, but served as a model for later efforts.
1765	Stamp Act Congress	Unified colonial opposition forced repeal of the Stamp Act.
1773	Committees of Correspondence	Colonial leaders coordinated unified action against British regulations.
1774	First Continental Congress	Twelve colonies met to petition the king to repeal the Intolerable Acts.
1775	Second Continental Congress	Provided a government for the colonies during the Revolutionary War.
1776	Declaration of Independence	Made formal declaration of the separation of the colonies from Great Britain; gave high moral purpose to the Revolution.
1781	Articles of Confederation.	Provided first constitutional government for the new nation.
1783	Treaty of Paris	Ended the Revolutionary War.
1787	Constitutional Convention	Instead of revising the Articles, delegates decided to write a new constitution.
1788	Constitution ratified	The new government came into legal existence after ratification by nine states.
1789	Washington inaugurated	The nation began its history as a republic.

up by the Constitution's ban on the issuing of paper money by the states.

The Federalists were quick to reply. In a series of brilliant newspaper articles, Alexander Hamilton, James Madison, and John Jay argued the case for supporting the Constitution. The articles were later published as a book called the *Federalist Papers*. The Fed-

The Battle for Ratification of the Constitution, 1787–1790

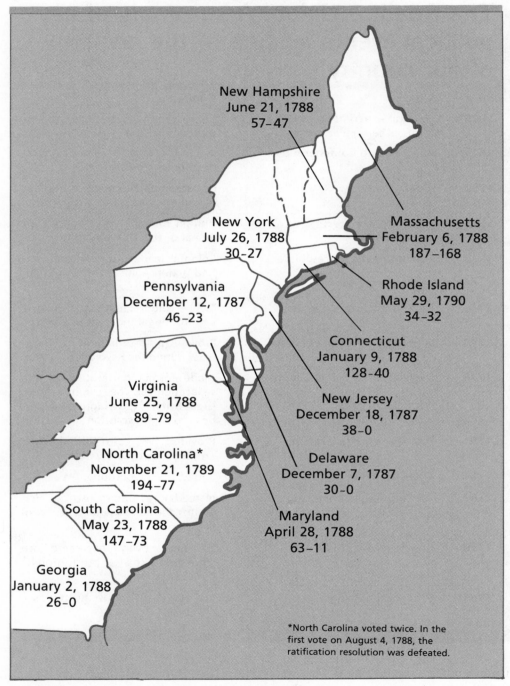

New Hampshire
June 21, 1788
57–47

Massachusetts
February 6, 1788
187–168

New York
July 26, 1788
30–27

Rhode Island
May 29, 1790
34–32

Pennsylvania
December 12, 1787
46–23

Connecticut
January 9, 1788
128–40

Virginia
June 25, 1788
89–79

New Jersey
December 18, 1787
38–0

North Carolina*
November 21, 1789
194–77

Delaware
December 7, 1787
30–0

South Carolina
May 23, 1788
147–73

Maryland
April 28, 1788
63–11

Georgia
January 2, 1788
26–0

*North Carolina voted twice. In the first vote on August 4, 1788, the ratification resolution was defeated.

■ The bitterness of the conflict over the acceptance of a strong central government can be seen in the closeness of the vote in a number of states.

eralists also promised to add a Bill of Rights to the Constitution as soon as it was ratified. The amendments were needed to guarantee everyone's fundamental rights and personal liberties.

CONSTITUTION RATIFIED

The *Federalist Papers* reassured many Americans. In addition, the support of Washington, Franklin, and other leaders tipped the balance in favor of the Constitution. Three states ratified the Constitution before the end of 1787. The ninth state added its approval in late June of 1788. The federal system would not have worked, however, without the largest and most important states. Only two of these, Pennsylvania and Massachusetts, were among the first nine to ratify. The other large states, Virginia and New York, finally ratified in the summer of 1788. In both states, the vote was close. The last two states finally made the ratification unanimous. North Carolina ratified in 1789, Rhode Island in 1790.

When the United States held its first presidential election, the 69 members of the Electoral College voted unanimously for George Washington. The first Congress under the new Constitution gathered in New York on March 4, 1789. On April 30, the members heard Washington recite the presidential oath of office.

The new nation finally had a government that worked. After 200 years, it still does.

Reviewing
what you've learned

1. The American colonial period was marked by two currents in British thought. One, the theory of *mercantilism*, insisted that the colonies existed for the benefit of the home country. The second was *salutary neglect*. Wrapped up in its own problems, Great Britain left the colonies free to develop a tradition of self-government.

2. The colonies can be classified as charter, proprietary, or royal. *Charter colonies* ran their own affairs and elected their own governors. *Proprietary colonies* belonged to companies or to wealthy proprietors who appointed the governor. These colonies were run as moneymaking enterprises. *Royal colonies* were ruled directly by the king, who appointed the governors.

3. The colonies developed legislative bodies with two houses. The upper house, or *council*, advised the governor and generally represented the colony's upper class. The lower house, or *assembly*, was popularly elected. The assembly held the purse strings and spoke for the colony's middle and lower classes.

4. After 1763, a series of harsh British laws drove the colonies together. Because the colonies hadn't been paying their way, the Stamp Act, Sugar Act, limits on westward migration, and the Townshend acts all seemed reasonable enough in London. Colonial resistance led to harsher British actions. Finally, the Intolerable Acts of 1774 set the colonies on the path to revolution.

5. The growing conflict created the need for a unified colonial government. At the *First Continental Congress* in 1774, the colonies pledged cooperation and sent a Declaration of Rights and Grievances to the king. In 1775, war with Great Britain began at Lexington and Concord.

6. The *Second Continental Congress* served as a national government from 1775 to 1781. Its members issued the *Declaration of Independence* and attempted to manage the economic and military problems of the Revolution. The Congress also wrote the *Articles of Confederation*, signed important treaties of alliance, and issued paper money to pay for the war.

7. The Articles of Confederation, ratified in 1781, established a weak, confederate form of government. On the positive side, the government gave Americans a chance to work together and to present a united front to foreign countries. The negatives, however, outweighed the positives. The government labored without an executive branch, a judicial system, and the power to tax or regulate interstate commerce. The confederation didn't have a good way of raising an army nor could it enforce laws or resolve conflicts between the states. The government did deal wisely with the public lands acquired in 1783. Also, the Northwest Ordinance of 1787 prepared the way for the admission of territories as new states.

8. In 1787, a convention met in Philadelphia to revise the Articles of Confederation. Wisely, the convention threw out the articles and created an entirely new federal system. The Framers reached major compromises on slavery, interstate commerce, and the legislature. The *Connecticut Compromise* created a Senate, in which each state has an equal voice, and a House of Representatives, in which seats are based on population.

9. During the ratification process, the *Federalists* supported the Constitution and the *Anti-Federalists* opposed it. The turning point came when the Federalists promised to add a Bill of Rights. The ninth state ratified the Constitution in the summer of 1788. In the spring of 1789, George Washington was sworn in as the first President.

Review questions and activities

TERMS YOU SHOULD KNOW

Albany Plan of Union	council	ratification
Anti-Federalists	Declaration of	royal colony
Articles of Confederation	Independence	salutary neglect
assembly	Federalist Papers	Second Continental
bicameral legislature	Federalists	Congress
charter colony	First Continental	Stamp Act Congress
common law	Congress	unicameral legislature
Connecticut Compromise	mercantilism	Virginia Plan
Constitutional Convention	proprietary colony	writs of assistance

REVIEW QUESTIONS

Select the response that best completes each statement or question.

1. Which of the following statements would *not* be true of a mercantile country's colonies during the seventeenth century? (*a*) No factories are permitted in the colony. (*b*) Gold, silver, and gems are sent back to the home country (*c*) All trade with the home country is carried in the home country's ships. (*d*) The colony is encouraged to develop its own form of self-government. (*e*) Trade between the colony and nations other than the home country is forbidden.

2. The part of the colonial system of government that most clearly spoke for the average colonist was the (*a*) governor. (*b*) council. (*c*) assembly. (*d*) Dominion of New England. (*e*) None of these spoke for the average colonist.

3. Which of the following statements most truly describes the colonial attitude before the 1760s? (*a*) Most colonists wanted complete independence from Great Britain. (*b*) The colonists thought that they should be granted more freedoms than the British people back home. (*c*) Most colonists accepted British rule but demanded that the monarchy be replaced by a republic. (*d*) Most colonists wanted to transfer their loyalties to the French government. (*e*) Most colonists wanted only the same rights and privileges enjoyed by the British people back home.

4. The existence of "salutary neglect" (*a*) gave the colonists time to develop their own way of life and government. (*b*) placed the colonists under the strictest possible British control. (*c*) strengthened the mercantile theory. (*d*) was a policy of the British government designed to help make the colonists independent. (*e*) had no effect on the colonies.

5. The colonists resisted the Sugar Act, the Townshend Acts, and the Stamp Act because (*a*) the colonists were not represented in the Parliament that passed the taxes. (*b*) the taxes placed a heavy financial burden on colonial businesses. (*c*) paying and collecting the taxes was a costly nuisance. (*d*) the taxes were thought to cut into colonial freedoms. (*e*) All of these were reasons for colonial resistance.

6. The *least* successful of early attempts at cooperation among the colonies was (*a*) the Nonimportation Agreements. (*b*) the Committees of Correspondence. (*c*) the Albany Plan of Union. (*d*) the Stamp Act Congress. (*e*) None of these were successful.

7. Which of the following identifies a major weakness of the Articles of Confederation? (*a*) No provision was made for an executive branch. (*b*) The government had no way of resolving conflicts between the states. (*c*) The government had no control over interstate commerce. (*d*) No sound taxing policy was established. (*e*) All of these were major weaknesses of the Articles.

8. When the Constitutional Convention accepted the Connecticut Compromise on the form of the new legislature, it resolved a conflict between (*a*) the North and South. (*b*) the two largest states. (*c*) slaveholders and those who wanted to abolish slavery. (*d*) the large and small states. (*e*) the western territories and the original 13 states.

9. The best description of the government created under the Constitution is that it was a (*a*) unitary system with all power given to a central government. (*b*) federal republic. (*c*) confederation with a stronger central government than under the Articles of Confederation. (*d*) totalitarian system. (*e*) modified parliamentary system based on the British model.

10. The states agreed to ratify the Constitution only after the Federalists agreed to return some of the federal government's powers to the states. This statement is (*a*) true. (*b*) false; the states agreed to ratify after the issue of protecting individual rights was solved by the promise of a Bill of Rights. (*c*) false; it was the Anti-Federalists who supported the Constitution.

CONCEPT DEVELOPMENT

1. In what ways did colonial governments duplicate the governmental institutions of Great Britain?

2. Summarize British attitudes toward the American colonies in the 1700s. Why did these policies and feelings seem logical to the king and Parliament?

3. The first attempts to unify the colonies were mostly failures. Explain why the colonists found it so difficult to work for the "common good" in the early 1700s.

4. What are the strengths and weaknesses of the confederate system of government? Use the Articles of Confederation and the Confederate States of America as examples in your argument.

5. Many critics attack government secrecy as a prime evil. What arguments can you find to support the need for secrecy? Use the strict secrecy rule imposed at the Constitutional Convention of 1787 as a reference point for your discussion.

HANDS-ON ACTIVITIES

1. Today's newspapers are filled with stories of revolutionary violence. Prepare an oral report for your class on the Sons of Liberty and their activities during the pre-Revolutionary period. Compare the Sons of Liberty with present-day organizations whose goal is the overthrow of an existing government. How are the groups alike, and how are they different?

2. Write and perform a skit that explores the British views of the American Revolution. Include the leading politicians of the day—Pitt, Grenville, Lord North, and the others who tried desperately to deal with a situation that quickly escaped their control. Remember that to most of the British people, the colonists were completely unreasonable in their demands. Excellent sources to draw on are such standard works on the Revolution as Knollenberg, *Coming of the Revolution;* Miller, *Origins of the American Revolution;* Commager and Morris, *The Spirit of Seventy-Six;* and Ward, *The War of the Revolution.*

3. If you can locate Richard Morris's interesting book *Seven Who Shaped Our Destiny: The Founding Fathers as Revolutionaries* (Harper & Row, 1973), select one of these seven outstanding Americans as the subject of a poster. Divide your poster into two parts: (1) sketch or paint a picture of the Founder; (2) summarize his life and work in a 100-word paragraph. Display your poster on the class bulletin board.

4. The Constitution was written by 55 delegates and ratified by conventions in each of the 13 states. As a result, the basic law of the land has never been officially approved by American voters. Do people still support a Constitution that was written two centuries ago? As an experiment, pick ten basic constitutional provisions and write them in question form. For example: Do you agree that members of the House of Representatives should be limited to two-year terms? Do you agree that Congress should have the power to "lay and collect taxes"? Do you agree that the President should be Commander-in-Chief of the armed forces? Once you have your list, ask at least ten people from your community to answer your questions. Share the results of your survey with your classmates.

3

"Wisdom and good examples": The broad principles of the Constitution

The heat lay heavy on Philadelphia in the summer of 1787. "A veritable torture," wrote a visiting Frenchman, "is the innumerable flies which constantly light on the face and hands, stinging everywhere." The 55 delegates who met in the State House that summer were forced to endure the heat and the insects. The young country badly needed a workable government.

George Washington spoke for all Americans when he wrote, "No morn ever dawned more favorably than ours did, and no day was ever

59

more clouded than the present! Wisdom and good examples are necessary at this time to rescue the political machine from the impending storm."

In *Miracle at Philadelphia*, Catherine Drinker Bowen describes the final days of the Convention:

> In spite of disagreement, indecision, threats of withdrawal and articles not settled, the Convention was ready [by early September] to put the Constitution into final form and present it to the country.... Madison recorded that a committee had been chosen by ballot to "revise the style of and arrange the articles which had been agreed to by the House." The five men selected were William Samuel Johnson, Alexander Hamilton, Gouverneur Morris, James Madison, and Rufus King. They were called the Committee of Style and Arrangement....
>
> During nearly four months Madison had been incredibly diligent and watchful. For the rest of his life he would be explaining and expounding the new Constitution—in Congress, as President of the United States, and years later at Montpelier, answering letters from all over the country. Now he sat in his place at the conference table, tired, serious, a person who had, wrote one who knew him, "a calm expression, a penetrating blue eye—and looked like a thinking man."
>
> . . . the committee made short work of their new preamble. *"We the People of the United States,"* wrote Morris boldly.... Better to avoid enumeration and let the various states ratify when and if they chose....
>
> No member of the committee has said he knew the significance of that phrase, or guessed it would arouse the bitter oratory of such men as Patrick Henry, to whom the Union meant the states, not the people as a nation.... Nor did the members of the committee foresee that in Europe the phrase would serve as an inspiration, a flag of defiance against absolutist kings....
>
> Having . . . got rid of the hazard of naming states that would not care to be named, Morris's pen proceeded . . . *"in Order,"* he wrote, *"to form a more perfect Union, establish Justice, insure domestic Tranquility, provide for the common defence, promote the general Welfare, and secure the Blessings of Liberty to ourselves and our Posterity, do ordain and establish this Constitution for the United States of America."*
>
> The seven verbs rolled out: to form, establish, insure, provide, promote, secure, ordain. One might challenge the centuries to better these verbs.

Gouverneur Morris went on to reduce the 23 articles agreed on by the convention to 7. Madison said that Morris had reason to be proud of his work, which was done with "finish and style." The convention debated and fine-tuned the language before approving the Constitution on September 15. Two days later, the Framers signed the Constitution and sent it to the Confederation Congress and, later, to the states for ratification.

Thomas Jefferson called the Constitution the "collected wisdom of our country." That wisdom has proven durable, for the document created in 1787 is now the oldest written constitution still in use. The seven sections spell out the duties and powers of the federal government. More important, the Preamble's single paragraph sums up the principles of American democracy. This chapter examines the meaning of those famous phrases, along with some additional constitutional concepts. The questions to be answered include:

1. How did the Constitution create "a more perfect union"?

2. What kind of system did the Framers set up to "establish justice"?

3. What is meant by "insure domestic tranquillity"?

4. How can the nation "provide for the common defense"?

5. How far should government go to "promote the general welfare"?

6. How does government "secure the blessings of liberty" for the people?

7. Why did the Framers provide for a separation of powers?

8. How does the system of checks and balances work?

9. What makes the Constitution a living, growing document?

10. What concepts did the Framers promote in the Constitution?

1. How did the Constitution create "a more perfect union"?

An English teacher might question the use of a phrase like "more perfect." If something is perfect, how can it be bettered? The Framers of the Constitution weren't worried about such matters. They believed that "a more perfect union" would solve the most critical problems created by the Articles of Confederation.

FEDERAL SYSTEM ADOPTED

In 1787, the 13 states were close to acting like separate countries. State legislatures regulated commerce, controlled their own militias, and jealously guarded their independence. If the new nation was to endure, the central government would need greater powers than those delegated under the Articles of Confederation. Out of the debates in Philadelphia came the answer: a federal government. The Framers believed that federalism would create a proper balance between the individual states and the national government. Each level of government was made responsible for the things it could do best.

Several sections of the Constitution, along with several amendments, spell out this division of powers. Most of the duties delegated to the national government are listed in Article I, Section 8. The responsibilities described in specific detail are called the *expressed powers*. In addition, the Constitution specifies that Congress may make all laws "necessary and proper" to carry out its expressed powers. This "elastic clause" has been affirmed by the courts and defined by usage as the basis for the *implied powers* exercised by Congress. (See

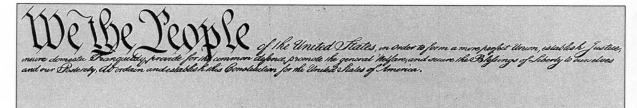

■ The preamble to the Constitution from the final hand-scribed document.

Chapter Eight, pages 172–196, for further discussion of this concept.)

FEDERAL–STATE RELATIONSHIP

Articles IV and VI, as well as a number of amendments, deal with the relationship between the federal and state governments. Federal treaties and laws passed by the U.S. Congress take priority over state laws. This concept is known as *federal supremacy*. The states that wished to raise the 55-miles-per-hour limit on interstate highways, for example, first had to persuade Congress to raise the national limit.

The federal government and the states share many of the same powers. These powers, such as the power to tax, are called *concurrent powers*. The Tenth Amendment in the Bill of Rights specifies that all powers not given to the national government remain with the states and the people. These are called *reserved powers*.

STATE–STATE RELATIONSHIPS

Relationships between states had gone from bad to worse under the Articles of Confederation. To overcome the problems, the Framers ordered that each state should give "full faith and credit to the public acts, records, and judicial proceedings of every other state." A marriage performed in New York, for instance, must be recognized in Ohio. A corporation chartered in Iowa must be allowed to open an office in Oregon. Conversely, both the married couple and the corporation must obey the laws of their new states.

Article IV, Section 2, states: "The citizens of each State shall be entitled to all the privileges and immunities of citizens in the several States." Simply put, this means that a state may not discriminate against nonresidents. This does not prevent a state from charging out-of-state fees for use of tax-supported facilites. Each state also has the right to establish its own residency requirements for voting in local and state elections.

2. What kind of system did the Framers set up to "establish justice"?

The absence of a court system under the Articles of Confederation caused serious problems for the new nation. Although each colony had adopted such British traditions as the common law and trial by jury, laws and courts varied widely from colony to colony.

COLONIAL COMPLAINTS

Colonial unhappiness with the court system helped bring about the Revolution. Protests began when the British shifted some tax trials to Admiralty Courts, where cases involving shipping were heard without a jury. Other colonial defendants were forced to stand trial in Britain, where they could not benefit from sympathetic juries. The Framers knew they had to devise a court system that would calm people's fears and gain their respect.

FEDERAL JUDICIARY CREATED

The problem was solved with the creation of a federal judiciary system (Article III). The

FYI . . .
The Constitution Corrects the Weaknesses of the Articles of Confederation

Weaknesses of the Articles	How corrected by the Constitution
1. No power to collect taxes.	Article I, Section 8, empowers Congress to "lay and collect taxes, duties, imports and excises."
2. No power over interstate and foreign commerce.	Article I, Section 8, gives Congress power to regulate commerce with foreign nations, among the several states, and with Indian tribes.
3. States were sovereign.	People of the whole nation were made sovereign. A federal union was created, and the federal Constitution was made the supreme law of the land.
4. No independent executive.	Article II provides for President chosen indirectly by the voters. President is given "the executive power"; is made commander-in-chief of the Army and Navy; and may take all steps necessary to see that laws are faithfully executed.
5. No federal courts. Federal laws enforced by state courts.	Separate systems of federal courts provided by Article III with authority to enforce federal laws and annul state laws inconsistent with federal Constitution or laws.
6. Congress was an assembly of delegates who were chosen by state legislatures, were expected to vote as instructed, and could be recalled. Each state possessed a single vote.	Congress composed of representatives who have definite tenure and can vote their consciences. House of Representatives chosen by direct vote of people, Senate by state legislatures (now by direct popular vote).
7. Articles could be amended only by consent of all the states.	Constitution can be amended with approval of Congress and three-fourths of states.
8. Congress had only specifically delegated powers.	Constitution gives implied powers to Congress along with a list of expressed powers.

■ Visitors who want to witness the Supreme Court hearings line up outside the Court building as a new term begins. Above the entrance to the building are the words: "Equal Justice Under Law." What does this mean? Over the years, the justices of the nation's highest court have gained the nation's respect and trust by serving as guardians of the people's fundamental liberties. How does the federal court system "establish justice"?

Constitution specifies only that the judicial branch should be composed of a Supreme Court and lower federal courts. Congress was assigned the task of creating the lower courts as needed. The First Congress moved quickly to do just that. The Judiciary Act of 1789 set up a nationwide system of district courts. In 1891, the federal courts of appeals were added to help the Supreme Court deal with its growing case load. (Chapter Fifteen describes the court system in detail.)

BILL OF RIGHTS

Many of the Framers believed that the Constitution was capable of protecting the people's traditional freedoms, but many other Americans disagreed. They had just fought a revolution against tyranny, and they wanted their rights spelled out in the country's basic law. As a result, the ten amendments that make up the *Bill of Rights* were added to the Constitution by the end of Washington's first term. (Chapter Four describes these freedoms in detail.) Similar protections were written into state constitutions.

AMERICAN JUSTICE AT WORK

The American system of justice depends on the people who administer it and the people who use it. Several key beliefs underlie the workings of the courts and the laws of the land: (1) All people are equal before the law. (2) Every person is entitled to treatment that reflects individual dignity and value. (3) Every person accused of a crime is presumed to be innocent until proven guilty.

The system of justice also needs a public that obeys the law, supports the work of the courts, and participates in the making of just laws. The Prohibition experience of the 1920s proved that laws work only when people are willing to obey them. The Eighteenth Amendment prohibited the manufacture and sale of alcoholic beverages, but many people ignored the law and drank "bootleg" liquor. Faced with almost universal resistance, the amendment was repealed in 1933.

3. What is meant by "insure domestic tranquillity"?

A common experience these days begins when a large, noisy party disturbs the peace of a neighborhood. Suddenly, out of the darkness comes the sound of a police bullhorn: "This is an unlawful assembly. You are disturbing the peace. Unless you leave the scene immediately, you will be arrested." The people who hear these orders sometimes claim that their First Amendment right to assemble peaceably has been violated. More accurately, the party goers' rights have come into conflict with the state's duty to preserve the "domestic tranquillity."

PROTECTION AGAINST DISTURBANCE

With every freedom comes an equal responsibility. The right of peaceable assembly does not include the right to trespass on other people's property or to disturb their rest. The Constitution requires that the government, from the President down to local law enforcement officers, insure domestic peace. State constitutions contain similar provisions.

FEDERAL RESPONSES TO DISORDER

Today, the federal government can take any number of actions when faced with civil unrest. The Federal Bureau of Investigation can be called on to provide highly professional law enforcement services. Federal marshals have been used to enforce civil rights laws when local officials refused to act. If riots threaten to get out of control, state governors can ask the President for U.S. Army troops to back up their own National Guard. Most disturbances, however are handled by the regular local and state police.

Natural disasters also upset the domestic tranquillity. State and federal governments provide aid to the victims of such catastrophes as fires, tornados, hurricanes, earthquakes, or floods. The President declares the region a disaster area, sends emergency aid, and provides for low-interest reconstruction loans.

4. How can the United States "provide for the common defense"?

The task of providing for the common defense is divided between Congress and the President. The Constitution gives Congress the power to declare war, ratify alliances, and raise an army and navy. As commander-in-chief of the armed forces, the President makes the decisions that guard our national security. Every President knows that a nuclear attack could destroy America's population centers in the first hours of an all-out war. In an uncertain world, Americans must be prepared for war even as they work for peace.

COSTS OF NATIONAL DEFENSE

Until the 1950s, the United States often retreated into isolationism between wars. At the same time, the armed forces were allowed to deteriorate. In an era of nuclear-tipped missiles, however, the nation can no longer afford to ignore its defenses. The 1980s were a time of relative peace, but the armed forces kept more than two million men and women in uniform. Even though the danger of war with the Sovet Union diminished as the 1990s began, the costs of maintaining a strong defense still run about $300 billion each year. That figure works out to over $1,200 per citizen.

■ To "provide for the common defense," the U.S. government has spent billions to develop weapons such as the controversial B-2 (Stealth) bomber. Should the United States continue to develop such costly weapons now that the cold war appears to be over?

COMPONENTS OF NATIONAL DEFENSE

Modern war, hot or cold, demands more of a country than keeping soldiers in uniform. National defense also requires:

1. *National will.* America's involvement in the nation's most unpopular war ended in 1973, when U.S. troops left Vietnam. This retreat came after a large number of Americans demanded an end to the war. As that experience proves, an informed, patriotic population, proud of their country and its ideals, is the first requirement for an effective national defense. People sometimes lose faith in their leaders because of misguided national policies or the propaganda efforts of their enemies. When that happens, raw military strength may not be enough to win a victory.

2. *Technology.* With scientific breakthroughs coming so fast, today's weapons may be obsolete tomorrow. Fortunately, this country has the scientists, raw materials, and factories to support a vast program of research and development. Some people say that this investment in military hardware is both wasteful and unnecessary. The defenders of the policy answer that the nation cannot afford to reduce its defense spending until the United States and the Soviet Union find a way to eliminate all nuclear arms.

3. *Foreign alliances.* The economy of this country depends on access to foreign raw materials and factory products from many areas. For example, we import oil from the Middle East and Mexico, aluminum ore from Jamaica, and electronic gear from Japan. We also need to export goods to other countries. Relations with our trading partners are sometimes difficult, but the United States depends on its economic alliances. Without certain imports, the nation's ability to defend itself would be in danger. If we cannot export the products of our industries, our high standard of living would also decline.

The U.S. armed forces are very strong, but they cannot defend every corner of the globe. The solution to that problem lies in military alliances. Should global conflict begin, the United States will combine its military and economic strength with that of its allies. Our allies, in turn, expect the United States to honor its treaty obligations. Despite their importance, these treaties are not always popular with Congress and the American people.

FYI . . .
Where Did the Framers Get Their Ideas?

Colonial leaders were familiar with the great ideas of Western civilization. When the Framers set out to write the Constitution, they drew upon the wisdom of philosophers, historians, and economists. Here are a few of the people whose words influenced the content of that remarkable document.

Concept: *The people have the right to rule themselves.*

Aristotle (384–322 B.C.). An argument for the concept of rule by the people comes from the words of a Greek philosopher. Aristotle wrote, "That the people at large should be sovereign rather than the few best would appear to be defensible. . . . There is this to be said for the Many. Each of them by himself may not be of a good quality; but when they all come together it is possible that they may surpass . . . the quality of the few best." (from *Essays on Politics*.)

Concept: *The rights of the individual are supreme.*

John Locke (1632–1704). In an age when many people believed that monarchs ruled by divine right, John Locke spoke out for individual rights. The Englishman believed that government was a compact between a people and their rulers. If the government violated this agreement, he wrote, "they forfeit the Power the People had put into their hands . . . and it [returns] to the People, who have a Right to resume their original Liberty . . ." (from *Two Treatises of Government*.)

Concept: *The separation of powers ensures a free government.*

Baron Charles de Montesquieu (1689–1755). The words of Montesquieu, a French philosopher, pointed the Framers toward the concept of the separation of powers. Montesquieu wrote, "When the legislative and executive powers are united in the same person, or in the same body of magistrates, there can be no liberty; . . . Again, there is no liberty if the judiciary power be not separated from the legislative and executive." (from *Spirit of Laws*.)

Concept: *A free economy provides the highest standard of living.*

Adam Smith (1723–1790). Adam Smith was a Scottish economist who believed that the true wealth of a nation is measured by the goods and services that business makes available to its people. Government can best promote business, he said, by leaving it alone. Smith explained, "The businessman intends only his own gain; however, . . . By pursuing his own interest, he frequently promotes that of society more effectually than when he really intends to promote it." (from *Wealth of Nations*.)

5. How far should government go to "promote the general welfare"?

When the Constitution was written, social welfare was thought to be mostly a private responsibility. In this century, the federal government has taken a much more active role to "promote the general welfare."

Today the United States spends billions of dollars for the nation's medical, educational, and economic needs. Because of these huge costs, more and more people are asking a critical question: How far should government go in promoting each citizen's general welfare? That question leads to a second: How much are people willing to pay to provide these services?

To some degree, the first question has already been answered. Most Americans want the federal government to act as the primary force in maintaining our quality of life. Every day, Americans come into contact with the work of government's many agencies. People's health, education, working conditions, and recreation all depend heavily on the work of the men and women we pay to "promote the general welfare."

COSTS OF GOVERNMENT SERVICES

A government that is growing in size and influence costs more and more money. (See the table on page 68 for a look at how the cost of social services has increased in just 50 years.) The average taxpayer in the United States works almost two days out of five to pay for the services of local, state, and federal government. Of all of the items in each American's budget (food, housing, transportation, and the like), taxes have grown faster than any other.

The cost of public services can also be measured by the government's growing influence on how Americans live. For example, federal agencies set safety standards, regulate working hours, and protect the environment. Federal programs support scientific research, help students attend college, and keep farmers from going bankrupt. To provide all of these services, the government employs more people than any single business or industry in the country.

ECONOMIC ASSISTANCE

The federal government provides economic assistance for those who cannot support themselves. Welfare programs care for the aged,

FEDERAL SOCIAL WELFARE PROGRAMS GROW MORE EXPENSIVE EVERY YEAR

	Old Age and Survivors Insurance	Disability Insurance	Federal Civil Service Retirement	Hospital Insurance	State Unemployment Insurance
	(IN BILLIONS OF DOLLARS)				
1940	$ .6	—	$ .1	—	$ .9
1950	2.1	—	.7	—	1.1
1960	9.8	$ 1.0	1.5	—	2.2
1970	30.0	4.1	3.7	$ 4.9	2.6
1975	56.0	7.4	9.3	11.3	5.3
1980	97.6	16.8	19.5	23.5	11.9
1984	158.7	15.4	25.8	42.7	19.4
1990	224.4	22.3	55.2	94.9	16.0

Note: This chart does not list all government social programs. The costs of social welfare programs have increased from under five percent of the gross national product in 1945 to over twenty percent in the 1980s. Social welfare services now take more than three dollars out of every five collected by the national, state, and local governments.

the handicapped, the unemployed, the poor, the hungry, the sick, and the uneducated. About half of every federal budget dollar goes to health, education, and welfare services.

How much more is the American public willing to be taxed to pay for economic assistance? Critics charge that the system tends to discourage individual effort. The American business system is based on the idea that most adults will take care of their own needs. People who don't work and who don't pay taxes become a burden for those who do. Moreover, the growing federal budget deficit sets limits on how much the government can spend to provide for the general welfare.

Let's review for a moment

In the brief Preamble to the Constitution, the Framers summed up the objectives of American government:

> We, the People of the United States, in Order to form a more perfect Union, establish Justice, insure domestic Tranquility, provide for the common defence, promote the general Welfare, and secure the Blessings of Liberty to ourselves and our Posterity, do ordain and establish this Constitution for the United States of America.

How close has this country come to achieving these goals? Although opinions differ, a majority would probably say that we've come a long way—but there's still a distance to go.

The Constitution attempted to form "a more perfect union" by establishing a federal system of government. Under that concept, the national government shares power with the individual states. The Constitution gives the national government the right to do many things—the *expressed* and *implied powers*. All other government powers are reserved to the states.

In order to "establish justice," the Constitution created a Supreme Court and gave Congress the power to establish a federal

court system. The Framers believed that the Constitution's original seven articles would be sufficient to protect traditional freedoms. The Bill of Rights was added soon after ratification as a way of spelling out these protections in greater detail.

To "insure domestic tranquility," the government tries to create a safe environment, protect people's rights, and provide aid when natural disasters occur. On the international level, the government spends billions of dollars on the American military in order to "provide for the common defense."

The meaning of "promote the general welfare" has changed greatly since 1787. The American people today demand more and more services from their government. These include food stamps, Medicare, social security, veterans' benefits, aid to education, rent subsidies, and environmental protection. Not everyone agrees on how much the federal government should spend on social welfare programs.

6. How does government "secure the blessings of liberty" for the people?

The media often run stories that ask questions about individual liberties. What are the rights of a person accused of a crime or an anti-nuclear protest? What happens when the individual's right to self-expression conflicts with the will of the community? Americans have usually sided with the cause of individual rights. The nation has never forgotten Patrick Henry's ringing cry of "Give me liberty or give me death!"

The addition of the Bill of Rights to the Constitution guaranteed the new country's freedoms. The people's rights were also protected by the British system of common law. Foreigners who visited the United States during the 1780s returned home to report that Americans were the freest people in the history of the world.

Rights Guaranteed in Constitutions Throughout the World

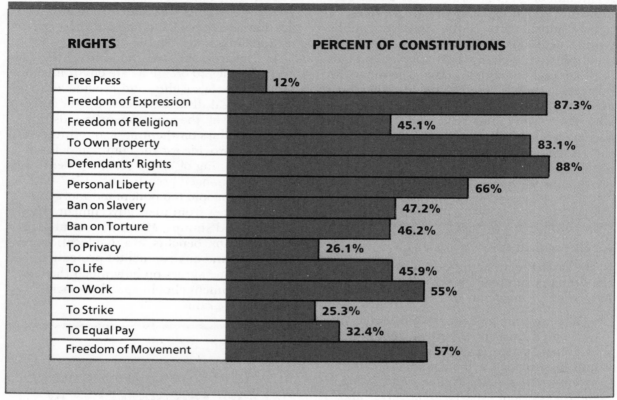

RIGHTS	PERCENT OF CONSTITUTIONS
Free Press	12%
Freedom of Expression	87.3%
Freedom of Religion	45.1%
To Own Property	83.1%
Defendants' Rights	88%
Personal Liberty	66%
Ban on Slavery	47.2%
Ban on Torture	46.2%
To Privacy	26.1%
To Life	45.9%
To Work	55%
To Strike	25.3%
To Equal Pay	32.4%
Freedom of Movement	57%

■ The freedoms Americans take for granted are often lacking in the constitutions of other countries. As this graph shows, only 12 percent of the world's constitutions guarantee freedom of the press. Fewer than half ban slavery and torture outright. Some governments may grant certain rights in their constitutions and then ignore these rights in their treatment of their citizens. What rights are essential in a healthy democracy?

LIBERTY IS NOT ABSOLUTE

An entire society benefits when its people have freedom of thought, freedom of choice, and freedom of movement. Some people, however, accept—even demand—liberty for themselves and do not consider extending it to others. The colonists who fought for their independence from Great Britain saw little reason to give full rights of citizenship to women, blacks, and Indians.

Most Americans now think of liberty in terms of their interactions with others. Liberty, they say, is the right to pursue one's own life-style, occupation, and personal philosophy. No one's freedom, however, should interfere with the right of others to enjoy their own lives and property.

To secure the "blessings of liberty," the government has designed a series of safeguards. Some of them protect the individual. Others limit individual freedom in order to promote the greater social good. The right to drive a car is a good example of this principle. Everyone who qualifies for a license has the right to drive a car, but the government cannot allow reckless drivers to endanger other people. If convicted of drunk driving, people can lose their licenses and may go to jail.

History shows that the breakdown of social controls can destroy a society. Indeed, most people feel more comfortable when they have rules to govern their behavior. True freedom exists only when a country's citizens support a democratic government that acts for the common good.

LIBERTY VERSUS REGULATION

American society is always making difficult choices. On one hand, the demand for more and better government services is growing stronger. On the other hand, many people are demanding more personal freedom. As you learned earlier, increased government services may mean increased government regulation. Local, state, and federal governments now regulate some part of almost every phase of life, from marriage and childbirth to death and burial.

The national debate over the use of nuclear power has created a serious dilemma. How do we balance the need for more power sources with the responsibility of protecting the health of our citizens? Pronuclear forces defend the right of private companies to build and operate nuclear plants. The antinuclear forces argue that the dangers of radiation and nuclear accidents outweigh the benefits. Government is caught in the middle. Thus far, the Nuclear Regulatory Commission has allowed nuclear plants to operate but only under strict rules. The debate over the degree to which individual and corporate rights should be subordinated to the welfare of the larger community is likely to go on for a long time.

7. Why did the Framers provide for a separation of powers?

In the 1700s, a French philosopher named Montesquieu (MON-*tes*-cue) developed a theory known as the *separation of powers*. Montesquieu believed that tyranny results when a single government body holds all the power. In a democracy, he said, power must be divided among an *executive branch* (to administer the laws), a *legislative branch* (to make the laws), and a *judicial branch* (to interpret the laws). Only then, Montesquieu concluded, will a political system remain responsible, limited, and free.

THREE BRANCHES OF GOVERNMENT

The First Continental Congress accepted the idea of separation of powers. State constitutions written during the Revolutionary War also reflected the theory. When the Constitutional Convention met, Madison argued that separation of powers was a "fundamental principle of free government."

As a result, the Framers created three separate-but-equal branches of government. The power to make laws was placed in a legislative branch composed of the two houses of Congress. The power to enforce the law was given to an executive branch headed by the President. The power to interpret the law was located in a judicial branch headed by the Supreme Court. The separation of powers has been successful. Each branch acts to keep the other two from becoming too powerful.

SHIFTING POWERS OF THE THREE BRANCHES

Over 200 years, the federal government has evolved in ways the Framers could never have imagined. Some of the most controversial changes have brought increased power to the executive and judicial branches.

1. *The "imperial presidency."* Ever since the administration of Franklin Roosevelt (1933–1945), some critics have charged that the presidency has outstripped the other two branches in its ability to make and carry out policy. They believe that this "imperial presidency" has created a type of American "emperor." Congress attempted to restore the balance of power after the Watergate scandal led to the end of Richard Nixon's presidency in the 1970s. These efforts were only partially successful. Popular Presidents, with their

The Three Branches of the Federal Government, 1790 and 1990

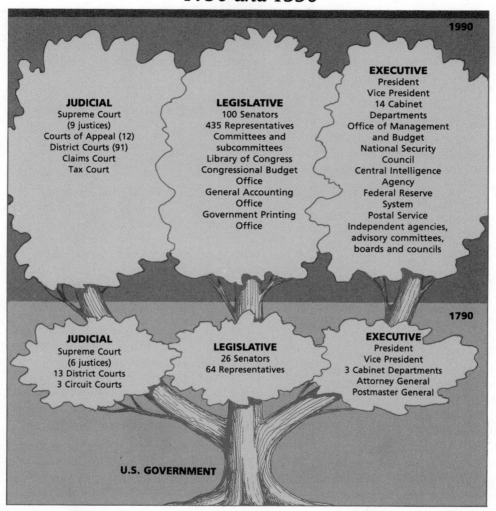

1990

JUDICIAL
Supreme Court
(9 justices)
Courts of Appeal (12)
District Courts (91)
Claims Court
Tax Court

LEGISLATIVE
100 Senators
435 Representatives
Committees and
subcommittees
Library of Congress
Congressional Budget
Office
General Accounting
Office
Government Printing
Office

EXECUTIVE
President
Vice President
14 Cabinet
Departments
Office of Management
and Budget
National Security
Council
Central Intelligence
Agency
Federal Reserve
System
Postal Service
Independent agencies,
advisory committees,
boards and councils

1790

JUDICIAL
Supreme Court
(6 justices)
13 District Courts
3 Circuit Courts

LEGISLATIVE
26 Senators
64 Representatives

EXECUTIVE
President
Vice President
3 Cabinet Departments
Attorney General
Postmaster General

U.S. GOVERNMENT

■ From its modest beginnings in 1790, the federal government has grown in size and scope as the needs of the nation have changed. In spite of their huge growth, the three branches still maintain the separation of powers written into the Constitution. Which branch appears to have expanded the most? How has this affected the system of checks and balances?

enormous budgets and their control of influential executive branch departments, still outbalance the legislature and the courts.

2. The "fourth branch." Congress has delegated more and more responsibility to independent regulatory agencies. These agencies, which regulate specific business and social activities, have become so important that they are sometimes called the "fourth branch" of government. Some agencies, such as the Interstate Commerce Commission and the Federal Communications Commission, exercise both legislative and judicial powers. Even though the agencies affect our business and private lives, their directors do not run for election. Presidents appoint these powerful men and women, but they can't control the decisions made by the directors.

3. *"Judicial legislation."* The courts have received their own share of the criticism. The hottest debate grows out of the charge that judges practice "judicial legislation"—making the law instead of interpreting it. The criticism was loudest during the 1950s and 1960s when the Supreme Court under Chief Justice Earl Warren struck down a series of segregation laws. Opponents of judicial legislation believe that Congress should settle such problems by passing new laws. If the voters don't like the way their representative votes, they can elect someone else. Supreme Court justices, the critics point out, do not have to face the voters.

8. How does the system of checks and balances work?

In addition to the idea of separation of powers, Montesquieu contributed the concept of *checks and balances*. The philosopher believed that each of the three branches of government should check, or limit, the powers of the other two. In that way, no one branch would be truly independent of the other two. This system creates six basic relationships. (See the illustration on page 74.)

1. THE EXECUTIVE CHECKS THE JUDICIARY

From the Supreme Court down to the district courts, the President appoints all federal judges. By choosing judges who share a common philosophy, the Chief Executive can influence the decisions of the courts for a generation or longer. It should be noted, however, that a President may not interfere in any case that is being heard by a judge. Similarly, justices never confer with the President before handing down their decisions.

2. THE EXECUTIVE CHECKS THE LEGISLATURE

The President can veto (refuse to sign) any bill passed by Congress (see Chapter Nine, pages 197–218). This check on legislative action can be overcome but only by a hard-to-get two-thirds vote of both houses of Congress. The President also checks the power of Congress by (a) proposing new legislation, (b) refusing to use powers delegated by Congress, (c) refusing to spend money voted by Congress, (d) campaigning for or against members of Congress, (e) appealing directly to the people for support, and (f) calling special sessions of Congress.

The Constitution specifies only the first and last powers, (a) and (f). The others are practices that have developed through usage. Each has been tested in the courts. The Supreme Court ruled in early 1975, for instance, that the Constitution does not give the President express authority to "impound" funds properly voted by Congress (item (c) in the previous list). Does the President have the implied power to do so? That question awaits further court tests.

3. THE LEGISLATURE CHECKS THE JUDICIARY

Except for the Supreme Court, the entire federal court system was established by Congress. The legislature could change or do away with the lower courts if it decided to do so. In addition, the Senate must approve the appointment of all federal judges. Two of President Nixon's candidates for the Supreme Court failed to gain Senate confirmation, and President Reagan lost two similar battles in 1987. Congress also sets the salaries of all federal judges, but it cannot punish judges by lowering their pay while they're serving on the bench. Finally, Congress has the power to *impeach* (accuse), try, and remove from office a federal judge whose conduct on the bench violates the public trust.

4. THE LEGISLATURE CHECKS THE EXECUTIVE

Congress holds one major advantage in its relations with the President—the power of the purse. Only Congress can appropriate funds for the operation of the executive branch. Each year, administration officials must go to the Capitol to explain their programs and to plead for their budgets. In the battle for funding that follows, Congress rarely gives the executive branch everything it requests.

Checks and Balances in American Government

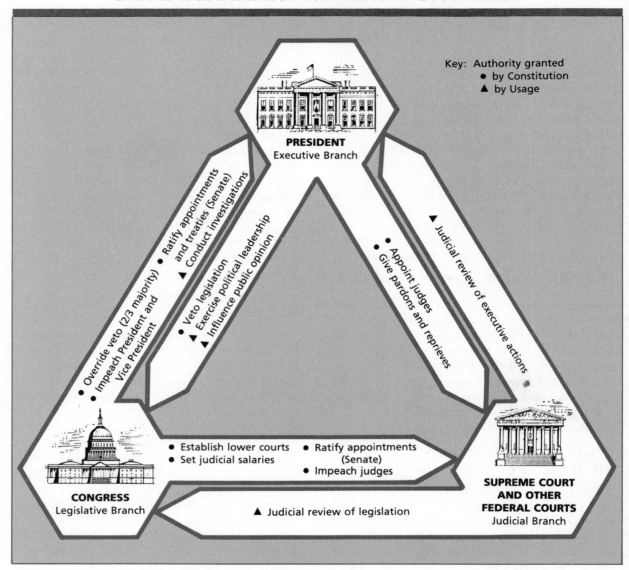

Key: Authority granted
- ● by Constitution
- ▲ by Usage

PRESIDENT
Executive Branch

- Ratify appointments and treaties (Senate)
- ▲ Conduct investigations
- Override veto (2/3 majority)
- Impeach President and Vice President
- Veto legislation
- ▲ Exercise political leadership
- ▲ Influence public opinion
- Appoint judges
- Give pardons and reprieves
- ▲ Judicial review of executive actions

- ● Establish lower courts
- ● Set judicial salaries
- ● Ratify appointments (Senate)
- ● Impeach judges

CONGRESS
Legislative Branch

▲ Judicial review of legislation

SUPREME COURT AND OTHER FEDERAL COURTS
Judicial Branch

Congress also plays a role in foreign policy through its power to declare war, grant foreign aid, determine the size of the military, and (in the Senate) approve treaties. The Senate has the additional right of confirming presidential appointees—Cabinet members, ambassadors, members of commissions, and the like. As a final check, the Constitution gives Congress the power to impeach all officials in the executive branch, from the President on down.

5. THE JUDICIARY CHECKS THE EXECUTIVE

The power of *judicial review* gives the courts the right to examine the actions of the executive branch. An executive order or regulation that is found to be unconstitutional will be set aside by the courts. Federal judges also use court orders called injunctions to forbid some actions and to modify others.

6. THE JUDICIARY CHECKS THE LEGISLATURE

Judicial review also applies to all federal laws and those state laws that involve federal questions. The process works slowly, for someone must challenge a particular law before the courts can examine its legality under the Constitution. A court test usually begins in the lower courts and works its way up to the Supreme Court in a series of appeals. Any federal court may declare a law unconstitutional. The decision stands unless someone appeals it. Once a law has been found unconstitutional, it loses its legal force everywhere in the United States and its possessions.

9. What makes the Constitution a living, growing document?

The two-centuries-old Constitution still gives this country a fresh and vigorous blueprint for government. Historian Charles Beard tried to explain the Constitution's ability to adjust to change. Beard said, "The Constitution . . . is what living men and women think it is." Reaching agreement on what the Constitution means, however, has not been easy.

STRICT CONSTRUCTION AND LOOSE CONSTRUCTION

At first, many Americans feared that the federal government was too strong. The courts tended to agree, and gave the Constitution a *strict construction*. Strict constructionists say that the government cannot do anything that is not expressly allowed by the Constitution. Jefferson and Madison led the strict constructionists during the first years of the new government. Today, people who follow that point of view are labeled conservatives.

Over the years, the strict constructionists began to lose ground. A new belief arose that favored the federal government's use of its implied powers to meet changing social and economic conditions. This *loose construction* of the Constitution has led to increased government influence in many areas of American life. Today's loose constructionists are called liberals. Time, however, alters the meaning of political labels. Views thought to be liberal in the early 1800s seem quite conservative today.

Loose construction has enabled Congress to pass laws needed by a changing country. The courts approved the use of implied powers in the case of *McCulloch* v. *Maryland* in 1819 (see pages 390–391). Those opposed to the use of implied powers charge that expanded federal regulation means fewer personal liberties. One of the important challenges facing today's courts is to define the proper balance between personal freedoms and the power of the federal government.

BRIEF AND CLEAR

Another strength of the Constitution lies in the fact that it's quite short. Many state constitutions are hundreds of pages long, but the U.S. Constitution is short enough to be read in half an hour. Its language is clear and direct. The Framers did not use confusing phrases or unnecessary words.

Being short isn't always a virtue. The Framers sometimes created problems by failing to address an issue. What if a state wants to secede from the Union? The Constitution's silence on the issue of secession helped lead the nation into the Civil War.

UNWRITTEN CONSTITUTION

Custom and usage have created a body of political traditions that form an *unwritten constitution*. Political parties, primary elections, and conventions have become important parts of the political process even though none of them is mentioned in the Constitution. The President's Cabinet is not mentioned by name nor is its structure described. Similarly, outgoing Presidents are guided only by custom when they work with a President-elect to ensure an orderly transition of power.

10. What concepts did the Framers promote in the Constitution?

The Framers created a government that reflected their own philosophy and the colonial experience. They based the Constitution on four important concepts:

1. CAPITALISM

The Framers believed in capitalism. As Thomas Jefferson explained, "Agriculture, Manufacture, Commerce, and Navigation, the four pillars of our Prosperity, are the most thriving when left to individual Enterprise." With that encouragement, the American free enterprise system grew and prospered.

Left to develop on its own, business sometimes lost sight of its social responsibilities. Americans recoiled from the excesses of unrestricted free enterprise and agreed that some degree of regulation was needed. Alexander Hamilton didn't particularly love the common people, but he spoke of the Constitution in a way most Americans would approve. "It is by this [Constitution], . . . ," Hamilton said, "that the rich and the powerful are to be restrained from enterprises against the common liberty."

2. STABILITY

Judged by today's standards, the Framers were not interested in a broad-based democracy. They attempted to keep the country

Learning Skills

Using the Library

Some students become discouraged when they walk into a library. They see thousands of books, magazines, tapes, catalogs, indexes, and other materials. Where do you start? Is it possible to find anything in that huge haystack? Luckily, libraries are organized to make finding things easy. Here are the basic rules for doing library research:

1. *Know what you're looking for.* You'll save time and effort if you know what you want when you go into the library. Some people waste time by wandering around, hoping that the books they need will fall into their hands.

2. *If you need help, ask for it.* A librarian's primary job is to help people find what they need. You can't expect the librarians to do your work for you, but they can point you in the right direction. In addition, if you don't know how to use the card catalog or the microfilm reader, they'll give you a quick training course.

3. *Use the card catalog.* Imagine that you're doing research for a paper on amendments to the U.S. Constitution. Go to the card catalog and check the subject heading for that topic. The older catalogs are made up of trays of 3 × 5 cards, but the newer ones have been computerized. If you don't find the topic under the first heading you try, keep digging. Try *Amendments, U.S. Constitution* or *U.S. Constitution—Amendments.* Each library has a slightly different way of organizing subject headings, so don't give up too soon. If you already have a list of books that sound useful, you can find them in the catalog by the author's name or by the title. Write the entire number down before you leave the catalog. Once

stable by preserving the existing social values. The vote, they believed, should be entrusted only to property owners. Such people were thought to have the strongest interest in good government. Far from locking the United States into a repressive system, however, the Constitution left each state free to define its own voter qualifications. As the demand for the right to vote grew, the system gradually broadened the franchise.

3. OPTIMISM

American government reflects the Jeffersonian view that people are rational. Clear-thinking men and women, the Framers believed, will keep themselves well informed. They will be concerned about the well-being of both their country and their fellow citizens. The Constitution thus reflects the beliefs of the late 1700s, when people were optimistic about humanity's future.

4. CHANGE

Even as they wrote the best Constitution they could, the Framers allowed for change. Several methods of amending the basic document were included:

1. An *amendment* may be proposed by a two-thirds vote in both houses of Congress. It must then be ratified by three-fourths of the state legislatures. Twenty-five out of twenty-six amendments were enacted in this way.

2. An amendment may be proposed by a two-thirds vote in both houses of Congress. It must then be ratified by three-fourths of the

---

you're back in the stacks, it's easy to forget a long call number.

4. *Find the books on the shelves.* Libraries shelve their books according to a numbering system. The Dewey Decimal system is the most common, but large university libraries use the Library of Congress system. Both systems assign a specific number to each book, and the books are shelved according to those numbers. If you're researching American government in a library that uses Dewey numbers, you'll probably find your books under call number 320.973.

5. *Try the magazine indexes.*
you've exhausted the card catalog, try the magazine indexes. Year by year, *Readers' Guide to Periodical Literature* lists the articles published in many national magazines. Look for your subject heading, just as you did in the card catalog. Once you find useful references, check to see if the library has those magazines on file. Sometimes you'll find the actual magazine, either as a loose issue or bound into yearly volumes. More often, you'll find the magazines copied onto microfilm or microfiche. The librarian can introduce you to other, more specialized indexes, too.

Once you've struck pay dirt, the rest is up to you. You can check the books out and take them home, or you can do your note taking in the library. Reference materials don't circulate, so you'll have to use them in the library. If you have some change in your pocket, you can photocopy the most important pages.

The more you use your library, the better you'll get at finding the treasures it holds. Happy hunting!

How Do You Change the Constitution?

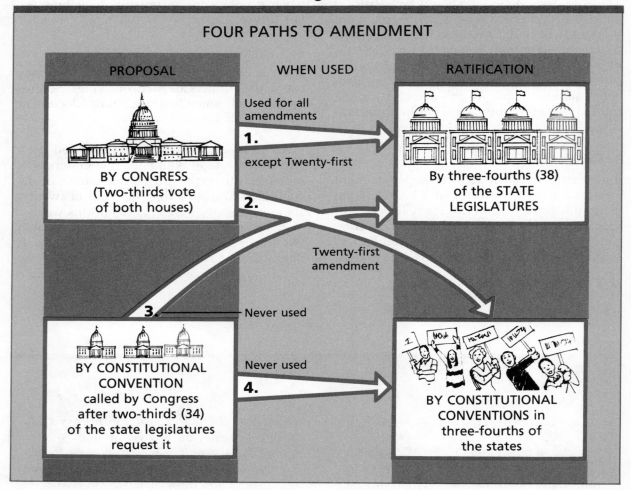

FOUR PATHS TO AMENDMENT

PROPOSAL	WHEN USED	RATIFICATION

PROPOSAL

BY CONGRESS
(Two-thirds vote
of both houses)

BY CONSTITUTIONAL
CONVENTION
called by Congress
after two-thirds (34)
of the state legislatures
request it

WHEN USED

Used for all amendments
1.

except Twenty-first
2.

Twenty-first amendment

3. — Never used

Never used
4.

RATIFICATION

By three-fourths (38)
of the STATE
LEGISLATURES

BY CONSTITUTIONAL
CONVENTIONS in
three-fourths of
the states

states at special conventions called for that purpose. The Twenty-first Amendment, which repealed Prohibition, was passed in this way.

3. If two-thirds of the state legislatures request it, Congress can call a national constitutional convention to propose amendments. Approval by three-fourths of the state legislatures must ratify any amendments proposed by the convention. Political scientists fear that a constitutional convention might "run wild," passing amendments that could damage the Constitution and our system of government.

4. A convention similar to the type noted in method 3 may also propose amendments, but these would be considered by individual state conventions. The amendments would become law if ratified by a three-fourths majority of the state conventions. The Constitution was ratified under a similar plan.

Additional change has come through a process called *informal amendment*. Two hundred years of solving problems unforeseen by the Framers have added an invisible network of laws, regulations, court decisions, and custom to the Constitution. As problems have arisen, government has found ways to meet the challenges. Typically, informal amendment begins when the legislature passes a new law to deal with a specific issue. If someone challenges the law, the case works its way up to the Supreme Court, which rules on the law's constitutionality. In some cases, the Court has restricted federal activities; in others, it has expanded the scope of federal control.

A good example of informal amendment can be found in the field of civil rights. Civil War-era amendments to the Constitution began the process of freeing America's blacks and guaranteeing their civil rights. Later, Congress passed laws that extended those rights in specific areas, such as voter registration. Finally, the courts ordered the President to enforce the civil rights protections provided by the Constitution. In this way, all three branches of the federal government contributed to the drive for racial equality.

Reviewing
what you've learned

1. In the Preamble to the Constitution, the Framers outlined the basic goals of the new government:

a. *Create "a more perfect union."* By establishing a federal system of government, the Constitution eliminated the weaknesses of the Articles of Confederation. The expressed and implied powers gave the national government the authority it needed to govern effectively.

b. *"Establish justice."* The Constitution established a federal judiciary as an equal branch of government in order to hear cases involving federal laws. The Bill of Rights was added to the Constitution in order to provide further guarantees of individual rights.

c. *"Insure domestic tranquillity."* Limited police powers were written into the Constitution so that government could protect its citizens from domestic disturbances. The government also gives aid to victims of natural disasters.

d. *"Provide for the common defense."* Despite the heavy costs in money and resources, the United States must maintain strong defense forces. Our defense depends on (1) a strong national will, (2) advanced weapons technology, and (3) trustworthy foreign alliances.

e. *"Promote the general welfare."* Most Americans today look to the federal government to maintain a high quality of life for all. The "general welfare" has come to include care for the aged, disabled, young, and unemployed; aid for education and health programs; and protection of the environment. Aid is targeted for people who cannot escape poverty or illness without help. Social welfare programs consume a large part of all government spending.

f. *"Secure the blessings of liberty."* With government services comes government regulation—of both individual and business life. The nation is still trying to find a balance between protecting personal liberties and meeting the needs of society.

2. The Framers adopted the theory of *separation of powers* in order to prevent any one branch of the government—*legislative, executive,* or *judicial*—from assuming tyrannical control. Some critics believe that the presidency has grown so powerful that it overshadows the other two branches.

3. The idea of *checks and balances* gives each branch of government the responsibility for performing its own duties while also "checking" the activities of the others. For example, the President checks Congress through the veto power and the judiciary through the power of appointment. The judicial branch exercises the power of *judicial review* over the actions of both Congress and the President. Congress checks both of the other branches through its control of the federal budget and the power of impeachment.

4. The Constitution is alive and flexible. The Framers made this possible through the *implied powers* clause and by writing a short, clear document. *Loose constructionists* make full use of the government's implied powers. An unwritten constitution has also come into existence. It is made up of customs, practices, and institutions—the President's Cabinet, for example—that have proven their worth.

5. Underlying the language of the Constitution are four assumptions held by the Framers: (a) the capitalistic system of private enterprise, (b) the preservation of traditional social values, (c) optimism regarding human society, and (d) the expectation that amendments would be needed in the future.

6. Only 26 formal amendments have been added to the Constitution despite the great changes that have taken place in American society. Flexible, farsighted, and free of excess words, the Constitution deserves the praise given it by a famous British politician, William Gladstone. He said, "I have always regarded that Constitution as the most remarkable work known to me in modern times to have been produced by the human intellect."

Review questions and activities

TERMS YOU SHOULD KNOW

Bill of Rights	impeach	loose construction
checks and balances	implied powers	reserved powers
concurrent powers	informal amendment	separation of powers
domestic tranquillity	judicial branch	strict construction
executive branch	judicial review	unwritten constitution
expressed powers	legislative branch	

REVIEW QUESTIONS

Select the response that best completes each statement or question.

1. Which of the following can a state refuse to a family that recently moved there from another state? (*a*) The right to vote in local elections until the adults have established residency. (*b*) The right to send children to the public schools. (*c*) Recognition of the legality of the parents' marriage. (*d*) The right to run a business that competes with local businesses. (*e*) None of these matters can be regulated by a state.

2. Which of the following is *not* true about U.S. justice? (*a*) An individual is presumed innocent until proven guilty. (*b*) All people are equal before the law. (*c*) Every person must be treated with dignity and respect. (*d*) Law enforcement officers cannot interfere with activities carried on in the privacy of one's home. (*e*) The U.S. legal system adjusts to meet changing social values and needs.

3. The largest single share of the federal budget goes toward (*a*) defense. (*b*) social welfare. (*c*) highway construction. (*d*) foreign aid. (*e*) interest on the national debt.

4. The average taxpayer works how many days out of five in the normal workweek to pay for the services of local, state, and federal governments? (*a*) one-half day. (*b*) one day. (*c*) almost two days. (*d*) two and a half days. (*e*) three days.

5. A useful definition of personal freedom in a democracy would be the (*a*) right to make one's own decisions as long as those choices don't interfere with anyone else's rights. (*b*) right to do anything one wishes to do. (*c*) obligation to serve the government in the best way possible. (*d*) obligation to take orders without asking questions. (*e*) right to do anything one can afford to do.

6. The Constitution makes no provision for the independent regulatory agencies. In creating them, therefore, Congress used its (*a*) power of judicial review. (*b*) implied powers. (*c*) veto override power. (*d*) power of *habeas corpus*. (*e*) power of the purse.

7. The President checks the actions of the legislative branch through formal and informal means, including (*a*) the veto. (*b*) public opinion. (*c*) influence over congressional election campaigns. (*d*) refusal to spend money appropriated by Congress. (*e*) all of these.

8. Once the Supreme Court has declared a law unconstitutional, the legislative and executive branches (*a*) can ignore the Court's decision. (*b*) can fire the judges and appoint new ones who will agree with their position. (*c*) can punish the judges by lowering their salaries. (*d*) must accept the decision as final. (*e*) can make the law legal by asking the state legislatures to pass it as a state law.

9. Which of the following American institutions or traditions would be considered part of the unwritten constitution? (*a*) A bicameral Congress. (*b*) Political parties and national conventions. (*c*) The Vice President. (*d*) Freedom of religion and speech. (*e*) The system of checks and balances.

10. Despite the many changes that have taken place in American society since 1787, the Constitution has been amended only (*a*) 10 times. (*b*) 20 times. (*c*) 26 times. (*d*) 34 times. (*e*) 42 times.

CONCEPT DEVELOPMENT

1. Imagine that you have been asked to establish a system of government that provides justice for all citizens. What features would you insist on in such a government?

2. What limits on individual liberties are necessary in a modern, urban society?

3. What arguments can you think of in favor of putting less emphasis on defense spending (missiles and submarines) and more on spending for social welfare (education and health care)? What arguments lead to the opposite conclusion?

4. Explain the thinking behind the system of checks and balances. Why doesn't this system automatically cause government to come to a standstill, with each branch keeping the others from working?

5. Read a history of the Constitutional Convention. What issues took the most time to resolve? What alternatives to our present form of government did the Framers consider?

HANDS-ON ACTIVITIES

1. The system of checks and balances is one of the keystones of our government. Make a poster or a bulletin board display that illustrates this concept. The diagram on page 74 can serve as a guide, but use illustrations (either your own drawings or pictures clipped from magazines) to add interest. The finished display will serve as a quick and dramatic reminder of how this important process works.

2. Two excellent books on the Constitutional Convention are Clinton Rossiter's *1787: The Grand Convention* and Catherine Drinker Bowen's *Miracle at Philadelphia.* Using these books as sources, write a dramatic skit that focuses on one of the major issues faced by the convention. Some sample topics: federation versus confederation, proportional representation, role of the executive, three-fifths compromise. With the help of volunteers, act out the skit for the class. (Remember that much of the work of the convention was done in the evenings, when delegates met to talk quietly and informally about the issues.)

3. Write a short paper comparing separation of powers in the British parliamentary system and the American federal system. What advantages and disadvantages can you find in each? How have the British resolved the weaknesses in their system that the Framers saw and tried to avoid in 1787?

4. Amending the Constitution of the United States is a long, difficult process. You'll find the process easier to understand if you look into the possibility of amending your student government's constitution. Begin by studying the constitution. How might it be improved? How does one go about amending it? How many times has it been amended, if ever? Ask the student government adviser to tell you about any amendment campaigns that failed. After putting your information together, look for an issue that the constitution doesn't address, and where an amendment is needed. Then, organize a campaign to amend the constitution. You'll have some fun, and you'll learn the mechanics of the political process firsthand.

Unit Two

The American Political Process

> **The justices refused to permit even the smallest intrusion on the First Amendment.**

4 Defining individual rights: The American citizen today

▲ The no-prayers-in-schools decision in 1962 affected students throughout the nation.

Because the Constitution is highly protective of civil rights, Americans have the freedom to speak and act almost as they please. As a result, many people are surprised to discover that there are limits on what they can do. Even the simple act of asking school children to say a short prayer can arouse a determined minority to challenge a practice that it feels violates its rights. A good example of such a conflict can be found in the case of the New York State Board of Regents' classroom prayer.

Ever since 1837, New York State had permitted prayer in the public schools. In 1951, the State Board of Regents adopted a nonsectarian prayer for classroom use. The Regents recommended that schoolchildren recite the prayer each school day after they finished the flag salute. This is the prayer:

> Almighty God, we acknowledge our dependence upon Thee, as we beg Thy blessings upon us, our parents, our teachers, and our country.

Because the prayer was optional, local school boards were free to make their own decisions about its use. In 1958, the Union Free School District Number Nine, Town of North Hempstead, Long Island, voted to require the daily use of the prayer. The school board's decision was challenged the following year. Five parents filed suit against the board, charging that adoption and use of the prayer constituted "establishment of religion" in violation of the First Amendment to the Constitution. The parents represented several different religious beliefs: two were Jewish, one was Unitarian, one belonged to the Society for Ethical Culture, and one was a nonbeliever.

The suit involved the state constitution as well as the Constitution of the United States. For that reason, a state court agreed to hear the case. After hearing arguments from both sides, the lower court ruled in favor of the school board and the use of the prayer. The decision noted that neither the Constitution nor its writers discussed the use of prayer in public schools. Therefore, the judges ruled, earlier court decisions provided the only means of deciding the suit.

Analyzing the case further, the judges noted that the prayer did not fall into the same category as Bible readings or religious instruction in public schools. These had already been found to be unconstitutional. In the Hempstead case, the school did not force anyone to recite the prayer nor did it discriminate against those who did not. Therefore, the court concluded, the prayer was permissible so long as it did not become compulsory or sectarian.

The New York Court of Appeals reviewed the case and upheld the lower court. In a 5–2 decision, the court said that the ban on the establishment of a state religion in the Constitution was never intended to forbid a simple expression of belief in God.

The parents appealed the decision to the United States Supreme Court. The school board based its defense on the lower court rulings as well as on custom and tradition. Attorneys pointed out that the United States had been built by God-fearing, religious people. They pointed to the use of "In God We Trust" on the nation's coinage and the phrase "one nation, under God" in the Pledge of Allegiance.

Despite these arguments, a 6–1 Supreme Court majority declared in June 1962 that the New York prayer violated the First Amendment. No matter how brief, the *Engel* v. *Vitale* decision stated, a prayer must be defined as a religious activity. Neither the nonsectarian nature of the prayer nor the lack of compulsion mattered. Similarly, in 1985 the

Supreme Court ruled in *Wallace* v. *Jaffree* that an Alabama law permitting silent prayer in the schools was also unconstitutional.

The justices refused to permit even the smallest intrusion on the First Amendment. Although the rulings related to only two states, the decisions affected school districts in all the states. As a result, some religious groups have turned to Congress. They are lobbying for a constitutional amendment that would permit silent prayer in the nation's public schools.

Those who oppose the school prayer decision claim that a vocal minority is using the cover of religious liberty to deny the wishes of the majority. Should that be permitted in a democracy? This chapter will explore that basic issue. One way to state the problem is as follows: What rights do individuals possess that cannot be denied by a majority vote of their fellow citizens or by the powers of government?

In particular, these questions will be explored in this chapter:

1. **What civil rights are guaranteed to all citizens by the Bill of Rights?**

2. **Where did American civil rights originate?**

3. **What basic rights does the Constitution protect?**

4. **How do the states guarantee individual rights?**

5. **How did the "civil liberties" amendments enlarge individual rights?**

6. **How does a person gain—and keep—citizenship?**

7. **When may civil liberties be limited or suspended?**

1. What civil rights are guaranteed to all citizens by the Bill of Rights?

When the Constitution was written in 1787, its authors laid down a framework for federal government that was general enough to gain wide acceptance. The Framers believed that the American people would have faith in their national government. In the years to come, they said, the federal government would write new laws as they were needed. With that in mind, they didn't think it was necessary to spell out every safeguard and liberty.

PROMISE OF A BILL OF RIGHTS

During the struggle for ratification in 1787–1788, opponents pointed out that the Constitution lacked a Bill of Rights. After all, they argued, Americans fought the Revolutionary War because their traditional rights as British subjects had been ignored. A compromise developed, based on the promise that the new government would add a Bill of Rights soon after the Constitution was adopted. The promise was kept.

The Bill of Rights that emerged was largely the work of James Madison. Twelve amendments were proposed in 1789, the first year of

Washington's administration. Ten were ratified by the states and became part of the Constitution in 1791.

FREEDOM OF RELIGION (FIRST AMENDMENT)

In a few words, the Constitution says all that it has to say on the subject of religion: "Congress shall make no law respecting an establishment of religion or prohibiting the free exercise thereof." By "establishment of religion" the First Amendment means that government may not require citizens to accept any specific religion, engage in any religious activity, or satisfy any religious qualification for public office. Thus, Congress may not adopt an official church, as Great Britain has done with the Church of England. Nor may government funds be spent to support church activities, as is often the case in Scandinavian countries.

The guarantee of *free exercise of religion* gives people the right to hold any religious belief, no matter how unusual it may be. The amendment does not, however, give people the right to disregard the public safety, violate criminal laws, or offend public morals in the name of their religion. When that happens, government has the right to pass and enforce laws regulating such behaviors.

Despite what appears to be a clear-cut restriction, the relationship between church and state still raises many constitutional questions.

■ Americans with strong religious beliefs have sometimes clashed with the state over compulsory school attendance. The Amish, who cherish their simple, agricultural way of life, believe that exposure to public schools will interfere with their children's religious upbringing. Faced with this conflict between faith and the need to educate children, the Supreme Court ruled that Amish children must go to school until the eighth grade.

■ A union-organized rally in Albany, New York, the state capital. The demonstrators are calling for more access to health care. What freedoms guaranteed in the First Amendment are these people exercising?

Should religious beliefs take precedence over federal authority? For example, should the government be able to draft pacifists even though their antiwar feelings are based on religious beliefs? Can the state force a Christian Scientist couple to allow a hospital to give a lifesaving blood transfusion to their child? (Christian Scientists do not believe in the need for certain kinds of medical treatment.) The courts' responses have been mixed. Judges have answered "no" to the drafting of pacifists, "yes" to the question of a dying child's constitutional right to life.

Should church income be free from taxation? Organized religious groups, such as churches, monasteries, and religious schools, are not required to pay income taxes. Many people believe that this exemption is really an "establishment" of organized religion by the government. Because religious groups are exempt from taxes, they point out, individual taxpayers must pay higher tax bills.

Should government provide support for church schools? Rising costs have led many church schools to seek financial support from local and state governments. Even if local voters wish to provide this subsidy (usually in the form of textbooks or transportation), does the Constitution allow such payments? The Supreme Court has ruled against most forms of state support for church schools, but the loan of state textbooks has been permitted in certain cases.

FREEDOM OF SPEECH (FIRST AMENDMENT)

Freedom of speech, like every other freedom, is not absolute. As Supreme Court Justice Oliver Wendell Holmes pointed out, "The most stringent protection of free speech would not protect a man in falsely shouting fire in a theater and causing a panic."

Justice Holmes meant that individuals must accept legal responsibility for what they say or write. Oral statements that damage someone's reputation may lead to a lawsuit for *slander*, in which the injured party attempts to collect damages. If a newspaper or magazine publishes the slanderous statement, the injured party may sue for *libel*. The best defense in libel and slander suits is to show that the statements are true.

Radical thinkers are free to say that the government should be overthrown. Their freedom stops, however, when their speeches actually call for violence or revolution. The courts have the job of deciding the point at which unpopular beliefs become a "clear and present danger" to public safety. Thus, asking people to vote for a radical idea is permitted. Asking them to attack police stations is not.

Outside of these obvious limits, the constitutional guarantees of freedom of speech are absolute. The government is forbidden to pass laws or take action against people whose only fault is that their opinions are unpopular or contrary to government policy.

FREEDOM OF THE PRESS
(FIRST AMENDMENT)

The right of the press to publish without fear of government censorship is one of America's oldest freedoms. This right was severely tested during the colonial period, as illustrated by the case of John Peter Zenger, a newspaper publisher. The conflict started in 1734, when the royal governor of New York had Zenger put in jail. The publisher was charged with printing treasonous statements that could have led to rebellion. The real reason for the imprisonment was that Zenger published articles criticizing the governor. When the case went to trial in 1735, the jury found Zenger innocent on the grounds that his newspaper had printed the truth. Zenger's brave stand helped establish the tradition of a free press in this country.

FREEDOM OF ASSEMBLY AND PETITION
(FIRST AMENDMENT)

The First Amendment also guarantees Americans the right "peaceably to assemble" in order to exchange opinions and ideas. The key word is "peaceably." Should a meeting clearly show signs of turning into a riot or threatening the public safety, the police may move in to break it up. If people wish to challenge the actions of the police, they may refuse to disperse and take their chances with the courts. The exercise of this right, as with all individual rights, should be guided by common sense and a concern for public safety.

Right to petition. The right to "petition the government for a redress of grievances" includes far more than the word *petition* seems to indicate. Any citizen may collect signatures on a petition and send it to the proper government official. An individual letter or a request to testify before a government body also counts as a petition. Similarly, when people knock on an official's door to ask for help or to suggest action in the public good, they are exercising their right to petition.

Picketing. Long lines of pickets marching in front of government buildings symbolize the protest movements of the past several decades. *Picketing* combines the right of assembly with the right of petition. Even though the rights of protestors are guaranteed under the First Amendment, most city governments have set up procedures that pickets must follow. People who want to picket must take out a permit, keep public walkways clear, and obey lawful orders of the police.

RIGHT TO BEAR ARMS
(SECOND AMENDMENT)

The right to bear arms was a necessity when the Constitution was written. Americans who lived on a wild frontier needed guns to defend themselves and to obtain food. The Founders also believed that the United States should depend on a civilian militia for defense rather than a permanent standing army. Today, the frontier has disappeared, and the armed forces protect us with a full-time corps of highly trained men and women.

Does the Second Amendment right to bear arms still apply under these changed conditions? Some citizens say yes while others say no. Federal law already forbids the ownership of automatic and heavy weapons, such as machine guns. In addition, most states (the Second Amendment does not apply to state law) require permits to own handguns and regulate the carrying of concealed weapons with special permits. Even so, the pros and cons of gun control still fuel a national debate.

FREEDOM FROM QUARTERING TROOPS
(THIRD AMENDMENT)

Time has robbed the Third Amendment of its importance. In colonial times, private citizens were often forced to take British troops into their homes, mostly because suitable barracks were not available. Their resentment over this invasion of their privacy found its way into the Bill of Rights. Today, members of the armed forces live on military bases or find quarters in nearby communities like any other renter or home owner.

■ Two contrasting views on the topic of gun control can be seen in these cartoons. What point of view does the cartoon by Mauldin (below) express? What is the thief saying to the homeowner? What is cartoonist Wicks saying about the availability of weapons? Which cartoonist would probably support strong gun control laws? Which probably feels that the right to "keep and bear arms" is restricted? What does the Second Amendment guarantee?

"BUDDY, IF THAT GUN AIN'T REGISTERED, YOU'RE IN WORSE TROUBLE THAN I AM."

FREEDOM FROM UNREASONABLE SEARCH AND SEIZURE (FOURTH AMENDMENT)

The Constitution guarantees that everyone's person, home, papers, and possessions should be secure. In practice, the courts do not deny police the right of "search and seizure"—as long as the action is reasonable. Common sense requires that law enforcement officers must stop suspects or search homes in the interest of public safety. When sufficient evidence exists to charge a person with a crime, the court may issue a warrant for that person's arrest.

Even so, cases questioning the legality of police searches keep the courts busy. Many arrests for violations of narcotics laws, for example, are thrown out because the arresting officer failed to follow court-ordered limits on searches of homes, cars, or individuals. Police officials argue in favor of "no-knock" laws, claiming that if they must first obtain a search warrant, the suspects will have time to destroy the evidence. In 1984, the Supreme Court ruled in *U.S.* v. *Leon* and in *Massachusetts* v. *Sheppard* that prosecutors have the right to introduce evidence that the police seized "in good faith," even though they were using a faulty search warrant. On balance, however, the courts still uphold the safeguards against unreasonable search and seizure as one of our most important freedoms.

FREEDOM TO OWN PROPERTY (FIFTH AMENDMENT)

The right to own and use private property forms the keystone of the capitalist system. As with other freedoms, this right is not absolute. For example, property owners may not use their homes for illegal purposes. In addition, an individual's private property may be taken away through *due process*—that is, through proper legal procedures. For example, a bank or other mortgage holder may legally foreclose on a home, farm, or business when the borrower falls behind in the payments.

Another restriction on the right to own property can be seen when a community needs the land to build a freeway, school, or other public facility. Under the *right of eminent domain*, private property may be taken when it's needed for the greater public good. The Fifth Amendment guarantees that the property owners will receive "just compensation" for giving up their land.

FREEDOM FROM PROSECUTION WITHOUT INDICTMENT (FIFTH AMENDMENT)

The police have the right to arrest someone who is suspected of committing a crime. Under the Fifth Amendment, that person cannot be brought to trial unless a grand jury issues a formal charge, called an *indictment*. Grand juries are made up of a cross section of citizens from the community (see page 379). Unless the prosecutor convinces these jurors that there is enough evidence to provide a reasonable chance of conviction, they will refuse to hand down the indictment. This procedure protects accused persons who might otherwise be put through the ordeal of a trial on the basis of weak evidence or careless police work.

FREEDOM FROM DOUBLE JEOPARDY (FIFTH AMENDMENT)

The Fifth Amendment states that no person shall "be twice put in jeopardy of life or limb" for the same offense. This means that if defendants are found not guilty by judge or jury, they may not be tried again for the same crime. This immunity from *double jeopardy* remains in effect even if new evidence of the suspect's guilt emerges later.

GUARANTEE OF PRESUMED INNOCENCE (FIFTH AMENDMENT)

Some crimes are so horrible, and the evidence of guilt so overwhelming, that the public is tempted to condemn the suspect before a trial is held. The courts, however, must presume that everyone charged with an offense is innocent until proven guilty. The Bill of Rights spells out this protection in the due process clause of the Fifth Amendment. To reinforce this heritage from English common law, the courts have put strict limits on the ways in which the police may gather evidence. The use in a trial of facts or testimony gained by nonlegal means is forbidden, no matter how damaging the information may be to the accused.

FREEDOM FROM SELF-INCRIMINATION (FIFTH AMENDMENT)

People accused of crimes cannot be forced to testify against themselves. The use of the "third degree" (an intense, often violent method of questioning a suspect) is forbidden. Even if they go to trial, defendants need not testify in their own behalf, nor is their silence considered a sign of guilt.

In complex prosecutions, such as those involving organized crime, the courts have worked out a system known as *immunity from prosecution*. Once a witness receives immunity, the normal rules relating to self-incrimination no longer apply. The person must testify under oath about the case. Any witness who refuses to testify under these conditions faces contempt of court charges.

Innocent Until Proven Guilty

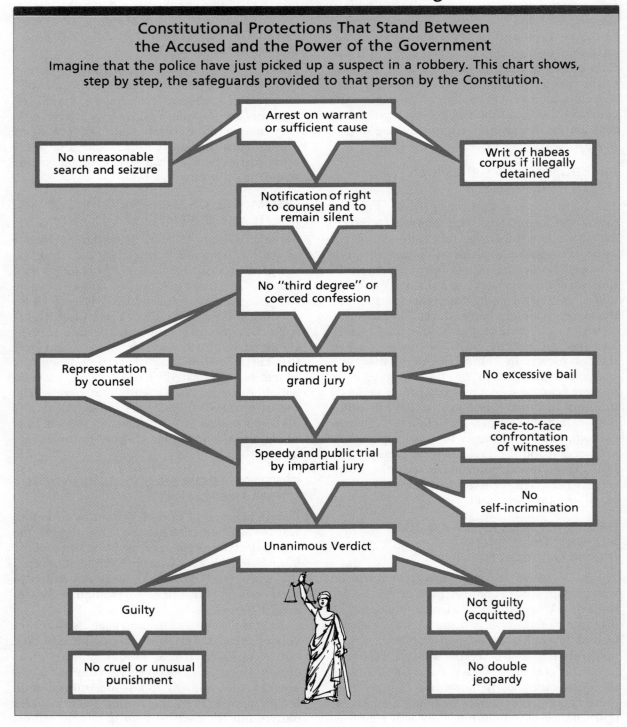

Constitutional Protections That Stand Between the Accused and the Power of the Government

Imagine that the police have just picked up a suspect in a robbery. This chart shows, step by step, the safeguards provided to that person by the Constitution.

Arrest on warrant or sufficient cause

No unreasonable search and seizure

Writ of habeas corpus if illegally detained

Notification of right to counsel and to remain silent

No "third degree" or coerced confession

Representation by counsel

Indictment by grand jury

No excessive bail

Speedy and public trial by impartial jury

Face-to-face confrontation of witnesses

No self-incrimination

Unanimous Verdict

Guilty

Not guilty (acquitted)

No cruel or unusual punishment

No double jeopardy

GUARANTEE OF DUE PROCESS
(FIFTH AMENDMENT)

The Fifth Amendment states that no person shall be "deprived of life, liberty, or property without due process of law." The concept of due process started centuries ago in English common law. Despite hundreds of years of legal precedent, however, the courts have not reached a final definition of the rights included under due process.

Today the main emphasis falls on the rights of an individual accused of a crime and facing trial. As illustrated in *Miranda* v. *Arizona* (see pages 404–406), any police action that denies a suspect's court-defined rights makes all further legal action impossible. In recent years, the courts have also set aside many local and state regulatory laws because they denied owners of property the right of due process. A state regulation that made it impossible for a legitimate business to make a fair profit would fall into this category.

GUARANTEE OF JURY TRIAL
(SIXTH AND SEVENTH AMENDMENTS)

Guilt or innocence in a criminal case must be decided by the 12 men and women of the trial jury. Whether the offense is first-degree murder or jaywalking, everyone who is accused of breaking the law has the right to request a jury trial. Most civil cases involve disputes between two or more people. Except for the simplest of suits (such as those heard in small claims court), civil cases may be tried before juries as well. Defendants have the right to a jury that is fair-minded and free of bias. If the 12 people of the jury do their job properly, their verdict will be based strictly on the facts presented in the courtroom.

A trial must be both "speedy and public." The law also requires that the trial be held in the city or county where the crime was committed. Should a defendant believe that publicity has made a fair hearing impossible, the defense attorney may ask that the trial site be changed. In a few cases, a judge may close the courtroom to the public and press if the welfare of the defendant, the witnesses, or the jury is threatened by too much publicity.

The right to a "speedy" trial does not mean that the trial must move quickly. Rather, it means that the trial should begin as soon as possible after the indictment has been handed down. If the case moves quickly to trial, witnesses are less likely to forget important details when they testify. In addition, if bail is denied, the defendant won't have to spend a long time in jail waiting for trial. Despite this constitutional protection, crowded court calendars force many defendants to wait long weeks and months for their trials to begin.

RIGHT TO BE INFORMED
OF CHARGES (SIXTH AMENDMENT)

A defendant in a civil or criminal action must be told the nature of the charges so that a proper defense can be prepared. The charges must be spelled out in detail. The defense also has a right to know what evidence will be used at the trial.

The Sixth Amendment provides several additional rights:

Right to confront witnesses. All accusers and witnesses must face the defendant in open court.

Right to secure witnesses. Defendants have the right to secure witnesses to testify in their behalf. At the defendant's request, the court will issue subpoenas to insure that the witnesses will appear.

Right to counsel. If the defendant cannot afford to pay an attorney's fees, the court will appoint a public defender. The government pays the costs of these defense attorneys. A 1975 Supreme Court decision (*Faretta* v. *California*) also gave defendants the right to serve as their own attorneys. Lawyers caution that people who defend themselves run the risk of having "a fool for a client."

GUARANTEE OF REASONABLE BAIL
(EIGHTH AMENDMENT)

Without the right to post bail, an accused might spend months in jail waiting for the trial to begin. By putting up a sum of money (or its equivalent in property), defendants guarantee their appearance for trial. Release on bail also gives the accused a chance to prepare a defense for the coming trial.

'PARDON ME, SIR! WE'RE DOING A SURVEY ON FEAR IN AMERICA...'

■ Rising crime rates have left their mark on many Americans. Victims of crime, in fact, often claim that the Constitution and the Bill of Rights give more protection to criminals than to law-abiding citizens. Why does the Bill of Rights give so many protections to people accused of crimes?

In minor traffic cases, the court establishes the amount of the bail as equal to the fine. If the defendant fails to appear, the bail is forfeited and that ends the case. In the most serious felonies, or when the defendant cannot be trusted to return for trial, the judge may deny the right to post bail.

FREEDOM FROM CRUEL AND UNUSUAL PUNISHMENT (EIGHTH AMENDMENT)

In the 1700s, convicted criminals were often whipped or tortured. The Eighth Amendment to the Constitution ended the use of "cruel and unusual punishment." Along with outlawing physical punishment, the amendment outlaws unfair sentences, such as a 20-year prison term for stealing a loaf of bread. Modern court decisions have broadened the Eighth Amendment to forbid the death penalty, except when state laws apply the punishment equally to all criminals convicted of capital crimes. In addition, the courts have used the Eighth Amendment to force improvements in prisons where inmates live in overcrowded, unsanitary conditions.

LIMITS ON THE POWER OF THE FEDERAL GOVERNMENT (NINTH AND TENTH AMENDMENTS)

The final two amendments of the Bill of Rights establish limits on the power of the federal government. The Ninth Amendment reminds federal officials that even though the Constitution does not spell out a particular right, that right still exists and must be protected. Similarly, the Tenth Amendment relates to the limited nature of the federal government. The last amendment of the Bill of Rights states that all powers not delegated to the federal government are reserved to the states or to the people. In brief, these amendments mean that the national government cannot enlarge its powers beyond those granted by the Constitution.

Let's review for a moment

The Framers of the Constitution strongly believed that the individual citizen must be protected from the abuse of power by government. The absolute guarantees hammered out in the Bill of Rights and in the court decisions that have broadened them shelter all Americans. But nothing is truly absolute. The courts are still attempting to strike a balance between the rights of individuals and society's need to protect itself against lawbreakers. Recent Supreme Court decisions have strengthened the authority of the police while still upholding free speech and the power of the press.

How many of the 18 rights described in this chapter can you remember? Close your eyes for a moment and try to count them off. How many was that—eight, nine? Not bad. Here's the full list:

1. Freedom of **RELIGION**
2. Freedom of **SPEECH**
3. Freedom of the **PRESS**
4. Freedom of **ASSEMBLY AND PETITION**
5. Right to bear **ARMS**
6. Freedom from **QUARTERING TROOPS** in your home

7. Freedom from unreasonable SEARCH AND SEIZURE
8. Right to own PROPERTY
9. Freedom from prosecution without an INDICTMENT
10. Freedom from DOUBLE JEOPARDY
11. Right to PRESUMPTION OF INNOCENCE
12. Freedom from SELF-INCRIMINATION
13. Right to DUE PROCESS OF LAW
14. Right to a JURY TRIAL
15. Right to be INFORMED OF CHARGES
16. Right to reasonable BAIL
17. Freedom from CRUEL AND UNREASONABLE PUNISHMENT
18. Limitations on the POWER OF THE FEDERAL GOVERNMENT

Where did these rights get started? Let's take a look.

---

2. Where did American civil rights originate?

As you learned in Chapter Two, the U.S. legal system and its emphasis on individual rights developed during the colonial period. During the years between 1607 and 1776, the English colonists—unlike their French and Spanish counterparts—lived under a government that accepted centuries-old limits on its power. As early as 1215, the Magna Carta declared that the law was greater than the monarch. Four centuries later, the charter of the Jamestown colony clearly spelled out the rights of English colonists in the New World. They were granted all the rights, liberties, and privileges of English subjects, just as if they had been born and were living in England. The English people gained their own Bill of Rights after King James II fled the country in 1688. William and Mary replaced James on the throne but only after they agreed to share power with Parliament.

■ One of the most important principles of democratic government began in 1215, when England's King John signed the Magna Carta. The "great charter" said that the "law is greater than the king." The Framers wrote this concept into the U.S. Constitution. Why did they do this?

SALUTARY NEGLECT

The English government was too far away to keep a tight rein on its American colonies. This gave the 13 colonies the chance to add a tradition of self-government to the rights granted under their charters. Colonial legislatures interpreted the laws passed by Parliament to suit themselves, much to the dismay of the royal governors. In addition to distance, England's wars with France, Spain, and the Netherlands kept the government from closely supervising the colonies. All of these factors led the monarch and Parliament to practice a policy of salutary neglect. While England (more properly known as Great Britain after the 1707 union of England and Scotland) was busy elsewhere, Americans learned to govern themselves.

RESISTANCE TO BRITISH RULE

Over a century of salutary neglect ended in the 1760s. By then, the colonists were passing their own tax laws, regulating their own courts, and safeguarding their own liberties. Americans were shocked when Parliament passed a new series of revenue bills. The new taxes were meant to force the colonists to pay a fair share of the costs of the French and Indian War. To Parliament's surprise, Americans refused to pay the new taxes.

When British troops were sent to the colonies to enforce the tax laws, the colonists treated the soldiers like foreign invaders. The royal governors tried tax-law violators in colonial courts, but juries refused to convict their fellow Americans. When special search warrants and other legal maneuvers seemed to be chipping away at their liberties, Americans began to organize a resistance movement.

THE DECLARATION OF INDEPENDENCE

The British abuse of American liberties led colonial leaders to write the Declaration of Independence in 1776. This document summarized the injustices that the colonists said the king had inflicted upon them. They objected to the dissolving of colonial legislatures, the keeping of British troops in the colonies in time of peace, the lack of colonial representation in Parliament, the denial of trial by jury, and other acts considered to be threats to colonial liberties. The Declaration argues that these rights were God-given and that when they were denied, the only option was revolution against British rule. Later, when they formed their own government, Americans demanded that their rights be protected in the new Constitution.

3. What basic rights does the Constitution protect?

Even though a Bill of Rights was needed to complete the Constitution, the Framers did not neglect the subject of individual rights. They wrote five important safeguards of personal freedom into the body of the Constitution itself.

WRIT OF HABEAS CORPUS (ARTICLE I, SECTION 9)

Without the right to a *writ of habeas corpus*, a prisoner might be held for weeks or months without being arraigned (charged with the crime). This often happens in a dictatorship. A writ of *habeas corpus* leaves the arresting agency with only two choices: (1) to bring the prisoner into court to be arraigned or (2) to release the prisoner. The restriction is absolute, and the interval between arrest and arraignment must not exceed a day or two. The writ may be requested by the prisoner or an attorney, and it is issued by the appropriate court (a sample writ is reproduced on page 97). This protection against lengthy imprisonment without a trial can be suspended only in time of rebellion or invasion.

NO BILL OF ATTAINDER (ARTICLE I, SECTION 9)

Passage of any *bill of attainder* is forbidden by the Constitution. A law that allows the police to collect fines for drunk driving at the time the arrest is made would be a bill of attainder. If a law of this type was permitted, an individual could be found guilty without going through a court trial. Such laws were common in the colonial period. They violated the American concept of limited government and the right to trial by jury.

NO *EX POST FACTO* LAWS (ARTICLE I, SECTION 9)

An *ex post facto* law makes a crime of an act that was not illegal at the time it was performed. Suppose a state law that will take effect next January 1 says companies cannot make political donations of more than $1,000. Any attempt to prosecute Company X for making a contribution of $2,000 *this* year would be *ex post facto* and, therefore, illegal.

Three factors define an *ex post facto* law: (1) It must be retroactive (the law applies to acts that took place before it went into effect). (2) It must impose harsher penalties than existing laws do. (3) It must deal with a criminal matter (as opposed to a civil procedure). For example, a new law making penalties more severe for the criminal offense of arson could only apply to crimes committed after the new law took effect. In noncriminal matters, such as a zoning change, a dairy farm can be forced to leave a residential area. This is true even though the farm was there before the houses were built and the new zoning law was passed.

■ A sample Writ of *Habeas Corpus*.

SUPERIOR COURT OF THE STATE OF CALIFORNIA FOR THE COUNTY OF LOS ANGELES

In the Matter of the Application of	CASE NUMBER
JOHN DOE, Petitioner	H. C. 0000–00
On Behalf of SAM DOE	WRIT OF HABEAS CORPUS 1474 Penal Code Criminal

THE PEOPLE OF THE STATE OF CALIFORNIA, TO:

_____ HARRY DOE _____ SHERIFF. CHIEF OF POLICE.

GREETINGS:

We command you to have the body of ___ Sam Doe _____

_____

who is now imprisoned and detained by you, together with the reasons for such imprisonment and detention and the length of time imprisoned, by whatever name said prisoner shall be called or charged before the

Honorable ___ Peter Doe _____ , Judge of the Superior Court, for the

County of Los Angeles, State of California, in Department No. _24_____ , located at _Big_____

_____ Town, USA _____ , on _June 20_____ , 19 _--_ , at _10 A_ M.,

for proceedings concerning the said prisoner; and have with you this writ.

Said prisoner may be released upon the posting of $ ___500.00____ Bail plus penalty assessment of

$___none_____ .

NO BAIL FIXED.

Dated: **June 19, 19--**

WILLIAM G. SHARP, County Clerk and Clerk of the Superior Court of the State of California for the County of Los Angeles.

By _____ Deputy

NARROW DEFINITION OF TREASON
(ARTICLE III, SECTION 3)

The Constitution defines *treason* (betrayal of one's country) very narrowly. The Framers knew that if they had lost the Revolutionary War, many of them would have been tried as traitors by the British government. Because treason carried the death penalty at that time, the Constitution requires three proofs of the crime: (1) Two or more witnesses must testify to having knowledge of the act. (2) The treason must be a definite physical act rather than just casual talk or attendance at a meeting where people talked about treason. (3) A confession is admissible only if the accused person admits guilt in open court.

RIGHT TO TRIAL BY JURY
(ARTICLE III, SECTION 2)

Except in cases of impeachment, the Constitution guarantees a trial by jury in all criminal cases. As you read on page 93, the Bill of Rights defines this process more fully.

4. How do the states guarantee individual rights?

Each state operates under a contract with its people that is defined by a state constitution. Indeed, Congress examines the constitution of each new state as part of the process by which it decides if a territory is ready for statehood. Although every state constitution is different, each one spells out such matters as how the legislature is to be organized, separation of powers, educational rights, and tax procedures.

Many of the rights written into the U.S. Constitution were not originally binding on the states. Each state, therefore, included a bill of rights in its own constitution that protected its citizens from abuses of power by state, county, or city government. Most—but not all—of the freedoms defined by the national Bill of Rights appear in the state constitutions.

The basic freedoms contained in the U.S. Constitution were extended to the citizens of each state in 1868 by the Fourteenth Amendment. This amendment gives federal judges the authority to enforce these rights. The power lies in a simple statement: "No State shall make or enforce any law which shall abridge the privileges or immunities of citizens of the United States." (Fourteenth Amendment, Section 1.)

5. How did the "civil liberties" amendments enlarge individual rights?

The authors of the Constitution and the Bill of Rights did not solve all of the nation's civil rights problems. Changing social conditions in the years after the Civil War required additional amendments to the Constitution. Some of these amendments corrected old injustices. Others extended the right to vote to Americans who had previously lacked that right.

THIRTEENTH AMENDMENT (1865)

This brief amendment formally abolished slavery and involuntary servitude in the United States. The restriction on involuntary servitude does not apply when a court punishes convicted criminals by sending them to jail.

FOURTEENTH AMENDMENT (1868)

Southern resistance to the acceptance of black people as full citizens under the law did not end with the Civil War. Congress passed the first section of the Fourteenth Amendment as a means of eliminating "black codes" and other postwar restrictions on the civil rights of the former slaves. The amendment says that no state may deprive its citizens of "life, liberty, or property, without due process of law." At the time, this phrase was interpreted as applying Fifth Amendment protections to every citizen. In recent years, the Fourteenth Amendment has been used to guarantee full constitutional rights to all Americans, whatever their color, religion, financial status, or place of residence.

Under this amendment, no state may deny its citizens "the equal protection of the laws." This does not compel government to treat all people alike, however. Age limits on the purchase of tobacco or alcohol, for example, are perfectly legal. *Equal protection of the laws* means that the rights given to any citizens within a certain category must not be denied to others within the same category because of arbitrary state standards. In 1978, this philosophy led to the Supreme Court's decision in *Regents of the University of California* v. *Allan Bakke*. In *Bakke*, the court ruled that colleges could not use strict racial quotas as

a way of granting admission to minority students. Race may be considered but only in combination with other factors. Otherwise, racial quotas are a form of reverse discrimination that violates the Fourteenth Amendment.

FIFTEENTH AMENDMENT (1870)

The brief Fifteenth Amendment extended state and federal voting privileges to all adult male citizens. The states are still permitted to set minimum requirements of age and residence, but the right to vote cannot be denied "on account of race, color, or previous condition of servitude." Faced with this clear language, some southern states turned to poll taxes and

■ The nation's debate over the status of blacks did not end with the Civil War. For a long time, many communities in the South maintained "separate but equal" facilities that were surely separate but seldom equal. In the 1950s, the Supreme Court began striking down the "black codes" that had violated the civil rights of blacks for almost 100 years.

unfair literacy tests as a way of denying voting rights to blacks and other minorities. The Twenty-fourth Amendment ended the use of poll taxes in 1964.

NINETEENTH AMENDMENT (1920)

Even after men were given the vote, women remained powerless to influence the course of American politics through the use of the ballot. The suffrage movement of the late 1800s and early 1900s finally led to the ratification of the Nineteenth Amendment. This amendment states that the right to vote shall not be denied in any federal or state election "on account of sex."

The right to vote did not bring the equality that the suffrage movement promised. Over the years, women pressed for an equal rights amendment (ERA), which Congress finally passed in 1972. In 1982, the extended deadline for ratification of the ERA expired before the required number of states had ratified it. Passage of the ERA is still a major goal of the feminist movement.

TWENTY-SIXTH AMENDMENT (1971)

A long dispute over the age at which citizens should be allowed to vote for the first time ended in 1971 with the ratification of the Twenty-sixth Amendment. Under the terms of this amendment, citizens who are 18 years of age or older may not be denied the vote in federal or state elections "on account of age."

6. How does a person gain—and keep—citizenship?

The Fourteenth Amendment defines *citizenship* in precise legal terms: "All persons born or naturalized in the United States . . . are citizens of the United States and of the State wherein they reside." The main body of the Constitution does not define the term, although the word "citizen" is used several times.

RIGHTS AND PRIVILEGES

United States citizenship carries with it a number of rights and privileges. Only citizens are allowed to vote in state and national elections, for example, and only citizens may serve on juries. In addition, many jobs are limited to citizens, including elective offices and sensitive positions in defense industries. *Aliens* (noncitizens living in the United States) receive most of the civil rights protections enjoyed by citizens. In return, aliens must accept the responsibilities that go with living in this country. These include such duties as obeying state and federal laws, paying taxes, and serving in the armed forces.

BECOMING A CITIZEN

Citizenship may be acquired in any one of three ways:

1. *Birth to American parents.* If either of a child's parents holds U.S. citizenship, the child is automatically an American citizen at birth.

2. *Birth within the United States to alien parents.* Why would pregnant women from foreign countries travel to the United States to give birth to their children? By doing so, the women give their babies the right to U.S. citizenship no matter where they and their husbands were born. Most of these children grow up holding *dual citizenship.* This means that they are citizens of two countries at the same time. Dual citizenship usually ends when the individuals become adults. Then they must choose the country in which they wish to claim citizenship.

3. *Naturalization.* Aliens who wish to become citizens of this country go through a process called *naturalization.* To become a naturalized citizen requires three steps:

a. *Statement of intent.* The citizens-to-be first file a statement of intent (called "first papers"). This statement declares that the individuals are over 18 years of age, are ready to give up their former citizenship, and intend to become United States citizens.

b. *Second statement.* After five years of res-

■ U.S. Navy personnel taking the oath of citizenship on board the U.S.S. *Constitution* in Boston. This ceremony was part of the celebration of the bicentennial of the Constitution in 1987. One need not be a citizen to serve in the armed forces.

idence in this country (three years for foreign-born spouses of American citizens), the citizens-to-be file a second statement. These papers include personal data and two statements from U.S. citizens testifying to the applicants' good character. In addition, they must sign statements renouncing their former citizenship and swearing that they have never belonged to any group that advocates the violent overthrow of the government of the United States.

c. *Taking the oath.* Finally, the citizens-to-be appear before a federal judge. They are asked to demonstrate their ability to read and write English and their knowledge of the American system of government. After passing this test, the applicants recite the oath of allegiance to their new country. In what is often an emotional ceremony, the judge awards a certificate of citizenship to each new Amer-

ican. Children under the age of 16 automatically become citizens at the same time their parents are naturalized. The new citizens have equal status with natural-born citizens in every way except one. No one not born to U.S. citizenship may become the President of the United States.

LOSS OF CITIZENSHIP

Citizenship can be lost as well as gained. United States citizens may lose their citizenship (1) by deliberately renouncing it; (2) by being convicted of treason or of attempting to overthrow the United States government by force; (3) by serving in the armed forces of a foreign country without written permission from the Secretary of State or the Secretary of Defense; or (4) by becoming a naturalized citizen of another country. Americans with dual citizenship may lose their U.S. citizenship by choosing the foreign country over this one or by not maintaining residence in this country. Finally, naturalized citizens may lose their citizenship if it is proved in a federal court that they gained their final papers by lying or misstating the facts.

Convicted felons do not lose their citizenship, but they do lose some of its privileges. Even after "paying their debt to society" by serving prison terms, convicted felons may not vote, serve on juries, or hold most public offices.

Learning Skills

Note Taking From a Textbook

Now that you've read the chapter, can you remember all that information about civil rights and citizenship? Unless you're lucky enough to have a photographic memory, learning about government is hard work. You can read the material over and over, but that's not very efficient. An excellent way to improve retention is to take notes on what you've read. Note taking forces you to dig out the most important ideas in order to write them down. In addition, the act of writing reinforces the learning process. As a final bonus, you can use your notes for a quick review when it's time for chapter and unit tests.

Here are some useful rules for note taking:

1. Take your notes in outline form.
2. Write down only the important ideas and facts.
3. Use shortcuts whenever possible. This means writing "gov't" for government, "US" for United States, and so on. In addition, use short sentences and phrases.
4. Write legibly. You'll have to read your own writing days or weeks from now.

Now, look at pages 100–102, "How Does a Person Gain—and Keep—Citizenship?" Try taking your own notes for that section.

Then compare your notes with the sample that follows.

A. C'ship defined—all persons born or naturalized in US have rights under Const.
B. Rights of c'ship: (1) voting, (2) serve on juries, (3) hold gov't office, (4) do secret defense work.
C. Aliens have same civil rights as citizens. Must pay taxes & serve in mil.
D. 3 ways to become citizen: (1) born to US parents; (2) born in US to non-citizens; (3) naturalized.
E. To become naturalized:

1. Step 1—over 18, live in US, ready to give up old c'ship (1st papers).
2. Step 2—5 yr. resident, good char., not planning revol. (2nd papers).
3. Step 3—pass test on US gov't and Eng. lang., swear allegiance.

F. Loss of c'ship: (1) if renounce c'ship; (2) dual cit. chooses other country; (3) nat. cit. lies on appl.
G. Felons lose right to vote & hold office.

Do your notes look anything like these? Don't worry if you left out a few facts. The important thing is to practice. After a while, you'll be able to make note-taking decisions almost as fast as you can write.

■ After Japan attacked Pearl Harbor in 1941, a panicky nation suspected all Japanese-Americans of disloyalty. President Franklin Roosevelt ordered their "relocation" from the West Coast to internment camps. Even though no proof could be found that these people were "a clear and present danger," the Supreme Court upheld the order. In later years, most Americans realized that a great injustice had been done. This photo shows U.S. Army personnel escorting Japanese-American families from Seattle to trains for the trip to an internment camp in central eastern California. In 1990, compensation was given to people who had been relocated.

7. When may civil liberties be limited or suspended?

The civil liberties guaranteed by the Constitution and the Bill of Rights stand as a firm shield against the misuse of governmental power. The need to maintain public safety, however, sometimes justifies the temporary suspension of civil liberties. In times of emergency, the governors of the individual states have the power to declare *martial law*. This act places an area hit by a tornado, for ex-ample, under military control to prevent loot-ing. National emergencies allow the President to suspend individual freedoms in a similar way. If the United States were attacked, the rights of *habeas corpus* and freedom of move-ment could be set aside by a presidential order.

THE "CLEAR AND PRESENT DANGER" DOCTRINE

Justice Oliver Wendell Holmes wrote the for-mula by which the courts determine the right of the government to suspend civil liberties.

Holmes specified that a "clear and present danger" to public safety or to national security must exist before the government may restrict any freedom. The Smith Act of 1940, for example, makes it illegal for any person to teach or advocate the violent overthrow of the government of the United States. The law bases its restriction of the First Amendment right to free speech on the belief that "words can be weapons" in any effort to arouse people to violent revolutionary action.

APPEAL TO THE COURTS

Any suspension of civil liberties may be appealed to the courts. President Lincoln's suspension of *habeas corpus* at the onset of the Civil War was declared illegal soon after the war ended in the case of *Ex parte Milligan* (1866). Convictions under the Smith Act are allowed to stand only if a defendant has actually urged people to commit a violent act. An attempt to change the way someone thinks does not violate this law.

Reviewing
what you've learned

1. The Bill of Rights provides an enduring heritage for all American citizens. The first ten amendments to the Constitution secure for us such important rights as freedom of religion, speech, and the press; the right to assemble and petition for change; freedom from unreasonable search and seizure; guarantee of a fair trial before a jury of one's peers; and protection from cruel and unusual punishment.

2. Building on traditions of English common law and self-rule, the American colonists developed workable concepts of the role of government and the importance of individual rights. As a result, the Constitution guarantees the right to a *writ of habeas corpus*, bans bills of attainder and *ex post facto* laws, restricts the definition of treason, and guarantees the right to trial by jury.

3. At first, the Constitution's civil rights guarantees did not apply to the individual states. State constitutions provided some rights, but others were overlooked. The Fourteenth Amendment solved this problem. The guarantees of *due process* of law and of *equal protection under the law* were extended. Anyone whose rights are violated may seek protection under federal law.

4. Not only have the courts extended personal freedoms, the Constitution has also been amended to meet new problems. The Thirteenth, Fourteenth, and Fifteenth Amendments granted full citizenship to freed blacks after the Civil War. Voting rights have also been broadened. The Nineteenth Amendment extended the franchise to women, and the Twenty-sixth did the same for 18-year-olds.

5. The rights and privileges of *citizenship* are given to all persons born or naturalized in this country. Most Americans gain their citizenship by being born to American parents, but a child born in this country to *alien* parents is also considered to be a citizen. The foreign-born may elect to become naturalized citizens after meeting residence, language, and loyalty requirements.

6. Civil rights may be suspended during emergencies, such as natural disaster, foreign invasion, or rebellion. The rise of totalitarian systems in the 1930s also led the courts to confirm certain restrictions that Congress placed on First Amendment freedoms. The rule established by the Supreme Court permits suspension of these rights if a "clear and present danger" can be proven.

Review questions and activities

TERMS YOU SHOULD KNOW

alien	*ex post facto* law	petition
bill of attainder	immunity from prosecution	picketing
citizenship	indictment	right of eminent domain
double jeopardy	libel	slander
dual citizenship	martial law	treason
due process	naturalization	writ of *habeas corpus*
equal protection of the laws		

REVIEW QUESTIONS

Select the response that best completes each statement or question.

1. In a democracy like the United States, the wishes of the majority always outweigh the wishes of a minority. This statement is (*a*) true. (*b*) false; the minority must always come first. (*c*) false; certain basic rights must be safeguarded no matter how unpopular their expression might be.

2. Statements printed in a newspaper that maliciously injure someone's good name may be cause for a lawsuit under the laws against (*a*) slander. (*b*) sedition. (*c*) libel. (*d*) treason. (*e*) malicious mischief.

3. In order for a revolutionary speech to be considered cause for arrest, the government must prove that it constituted (*a*) a clear and present danger. (*b*) a violation of public morality. (*c*) a view contrary to that held by the majority of U.S. citizens. (*d*) an offense against tradition or custom. (*e*) praise for a foreign system of government.

4. The right to "keep and bear arms" is an absolute privilege granted under the Bill of Rights. This statement is (*a*) true. (*b*) false; the government places many restrictions on the use of arms. (*c*) false; the government has the right to decide on all matters of public safety without worry about constitutional restrictions.

5. A judge is most likely to issue a search warrant (*a*) when the police request one. (*b*) when possession of narcotics is suspected. (*c*) when the police have good reason to believe that a crime has been committed. (*d*) when the crime involved is murder. (*e*) when suspects refuse to let the police enter their home.

6. The due process clause in the Fifth and Fourteenth Amendments defines a citizen's right to fair and equal protection under state and federal laws. This statement is (*a*) true. (*b*) false; "due process" refers to the process by which an alien becomes a citizen. (*c*) false; the Constitution makes no mention of "due process" in any amendment.

7. The American colonists based their decision to revolt against British rule on (*a*) their dislike of being British subjects. (*b*) the belief that they were being denied their rights as British subjects. (*c*) their desire to do away with all government control over their lives. (*d*) the wish to do away with taxation. (*e*) the wish to become part of the French colonies in the New World.

8. Federal protections written into the Bill of Rights have always applied to state law as well. This statement is (*a*) true. (*b*) false; the Constitution forbids the federal government to interfere with state laws. (*c*) false; not until 1868 did the due process clause of the Fourteenth Amendment give the courts the legal means of extending federal civil rights guarantees to cases involving state laws.

9. Noncitizens living in the United States receive equal protection under the guarantees of the Constitution. This statement is (*a*) true. (*b*) false; aliens may be tried in special government courts that do not allow trial by jury. (*c*) false; aliens do not pay taxes, so they do not receive civil rights protections.

10. A child would *not* have United States citizenship who was born to (*a*) U.S. citizens living in Russia. (*b*) Mexican citizens living in San Diego, California. (*c*) an American citizen married to a Japanese and living in Afghanistan. (*d*) parents who had become naturalized citizens two years before. (*e*) a British couple who worked at a U.S. consulate in London.

CONCEPT DEVELOPMENT

1. Why did Americans demand the addition of a Bill of Rights to the Constitution? Are any further protections needed today?

2. Discuss Lincoln's suspension of *habeas corpus* during the opening days of the Civil War. Do you believe this was justified? Why or why not?

3. Which four constitutional rights are most important to you? Why?

4. Why does the American system of government work so hard to maintain the separation of church and state? Explain your own feelings about the questions of school prayer and federal aid to religious schools.

5. The struggle for civil rights by minority groups in the United States has been a long and difficult one. Summarize the conflicts involved in obtaining full civil rights by blacks, Hispanics, or any other significant minority group.

HANDS-ON ACTIVITIES

1. Do Americans really believe in the Bill of Rights? Try this experiment to find out. Write up the guarantees provided by the Bill of Rights in the form of a petition. The petition should demand that these freedoms be granted to representatives of any cause that is unpopular in your community. Circulate the petition in a local shopping center or other public place, asking people to read it and to sign it if they agree with it. Keep a record of each person's response to your request to sign. Report the results of your survey to your class.

2. Ask your parents, relatives, and friends to help you locate several naturalized citizens. Interview these people and record (a) their experiences in immigrating to this country and obtaining citizenship and (b) their attitudes toward the United States and the value of their citizenship.

3. Invite a member of a local civil rights organization to speak on the work the group does in the community. Groups that you're likely to find in your area are the American Civil Liberties Union (ACLU), the National Association for the Advancement of Colored People (NAACP), the National Organization for Women, Common Cause, and the American Association of University Women.

4. Research several civil rights cases (see that listing in your library's card catalog or computerized catalog). Extract the basic facts of each case. Present these to your class, either orally or in written form. Ask the class to decide the cases. How do the decisions made by your classmates compare with the actual decisions? Why is it so difficult to predict the direction the courts will take?

5 The American political system

Who says young people don't count in politics? Take a look at the unexpected events that took place early in 1968.

The scene: The icy streets of the towns and cities of New Hampshire.

The event: New Hampshire's presidential primary election, the first in the nation.

The question: Can an army of college students, political amateurs all, unseat an incumbent President of the United States?

Only a movie script writer would have dared to write such a scenario. Still, the conditions were special. Many Americans no longer believed that democracy's future depended on winning the war in Vietnam. Lyndon Johnson, the Democratic President, had become the symbol for a growing national tragedy.

▲ College students working for McCarthy's presidential primary campaign in New Hampshire in early 1968.

Senator Eugene McCarthy, Democrat from Minnesota, stepped forward as an antiwar candidate. More then 3,000 enthusiastic college students joined him in New Hampshire for the first primary campaign of that election year. The young people gave freely of their time and put their beliefs on the line for McCarthy. In the two weeks before the election, they spoke to 30,000 voters and left leaflets for 10,000 more. By election eve, their personal appeals had reached over one-half of the homes in the state.

Political polls traced the growing impact of this youth-oriented campaign. In January, the Gallup poll had shown that McCarthy's chances for winning in New Hampshire were practically nil. The poll predicted that only 12 percent of the state's Democrats would vote for him. In February, President Johnson's private poll revealed that the antiwar vote had increased to 18 percent. New Hampshire's governor predicted that McCarthy's strength would peak at 25 percent. Only Eugene McCarthy and his "kids" believed that Johnson's presidency had begun to collapse.

The election on March 12 proved that the polls had misjudged the mood of the voters. When precinct workers added Republican write-in ballots to the Democratic tally, President Johnson's lead over McCarthy shrank to a razor-thin margin of 230 votes. The McCarthy forces celebrated briefly, then headed for Wisconsin to fight the next primary battle.

All through March, the college students continued to work their political magic. In the hard, daily grind of the American political process, their energy and determination made a difference. New polls forecast an overwhelming McCarthy victory in Wisconsin. What would the President do?

The answer came with dramatic suddenness. On Sunday, March 31, President Johnson startled the nation by announcing, "I shall not seek and I will not accept the nomination of my party for another term as your President."

The thousands of antiwar students had succeeded in mobilizing public opinion against the war and the President who was blamed for it. They demonstrated that citizens who understand the workings of the American political system can win major victories. The victory over Lyndon Johnson was especially impressive because it came against a powerful incumbent President.

Although the students won these early battles, they lost the war. The bitterly divided Democratic convention turned away from McCarthy and nominated Hubert Humphrey. Four years later, George McGovern carried the antiwar banner to a convention victory, much to the joy of the former McCarthy supporters. Both Humphrey and McGovern were defeated by Richard Nixon. Humphrey lost by a narrow margin in the 1968 election, McGovern by a landslide in 1972.

Before you can elect a President, you have to know how the political system works. This chapter answers the following questions about American politics:

1. What is a political party?

2. What do political parties try to accomplish?

3. Why does the United States keep the two-party system?

4. How did the American two-party system develop?

5. How have third parties affected the American political system?

6. What do political labels really stand for?

7. How is a political party organized?

8. What happens at a party convention?

9. What are the steps in the presidential election cycle?

---

1. What is a political party?

In a democracy, the people select their government and influence its policies through their votes. These same people differ greatly when it's time to decide the direction that government should take on any given issue. When like-minded people join together to achieve common political goals, they often form a *political party*.

REQUIREMENTS FOR A POLITICAL PARTY

Before a group of citizens may be considered a true political party (as opposed to a pressure group), three elements must exist:

1. *Shared beliefs.* The members should believe in the same political philosophy and be willing to work for the same goals.

2. *Program.* The members should agree on a program for turning their beliefs into law after their candidates have been elected.

3. *Chance of success.* The members should have a realistic chance of winning an election or gaining support for their programs, either now or in the future.

Minor parties seldom satisfy these qualifications. In the American system, they should more properly be classified as *pressure groups*. True political power belongs to those parties that have a realistic chance of winning control of a local, state, or national government on election day.

HISTORICAL DEVELOPMENT

Political parties are a relatively new invention. Although British politicians called themselves Whigs and Tories, parties did not exist in Great Britain before 1776 in a form we would recognize today. Nor were parties thought to be desirable. George Washington warned against the development of political parties in his Farewell Address:

> Let me now . . . warn you in the most solemn manner against the baneful effects of the Spirit of Party, generally. . . . It serves always to distract the Public Councils and enfeeble the Public administration. It agitates the Community with ill-founded jealousies and false alarms, kindles the animosity of one part against another. . . .

The advice went unheeded. By the time Washington wrote these words, in 1796, the United States had already begun to build a two-party system. Since then, politicians in democracies around the world have copied the structure and organization of American political parties.

2. What do political parties try to accomplish?

In a democracy, the needs of many competing interests must be balanced before worthwhile ideas can be enacted into law. Political parties play a major role in that process.

1. ORGANIZE A POLITICAL MAJORITY

People join the political party that best reflects their ideas about economics, foreign policy, social welfare, personal freedom, and the like. In a two-party system, neither political party can support positions that satisfy every voter. Political power, therefore, falls to the party that comes closer to representing the majority's wishes at any given time.

2. PROVIDE ELECTABLE CANDIDATES

Political parties serve as a screening device. Each party's candidates must appear before

■ Senator Robert Dole of Kansas campaigning for the Republican presidential nomination in 1988. He lost out to George Bush, who also won the presidency.

■ Democrat Walter Mondale campaigning for the presidency in 1984. With him is Geraldine Ferraro, the first woman nominated for the vice presidency by a major party.

the public to state their positions on the issues. Public opinion, the media, and the party leadership combine to weed out candidates who hold unpopular, unworkable, or extremist views. When election time arrives, the party and its candidates usually have adjusted their positions to what they hope will be the wishes of a majority of the voters.

3. EDUCATE VOTERS

Each political party begins a campaign by writing a *platform* that sums up its position on national priorities. The party's candidates then carry that message to the voters. The candidates describe the specific things they will do if they are elected. Ideally, by the time voters reach the polling place, they will have heard and read enough to make intelligent choices.

4. FINANCE ELECTION CAMPAIGNS

National in scope, political parties can raise the large sums of money needed to conduct an election campaign. Few candidates, even the wealthiest, can pay the millions of dollars eaten up by political advertising, television, travel, staff salaries, and the other expenses of a modern campaign. Candidates in local elections, despite their smaller budgets, also need the organization, loyalties, and financing a party can offer.

5. WINNERS TO RUN THE GOVERNMENT

When the United States was young, a political party that won a national election quickly staffed the government with its own loyal members. Today, the civil service laws prevent a repetition of the spoils system that was common in the 1800s. The winning party

Learning Skills

Writing a Summary

In Chapter Four, you practiced your note-taking skills. Quick, concise notes in outline form work well when you're working with a textbook. There are times, however, when you'll want to sum up a lengthy passage in a few sentences. Perhaps you're getting ready for an oral report, or you're writing a term paper. That's when writing a summary comes in handy.

The dictionary defines a summary as *a shortened version of a longer document or speech*. You've already done a lot of summarizing, probably without knowing it. Every time you tell your friends about a movie or a ball game, you summarize it for them, don't you? No one wants to hear every detail. The way to write good summaries is to discard all but the most important information. It's easier than it sounds. Go

back and reread the account of the primary elections of 1968 on pages 108–109. Then summarize it in no more than three sentences. When you're finished, compare your summary with the one that follows.

Sample: College students who were against the war in Vietnam helped Eugene McCarthy's campaign for the presidency in 1968. McCarthy's successful showing in New Hampshire and Wisconsin forced President Johnson to withdraw. Citizens who get involved can make a difference in the American political process.

How does your summary compare with the sample? When you watch television tonight, try summarizing the story of one of your favorite shows. As with note taking, practice makes perfect!

cannot fire the bureaucrats who keep the business of government moving. The party can—and does—fill many top executive and judicial openings with its supporters.

In Great Britain, when the ruling party loses an important vote in Parliament, the prime minister resigns and calls a new election. By contrast, American Presidents remain in office even if they lose many votes in Congress. The public, however, holds a party responsible for what happens during its term in office. Herbert Hoover and the Republican party, for example, were blamed for the Great Depression that followed the Stock Market Crash of 1929. When such a disaster occurs, the party in power almost always loses the next election.

3. Why does the United States keep the two-party system?

The American two-party system has some obvious flaws. Each party, for example, must span a wide range of political beliefs. Even so, there are four logical reasons why social scientists predict a long life for our political system.

1. DESIRE FOR STABILITY

The voters in many countries, Italy and Israel among them, support numerous political parties. With the vote split six or eight ways, it often happens that no single party gains a legislative *majority* (more than one-half of the seats in the lawmaking bodies). When this occurs, a *coalition*, or union of cooperating parties, must be formed. Only then can the ruling coalition choose a chief executive. If one or more small parties drop out of the coalition, the government collapses. Thus, the multiparty system sometimes results in unstable governments that change almost monthly.

The U.S. two-party system provides more stability. One major party or the other always holds a majority in the House or the Senate—and sometimes controls both houses. Further,

a President can still be effective even though the executive's own party controls neither of the two houses. The President's veto power keeps a hostile Congress from totally dominating the political scene.

2. NATIONAL ELECTION LAWS

American election laws favor a two-party system. Most elected positions are contested on the basis of "winner take all." A major party's candidates may win only 51 percent of the vote in each district, but it will still elect all of the congressional representatives from that state. Smaller parties, therefore, stand little chance of gaining national representation.

3. SIZE OF THE FEDERAL SYSTEM

The very size of the United States has helped to create the two-party system. Many *third parties* (also known as *minority parties*) have developed strong local or regional appeal. These parties have carried cities and even an occasional state. Before a minority party can succeed on the national level, however, a major party adds the smaller party's ideas to its platform. Such a move robs the minority party of its reason for existence.

4. TRADITION OF ALTERNATION IN OFFICE

No American political party has ever "owned" the federal government. Democrats and Republicans have each enjoyed long periods of success. But after a while, the voters tire of the old policies and return the other party to power. The Democrats, for example, held the presidency for most of the years between 1800 and the Civil War. Beginning in 1860, the Republicans won 14 of the next 18 national elections.

4. How did the American two-party system develop?

Modern U.S. political parties began to form in 1787 during the campaign to ratify the Constitution. Many of the new country's leaders wanted a strong federal government. Call-

■ A souvenir from the presidential campaign of 1888. Republican Benjamin Harrison (left) is weighing in against Democrat Grover Cleveland. Harrison won.

ing themselves Federalists, they set out to convince the legislatures of the 13 states that the Constitution should be ratified. The opposition, known as the Anti-Federalists, believed that the state governments should keep their independence. The Anti-Federalists also objected to the absence of specific guarantees of personal freedom in the Constitution. The ratification of the Constitution in 1788 and the later addition of the Bill of Rights failed to end the division between the Federalists and Anti-Federalists.

DEVELOPMENT OF THE DEMOCRATIC PARTY

Thomas Jefferson led the Anti-Federalists, who were soon known as the Democratic-Republican party. Jefferson's political ideas appealed to the country, and he defeated John Adams, the second and last Federalist President. The Federalist belief in government by an aristocracy, plus a continuing distrust of strong national government, helped ensure Adams's defeat.

The Era of Good Feelings was dominated by the Democratic-Republican presidency of James Monroe. This period was marked by an absence of serious political strife. It ended when John Quincy Adams and Andrew Jackson fought the bitter campaign of 1824. In the 1830s, Jackson rebuilt the Democratic party ("Republican" had been dropped from the party name in 1825). After the Civil War, the Democrats gradually changed from a states' rights party to one that believed in a strong federal authority. The modern Democratic party emphasizes its ties to the "common people." It dedicates itself to using government to solve a variety of problems that neither individuals nor the states can solve for themselves.

DEVELOPMENT OF THE REPUBLICAN PARTY

Today's Republican party traces its history back to the original Federalists. The Federalist party had largely broken up by the end of the War of 1812. The short-lived National Republican party took its place, only to be absorbed by the Whig party in the 1830s. The Whigs won the presidency with William Henry Harrison in 1840 and with Zachary Taylor in 1848. Despite those victories, the Whigs were divided by the slavery question and disappeared in the 1850s.

The heritage of the Federalist-Whig party fell to a minority party that was organized in 1854 to oppose slavery. Abraham Lincoln led the new Republican party to its first national victory in 1860. That election began a Republican domination of national politics that lasted until the election of Franklin Roosevelt in 1932.

Like the Democratic party, the Republicans have undergone a major change in their basic political philosophy. The original Federalists believed in a strong federal authority. Modern Republicans favor states' rights and freedom from government control.

PARTIES CHANGE WITH THE TIMES

A word of caution should be added regarding the dangers of comparing political beliefs over a span of two centuries. Despite the apparent shift in philosophy noted above, most modern Republicans accept more government control over the lives of the American people than any old-time Federalist would have believed possible. Times change and so do politics.

5. How have third parties affected the American political system?

The modern Republican party began as a minority, sectional party. In 1860, however, it emerged as the country's second major party. No other third party has made that leap. Most of America's third parties, in fact, have played only a minor role in the nation's history.

The American campaign trail has been well traveled by third parties, as the table on page 117 demonstrates. In those states in which it's easy to add a party's candidates to the ballot, voters may be faced with six or more choices for President. Once their candidates qualify to be put on the ballot, most minority parties do not have the resources to challenge the major parties. They use the publicity generated by the campaign to advance their special causes.

ECONOMIC GOALS

A few third parties have done more than satisfy private enthusiasms. The Populist party, active in the late 1800s, consisted mainly of discontented farmers from the West and South. The Populists stood for federal ownership of the railroads and the telegraph and telephone systems, an income tax system that called for higher rates for higher income brackets, and unlimited coinage of silver to increase the money supply. On this platform, the Populist party won some city elections, elected state legislators, and sent representatives to Congress. Nevertheless, the Populists disappeared when the Democratic party added many of their policies to its own platform.

SECTIONAL DISCONTENT

Some third parties have reflected sectional discontent rather than economic ideas. The

■ Campaign buttons from the presidential race in 1900. Republicans William McKinley and Theodore Roosevelt promised four more years of prosperity. They won.

States' Rights party, for example, polled more than a million votes in the 1948 presidential election. Its members were mostly Southern Democrats. These voters disliked the liberal civil rights platform supported by the regular Democratic candidate, Harry S Truman.

A similar southern movement produced the American Independent party of George Wallace in 1968. Heavy southern support for the AIP stripped enough votes from the Democrats to send Richard Nixon to the White House with less than 50 percent of the popular vote.

NOW LET THE SHOW GO ON!
ARRIVAL OF THE POLITICAL COLUMBINE TO JOIN THE POLITICAL CLOWN.

■ Cartoon from the 1884 presidential campaign features Belva Lockwood, nominee of the Women's Rights party. One of the few women who have run for the presidency, Lockwood was a reformer and woman suffrage leader.

RADICAL POLITICS

Many third-party movements pursue radical political beliefs. On the far left, the Socialist party has participated in national politics for many years. Similarly, the Peace and Freedom party became active in 1968, primarily in opposition to the war in Vietnam. On the far right stand parties such as the Know-Nothings of the 1800s and the American Nazis of today. Both right-wing parties have tried to use political means to promote their extremist goals, but they have met with little success.

SINGLE-ISSUE PARTIES

Occasionally, a party emerges that focuses attention on a single issue. The Prohibition party, which helped promote the Eighteenth Amendment, built its strength by opposing the sale and use of alcoholic beverages. Theodore Roosevelt created the Progressive (Bull Moose) party in 1912 in a vain attempt to win the presidency after being denied the Republican nomination.

Let's review for a moment

A *political party* may be defined as an organization of people who attempt to elect government officials and influence policies. To be a true party, as distinct from a *pressure group*, the party must demonstrate (1) common beliefs, (2) a program for running the government should its candidates be elected, and (3) a reasonable chance of success.

Can you remember five functions of political parties in a democracy? They serve to (1) organize a political majority, (2) provide electable candidates, (3) educate the public, (4) finance election campaigns, and (5) provide personnel for government service.

The two-party system took hold largely because the United States elects its officials on a "winner-take-all" basis. The desire for stability, the size of the federal system, and changes in policies by the major parties to keep themselves in power have also restricted the growth of *minority parties*.

Can you remember the different names the Republicans and Democrats have been known by during their history? The Federalists turned into Whigs, and were later absorbed by the antislavery Republicans. The Democrats started as the Anti-Federalists, who later became the Democratic-Republicans, and then the Democrats.

Now let's look at some of the political labels that are often pasted on members of our major parties.

6. What do political labels really stand for?

Can you imagine shopping in a market where none of the cans, bottles, and packages are labeled? Without some type of label, you couldn't tell a can of peas from a tin of sauerkraut. Politics isn't a supermarket, however, and the country doesn't ask its politicians to wear ID tags. Even so, people are more

FYI . . .
A Sampling of Third Parties in American Politics

Party	Dates	Description
Liberal party	1840–48	First antislavery party.
Free-Soil party	1848–56	Favored free territories in the West.
American party (Know-Nothings)	1852–60	Anti-immigrant, anti-Catholic party. Nickname grew out of members' claim, when questioned, to "know nothing" about the party.
Prohibition party	1869–	Based on opposition to use of alcohol. Worked for Eighteenth Amendment.
Greenback party	1876–84	Supported paper money, extension of federal power, and the income tax.
Socialist party	1890–	Favors government ownership of natural resources and of major industries.
Populist party	1891–96	Farmer and worker party; anti-monopoly.
Progressive ("Bull Moose") party	1912	Theodore Roosevelt's split from conservative Republicanism.
Progressive party	1924–46	Robert La Follette's semi-socialistic party; promoted government ownership of business and natural resources.
States' Rights party (Dixiecrats)	1948	Southern Democratic split over civil rights question.
American Independent party	1968	George Wallace's states'-rights party.
Peace and Freedom party	1968–	Antiwar, antidraft, left-wing movement.
National Unity/Liberal party	1980	Republican John Anderson led a unity movement that was conservative in economic matters and liberal in dealing with social problems.

comfortable when they can fit candidates into neatly labeled political pigeonholes.

The use of political labels can never be totally precise, of course. As the issues change and as society's values shift, the meaning of political labels changes as well. Many people react to terms such as "liberal" or "conservative" as if one were good and the other were bad. In reality, the meaning of these labels often depends on one's own political beliefs.

The diagram on page 119 shows how the most common political labels relate to one another. In general, liberals who want more government action are called *left wing*. They are placed on the left side of the diagram. Conservatives who want less government control are called *right wing*. They appear on the right side of the diagram. The terms date back to the French Revolution when liberals and conservatives in the National Convention seated themselves on the left or right side of the room, respectively, according to their political philosophies. Now let's discuss the political labels that show up in the diagram.

RADICAL

A *radical* might be described as someone who believes (1) that the problems of the country can be solved only through extreme measures and (2) that the change should take place immediately. Some radical groups are content to work within the structure of the democratic process. Others believe in revolutionary change.

The radical right consists of groups that sometimes gather under the flag of militant anticommunism. Often known as *reactionaries*, they denounce most forms of government regulation, including progressive taxation and restrictions on business and industry. Strangely enough, these radicals would not hesitate to use the government's police power to enforce the changes they desire. Examples of political groups on the radical right are the John Birch Society, the National States' Rights party, and the Christian Crusade.

The radical left, on the other hand, often marches under the banner of socialism. Groups such as the Socialist Workers party and the American Communist party believe that the problems of poverty, race relations, and unequal opportunity cannot be solved by the capitalist system. These parties want the government to take over the nation's "means of production." When Socialists use that phrase, they mean all natural and industrial resources.

LIBERAL

Liberals look to the government for solutions to the many problems of modern life. They accept increased government regulation as the price that must be paid if everyone is to have the basic necessities of life. Liberals believe in gradual change by democratic means rather than by revolution. Most liberals, for example, would not favor government takeover of the medical profession. Instead they would vote for government-guaranteed health insurance, extended Medicare programs, and greater supervision of the entire health industry.

MODERATE

A *moderate* occupies that political position called "the middle of the road." Politicians dare not ignore the moderates because a majority of the American people usually vote under this label. Although moderates largely accept government as they find it, they often favor new and better laws. In any given election, their loyalties may shift to the liberal or conservative side when it comes to individual issues.

CONSERVATIVE

Conservatives believe "that government governs best which governs least." They hold that most regulation by the federal government should be handed over to people at the state or local level. The conservatives' ultimate goal would be to give individuals a maximum amount of freedom. When this happens, responsibility for the public welfare will be removed from what conservatives see as government's costly and inefficient hands.

INADEQUACY OF LABELS

Even though terms like "liberal" and "conservative" make handy labels, they cannot

The American Political Spectrum

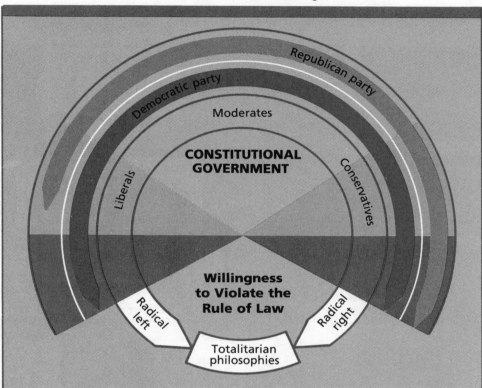

describe anyone's total political beliefs. Sharp breaks do not exist from one philosophy to the next. Instead, moderates gradually merge with conservatives on the right and with liberals on the left (as the diagram on page 119 indicates). When you hear a politician described as a "liberal" or a "conservative," look to see who is applying the label. To someone on the radical right, a moderate Republican may seem much too liberal. To the radical left, the same moderate may seem too conservative.

To make matters more confusing, Americans wear their party labels rather loosely. It isn't until after an election that a party learns how many of its members used the secrecy of the voting booth to cast their votes for the other side. This type of political independence takes several forms. Some people vote a *split ticket*, which means that they support candidates from both parties. Others practice *crossover voting* and support the opposition party's full slate of candidates.

7. How is a political party organized?

Today, approximately three voters in ten claim to be Republicans. About two in five call themselves Democrats. Except for a scattering of minority party members, the remaining 30 percent think of themselves as *independents*. Independent voters do not always vote in predictable patterns—and neither do registered Republicans and Democrats. The major parties, therefore, cannot win an election unless they have a party organization strong

Organization of a Political Party

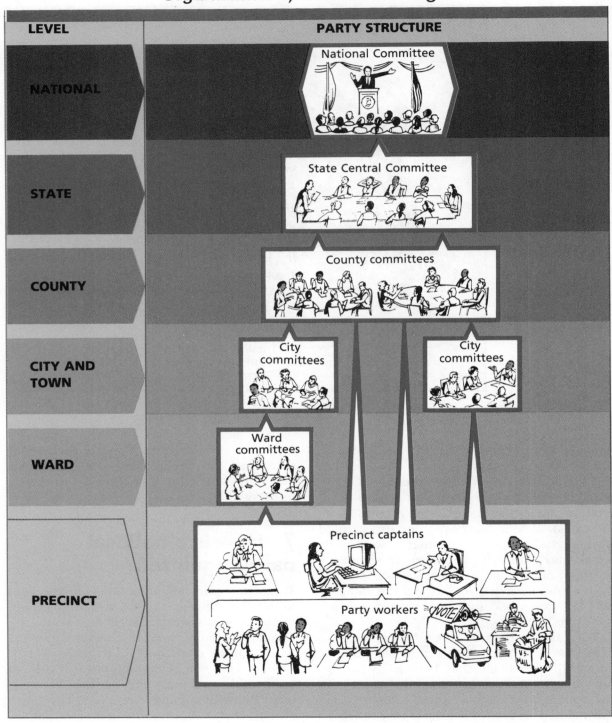

■ The man standing behind the table is a poll watcher at a local election in Chicago. What responsibility does a poll watcher have? Why are police officers present in polling places?

enough to build support for their candidates at every level of government. The illustration on page 120 shows a typical party structure.

NATIONAL COMMITTEE

American political parties maintain a national organization, but they are most active at the state level. The activities of the *national committee* become most noticeable when it's time for a presidential election. The role of the committee includes (1) planning the national convention every four years, (2) raising money to finance party activities, (3) writing the party platform, and (4) running the presidential election campaign. State committees select the members of the national committee, who then elect the national party leader. National committee members, who are often the leaders of the state committees, must be confirmed by action of the delegates to the national convention.

STATE CENTRAL COMMITTEE

The structure of political parties reflects the federal-state relationship. Within each state, the party develops policies independent of the national committee. Members of the powerful *state central committee* gain their positions by (1) election in a state primary, (2) appointment by county or city committees, or (3) election at a state convention.

The state central committee and its leader supervise the writing of party policies and programs. The leader tries to keep county organizations working together. Other duties of the state central committee include (1) supervising the selection of candidates, (2) fund-raising, (3) organizing conventions, (4) coordinating the work of county committees, and (5) supervising party political activities throughout the state. The state central committee also supervises the distribution of party *patronage*. Patronage refers to the handing out of jobs, contracts, and other favors to party supporters.

COUNTY COMMITTEE

The *county committee* is the basic party unit below the state level. Led by a county leader, the committee members supervise the daily political life of their district. Not only does the committee direct party workers during election campaigns, it also expects to influence zoning decisions, business licensing, and other sensitive political matters. Many county leaders build up disciplined party followings called *political machines*. Their power rests on their ability to do political favors. A party boss can influence the awarding of county contracts and the hiring of non-civil-service workers.

PRECINCT ORGANIZATION

In some states, another layer of organization exists below the county committee. The party unit at the town or neighborhood level is commonly called the *ward committee* or *precinct committee*. If these committees exist, they supervise the work of the local precinct captains. These local workers, known as the political *"grass roots"* of the party have the vital job of ensuring a strong voter turnout on election day. The precinct committee represents the party in the minds of most voters. Their loyalty to the party is often measured by how well the precinct captain helps them work out their problems with local government agencies.

8. What happens at a party convention?

Every four years, each of the major parties holds a widely publicized convention. State committees meet in convention more frequently but without the same attention from the media. Whether they are held at the state or national level, conventions engage in three important political activities: (1) The convention nominates candidates for political office. (2) The convention hammers together a plat-

form, which sets forth the positions that the party will support in coming elections. (3) The convention votes on rules for the operation of the party.

CONTROL OF THE CONVENTION

The convention system has replaced the old *party caucus*. These were closed meetings run by party officials. In the "smoke-filled rooms" of the caucus, political bosses selected candidates and wrote party policy. Faced with the loss of voter confidence, party leaders in most states finally gave up the undemocratic caucuses in favor of open conventions.

Delegates to the national convention are selected in two ways: (1) Many states hold statewide party elections, called *primaries*. In these special elections, voters select slates of delegates, each pledged to support a particular candidate for the party's nomination. (2) Other states hold a *nominating convention*, which selects the delegates to the national convention. Quite often, these delegates are not required to vote for any particular candidate.

Despite these reforms, powerful political leaders maintain control of many aspects of the convention. Mayors, governors, state central committee leaders, members of Congress, special-interest groups, and candidates all try to use their influence to accomplish their own political ends. Groups of uncommitted delegates from non-primary states can often be pressured to support a particular candidate or sectional interest. If none of the candidates can win an early victory in convention voting, the party leaders begin to "wheel and deal." A state governor, for example, might promise to deliver a block of delegate votes in exchange for favors to be collected at a later date.

In recent years, front-running candidates have often won enough votes in the primaries to ensure their victory at the convention. With most of the suspense of choosing a nominee removed, the convention then turns into a media event. Party leaders take advantage of the television and newspaper coverage to make their policies and candidates better known to the American public.

■ An enthusiastic demonstration after a rousing speech by Ann Richards of Texas at the 1988 Democratic National Convention in Atlanta. Delegates hope such activities will win voter support.

EARLY CONVENTION BUSINESS

In the early days of the convention, two seldom-noticed activities take place.

Committee on credentials. The committee on credentials settles disputes over which slate of delegates from a particular state should be seated. Credentials disputes arise when each rival camp within a state party sends its own delegates to the convention.

Platform committee. The platform committee decides what positions the party will support in the coming election. Sharply opposing views often make compromise impossible. When that happens, the committee may send a majority and a minority report to the floor of the convention. In that case, the entire body of delegates makes the final decisions.

CONVENTION BALLOTING

The drama of the national convention reaches its peak with the balloting on the nominations for President. One after another, speakers nominate the candidates. The presiding officer of the convention then asks for a roll call of the states. Some state delegations vote as a bloc, but others split their votes. The roll calls continue until one candidate wins a majority. At that point, the delegations scramble to switch their votes so that the nomination will seem to be unanimous. In this way, the party can appear to be united when it goes before the voters in the coming campaign.

■ Candidates for the Democratic presidential nomination in 1988 at a televised debate in New Hampshire. From the left, Sen. Albert Gore, Jr., of Tenn., Gov. Michael Dukakis of Mass., Moderator Sander Vanocur, Sen. Paul Simon of Ill., former governor Bruce Babbitt of Ariz., and the Rev. Jesse Jackson of Ill.

9. What are the steps in the presidential election cycle?

The conventions are only one step in the election cycle. Before a citizen walks into a voting booth in early November, the candidates and parties have invested months of costly effort. The length of local and state campaigns varies widely from state to state and from election to election. Presidential election campaigns, however, dominate the nation's political life for well over a year. Within that long campaign, the voter can expect to see several traditional milestones.

1. THE ANNOUNCEMENT

Candidates often announce their candidacy a year or more in advance of an election. The announcement generates an initial surge of useful publicity. There is, however, some danger in starting out this early. A front runner often becomes a highly visible target for attacks by opponents, the media, and the opposition party. In the summer of 1987, news about a possible extra-marital affair forced Democratic front-runner Gary Hart to drop out of the race for several months before the

first primary. If Hart hadn't been an announced candidate, the media wouldn't have been watching his private life so closely.

2. NOMINATING CONVENTIONS AND PRIMARY ELECTIONS

In states without primary elections, the party organization holds a nominating convention in the spring. At the convention, state political leaders play a major role in selecting candidates for local, state, and national office. In this century, presidential primary elections have replaced nominating conventions in well over half the states and in the District of Columbia.

Primary elections allow voters registered as members of a particular party to select their party's candidates for the general election. Primaries open only to registered members of a particular party are called *closed primaries*. A few states hold *open primaries*, in which voters do not declare their choice of party until they are in the privacy of the voting booth. Then they mark the appropriate party ballot. To make matters even more complicated, some states permit crossover voting. This allows Democrats to vote in the Republican primary and vice versa.

Finally, many states run *presidential pref-*

erence primaries (sometimes called "beauty contests"). In these primaries, the election of delegates is separate from the voting for a presidential candidate. These contests give candidates useful publicity, but the results are not binding. The delegates are not selected until later, when the party holds its state convention.

Until recently, some states awarded delegates on a "winner-take-all" basis. The candidate who won the preference vote walked off with all of the state's delegates. Today, these winner-take-all primaries have all but disappeared. In 1976, 1980, and 1988 (but not 1984), the Democratic party imposed a proportional representation rule that awarded delegates according to the percentage of the primary vote won by each candidate. Most states have now adjusted their primary laws to reflect this rule.

Some critics think that the entire primary process should be overhauled. They say it's too long, too expensive, and too hard on the candidates. To replace it, they suggest that each party should hold a single, nationwide presidential primary. Along with simplifying the long primary campaign, it would eliminate much of the need for national conventions. Supporters of the primary system argue that the primaries serve three purposes: they weed out weak candidates, bring candidates closer to the voters, and help the country focus its attention on important national problems.

3. NATIONAL CONVENTION

National conventions are one of the great spectacles in American politics. Large cities are happy to host the conventions, which generate publicity as well as business. The conventions bring candidates and delegates together for a week of summer madness. The political tensions built up during the long primary campaign are worked out in wild floor demonstrations. Delegates shout, sing,

■ The delegates to the Republican National Convention in 1988 cheer the presidential and vice-presidential nominees and their wives. From the left, Barbara and George Bush and Dan and Marilyn Quayle. After the convention, the nominees campaign throughout the country.

march, and wave placards. Behind the scenes, candidates and party leaders carry on a frenzied search for the votes they need to lock up the nomination.

After an orgy of oratory and demonstrations, the delegates finally choose their presidential candidate. Incumbent Presidents and highly popular candidates are often nominated on the first ballot. If no clear winner has emerged from the primaries, several candidates may divide the vote, and no one will gain a majority. To break this deadlock the convention may take dozens of roll-call votes before agreeing on a candidate. In these cases, a compromise "dark horse" sometimes emerges as the party's nominee.

The nominee's first task is to choose a candidate for Vice President. Candidates who have locked up the nomination early sometimes choose their running mates before the convention begins. At other times, the choice of a vice presidential candidate is kept secret so as to build suspense. Even though some delegates may not approve of the candidate's choice, the convention's approval is given automatically.

4. THE CAMPAIGN

Presidential campaigns traditionally begin on Labor Day, when the American public ends its summer vacation and returns to work. In truth, the campaign starts the day the national conventions end. The pace simply increases in September and October as each major party attempts to build support for its candidate. The tiring, expensive campaign dominates national attention until election day. (The campaign and the election itself are discussed in greater detail in Chapter Six).

5. ELECTION DAY

On the first Tuesday after the first Monday in November of an election year, Americans go to their polling places. After all the excitement

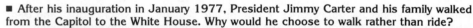

■ After his inauguration in January 1977, President Jimmy Carter and his family walked from the Capitol to the White House. Why would he choose to walk rather than ride?

and controversy of the campaign, the decisive moment comes when the voters mark their secret ballots. Government agencies, whether city, country, or state, manage the election process. Voting may be by machine, computer punch card, or hand-marked paper ballot. The counting goes quickly in most cases. Officials often announce preliminary results within a few hours after the polls close.

6. INAUGURATION

The election cycle ends when the victorious candidate takes the oath of office. The weeks between the election and the swearing-in ceremonies are called the outgoing administra-tion's *lame-duck period*. The newly elected President must wait more than two months to be inaugurated. The results of the election aren't official until the new Congress meets and certifies the vote of the Electoral College (see Chapter Eleven). The interval between November and January allows the President-elect to assemble an administration, particu-larly an executive staff and Cabinet. At one time, outgoing Presidents did little to help their successors prepare for their first day in office. Fortunately, that practice has changed. Recent changeovers have been notable for the cooperation between the old and the new administrations.

Reviewing
what you've learned

1. Whenever a large number of people join together to elect candidates or promote their political beliefs, a *political party* is born. Parties serve to organize a political *majority*, provide reasonable choices at election time, educate voters, make election to office possible, and provide personnel to run the government.

2. The Democratic party traces its roots back to Thomas Jefferson and Andrew Jackson. The Democratic philosophy moved from a belief in states' rights to today's emphasis on using government to solve society's problems. The Republican party was born out of the antislavery movement of the pre-Civil War period. It can trace its heritage back to the Federalist and Whig parties. Like the Democrats, the Republicans have revised their beliefs. Once they believed in expanding the powers of the federal system, but now they distrust "big government."

3. *Third parties* have made little impression on American politics. Although they often appear on state ballots, they seldom achieve national importance. One reason is that one of the major parties usually adopts their most popular goals. When third parties do arise, they usually have special economic, sectional, or political goals.

4. Political labels serve as a shorthand method of identifying candidates and issues. Labels like *reactionary, conservative, moderate, liberal,* and *radical left* or *right* possess limited accuracy. Meanings and beliefs change as the times change. American voters, moreover, wear party labels lightly, sometimes changing them on their way to the voting booth.

5. Each major party is guided by a *national committee* that is made up of representatives from each state. This committee stages national conventions and manages the party's general election campaigns. Much of the power within each party is held at the state level. *State central committees* work year-round to coordinate party activities, raise money, and mend political fences. *County* and *ward* (or *precinct*) committees complete the party structure.

6. *Primary elections* allow the voters to select their party's candidates for office. Party *nominating conventions* still pick many state-level candidates and delegates to the national convention. Political pressure pays off at these conventions, where special-interest groups, political bosses, and powerful elected officials compete for the privilege of choosing the party's nominees.

7. The long cycle of a presidential campaign begins when the first candidates announce that they're running for office. In the spring of an election year, the states hold *primary* elections and conventions to choose delegates who support one candidate or another. At the national conventions in the summer, the delegates choose their party's presidential candidate. The fall campaign runs through September and October, and the election is held in early November. *Inauguration* of the newly elected President takes place in January of the following year.

Review questions and activities

TERMS YOU SHOULD KNOW

closed primary	minority party	presidential preference
coalition	moderate	primary
conservative	national committee	pressure group
county committee	nominating convention	primary
crossover voting	open primary	radical
"grass roots"	party caucus	reactionary
independent voter	patronage	right wing
lame-duck period	platform	split-ticket voting
left wing	political machine	state central committee
liberal	political party	third party
majority	precinct	ward

REVIEW QUESTIONS

Select the response that best completes each statement or question.

1. Political parties are needed in a democracy in order to   (*a*) organize the political majority.   (*b*) educate the people about the issues of the day.   (*c*) provide personnel to run the government.   (*d*) provide candidates to run for office.   (*e*) all of these reasons.

2. A two-party system holds an advantage over the multiparty European systems in that   (*a*) it makes coalition government possible.   (*b*) it provides stable governments that change only at election time.   (*c*) all minority parties gain equal representation.   (*d*) multiparty governments work well only when people don't care about their form of government.   (*e*) all of these reasons.

3. The modern Republican party inherited the political tradition of the (a) Federalists and Democratic-Republicans. (b) Anti-Federalists and Whigs. (c) Federalists and Progressives. (d) Federalists and Whigs. (e) none of these.

4. The failure of third parties to win national elections can be traced to (a) the tendency of the major parties to take over the ideas of third parties once these ideas become popular. (b) their failure to present programs that appeal to voters. (c) laws that prevent third parties from appearing on the ballot. (d) voter dislike of parties that have a great deal of money to spend. (e) all of these reasons.

5. A right-wing politician would most likely believe in (a) increased welfare payments to the poor. (b) a program of national health care. (c) less government control over auto manufacturers. (d) government takeover of the arms and munitions industry. (e) stricter controls over industrial pollution.

6. The majority of American voters can usually be found in the political camp of the (a) radical left. (b) liberals. (c) moderates. (d) conservatives. (e) reactionaries.

7. Which of the following is *not* a job handled by the Democratic and Republican national committees? (a) Planning the national convention. (b) Selecting the presidential nominee. (c) Raising money to finance party activities. (d) Writing the party platform. (e) Running the presidential election campaign.

8. Of the following party activities, the most democratic is the (a) party caucus. (b) giving of party patronage. (c) primary election. (d) state convention. (e) national convention.

9. The most important task of the national convention is to (a) select the party's candidate for President. (b) raise money to run the campaign. (c) write a platform that states the party's position on important issues. (d) check the credentials of the delegates. (e) select the party leaders who will guide the party for the next four years.

10. A "lame-duck" politician is one who (a) was careless while on a hunting trip. (b) is waiting to take office after winning an election. (c) lost the party nomination at the convention. (d) is waiting to leave office after a successor has been elected. (e) none of these.

CONCEPT DEVELOPMENT

1. Why do most Americans prefer not to become involved in politics? What are the long-range consequences of this attitude?

2. What differences can you find in the goals supported by today's Republican and Democratic parties?

3. Why have third parties failed to establish themselves as lasting political forces in the United States? Would our country be better off with more than two major parties? Why or why not?

4. Describe the structure of a typical political party. Why are "grass roots" so important to the success of a party's candidates?

5. What reforms would you suggest for the American political system? How would you put these changes into effect?

HANDS-ON ACTIVITIES

1. "Grass roots" politics begins with local party officials. Invite both the Republicans and Democrats to send staff members to your class to talk about their jobs and their parties. Ask them to emphasize the role individual voters can play in the political process at the community level. Political party headquarters are usually listed in the telephone book—and they'll be happy to talk to young voters.

2. Set up a round-table discussion among five students from your class. Assign the roles of a reactionary, a conservative, a moderate, a liberal, and a radical leftist. Use a current topic that will bring out contrasting viewpoints. For example: "Should the U.S. government return to strict regulation of the airlines?" or "Should the U.S. offer health insurance to all citizens?" or "Should the federal government be required to have a balanced budget?"

3. Arrange to visit a meeting of your local Republican or Democratic central committee (county or city). Report back to your class on the business conducted by the committee and its membership. If that's not possible, try to attend a ward or precinct meeting.

4. Dramatize a scene from a "smoke-filled room" at a national political convention. Through the dialogue, show how powerful politicians trade votes in order to gain influence over a candidate. Useful background information from America's political past can be found in three influential novels: Edwin O'Connor's *The Last Hurrah*, Robert Penn Warren's *All the King's Men*, and Allen Drury's *Advise and Consent*.

5. Involve yourself (and your class, if possible) in a local political campaign. Volunteer for precinct work: stuff envelopes, ring doorbells, answer phones. All the while, note what is going on around you. Write about your experience for the class or the school paper. Include your honest opinion as to the value of joining in the political process at the grass roots level.

❝ **. . . your vote does count. Elections often turn on a handful of votes.** **❞**

6 The voter's role in the electoral process

Over 91 million Americans cast ballots in the 1988 presidential election. Millions more will vote in future elections. Does your vote really count when it's mixed in with all those others? What if you're a concerned citizen who makes the effort to go to the polls. How can you be sure that political bosses won't "steal" the election?

The record shows that your vote does count. Elections often turn on a handful of votes. Political scientists point to 1960 as a good example. If one or two more Republicans had voted in each of the nation's election precincts, John Kennedy never would have been elected. Richard Nixon lost by only 118,000 votes. That's less than two-tenths of one percent of

▲ Lyndon Johnson in 1941, campaigning in Texas for a seat in the U.S. Senate.

the 68 million votes cast! Many elections are determined by the nonvoters whose only election day activity is watching the returns on television.

Voting is important, but it may not be enough. Election officials must count the ballots honestly. A young Texas politician named Lyndon Johnson, for example, mysteriously lost one recount and won another during the 1940s.

In 1941, Johnson apparently led Governor W. Lee "Pappy" O'Daniel by a safe 5,000 votes in a special election for a seat in the U.S. Senate. By the next day, the situation changed. "Corrected" votes had poured in from rural counties controlled by the governor's party organization. O'Daniel was elected to the Senate by a margin of 1,311 out of more than 600,000 votes cast.

Seven years later, Johnson opposed another Texas governor, Coke Stevenson, in the Democratic primary for the U.S. Senate. Again the election was close. Election day returns favored Stevenson. It looked as though Johnson's Senate hopes had been defeated a second time. A few days later, the tiny town of Alice, in Jim Wells County, "found" 202 additional votes. Two hundred and one of the new votes were for Johnson. The Stevenson camp screamed that Archie Parr, the county's political boss, was a Johnson supporter. That was true, but the revised count stood up in court. "Landslide" Lyndon's edge of 87 votes out of the 988,000 cast paved the way for his victory in the general election.

These examples of close elections, even when distorted by vote counting hanky-panky, underline a major thesis in American politics: *Individual votes do matter.* The American system depends on every citizen's participation. Every time we vote and count the ballots honestly, we renew the vitality of our government and its ability to serve our needs.

Where do you fit in the electoral process? Your duties as an American voter are explored in this chapter. You'll learn the answers to these questions:

1. What limits were once placed on the right to vote?

2. What limits on the right to vote remain today?

3. What does party membership have to do with voting?

4. How does the American secret ballot work?

5. How do Americans select their party and their candidates?

6. Why do so many Americans choose not to vote?

7. Who pays for American election campaigns?

■ A women's suffrage parade in New York City in the early 1900s. The struggle by U.S. women to win the right to vote in all elections officially began in 1848. The Nineteenth Amendment in 1920 finally gave them that right. Women now strive for equal rights in the workplace.

1. What limits were once placed on the right to vote?

Today's citizens enjoy the *franchise* (the right to vote) with fewer limitations than at any other time in America's history. Most of the restrictions that were accepted in colonial times have been erased by constitutional amendments, congressional action, or court decisions.

The limits on the franchise that were accepted during the nation's early years grew out of laws written by each colony. Probably not even 1 American in 15 qualified to vote for Washington in 1789. In the early years of the republic, the following restrictions affected a person's right to vote.

PROPERTY OWNERSHIP

All 13 colonies required property ownership as a qualification for voting. The reasoning behind that restriction was that people who didn't own property lacked independence, judgment, and virtue. Without these qualities, they couldn't make proper decisions regarding government in a free republic.

RELIGIOUS BELIEF

Because many colonies were founded by religious groups, would-be voters were required to swear that they believed in a Supreme Being. Others, like the Massachusetts Bay Colony, went a step further and required church membership.

POLL TAX

A tax on the right to vote is called a *poll tax*. Poll taxes produced revenue for some states much as a property tax does today. Sometimes the tax added up year by year. If a voter didn't pay one year's tax, it was doubled the next. When used in this way, the poll tax took the vote away from those who couldn't pay. Many southern states imposed poll taxes until 1964, when they were abolished by the Twenty-fourth Amendment to the U.S. Constitution.

SEX DISCRIMINATION

In 1869, Wyoming became the first state to give women the franchise. Until then, American women had been barred from voting at every level of government. Male politicians used three arguments to justify the lack of women's suffrage. First, they said, women were not interested in politics. Second, they claimed that women could not vote wisely because they were poorly educated. Finally, they argued, giving married women the vote would be foolish because wives would vote the way their husbands told them to vote.

Suffragist leaders began the struggle for the franchise in the years before the Civil War. The early efforts were led by Elizabeth Cady Stanton and Susan B. Anthony. Slowly, following Wyoming's lead, more states joined the suffrage movement. The fierce debate ended in 1920, when the Nineteenth Amendment awarded the vote to women on the same basis as men.

CONDITION OF SERVITUDE

The slavery issue created controversy from the earliest days of the nation's history. By including the Three-fifths Compromise in the Constitution, the Framers allowed a state to count three-fifths of its slaves as part of its population for the allocation of seats in the House of Representatives. Slaves themselves could not vote. The Fourteenth and Fifteenth amendments finally corrected this injustice. After 1870, a previous condition of servitude (slavery) could no longer bar a man from voting.

INDIRECT ELECTIONS

The Framers believed that full democracy could lead to rash and impulsive action. As a result, they created the Electoral College to choose the President and directed that senators should be elected by the various state legislatures. After the Seventeenth Amendment was ratified in 1913, Americans were allowed to vote directly for their state's two senators. See pages 244–245 for further discussion of the Electoral College.

2. What limits on the right to vote remain today?

The franchise has been extended to all American citizens of voting age. After basic constitutional protections have been met, however, the states have the right to limit the right to vote in several specific ways.

CONSTITUTIONAL PROTECTION OF VOTING RIGHTS

A state's voting regulations may not violate the Constitution's four major guarantees:

1. *Voting equality.* Any voter who is eligible to vote in an election for a state's larger legislative house (the state assembly, for example) must be allowed to vote in federal elections.

2. *No racial discrimination.* No state may deny the right to vote on the basis of race, color, or previous condition of servitude.

3. *No sex discrimination.* No state may deny the right to vote on the basis of sex.

4. *No poll tax.* No state may require the payment of a poll tax or any other tax in order to vote in a federal election. Supreme Court decisions have applied this principle to local and state elections as well.

REMAINING LIMITATIONS

Within these constitutional restrictions, the states have imposed a number of realistic limits on the right to vote.

1. *Citizenship.* Every state requires that voters must be citizens before they take part in local, state, or national elections. These laws do not distinguish between naturalized and native-born citizens. Early in this century, resident aliens were allowed to vote. The last state to permit the practice was Arkansas, which barred noncitizens from voting in 1926.

2. *Residency.* Every state requires that new voters must live within the state for a certain length of time before they become eligible to register. A shorter period of *residency* is often required for local elections than for state and national elections. One year's residence within a state and 30 days within a precinct are common requirements, but the rules vary from state to state.

Residency requirements have two major purposes: (1) They prevent political bosses from "importing" voters into their districts in order to win a close election. (2) They try to ensure that voters will be familiar with the local issues and candidates. Almost all states bar temporary residents from voting. People who are away from their permanent home, such as members of the Armed Forces and college students, fit into this category. Temporary residents must cast absentee ballots in their home precincts if they wish to vote.

3. *Age.* In 1971, the Twenty-sixth Amendment lowered the voting age to 18. Supporters of the amendment argued that if young people could legally marry and be drafted at 18, they were adults and should be allowed to vote. The movement began in Georgia (which changed its law in 1943) and Kentucky (1955).

Except in a few places, such as the college town of Berkeley, California, the effect of the Twenty-sixth Amendment has been minimal. In Berkeley, college-age voters took control of the city council, but in most places younger voters are staying away from the polls. In a recent congressional election, only 25 percent of the eligible voters in the 18–21 age group cast their ballots. This contrasted with a 45 percent turnout in the 25–44 age bracket.

4. *Registration.* Even though citizens meet all other requirements, they may not vote until they are *registered*. This means that they've gone to election officials and formally added their names to the list of voters. Registration prevents people from voting more than once. In a number of states, precinct workers post the voting list outside the polling place. As people vote, their names are crossed off.

A new voter may register at any time. To vote in a particular election, however, the new voter must register a certain number of days in advance. This gives registrars time to check the voting lists to ensure that all requirements have been met. In some states, registration

■ A sample voter registration form.

ORIGINAL

2 I am not currently registered to vote in Los Angeles County.
Actualmente no estoy registrado para votar en el Condado de Los Angeles.

☐ 1st of age / Mayoría de edad   ☐ 1st in State / 1ra Vez en Calif.   ☐ 1st in County / 1ra Vez en el Condado

CC _____   PCT _____

3 I am currently registered to vote in Los Angeles County / or
Estoy registrado para votar en el Condado de Los Angeles / o

_____ County

and hereby request said registration be cancelled.
y por la presente pido que se cancele dicho registro.

☐ CHANGE OF NAME / CAMBIO DE NOMBRE
Former Registered Name/Nombre Previamente Registrado

☐ CHANGE OF ADDRESS / CAMBIO DE DIRECCION
Former Registered Address/Dirección Previamente Registrada

☐ CHANGE OF PARTY / CAMBIO DE PARTIDO
City / Ciudad

☐ CHANGE OF OCCUPATION / CAMBIO DE OCUPACION

OFFICE USE

☐ FAILED TO VOTE LAST GENERAL ELECTION / NO VOTE EN LA PASADA ELECCION GENERAL

☐ OTHER / OTRO _____

1

STATE OF CALIFORNIA
COUNTY OF LOS ANGELES
AFFIDAVIT OF REGISTRATION

ESTADO DE CALIFORNIA
CONDADO DE LOS ANGELES
AFIDAVIT DE REGISTRO **GK** 000-000

I CERTIFY THAT I AM A CITIZEN OF THE UNITED STATES AND RESIDE AT THE ADDRESS STATED BELOW. I AM NOT CURRENTLY IMPRISONED OR ON PAROLE FOR THE CONVICTION OF A FELONY. ALL INFORMATION GIVEN BY ME ON THIS AFFIDAVIT IS TRUE AND CORRECT UNDER PENALTY OF PERJURY.

CERTIFICO QUE SOY CIUDADANO DE LOS ESTADOS UNIDOS Y QUE RADICO EN LA DIRECCION ABAJO CONSTATADA. NO ESTOY EN PRISION O EN LIBERTAD PROVISIONAL POR HABER SIDO JUZGADO CULPABLE DE UNA FELONIA. TODA LA INFORMACION DADA EN ESTE AFIDAVIT ES CIERTA Y CORRECTA BAJO PENA DE PERJURIO.

SPECIMEN

4 ☐ Mr/Sr ☐ Mrs/Sra   ☐ Ms ☐ Miss/Srta ☐ None/Ninguno   FIRST & MIDDLE NAME OR INITIAL/NOMBRE(S)   LAST NAME/APELLIDO PATERNO   ☐ Jr/Hijo ☐ Sr/Padre

5 RESIDENCE ADDRESS/DIRECCION RESIDENCIAL   AV ☐ PL ☐ BL ☐ ST ☐ DR ☐ Apt. No./No. de Apt.
CITY/CIUDAD   ZIP CODE/ZONA POSTAL

6 I LIVE BETWEEN THESE CROSS STREETS / VIVO ENTRE ESTAS CALLES   Street/Calle   AND/Y   Street/Calle

7 MAILING ADDRESS IF DIFFERENT / DIRECCION POSTAL SI DISTINTA   P. O. Box/Apartado Postal   Street/Calle   City/Ciudad   Zip Code/Zona Postal

8 OCCUPATION/OCUPACION   9 POLITICAL AFFILIATION/AFILIACION POLITICA   (CODE)

10 HEIGHT / ESTATURA Ft./Pies In./Pulgadas   11 DATE OF BIRTH / FECHA DE NAC. Mo./Mes Day/Día Yr./Año   12 SOC. SEC. NO./NO. DE SEGURO SOCIAL (May Omit) (Opcional)

13 RESIDENCE PHONE (May Omit) / TELEFONO RESIDENCIAL (Opcional)   14 PLACE OF BIRTH/LUGAR DE NACIMIENTO

15 SIGNATURE OF WITNESS/FIRMA DEL TESTIGO   16 VOTER'S SIGNATURE/FIRMA DEL VOTANTE   Date/Fecha

18 CERTIFIED BEFORE ME/AFIRMADO ANTE MI   17 RESIDENCE ADDRESS/DIRECCION RESIDENCIAL

THIS _____ DAY OF _____ 19___
ESTE _____ DIA DE _____

19 LEONARD PANISH, REGISTRAR-RECORDER / REGISTRADOR DE VOTANTES

BY / POR _____ DEPUTY REGISTRAR OF VOTERS / DIPUTADO DEL REGISTRADOR DE VOTANTES   ACCT. NO.

GK 000-000

76A33ZQ RR 10.22.13 ES

18th BIRTHDAY / CUMPLE 18 AÑOS   Yr./No   Day/Día   Mo./Mes

CANCELLED Date _____ 19___ ☐ OTHER _____
☐ TRANSFER ☐☐☐
☐ DEATH by _____   ELECTIONS DEPUTY

---

stays in effect as long as the voter participates in all general elections or does not move to a new voting district. In other states, registration must be renewed every few years.

5. *Legal disfranchisement.* Some U.S. citizens are legally barred from voting. Typical of the people who may be *disfranchised* are vagrants, the severely mentally retarded, convicted felons, and other inmates of public institutions. Voting rights lost for any of these reasons can be restored only by an act of the state legislature or by a pardon from the governor of the state.

3. What does party membership have to do with voting?

General elections are held in November of each even-numbered year. At this time, the nation's registered voters select the officials who run our local, state, and national governments. All eligible voters, whether or not they belong to a political party, may also take part in *special elections*. Special elections are called to meet specific state or local needs. At a typical special election, the voters may be asked to approve sewer bonds, raise tax rates, or elect city council and school board members.

In a *primary election*, citizens have a chance to select their party's candidates for the general election. Primary elections are usually restricted to voters who have registered as members of a political party.

In most states, voters name their party preference when they first register to vote. A political party counts on its registered members to support its candidates. Each party spends large sums of money to attract, register, and hold its members. Voter registration drives seek out nonvoters at home, at work, at school, and even in shopping centers.

Many Americans change their party registration as candidates and issues change. A change of registration requires only a brief visit to the registrar of voters. Because of the time needed to change the voting lists, the law sets a cutoff date for changes before each election. A typical registration form is shown on page 136.

Voters may decline to state their party preference, or they may list themselves as independents. People who register in this way may not vote in closed primaries. Closed primaries are limited to voters who are members of the parties that have candidates on the ballot. Although over a third of the nation's voters call themselves independents, most declare a party choice. They want to be eligible to vote in closed primaries.

4. How does the American secret ballot work?

When Americans step into a voting booth, they use one of many types of ballots. Some towns still use paper ballots on which voters mark their choices with a rubber stamp or a pen. When the polls close, election officials count the ballots by hand. Other towns and cities

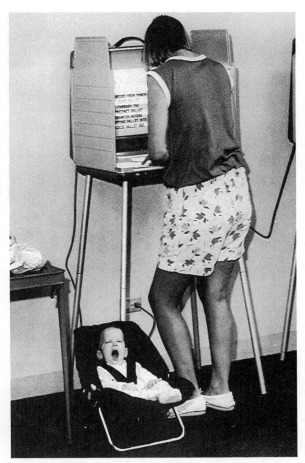

■ A Texas voter recording her choices. Technological innovations are changing the act of voting. Soon computers will be common sights in voting booths. The newer devices protect a voter's privacy while speeding up the process of counting ballots. How will electronic devices affect voter frauds and close counts?

use voting machines that allow voters to flip levers next to the printed names of the candidates. The machine then records all the votes automatically when the curtain to the voting booth is opened. Another automated voting method involves the use of computer punch cards. Once fed into a computer, the cards speed up vote counting by many hours.

DESIGNING A SECRET BALLOT

Whatever system a local precinct uses, it features the *secret ballot*. First developed in Australia, the secret ballot has not always been used in American elections. In the early years of the republic, people called out their votes in public. When paper ballots came into use, the parties printed ballots of different sizes and shapes. This allowed an observer to see which ballot each voter selected. Powerful political bosses then could pressure people to pick the "right" ballot.

The secret ballot guarantees that the voter's privacy will not be violated. It goes a long way toward ensuring an honest vote count. Common features of the secret ballot include:

Learning Skills

Making a Time Line

If you're like many people, historical dates are hard to remember. You see them in the text, and then you promptly forget them. One way to make dates stick in your mind— and to remember the events that make the dates important—is to construct a time line. In the last two chapters, for example, you've learned about the step-by-step expansion of the franchise. If you put those dates and events onto a time line, you'll have a visual picture of what's been happening to voting rights over the last 200 years.

Start your time line by drawing a six-inch by one-inch box on a sheet of paper. Divide the box into half-inch sections. Let each section stand for a 20-year period, starting with 1780. It will look like this:

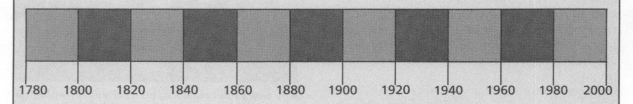

1780 1800 1820 1840 1860 1880 1900 1920 1940 1960 1980 2000

Now, put a dot where the date for each major event in the struggle to extend the franchise would fall. Label each dot with the date, and draw a line up or down from the box to a brief note that explains the importance of the date. Here are some key dates and events that should be on your time line:

1788—Constitution ratified. Franchise limited to about one in fifteen adult Americans.

1810—Last states give up religious qualification to vote. Requirements of property ownership fall soon after.

1870—15th Amendment gives vote to former black slaves.

1913—17th Amendment allows direct vote for U.S. Senators.

1920—19th Amendment gives women the right to vote.

1964—24th Amendment does away with poll tax.

1970—Voting Rights Act ends literacy requirements.

1971—26th Amendment gives vote to 18-year-olds.

19??—The first year you're eligible to vote!

When you're finished, your time line will show you the history of American voting rights in graphic form. Make a similar time line any time you need to learn a sequence of dates.

1. *Uniform ballots.* Election official print all ballots at public expense. Every ballot is identical in size, shape, and color. Each general election ballot lists all of the candidates and their parties. In primary elections, separate ballots are printed for each party.

2. *Numbered ballots.* Each polling place receives a series of ballots numbered in consecutive order. The number of votes cast must match the number of registered voters signing the tally book. All voters sign the book when they receive their ballots. Their names are then crossed off on the registry sheet to prevent multiple voting. When a voting machine is used, election officials do not issue ballots. Instead, they check the number of votes cast against the list of those who have voted.

3. *Detachable ballot* Before voters drop their completed ballots into the ballot box, an official tears off the ballot numbers and returns them to the voters. From that point on, every completed ballot looks like the next. No one could possibly match a ballot to a particular voter.

4. *Write-in votes.* Most ballots provide space for *write-in votes* for candidates whose names are not printed on the ballot. Some voting machines also provide a place for write-in votes. When using machines that don't, voters may ask for special paper ballots so they can add a name not on the official list.

SUPERVISING THE POLLS

Every county elects or appoints a registrar of voters. This official prepares the ballots, supervises the election, and oversees the counting of the ballots. In addition, every party has the right to place observers in each polling place and at locations where votes are counted.

By law, voters must be notified of the location of their polling place. The registrar of voters usually sends this notice by mail well before the election. In many places, the voter's packet also includes a sample ballot and summaries of the arguments for and against issues to be decided at the election.

CONTESTED ELECTIONS

It's not unusual for individual citizens or party officials to claim that a vote count was inaccurate or dishonest. In such a case, they may appeal to the courts to investigate. Some states require an automatic recount in very close elections (the definition of "very close" varies from state to state). A candidate who loses a close election also has the right to ask for a *recount.* A number of elections have been won in recounts because a few ballots were overlooked or miscounted. In cases of contested congressional elections, each house has a committee to investigate the dispute. The full house must vote on the committee's recommendation before the winner may be seated.

Most observers believe that recent American elections accurately report the wishes of the voters. That has not always been true. All too often during the nineteenth century, *vote frauds* mocked the democratic process. These frauds included such tricks as registering dead or imaginary voters, multiple voting, ballot-box stuffing, and dishonest vote counts. Vote frauds still happen, but the safeguards in the system have made the rigged election extremely rare.

Let's review
for a moment

The privilege of voting, which many Americans take for granted, was limited to a few select citizens when the country was founded. Property requirements, religious qualifications, *poll taxes*, and discrimination on the basis of age, sex, and race limited the franchise. How do you qualify to vote today? If you meet the age, residency, citizenship, and registration requirements of your state, you're a potential voter.

General elections, held every two years, give you a chance to vote for legislators and officials at the local, state, and national levels. From time to time, you will also find notices in your mailbox for *special elections*. In March, you might be asked to vote for the local school board. In June, the ballot might list the candidates for city council along with a bond issue for a new city library. If you registered as a member of a specific party, you will also be eligible to vote in

primary elections. That's when you help select your party's candidates for the general
election.

Many colorful stories are told of historic
vote frauds, but they have almost disappeared. The *secret ballot,* with its careful
double checks of each step in the voting
process, makes sure that only one ballot is
cast—and counted—per voter.

The official responsible for supervising
elections is the registrar of voters. Candidates who lose a close election are entitled
to call for a *recount.* They may not win, but
they have the satisfaction of knowing that
the tally was accurate.

5. How do Americans select their party and their candidates?

Scientists and politicians alike have studied
the behavior of that strange species, *voter
Americanus.* Their findings show that Americans often exhibit *bloc voting* tendencies. This
means that people with similar characteristics
tend to vote the same way.

CHARACTERISTICS OF BLOC VOTING

Some of the situations that lead to bloc voting
include:

1. *Parents' voting patterns.* Two out of
three Americans have the same political beliefs as their parents.

2. *Place of residence.* Small-town and
rural voters tend to support Republican candidates. City dwellers more often vote Democratic. Suburban residents have tended in
recent years to join their rural neighbors in
voting Republican.

3. *Section of the country.* Certain regions
have expressed a historical preference for one
party over the other. For instance, the South
remained almost solidly Democratic for a
century after the Civil War.

4. *Religion.* Although many variables exist in this category, Catholic and Jewish voters

have been more likely to vote Democratic.
Protestants more often vote the Republican
ticket.

5. *Race.* Although white voters divide their
loyalties about equally between the two major
parties, they are much more likely to vote
Republican than nonwhites. Blacks and Hispanics overwhelmingly prefer the Democratic
party.

6. *Age.* Voting preferences sometimes divide along lines of age rather than family
tradition. Younger voters (under 35) tend to
vote Democratic. Their parents (over 55) often
support Republican candidates. Despite this
pattern, a higher percentage of young people
are voting Republican these days.

7. *Income level.* Many low-income voters
believe that the Democratic party best supports their interests. People with higher incomes tend to identify with the Republicans.

8. *Education.* Americans who ended their
education at the elementary- or high-school
level tend to register as Democrats. The college
educated are more likely to call themselves
Republican.

9. *Occupation.* Business owners, farmers, professional people, and white-collar
workers tend to support Republican candidates. Blue-collar workers, both skilled and
unskilled, usually stick to the Democratic party.

VALUE OF STUDYING VOTER TENDENCIES

Many Americans refuse to believe that their
party choice was influenced by parents, age,
income, or any other bloc characteristic. Be-
sides, you probably know voters who cannot
be jammed into neat categories. A voter may
be under 30, college educated, Jewish, live in
a city, make $50,000 a year, and belong to a
labor union—all at the same time.

The key idea, in any case, is the concept of
voter tendencies. The preferences described
above may amount to only a few percentage
points, but these patterns have repeated themselves in election after election.

■ Youngsters and adults demonstrating to pressure the local government to put a traffic light at a busy intersection. How do parents influence the political and civic values of their children?

TRENDS IN AMERICAN VOTING

Politicians know that familiar voting patterns don't last forever. Several new trends in Americans politics have begun to blur the old certainties.

Voting a split ticket. Individual Americans increasingly vote a *split ticket* in general elections. This means they may vote for a Republican candidate for President and for a Democrat to represent them in Congress. Voting machines (with a separate lever for each candidate) and computer punch cards make it easy to ignore party labels. As a result, the President often represents one party, while Congress is controlled by the opposition. The same thing happens to state governors and their legislatures.

Voting for the person. Ticket splitting usually takes place when people vote for a candidate's personality rather than a party label. The voter, who may be confused by party platforms and political controversy, selects a candidate on the basis of the "image" that the politician projects. Knowing this, candidates work hard to appear dynamic, sincere, honest, dedicated, and likable. If successful, they may ride into office on the mix of inspiring personal qualities that is known as "charisma."

Political campaigns, therefore, have been increasingly taken over by "image makers." Public relations firms produce commercials that emphasize a candidate's speaking voice, physical appearance, and family. Candidates are coached to make speeches filled with a something-for-everybody philosophy. This approach has turned many elections into popularity contests.

Voting for the person tends to turn the public's attention away from hard political issues. Well-known astronauts and actors can be packaged into popular candidates, but they may not prove equally successful at writing legislation or running a state. Historically, most major wars have produced at least one President from among the generals who won fame for their military skills. Good generals sometimes make good Presidents, as George Washington proved. The opposite may also be true, as Ulysses S. Grant's scandal-ridden administration reminds us.

6. Why do so many Americans choose not to vote?

How many people voted in your community's last election? If your neighbors followed the usual pattern, about 56 percent voted in the general election and far fewer in special elections. As the FYI feature on page 144 shows, Americans are near the bottom of the list of Western democracies when it comes to turning out to vote.

GENERAL ELECTION TURNOUT

Every four years, the excitement of the presidential sweepstakes creates the highest voter turnout this nation can muster. When the returns flash across our television screens, the millions of votes look impressive. Even so, the figures are misleading. Let's see how George Bush was elected in 1988:

—182 million Americans were of voting age.

—Of these, only 127 million (70 percent) registered to vote. More than one potential voter in four was lost before election day.

—91.6 million people voted (about 50.2 percent of those old enough to vote). Bush was elected with 47.9 million votes, or 54 percent of the votes cast. The low voter turnout meant that the new President was sent to the White House by only 26.6 percent of the nation's voting-age population.

OFF-YEAR AND SPECIAL ELECTIONS

Congressional elections held in *off years* (when no presidential race is scheduled) attract even lower numbers. Over the past 20 years, the turnout has averaged about 40 percent of the eligible voters. Special elections at the local level often find less than 20 percent of the registered voters going to the polls.

CAUSES OF LOW VOTER TURNOUT

Ask any group of nonvoters why they didn't make it to the polls. It's likely the answers will fall into these categories.

1. *Reasons beyond the voter's control.* Experts estimate that up to ten percent of the eligible voters fail to vote because of reasons beyond their control. They may be ill, on a vacation or business trip, or unable to take time off from work or school. This happens even though polls stay open in many states from 7:00 A.M. to 8:00 P.M. Many of these ill or on-the-move people could have applied for and mailed in an *absentee ballot* if they wanted

---

Application for Absent Voters Ballot—Primary Nominating Election—APRIL 1

Do not use this form if you have already requested an absent ballot for this election

I, _____, am a registered voter in the
(Print full name — women use own first name and Miss or Mrs.)

City of Los Angeles, the Los Angeles Unified School District, or the Los Angeles Community College District.
I am registered at my present home address, which is

_____ _____ _____ _____
(Number and Street)   (City)   (Zip Code)   (Phone: Res. or Bus.)

The only reasons a voter may vote an absent voters ballot are the following:

(Check the reason applicable to you.)

☐ 1. Because of physical disability I will be unable to go to the polls on the day of election.

☐ 2. The tenets of my religion will prevent me from attending the polls throughout the day.

☐ 3. I reside more than 10 miles from polling place by the most direct route for public travel.

☐ 4. I expect to be absent from my election precinct. I will be leaving _____ ;
(Date)

after this date mail my ballot to: _____

_____

_____

Mail to: **Los Angeles City Clerk
Election Division
P.O. Box 54377, Terminal Annex
Los Angeles, California 90054**

_____
(Signature of Applicant as Registered — DO NOT PRINT)

_____
(Date of Signing)

APPLICATION MUST BE MADE NO LATER THAN MARCH 25

■ A sample application for an absentee ballot.

FYI . . .

Americans Are Careless About Registering and Voting

Reasons for failing to register

1. Unable to register
   a. Moved recently
   b. Illness or disability
   c. Inconvenient
   d. Other reasons
2. Didn't bother to register
   a. Didn't like any of the candidates
   b. Just not interested
3. All other reasons (forgot, didn't know how, etc.)
4. Don't know why

Approximate percentage of the voting-age population who vote in national elections

Australia	94.4
Belgium	94.2
Sweden	91.6
Austria	91.5
West Germany	88.4
Netherlands	87.0
Great Britain	76.1
France	70.7
Canada	69.2
United States	50.2
Switzerland	48.7

Reasons for not voting

1. Wasn't able to vote
   a. Couldn't get to polls
   b. Couldn't take time off from work
   c. Out of town
   d. Illness
   e. Family emergency
2. Didn't want to vote
   a. Didn't like any of the candidates
   b. Just not interested
3. All other reasons (forgot, went to polls at wrong time, went to wrong polling place, etc.)
4. Don't know why

Who Votes in Presidential Elections?

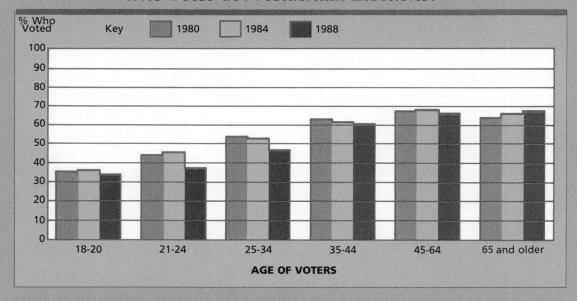

to make the effort. As the application form on page 143 shows, a voter had until six days before this primary election to request an absentee ballot.

2. Difficult registration procedures. In some states, registration procedures make it hard for citizens who want to sign up to vote. Election officials used to keep people from registering by using unfair literacy tests. The biggest problem today is that the registrar's office may be difficult to reach, or it may be closed during the hours when most people are off work.

3. Complex election issues. Some voters look at a long, complicated ballot and give up. Others listen to the barrage of arguments that fill the airwaves as the election approaches and become confused. A final group of voters ignore the election until the last minute. Then they decide not to vote on the grounds that they haven't had time to make a proper judgment on the issues or candidates.

4. One-party domination. In the South or Midwest, where one party has long dominated congressional races, some people miss the excitement of a hot campaign. Seeing little chance that their party will lose (or that their minority views will win) they forget to register or don't take the time to vote.

5. Voter alienation. Some Americans believe that it doesn't matter who wins an election. They feel that the results won't make any difference in their lives. This feeling reveals a deep and growing distrust of politics and politicians by people who feel powerless to change things. Political scientists call them the *alienated voters*. Some of these nonvoters simply drop out of the political process. Others believe themselves morally superior to those who do vote. Casting a ballot, they claim, means that you approve of the existing system.

WHAT EFFECT DOES NONVOTING HAVE?

Nonvoters are often the first to complain about the faults they see in our society. If they refuse to seek change within the system, however, they leave themselves only two choices. First, they can endure the conditions they believe are unjust. If that doesn't suit them, they can join a revolutionary movement. To do so, however, goes against the American tradition of peaceful, legal change.

If citizens who do not vote harmed only themselves, we could leave the matter to their own consciences. Nonvoters, however, endanger everyone's freedom. Back in the 1700s, a British politician named Edmund Burke told us very clearly what nonvoting means to a democracy. "The only thing necessary for the triumph of evil," he warned, "is for good men to do nothing."

7. Who pays for American election campaigns?

State and local governments pay the visible costs of holding an election. These expenses, which include such items as printing ballots and paying election workers, are only the tip of the iceberg. The huge, hidden costs are the bills run up by office seekers during their campaigns. A national campaign for the presidency costs many millions of dollars. Even at the local level, a council race in a large city forces the candidates to spend tens of thousands of dollars. Television spots, campaign literature, postage, office rent, billboards, bumper stickers, telephone lines, opinion polls—these and dozens of other expenses make running for office extremely costly.

Most Americans do not have a passionate loyalty to their party. For that reason, the European system of collecting dues from party members probably would not work in the United States. By checking an optional $1 contribution on their income tax forms, taxpayers can help pay for presidential elections. Even with this aid, some candidates are left with large campaign debts long after the election is over.

The enormous increase in the cost of running for office has raised some important issues. For one thing, some critics warn that only rich people or those with the support of wealthy special interests will be able to campaign for state or national offices. Second,

■ **U.S. Representative Jolene Unsoeld of Vancouver, Wash., (right), started soliciting campaign funds and promoting voter registration drives shortly after she was elected to Congress in 1988. Why is money so important to a candidate?**

losing parties and candidates have trouble paying off their debts. If the party is short of cash when the next election rolls around, it won't be able to mount the type of campaign that wins elections.

SOURCES OF CAMPAIGN FUNDS

Political parties can't afford to overlook any source of money. Most of their campaign contributions come from five sources.

1. *Families and individual supporters.* Party members receive frequent mailings that ask them to donate money to the party and its candidates. Parties welcome even the smallest donations. They know people will feel a greater loyalty to a party that they help finance. Some wealthy people give large sums of money to the party and its candidates. By making donations in the names of family members and friends, they evade the federal laws that limit the amount one person can contribute.

2. *Officeholders and office seekers.* The lure of public office is so powerful that some politicians willingly pay most of their own campaign expenses. Primary campaigns, in which little-known candidates may be running without a political following, often cannot be paid for in any other way. Officials running for reelection have an easier time raising campaign money. Even so, both incumbents and challengers sometimes pay many of their own expenses. In 1976, the Supreme Court struck down a section of the 1974 law that kept presidential candidates or their families from giving more than $50,000 to their own campaigns.

3. *Special-interest groups.* Restrictions on the size of campaign contributions led to the creation of *political action committees.* Most people know them as PACs. Labor groups (such as the AFL-CIO), business and industrial associations (such as the National Association of Manufacturers), and professional groups (such as the American Medical Association) are not allowed to make political contributions. As a result, their members have formed PACs that funnel money to their favorite candidates. PACs solve one problem but create another. Even honest politicians may find it difficult to forget generous campaign gifts when they're making a decision that affects a PAC's special interests.

4. *Fund-raising events.* Campaign committees, often formed only for the purpose of raising money, hold special events to support their candidates. Banquets and dinners, with tickets selling for $100 a plate and up, bring supporters and candidates together for an evening of entertainment and speech making. Stars from the sports and entertainment worlds often make an appearance. This guarantees a bigger turnout and creates more publicity for the candidates.

5. *Public financing.* The federal government uses the money donated $1 at a time by taxpayers to support presidential candidates. To qualify, candidates must prove that they have support in many different sections of the country. The law requires that they raise at least $5,000 (in contributions of $250 or less) in 20 states or more. Candidates who qualify and who agree to a spending limit in the primaries are eligible for up to $5 million each.

The major parties also receive federal funds to stage their national conventions. After they nominate a candidate, both parties receive more federal money for their campaigns. A minority party that gains five percent of the vote in a presidential race also qualifies for public funding.

REGULATION OF CAMPAIGN SPENDING

Large sums of money sometimes bring out the worst in people. With that in mind, federal laws try to prevent the misuse of party campaign funds. Controls have been imposed in three areas:

1. *Financial reports.* Campaign committees must file detailed reports on what they take in and what they spend. These reports go to Congress after federal elections and to the proper state officials after state and local elections.

2. *Limits on spending.* Attempts have been made to set limits on what candidates may spend in running for many federal offices. The 1974 campaign law, for example, limited presidential candidates to a maximum expenditure of $20 million during the general election campaign. In 1980, the limit was raised to $29.4 million. It then jumped to $40.4 million in 1984 and to $54.4 million in 1988. When they accept the federal money, the candidates agree not to spend additional funds donated by private supporters.

3. *Limits on the source of funds.* Since 1907, corporations have been forbidden to contribute to a candidate for federal office. Labor unions have operated under a similar ban since 1943. Some company officials and special union election committees have evaded the intent of the law. For instance, many corporations contributed heavily—and illegally—to the Nixon reelection campaign in 1972. The courts have imposed fines and suspended sentences on a number of business executives as a result of these activities.

The Federal Election Commission (FEC) was established in 1974 to administer the laws dealing with campaign financing. This independent agency has six members appointed by the President and confirmed by the Senate. The FEC collects information relating to campaign finances and monitors the public funds that the government makes available for presidential election campaigns. In addition, the commission oversees laws that place limits on campaign contributions and campaign spending. Candidates for federal office have been forced to hire accountants to make sure that they remain in compliance with these rules.

People who wish to donate money to candidates for federal office are bound by similar restrictions. A citizen may give $1,000 to each

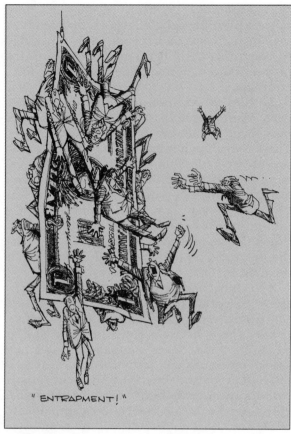

" ENTRAPMENT! "

■ The never-ending quest for campaign money has led to a long series of scandals in Washington, D.C. The cartoon refers to an FBI "sting" operation in the 1980s that offered U.S. legislators money in return for political favors. Politicians are shown to be people who are irresistibly drawn to money. Then they are "stuck" to it much as flies are caught by sticky tape.

a political party. However the donors divide up the gifts, they are limited to $25,000 in donations in any one year. When people donate funds for state and local campaigns, there is no limit on what they may give. The only requirement is that donations of over $100 must be reported to the proper election commission.

Interest groups, such as PACs, may donate up to $5,000 per candidate in both the primary and general elections. With over 3,000 PACs in operation, there is rising concern over the role these groups play in the election process. A PAC can give only $5,000 to any one candidate, but it can give that amount to as many different candidates as it wishes. Thus, there is no overall limit on how much a PAC can donate to candidates who share its political or economic goals.

REFORM OF CAMPAIGN SPENDING

As campaigns become more expensive, the problem of paying for them will grow even more difficult. A number of reforms have been suggested. These changes include: (1) Free air time for candidates on radio and television. (2) Government funding of all federal campaigns (perhaps based on the taxpayer check-off system). (3) Strict limits on the amount spent per voter by each candidate. (4) Much tougher financial reporting procedures for campaign committees. (5) Creation of a non-political agency to raise and distribute funds equally to all qualified candidates.

As might be expected, the candidates who have the most trouble raising money tend to favor these reforms. Wealthy, well-financed candidates see little reason to change the system.

candidate for Congress and the presidency in both the primary and general elections. Individuals may not donate more than $5,000 a year to a PAC or more than $20,000 a year to

Reviewing
what you've learned

1. Despite voter apathy, campaign funding scandals, and occasional *vote frauds*, the American electoral system still works. Old limits on the *franchise* have been removed. Today's voters don't have to face restrictions based on property ownership, religion, race, or sex. Unfair requirements such as *poll* *taxes* and literacy tests have also been removed by federal law. Any person who qualifies on the basis of citizenship, *residency*, and age may register to vote.

2. Most voters join a political party. Some do so out of party loyalty, others in order to vote in *primary elections*. Party labels mean little when voters step into the privacy of the voting booth. There, protected by the *secret ballot*, they freely choose the candidates and issues they wish to support. The *recount* process allows a double check of the accuracy of the tally.

3. Researchers have learned that Americans with similar backgrounds tend to vote alike. Many exceptions to this pattern exist, but the politics of one's parents seems to have a strong influence on young voters. Other influences include place of residence (rural, urban, or suburban), section of the country, religious background, race, age, income, education, and occupation. The influence of any single factor on anyone's voting tendencies varies greatly.

4. Americans tend to separate the candidates from their parties. This habit of "voting for the person" leads candidates to substitute attractive public images for specific stands on the issues. Public relations agencies that manage this "packaging" of candidates have become a strong political force.

5. Whether America's nonvoters are forgetful or alienated, their lack of participation spells trouble. Change and improvement in a democracy can take place only when all citizens share in the decision making.

6. The growing cost of American elections has led to many problems. Some good candidates cannot afford the high cost of running for office. Others end up owing favors to powerful individuals or special-interest groups. To pay the costs, candidates solicit contributions, accept money from PACs, hold fund-raising dinners, and dig into their own pockets when necessary. The taxpayer checkoff helps equalize spending in presidential campaigns. Campaign finance laws have tightened financial reporting and set limits on the amount of money individuals and groups can contribute.

Review questions and activities

TERMS YOU SHOULD KNOW

absentee ballot	off-year election	residency
alienated voter	political action committee (PAC)	secret ballot
bloc voting	poll tax	special election
disfranchise	primary election	split ticket
franchise	recount	vote fraud
general election	register (to vote)	write-in vote

REVIEW QUESTIONS

Select the response that best completes each statement or question.

1. Imagine that you're living in the early 1800s. You want to register to vote. Which of these is *not* a requirement you would likely have to meet? (*a*) Being a male. (*b*) Owning property. (*c*) Paying a poll tax. (*d*) Being a church member. (*e*) Swearing a loyalty oath.

2. A residency requirement for voting is intended to ensure that (*a*) voters will pay local taxes. (*b*) voters will approve tax increases for local projects. (*c*) local candidates will have a better chance of winning. (*d*) nonresidents will be prevented from coming into a neighborhood on election day just to vote. (*e*) nonvoters can be found and fined.

3. Disfranchisement would most likely result if a citizen (*a*) were found guilty of a felony. (*b*) filed for bankruptcy. (*c*) lost a civil suit for damages resulting from an automobile accident. (*d*) failed to vote in five local elections in a row. (*e*) all of these.

4. Many independent voters register as members of a party because (*a*) voter registration forms force them to make a party choice. (*b*) as independents they cannot vote in closed primary elections. (*c*) party membership gives them special tax advantages. (*d*) general elections are open only to registered party members. (*e*) many government jobs require party membership.

5. The secret ballot tries to guarantee that (*a*) every voter's ballot remains totally private. (*b*) all candidates will receive a minimum percentage of the vote. (*c*) vote counting will be fast and efficient. (*d*) voters will not make mistakes in filling out their ballots. (*e*) minority parties do not receive the same ballot space as the major parties.

6. The most important factor influencing a typical American voter is probably (*a*) place of residence. (*b*) occupation. (*c*) parents' politics. (*d*) income level. (*e*) religion.

7. Low-income, urban, minority voters would most likely support (*a*) Republican candidates. (*b*) Communist candidates. (*c*) conservative candidates. (*d*) Prohibition candidates. (*e*) Democratic candidates.

8. Which of the following is *not* a problem created by the tendency to vote for the person and not the party? (*a*) Charisma does not guarantee a good performance in office. (*b*) Candidates may be "packaged" to appear different from what they really are. (*c*) Issues may be ignored. (*d*) It's almost impossible to find candidates to run for office. (*e*) Elections become popularity contests.

9. In a typical general election, the percentage of Americans of voting age who can be expected to go to the polls is about (*a*) 20 percent. (*b*) 40 percent. (*c*) 60 percent. (*d*) 80 percent. (*e*) 90 percent.

10. When a candidate must rely on large campaign donations from individuals and special interests, a problem may result because (*a*) the candidate feels obligated to return the favor by voting for legislation favored by the donors. (*b*) only wealthy, well-known candidates have a chance to raise the money needed to run a campaign. (*c*) people lose faith in a government that seems too indebted to special interests. (*d*) all of these are possible problems. (*e*) none of these will happen.

CONCEPT DEVELOPMENT

1. How does a citizen become a registered voter? Do you believe that the restrictions on voting should be increased or further decreased? What changes would you make?

2. List a number of the factors that influence the way American voters cast their ballots.

3. What is the purpose of a presidential primary? Do the primaries usually lead to the nomination of the best available candidates? Why or why not?

4. Do you believe that the typical American voter can be "sold" a candidate by a high-powered public relations firm? Why have modern campaign tactics increased the tendency to "vote for the person"?

5. Why do political observers believe that the skyrocketing costs of running for office must be brought under control? What steps has the government taken to solve this problem?

HANDS-ON ACTIVITIES

1. How good a job of voter registration does your town or city do? Contact the registrar of voters and arrange for an interview. Ask about registration procedures, limitations, requirements, and voter turnout percentages. Report your findings to the class.

2. A surprising number of 18-year-olds have not registered to vote. Organize your class to run a voter-registration drive in your school. Ask the local registrar's office or the League of Women Voters for help in registering eligible juniors and seniors. Your social studies teacher and your principal can help you organize and publicize this service.

3. Survey a representative number of voters in your community. How many voted in the last general election? How many in the last special election? Compile the reasons people give for not voting. Can you think of any ways to increase the percentage of people who register and vote?

4. Organize a debate to be held in your class on the topic, "Resolved: that the United States should follow Australia's lead and establish a system of compulsory voting in state and national elections." You will find it interesting to research the Australian and Belgian experience with compulsory voting. If your library does not provide enough information, ask the nearest Australian and Belgian consulates for help.

5. Make a poster for your classroom showing the amount of money spent by the winning and losing candidates for office in the most recent election. Cover the offices of President, senator and representative, state governor, state legislator, and city council. Do you find any matchups between victors and big spenders? If so, what dangers does this present to our democracy?

7 American voters: How they influence the government

On December 1, 1955, Rosa Parks boarded the Cleveland Avenue bus in downtown Montgomery, Alabama. Parks, a seamstress in a department store, settled wearily into a seat in the first row of the section reserved for black passengers.

As the bus filled up, driver J. F. Blake enforced one of the city bus line's regulations. The rule stated that when the white section at the front of the bus was full, black passengers in the next row had to vacate their seats so that whites could sit down. Three of the blacks sitting in the first row moved at Blake's request. Only Rosa Parks refused to

▲ Rosa Parks on a Montgomery city bus after the boycott ended in 1956.

change her seat. When it was clear that she wouldn't move, Blake called for the police. Officers Day and Mixon answered the call and arrested Parks.

The Montgomery courts usually downplayed such protests by calling them "disorderly conduct." Parks insisted on being tried for breaking the segregation law. A judge heard the arguments, found her guilty, and fined her ten dollars plus court costs. Throughout her ordeal, Rosa Parks met every test with courage and dignity.

The civil rights leaders in Montgomery voted to support their new heroine. They announced that blacks would refuse to ride the buses until the transportation system was fully desegregated. A young Baptist preacher named Martin Luther King, Jr., emerged as the leader of the boycott. Inspired by King's eloquent words, the Montgomery Improvement Association spread word of the boycott across the city. Blacks formed car pools and cheered as the nearly empty buses rolled past.

As the months dragged on, the two sides fought a bitter battle on both the local and national levels. In Montgomery, those blacks who couldn't join a car pool got up early and walked to work. The bus company suffered severe financial losses. Violence flared as white segregationists tried to intimidate blacks with rifle fire and dynamite. At the same time, the two sides were also fighting in the courts. When the U.S. Supreme Court confirmed an appeals court judgment that struck down Montgomery's segregation laws, the city was forced to give in.

On December 21, 1956, King and some of his supporters rode on a newly desegregated bus. The entire nation witnessed the victory through its newspapers and television sets. By the 1960s, what had begun as one woman's demand for dignity and equality had grown into a national movement. Federal laws were passed that guaranteed equal treatment under the law to all Americans.

This example illustrates three important stages in correcting a social injustice. First, one brave person took a well-publicized stand against a violation of her civil rights. Second, a special-interest group joined the cause and used the courts to put pressure on local, state, and national governments. Finally, the American political system translated the protest into laws designed to end the injustice. That's the process that Rosa Parks set in motion that December day in 1955.

Can you, as an individual citizen, influence the actions of your government? In this chapter you will learn how public opinion, pressure groups, and other factors influence all levels of government. You will find answers to such questions as:

1. **What is public opinion?**

2. **What forces combine to create public opinion?**

3. **What is the role of pressure groups?**

4. Are pressure groups good for American society?

5. How can citizens create new laws?

6. How can voters confirm or reject new laws?

7. How can voters fire an elected official?

8. How can voters take a more active role in the political process?

1. What is public opinion?

Political scientists use the term *public opinion* to mean the public's attitudes toward any and all aspects of life in the United States. In this chapter, the term will be used to refer to the attitudes of citizens toward issues relating to government.

ASPECTS OF PUBLIC OPINION

Three factors affect our understanding of public opinion:

1. *Shifting public interests.* The issues that Americans worry about change as political, economic, and social climates change. Surveys taken during the 1960s showed that most people were worried about the dangers of nuclear war, crime, and narcotics. By the mid-1970s, crime was still a major concern, but new issues had also appeared: inflation, energy shortages, and conservation of natural resources. In the 1980s, people shifted their attention to fears of drugs and crime, the budget deficit, AIDS, environmental pollution, and the threat of Communist expansion in Latin America. The problems of earlier decades still exist, but the public tends to focus on a few major issues at a time.

2. *Lack of consensus.* Even when public opinion spotlights an issue, few people can agree on what to do about it. Many Americans worry about the imbalance in foreign trade, for example, without having any practical solutions to offer. Most of us expect others to buy the higher-priced goods made in this country—while we purchase lower-priced imports. Whether the issue is higher taxes, capital punishment, or conservation, about as many Americans will be on one side as on the other.

3. *Time lag.* Even after public opinion solidifies into a consensus, many months may pass before the government acts on that agreement. For example, a majority of the American people wanted to end the Vietnam War long before the government closed out its political and military involvement in Southeast Asia. One reason for this delay is that the President and the Congress often claim that the public's wishes are too impractical to turn into law. Finally, a party that has been elected on a popular issue may find that public opinion has turned against its position. It usually takes another election to resolve this type of conflict.

MEASURING PUBLIC OPINION

The taking of the public pulse has become something of a science. Poll takers try to measure opinions, chart changes in public opinion, and predict future trends. Two common polling techniques are straw polls and scientific samplings.

ature. The first measurements of public opinion were called *straw polls*. In the early straw polls, magazine and newspaper readers (or radio audiences) were asked to send in ballots for or against a candidate or policy. Some newspapers and television and radio stations still use straw polls to survey opinions on everything from politics to football games. The weakness of a straw poll is that most of the people who respond already have strong feelings about the issue. The results are often distorted by this narrow sample, as when a radio station reports that "92 percent of the callers in our poll support the death penalty."

Scientific sampling. In the 1930s, experts began to take polls based on a scientific *cross sample* of the population. Using census data, the poll takers first figure out how many people make up each major segment of the public. They know, for example, how many southerners, white-collar workers, Catholics, married couples, 18-year-olds, and other groups to include in the survey. In this way, a sampling of only a few thousand people produces results that are reasonably accurate for all Americans.

Improved poll-taking techniques. Even the best polls make embarrassing mistakes. A good example is the Gallup poll that predicted a landslide victory for Republican challenger Thomas E. Dewey in the presidential election of 1948. A late voter swing to President Harry Truman went unnoticed by the Gallup surveys. When Truman returned in triumph to the White House, the nation had a good laugh at the expense of the poll takers.

Today's polls wouldn't make exactly the same mistake. The poll takers now use computers, follow-up surveys, and cross-checks on voter responses. In addition, no polling service claims 100 percent accuracy. The results can be off by plus-or-minus two percent or more. In a close election, that leeway can represent the difference between victory and defeat. The table on page 156 reviews the growing accuracy of the Gallup poll in pinpointing voter choices.

IT'S DIFFICULT TO PIN DOWN PUBLIC OPINION

Many people see themselves as typical Americans. They believe that their solutions to national problems reflect public opinion across the country. With so many "publics" influencing American political and social views, it is difficult for politicians to achieve a consensus. Somehow, they must transform a hundred competing ideas into effective legislation.

Public opinion has many components. Voters' beliefs are conditioned not only by where they live and how they make a living but also by changing factors such as recent news sto-

■ Poll takers use many approaches to find out what Americans think about issues. Here a shopper in a mall is being asked a series of questions. A large portion of surveys are conducted over the telephone. Many politicians base their public stands on opinion polls.

ries. Many people don't have an opinion on a given issue or remain unaware of serious issues. Like a chameleon, public opinion constantly changes its colors, defying even the best efforts to pin it down.

2. What forces combine to create public opinion?

Americans base their opinions on many different influences and experiences. In time, their opinions harden into a set of beliefs that they think are right. Most people have only a vague idea of how they developed these beliefs.

RECORD OF ACCURACY FOR GALLUP POLLS IN PRESIDENTIAL ELECTIONS

Year	Election winner	Gallup prediction of winner's percentage	Winner's actual percentage	Percentage of error
1936	Roosevelt	55.7	62.5	6.8
1940	Roosevelt	52.0	55.0	3.0
1944	Roosevelt	51.5	53.9	1.8
1948	Truman	44.5	49.9	5.5
1952	Eisenhower	51.0	55.4	4.4
1956	Eisenhower	59.5	57.8	1.7
1960	Kennedy	51.0	50.1	0.9
1964	Johnson	64.0	61.3	2.7
1968	Nixon	43.0	43.4	0.4
1972	Nixon	62.0	60.7	1.3
1976	Carter	46.0	51.0	5.0
1980	Reagan	42.0	51.7	9.7*
1984	Reagan	59.0	59.1	0.1
1988	Bush	56.0	53.9	2.1

In the five elections between 1936 and 1952, the polls produced an average error of 4.3 percent. Between 1956 and 1968, the Gallup organization cut its prediction error to an average of 1.4 percent. The improvement could be credited mostly to improved polling techniques.
*The three-way race of 1980 complicated the polling greatly. People who expressed support for the third party candidate did not always vote for him.

PROPAGANDA

Information designed to persuade people to think a certain way is called *propaganda*. Depending on your point of view, propaganda may be either good or bad. The cigarette ad that encourages people to smoke is called "evil" by those who worry about the public health. People in the tobacco industry say that the same ad is socially responsible because it contains a health warning.

1. *Mass media.* Much of our information regarding the world comes to us through the *mass media*. Designed to reach large numbers of people quickly and cheaply, the mass media are composed of the broadcast media (radio and television) and the print media (newspapers, magazines, and other publications).

Tens of millions of Americans tune in to radio and television news programs daily. People report that they receive more of their news from the broadcast media than from the press. Although radio and television newscast-ers claim to present information fairly, even the best programs cannot maintain a perfect balance. Conservatives, for example, have charged repeatedly that the broadcast media have a liberal slant. Whether that's true or not, the pressures of time limits and the need to entertain viewers force television news to limit most stories to a simple, brief summary. Programs that give a full hour to an issue (the budget deficit, for example) can't compete for viewers with shows that entertain (such as football games or daytime soaps).

Newspapers and magazines provide the in-depth news analysis seldom found on television. In addition, the print media claim that they publish the news in a factual, unbiased way. That doesn't always happen. Editors can "slant" the news by playing up one story and burying another on a back page or by leaving out certain parts of a story. When they're playing fair, newspapers run information and opinions designed to convince or persuade on the *editorial pages*. These pages, with their

■ The print and visual media have a profound impact on our opinions. Our views are shaped by the type of newspapers and magazines we read and the television programs we watch. How can newspaper editors and television program directors influence what we think? How can we try to learn about the many sides to an issue?

editorials and long "thought pieces," attract the better-educated, more influential readers. For this reason, newspaper editorials often have an influence beyond the size of their readership.

Most major cities once supported several highly competitive newspapers. Rising production costs, mergers, and bankruptcies have reduced the number of papers. A few national chains now control most urban newspaper markets. This means that many newspaper readers are exposed to only a single editorial viewpoint.

Readers who are surrounded by incomplete or slanted news must work hard at staying informed. Many citizens find this a difficult chore. It takes time to read more than one newspaper or magazine and to follow several television news programs. Even so, American voters must do just that if they are to be properly prepared for decision making.

2. *Motion pictures.* Filmmakers, who deal primarily in entertainment, do not exercise the self-restraint expected of the news media. Unless they're careful, viewers may become so wrapped up in the action on the screen that they do not realize how strongly they are being influenced. Television entertainment, whether it's a talk show, situation comedy, or variety program, can also carry the same impact.

3. *Advertising.* The advertising industry, by definition, openly promotes a point of view. Most often, the message tries to sell the public on the merits of buying Kwispy Kwackers or the new Torpedo sports car. A growing number of commercials and advertisements, however, try to "sell" political and economic viewpoints. Political candidates openly praise themselves and promote their programs. Not to be outdone, public utilities (such as the telephone company) buy air time to tell us what a marvelous job they do. In time, a brainwashed public may come to believe what the television ads tell them.

4. *Government.* Politicians also try to mold public opinion. Presidents, governors, members of Congress, and civil servants all use press conferences, televised speeches, and computerized mailings to promote themselves and their causes. Legislators, for example, may make the evening news by opening their re-election campaigns at the Lincoln Memorial. Similarly, a governor may use a press conference to build support for a bill aimed at controlling drug abuse.

5. *Other sources of propaganda.* Propaganda designed to influence public opinion also comes from business, charitable, and professional organizations. Pressure groups (see the following section) conduct local and national campaigns via mailings, telephone calls, and media publicity.

ECONOMIC FORCES

People tend to support viewpoints that make them feel more economically secure. Conflicts arise when policies that help one group seem to deny equal advantages to another. Sponsors of competing programs crank up the propaganda machines in an effort to convince voters that they're the only ones who can solve the problems of inflation, recession, poverty, and high taxes. For example, the American people tend to support affirmative-action hiring programs for women and minorities. But the support dies quickly when such programs affect the individual's own job opportunities.

CULTURAL INFLUENCES

The community in which people live serves as a third major factor in shaping opinion. Research shows that Americans tend to reflect the opinions of their own geographic, religious, social, and educational groups. Oregonians may look and dress like Georgians, for example, but their political attitudes often differ. Because the people of Oregon wanted to clean up their parks and roadways, they were the first to require a deposit on soft-drink cans and bottles. Georgians attack their litter problem in other ways.

3. What is the role of pressure groups?

Citizens who join together in an effort to influence public policy are known as a *pressure group.* Such groups may have anywhere from a few dozen members to several million. Pressure groups are most active in the state and national capitals, but they are found anywhere a governmental body meets. Pressure groups support political parties, candidates, and officeholders at all levels of government. In return, they ask for political favors when decisions are being made that affect their own interests.

Many of the most influential pressure groups represent economic interests: labor groups, professional organizations, chambers of commerce, or farm and business organizations. Political pressure groups also compete for public attention: the League of Women Voters, Common Cause, and the American Civil Liberties Union are examples. Specific issues, such as ecology, may give birth to other groups: the National Air Pollution Committee and the Sierra Club. Religious, racial, and ethnic groups form their own organizations if they need public support: the NAACP, the B'nai B'rith Anti-Defamation League, the National Association of Arab Americans.

REASONS FOR THE GROWTH OF PRESSURE GROUPS

Several factors have led to the growth of pressure groups in the United States:

1. *Free speech and assembly.* The Constitution guarantees the rights of free speech and assembly. Because of these safeguards, legitimate groups need not fear government opposition or repression. An exception to this rule, revealed in 1976, was the harassment by law enforcement agencies of the Black Panthers and the Socialist Workers party. More recently, religious groups who give sanctuary to refugees from Central America have complained of being harassed by federal authorities. Liberals and conservatives alike often speak up for the right of left-wing groups to pursue their goals—as long as they do it in a peaceful way. If two or more people believe as you do about an issue, you are free to form a new pressure group.

2. *Responsive political system.* In many countries, pressure groups gain influence by forming their own political parties. Under the American two-party system, people who have strong opinions about an issue find it more effective to work with one of the major parties. Politicians, for their part, welcome the support of the various pressure groups for at least three reasons: (1) These organizations often give generously to election campaigns. (2) By listening to the leaders of these groups, politicians keep themselves informed about the needs and wishes of the voters. (3) Lawmakers can rely on pressure groups for expert help when they're drafting new legislation.

3. *Growing size of government.* As government grows larger, it affects our lives more and more. Individual citizens feel powerless to fight back, but they can increase their influence by joining a pressure group. Instead of letting others decide important policy and legislative matters, they become active participants in the national debate.

4. Are pressure groups good for American society?

Most Americans realize that pressure groups play a useful role in the democratic process. Still, the suspicion remains that there is something underhanded about the way some pressure groups promote their special interests.

Historical abuses by pressure groups. In the 1800s, pressure groups sometimes deserved this distrust. Big business trusts and monopolies hired *lobbyists* who used fair means and foul to influence public officials. As a result, they often corrupted the political process. (See Chapter Nine for a full discussion of lobbyists and their activities.) Once in office, politicians elected by special interests tended to sell their votes and ignore the public welfare.

Modern limits on pressure groups. Laws that vary from state to state now limit the activities of pressure groups. Generally, lobbyists are allowed to take legislators out to dinner and to provide limited secretarial and publicity services. On the other hand, they may not pay legislators for their votes (which

"It's Awful The Way They're Trying To Influence Congress. Why Don't They Serve Cocktails And Make Campaign Contributions Like We Do?"

would be bribery), contribute money for the legislators' private use, or make illegally large donations to their campaign funds (as you learned in Chapter Six). Strict reporting rules help the state and federal governments keep watch over the financial dealings between lawmakers and pressure groups.

The law also forces most high-level government officials to make public disclosure of their personal wealth. The people have a right to know, for example, if lawmakers have a financial interest in the bills they support. A legislator who owns stock in a coal company might find it difficult to vote for a law that restricts mining operations. If these *conflicts of interest* aren't controlled, they can destroy the public's confidence in its elected representatives.

Success of pressure groups. Despite continued suspicion, pressure groups play a useful role in the American system. Not too surpris-

What Can You Do to Influence Your Elected Officials?

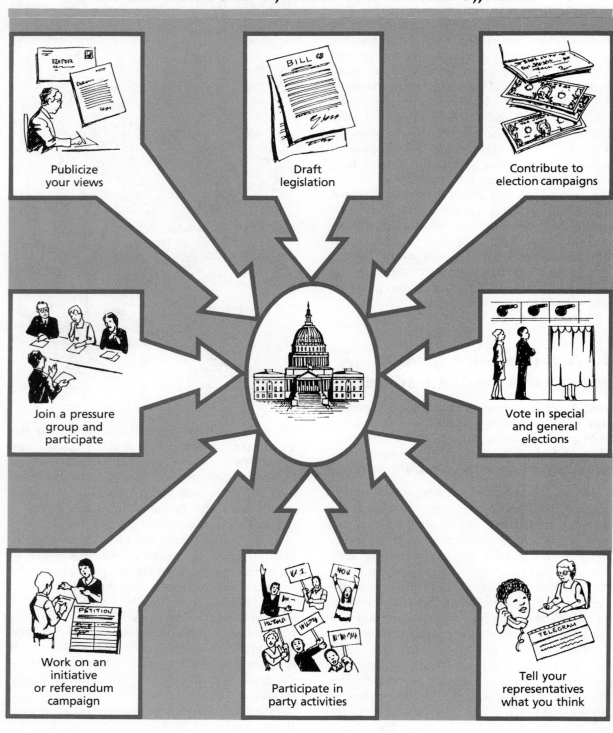

ingly, they frequently win important benefits for their members. In addition, they provide information, research, and guidance at all levels of government. Faced with a bill that would benefit farmers, for example, a member of Congress will be reminded that the same law may harm food processors, retailers, and consumers. By listening carefully to all the pressure groups involved, the lawmaker can modify the legislation to achieve the greatest good for all.

Let's review for a moment

Can you really change anything in this country? Rosa Parks helped put an end to segregated seating on buses in Montgomery, Alabama. She couldn't have done it alone, however. Find enough dedicated supporters, as Rosa Parks did, and you can make things happen.

The term *public opinion* refers to the sum of all views held by Americans on any given issue. Everyone's view counts but in varying degrees. To further complicate things, the public's priorities change, and not everyone cares about every issue. Politicians depend on scientific opinion polls to measure *public opinion.*

Where do your own opinions come from? Your economic and cultural background are key factors in forming your opinions. What else? The broadcast media, along with the press, bombard you daily with *propaganda* designed to influence you. Motion pictures, the advertising industry, government, and your friends and family also affect your thinking.

The Constitution guarantees us the right to join any *pressure group* that pursues its goals in a peaceful, legal manner. Many pressure groups hire *lobbyists* to promote their views. You don't have to travel to Washington or your state capital to find pressure groups at work. A local homeowners' association working to keep apartments out of an area of one-family homes demonstrates the principle quite well.

5. How can citizens create new laws?

Most people think of "writing to their representative" when they see the need for a new law. At the state and national levels, this makes sense. In some states even ordinary citizens have the power to write their own laws. This form of direct democracy dates back to the New England town meetings of colonial times. Today's cities are too large for town meetings to be truly effective, but direct democracy still exists. In over one-third of the states (and in many cities and counties), general election ballots often contain new laws proposed by the people. These laws, which take effect if passed by the voters, are known as either *initiatives* or *propositions.*

THE INITIATIVE PROCESS

Because many people believe government has lost touch with the people, the initiative process holds great appeal. Voters use the initiative to bypass slow-moving legislatures in matters of tax relief, school reform, and protection of the environment. A group that wishes to pass an initiative usually follows a seven-step procedure:

1. *Drafting the proposal.* Any individual or group may write an initiative. The language of the proposed law must meet legal and constitutional requirements.

2. *Preliminary filing.* Sponsors must file the proposal with the proper official. This is usually the secretary of state if a state law or state constitutional amendment is involved.

3. *Circulation of petitions.* A specified number of registered voters must sign printed copies of the initiative, called *petitions.* This verifies that the public is interested in the new law. Requirements vary from state to state. Some call for the signatures of three to ten percent of the vote cast for governor in the last general election. Others set a fixed number, running from 10,000 to 50,000 signatures. The sponsors also must meet a deadline for circulating their petitions.

4. *Verification of signatures.* As the deadline for filing approaches, election offi-

■ Citizens of Boston, Mass., sign petitions calling for the recycling of bottles. Campaigns for and against initiatives and referendums are among the hardest fought of all election battles. Supporters and opponents often appeal more to emotion than to reason.

cials check the signatures on the petitions. Initiative sponsors must expect to lose a number of signatures through duplication, faulty petitions, or the discovery that some signers were not properly registered. The sponsors allow for this shrinkage by gathering more signatures than the actual number required. If the petitions pass, officials certify the initiative for the next general election ballot.

5. *Educating the public.* Circulating petitions is only the beginning of the battle to pass an initiative. Individuals and groups supporting (or opposing) the measure must try to convince the public that they should vote for (or against) the proposition. Billboards, television spots, and direct mailings urge the public to "Vote YES on Proposition 12," and to "Save the Whales! Vote NO on Proposition 5." In several states, balanced arguments for and against the initiatives are included in information packets mailed to the voters.

6. *Decision by the voters.* Qualified initiatives receive a place on a primary or general election ballot. In most cases, a simple majority is enough either to pass or reject the initiative.

7. *Promulgation of the new law.* If the intiative passes, officials *promulgate* the new law. This legal term refers to the proclamation that gives the initiative measure the force of law in the city, county, or state where the election took place.

ARGUMENTS AGAINST THE INITIATIVE

Opponents of the initiative process point to a number of possible abuses. These include: (1) Special-interest legislation is passed by voters who are misled by high-powered campaigns. (2) Firms hired to circulate petitions use dishonest methods to gain signatures. (3) The normal work of the legislature is disrupted by poorly planned initiatives. (4) Voters are confused by long and complicated ballots. (5) Initiative campaigns add to the already high cost of elections. (6) Poorly drafted legislation leads to long and expensive court battles.

ARGUMENTS FOR THE INITIATIVE

Supporters of the initiative process admit that problems exist. They argue, however, that the merits of the system outweigh the dangers. Their arguments say: (1) The initiative process strengthens *popular sovereignty* (rule by the people). (2) The initiative process counteracts the influence of special-interest groups, which might otherwise dominate a legislative body. (3) The initiative process awakens the public to important issues. (4) The threat of an initiative forces the legislature to pass laws that would otherwise die. If a poorly written initiative is passed, supporters argue, the city council or state legislature can amend or repeal it later.

6. How can voters confirm or reject new laws?

Along with the initiative, a number of states give their citizens a second type of direct power. Certain kinds of laws, even though passed by city councils or state legislatures, may not be enforced until they are ratified by the voters. This process of voter approval or rejection of legislation is called the *referendum*. Like the initiative, the referendum began more than 200 years ago. Massachusetts, for example, submitted its own constitution to its voters for approval in 1780.

THREE TYPES OF REFERENDUMS

Where permitted by law, three types of referendums exist:

1. *Mandatory referendum.* Mandatory referendums are those required by law. Amendments to the state constitution must be submitted to the voters to be approved or rejected. Similarly, cities and states cannot issue new bonds without asking the voters for approval.

2. *Optional referendum.* If a new law is important or controversial enough, a legislature may ask the people to vote on it. An optional referendum might be appropriate when emotional issues such as funding for schools or welfare laws are involved.

3. *Petition (or protest) referendum.* Even though a law has passed the legislature, some states still allow the voters to approve or disapprove. Most laws do not take effect until a definite time period has passed (usually 60 or 90 days after the legislature adjourns). During this time, any interested group may initiate a petition referendum (sometimes called a protest referendum) that can lead to a popular vote on the law.

QUALIFYING A REFERENDUM

In most of the states that allow it, a referendum petition requires fewer signatures than an initiative. If a group wants to qualify a referendum, it generally needs enough signatures to equal five percent of the vote for governor in the last general election. The steps necessary to pass a referendum (except for the qualifying process itself) repeat those of the initiative. States that use the referendum usually accept a simple majority vote as binding. The exception is for some bond issues, which require a two-thirds majority.

7. How can voters fire an elected official?

What can you do when public officials fail to do their jobs properly? If they're guilty of "high crimes and misdemeanors," many federal and state officials—both elected and appointed—can be removed from office through impeachment (see page 190). Even if state or local officials haven't committed an impeachable offense, they can still be sent back to private life. Officials who have lost the confidence of the voters can be "fired" through a process known as a *recall* election.

The recall appeared well after the initiative and referendum. Los Angeles first used the procedure in 1903, and Seattle followed in 1906. Oregon adopted the recall at the state level in 1908. About a third of the states and several hundred cities now permit its use.

STEPS IN THE RECALL PROCESS

The legal steps leading to a recall election parallel those of the initiative, but many more signatures are needed on the recall petition. Recall supporters must gather the signatures of 25 percent of the vote cast for a particular office in the previous election. Once the signatures have been certified, the recall vote must be held by a specific date. Officials facing a recall sometimes resign before the election is held.

The voters mark their recall ballots "yes" or "no." Sometimes the people vote for a successor in the same election. In other cases, a second election is held, usually within 30 days. Even though state governors are occasionally threatened with recall, only one governor has been successfully removed from office. In 1921, the people of North Dakota recalled Governor Lynn J. Frazier. More recently, Governor Evan Mecham of Arizona was impeached and removed from office in 1988 before a scheduled recall election could be held. Recalls are more common at the local level. Many corrupt or incompetent mayors, city council members, and school board trustees have had their careers ended by recall elections.

DEBATE ON THE USE OF RECALL

The recall process has always created controversy. Some critics once predicted that every public official who takes an unpopular stand would be recalled. In the states where the recall is used, however, officeholders cannot normally be recalled until they have been in office for six months or longer. Further protection exists in the rule that only one attempt at recall may be made during an official's term in office.

Events have not justified the fears that minority and special-interest groups would abuse their power. Voters, in fact, have proven reluctant to use the recall. Most Americans seem content to wait until the next regular election to remove a politician from office. Some people would like to extend the initiative, referendum, and the recall to the federal level, but it would require a constitutional amendment to do so.

8. How can voters take a more active role in the political process?

As an alert, concerned citizen, you can make your political presence felt in a number of ways. Participation is the key. You can join in the activities of a political party or pressure group; you can vote in general and special elections; you can take part in initiative, referendum, or recall campaigns. The truly committed person can go the final mile and run for office.

Even if you don't want to become a candidate, you can still play a role in American politics. For one thing, every time you express an informed opinion, you influence others. The problem is that you can't see the change that results from private debates. With just a little extra effort, you can make your voice heard in a much larger forum.

WRITE TO YOUR REPRESENTATIVES

A letter directed to local, state, or federal officials almost always receives a prompt reply. Personally written letters that express your opinions in your own words work best. Pressure groups often organize mass mailings, but these letters and cards usually end up in the hands of a clerk. Only the totals reach the legislator.

When you write to your representative,

Learning Skills

Getting Involved in Politics

Do you feel left out of the political process? If you do, many Americans share your feelings. Some of them have "dropped out" of politics, except for griping when they don't like what's going on. That's sad, because our political system is only as good as the people who take an active part in making it work.

The best way to sharpen your political skills is to join a political campaign at the "grass roots" level. That's just a way of saying that the real work of electing a candidate takes place in your own neighborhood. Political parties are active throughout the year, but they're most visible during the weeks leading up to an election. If you want to join in, all you have to do is let the right people know you're interested. Someone will put you to work. You won't be paid (except with soft drinks, sandwiches, and an invitation to the victory party), but you will learn a great deal about the wonderful and fascinating game of politics.

How do you get into the game? The rules are few and easy to remember:

First, pick your party or candidate. You can work for a friend who's running for city clerk, or you can join a national presidential campaign. You'll be welcome at any level.

Second, don't wait until the day before the election. Join early. You'll see more and be given more varied jobs to do. You may end up supervising the volunteers who join later.

Third, inventory your skills. What can you offer the campaign? Don't be afraid to let people know that you can type, use a computer, drive a car, manage a switchboard, and so on. Even if your skill doesn't seem related to politics, offer it. If you're a great skateboarder, maybe you can organize a skateboard crew to distribute flyers for your candidate.

Fourth, be ready to do anything. Some jobs are more fun than others, but all of them are important. You may find yourself addressing envelopes, making phone calls, decorating the headquarters, running errands, passing out handbills on the street, or driving voters to the polls on election day. The more tasks you take on and do well, the more you'll be given to do.

Fifth, don't expect to run the campaign. If you have good ideas, the campaign staff will probably listen to them. Don't be disappointed, however, if your great plan is turned down. With so much riding on the results, politicians tend to put their faith in experts.

That's about all there is to it. If an election campaign is in the air, find the local headquarters for the party you prefer. Walk in and say, "I'm here to work for your candidate. What can I do?" You'll have a job before you can take another breath!

■ U.S. Representative Illeana Ros-Lehtinen of Florida greeting supporters after her election. Lawmakers like to keep in touch with voters. What can a national legislator do when local concerns are at odds with what may be best for the country as a whole?

address yourself to a specific subject. Explain your concerns, and explain what you want done about them. Your letter may deal with any matter that involves you and your government. Representatives and their staffs will dig out information for you, or they will refer your request to the appropriate agency. If you need help in dealing with the Small Business Administration, for example, a nudge from your representative or senator will speed up the process.

Tradition suggests that telegrams carry a greater impact than letters. If you wish to take advantage of this, the telegraph company provides a next-day delivery service.

Don't be upset if you receive a form letter in reply. When a major issue touches off a large volume of mail, a busy official cannot respond personally to each letter. Most letters are answered by legislative assistants. While that may seem rather impersonal, remember that your representative's legislative tasks come first.

What is true in Washington is also true at state and local levels of government. A member of the House of Representatives speaks for about half a million people—but a state legislator or a city council member is responsible to far fewer voters. Your letters to these officials, therefore, may carry even greater weight. For your convenience, many newspapers and telephone directories regularly print the addresses of your representatives. Reference books available in your local library also contain this information.

VISIT YOUR ELECTED OFFICIALS

A personal visit is better than a letter. You probably won't have to travel to Washington because all members of the House of Representatives maintain offices within their districts. Write or phone for an appointment. If your request merits the legislator's attention, the staff will set aside time for you. If you're an expert in your field, you may be asked to testify before a legislative committee. Before that happens, you'll be interviewed by a member of the committee staff. To speed up the process, you may be asked to write out your testimony so that the committee members can study it ahead of time.

Within your own city or town, boards of supervisors, city councils, school boards, and other elected bodies hold open meetings. Sometimes people from the audience are invited to speak. More often, you must go in ahead of time to ask for a place on the agenda. When you do speak up, you will learn that very few citizens take advantage of this op-

portunity to meet face-to-face with their elected representatives.

SPEAK OUT IN THE MASS MEDIA

Most newspapers and many radio and television stations welcome your views. Almost all newspapers print a cross section of the letters they receive, even those that disagree with the paper's editorial position. If a radio or television station takes an editorial stand, the Federal Communications Commission requires that the station provide free time for qualified speakers for opposing views. The increasing number of radio talk shows also provide average people with a chance to tell the community how they feel about any subject under the sun. You can't make people listen, but you have plenty of chances to voice your opinions.

Reviewing
what you've learned

1. *Public opinion* represents the public's attitude about all aspects of life in this country. It changes often, and many people disagree as to how government should solve the nation's problems. Once public opinion has been mobilized behind a cause, however, the American political process usually responds.

2. The task of measuring public opinion falls to the poll takers. *Straw polls*, with their built-in inaccuracies, have given way to scientific sampling. A scientific sampling uses a carefully selected *cross sample* of the population. Despite all their care, poll takers still find that shifting tides of public opinion make exact predictions almost impossible.

3. Public opinion is shaped by many forces. The mass media bombard us with *propaganda*—information designed to influence our views. Moviemakers, the advertising industry, and government leaders also spend time and money to persuade us to accept their viewpoints. Economic forces and cultural influences also build public opinion.

4. Many Americans join *pressure groups* with other people who share their opinions. The Constitution protects these organizations, and our political system responds to them. Most pressure groups represent economic, political, religious, or ethnic interests. Others support specific issues, such as ecology or consumer interests.

5. Past abuses by pressure groups and their hired *lobbyists* have led to strict laws controlling their activities. Despite scandals and conflicts of interest growing out of their lobbying practices, pressure groups still serve a useful purpose. They give individual citizens a voice in national affairs, and they furnish useful information that legislators can use for writing better laws.

6. In a number of states, voters can create their own laws through the *initiative* process. Once the initiative has been drafted, signatures must be gathered on *petitions*. After the signatures are verified, the proposed law appears on the general election ballot. A *referendum* gives voters a chance to approve or reject a new law. Some referendum measures appear on the ballot when mandated by law. Others appear when either the legislature or the people have asked for public approval of a new law. Incompetent or corrupt public officials may be removed from office by a *recall* election.

7. Public officials pay attention to letters and telegrams from the public. When schedules permit, citizens can talk to their elected officials in person. Local and national publications welcome letters to the editor, and talk shows provide a public forum for your opinions.

8. If you're a concerned citizen, voting in elections is the least you can do. Unless everyone participates, a few powerful leaders may emerge to claim to speak for all of us. A democracy cannot afford to run that risk.

Review questions and activities

TERMS YOU SHOULD KNOW

conflict of interest	mass media	proposition
cross sample	petition	public opinion
editorial page	popular sovereignty	recall
initiative	pressure group	referendum
lobbyist	promulgate	straw poll
	propaganda	

REVIEW QUESTIONS

Select the response that best completes each statement or question.

1. The Montgomery bus boycott illustrates an important principle of American democracy: (*a*) All bad laws will be changed someday. (*b*) Conflicts between blacks and whites cannot be avoided. (*c*) The American system responds to a strong expression of public opinion. (*d*) When their economic interests are threatened, the rich and powerful always win. (*e*) The use of violence is the only way to change unjust laws.

2. The most accurate poll on a major question of national policy would be (*a*) a straw poll taken among listeners to a popular radio station. (*b*) an interview survey of people in a shopping center. (*c*) a cross sampling of the population of a big city. (*d*) a cross sampling of people from several widely scattered states. (*e*) all are about equal.

3. The biggest problem facing someone who wants to conduct an accurate poll is that (*a*) people's opinions change too rapidly to measure. (*b*) a good cross sample is impossible to obtain. (*c*) most people never tell the truth to a poll taker. (*d*) people don't pay much attention to the results of a poll. (e) all of these have an equally bad effect on a poll's accuracy.

4. The best place to look in a newspaper for articles designed to both inform and persuade would be (a) the front page. (b) the editorial page. (c) the society page. (d) the entertainment section. (e) the business section.

5. The primary job of a pressure group is to (a) elect its members to public office. (b) obtain favorable action from government for the cause it supports. (c) furnish campaign money to candidates running for office. (d) change the political system to reflect some extremist philosophy like communism or fascism. (e) win publicity for its members.

6. An example of improper conduct by a pressure group or its lobbyist would be (a) making a large, secret donation to a candidate's congressional campaign fund. (b) sponsoring a dinner for a congressional candidate. (c) providing expert testimony before a congressional committee. (d) helping its members obtain appointments to see an important legislator. (e) helping a legislator write a piece of legislation.

7. An initiative permits the people of a state to (a) approve or reject a law passed by the legislature. (b) remove an unpopular official from office. (c) approve or reject a bond issue. (d) propose and pass a law without any action by the legislature. (e) pass an *ex post facto* law as part of the state's criminal code.

8. The most common measures submitted to voter approval by referendum are (a) laws involving the way the state government conducts its business. (b) constitutional amendments and revenue bonds. (c) confirmation of general election results. (d) bills relating to business practices, such as fair trade laws and safety codes. (e) changes in the election code.

9. The public official who is most likely to be subject to removal from office by a recall vote is a (a) state governor. (b) justice of the United States Supreme Court. (c) United States Senator. (d) member of the U.S. House of Representatives. (e) member of a city council.

10. Citizens who want to influence government policy are *least* likely to be successful when they (a) organize a letter-writing campaign directed at Congress. (b) complain loudly to their friends and co-workers. (c) study the issues and vote intelligently. (d) join special interest pressure groups. (e) take an active part in party politics.

CONCEPT DEVELOPMENT

1. What is a lobbyist? Discuss the positive and negative results of allowing lobbyists to influence legislation.

2. How can the voters remove incompetent or corrupt officials from public office? Why aren't these procedures used more often?

3. What do we mean by the phrase "public opinion"? Why do politicians and pressure groups spend so much time and money attempting to influence it?

4. Write out a list of the alternatives open to a person who wishes to change a governmental policy. Evaluate the effectiveness of each method listed.

5. Pick out a social issue that you feel is important to most Americans—the cost of living, civil rights, crime, or any similar topic. What forces have helped shape public opinion on this issue?

HANDS-ON ACTIVITIES

1. Forming a pressure group isn't as difficult as you might think. Select an issue that currently concerns your community. Organize a letter-writing campaign to the appropriate public officials asking for prompt and effective action. Visit their offices to reinforce your ideas. If you can zero in on a situation that is both local and immediate, you might accomplish something worthwhile. Examples include (a) installation of traffic signals or stop signs at a dangerous intersection near the school; (b) funding of summer recreation programs; (c) addition of long-needed courses to your school's curriculum.

2. Select a current national or local issue that has aroused controversy in your school. Organize your class to conduct a scientific survey of the student body to obtain a valid sampling of opinion. This will mean analyzing students on a number of criteria—sex, age, grade level, ethnic background (if appropriate to the issue), and so on. (Your registrar or attendance office can help you to develop an accurate sampling.) Can you find differences of opinion that seem based on these factors?

3. Ask to have your name placed on the agenda of the next school board meeting. Use your allotted time (a) to speak for a project you feel is important to you and your school or (b) to question the board about policies and decisions you wish to know more about. Afterward, report to your class on the experience. Remember, board members have serious business to conduct. Don't use valuable time to pursue unrealistic projects, such as asking the board to cut your school day by half.

4. Research the history of protest movements in the United States. You will discover that the early labor movement was often awash in violence. Even Martin Luther King, Jr.'s nonviolent philosophy could not prevent some bloody conflict. Can true change be brought about peacefully, or does it come only through confrontation? Discuss this with your class, perhaps in the form of a panel report or debate.

Unit Three

The Legislative Branch of American Government

8 The organization and power of Congress

▲ The U.S. House of Representatives in session in 1848.

The newly elected congressman was arguing against the war. Speaking in the House of Representatives, he attacked the President without seeming to do so:

> When the war began, it was my opinion that all those who . . . could not conscientiously oppose the conduct of the President in the beginning of it because of knowing too much or too little . . . should, nevertheless, as good citizens, remain silent on that point, at least till the war should be ended.

The President quickly answered the young legislator's implied criticism. His counterattack, full of partial truths, created a wave of protest against the congressman in his home district. Political opponents labeled him a traitor.

Undaunted, the congressman refused to back down. "The President should answer fully, fairly, and candidly," he said. "Let him answer with facts and not with arguments." If the President couldn't explain why the country had gone to war, he went on, "then I shall be fully convinced of what I more than suspect already . . . that he feels the blood of this war, like the blood of Abel, crying to heaven against him."

Passionately, the young politician charged that the President must have had some strong motivation for involving two countries in a war. He went on to say that "trusting to escape scrutiny by fixing the public gaze upon the exceeding brightness of military glory—that attractive rainbow that rises in showers of blood—he plunged into it, and has swept on and on till, disappointed in his calculations . . . he now finds himself he knows not where."

Was the President's critic talking about Vietnam? No? Then perhaps he was criticizing the invasion of Grenada or Panama. Was he attacking President Lyndon Johnson? Richard Nixon? Ronald Reagan? George Bush? Those are good guesses, but none is correct. The "showers of blood" took place in 1847. The "enemy" was Mexico. The President under attack was James K. Polk, and the fiery speaker was Abraham Lincoln.

Today, many voters admire politicians who oppose decisions by a President that might lead to bloodshed or war. Lincoln, however, paid a high price for speaking out against the Mexican War. After he ended his term in Congress, his Illinois constituents did not support him for nomination to a second term.

Lincoln may have made a political mistake, but he was on firm legal ground. The Framers of the Constitution gave Congress—not the President—the right to declare war. Like Lincoln, many Americans still object to presidential decisions that send troops into combat without asking for approval from Congress.

The Constitution gives Congress far more than the right to declare war. The Framers, in fact, devoted more words to the legislative branch than to the other two branches combined. Today's senators and representatives have inherited these wide-ranging powers and duties. Their role in American government is discussed in the answers to the following questions:

1. **What are the requirements for election to Congress?**

2. **Why do we have two houses of Congress?**

3. **What is the term of Congress?**

4. **How are congressional seats apportioned?**

5. **How does Congress organize itself?**

6. **How is the committee system organized?**

7.   What is the basis of congressional power?

8.   What are the nonlegislative tasks of Congress?

9.   How has the power of Congress grown?

10.   What does it mean to be a member of Congress?

1. What are the requirements for election to Congress?

Lincoln was elected to Congress in 1846 and decided not to run for reelection in 1848. As his brief stay illustrates, members of the House of Representatives serve two-year terms. All members of the House who seek reelection must return to their home districts to face the voters in November of each even-numbered year.

By contrast, a senator serves a six-year term. Only one-third of the Senate membership stands for election (or reelection) at any one time. Political scientists say that the Senate's longer term is important to our legislative system. Senators stay in office long enough to give stability and long-term direction to the lawmaking process.

QUALIFICATIONS FOR OFFICE

To run for Congress, a candidate must satisfy the requirements listed in the Constitution. These basic qualifications are summarized in the table on page 174.

NOMINATION AND ELECTION

Candidates for Congress are normally selected by their political parties. Membership in a party isn't required, but very few candidates can afford to run without their party's financial support. From state to state, Republicans and Democrats nominate their candidates in a variety of ways. In some states, party nominating committees meet in each congressional district to pick the candidates. In others, party officials select the candidates at state conventions. A third method is to allow voters to choose their own candidates in primary elections.

For 125 years, senators were elected by the legislatures of their home states. This practice ended when the Seventeenth Amendment was ratified in 1913. Today, both senators and representatives are elected by the voters in their home states and districts.

In many states, the governor has the power to appoint a replacement when an incumbent senator resigns or dies. The new senator serves until the next regular election. By contrast, special elections are usually called to fill vacancies in the House.

CONSTITUTIONAL QUALIFICATIONS FOR ELECTION TO CONGRESS

Requirement	House of Representatives	Senate
Age	Twenty-five years or older.	Thirty years or older.
Citizenship	Must have been a United States citizen for at least seven years.	Must have been a United States citizen for at least nine years.
Residence	Must be a resident of the state in which he or she is elected. By custom, a representative is also expected to live in the district represented.	Must be a resident of the state he or she represents.

■ The members of the House and Senate pursue their legislative activities separately, coming together only for ceremonial occasions. One such event takes place each January, when the members gather in the chamber of the House of Representatives to hear the President give the State of the Union Address.

2. Why do we have two houses of Congress?

The Framers created a bicameral Congress (a legislature made up of two houses) to serve as the nation's lawmaking branch. Several reasons, some historical and some practical, explain this choice. The British Parliament, with its House of Lords and House of Commons, served as the original model. Similarly, most of the colonial legislatures had two houses. By the time the delegates met to write the Constitution in 1787, almost all the state legislatures were bicameral.

The practical reasons that led to a bicameral legislature were more important than the historical traditions. The reasons are as follows: (1) Unicameral, or one-house, legislatures under the Continental Congresses and the Articles of Confederation had not worked well. (2) Several of the Framers believed that a two-house lawmaking body was essential to the system of checks and balances they were building into the new government. (3) The dispute over representation between the large and small states was solved by the Connecticut Compromise (see page 52). First, the interests of the small states were protected in the Senate, where every state was given two seats. Second, that decision allowed the Framers to recognize the greater economic and political weight of the large states by allocating House seats on the basis of population.

Most critics believe that the system has worked well. A bicameral Congress:

1. *Serves as a brake.* Because a bill must be approved by both houses meeting separately, there's less chance that hasty and unwise legislation will be passed. (You'll learn how a bill becomes a law in Chapter Nine.)

2. *Prevents sectional legislation.* A bill passed by the House that favors a single, heavily populated region of the country can be killed in the Senate. This prevents the passage of laws that might work against the best interests of other sections of the country.

3. *Provides differing viewpoints.* The members of the House, who must run for reelection every two years, are forced to respond to the immediate wishes of the people. Senators, who have the security of six-year terms, can examine legislation from a longer-range view.

4. *Provides time for review.* Most new bills take a long time to go through both houses. This slow progress gives everyone—the public, the media, pressure groups, and Congress itself—time to study and criticize a bill before it becomes a law.

Critics of bicameralism believe that the system's slow pace is a fault, not a strength. They say that important legislation often is delayed or weakened by amendments as it makes its way through Congress. That same slowness, they also claim, gives special interests too many chances to delay or defeat the bills they oppose.

Despite these problems, bicameralism is here to stay. No one has made a serious effort to change the makeup of Congress since it was approved by the Framers.

3. What is the term of Congress?

The *term of Congress* is the period during which a Congress remains in session between elections. Each Congress is numbered in sequence and has a life span of two years. The first Congress convened in 1789, the 101st in January 1989.

Custom divides each term of Congress into two yearly *sessions*. Before World War II, Congress stayed in session for only four or five

months each year. Today's sessions last almost a full calendar year. This complicates the lives of members who are running for reelection. Senators and representatives often miss important votes because they've gone home to conduct business or to campaign.

Congress may be recalled by the President for a special session. This can happen even though the regular session has ended and the members have scattered. President Truman used this constitutional power in 1948. He recalled the legislators to work on a series of education, health, and civil rights bills. Special sessions, however, are rare.

4. How are congressional seats apportioned?

By law, the Congress of the United States contains 535 members—100 senators and 435 representatives. The Constitution does not fix the number of representatives; the original House met in 1789 with only 65 members. As the nation's population grew, the number of representatives increased. In time, it became clear that the House wouldn't be able to do its work if it had too many members. After much debate, Congress passed the Reapportionment Act of 1929. This law fixed the membership of the House at its present size.

With membership fixed, population growth has increased the number of people in each congressional district. Each representative now speaks for an average of over 500,000 citizens. The number of representatives (out of the 435) that each state sends to the House is set by the ratio of the state's population to the national population. Those states with small populations are guaranteed at least one representative. Alaska, Delaware, South Dakota, North Dakota, Vermont, and Wyoming each send a single representative to Washington. By contrast, California sends 45.

The people of Washington, D.C., are not fully represented in Congress because of the city's unique federal status. At the present time, the capital's 600,000 residents are allowed to send only a single nonvoting delegate

Changing Patterns of Congressional Representation
Projected Reapportionment Based on the 1990 Census

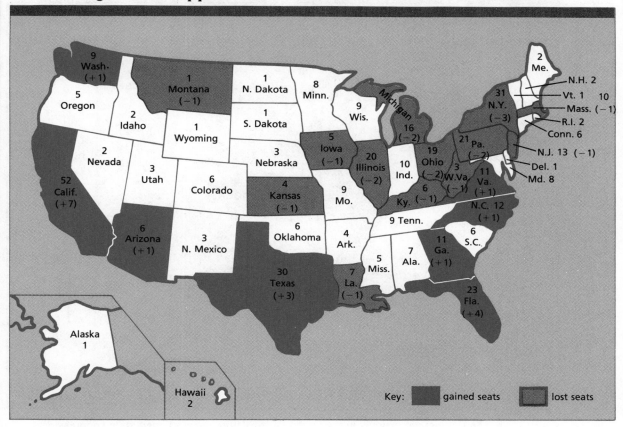

Key: ■ gained seats □ lost seats

to Congress. Vermont, Alaska, and Wyoming all have fewer people than Washington, but each is represented by two senators and a representative. A Constitutional amendment was proposed in 1978 that would allow the city's representative to vote along with the other 435 members of Congress. The amendment attracted little support and fell far short of passage by the 38 states needed for ratification.

REAPPORTIONMENT

The population of the United States grows larger every year. Americans also move frequently. The greatest migration today is from cold weather states to the jobs and warm weather of the "sunbelt." The national census

(taken every ten years in years ending in "0") measures this mobile population. The announcement of the census figures is of great interest to the states, because the size of their delegations to the House can be affected. States that have lost population may lose seats. States that are growing may gain seats. The Bureau of the Census prepares the *reapportionment* plan for the President, who forwards it to Congress for action. Unless Congress changes it, the plan becomes law after 60 days.

Each state legislature then begins the tricky task of drawing the lines for its congressional districts. Many stormy political battles have been fought over the placing of these boundaries. The majority party in each legislature tries to draw the lines to favor its own mem-

The Gerrymander Lives!

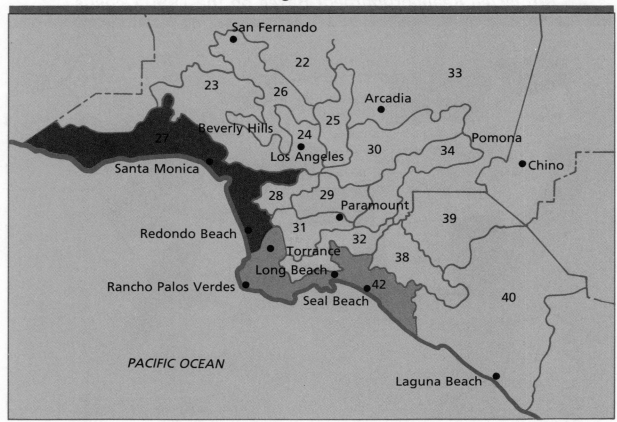

San Fernando

22

23

26

Arcadia

33

25

Beverly Hills

27

24

Pomona

Los Angeles

30

34

Chino

Santa Monica

28

29

Paramount

39

31

Redondo Beach

32

38

Torrance

42

Long Beach

Rancho Palos Verdes

Seal Beach

40

PACIFIC OCEAN

Laguna Beach

■ The Democratic majority in the California legislature reapportioned state congressional districts in 1981. The 27th included a "safe" Democratic majority. The next-door 42nd, by contrast, was allowed to tilt toward the Republican camp. New lines will be drawn in 1991.

bers. Such political self-interest often results in the creation of oddly shaped districts. The only reason for their shape is that a majority of the voters who live in them are registered as members of the party in power. This process provides "safe" seats for the majority party's candidates. The majority party sometimes "sacrifices" a few districts by including large numbers of the minority party's voters within their boundaries (see the map on page 178).

The process of creating strangely shaped districts that favor the party in power is known as *gerrymandering*. The name comes from an early Massachusetts governor named Elbridge

Gerry. When Gerry was finished with his reapportionment in 1812, one salamander-shaped district was quickly dubbed a "gerrymander."

"ONE MAN, ONE VOTE"

Starting in 1962, the U.S. Supreme Court heard a series of cases that led to reforms in reapportionment. The justices handed down the key decision in the case of *Wesberry* v. *Sanders* (1964). The Court ruled that "as nearly as is practicable, one man's vote in a congressional election is to be worth as much as another's." The Court demanded (1) that congressional districts be of a reasonably compact shape and (2) that each district in a state contain roughly the same number of people.

Since then, the courts have examined many reapportionment plans to make sure that each district falls within allowable limits. In practice, the majority party in each state still tries to reapportion so as to keep itself in power. The "one man, one vote" rule, however, has prevented the worst excesses of the old-fashioned gerrymander.

5. How does Congress organize itself?

Congress has organized itself to conduct "the people's business" as efficiently as possible. Members of each house elect their own officers to supervise the ongoing work of the legislature.

SPEAKER OF THE HOUSE

The House of Representatives is led by a presiding officer known as the *Speaker*. Traditionally, the leader of the majority party holds this powerful post. The Speaker conducts House business according to rules called parliamentary procedure. Among the Speaker's powers are:

1. *Power to recognize members.* House members cannot take the floor to speak unless they are recognized by the Speaker. In practice, the Speaker may recognize those who favor the majority party's position while "overlooking" legislators who want to speak in opposition. By controlling debate on a particular bill, the Speaker can influence its passage or defeat.

2. *Power to interpret House rules.* The Speaker also interprets and applies the rules of the House. This power enables the Speaker to (1) refer bills to favorable committees, (2) appoint special and conference committee members, and (3) delay or speed up the passage of legislation.

The majority party elects the Speaker at a special party conference, or *caucus*. This important caucus is held at the beginning of each

■ In 1812, the Massachusetts legislature and governor, Elbridge Gerry, redrew the map of the state's election districts. The new boundaries favored the Democratic-Republicans. To poke fun at the results, an artist added a head, wings, and claws to one odd-shaped district and created the gerrymander.

new term. Once elected, the Speaker serves for two years and must stand for reelection when the next Congress convenes. Along with presiding over the House, the Speaker sometimes joins in a debate (after appointing a temporary presiding officer to fill the chair). The Speaker may also vote on any issue but seldom does so except to break a tie. If both the President and Vice President die at the same time, the Speaker is next in line for the presidency.

PRESIDENT OF THE SENATE

The Vice President of the United States serves as the President of the Senate. This is one of the few specific tasks that the Constitution gives to the Vice President. In practice, Vice Presidents seldom preside over the Senate unless a close vote on an important bill is expected. The Vice President may not take part in debates but casts the deciding vote in case of ties.

Organization of the Congress of the United States

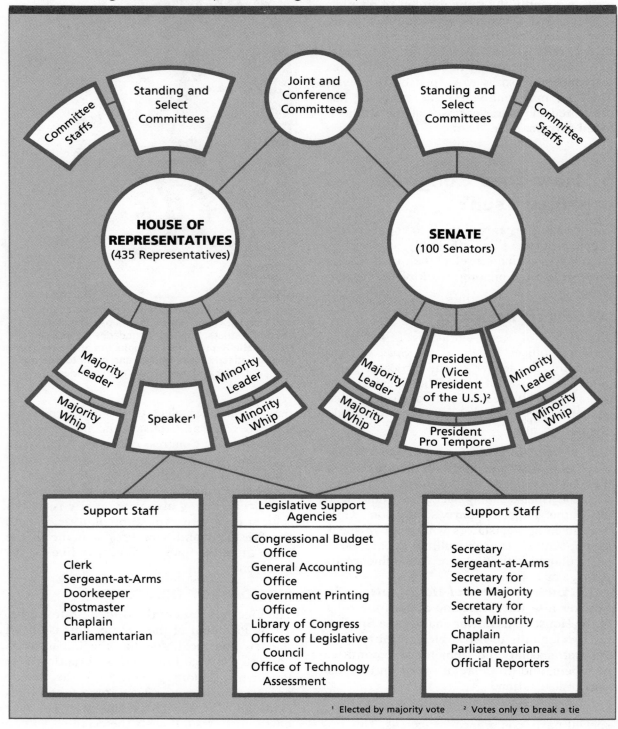

Committee Staffs

Standing and Select Committees

Joint and Conference Committees

Standing and Select Committees

Committee Staffs

HOUSE OF REPRESENTATIVES (435 Representatives)

SENATE (100 Senators)

Majority Leader

Majority Whip

Speaker[1]

Minority Leader

Minority Whip

Majority Leader

Majority Whip

President (Vice President of the U.S.)[2]

President Pro Tempore[1]

Minority Leader

Minority Whip

Support Staff	Legislative Support Agencies	Support Staff
Clerk Sergeant-at-Arms Doorkeeper Postmaster Chaplain Parliamentarian	Congressional Budget Office General Accounting Office Government Printing Office Library of Congress Offices of Legislative Council Office of Technology Assessment	Secretary Sergeant-at-Arms Secretary for the Majority Secretary for the Minority Chaplain Parliamentarian Official Reporters

[1] Elected by majority vote   [2] Votes only to break a tie

The Senate also elects one of its members to the post of *President pro tempore*. This senator presides over the Senate when the vice presidency is vacant or when the Vice President is absent. The majority party picks one of its senior members as President *pro tem*, but it doesn't usually elect its majority leader to fill this post. The majority leader's skills are needed on the floor, where battles over key legislation are won and lost. On days when business is routine, junior members of the majority party (those with little seniority) sometimes are called on to preside.

PARTY LEADERS

Each house has a *majority* and a *minority party leader*. These floor leaders head *steering committees* that supervise the legislative business in each house. Those leaders who belong to the President's party work with the White House to pass the administration's legislative program. Each party awards its floor leadership positions to senior members who have demonstrated superior political skills.

The majority and minority party leaders work with the Speaker of the House and the President of the Senate. They have several important jobs: (1) To manage debate on all business before the House and Senate. (2) To coordinate the work of congressional committees. (3) To choose the speakers who are going to debate a particular bill. (4) To work with the Rules Committee to move bills onto the floor. (5) To organize party members so that the party is unified on important votes.

Party whips assist the floor leaders in each house. The whips are usually selected by the party leader. They act as assistant floor leaders to line up votes for or against a given bill. The whips must be accurate judges of how each party member is going to vote. They also must be capable of delivering the votes of party members when a vote is taken. Party whips use many methods to get the job done, from polite debate to political arm-twisting.

OTHER OFFICIALS

In addition to party leaders, each house is served by a staff of nonelected officials. These include a sergeant-at-arms (who maintains order and organizes security) and a legislative counsel (who helps write and review new bills). In addition, official reporters, parliamentarians, chaplains, and a number of others carry on the daily "housekeeping" tasks of the Congress.

6. How is the committee system organized?

Every year, Congress staggers under a work load that is increasing in size and complexity. A single energy bill, for example, might run to 400 pages or more. Members cannot be fully informed on every issue, nor can members study every problem in depth. Congress solves this dilemma by using the committee system. Serving on committees gives legislators a chance to concentrate on one or two areas of legislation that especially interest them. Senators and representatives still come together to debate and vote, but they carry on much of their business in committees.

COMMITTEE FUNCTIONS

Except for the Rules Committee in each house, the standing committees serve as tiny legislatures. Each holds hearings on matters related to its area of authority. A bill that would set up a new foreign aid program, for example, would be heard before the Senate Committee on Foreign Relations and the House Committee on Foreign Affairs.

Many committee hearings take the form of investigations. The information gathered during these sessions may (1) aid in the writing of new laws; (2) spotlight a social problem, such as health care for the poor; or (3) provide insight into the activities of the executive and judicial branches. Recent committee hearings on organized crime, stock market trading, and the conduct of foreign affairs in the Middle East were held in order to fulfill these duties. As a result of committee investigations, Congress may pass corrective legislation or force the executive branch to change the way it conducts its business.

THREE TYPES OF COMMITTEES

Congressional committees fall into three major categories:

1. *Standing committees.* Much of the legislative work of Congress takes place in *standing committees*. (See the list on page 182, which arranges the committees in the order of their importance.) Each of the permanent committees studies new bills that fall under its jurisdiction. These committees also investigate problems that need legislative attention. Congress once labored under the weight of 81 standing committees, but the number has now been streamlined to 38. The House has 22, and the Senate has 16. Each standing committee further divides itself into *subcommittees* that handle specialized committee business. Congressional committees also depend on expert staffs to aid them in their work.

2. *Special committees.* When a situation develops that cannot be handled by normal committee procedures, Congress creates *special committees*. These "select" committees, as they are sometimes known, disband after their particular tasks are finished. Most special committees last for less than a year. Members of the special committees are appointed by the Speaker of the House or by the President of the Senate. In recent years, special committees have looked into the problems of ageing, hunger, Indian affairs, and government intelligence agencies.

3. *Conference committees.* The House and Senate versions of the same bill often differ. When this happens, the leadership appoints a temporary *conference committee*. Conference committee members meet, settle their differences through compromises, and write a conference report. Both houses must accept

---

STANDING COMMITTEES OF CONGRESS, 1990
RANKED BY GROUPS IN RELATIVE ORDER OF IMPORTANCE

House of Representatives	Senate
Rules	Appropriations
Appropriations	Foreign Relations
Ways and Means	Finance
Armed Services	Armed Services
Judiciary	Judiciary
Agriculture	Agriculture, Nutrition, and Forestry
Energy and Commerce	Commerce, Science, and Transportation
Foreign Affairs	
Government Operations	
Banking, Finance, and Urban Affairs	Banking, Housing, and Urban Affairs
Budget	Budget
Education and Labor	Labor and Human Resources
Interior and Insular Affairs	Energy and Natural Resources
Science and Technology	Environment and Public Works
Public Works and Transportation	
Post Office and Civil Service	Government Affairs
Merchant Marine and Fisheries	Veterans' Affairs
Veterans' Affairs	Rules and Administration
Small Business	Small Business
District of Columbia	
House Administration	
Standards of Official Conduct	

■ A meeting of the House Budget Committee headed by Leon Panetta of California. Before a bill reaches the floor of Congress to be voted on, it must be studied in committee. Often, expert witnesses are called to give their views on the legislation. Most committee hearings receive little public attention, but important bills sometimes attract the attention of the entire nation. Why are some committee assignments more desirable than others?

or reject the report without amendment. The conference committee thus plays a key role in deciding a bill's final form.

COMMITTEE MEMBERSHIP

The membership of standing committees reflects the strength of each party in the House and Senate. If there were 60 Republicans and 40 Democrats in the Senate, the Republicans would be entitled to three-fifths of the seats on each committee. If the Democrats were in control of the House, they would reserve a majority of the lower chamber's committee seats for themselves.

Committee assignments usually reflect (1) the legislator's personal interests, (2) the seniority (length of service) the legislator holds in Congress, and (3) the leadership's opinion of the legislator's abilities. From their first days in Congress, senators and representatives compete for assignments to the most presti-

gious committees. A lawmaker who serves on a committee that handles money bills, foreign relations, or military matters often receives favorable national attention. In the House, for instance, three of the most desirable committees are Appropriations, Foreign Affairs, and Armed Services. Seats on the Rules Committee are also highly prized. This committee receives little public notice but exercises great influence within the House.

Senate rules allow senators to serve on a maximum of two major committees and one minor committee. In the House, party caucuses have established even stricter limits. House rules permit Democrats to serve on one major and one minor committee *or* two minor committees. House Republicans (who have been the minority party since 1955) have fewer seats to distribute. They are limited to service on a single major or two minor committees.

Despite these rules, exceptions sometimes

occur. Some representatives content themselves with a single major committee assignment. Conversely, a few members of the House are permitted to hold as many as three committee seats. Each of the legislators also sits on several subcommittees. Some of these subcommittees are as important as their parent committees.

Each party has chosen a slightly different method for assigning its members to committees. In the Senate, the Democratic Steering Committee and the Republican Committee on Committees draw up the committee assignments. The Democratic party caucus then meets to approve the Steering Committee's choices. The Republican caucus does not vote on the decisions made by the Committee on Committees. In the House, the Democratic Steering and Policy Committee makes the assignments, subject to the approval of the party caucus. The Republican Committee on Committees performs a similar task, but the party caucus votes only on the choice of the ranking Republican member of each committee. Meetings of the party caucuses are usually held before Congress convenes in January. After committee assignments are drawn up, each house adopts the lists with little or no debate.

The majority party in each house always appoints its own members as committee chairmen.* Traditionally, these key posts have gone to those senators or representatives who have the greatest seniority. Every lawmaker's vote is equal, but committee chairmen are "first among equals." Chairmen can call (or refuse to call) committee meetings. They schedule hearings, establish rules of procedure, and assign members to subcommittees. Bills that don't meet with the chairman's approval usually die in committee. When a bill does reach the floor, the chairman manages the debate and works for its passage.

A major change occurred in 1975 when the Democratic party caucus refused to return three senior members to their former chairmanships. Younger, more liberal members said that these older, more conservative representatives did not reflect the liberal views of the Democratic majority. The revolt shook up the seniority system. Committee chairmen still enjoy great prestige and power, but they no longer rule as dictators.

Let's review for a moment

Thus far you've learned some basic facts about Congress. You know that Congress is bicameral—divided into two houses. You also know that to run for either the Senate or the House of Representatives, you must meet the minimum qualifications spelled out in the Constitution. Further, you must be elected by the voters of your state or district. If you're a representative, you'll be elected to serve for two years. If you're a senator, you'll serve for six years. All states are equally represented by two senators. The population of each state determines how many representatives it can send to the House.

Now, who will call you to order when you take your seat as a new member of Congress? In the House, the *Speaker* runs the show. In the Senate, the Vice President presides. The Senate also elects a *President pro tem* to conduct business during the Vice President's frequent absences. *Majority* and *minority leaders* and their assistants (the party *whips*) regulate the flow of legislation through the two houses.

The various *standing committees* allow Congress to cope with its heavy work load. If you're the new representative from Iowa, you would likely ask for assignment to the Agriculture Committee. Don't be surprised, however, if you end up on the committee on Merchant Marine and Fisheries. The party *caucus* may have assigned all the open seats on the Agriculture Committee to its more senior lawmakers. Your *standing committee* will probably be divided into *subcommittees* so that members can take a closer look at complex issues.

When a "hot" political debate develops,

---

* Congress uses the masculine form for any head of a committee, whether a male or female.

you might be appointed to a *special committee* that has the job of investigating the issue. Senior members dominate the *conference committees*. These committees iron out the differences in bills passed separately by the House and Senate.

Now let's take a closer look at the actual legislative powers of Congress.

7. What is the basis of congressional power?

One of the nation's first political battles took place between the supporters of Alexander Hamilton and Thomas Jefferson. The conflict grew out of a basic question: How much power does the Constitution give to Congress? The Hamiltonians formed the Federalist party, which believed in a loose construction of the Constitution. The Jeffersonians (later known as the Democratic-Republicans) stood for a strict construction.

A strict interpretation meant that the government, and particularly Congress, was limited to those activities that were spelled out in the Constitution. Loose constructionists, on the other hand, insisted that the intentions as well as the words of the Framers should be considered. They also believed that the government possessed all the authority it needed to carry out the specific powers granted by the Constitution.

History has seen the victory of the loose construction interpretation. The influence of government now extends into almost every nook and cranny of our lives.

DELEGATED POWERS: INHERENT, EXPRESSED, AND IMPLIED

The Framers of the Constitution began by deciding on the type of democratic government they wanted for the United States. Then they gave the national government the powers it would need to govern. These are the *delegated powers* found in the Constitution. Delegated powers are of three kinds: inherent, expressed, and implied.

Inherent powers. *Inherent powers* are those that belong to any national government. Without these powers the government could not rule a sovereign nation-state. Inherent powers include such rights as protecting the nation against invasion, regulating immigration, and gaining new territory.

Expressed powers. Most congressional powers are either *expressed* (those named in Article I, Section 8 of the Constitution) or *implied* (justified as necessary to carry out the government's constitutional duties). Another named for expressed powers is *enumerated powers*; a list can be found on page 187.

The expressed powers of Congress relate to broad areas of our national life. Congress sets tax rates and regulates interstate commerce. The legislative branch authorizes the spending of our money, and it has the power to borrow it back again. Congress regulates bankruptcy, oversees the postal system, controls the patent and copyright systems, and governs U.S. territories. In addition, the House and Senate establish federal courts, declare war, and share with the President the conduct of foreign affairs.

War powers. Of all the expressed powers given to Congress, the right to declare war has created some of the most explosive arguments. During the Vietnam conflict of the 1960s, for example, the legislative and executive branches clashed over their respective war-making powers. Critics charged that President Johnson's handling of the fighting in Vietnam was illegal because Congress had not passed a declaration of war. Congress tried to resolve the debate by enacting the 1973 War Powers Resolution. The resolution states that the President must ask for congressional approval of any emergency military action. Since then, every President has argued that the law severely limits his ability to respond to quick-breaking, "brushfire" wars.

The legality of the War Powers Resolution will remain in doubt until a President disobeys it and the Supreme Court decides the matter. Acting in a separate case, the Court declared in 1983 that a "legislative veto" on a President's legal actions was unconstitutional. (A

Learning Skills

Compiling Lists

Imagine that your best friend's parents have invited you to go to Tahiti with them. What's the first thing you'd do to get ready (after you calmed down a little)? If you're like most people, you'd start by making a list—clothes, equipment, toilet items, and the like. That makes sense, because otherwise you might forget something important.

The same lesson holds true when it comes to carrying out any complicated task. If you're studying this chapter, for example, you'll find it helpful to make lists of important items, such as the expressed powers of Congress. The process is a little like making an outline. Write down all the items that fall under a particular heading, one item per line. Think of it as a shopping list—a shopping list of ideas.

Now, let's apply the principle of listing to a project that has long-term value. Concerned citizens know they should tell their elected representatives how they feel about important issues. Most people never get beyond thinking about it, because they don't know where to send their letters. With the help of the phone book and the reference section of your library, you can compile a list of the local, state, and national officials who serve your community. Here's a useful number to get you started: U.S. Congress information switchboard, (202) 224-3121.

At a minimum, list the following addresses and phone numbers.

Office	Name and Party	Address	Phone
School board			
City council			
County board			
State legislature (lower house)			
State legislature (upper house)			
State governor			
U.S. House of Rep.			
U.S. Senate			
U.S. Senate			
President of the U.S.			

Now, put that list to use. Is there a serious problem that you want to see fixed? Is Congress about to vote on an issue that concerns you? Write letters to the appropriate people on your list, telling them what you want them to do. See pages 422–423 for a Learning Skills feature on writing to an elected official.

EXPRESSED POWERS DELEGATED TO CONGRESS BY ARTICLE I, SECTION 8 OF THE CONSTITUTION

1. To lay and collect taxes, duties, imposts, and excises for the purpose of paying the debts and providing for the common defense and general welfare of the United States.

2. To borrow money.

3. To regulate foreign and interstate commerce.

4. To formulate rules for bankruptcies and naturalization.

5. To coin money and set standards of weights and measures.

6. To punish counterfeiting.

7. To establish post offices and post roads.

8. To grant copyrights and patents.

9. To set up federal courts below the Supreme Court.

10. To punish piracy and offenses against the law of nations.

11. To declare war.

12. To raise and support armies.

13. To provide and maintain a navy.

14. To enact a code of military law.

15. To call out the national militia.

16. To regulate, arm, and discipline the militia.

17. To govern the District of Columbia.

18. To make all laws necessary and proper for carrying out the foregoing powers (the "elastic clause").

"legislative veto" is a law through which Congress tries to prevent the President from using a specific executive power.) Even without the legislative veto, Congress can still control the military budget. If lawmakers want to force the President to withdraw troops from a foreign battlefield, they can cut off funding for the operation.

Judicial and police powers. The judicial powers of Congress include the right (1) to establish federal courts, (2) to define federal offenses and their punishments, and (3) to impeach and remove federal officials guilty of violating their oath of office. Laws passed to promote public health, safety, and welfare are part of the police power of Congress. The United States does not have a national police force, however. The Justice Department and the Department of the Treasury have special marshals and agents who protect the public interest when federal laws are violated.

Implied powers. The battle over implied powers began as early as 1790. In that year, Hamilton proposed a Bank of the United States to regulate the nation's currency. The Federalists found the constitutional authority they needed in Article I, Section 8, Clause 18—the *"necessary and proper"* clause. This *"elastic" clause* states that Congress shall have power "to make all laws which shall be necessary and proper for carrying into execution the foregoing powers . . ."

Congress determines what is "necessary and proper" in the course of writing the laws. That power is not absolute, for all legislation is subject to presidential veto and to judicial review by the courts. The Supreme Court approved the concept of implied powers in *McCulloch* v. *Maryland* in 1819 (see pages 390–391).

LIMITS ON CONGRESSIONAL POWER

The elastic clause does not provide Congress with unlimited power. Limits on legislative authority appear at several points in the Constitution, particularly in Article I, Section 9, and in the Bill of Rights. These *forbidden powers* include the peacetime suspension of *habeas corpus* and the enactment of a bill of attainder or *ex post facto* law (see pages 96–

FYI . . .

Congressional Investigations Serve as the "Eyes and Ears" of the Legislative Branch

Congressional investigations have four purposes: (1) to gather facts on which legislation can be based, (2) to "watchdog" government operations, (3) to inform the public, and (4) to look into questions regarding the conduct of government officials. The first investigation was launched in 1792, and every Congress since then has continued the practice. Out of thousands of investigations, a few have left permanent imprints on American history.

ST. CLAIR INQUIRY

In 1792, the House authorized the first congressional investigation. The target was the 1791 defeat of American troops by Indians in the Northwest Territory. The inquiry cleared General Arthur St. Clair of blame in the deaths of about 600 men. The committee found that the War Department and its contractors had been guilty of mismanagement and delay.

JOINT COMMITTEE ON THE CONDUCT OF THE [CIVIL] WAR

The first joint House-Senate investigating committee was formed in 1861. After looking into the Union's early defeats at Bull Run and Ball's Bluff, Radical Republicans used the committee to examine Lincoln's conduct of the war. Committee members forced Lincoln to fire generals they disliked and often leaked information. Confederate General Robert E. Lee said that the committee was worth two divisions of troops to his cause.

INVESTIGATION OF THE MONEY TRUST

In 1912, a House subcommittee began an inquiry into the U.S. banking system. The committee found that many leading industries and banks were being run by interlocking directorates. By serving as directors on many boards, financial giants such as J. P. Morgan, Sr., were able to reduce competition and increase their profits. The committee's work led to the Federal Reserve Act of 1913, the Clayton Antitrust Act of 1914, and the Federal Trade Commission Act of 1914.

THE TEAPOT DOME INQUIRY

In 1922, the Department of the Interior leased naval oil reserves at Elk Hills (California) and Teapot Dome (Wyoming) to two oil companies. The leases put the companies in a position to make enormous profits. A Senate committee investigated the leases, which had been approved by President Warren Harding's Secretary of the Interior, Albert B. Fall. The committee revealed that Fall had accepted $300,000 in bribes from the oil companies. The courts sent him to prison and canceled the leases.

THE WATERGATE HEARINGS

The most sensational investigation in recent history began in 1973. A Senate committee was given the task of looking into illegal campaign practices after the White House tried to cover up its role in a break-in at Democratic campaign headquarters. The committee's hearings uncovered a trail that led directly to President Richard Nixon's office. The tales of "dirty tricks" and campaign finance abuses helped to drive Nixon from office and led to the reform of election laws.

THE IRAN-CONTRA AFFAIR

The White House was again shaken by a congressional investigation in 1987, but President Ronald Reagan survived the Iran-Contra inquiry. The joint House-Senate hearings revealed that the administration had used the National Security Council to sell missiles to Iran. The money raised by the sales was used to support the Contras fighting in Nicaragua. Reagan convinced the committee that he was unaware of the illegal activities carried on in his name.

97). In case these limitations fall short of their purpose, the Tenth Amendment includes the reserved power clause. It states that "The powers not delegated to the United States by the Constitution, nor prohibited by it to the States, are reserved to the States respectively, or to the people."

8. What are the nonlegislative tasks of Congress?

The enactment of new laws is only one of the major tasks given to Congress. Indeed, much of our lawmakers' work can be classified as nonlegislative in nature.

INVESTIGATION

The committees and subcommittees of the House and Senate often investigate (1) the need for new laws, (2) scandalous events or behavior contrary to the public interest, or even (3) the changing patterns of American life. Ever since the Civil War, Congress has kept close watch over the executive branch's conduct of the country's wars. More recently, congressional investigations have led to changes in the way the executive branch gathers intelligence and conducts foreign policy.

SEATING AND CONFIRMATION

Congress exercises final authority over the seating of its own members. The House and Senate use this power most often (1) when election results are contested and cannot be resolved at the state level or (2) when a member of Congress is accused of improper conduct in office.

More important, the Senate must approve White House appointments at many levels. This *confirmation process* affects officials as varied as the members of the President's Cabinet, federal judges, ambassadors, and the heads of independent agencies. This process gives Congress a voice in the selection of the people who interpret and administer our laws.

After the President nominates an official, the nominee testifies under oath before the proper Senate committee. The committee probes the nominee's political philosophy, personal finances, and administrative ability. The members then send their recommendations to the Senate, where a final vote is taken. If the Senate does not approve the nomination, the President must find another nominee. The administration often withdraws a candidate's name if White House officials foresee a close vote that might embarrass the President.

CONSTITUTIONAL AMENDMENT

Congress plays a key role in amending the Constitution. Any proposed change in the nation's basic law must pass both houses by a two-thirds majority. In addition, Congress usually sets a date by which three-fourths of the state legislatures (38 states) must have

Herblock © 1979 The Washington Post Co.

■ A drive to pass a constitutional amendment mandating a balanced federal budget gained strength in the 1980s. More than 30 state legislatures sent resolutions to Congress calling for a new constitutional convention. Political scientists fear that if a new convention is called, the delegates might go on to rewrite other sections of the Constitution—with disastrous results.

ratified the amendment. If the amendment is not approved by the deadline, Congress can give the states more time to act.

Although the process has never been used, Congress may call a constitutional convention to consider further amendments at the request of two-thirds of the states. Legal experts warn that a new constitutional convention might not stop with a single amendment. Once started, the delegates could revise large sections of the Constitution. That's what happened at the last Constitutional Convention in 1787. The Framers threw out the Articles of Confederation and created a new system of government.

IMPEACHMENT

The House of Representatives has one judicial power. After a careful investigation, the House can accuse federal officials (including the President) of high crimes and misdemeanors. This rarely used process is called *impeachment*. Articles of impeachment have been voted only a dozen or so times in 200 years. An impeachment action by the House is similar to indictment by a grand jury in a criminal case. It means only that sufficient evidence exists to justify prosecution of the accused. The trial itself takes place in the Senate. Only four impeached officials, all federal judges, have been convicted.

Other nonlegislative jobs of Congress include (1) election of a President and Vice President when no candidate wins a majority in the Electoral College, (2) approval of treaties by the Senate, and (3) admission of new states and territories.

9. How has the power of Congress grown?

Much of the influence that Congress exercises over the lives of the nation's citizens can be traced to two expressed powers: (1) the power to tax and (2) the power to regulate interstate commerce. After their experience with the Articles of Confederation, the Framers realized that a national government could not function without these powers.

THE POWER TO TAX

During the early 1980s, President Reagan persuaded Congress to expand the nation's military budgets. At the same time, Congress continued to fund most federal social programs. The lawmakers know that millions of Americans depend on the federal government for economic security. The nation's "safety net" of social services includes old-age benefits, unemployment insurance, health care, and a thousand other programs unknown when the Constitution was written. These costly services can be funded in only one way: from the pockets of America's taxpayers.

The federal government collects hundreds of billions of tax dollars every year. Although Americans pay a wide variety of taxes (see Chapter Ten), income taxes are the major source of federal income. The income tax was made possible by the Sixteenth Amendment in 1913. It allows the government to take a share of people's paychecks, investment profits, interest payments, and stock dividends.

Each year, Congress and the White House conduct a vigorous tug-of-war over the federal budget. There are never enough dollars to fund every worthwhile program. The President makes the first move by sending a budget to Congress that spells out the administration's spending plans. Congress then cuts some programs (a new missile, perhaps) and adds others (a regional waterway, for example). If

■ One of the most difficult tasks facing Congress is the yearly wrestling match with the budget. Why is balancing the budget such a problem?

the budget doesn't balance, Congress can take the politically risky step of increasing taxes. More often, the budget remains unbalanced, and the Treasury borrows money to make up the difference. (Chapter Ten describes the federal budget in greater detail.)

THE POWER TO REGULATE INTERSTATE COMMERCE

Congress has enacted many laws that regulate the conditions under which Americans live and work. Whether you dig coal, drive a truck, publish a newspaper, or cook hamburgers, your job has been influenced by Congress.

The development of the nation's transportation system in the nineteenth century brought more and more goods into interstate commerce. At first, the term was applied only to the movement of goods across state lines. Today, the courts define interstate commerce to include anything that influences such movement. Along with the goods themselves, the means of transporting and trading them have come under regulation. The Court decision that made this possible came in 1824 (see *Gibbons* v. *Ogden*, pages 391-393). New industries, such as telecommunications and air travel, have automatically fallen under this regulatory power.

In the 1950s, Congress began using its power to regulate interstate commerce as a way to attack racial discrimination and other social injustices. On the surface, the refusal of a small barbecue restaurant in Birmingham, Alabama, to provide service to black Americans may seem far removed from interstate commerce. The Supreme Court ruled, however, that Congress has the authority to end discrimination even by small, local businesses (*Katzenbach* v. *McClung*, 1964). The Court said that once a small business buys supplies that cross state lines, it is involved in interstate commerce.

The power to regulate interstate commerce has also been used to fight monopolies and other operations that limit competition. Government regulation tries to promote the free flow of goods, services, and people across state lines.

LIMITS ON THESE POWERS

Despite what many taxpayers believe, there are limits on the power to tax and to regulate commerce. Congress may not tax exports, for example, nor may taxes be levied on organized religions. Although the Constitution guarantees free passage of goods across state lines, the states have the right to restrict these movements when the public's health and safety are involved. This is particularly true of raw farm products and dangerous chemicals.

10. What does it mean to be a member of Congress?

Members of Congress fulfill two main roles: (1) They serve as legislators, writing the laws needed to govern a complex society. (2) They help their *constituents* (people who live in their districts) solve problems, especially those that bring people face-to-face with government agencies.

■ **U.S. Representative Pat Schroeder of Colorado and some of her staff. Without competent aides, a member of Congress would have difficulty handling government responsibilities and taking care of constituents' needs.**

FYI . . .
Salary and Privileges of a Member of Congress

Category	Benefit
Salary	House members earn $125,100 per year; they may not accept payments (known as honoraria) for making speeches or personal appearances. Senators earn only $101,900, but they may keep up to $23,568 in honoraria. All members of Congress receive a 3 percent cost-of-living adjustment each year.
Expenses	Members submit yearly claims ranging from $88,000 to $280,000. The expense allowance covers travel, telephones, telegrams, newsletters, and other official costs.
Travel	Free use of government transportation when on official business. Foreign spending allowance of $75–$108 a day.
Publications	Free publication and distribution of speeches and other materials. Free copies of the Congressional Record. Free maps, calendars, and pamphlets for the voters back home.
Mailing	Free postage for official mail (the franking privilege).
Offices	Fully equipped office in House or Senate office buildings, plus offices in members' home states.
Staff	Each Senator is allowed $875,896 to $1,550,560 for staff salaries, based on the state's population. Representatives are allowed $379,488 a year for their staffs.
Communications	Free, unlimited long-distance telephone calls. Low fees for use of government radio and television studios.
Pension	Generous pension after a minimum of five years of service in Congress. Pension after 32 years of service: $54,000.
Tax benefits	Tax exemption based on need to maintain a home in Washington (if occupied less than six months a year).
Miscellaneous	Free hospital benefits, legal counsel, photography service, swimming pools, gym facilities, and potted plants. Low cost life insurance, barber and beauty shops, and cafeteria service. Special parking privileges.

SERVICE TO CONSTITUENTS

What do you do if you're upset about pollution, foreign aid, or the route of the new interstate highway? Don't wait. Write your senators and your representative. After all, you and your community sent them to Washington as your personal representatives. They can provide information, assistance, and advice about government's actions or inactions. Moreover, when enough people speak out about important matters, legislators take action.

The members of Congress have a duty to serve as the voice of their constituents in Washington. Through those voices, the will of the voters gains expression on a national level. It doesn't matter whether the issue affects one person or the entire country. Constituents also want their representatives to make sure that part of the government's huge annual budget is spent in their state and district.

THE LEGISLATORS' DILEMMA

Despite this apparently clear-cut mission, the members of Congress face a constant dilemma. When the Clerk of the House or Senate calls for their votes, each member must make a moral decision. Which of the many interests tugging at them should they follow? Their party may demand that they vote one way, while their constituents may expect an opposite vote. On another occasion, they may have to take the hard road of voting against a popular bill because it violates their own sense of what is right. Whatever they decide, their decision will surely offend someone.

BENEFITS AND PRIVILEGES

Members of Congress receive a number of benefits and privileges. In addition, election to Congress can be a stepping-stone to higher office. Many lawmakers go on to become state governors, and a few reach for the presidency. To encourage freedom of debate, members of Congress may not be sued for what they say in the halls of Congress. In addition, they may not be arrested while on congressional business. This privilege usually amounts to little more than an immunity from traffic tickets.

Members of Congress are not paid by the hour. No regulations require their presence on the floor of Congress, or even in Washington, for any specific number of days. As a result, Congress is full of tales of absentee lawmakers who spend long weekends on Bermuda beaches. Others find excuses to run off on "fact-finding" trips to Hong Kong, London, or Rio de Janeiro.

Serving in Congress isn't all fun and games, however. The members must find time for committee work, floor debates, serving the interests of their home districts, making speeches, and raising money for the next election campaign. At election time, members of Congress must take time from their legislative duties while they campaign. In addition, most lawmakers must bear the expense of maintaining two homes—one in their home district and one in Washington, D.C. Family relationships sometimes suffer when spouses are unwilling or unable to follow the members to the capital.

Reviewing
what you've learned

1. The United States Congress is the lawmaking branch of our government. The Constitution spells out in great detail what it may do and what it may not do. Members of the House of Representatives and the Senate are elected by voters in their home states, with two-year terms in the House and six-year terms in the Senate. A two-house (bicameral) legislature allows new legislation to be carefully studied and voted on. Bicameralism also solves the problem of striking a power balance between large and small states. Every state has equal representation in the Senate, but seats in the House are allocated on the basis of population.

2. Congress meets for a two-year term, which is divided into two annual sessions. One hundred senators, two from each state, sit in the upper chamber.

The 435 members of the House of Representatives are chosen from individual districts. House districts are reapportioned every ten years, after the national census measures changes in the nation's population.

3. Each house elects a *majority* and a *minority leader,* along with other officials who organize and schedule the work load of Congress. The Constitution provides for a *Speaker of the House* as presiding officer. The post is held by the leader of the majority party. The Vice President of the United States serves as the President of the Senate but has little real influence except when called on to cast the deciding vote that breaks a tie.

4. Congressional *standing committees* and their *subcommittees* do most of the legislative work. Members of Congress are assigned to these committees according to their party's strength in each house. Chairmen are usually selected on the basis of their seniority. Standing committees hold hearings on new legislation and also hold investigative hearings. *Special committees* are appointed to study unusual problems. *Conference committees* meet to iron out differences when the two houses pass different versions of the same bill.

5. Congress operates under a loose construction of the Constitution, which has given it wide powers. The three main sources of congressional power derive from Article I, Section 8 and include (1) the *elastic clause* of the Constitution, (2) the power to tax, and (3) the power to regulate interstate commerce. In addition, Congress carries out nonlegislative functions such as confirmation of presidential appointments, investigations, and *impeachment* proceedings.

6. The pay and privileges given to senators and representatives reflect the importance of Congress. The presidency often dominates the headlines, but the executive branch can still be checked by Congress through its control over the federal budget. Thus, Congress continues to play a major role in the U.S. system of government—just as planned by the Framers of the Constitution.

Reviews questions and activities

TERMS YOU SHOULD KNOW

caucus	gerrymandering	reapportionment
conference committee	impeachment	session of Congress
confirmation process	majority leader	Speaker of the House
constituents	minority leader	special committee
delegated powers	"necessary and proper"	standing committee
elastic clause	clause	steering committee
enumerated powers	party whip	subcommittee
forbidden powers	President *pro tempore*	term of Congress

REVIEW QUESTIONS

Select the response that best completes each statement or question.

1. The Constitution requires that ——— of the membership of the House of Representatives stand for election every two years. (*a*) one-third. (*b*) one-half. (*c*) two-thirds. (*d*) three-quarters. (*e*) all.

2. Bicameralism was chosen as the principle for the United States Congress because (*a*) the British Parliament set the example. (*b*) one-house legislatures under the Continental Congresses and the Articles of Confederation were unsuccessful. (*c*) there was a need to resolve the conflict between the small and large states. (*d*) colonial legislatures had been bicameral. (*e*) all of these.

3. National reapportionment serves the purpose of (*a*) assigning congressional seats according to the wealth of a state. (*b*) setting the boundaries of individual congressional districts. (*c*) rewarding the states that voted for the President in the previous election. (*d*) assigning seats in the House of Representatives according to changing population patterns. (*e*) raising taxes in the wealthy districts of each state.

4. The "one man, one vote" philosophy would tend to prevent (*a*) a rural congressional district being drawn the same size as an urban district. (*b*) politicians from "selling out" to special interests. (*c*) the reelection of the same person to Congress year after year. (*d*) favored districts from receiving more than their share of defense contracts. (*e*) members of Congress from raising their own salaries.

5. The major part of congressional business is handled (*a*) by debate on the floor of Congress. (*b*) through closed-door conferences between White House representatives and members of Congress. (*c*) by special investigative committees. (*d*) by the standing committees. (*e*) by consultation with the President.

6. The "elastic clause" in the Constitution has been used to (*a*) establish the presidency as the dominant branch of government. (*b*) hold Congress to a strict construction of the Constitution. (*c*) give Congress the power to make whatever laws are necessary and proper. (*d*) stretch out the term of Congress during wartime. (*e*) give Congress the power to impeach.

7. The power of Congress to declare war is (*a*) an expressed power. (*b*) an implied power. (*c*) a judicial power. (*d*) a forbidden power. (*e*) a reserved power.

8. The confirmation process allows the Senate to (*a*) propose amendments to the Constitution. (*b*) sit as a jury to hear charges of impeachment brought by the House. (*c*) set up investigative committees to probe national problems. (*d*) judge the abilities of the President's appointees to the Cabinet and to the Supreme Court. (*e*) accept or reject the President's yearly budget.

9. The biggest source of federal tax revenue is from (*a*) the sales tax. (*b*) the income tax. (*c*) import taxes. (*d*) excise taxes. (*e*) the sale of federal lands.

10. Members of Congress do *not* receive (*a*) free postage for official mail. (*b*) travel allowances while on government business. (*c*) allowances for maintaining an office. (*d*) a tax-free salary and expense account. (*e*) free phone calls.

CONCEPT DEVELOPMENT

1. A friend wants to run for the House or Senate. Explain the minimum requirements set up by the Constitution for representatives and senators. What training and experience do you think your friend needs in order to be a good legislator?

2. Describe the reapportionment process that determines how many members each state can send to the House of Representatives.

3. What is meant by gerrymandering? How have Congress and the courts tried to limit this practice?

4. Why does Congress place so much emphasis on the committee system? What changes would you make in it?

5. How has Congress made use of the Constitution's elastic clause? Use the power to tax and the power to regulate interstate commerce as examples to support your explanation.

HANDS-ON ACTIVITIES

1. Organize a panel discussion or debate on the topic, "Congress should return to a strict construction of the Constitution." Let each side present its argument. Then let the class vote on whether or not it would accept the consequences of this decision.

2. Prepare a research report for your class that compares the British parliamentary system with our own Congress. Point out the strengths and weaknesses of each. You'll probably discover that British politicians are envious of our committee system. Why do you think that might be true?

3. Write to your representative or senator to ask for a copy of the legislator's daily schedule for several weeks. After analyzing it, prepare a chart showing the percentage of time the legislator spent on various official duties. Do you feel that the legislator's time was spent appropriately?

4. If this is an election year, invite several local candidates for congressional office—or their campaign managers—to speak to your class. Be prepared to question them on their political philosophy, their understanding of the role of Congress, and their opinions on special issues that are important to you and your classmates.

5. Survey 30 people in a local shopping center. Ask them (a) to identify their representative and at least one of their two senators and (b) whether they voted in the last congressional election. Analyze the results and present them to your class.

9 How laws are made: Congress at work

▲ Worried bank customers in the early 1930s line up to withdraw their money.

Have you ever ordered a gadget through the mail that didn't work properly? Remember that time you were stuck behind a big truck that was poisoning the air with exhaust fumes? Perhaps you've read about cases in which the Internal Revenue Service took away a child's savings account because the parents were involved in a tax dispute. Injustices like these make us angry. The more you think about them, the more you feel like shouting, "There ought to be a law against that!"

Maybe there should be, but getting a law passed isn't easy. The problem lies in the slow and uncertain process by which government turns public concerns into public laws. For example, the United States has run up huge federal deficits in the past few years. It took a sharp stock market drop in 1987 to force the President and the Congress to work together to reduce the deficit. Great emergencies, however, can push the legislative process into moving with lightning speed.

In March 1933, the United States faced a great emergency. The nation lay helpless in the iron grip of the Great Depression. As President

197

Franklin Roosevelt waited to take his oath of office, at least 15 million Americans were out of work. Wall Street was in panic. Farmers were fighting to keep the banks from foreclosing on their land. To add to the danger, many banks were facing ruin. Nervous depositors were withdrawing their savings, fearful that they'd lose their money if the banks failed. A large number of banks had closed. Others were open only part-time.

Roosevelt tried to strike an optimistic note in his inaugural address on March 4. "The only thing we have to fear is fear itself," he told the nation. Even as he spoke, new laws were being prepared to save the banking system from complete collapse.

Working quickly, the new Secretary of the Treasury drafted an emergency banking bill. Meanwhile, President Roosevelt declared a national bank holiday. The "holiday" closed the banks in order to prevent panic withdrawals. The breathing space gave bankers a chance to assure the people that their savings were safe. The country relaxed and the panic subsided.

A message from the President awaited the new Congress when it convened on March 9: "I cannot too strongly urge upon the Congress the clear necessity for immediate action," Roosevelt told the legislators. No one argued with him.

In the House, representatives scrambled to find their seats while the Speaker of the House read aloud the text of the emergency bill. He was holding the only available copy. Debate was limited to 40 minutes, but the House didn't need that much time. When the bill came to a vote, it was passed by a thunderous voice vote. The representatives didn't want to wait for a slower roll-call vote.

The Senate, too, was in a hurry that March 9. Unwilling to wait for printed copies of the proposed law, the Senators debated the House version. Despite heated discussion, the bill passed without amendment. The vote was 73 to 7.

By 8:30 of the same evening, the Emergency Banking Relief Act of 1933 lay on the President's desk. It became law as soon as he signed it. The whole process, from introduction to signature, had taken less than eight hours. In addition to ending the banking crisis, the swift passage of the law left people with the hope that the new administration would act decisively to end the Depression.

Congress usually doesn't act this quickly. Of the 20,000 bills and resolutions introduced during each session of Congress, only a handful are rushed through without careful study and debate. Most bills follow a slow, tortuous route, and many die along the way. This chapter will answer these basic questions about the process:

1. **Who originates bills?**

2. **What is the role of committee staffs?**

3. **What is the role of the lobbyist?**

4. What happens when a bill is introduced?

5. What happens to bills during committee hearings?

6. What is the special role of the Rules Committee?

7. What happens when a bill reaches the floor?

8. How do the House and Senate work out their differences on a bill?

9. What choices does a President have when a bill reaches the White House?

1. Who originates bills?

When a law is first proposed, it's called a *bill*. Only a member of Congress can formally introduce a bill into the House or Senate. Legislators and their staffs write some of the bills themselves. More often, they introduce bills that have been written by private citizens, special-interest groups, the executive branch, or a congressional committee (see the table on page 199).

A bill must be carefully written in exact legal language. The Library of Congress provides a Legislative Reference Service to assist

FYI . . .
Where Bills Originate

Source of bills	Description of procedure
Private individuals and special-interest groups	The largest number of bills are written by these groups, then given to individual members of Congress for introduction. The proposed legislation is intended to promote the cause of the person or group proposing it.
The administration (the White House and other agencies of the executive branch)	The executive branch suggests laws and regulations that will assist it in carrying out its constitutional and legislatively ordered responsibilities. A new administration often proposes a package of laws designed to carry out the promises made during an election campaign.
Congress	Individual members of Congress write legislation in their areas of specialization and concern. The bills may be introduced on behalf of constituents, or they may reflect the legislator's own assessment of national needs.
Congressional committees	A committee or subcommittee, with the aid of its staff, may initiate legislation aimed at solving specific problems uncovered during committee hearings and investigations.

members of Congress in the task of researching and writing their bills. Each house of Congress maintains a legislative counsel for the same purpose. A corporation, labor union, or other special-interest group that wants to propose legislation will hire an expert to do the job.

The Government Printing Office (GPO) prints copies of all bills. The copies are available to senators and representatives, the administration, and the general public. Each line of the printed bill is numbered. The numbering lets

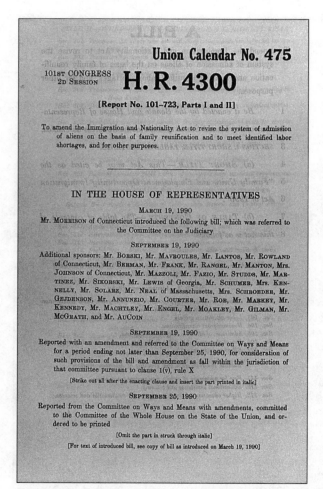

Union Calendar No. 475

101st CONGRESS
2d SESSION

H. R. 4300

[Report No. 101–723, Parts I and II]

To amend the Immigration and Nationality Act to revise the system of admission of aliens on the basis of family reunification and to meet identified labor shortages, and for other purposes.

IN THE HOUSE OF REPRESENTATIVES

MARCH 19, 1990

Mr. MORRISON of Connecticut introduced the following bill; which was referred to the Committee on the Judiciary

SEPTEMBER 19, 1990

Additional sponsors: Mr. BOSKI, Mr. MAVROULES, Mr. LANTOS, Mr. ROWLAND of Connecticut, Mr. BERMAN, Mr. FRANK, Mr. RANGEL, Mr. MANTON, Mrs. JOHNSON of Connecticut, Mr. MAZZOLI, Mr. FAZIO, Mr. STUDDS, Mr. MARTINEZ, Mr. SIKORSKI, Mr. LEWIS of Georgia, Mr. SCHUMER, Mrs. KENNELLY, Mr. SOLARZ, Mr. NEAL of Massachusetts, Mrs. SCHROEDER, Mr. GEJDENSON, Mr. ANNUNZIO, Mr. COURTER, Mr. ROE, Mr. MARKEY, Mr. KENNEDY, Mr. MACHTLEY, Mr. ENGEL, Mr. MOAKLEY, Mr. GILMAN, Mr. McGRATH, and Mr. AuCOIN

SEPTEMBER 19, 1990

Reported with an amendment and referred to the Committee on Ways and Means for a period ending not later than September 25, 1990, for consideration of such provisions of the bill and amendment as fall within the jurisdiction of that committee pursuant to clause 1(v), rule X

[Strike out all after the enacting clause and insert the part printed in italic]

SEPTEMBER 25, 1990

Reported from the Committee on Ways and Means with amendments, committed to the Committee of the Whole House on the State of the Union, and ordered to be printed

[Omit the part in struck through italic]

[For text of introduced bill, see copy of bill as introduced on March 19, 1990]

■ Before H.R. 4300 could go to committee for hearings, it had to be written in proper legal language. Busy lawmakers depend on their staffs to handle this type of detail work. Note the committees to which the bill was referred and the calendar it was put on. What act does the bill amend? The House passed the bill in October 1990. What other steps did it have to go through before it could become a law?

speakers refer to specific lines while the bill is being studied and debated.

Congressional committees turn to staff members and lobbyists for advice and information during the hearings on a new bill. The bill's language is often modified during the give-and-take of the hearings. Very few bills move to final passage without being changed in the process.

2. What is the role of committee staffs?

America's lawmakers lead busy lives. On a typical day, they must attend committee meetings, greet visitors, answer mail, and debate important issues on the floor of Congress. They have staffs to help them, but they have little time to study personally the flood of bills that Congress must consider during each session. As a result, the members of Congress rely on the committee system. Every bill must pass through one or more standing committees, each of which has its own professional staff. These staffs play a major role in helping lawmakers write and evaluate legislation.

MAKEUP OF THE STAFFS

Since 1946, a typical committee staff has been made up of a director, three staff members, and six clerks. The largest and busiest committees, such as Foreign Relations, have much larger staffs. Because of political differences, the majority and minority members of each committee have separate staffs. Even though Congress now has over 1,500 committee staff members, observers believe that more are needed. When staff members cannot handle the work load, Congress is forced to rely on the executive branch for research and evaluation of new bills.

FUNCTIONS OF THE STAFFS

Congressional committee staffs do not establish policy nor do they introduce legislation. These duties are reserved to the members of Congress and to the committees on which they serve.

1. *Research.* Staff members collect the data needed by their committees. The Library of Congress, with its fine research facilities, was set up to provide this information.

2. *Drafting of bills.* Staff members furnish the technical writing skills needed when new bills are being drafted. They work closely with the Office of Legislative Counsel.

3. *Investigation.* Staff members plan the public hearings that are an important part of the legislative process. Their investigative role includes (a) interviewing witnesses, (b) drawing up questions for committee members to ask during the hearings, and (c) analyzing the statements of those who testify.

4. *Expertise.* Staff experts provide technical analyses of complex matters such as taxation or the defense budget. If the staff lacks the necessary expertise, the committee calls in specialists from executive agencies, universities, business, or labor.

The staff directors supervise the day-to-day operations of their staffs. In addition, they work with committee heads to plan hearings and to make recommendations to committee members. When public and private organizations have business with a committee, their first contact is usually with the staff director.

3. What is the role of the lobbyist?

Special-interest groups play an important role in American politics. These organizations try to exert pressure on Congress (or on any governmental body) to pass, defeat, or interpret legislation to their own advantage. Groups that play this political game are called pressure groups or *lobbies*.

People join pressure groups because they share a common interest. Business, farming, and professional organizations, for example, send people called *lobbyists* to Washington to promote their economic interests. Pressure groups that share a common social goal, such as the passage of gun-control laws, also lobby for their causes.

■ Consumers have an effective lobbyist in Ralph Nader. He has spoken out for safer products, truth in advertising, fair prices, and other consumer interests for over 20 years. With the help of an enthusiastic staff, he has pushed dozens of consumer protection laws through the lawmaking process.

Pressure groups work hard to elect members of Congress who are favorable to their causes. Because of this, the law limits the amount of money a pressure group can give to a political campaign (see pages 147–148). This limitation has led to the creation of separate money-giving groups called political action committees (PACs). At the present time, PACs are pouring millions of dollars into the campaign chests of congressional candidates. Typical PACs represent realtors, doctors, tobacco farmers, auto workers, and about 3,000 other special-interest groups.

LOBBYISTS AT WORK

Lobbyists try to obtain favored treatment for their clients. They may work to create tax breaks for oil companies, protect Social Security benefits, or increase subsidies for tobacco farmers. In 1988, for example, Congress had to decide whether or not to spend $180 million on an antiradar missile (the Tacit Rainbow) built by a major defense contractor.

The Tacit Rainbow's critics pointed out that the expensive missile had failed its four test flights. With the help of lobbyists and $286,517 in PAC contributions, the defense contractor overcame the opposition. Congress funded the missile for another year. To accomplish tasks like these, the lobbyist plays a number of roles.

1. *Drafting new legislation.* Lobbyists provide expert help in drafting bills favorable to their clients' interests. Lawmakers who sponsor these bills sometimes label them as being introduced "by request of" one special-interest group or another.

2. *Expert testimony.* As experts in their special fields, lobbyists are often called to testify about legislation that affects their clients.

3. *Application of pressure.* Lobbyists know the legislative process inside out. They work tirelessly to influence Congress from the first hearings on a new bill to the last minutes before the final vote. Even if Congress passes a law they think is unfavorable to their clients, lobbyists don't give up. By putting pressure on the President, they try to force a veto that will keep the bill from becoming a law.

LOBBYING TECHNIQUES

Lobbyists employ a variety of methods to influence legislation. Some of their techniques are as follows:

1. *Communications.* Lobbyists often organize campaigns to flood Congress with telegrams, letters, personal visits, and telephone calls. These communications are meant to convince the lawmakers that the public supports the lobbyists' position on a particular bill.

2. *Contributions.* Someone once said that "money is the mother's milk of politics." Thus, a good lobbyist knows how to keep friendly lawmakers well nourished. Along with cash donations to their campaigns, lobbyists often provide a variety of useful services. Legislators running for reelection, for example, may receive help for their campaigns from "volunteers" lined up by lobbyists.

3. *Social contacts.* Entertaining politicians has always been a favorite lobbying technique. Parties, dinners, and "nights on the town" help cement the friendships and create the obligations that are the stock-in-trade of the lobbyist.

4. *Sanctions.* Lobbyists have ways of "punishing" members of Congress who refuse to cooperate. They can cut off campaign contributions or throw their support to a lawmaker's opponent.

5. *Demonstrations.* Pressure groups often organize protest marches and picket lines to enforce their demands. If that doesn't work, they invent more dramatic ways of attracting attention. Farmers have dumped surplus milk and truck drivers have blocked highways to make sure that Congress is aware of their needs.

6. *Formation of alliances.* Lobbyists from different pressure groups sometimes join forces to multiply their influence. A united front can create the impression that the public strongly favors their position.

In order to be welcome in a lawmaker's office, lobbyists must do more than hand out gifts and services. They must develop an expertise in their field that makes their opinions valuable. The success of a pressure group also depends on its size, prestige, leadership skills, and financial resources.

IS "LOBBYING" A BAD WORD?

In U.S. politics, lobbyists have been linked to phrases like "corrupt politicians" and "influence-peddling." Scandals do break from time to time, usually involving unethical lobbyists and weak-willed legislators. Each time this happens, lobbying comes under attack. In reality, the lobbyists on Capitol Hill are well policed. They must file reports that disclose the names of their clients, their fees, the nature of the legislation they lobby for or against, and any expenditures over $100.

Clever lobbyists do not need to "buy" votes. They know that members of Congress must serve the best interests of the people back

FYI . . .
Pro & Con: Should Lobbying Be Illegal?

The history of lobbying to influence legislation is older than the Republic. Representatives for special interests (the word "lobbyist" wasn't used until the 1830s) flocked to Philadelphia when the First Continental Congress met there in 1774. Arguments over the value (or threat) of lobbying are almost as old. If Congress held a debate on the issue of outlawing lobbying, the Pro and Con might go something like this:

Pro: Get Rid of Lobbyists!	*Con: Lobbyists Are Useful!*
1. Congress has enough staff and enough contact with the public to keep itself informed without the help of lobbyists.	1. Lobbyists bring matters of public interest before Congress and make sure that lawmakers have all the information they need.
2. The danger of allowing free-spending lobbyists to influence Congress is far greater than any informational service they provide.	2. Lobbyists give companies and organizations an effective way of publicizing their views as well as making personal contact with their representatives.
3. Lobbyists scream when their pet interests are threatened. They seldom count the costs to others of legislation they favor.	3. Lobbyists help lawmakers judge the effects of proposed bills. This prevents the passage of laws that might otherwise harm some segment of society.
4. Congress has staff experts who can be relied upon to draft legislation properly.	4. Lobbyists provide much-needed technical help in drafting legislation.
5. In a very real sense, lobbyists do "buy" votes. By contributing to the campaign funds of key lawmakers, they insure favorable treatment when their pet bills come up for a hearing or a floor vote.	5. Lobbyists, despite their reputations, don't try to "buy" votes. When they're successful in promoting or defeating a bill, it's because they've done a good job of presenting their views to Congress.

home. Senators from wheat-growing states, for example, cannot vote against farm subsidies if they wish to stay in office. Lobbyists for farm interests, therefore, make sure that farm-bloc legislators receive a steady flow of mail, personal visits, and research data. A *bloc* is made up of all the members in a legislative body who share common economic interests. Blocs often cut across party lines and include interests such as farming, defense, electronics, and textiles.

When Congress is ready to vote on a major farm bill, for example, lobbyists see to it that all farm bloc legislators know how the voters back home are feeling. Then, when election time comes, lobbyists "repay" cooperative politicians with campaign contributions and other assistance.

4. What happens when a bill is introduced?

After a bill has been written, the legislative process can begin. Before the bill goes to the President for signature, however, it must survive a long and difficult journey through the two houses of Congress. Even though lawmakers sometimes introduce the same bill at the same time in both houses, each house considers legislation in its own way and on its own schedule.

PROCEDURE FOR INTRODUCING A BILL

In the House, the representative who introduces a bill begins the process by signing it. The lawmaker then drops the bill into the "hopper," a box on the desk of the Clerk of the House. A clerk assigns it a number according to its place in line. A bill introduced in the House might be called H.R. 1776. The Senate version of the same bill will have a different number, perhaps S. 85. The bill is then registered in the House *Journal* and sent to the Government Printing Office. The GPO prints copies for the members of Congress and for interested agencies. Citizens who want to see the bill may ask for their own copies.

Senators introduce bills by making a formal announcement of the fact during the "morning hour." This "hour" lasts from noon until 2:00 P.M. Senators also introduce bills by giving them to clerks at the desk of the presiding officer.

Major bills are often introduced at the same time in both houses. In this way, committee work can begin without waiting for the other house to complete action on the bill. The legislators who draft the bills and introduce them are called "sponsors." Popular bills sometimes attract dozens of sponsors. Even though they have a number, important bills are known by the names of their major sponsors. The 1985 Gramm-Rudman-Hollings balanced budget law, for instance, was sponsored by Senators Phil Gramm of Texas, Warren Rudman of New Hampshire, and Ernest Hollings of South Carolina.

Printing a bill's number and title in the *Congressional Record* and in the *Journal* gives the bill its *first reading*. This step serves notice on interested parties that Congress is studying legislation that might concern them.

REFERRAL TO COMMITTEE

The pressures of time make it impossible for the entire House or Senate to consider every bill that is introduced. That's where the committee system shines. Committee members whittle down the number of bills and refine the content of those that survive.

After the introduction and first reading, a bill is almost always referred to the appropriate committee. At one time, the power of the Speaker of the House was magnified by the right to name the committee that would study a particular bill. Since it's common for one committee to oppose a bill and for another to favor it, the Speaker was able to determine a bill's future by choosing the "right" committee. That process changed in 1946, when committee jurisdictions were defined more precisely. Assigning a bill to a committee is now a routine job for legislative clerks.

RESOLUTIONS

Some bills are introduced as *resolutions*. These bills set up "housekeeping" rules for the House or the Senate, express the opinions of one house or the other, or call on the executive branch for information.

A resolution agreed on by both houses of Congress is called a *joint resolution*. The President must sign a joint resolution before it has the force of law. *Concurrent resolutions* are also passed by both houses, but they usually deal with congressional business. Typical concurrent resolutions set a date for adjournment or launch a joint investigation. They do not require the President's signature.

Let's review for a moment

Suppose you've become convinced that there should be a new law to bring computer data banks under public control. The first step is to draft a *bill* that spells out the new legislation. Writing a bill isn't easy, however. How do you translate everyday needs into legislative language? How can you be sure that your law doesn't conflict with laws that are already on the books? The legislative experts on the committee staffs of Congress can check—or a civil rights group might help.

Next, you'll have to find a member of Congress who will introduce your draft bill. If you are really serious, you can enlist the aid of a *lobbyist* who knows how to line up support for new bills. Many people are suspicious of lobbyists, but they play a useful role in the complex process of writing, studying, and passing legislation.

Congratulations! Your bill has been introduced and numbered. It has received its *first reading*, and it's been referred to the proper committee. What happens in committee? Let's find out.

5. What happens to bills during committee hearings?

The complete legislative journey shown in the diagram on page 210 can only take place after a committee decides that a bill merits a hearing. Many bills are set aside in committee never to reappear. These bills are said to be *pigeonholed*. This action usually happens because (1) the committee chairman doesn't like a bill, (2) lobbyists put pressure on the committee, or (3) committee members ask that a bill be pigeonholed.

THE HEARING PROCESS

A committee *hearing* is meant to serve as an information-gathering process. The American public sometimes misunderstands this fact. The courtroom-like setting, the testimony given under oath, and the sharp exchanges between committee members and witnesses often make hearings look and sound like a trial.

Each committee runs hearings in its own way. Some hearings are fair to both sides of an issue. Other committees may restrict testimony to witnesses who represent mainly one side of an issue. Despite this, it's during congressional hearings that the American people have their best chance to debate the value—or danger—of new bills. It's much harder to change a bill after it becomes a law.

Hearings are open to the public unless the committee votes to close the meeting. In recent years, about one out of three hearings have been held behind closed doors. Normally, sensitive matters relating to national security are heard in secret.

The chairman, with the help of the committee staff, chooses the witnesses and schedules the meetings. Because lawmakers serve on several committees and subcommittees, only the most important hearings draw all of the committee's members. The daily schedule of hearings is published in Washington's newspapers. Witnesses usually read a prepared statement before they answer questions asked by committee members. A hearing on a minor bill may last only a few hours. Hearings on the budget or on a complex welfare reform bill may drag on for several months.

Clerks keep an exact record of everything said during a hearing, but committee members often edit their remarks before the report is printed. The final report, which may run to hundreds of pages, is printed by the GPO for the committee. It is also distributed to other members of Congress and to the public.

THE PURPOSES OF A HEARING

Congressional hearings have several purposes:

1. *Information.* Witnesses present technical, economic, and political information relating to a bill. In the give-and-take of the hearing, all points of view can be heard and evaluated.

2. *Propaganda channel.* New or controversial ideas can be "sold" to Congress and the public through exposure during a hearing.

3. *Safety valve.* Hearings ease tensions and resolve differences. They give both sides of an issue a way of working out political and social conflicts.

FYI . . .

Congress Records Everything It Says

Congress compiles a careful and complete record of everything that happens in its sessions. Each house keeps the minutes of its proceedings in a daily *Journal*. Although both houses are supposed to start each session with a reading of the *Journal*, the members usually agree unanimously to skip the reading.

As each day ends on Capitol Hill, the Government Printing Office goes to work on a daily publication called the *Congressional Record*. The CR prints every word spoken on the floor of Congress (and many that are not). House and Senate reporters write down everything that's said, type up their notes, and show them to the lawmakers. Members then have the privilege of revising their speeches and comments to make them look better in print. The reporters also compile a "Daily Digest" section that summarizes the work of House and Senate committees. A final section, called "Extensions of Remarks," gives legislators a chance to put anything they want into the record. Typically, this section prints speeches given outside of Congress, letters, magazine articles, memorials, editorials, and so on. A typical day's 200-page CR is as long as a novel, but the GPO has never missed its 8 A.M. delivery schedule.

Congressional Record

United States of America

PROCEEDINGS AND DEBATES OF THE *101ˢᵗ* CONGRESS, SECOND SESSION

Vol. 136   WASHINGTON, MONDAY, OCTOBER 1, 1990   *No. 125*

Senate

(Legislative day of Monday, September 10, 1990)

The Senate met at 3 p.m., on the expiration of the recess, and was called to order by the Honorable JOSEPH I. LIEBERMAN, a Senator from the State of Connecticut.

PRAYER

The Chaplain, the Reverend Richard C. Halverson, D.D., offered the following prayer:

Let us pray:

He hath shewed thee, O man, what is good; and what doth the Lord require of thee, but to do justly, and to love mercy, and to walk humbly with thy —Micah 6:8.

author-

LIEBERMAN, a Senator from the State of Connecticut, to perform the duties of the Chair.

ROBERT C. BYRD,
President pro tempore.

Mr. LIEBERMAN thereupon assumed the chair as Acting President pro tempore.

RECOGNITION OF THE MAJORITY LEADER

The ACTING PRESIDENT pro tempore. Under the standing order, the Senate majority leader is recognized.

dent, I that

morrow sometime prior to the close of business. I hope that proves to be possible.

Mr. President, I reserve the remainder of my leader time, and I am pleased now to yield to the distinguished Republican leader.

RECOGNITION OF THE REPUBLICAN LEADER

The ACTING PRESIDENT pro tempore. Under the standing order, the Republican leader is recognized.

Mr. DOLE. Mr. President, I would say in response to the majority leader's statement. I see no problem

PARTISANSHIP

Whenever a committee meets, whether in open hearings or in executive sessions, its members often vote according to their party's position on the issues. Committee chairmen offer the most visible examples of this political partisanship. They have the power to schedule (or not schedule) hearings, to select witnesses, and to refer a bill to a favorable or unfavorable subcommittee. Thus, from the time a bill is referred to committee until it comes up for debate on the floor, partisan politics plays a major role in determining a bill's success or failure.

EXECUTIVE SESSIONS

Public hearings do not end in a dramatic roll-call vote. Committee members make their decisions in closed meetings called *executive sessions*. These closed meetings allow the informal give-and-take that produces legislation acceptable to both parties. Here, committee members can change their minds or accept compromises without public embarrassment.

Executive sessions are often referred to as "markups." Like the formal hearings, they are dominated by the committee chairman. The committee staff sits in to provide information and analysis. As the committee examines the bill line by line, it takes on the form it will have when sent to the floor of the House or Senate for debate.

COMMITTEE REPORT

At the end of the executive session, the committee prepares a *report on the bill*. The report summarizes the evidence heard by the committee and reveals the committee's vote on the bill. If the committee votes against reporting a bill, its decision is almost always final. Both houses do have rules (called discharge procedures) that make it possible to force a bill out of committee, but this procedure is rarely used. Most members of Congress are reluctant to challenge the committee system. As a result, the discharge procedure is seldom successful.

Only rarely do committees report out a bill that a majority of the members want killed. When they do, it usually means that the committee has decided not to pigeonhole a bill that the entire house wants to debate. Committee reports usually delete any evidence of disagreement within the committee. Once in a while the minority members file a dissenting report that brings the conflict into the open.

TODAY IN CONGRESS

SENATE

Meets at 3 p.m.
Committee:
Foreign Relations—10:30 a.m.
Closed. Nomination of Frederic Vreeland to be ambassador to Myanmar. 419 Dirksen Office Building.

HOUSE

Meets at noon.
Committees:
Appropriations—1 p.m. Open. Mark up FY91 Interior approps. 2360 Rayburn House Office Building.
Banking, Finance and Urban Affairs—10 a.m. Open. Impact of economic and regulatory policies on the savings and loan industry in the late 1970s and the 1980s. 2128 RHOB.
Energy and Commerce—1 p.m. Open. Energy and power subc. Automotive fuel efficiency. 2322 RHOB.

■ A list of hearings in Congress for one day.

6. What is the special role of the Rules Committee?

When a House committee reports a bill, it is placed on one of four main calendars. In theory, assignment to a calendar determines the order in which Congress will consider new bills. In practice, the Rules Committee often modifies the calendar.

Appropriation bills—bills that will either raise or spend money—go on the Union Calendar. *Public bills*, which affect the country as a whole, are assigned to the House Calendar. *Private bills*, which affect only one person or a few citizens, go on the Private Calendar. Minor bills, those with little or no opposition, go on the Consent Calendar. Bills assigned to the Private Calendar and the Consent Calendar usually become law without debate.

THE RULES COMMITTEE REGULATES THE FLOW OF TRAFFIC

The existence of the four calendars tells little about the order in which bills will be taken

"Come In — Come In"

■ Although the Rules Committee performs a useful service in scheduling bills for debate, its power and generally conservative leadership have often been criticized.

up by the House. Bills from a few committees (Ways and Means or Appropriations, for example) receive top priority and are always debated promptly. Conference committee reports and bills vetoed by the President also receive special treatment.

Aside from these few exceptions, the fate of thousands of bills is controlled by the members of the powerful *Rules Committee*. The committee screens out all but a hundred or so bills during each session. These are the bills judged important enough to merit debate on the floor of the House. Of these, a little over 50 percent are debated under special resolutions drawn up by the Rules Committee. Bills that lack this privileged status cannot be brought to the floor without a special ruling.

The Rules Committee's "traffic control" makes political sense. Without it, important legislation might be lost in the logjam of bills

that clog the calendars. The price of efficiency is that the Rules Committee can—and does—decide which bills will appear on the House agenda.

FOUR KINDS OF SPECIAL RULES

The Rules Committee uses four types of special rules to govern the flow of bills to the floor of the House.

1. *Open rules.* Most bills are debated under open rules, which permit members to amend the legislation.

2. *Closed rules.* The committee uses closed rules to limit or prohibit amendments. Only a handful of bills are debated under closed rules during a session.

3. *Waiving points of order.* This rule limits technical objections to a controversial bill. Instead of raising parliamentary "points of order," the House must debate the bill on its merits.

4. *Arranging a conference.* If the House and Senate have passed different versions of the same bill, a conference must be held to work out the conflicts.

In its role as "traffic cop," the Rules Committee may turn down a committee's request for a special rule. Even if it holds a hearing, the members may decide not to grant the rule. Such refusals usually mean that the bill is dead for that session of Congress. At other times, the Rules Committee bargains with a committee that wants a special rule. If it wants to save the bill, the committee may have to change the bill to a form more acceptable to Rules Committee members.

SIDESTEPPING THE RULES COMMITTEE

Bills that fail to gain a special rule aren't quite dead. If the sponsors can round up enough votes, there are several ways of moving the bill to the floor. They can ask for *suspension of the rules, unanimous consent,* or a *discharge procedure.* As the names suggest, these procedures force the Rules Committee to send the pigeonholed bills to the floor.

A fourth procedure is known as *Calendar Wednesday.* This is a time when standing committees are permitted to bring to the floor bills that lack privileged status. In practice, members seldom use this method of bypassing the Rules Committee. The majority leader usually requests that Calendar Wednesday be ignored, and the House almost always accepts the motion.

THE SENATE'S SIMPLER PROCEDURES

The Senate uses a simpler procedure to bring bills to the floor. All bills reported out of committee are assigned to a single calendar. The majority leader schedules debate on the bills after consulting with the party's policy committee. In many cases, the majority leader also listens to the wishes of the minority leader.

7. What happens when a bill reaches the floor?

Many first-time visitors to the House or Senate are shocked by what they see. Most congressional business is conducted with only a few members present. The scene that stays in one's mind is of empty desks, casual conversation, and constant movement into and out of the chamber. Visitors leave with the impression that Congress pays little attention to the people's business.

A more careful study, however, shows that these first impressions are wrong. Much of a member's time is taken up by committee hearings, meetings with constituents, and trips to the home district. These activities help prepare lawmakers for floor debate on new legislation by exposing them to a variety of opinions.

DEBATE IN THE HOUSE

Only a few bills survive the hearing process and earn a special rule from the Rules Committee. Those that do are debated on the floor of the House, with debate limited to one hour. Speakers from the majority and minority parties divide the time equally, as scheduled by their party leaders. If the bill is highly controversial, House members sometimes vote to extend the debate. Suspension of the rules requires a two-thirds majority of the members voting.

After the general debate, the bill receives a section by section *second reading*. The House often turns itself into a *Committee of the Whole* at this time. By sitting as one large committee, the members can make decisions more quickly. If amendments are permitted, debate on each amendment is usually limited to five minutes. When the reading is finished, the Committee of the Whole turns itself back into the House.

DEBATE IN THE SENATE

The Senate's smaller size results in fewer bills and simpler rules. The 100 members guard one right jealously—the tradition of unlimited debate. On occasion, a senator or group of senators uses unlimited debate to keep the Senate from voting on a bill. This tactic is known as a *filibuster*. In order to keep the floor, senators must remain standing and speak continuously.

A filibuster soon uses up a speaker's prepared speeches. The senator then reads novels, newspapers, recipes, and other unrelated materials to a nearly empty chamber. Exhausted senators often yield the floor to other members of the filibuster team in order to gain time for a quick nap. This delaying tactic can go on and on and on. A filibuster against the Civil Rights Act of 1964 lasted three months before it was ended. Another filibuster, aimed at the 1953 Tidelands Oil Bill, added 1,241,414 extra words to the *Congressional Record*.

The Senate can end a filibuster by invoking the *closure rule* (also spelled "cloture"). A closure motion requires the signature of 16 senators followed by a "yes" vote from three-fifths of the Senate. Despite the frustration caused by filibusters, the Senate rarely votes for closure. Most senators vote against closure motions because the next filibuster might be their own.

DELAYING TACTICS

The filibuster is a delaying tactic available only to senators. Other tactics can be used in either house of Congress.

The Perilous Journey of a Bill Through the U.S. Congress

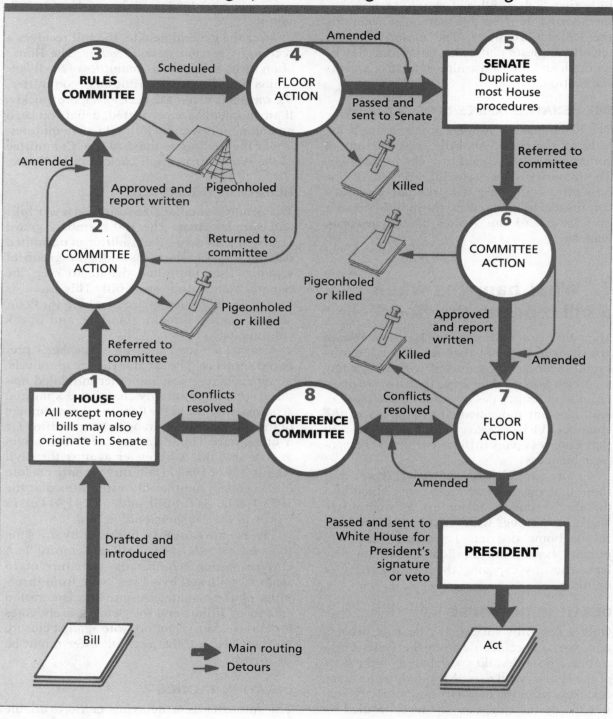

Members of Congress often use amendments as a way of delaying action on a bill they oppose. Amendments meant to delay a bill are often tacked on as *riders*—amendments that have little or no relation to the main bill. Members who might have voted for the bill may withdraw their support because they object to the riders. In addition, each rider must be debated. This further delays the final vote on the original bill.

Another delaying tactic is the *quorum call*. A quorum is the number of legislators who must be present before the body can vote on a bill. If a member counts heads and announces that the body doesn't have a quorum, all debate stops. Bells ring in offices all around the Capitol and in the congressional office buildings. Members scurry onto the floor to have their attendance recorded. Meanwhile, the side that is losing the debate has a chance to round up additional support.

VOTING ON A BILL

The members of Congress cast their votes in a number of ways. Many nonpartisan bills are decided by *voice vote*. The presiding officer listens to the "ayes" and "nays" and then decides which side clearly has the most support. If a member questions the result, a *rising vote* may be called for. In this case, the presiding officer "counts heads" when the members stand to support or oppose the bill. Most lawmakers prefer voice votes and rising votes because no public record is kept of how they voted.

If one-fifth of the members present demand it, the presiding officer calls for a *roll-call vote*. A roll-call vote puts each lawmaker's "aye" or "nay" into the public record. Most major bills are voted on in this way. In the Senate, a clerk reads the senators' names one at a time and records their votes. In the House, an electronic voting system replaced the roll call in 1973. Representatives now insert personal ID cards into a small box near their seats. Then they punch either the "yea," "nay," or "present" button. A master board at the front of the chamber records the votes.

When members of Congress know they will

■ Members of the House Public Works Committee and their aides discussing amendments to a bill being debated on the House floor. When the representatives vote on the bill, they will most likely press one of the buttons pictured—yea, nay, or pres (present). By voting present, they signal a desire not to make a choice to support or reject the bill.

miss a roll-call vote, they often "pair" their votes. Pairing matches an "aye" voter with a "nay" voter who will also be absent (or vice versa). Since the paired votes cancel each other out, no one can accuse the absent members of affecting the fate of an important bill. The practice also allows "paired" lawmakers to go on record with their votes.

More battles lie ahead for bills that pass the House or Senate. A new set of obstacles awaits in the committees and on the floor of the other house. Only after bills pass both houses can the conference committees go to work.

8. How do the House and Senate work out their differences on a bill?

The House and Senate often pass different versions of the same bill. Amendments added in one chamber may not be acceptable to the other. This creates new problems, for a bill cannot be sent to the President until both houses agree on its content and language. Resolving these conflicts is the job of a temporary *conference committee*.

The leaders of the House and Senate each appoint three to nine "conferees" to a conference committee. A typical committee includes the chairmen and the leading minority members of the standing committees that held hearings on the bill, plus other legislators who fought to pass it. The conferees are expected to support their own version of the bill. They also know how much they can give up in order to reach a compromise.

The rules limit conference committees to rewriting sections of the two bills that are different. Nevertheless, the conferees often make additional changes that they think are needed to gain passage in both houses. Once in a while, the committee's efforts to find a compromise end in deadlock. When that happens, floor leaders from both parties are called in to solve the problem.

After a final compromise has been hammered out, the bill is reported back to both houses. Neither house is allowed to amend the conference committee's bill. Although the bill is offered on a "take-it-or-leave-it" basis, Congress seldom rejects the work of a conference committee.

Once it has passed both houses, the bill is printed on parchment and signed by the Speaker of the House and the President of the Senate. Months of hearings, debate, compromise, and voting are over, but the bill is not yet a law. The President must make the next decision.

■ Although hundreds of pieces of legislation make it to the President's desk each year, only a few change the course of history. One such occasion was the Declaration of War that President Franklin Roosevelt signed in 1941. Even though Japan had already attacked Pearl Harbor, the United States wasn't officially at war until Congress passed the declaration and Roosevelt signed it.

9. What choices does a President have when a bill reaches the White House?

The bills that reach a President's desk often began their life in the executive branch. Presidents suggest legislation to Congress or talk members into sponsoring bills drafted by the White House staff. Once the bills they favor have been introduced, Presidents use their enormous political power to push for the bills' adoption.

One favorite technique is to prepare a legislative "package" made up of several related bills. The White House then tags the "package" with a catchy title, such as "War on Poverty." Using speeches and press conferences, the President tells the public that the country

Learning Skills

Making Good Decisions

Experienced decision makers are good at analyzing the consequences of their choices. Decisions made in haste can lead to unexpected, even disastrous, results.

Imagine that Mike Jones wants to buy a car. He's so anxious to show off his new wheels, in fact, that he hasn't thought through the consequences of his purchase. Any car owner can tell him about the costs of insurance, upkeep, licensing, gas and oil, and so on. Those are serious issues, but there's another problem. If Mike has a car, will he have to find a job to support it? If he takes a job, will he neglect his schoolwork? Mike has some careful thinking to do before he picks out his dream car.

Here's a way to analyze any big decision. It works whether you're buying a car or deciding on which candidate you'll support for President.

1. State the problem clearly and exactly. Mike's problem isn't "Do I want a car?" It's really "Can I afford to take on the responsibilities of owning a car at this time?"

2. Now, do some additional research. Talk to experts, check out some books, and ask for opinions from your friends and family. You'll probably learn some things you hadn't thought about, both negative and positive. A negative, for example, is the unexpectedly high cost of insurance. A positive might be the opportunity to take a part-time job that requires the use of a car.

3. What alternatives do you have? List them all. Mike's alternatives include (a) buying a car, (b) continuing to depend on friends and family for transportation, (c) buying a bicycle or moped, (d) jogging everywhere as part of an exercise program. You can probably think of some more.

4. List three positive and three negative consequences that grow out of each alternative. These are the rewards and penalties that go with a decision. Be honest. Don't overlook some negative consequences just because you favor a particular choice. A positive for Alternative D, for example, is that it will help Mike lose some weight. On the negative side, he'll be hot and sweaty when he gets to school each day.

5. Study your list carefully. Rank each consequence in order of its importance. It's possible that one positive consequence may outweigh three negatives—or vice versa. If social status based on owning a car is important to Mike, he'll give that fact a high ranking.

6. Make your decision based on your best analysis of your alternatives and their consequences. Remember, it's easy to find reasons to do what you wanted to do in the first place. Mike may discover that keeping his grades up and getting into college are his highest priorities right now. Buying a car he can't afford without taking on many hours of part-time work will interfere with that goal.

Using this decision-making technique doesn't mean that you'll never make a mistake. It does mean that you'll be making the best decisions you're capable of making.

FYI . . .
Presidential Vetoes: The "Batting Averages," 1901–1989

The veto is one of a President's strongest weapons. Some Presidents have used it sparingly, while others have engaged in veto warfare with Congress. Each veto and override listed in this chart represents a tough political struggle for both sides.

President (Years Served)	Vetoes (including Pocket Vetoes)	Over-rides	Pct. Vetoes Sustained
Theodore Roosevelt (1901–1909)	82	1	.988
William H. Taft (1909–1913)	39	1	.974
Woodrow Wilson (1913–1921)	44	6	.864
Warren G. Harding (1921–1923)	6	0	1.000
Calvin Coolidge (1923–1929)	50	4	.920
Herbert Hoover (1929–1933)	37	3	.919
Franklin D. Roosevelt (1933–1945)	635	9	.986
Harry S Truman (1945–1953)	250	12	.952
Dwight D. Eisenhower (1953–1961)	181	2	.989
John F. Kennedy (1961–1963)	21	0	1.000
Lyndon B. Johnson (1963–1969)	30	0	1.000
Richard M. Nixon (1969–1974)	42	5	.881
Gerald R. Ford (1974–1977)	66	12	.818
Jimmy Carter (1977–1981)	29	2	.931
Ronald W. Reagan (1971–1989)	78	9	.897

desperately needs these bills. If public opinion responds favorably, Congress feels the pressure and is more likely to pass the legislation.

THE PRESIDENT'S CHOICES

Whatever the origin of a bill, the President has four choices once it reaches the White House.

1. *Sign it.* In most cases, the President will sign the bill, thus making it a law.

2. *Do nothing.* The President may allow a bill to become law without signing it. This happens automatically after ten working days, if Congress is still in session.

3. *Veto it.* A *veto* is a formal refusal to sign a bill. The President sends the legislation back to Congress, along with a message explaining the reasons for rejecting it.

4. *Use a "pocket veto."* If Congress plans to adjourn within ten days, a President can refuse to act on bills that have been sent to the White House. When a President puts a bill into his "pocket" and holds it until Congress adjourns, the bill dies. Known as a *pocket veto*, this action has several advantages. For one thing, it allows a President to veto a bill without announcing the reasons for the veto. More important, the pocket veto makes it unnecessary for a President to spend political capital to sustain a veto in Congress.

Can the President use the pocket veto when Congress is on vacation rather than adjourned between sessions? President Gerald Ford tried to use the pocket veto during a vacation period. His action led to a court battle that forced him to accept the strict constitutional definition of the procedure. Henceforth, President

Ford promised, he would use the pocket veto only when Congress was formally adjourned.

One veto power denied to the President is the *item veto*. A chief executive who has the item veto can strike out parts of a bill without vetoing the entire measure. Lacking this power, Presidents often use veto messages to list the sections of a bill that they can't approve. The bill will be signed, the message usually says, once those sections are deleted or changed.

DEALING WITH A VETO

A vetoed bill returns to the house in which it was first introduced. If two-thirds of the members approve the bill as it stands, it goes on to the other house. A second two-thirds vote there completes the *override*, and the bill becomes law without the President's signature. If one-third-plus-one of the lawmakers in either house vote against the override, the veto is said to be sustained. The bill's sponsors can introduce it again, but they must repeat the entire hearing process.

Overrides make headlines, but they don't happen very often. An override is a blow to presidential pride and to party prestige. For these reasons, Presidents can usually find the one-third vote they need to sustain a veto. Dwight Eisenhower, for example, compiled a "batting average" of .989 when it came to sustaining his vetoes. Congress overrode only two of 181 vetoes during Eisenhower's eight years in office.

THE BILL BECOMES LAW

After the President signs a bill, aides send it to the Department of State. The Secretary of State preserves the original copy and publishes the law for the public record. Language written into the law determines when it will take effect.

Laws passed by Congress and signed by the President appear in *Statutes at Large of the United States*. These books are heavy reading, but they are the best single source of information on the federal government's official actions. The *Statutes* contain treaties, proclamations, and resolutions, as well as the laws that govern our nation. Most city libraries have up-to-date sets of these books on their shelves.

Reviewing what you've learned

1. Congress occasionally passes a new law in a few hours, but most bills take months to move from introduction to passage. Lawmakers sometimes draft their own bills. More often, bills are suggested by the executive branch or by special-interest groups. Whoever drafts a bill must write it in proper legal language. Only members of Congress can actually introduce bills into the House and Senate.

2. Each senator and representative is burdened by a great many political and legislative jobs. The committee system divides up the workload so that Congress can give proper attention to each new piece of legislation. It is in the daily grind of committee *hearings* that new laws are analyzed, rewritten, and shaped to national needs. Committee staffs play a backstage role in the committee process. Staff members do research, carry on investigations, provide technical expertise, and draft bills.

3. Members of Congress tend to follow the lead of their party and committee chairmen. They're also influenced by special-interest pressure groups and *lobbyists*. Lobbyists influence legislators by providing useful information, helping with election campaigns, and by organizing public opinion.

4. Once approved by the proper committee, a bill is put on a calendar to await its turn for debate on the floor of Congress. In the House of Representatives, the *Rules Committee* awards special rules to some bills and denies others. It's possible to move a bill to the floor without favorable action by the Rules Committee, but this doesn't happen very often. After the members debate a bill, they vote for or against it. *Voice votes* and *rising votes* do not put members on record as to how they voted. A *roll-call vote* forces lawmakers to record their "ayes" and "nays."

5. A bill must be approved by both houses of Congress before it can go to the President. Any differences in the versions of the bill passed by each house are resolved by a *conference committee*. After the conference committee does its work, it returns the bill to the House and Senate for final approval.

6. The President can approve a bill by signing it or by allowing it to become law without a signature. Rejected bills are returned to Congress with a *veto*. The House and Senate can *override* a veto by a two-thirds vote in each house, but overrides are rare. If the President receives the bill less than ten days before Congress adjourns and does not sign it, the bill dies. This is a *pocket veto*, and it cannot be overridden.

7. The machinery of Congress has been modified over the years. The power of the leadership and the iron rule of the committee chairmen have been limited by changes in rules and procedures. Most legislation still moves through Congress at a snail's pace, but there is little demand for major reform.

Review questions and activities

TERMS YOU SHOULD KNOW

appropriations bill	first reading	report on a bill
bill	hearing	resolution
bloc	item veto	rider
Calendar Wednesday	joint resolution	rising vote
closure (cloture) rule	lobby/lobbyist	roll-call vote
Committee of the Whole	override	Rules Committee
concurrent resolution	pigeonhole	second reading
conference committee	pocket veto	suspension of the rules
discharge procedure	private bill	unanimous consent
executive session	public bill	veto
filibuster	quorum call	voice vote

REVIEW QUESTIONS

Select the response that best completes each statement or question.

1. A proposal for a new law is properly called a (*a*) bill. (*b*) statute. (*c*) resolution. (*d*) proclamation. (*e*) rider.

2. Most bills originate with   (a) the executive branch.   (b) members of Congress.   (c) private individuals and pressure groups.   (d) congressional committees.   (e) the national committee of each political party.

3. Committee staffs provide a number of services to Congress, including   (a) investigative services.   (b) research.   (c) expert testimony.   (d) writing proposed bills in legislative language.   (e) all of these.

4. A member of the House introduces a bill by   (a) obtaining the approval of the Speaker.   (b) reading the bill aloud on the floor.   (c) giving the bill to the appropriate committee chairman.   (d) dropping the bill into the hopper.   (e) sending a printed copy of the bill to each House member.

5. Congressional committee hearings   (a) are conducted almost exactly like trials in a court of law.   (b) give Congress a way of reducing the number of bills introduced each session to a manageable number.   (c) do not permit witnesses who are not members of Congress to testify.   (d) are usually held in secret sessions.   (e) can only approve or disapprove a bill.

6. Executive sessions of congressional committees are closed to the public so that   (a) committee members may make compromises without public embarrassment.   (b) secret, illegal deals can be made.   (c) lobbyists can join the meetings and vote on the bill.   (d) information can be kept from the President.   (e) all of these.

7. When a House committee reports out a new bill, it is placed on a calendar. The next step is to   (a) begin floor debate.   (b) pigeonhole the bill.   (c) find out the President's wishes.   (d) send it to the Rules Committee to establish the bill's priority.   (e) read it into the *Congressional Record.*

8. Unlimited floor debate on a bill may take place in   (a) the House.   (b) the Senate.   (c) both houses of Congress.   (d) neither house.   (e) in either house if the Speaker is a committee chairman.

9. In order to record a senator's vote for all to see, the vote must be a   (a) rising vote.   (b) roll-call vote.   (c) voice vote.   (d) paired vote.   (e) none of these.

10. The President plays a major role in the legislative process by   (a) recommending new laws.   (b) applying pressure on Congress.   (c) using the veto.   (d) asking for public support of legislation sponsored by the executive branch.   (e) all of these.

CONCEPT DEVELOPMENT

1. List the different people and groups, in and out of the House and Senate, who would be expected to propose the bills introduced during a session of Congress.

2. Trace the progress of a new tax bill from the time it is introduced in the House of Representatives to the time it reaches the President's desk.

3. Write a plan of action for lobbying for or against a proposed law. Which parts of the plan do you think will have the greatest impact?

4. Discuss the following statement: "The President plays a larger role in creating major new laws than does Congress."

5. How does the chairman of a standing committee gain the position, and what powers go with the job? Why are legislators so anxious to be chosen to chair major committees?

HANDS-ON ACTIVITIES

1. Today's Speaker of the House possesses great power and influence. In 1910, however, it took a "revolution" to cut the Speaker's power down to its present size. Check up on the "Revolution of 1910" and report to the class on the events of that period. How did the old rules compare with today's procedures?

2. Organize a debate on the question: "Resolved, that lobbyists contribute greatly to the general welfare of the country." Along with doing library research, the debaters can contact the offices of their local representatives for firsthand information about lobbyists.

3. Write to your representative for copies of recently printed reports of committee hearings. Ask for reports on a topic that concerns you. After reviewing the reports with the class, discuss such questions as: (a) Were the hearings fair? (b) Did the committee members perform with intelligence and perception? (c) How useful were the hearings in gathering information about the bill the committee was studying?

4. Analyze a copy of the *Congressional Record*. Describe to the class the quality and depth of the debates recorded there. What do you think is the purpose of the material printed under "Extension of Remarks"?

5. Write a bill concerning a topic you feel strongly about, such as pollution or student rights. Obtain a sample bill to use as a model. After you've drafted your bill, organize a mock committee hearing. Assign class members to serve as witnesses, lobbyists, committee members, and committee staff. See what happens to your bill as it is attacked and defended from all sides. After the "hearings," send the rewritten bill to the office of your local member of Congress. Congressional staff members are busy people, but the chances are good that someone in the office will write back to comment on your proposal.

PROFILES IN COURAGE

10 Congress and the control of fiscal policy

Many people can remember the exact moment when they began to take an active interest in the federal government. "Where do all those tax dollars go?" they ask, looking sadly at their first paycheck. Nobody is ever fully prepared for the size of Uncle Sam's appetite when it comes to collecting income taxes.

Generally, Americans know that their taxes pay for military security and social welfare and all the programs in between. You may have been fed by a school lunch program that's partly paid for by the federal government. You and your friends may be using computers that were purchased by a federal grant. If tax money is spent on worthwhile services, who can object?

A little digging, however, reveals that federal money finances a number of surprising expenses. Chauffeured limousines, for example, cost the government several million dollars a year. Dining rooms for

▲ Juggling income and expenses is not an easy task for anyone.

219

the top brass in the Pentagon cost additional millions. The Secretary of State and the other Cabinet secretaries don't go hungry, either. The government pays the salaries of their personal chefs. The chauffeurs and chefs do provide a useful service, but what about the 94 elevator operators Uncle Sam hired in a recent year? These civil servants were kept busy pushing the buttons in the capital's automatic elevators! Annual cost: almost a million dollars.

The government also sponsors research projects. One study, for example, spent $222,000 to ask if drivers thought that large trucks helped cause traffic jams. (Yes.) Another $120,126 was invested to find out if a motorcycle could be steered with its rear wheel. (No.) Then there was the $140,000 survey that counted the number of Samoans living in Orange County, California. The number remains unknown, because the report disappeared four months later.

Many taxpayers look at these expenditures and grumble that no one is minding the store. As Congress rushes to pass its money bills each year, wasteful projects known as *boondoggles* do slip through. Stories about chauffeured limousines and useless elevator operators make for sensational reading in the national press. The money spent on such foolishness, however, is only a tiny fraction of the federal budget. Congress isn't asleep. It's just terribly busy.

The size of the federal budget makes money matters the largest single issue taken up during each legislative session. This chapter will look into the following questions about Congress and federal monetary policy:

1. How has the U.S. budget grown over the years?

2. Where does the money to pay bills come from?

3. What limits the power of Congress to impose taxes?

4. How does the federal government collect taxes?

5. Where do the federal tax dollars go?

6. Why does the United States have a national debt?

7. How is money appropriated by Congress?

8. How does Congress influence the U.S. economy?

1. How has the U.S. budget grown over the years?

President George Washington created the Treasury Department when he formed his first Cabinet. As the first Secretary of the Treasury, Alexander Hamilton designed the federal budget to be the cornerstone of the nation's financial stability. The *budget* is an outline of the government's spending program for the coming year. Today the Office of Management and Budget writes each budget to reflect the

President's ideas about national needs and priorities. The budget then goes to Congress, where spending bills must be debated and passed.

Government spending has increased enormously since Washington took office in 1789. The percentage of national income earmarked for federal use has also grown. In the 1790s, for example, the U.S. population numbered between 4 and 5 million. The annual federal budget at that time averaged less than $6 million—about $1.50 per person. By fiscal* 1990 federal spending had topped $1 trillion a year—over $4,000 for each of the nation's residents. The table on page 222 traces the increases over the decades, an upward trend broken only by cutbacks following major wars.

In the 1800s, Americans were content if the federal government defended the country, delivered the mail, and tended to its own housekeeping. *Tariffs* (taxes on imports) and sales of public lands provided most of the revenue needed to pay the government's expenses. In the 1890s, the role of government began to change. Americans wanted the federal government to regulate the large corporations. They also demanded more governmental services of all kinds. These new demands added thousands of public employees to the federal payroll.

Spending for social welfare programs grew rapidly in the years after 1932. As the 1980s came to a close, the federal government employed 2.9 million civilian workers (over 98 percent in the executive branch). Another 2.1 million men and women served in the armed forces.

The Reagan administration slowed the pace of the growth when it came to Washington in 1981. Savings in social programs, however, were canceled out by tax cuts and increased military spending. Revenue fell short of expenses. The richest nation on earth dropped deeper and deeper into debt.

---

* The *fiscal year* is the 12-month period the government uses for budgeting and financial management. The federal government's fiscal year runs from October 1 through September 30.

2. Where does the money come from?

In 1989, the total of all goods and services produced by the United States reached an astronomical $5.57 trillion (written in figures that's $5,570,000,000,000). Another name for this figure is *gross national product,* or *GNP.* The federal budget for that year amounted to just over $1.1 trillion. This figure represented about 20 percent of the GNP. When you add the costs of local and state governments, the growing size of the tax burden becomes apparent.

Today's tariffs supply only one percent of the revenue needed to run the federal government. Other tax sources have been developed to make up the difference. This federal tax "pie" yields receipts of about $1 trillion each fiscal year. As the graph on page 223 shows, the federal government depends on six main sources of income: (1) personal income taxes, (2) Social Security taxes, (3) corporate income taxes, (4) excise taxes, (5) estate and gift taxes, and (6) unemployment insurance taxes. A seventh group of miscellaneous taxes includes tariff duties, the sale of federal lands, and earnings on investments.

PERSONAL INCOME TAXES

The federal government uses the *personal income tax* to collect a percentage of each American's earnings. The first income tax law was passed during the Civil War, but it expired in 1872. In 1913, the need for greater tax revenues led the states to ratify the Sixteenth Amendment. This amendment states that "The Congress shall have the power to lay and collect taxes on incomes, from whatever source derived, . . ." Even though most Americans dislike the income tax, they accept it as the fairest way to pay for government services.

From the beginning, the federal income tax system was based on *progressive tax rates.* This means that the well-to-do pay a higher percentage of their earnings in taxes than do the poor. In recent years, the basic rates ranged from 12 to 50 percent of all taxable income. Beginning in 1987, however, the Tax Reform

INCREASE IN THE SIZE OF THE FEDERAL BUDGET, 1789–1994

(Yearly averages of federal expenditures in millions of dollars)

Year	Amount	Percent change	Events
1789–1800	$ 5.8		
1801–1810	9.1	+ 56.9	
1811–1820	23.9	+ 162.6	War of 1812
1821–1830	16.2	− 32.2	
1831–1840	24.5	+ 51.2	
1841–1850	34.1	+ 39.2	
1851–1860	60.2	+ 76.5	
1861–1865	683.8	+ 1235.9	Civil War
1866–1870	377.6	− 44.8	
1871–1875	287.5	− 23.9	
1876–1880	255.6	− 11.1	
1881–1885	257.7	+ 0.8	
1886–1890	279.1	+ 8.3	
1891–1895	363.6	+ 30.3	
1896–1900	457.5	+ 25.8	
1901–1905	535.6	+ 17.1	
1906–1910	639.2	+ 19.3	
1911–1915	720.3	+ 12.7	
1916–1920	8,065.3	+ 1019.7	World War I
1921–1925	3,579.0	− 55.6	
1926–1930	3,182.2	− 11.1	Depression begins
1931–1935	5,214.9	+ 63.8	
1936–1940	10,192.3	+ 95.4	New Deal
1941–1945	66,038.0	+ 547.9	World War II
1946–1950	42,334.5	− 35.9	
1951–1955	65,720.0	+ 55.2	Korean War
1956–1960	82,782.0	+ 25.8	
1961–1965	110,523.0	+ 33.5	
1966–1970	170,283.0	+ 54.0	Vietnam War
1971–1975	257,650.0	+ 51.3	
1976–1980	466,819.0	+ 81.2	
1981–1985	808,622.0	+ 73.2	
1986–1988	1,009,900.0	+ 24.9	
1990	1,151,800.0	+ 37.0	Estimated expenditures
1994	1,311,600.0	+ 13.9	Estimated expenditures

Act of 1986 reduced the rates. For most taxpayers the rates now range from 11 to 28 percent.

Not all income is taxable. *Exemptions* and *deductions* allow people to subtract many personal and business expenses from their earnings before they calculate their taxes. Some deductions encourage people to give to char-ities, for example. Others aid the economy by encouraging investment. Economists believe that exemptions and deductions are useful as long as they reflect the actual costs of keeping a family or of doing business.

Exemptions and deductions permit Americans to pay lower taxes than they would if their entire incomes were taxed. Some cate-

Sources of Federal Income, 1990

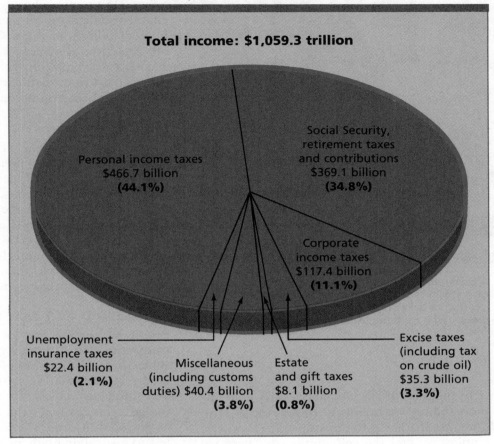

Total income: $1,059.3 trillion

Personal income taxes
$466.7 billion
(44.1%)

Social Security,
retirement taxes
and contributions
$369.1 billion
(34.8%)

Corporate
income taxes
$117.4 billion
(11.1%)

Unemployment
insurance taxes
$22.4 billion
(2.1%)

Miscellaneous
(including customs
duties) $40.4 billion
(3.8%)

Estate
and gift taxes
$8.1 billion
(0.8%)

Excise taxes
(including tax
on crude oil)
$35.3 billion
(3.3%)

■ The graph shows estimated figures. Total includes interfund and intragovernmental transactions and receipts, which are not shown on the graph.

gories of taxpayers are able to take advantage of *loopholes* in the tax law. Loopholes are special tax breaks that allow individuals and corporations to reduce or eliminate their taxes. A great many taxpayers have the impression that wealthy citizens benefit most by tax loopholes. It is possible, however, for anyone to escape taxes on interest by putting money into investments such as tax-exempt municipal bonds. The Tax Reform Act of 1986 did away with many special-interest loopholes. Most Americans applauded the action—as long as their own deductions were left alone.

SOCIAL SECURITY TAXES

The Social Security system was established in 1935. The system was designed to provide old-age benefits for America's factory and office workers. Survivors' benefits were added in 1939. Today, Social Security touches the lives of more than nine out of ten Americans. Social Security taxes are withheld from paychecks to cover (1) old-age and survivors' insurance, (2) disability insurance, (3) unemployment insurance, (4) medical insurance, and (5) retirement plans for certain groups of civil servants and railroad workers.

■ Some taxes are less noticeable than others. Americans pay indirect taxes on many items—phone service, theater tickets, cigarettes, gasoline, alcoholic beverages. Why are these taxes popular with lawmakers?

In the early 1980s, Social Security paid out more than it was taking in. To save the system, Congress increased the taxes paid by workers, employers, and the self-employed. These reforms, voted in 1983, also advanced the retirement age from 65 to 67 by the year 2027. The legislator's goal was to make Social Security self-supporting for another 75 years.

CORPORATE INCOME TAXES

Industries and businesses pay *corporate income taxes* on their profits. The corporate tax rates range from 15 to 34 percent. Companies pay their corporate income tax after subtracting their exemptions and deductions but before paying dividends to investors. Investment credits and other tax breaks make it possible for some large companies to make millions of dollars while paying almost no taxes.

Corporate income taxes have been criticized for drawing off funds that could be used to expand and modernize ageing factories. The critics believe that higher business profits would create more jobs and higher tax revenues. On the other hand, tax loopholes have enabled some giant corporations to avoid millions of dollars in taxes. The much debated oil depletion allowance is an example of a special tax exemption. The allowance gives a tax credit to petroleum companies for each barrel of oil they pump out of the ground.

EXCISE TAXES

Taxes levied on the sale of specific goods and services are known as *excise taxes*. Whenever Americans pay a telephone bill, buy cosmetics, visit a theater, or purchase a bottle of liquor, this tax is included in the price. Economists say that the excise tax is a *regressive tax*, one that forces rich and poor alike to pay the same amount. The excise tax is harmful to the poor because each dollar they pay represents a larger share of their income.

ESTATE AND GIFT TAXES

People pay estate and gift taxes when they transfer money or property to another person. When someone dies, the heirs receive a lifetime credit of $192,800 against combined estate and gift taxes. Once this figure is exceeded, the government taxes the value of the estate as personal income. The money and property left to a surviving wife or husband is exempt from estate taxes.

Gifts are taxed under a different system. Each year, a donor may give up to $10,000 tax-free to another person. After that limit is reached, Uncle Sam collects gift taxes at the same rates as for personal income. Gift taxes keep wealthy people from giving away their money in order to avoid estate taxes.

CUSTOMS TAXES

If you buy something imported from another country, the price probably includes a customs tax. This tax is also known as a tariff or duty. Customs inspectors determine the taxes due on imports according to their value and category. A number of items, such as art objects and books, pass through duty free. Many other items carry only a small customs tax.

During the 1800s, the United States used

high tariffs as a way of protecting its infant industries. Since World War II, the government's policy has been one of lowering tariff barriers. By reducing customs taxes, the United States has stimulated trade and opened new markets for U.S. exports.

American goods once outsold foreign competition because of this country's advantage in technology. That advantage has almost disappeared in many industries. Low-priced imports have driven some American companies out of business, and overseas markets for many U.S. goods have dried up. As a result, a number of American manufacturers are lobbying for higher tariffs and other restrictions on imports.

3. What limits the power of Congress to impose taxes?

The power of Congress to impose taxes is restricted by two main authorities: the Constitution and court decisions.

The Constitution forbids the imposition of

■ In the late 1980s, Japanese imports drove some American manufacturers out of business. Rather than see the last U.S. motorcycle maker collapse, Congress passed a bill that set high tariffs on large motorcycles (700 cc and above). The five-year tariff gave Harley-Davidson the time it needed to improve its product. As a result the new Harleys are holding their own in sales competition with the big Hondas and Kawasakis.

export taxes on goods shipped to other countries. It also provides that *indirect taxes*, the cost of which is passed on to the consumer, must be uniform throughout the country. For example, federal taxes on skateboard manufacturers must be the same in New York as in California. The employer of a well-paid accountant must pay the same Social Security tax rate as the employer of a cook who works for the minimum wage.

Governments often use taxes to achieve social goals. High excise taxes on alcoholic beverages limit consumption and raise money at the same time. Similarly, some economists want to reduce the country's dependence on imported oil. They argue that higher federal gas taxes will cause people to use less gasoline.

The use of taxes to bring about social reform cannot be carried to extremes, however. The Fourteenth Amendment requires that taxes be fair and that they be imposed only for public purposes. In addition, no tax may be set so high as to actually take away someone's property. In the early 1900s, for example, taxes meant to discourage the use of child labor

were thrown out by the Supreme Court. Today's Court would be more likely to approve taxes that regulate social and business behavior. These taxes, however, must meet the test of being fair and reasonable.

4. How does the federal government collect taxes?

The Treasury Department oversees the collection of the nation's yearly harvest of taxes. The job of administering and enforcing the taxes passed by Congress belongs to the Internal Revenue Service (IRS). A commissioner, appointed by the President and confirmed by the Senate, directs the IRS and its 62 districts. An IRS director supervises the collection of taxes in each district.

Americans, often to their own surprise, have a worldwide reputation for paying their taxes honestly and promptly. The IRS, however, reports that tax evasion is on the increase. The combined pressures of inflation and high tax rates are part of the problem. The belief that the tax system favors the rich and powerful also leads lower- and middle-class taxpayers to underreport their income. The Tax Reform Act of 1986 plugged many of the old loopholes. The act's sponsors predicted that the changes would increase tax revenues and reduce tax evasion.

The IRS does its best to keep American taxpayers honest. The most effective method is tax withholding. Employers subtract taxes from their workers' paychecks and pay the money directly to the Treasury. The IRS also collects information on the dividends and interest paid to investors. If they suspect tax evasion, IRS agents have the right to (1) inspect a company's books, (2) call witnesses to testify in tax cases, and (3) require a uniform method of accounting.

All Americans who earn more than the minimum amount set by law must file an annual tax return. If their employers do not withhold enough money, the taxpayers pay the difference. When the employers withhold too much, the IRS sends a refund. Many taxpayers wait until the April 15 deadline is closing in on them before they fill out their returns. In recent years, the media have also reminded taxpayers that May 4 is "Tax Freedom Day." The Tax Foundation bases this calculation on the fact that most Americans pay about one-third of their income in federal, state, and local taxes. Until early May, therefore, people are working for the government!

The IRS uses sophisticated computers to check returns. The computers verify the accuracy of the income reported and the deductions claimed. When the IRS suspects that people are cheating on taxes, it calls them in for an audit. If the taxpayers cannot prove that their tax returns are accurate, the auditor bills them for back taxes plus interest. People accused of tax fraud are tried in federal courts. If they are found guilty, they face heavy fines. Judges also send tax evaders to prison in more serious cases.

5. Where do the federal tax dollars go?

In 1900, some critics condemned the federal government for spending $500 million a year. In 1990, with the population a little more than three times what it was in 1900, total federal

How the 1990 Federal Budget Dollar Was Spent

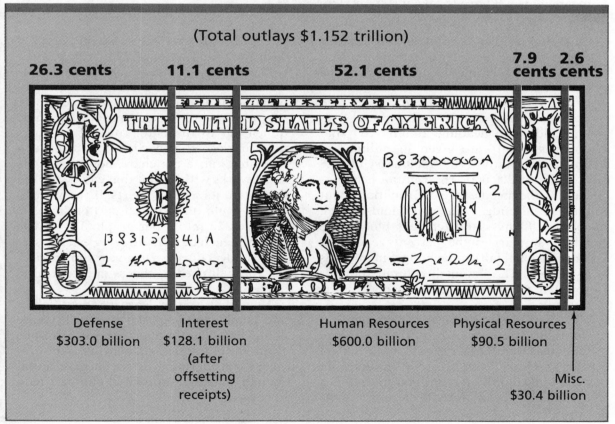

(Total outlays $1.152 trillion)

| 26.3 cents | 11.1 cents | 52.1 cents | 7.9 cents | 2.6 cents |

| Defense $303.0 billion | Interest $128.1 billion (after offsetting receipts) | Human Resources $600.0 billion | Physical Resources $90.5 billion | Misc. $30.4 billion |

■ The federal government spends about $3.2 billion a day. If you piled these dollar bills on top of one another, the stack would tower 212 miles high. That's up there with the space satellites that circle the earth. Put another way, the stack would be as high as 39 Mount Everests.

Learning Skills

Making Sense of Tables and Graphs

For an author, deciding what to do with a long list of statistics presents a real challenge. Filling a paragraph with dozens of numbers confuses the reader. It's tempting to forget about the statistics, but that means leaving out important information. The solution is to translate the numbers into a well-designed visual.

Now, turn back to the table on page 222. At first glance, it looks like a jumbled mass of numbers. If you're going to extract its meaning, you'll have to take it step by step.

1. *Find out what the table is trying to tell you.* The heading says it all: "Increase in the size of the federal budget, 1789–1994." All tables have headings of one form or another.

2. *Study the special data lines and column headings.* Note the special data line under the heading. It tells you that dollar amounts are given in millions of dollars. Thus, the 1789–1800 entry of $5.8 is really $5,800,000. The column headings identify the specific bit of information about the federal budget that you'll find in each column. In five- and ten-year blocks, the table summarizes the percentage growth (or occasional fall) of the budget in millions of dollars. The "events" column reminds you that a war or depression can affect the budget.

3. *Put it all together.* You can look at the table as a whole or at the individual sections. Overall, the increase in the budget shows clearly, from $5.8 million to $1,311,600.0 million (a million million is a trillion!). You can pick out the times of the largest increases—the Civil War, World War I, and World War II. The largest dollar increases, however, came at a different time. Can you find those years?

Next, look at the table on page 230. Apply the same three steps to this table. You'll see how the national debt has increased in the years between 1900 and 1990. If the total debt rises in the next eight years at the same percentage that it rose between 1986 and 1990, how large will it be in the year 1998?

Finally, compare the table on page 230 with the graph on page 223. Which of the two is easier to understand? Most people would vote for the pie chart (or circle graph) because the size of the "slices" makes them easy to compare. This chart adds a graphic dimension to the plain rows of numbers that you looked at earlier. You can't turn the table into a pie chart, however. A pie chart works with a total that can be broken down into its separate parts. If you wanted to, you could turn at least part of the table on page 222 into a bar graph. Try it. The length of each bar should represent the size of the budget during a five-year time period. So, you will need to choose only a portion of the table to work with.

Now that you've learned about tables and graphs, put your skill to use. If you're doing some career planning, for example, graph the pay scales and benefits of the jobs you're considering. The graph may reveal comparisons that individual numbers tend to conceal.

outlays were 2,000 times higher. Clearly, people today expect more services from the government than people did in 1900. As you can see in the graph on page 227, four major categories account for 99 cents out of each federal dollar spent.

DEFENSE

Military costs consume a large share of the budget, even in peacetime. The Pentagon's share of the budget rises and falls with the changing climate of international relations. Between 1960 and 1990, for example, defense costs as a percentage of total federal spending fell from 49 to 26 percent. The dollar investment, however, rose from $45 billion in 1960 to over $300 billion in 1990. That sounds like a tremendous increase, but inflation ate up many of the new dollars.

Most Americans understand the need for a strong national defense. The United States also shoulders peacekeeping responsibilities around the globe. As the danger of war with the Soviet Union lessened, Congress cut back the military budget. It was hoped that this "peace dividend" could be used to reduce the deficit and to fund social programs. But the war in the Persian Gulf may have destroyed this hope.

HUMAN RESOURCES

The federal government spends billions of dollars for education, medical care, antipoverty programs, food stamps, and other social welfare programs. These expenses make up the human resources segment of the budget. Between 1965 and 1990, the cost of such programs jumped from 30 to 52 percent of all federal spending. Human resources is now the largest category in the federal budget.

Spending on human resources reflects a change in American priorities. Citizens want the government to play a major role in improving the quality of life in the United States. If local or state governments cannot provide the services people want, they turn to the federal government. Even though most taxpayers grumble at the size of their tax bill, they understand that government cannot provide services unless they pay their taxes.

INTEREST ON THE NATIONAL DEBT

During the Great Depression of the 1930s, the government went into debt to help jobless and hungry Americans. Later on, World War II, the Korean and Vietnam wars, and the new social programs of the 1960s all required increased federal spending. As a result, the national debt skyrocketed. When tax revenues fall short of expenses, the Treasury borrows money by selling notes and bonds to raise the difference. Like any consumer, the government must pay interest on the money it borrows.

Higher interest rates and the fast-growing mountain of debt pushed interest payments from $1 billion in 1939 to $170 billion in 1990. That $170 billion amounts to one-sixth of the entire federal budget.

PHYSICAL RESOURCES

The government spends eight percent of its budget on physical resources. This money pays for programs that include interstate highways, public housing projects, NASA's space shots, farm subsidies, and office space. As the nation's largest landowner and landlord, the federal government's yearly housekeeping bill runs into the billions. To this must be added the costs of new construction and research projects.

MISCELLANEOUS

Miscellaneous expenses made up less than three percent of the 1990 budget. Support for the United Nations, disaster relief, and other useful programs are included in this category.

Let's review for a moment

Can you grasp the magnitude of government expenditures? If you somehow could spend one million dollars a day for 3,154 years, you would have run through only one year's *budget*—1990's $1.151 trillion. This remarkable sum of money reflects America's ever-increasing demand for governmental services.

Most of the money to finance the budget comes from taxes. Americans pay *personal* and *corporate income taxes*, Social Security taxes, excise taxes, estate and gift taxes, and customs taxes. Where does the money go? Defense, human and physical resources, and interest on the *national debt* take most of your federal tax dollar.

Congress does not have unlimited taxing powers. Exports cannot be taxed, for example, and federal tax rates must be equal for all sections of the country. The income tax is an example of a *progressive tax* because the tax rate increases as the size of a person's income increases. *Excise taxes*, on the other hand, are *regressive taxes*. Everyone, rich or poor, pays the same rate.

The Treasury Department's Internal Revenue Service supervises the collection of income taxes. The Tax Reform Act of 1986 simplified the tax laws and closed *loopholes*. Even with tax reform, federal, state, and local taxes consume one-third of an average citizen's income.

6. Why does the United States have a national debt?

Revolutions cost money, even those that happened in the 1700s. Thus, the United States was born with a *national debt* (the total amount owed by a country to its creditors). By 1900 the debt was $1.3 billion. World War II ballooned the debt sixfold, from $43 billion in 1940 to $257 billion in 1950. By today's standards, that debt was quite manageable. Between 1981 and 1990, the debt more than tripled—from $1 to $3.1 trillion. That amounts to a debt of over $12,000 for every man, woman, and child in the United States.

THE LUXURY OF BALANCED BUDGETS

The federal government creates the national debt by spending more money than it collects. This practice is called *deficit spending*. For example, the annual budget deficit for 1990 is estimated to be $93 billion. For economic reasons, the President and Congress would prefer to operate under a *balanced budget*, with income equal to outgo. A rare budget surplus, in which revenue exceeds spending, would allow the government to pay off some of the debt. The United States did have a few budget surpluses during the 1800s and in the 1920s.

Balanced budgets become a luxury when Congress and the President agree that the nation's needs cannot be met from current income. During a time of high unemployment, for example, the government borrows money and pumps it into the economy. If this practice succeeds, jobs are created and people go back to work. But the borrowed money adds to the national debt.

THE NATIONAL DEBT OF THE UNITED STATES, 1900–1990

Year	Total debt (billions)	Debt per capita	Interest paid (billions)	Percent of budget for interest
1900	$ 1.3	$ 17	$ *	7.7%
1910	1.1	12	*	3.1
1920	24.3	228	1.0	15.9
1930	16.2	132	0.7	19.2
1940	43.0	325	1.0	11.5
1950	257.4	1,697	5.7	14.5
1960	286.3	1,585	9.2	10.0
1970	370.9	1,811	19.3	9.8
1979	826.5	3,740	59.8	11.0
1984	1,600.0	6,768	149.5	17.5
1986	2,112.0	9,324	136.0	13.7
1988	2,509.0	10,909	139.0	13.6
1990 (est.)	3,107.2	12,653	170.0	16.0

* Less than half a billion dollars.

DEBT CEILING

Congress regularly places a limit on the national debt by setting a *debt ceiling*. Deficit spending pushes the debt up against the ceiling just as regularly. When that happens, the President must ask Congress to raise the ceiling. If the ceiling isn't raised, all but the most essential government activities come to a halt. The huge deficits of the 1980s forced the government to raise the debt ceiling to over $3 trillion in 1990.

PAYING INTEREST ON THE DEBT

The national debt creates problems far greater than trying to figure out ways to reduce its size. Interest payments on the debt take a big share of federal tax revenues every year. As the United States pays out more and more money in interest, two additional problems result:

1. *The dollar declines in value.* Huge deficits in the federal budget cause foreign investors to lose faith in the dollar. The nation's *balance of payments deficit* (the amount by which imports exceed exports) adds to the problem. A trade deficit of $36 billion in 1980 increased to an alarming $126 billion in 1988. Investors in Japan, Canada, and other countries fear that the budget and trade deficits will ruin the U.S. economy. To protect themselves, they exchange their dollars for "safe" investments such as Swiss francs or gold. When that happens, the dollar loses a little more of its value.

2. *Inflation increases.* Consumers, investors, corporations, and governments all borrow money. When the Treasury borrows billions of dollars to finance the federal deficit, competition for money forces interest rates upward. Higher interest rates mean that everything costs more to produce. The resulting *inflation* pushes prices higher and higher.

Defenders of deficit spending remind us that large companies borrow to expand and modernize. They believe that government should do the same. These economists point out that the nation's gross national product (GNP) has been growing faster than the debt. In 1950, for example, the national debt was equal to

the country's GNP for an entire year. In 1990, the debt is expected to amount to little more than a six-month share of the GNP.

7. How is money appropriated by Congress?

The Constitution states that "no money shall be drawn from the Treasury, but in consequence of appropriations made by law." Thus, the President may propose a budget, but Congress makes the final decision as to how much money will be spent. Each year, the President sends requests for budget *appropriations* (money bills to be passed by Congress) to Capitol Hill. The year's appropriations must cover continuing programs (veterans' benefits and aid to Latin America, for example) as well as any money needed to launch new programs. No money can be spent, however, until the appropriations process makes funding available.

THE APPROPRIATIONS PROCESS

The annual process of writing and funding the federal budget takes place in ten steps.

1. *Preliminary planning.* Each department and agency of government compiles data on the funding needed to support old and new programs for the coming year. Priorities established by the President and the Office of Management and Budget (OMB) guide the executive branch's planning during this stage. The OMB has the task of putting the huge federal budget into its final form.

2. *OMB review.* The OMB holds hearings at which each department defends its requests. The OMB then prepares a proposed budget and sends it to the White House. The President makes the final budget decisions after conferring with White House staff and department heads. All work on the proposed budget must be completed by the end of the calendar year. After the President signs off on the bulky budget document, the Government Printing Office prints it for the nation to examine.

3. *President's budget message.* In January, the President submits the budget to Congress. This budget message outlines priorities and gives the President's views on the nation's economy. The budget also includes an estimate of tax revenues expected during the year. If a budget deficit appears certain, the President must justify the borrowing needed to balance income and outgo.

4. *Congressional budget resolution.* Under the Congressional Budget Act of 1974, the House and Senate must adopt proposed budgets by May 15. Legislative committees in both houses study the President's budget and revise it in keeping with their own priorities. Their independence shows most clearly when the President's party has lost control of Congress to the opposition. Each house passes its own budget resolution, and a conference committee works out a final version. Congress is supposed to complete its work on the budget before October 1, but it often misses that deadline.

5. *House action.* The budget resolution sets up funding targets, but no money can be spent until Congress passes authorization and appropriations bills. All appropriations bills must originate in the House of Representatives. By this time, budget requests have been broken into separate bills dealing with the defense budget, aid to agriculture, the space program, and the like. Subcommittees of the House Appropriations Committee and other standing committees hold hearings on each spending bill. As the bills clear the committees, they go to the floor of the House. There, the full membership joins in the debate.

6. *Senate action.* Once the House has acted, the Senate begins work on its own appropriations bills. Agencies that have had budgets cut in the House use the Senate hearings to appeal for help. For every appropriation the Senate increases, it may cut another. After hearings close, the committees report the bills to the floor of the Senate. There, the dollar amounts are again subject to change. Finally, the full Senate votes on the amended legislation.

7. *Conference committee meetings.* A special conference committee meets to work out a compromise on the appropriations voted in the two houses. These bargaining sessions usually end with each side giving a little. The bills that emerge often contain far different figures from the ones with which the committee started.

8. *Final congressional action.* Conference committee members return their compromise bills to the House and Senate for final action. Because conference reports cannot be amended, the lawmakers usually accept them. Refusal to accept the report would greatly delay passage of the high-priority appropriations bills. Without this legislation, government operations would close down at the end of the fiscal year.

9. *The President's options.* The President may either sign or veto the appropriations bills. These bills are rarely vetoed. To do so would disrupt the work of the department or agency that has projects funded by the bill. When the President does veto an appropriations bill, it's often because Congress made major changes in the original budget request. In the battle that follows, Congress usually loses the fight to override the veto.

10. *Using the appropriations.* Each department or agency uses the funds Congress has appropriated to carry on its activities through the next fiscal year. The government has adopted a fiscal year that runs from October 1 to September 30 of the following year. Fiscal 1991 thus began on October 1, 1990. Fiscal years for state governments often begin on July 1, a date used by the federal govern-

The Appropriations Process

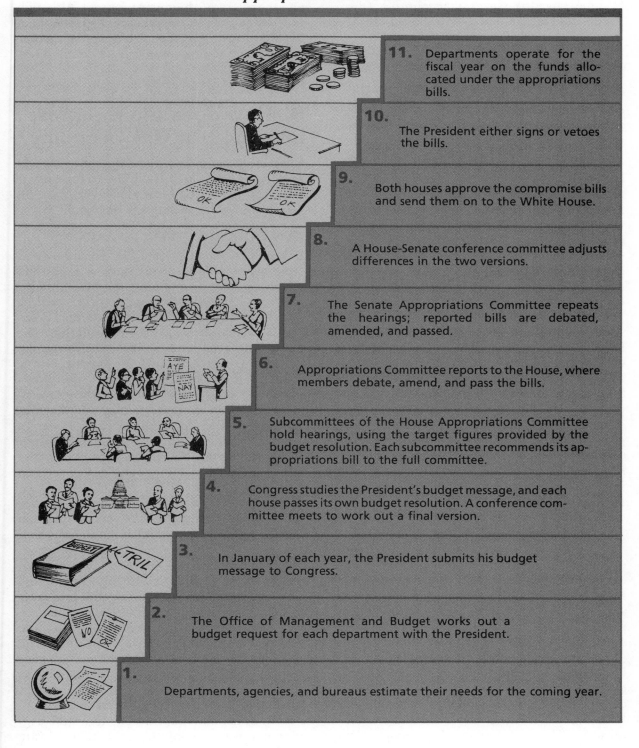

11. Departments operate for the fiscal year on the funds allocated under the appropriations bills.

10. The President either signs or vetoes the bills.

9. Both houses approve the compromise bills and send them on to the White House.

8. A House-Senate conference committee adjusts differences in the two versions.

7. The Senate Appropriations Committee repeats the hearings; reported bills are debated, amended, and passed.

6. Appropriations Committee reports to the House, where members debate, amend, and pass the bills.

5. Subcommittees of the House Appropriations Committee hold hearings, using the target figures provided by the budget resolution. Each subcommittee recommends its appropriations bill to the full committee.

4. Congress studies the President's budget message, and each house passes its own budget resolution. A conference committee meets to work out a final version.

3. In January of each year, the President submits his budget message to Congress.

2. The Office of Management and Budget works out a budget request for each department with the President.

1. Departments, agencies, and bureaus estimate their needs for the coming year.

ment until 1976. Once appropriations have become law, the General Accounting Office supervises the day-to-day spending of the money.

PROBLEMS CAUSED BY THE APPROPRIATIONS PROCEDURE

A procedure as complex as the appropriations process doesn't always work smoothly. Three major criticisms are often directed against it.

1. *Short-term commitments.* Many executive branch officials believe that appropriations should extend beyond a single year. Long-range programs cannot be developed, they claim, when Congress limits funding to a year at a time. Congress, for its part, does not wish to give up its yearly review of executive branch activities. Only a few agencies—notably international operations like the World Bank—receive multi-year funding.

2. *Porkbarreling.* Because the President seldom vetoes an appropriations bill, an unfortunate side effect has developed. Members of Congress often give in to political pressure and add vote-winning projects to general money bills. The total of costly special-interest appropriations passed each year is called that session's *porkbarrel*. Many porkbarrel riders pay for nearly useless construction projects (flood control levees on rivers that have never been known to flood) or financial aid for special interests (subsidies for the merchant marine). Even useful porkbarrel projects spend precious federal funds that the President might prefer to use elsewhere.

Members of Congress often support someone else's porkbarrel projects in return for support of their own. This exchange of votes is called *logrolling*. The President cannot veto special-interest projects tacked onto appropriations bills without vetoing the entire bill. Thus, the porkbarrel fills to overflowing.

3. *Complexity of the budget.* The printed budget that the President sends to Congress each year is hundreds of pages long. Even experienced economists find it difficult to analyze. Since 1968, the White House has submitted a "unified" budget. This budget lists all the money to be spent, including dollars from special funds such as Social Security and the interstate highway program. Although this format helps Congress see the full impact of federal spending, the job of juggling income and outgo remains complex and demanding.

8. How does the Congress influence the U.S. economy?

Congress uses its control of the purse strings to do more than pay the bills. By raising or lowering taxes, for example, lawmakers directly influence the nation's economy.

TAXATION TO COMBAT INFLATION

Inflation is often described by economists as "too many dollars chasing too few goods." In other words, if people have too much money and goods are in short supply, prices will be pushed upward. Traditional economics holds that taxes can be used to stop inflation. The theory states that money taken from the public in taxes is not available for buying scarce goods, so the price of those goods goes down. The theory does work—but only when government holds on to the excess dollars. If Congress and the President spend the extra tax revenues on new programs, they're substituting their own spending for that of the consumer.

TAXATION TO COMBAT RECESSION

High interest rates and limits on the money supply helped reduce the 12.4 percent inflation of 1980 to only 3.2 percent in 1983. But these tough anti-inflation measures sent the economy into a recession. A *recession* is a slowdown in the economy that causes high unemployment and lower production of goods and services. The government fought the recession with tax policies that put more money into the pockets of consumers and corporations. The economy responded by shifting into high gear in 1983–1984. Unemployment fell rapidly at first, then inched downward to less than six percent in 1989 and then began to edge up. Despite fears that federal deficits would trigger a new round of inflation, the inflation rate held relatively steady.

SAVINGS AND LOAN FAILURES INCREASE THE DEFICIT

Attempts to balance the federal budget suffered a serious blow when many of the nation's savings and loan banks failed in the late 1980s. A few of the banks failed because of inept or dishonest management. But most of them were guilty only of making too many risky loans that went bad. Whenever an S&L went under, the Federal Savings and Loan Insurance Corporation (FSLIC) stepped in and paid off its depositors on accounts up to $100,000. The banks that couldn't be saved were closed. Others were sold to new owners who agreed to keep them open by investing fresh capital.

Because of the drain on the FSLIC insurance fund, Congress had to pump billions of dollars into the banking system. To make sure that the problem didn't repeat itself, lawmakers wrote new laws for the industry. As before, deposits up to $100,000 were insured, but a new Savings Association Insurance Fund (SAIF) was created to replace the FSLIC. The remaining S&Ls will be forced to make at least 80 percent of their loans in the safer home mortgage market. Further, they must double their capital (the cushion they hold against loan losses) from 3 percent to 6 percent of their assets.

Under these strict rules, banking experts believe that two-thirds of the nation's 3,000 S&Ls will disappear within 10 years. Total government costs of the salvage plan are expected to run into the hundreds of billions of dollars.

REGULATION TO END THE DEFICITS

At the end of 1985, Congress passed the Gramm-Rudman Act in an attempt to eliminate deficits by 1991. If Congress fails to produce a balanced budget, Gramm-Rudman calls for automatic spending cuts. Half of the cuts must come from defense and half from domestic programs. In 1986, the Supreme Court declared that the act was unconstitutional because it gave budget-cutting powers to the General Accounting Office (a congressional agency). The Court ruled that only the executive branch could order the cuts.

In 1987, Congress passed a second version

■ Not since the 1930s have banks faced so many problems. This bank in Texas found new life after it received funds from the Federal Deposit Insurance Corporation (FDIC). The collapse of so many savings banks in the late 1980s weakened the FDIC. Congress passed legislation to restore confidence in the system.

of Gramm-Rudman. This time, the budget-cutting authority was given to the Office of Management and Budget (an executive branch agency). The target date for eliminating deficits was extended to 1993. Although Congress has fallen short of meeting the Gramm-Rudman targets, economists credit the bill with holding down federal spending for both military and social programs.

REGULATION OF THE CURRENCY

Congress also affects the economy by regulating the value of the currency. Congressional powers in this area include (1) regulating banking through the Federal Reserve System (see page 352) and (2) guaranteeing the safety of individual bank accounts up to $100,000 through the Federal Deposit Insurance Corporation. Two additional powers include (1) working with the President to set the international value of the dollar and (2) authorizing U.S. participation in world banking agencies such as the International Monetary Fund.

Reviewing
what you've learned

1. The Congress of the United States raises and spends astronomical sums of money each year. The power to regulate the economy enables the Congress to deal with the increased demand for government services and the upward and downward swings in the economy. Because Congress appropriates more money than the Treasury takes in, the government must borrow billions of dollars each year. Because money is being borrowed faster than it is being paid back, the United States has built up a huge *national debt*.

2. Four revenue sources provide over 90 percent of federal income: *personal income taxes*, Social Security taxes, *corporate income taxes*, and *excise taxes*. Taxes pay for government activities, but Congress also uses them to achieve social goals. The Internal Revenue Service enforces the complex tax laws.

3. The main items in the federal *budget* are defense, human resources, interest payments on the national debt, and physical resources. The Office of Management and Budget (OMB) coordinates the preparation of the budget, which the President submits to Congress for approval. Congress then passes its own budget resolution, which often differs from the President's budget.

4. *Appropriation* bills originate in the House of Representatives. The original budget requests often are greatly modified during committee hearings and floor debate. The Senate conducts its own hearings on the appropriation bills, after which a conference committee irons out the differences between the two houses. The President seldom vetoes a money bill, so members of Congress often load up the *"porkbarrel"* with projects that benefit special interests.

5. Congress exerts a major influence on the economy through its power to tax. Tax increases have been used as a brake on *inflation*, and tax reductions have been used as a stimulus during *recessions*. Congress also tries to stabilize the value of the dollar through its regulation of the currency and banking systems.

Review questions
and activities

TERMS YOU SHOULD KNOW

appropriations	deficit spending	logrolling
balanced budget	excise tax	loophole
balance of payments deficit	exemption	national debt
boondoggle	export tax	personal income tax
budget	fiscal year	porkbarrel
corporate income tax	gross national product (GNP)	progressive tax rate
debt ceiling	indirect tax	recession
deduction	inflation	regressive tax
		tariff

REVIEW QUESTIONS

Select the response that best completes each statement or question.

1. Federal spending has grown rapidly because (*a*) the American people have demanded more and more government services. (*b*) the United States population has continued to increase. (*c*) spending on social welfare has soared in the past 50 years. (*d*) larger expenditures were needed for defense. (*e*) of all of these reasons.

2. The largest single source of federal tax revenues is the (*a*) corporate income tax. (*b*) excise tax. (*c*) Social Security tax. (*d*) personal income tax. (*e*) import tax.

3. An example of a *regressive* tax would be a tax on (*a*) personal income. (*b*) corporate profits. (*c*) cigarettes and liquor. (*d*) the estate inherited by a person's children. (*e*) all of these are regressive taxes.

4. A *loophole* in the tax laws gives (*a*) the government a way of collecting extra taxes. (*b*) the average taxpayer a way of avoiding the payment of all income taxes. (*c*) Congress a means of changing the President's budget. (*d*) corporations and individuals a way of greatly reducing their tax payments. (*e*) foreign investors a way of buying U.S. companies without obeying U.S. laws.

5. Which is a *true* statement about the Social Security system? (*a*) Social Security was set up to provide old-age and survivors' benefits. (*b*) Social Security is a program designed to prevent recession. (*c*) Social Security will soon be bankrupt. (*d*) Only government employees can belong to Social Security. (*e*) Social Security pays only for hospital care.

6. The government agency established to collect taxes and deal with tax fraud is the (*a*) U.S. Secret Service. (*b*) Federal Bureau of Investigation. (*c*) General Accounting Office. (*d*) Office of Management and Budget. (*e*) Internal Revenue Service.

7. In recent years, federal fiscal policy can best be described as being marked by (*a*) balanced budgets. (*b*) lowered debt ceilings. (*c*) lower federal spending. (*d*) deficit spending. (*e*) repayment of the national debt.

8. The national debt continues to grow. As a percentage of the Gross National Product it has (*a*) increased. (*b*) remained the same. (*c*) decreased. (*d*) grown larger than the GNP. (*e*) no relation to the GNP.

9. All federal appropriations bills originate in (*a*) the White House. (*b*) the individual state legislatures. (*c*) the Senate. (*d*) the OMB. (*e*) the House of Representatives.

10. An example of true porkbarrel legislation would be (*a*) an increase in Social Security benefits. (*b*) establishment of a national health care program. (*c*) funding a cancer research project at a major university. (*d*) construction of a breakwater to protect pleasure boats at a Florida resort. (*e*) appropriating funds for a space probe to Mars.

CONCEPT DEVELOPMENT

1. Why has the federal budget grown so rapidly—much faster than this country's population—over the past 50 years?

2. List the major types of federal taxes. What percentage of government income does each produce? List the advantages and disadvantages of increasing the personal income tax.

3. If you were President, what taxes would you increase and which would you reduce? Are there any new taxes you would use to replace existing taxes? (No, you can't cancel all taxes. Without tax revenue, the government couldn't pay its bills.)

4. Why has the federal government allowed the national debt to increase year after year? How does the Gramm-Rudman Act propose to bring this mountain of debt under control?

5. As you've read in this chapter, federal deficits grew at an alarming rate in the 1980s. Some experts say the deficits reflect the difference between what people want from government and what they are willing to pay for its services. Is this a fair statement? Why or why not?

HANDS-ON ACTIVITIES

1. You'll need a set of tax forms for this activity. Pick them up from the IRS, the post office, a bank, a library, or a local accountant. Use a tax manual to help you fill out 1040 returns for three typical taxpayers. Give them income levels of (a) $10,000, (b) $40,000, and (c) $100,000. Each taxpayer is married and has two young children. Invent reasonable expenses that reflect their different incomes. When you're finished, attach the 1040s to a poster, along with an explanation of progressive taxation as it applies to these returns.

2. Look up the names and addresses of your representatives in Congress. Write to them and ask for lists of projects they have sponsored that have directly benefited your district. Study the lists carefully. Should any of them be labeled porkbarrel projects? Why or why not?

3. Inflation has taken a large bite out of the dollar since 1960. The raw numbers don't mean too much, however. To put inflation in its proper perspective, find out how the prices of everyday products have increased since 1960. Check out the cost then and now of such items as an American-made automobile, a pair of shoes, a quart of milk, a pound of chicken or ground beef, and so on. Construct a bar chart to display your research. Microfilm copies of old newspapers should contain ads that will be helpful.

4. Prepare a bulletin board display in collage form that demonstrates (a) the sources of the federal tax dollar and (b) the uses the government finds for that dollar.

5. Obtain a copy of the federal budget for the current fiscal year. After a brief examination, summarize its structure and priorities. Pay particular attention to any items that strike you as being wasteful. If you were the President, how would you cut these items in order to eliminate budget deficits? Why is it so hard to push such cuts through Congress?

Unit Four

The Executive Branch of American Government

11 The many jobs of the nation's President

"On Tuesday morning, October 16, 1962, shortly after 9:00 o'clock, President Kennedy called and asked me to come to the White House. He said only that we were facing great trouble. Shortly afterward, in his office, he told me that a U-2 [high-flying observation plane] had just finished a photographic mission, and that the Intelligence Community had become convinced that Russia was placing missiles and atomic weapons in Cuba.

"That was the beginning of the Cuban missile crisis—a confrontation between two giant atomic nations, the U.S. and the U.S.S.R., which brought the world to the abyss of nuclear destruction and the end of mankind."

▲ President John F. Kennedy signing an arms quarantine against Cuba in October 1962.

These doomsday words came from the pen of Robert Kennedy, the President's brother and the U.S. Attorney General, who played a key advisory role during those near-fatal two weeks. He went on to tell the story of how advice poured into the President's office from military and diplomatic officials. The "hawks" pushed for an immediate air strike to knock out the missiles or for an air-sea invasion of Cuba. "Doves" pointed out the dangers of a military solution and advised Kennedy to try for a diplomatic compromise.

President Kennedy knew he could not permit the missiles to remain 90 miles off the coast of Florida. The Soviets could use the threat of those weapons to force the United States to back down in other parts of the world. In his own mind, Kennedy had already decided that he would not touch off a war with the Soviet Union if any possibility of a peaceful settlement remained open. Listening, thinking, questioning, he considered the consequences of each step open to him.

"Those hours in the Cabinet Room that Saturday afternoon in October [the 27th] could never be erased from the minds of any of us. We saw as never before the meaning and responsibility involved in the power of the United States, the power of the President, the responsibility we had to people around the globe who had never heard of our country or the men sitting in that room determining their fate, making a decision which would influence whether they would live or die.

" 'We won't attack tomorrow,' the President said. 'We shall try again.' "

Communication links were opened between Kennedy and Nikita Krushchev, the Soviet Premier. At the same time, the country began to prepare for the worst. The Pentagon placed troops and planes on alert. Panic buying resulted in long lines and empty shelves at grocery stores. Families began digging backyard air-raid shelters. The leaders of both countries lived with the terrible knowledge that World War III was only a decision or two away.

Describing events on Sunday, October 28, Robert Kennedy wrote, "I went immediately to the White House, and there I received a call from Ambassador Dobrynin [Soviet Ambassador to the United States], saying that he would like to visit with me. I met him in my office at 11:00 A.M.

"He told me that the message was coming through that Krushchev had agreed to dismantle and withdraw the missiles under adequate supervision and inspection; that everything was going to work out satisfactorily; and that Mr. Krushchev wanted to send his best wishes to the President and to me.

". . . I believe our deliberations proved conclusively how important it is that the President have the recommendations and opinions of more than one individual, of more than one department, and of more than one point of view. . . .

"The possibility of the destruction of mankind was always in his [President Kennedy's] mind. Someone once said that World War III would be fought with atomic weapons and the next war with sticks and stones."

The awesome power that belongs to the President of the United States is clearly dramatized by the Cuban missile crisis. But Presidents don't wait for life-or-death emergencies to exercise their authority. This chapter will discuss the qualifications a person must have to become President and the many different roles the occupants of the White House play. The wide scope of the American presidency can be seen as these questions are discussed:

1. How does a person gain the presidency?

2. What are the President's duties as chief of state?

3. How does the President serve as chief legislator?

4. What powers does the President exercise as chief executive?

5. How does the President represent the United States as its chief diplomat?

6. How does the President serve as chief politician?

7. Why does the President serve as commander-in-chief of the armed forces?

8. How does the President function as chief jurist?

9. What is the role of the Vice President?

10. What is the job of the President's Executive Office?

1. How does a person gain the presidency?

Out of the hundreds of millions of Americans who will live and die during your lifetime, fewer than 20 will attain the office of the presidency. The odds on any one of us winning a million dollars in a state lottery are better than the odds of being elected President. Despite the tremendous difficulties they must overcome, however, ambitious politicians still set their sights on the White House. If elected, a handful of them will have the opportunity of leaving their mark on the history of this country and of the world.

QUALIFICATIONS FOR THE PRESIDENCY

Legal qualifications. Surprisingly, the legal qualifications for being President are very few. The Constitution merely requires that the candidate be 35 years of age, a natural-born citizen (someone who is a citizen by birth), and a resident of the United States for 14 years.

Personal qualifications. Tradition has created a second set of unwritten qualifications. No one under 40 has ever been elected (or succeeded) to the presidency. Most Presidents have been in their fifties or sixties when elected. All Presidents have been male, all but two have been married, and only one has been

FYI . . .
Nine "Rules" for Presidential Hopefuls

All serious candidates for President must play by these "rules" if they hope to be nominated by a major party. Of course, not all nine rules are applied at one time. Party differences, the demands of a particular election, and the personalities of the candidates will all influence the priorities of the delegates to a national convention.

1. The rule of political talent — Candidates should have some successful experience in government, in either appointed or elected office. Victorious generals can ignore this rule if they choose.

2. The rule of governors — Nominating conventions frequently choose their candidates from among the state governors. Governors control state delegations; governors do not normally take vote-losing stands on controversial issues, as do members of Congress.

3. The rule of big "swing states" — Candidates from big states have a better chance, particularly if they don't come from one-party states. The hope is that they can carry their own states and go to the national convention with a big bloc of votes that will sway others.

4. The rule of multiple interests — Conventions choose candidates who can command support from many different economic interests—agriculture, labor, commerce, and industry.

5. The rule of happy family life — Candidates must appear to lead ideal family lives. Showing off a photogenic spouse and wholesome looking children also helps.

6. The rule of character — The candidates' personal qualities are just as important as their policies. Presidents can and do change their policies, but the public believes that it is much harder for them to change their characters.

7. The rule of British stock — Candidates with British ancestors have been preferred. Up to 1989, 41 men had held the presidency, and 35 of them traced their ancestors back to the British Isles.

8. The rule of Protestantism — Only one non-Protestant (Kennedy, a Roman Catholic) has held the office, despite the Constitution's ban on religious tests for holding any office.

9. The rule of being male — Political scientists agree that a woman can and will be elected President some day—but no major party has yet nominated a woman for President.

divorced. Two-thirds have come to the office with legal training. Only one non-Protestant has been elected: John Kennedy, a Catholic, won the White House in 1960. At age 43, Kennedy was also the youngest person elected to the office of President.

Political qualifications. The candidates' political backgrounds play a major role in their race for the presidency. Most Presidents have come from large states with important blocs of electoral votes. Almost all were well-known public figures before the election, either

■ Members of the Electoral College in Virginia at the state capital in Richmond casting votes for President and Vice President in December 1988. Republicans George Bush and Dan Quayle were awarded Virginia's 12 electoral votes. How do they decide whom to vote for?

as a result of holding high office or commanding troops during a war. Many presidential hopefuls have served apprenticeships as state governors or as U.S. Senators before becoming candidates.

ELECTORAL COLLEGE

The Framers of the Constitution did not foresee mass communications and the emergence of two major national political parties. They thought that each state would support its own candidate for President. To deal with this situation, they set up a presidential election system designed to select a President from a field of many candidates. The institution the Framers created is called the *Electoral College.* This "college" has no campus and no students. Its only function is to elect a President.

The Electoral College process. When American voters go to the polls in November of a presidential election year, they do not actually vote for the President. The small print on each ballot reads, "For electors pledged to THEODORE ROOSEVELT," or whatever the candidate's name is that year. The number of electors from each state is equal to the number of representatives plus the two senators from that state. Thanks to the Twenty-third Amendment, ratified in 1961, the District of Columbia elects three additional electors.

Each state's electoral vote varies with changing population patterns, as determined by the national census. The slate of electors winning the highest number of votes in a given state wins all of the electoral votes from that state. The winning slate needn't receive a majority of the popular votes. If a state's voters divide their ballots among three or more popular candidates, whoever wins the most votes also wins the state's electoral votes.

On the first Monday after the second Wednesday in December of presidential election years, the winning electors gather at the state capitals to cast their ballots. In theory, the electors are free to vote for any of the candidates. Very few, if any, will vote for a candidate other than their party's nominee. After the vote is taken, each of the Electoral College meetings sends an announcement of the results to the President of the Senate. On the following January 6, Congress meets in joint session to tally the ballots. The count of the 538 electoral votes brings the election to an official conclusion. The American people are then officially informed of what they have known since the media reported the results on election night. In the deliberate manner required by the Constitution, the new President's election has been confirmed.

Weaknesses of the Electoral College system. Critics of the Electoral College claim that it has outlived its usefulness. They point out that the system is capable of selecting a candidate who did not win the most popular votes. Jackson (1824), Tilden (1876), and Cleveland (1888) all received the highest number of votes but lost in the Electoral College. That possibility still exists. By carrying the most populous states, a candidate can win the White House even though the opposing candidate polls more popular votes. This weakness of the Electoral College, which seems to deny the value of the popular vote, has led to vigorous cries for its reform or abolition.

Another problem develops when no candidate wins a majority of the electoral vote. That has happened only twice, in 1800 and in 1824, although the 1968 election came within a key state or two of repeating the experience. The Constitution provides that if no clear majority exists, the final election must take place in the House of Representatives. House members must choose from the top three candidates, with each state having only one vote. This procedure obviously favors the party that controls the House.

Every four years or so, the attacks on the Electoral College are renewed. Nevertheless, no one is predicting an early death for this two-centuries-old system of electing the President. Abolishing the Electoral College would require the ratification of an amendment to the Constitution. A reading of American history confirms that many amendments are proposed, but few are adopted.

TERM OF OFFICE

American presidents serve four-year terms. They are elected in years divisible by four—1792, 1860, 1976, 1988, and so on. George Washington began the tradition that no President would serve more than two terms. That tradition was unbroken until Franklin Roosevelt won a third term in 1940—and then a fourth term in 1944. The Twenty-second Amendment, ratified in 1951, now limits Presidents to two terms.

A Vice President who succeeds to the office may run for the presidency twice—but only if the first partial term was for less than two years. Under this rule, the maximum time in office for a former Vice President is now one day less than ten years: two regular terms plus less than half of the former President's term.

2. What are the President's duties as chief of state?

Delegates to the 1787 Constitutional Convention argued at length about the role to be played by the nation's head of government. One plan called for the creation of a constitutional monarchy. Some of the Framers wanted to enthrone a king or queen, stripped of political power, to represent the nation in ceremonial matters. A similar system exists today in Great Britain, Sweden, and the Netherlands. The majority of the delegates rejected that idea. Instead, they voted to add ceremonial functions to the many roles that the President must play. The diagram on page 248 pictures the President's many jobs.

A SYMBOL OF THE NATION

When acting as chief of state, the President is the symbol of the United States, its power, and its policies. While the American people look to the President as a symbol of their way

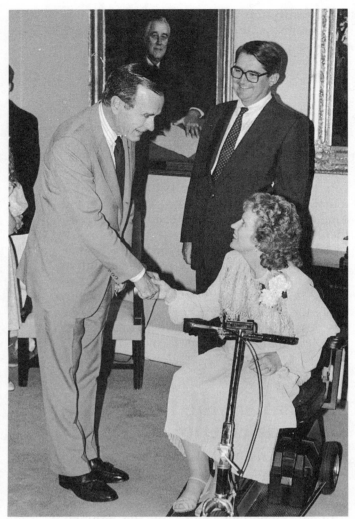

■ As chief of state, the President devotes a large portion of his time to ceremonial duties. Here President Bush greets the Multiple Sclerosis Mother and Father of the Year. The woman, mother of 10, is from Idaho. The man, from Massachusetts, is father of 3.

of life, the rest of the world sees the United States reflected in the President's image. People around the world look to the White House for leadership, particularly in times of crisis.

The President spends much valuable time in the role of chief of state. High-level foreign visitors, who sometimes stay in the White House, must be greeted and honored at formal banquets. Since World War II, American Presidents have made frequent trips to other coun-

tries. This form of personal diplomacy receives international attention. Less newsworthy activities also appear on the President's daily schedule. In a typical year, the President lights the national Christmas tree, appears at the Easter egg roll on the White House lawn, lays a wreath on the Tomb of the Unknown Soldier, and poses for countless photos to publicize various charity drives. The ceremonial duties go on and on.

The President also signs all commissions of office under the United States, including those of junior-grade officers in the armed forces. As far back as Thomas Jefferson, Presidents were complaining about this time-consuming task. Just signing the stacks of formal documents that cross the Oval Office desk can consume a big chunk of the President's workweek.

A NECESSARY ROLE

Despite all of these apparently negative factors, the importance of allowing the President to serve as a symbol for the ongoing life of the nation should not be overlooked. Even when standing in a reception line, the President is also serving as the country's chief legislator, chief executive, chief diplomat, chief politician, commander-in-chief, and chief jurist. A U.S. President can never be ignored.

3. How does the President serve as chief legislator?

Despite the separation of government into executive, legislative, and judicial branches, the President exercises broad legislative powers and responsibilities. Most Presidents enter office dedicated to a platform of specific programs that must be translated into legislation. At the same time, Congress looks to the President for suggestions and leadership in drafting new laws.

SOURCE OF THE PRESIDENT'S LEGISLATIVE POWER

The President's legislative powers derive from the Constitution. Article II, Section 3, states that the President "shall from time to time

■ Presidents find it necessary to consult with congressional leaders from time to time. Here President Bush meets in the White House with House and Senate leaders to work out the budget crisis in 1990. From the left, White House Chief of Staff John Sununu, House Minority leader Robert Michel of Illinois, Senate Minority Leader Robert Dole of Kansas, Speaker of the House Thomas Foley of Washington, President Bush, Senate Majority Leader George Mitchell of Maine.

give to the Congress information of the state of the Union, and recommend to their consideration such measures as he shall judge necessary and expedient. . . ."

Each January, the President delivers a formal State of the Union address to Congress, either in person or by special message. In this speech, the President outlines the economic and social problems of the country and suggests legislation to solve them. Early in the year, too, the President submits a budget message. The message asks Congress to appropriate the money thought necessary to run the federal government for the next fiscal year. The President sends additional suggestions and requests to Congress throughout the legislative session.

INFLUENCE ON CONGRESS

Presidents have many ways of pressuring Congress to pass the legislation they want. They wield this influence through speeches, press conferences, and by using the staff and resources of the executive branch. With the media reporting the President's every word, it is relatively easy to rally public support for the administration's programs.

The President may call special sessions of Congress to consider emergency legislation. Because today's congressional sessions run almost year-round, special sessions are seldom needed. In the past, when Congress usually adjourned for the year by midsummer, the special session made more sense.

The Seven "Hats" of the President

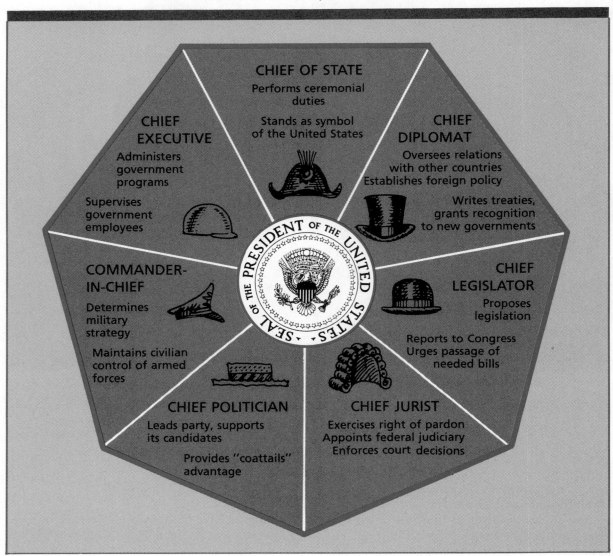

VETO POWER

After weighing the merits of a bill passed by Congress, the President may exercise the veto power and refuse to sign it. The veto (see Chapter Nine, pages 197–218), also gives the President a bargaining chip with Congress. Knowing that a bill faces a veto, congressional leaders often modify legislation to conform more closely with the wishes of the White House. Overriding a veto is a politically dif-

ficult task. Congress scored only 9 victories in 78 attempts when it tried to override President Ronald Reagan's vetoes during his eight years in office.

CHECKS AND BALANCES

As the veto power illustrates, the Framers gave Presidents an important voice in legislative matters. The executive branch can't dominate Congress, however. The President's

■ As the nation's chief executive, the President must work through the White House staff and the Cabinet to make sure that the vast mechanism of government does its job. The first meeting of President Bush's new Cabinet in January 1989 received a great deal of attention from the media. How are Cabinet heads chosen? Which Cabinet positions tend to have the most influence on the President? Has the Cabinet become too large to function well?

role as chief legislator provides an excellent example of the system of checks and balances.

4. What powers does the President exercise as chief executive?

The Constitution declares that the President "shall take care that the laws be faithfully executed." In fulfilling this duty as chief executive—the head of the vast administrative machinery of the federal government—the President affects the lives of all Americans. To help the President with this enormous task, Congress has created 14 *Cabinet* offices (see

Chapters Twelve and Thirteen). These departments employ some three million federal employees to enforce, administer, and direct the course of government. All of them work under presidential supervision.

THE PRESIDENT'S CABINET

Nowhere in the Constitution is there formal language that provides for a Cabinet to advise the President. When Washington formed the first Cabinet in 1789, he used Section 2 of Article II as his authority. This section allows the President to "require the opinion, in writing, of the principal officer in each of the executive departments." That first Cabinet brought together the heads of three depart-

FYI . . .
Development of the Presidency

President	Contributions
George Washington	The first President's every action set precedents that built a firm foundation for later Presidents. He brought dignity and authority to the office, and clarified the vague "executive power" as the President's right to take the initiative in both foreign and domestic affairs.
Thomas Jefferson	Not just a thoughtful contributor to the philosophy of American government, Jefferson left two practical legacies: (1) he was the first "party leader," thus providing the President with a source of political power; and (2) by making the Louisiana Purchase, he brought the doctrine of "implied powers" to life.
Andrew Jackson	The presidency first became a "people's" office under Jackson. By appealing to the public over the head of Congress, and by vigorously wielding the powers of appointment and dismissal, he gained total control of the executive branch. In the nullification dispute, he asserted the federal government's supremacy over the states.
Abraham Lincoln	Lincoln did much more than save the Union. He showed that the President had the authority to master crisis, manage the nation's growing strength, and establish policy that he felt was right, no matter what the opposition.

ments—State, War, and Treasury. Washington also added the Attorney General to the first Cabinet, although the Justice Department wasn't created until 1870.

The top official of 13 of the Cabinet departments carries the title of Secretary (as in Secretary of State). The head of the Justice Department is known as the Attorney General. Each Cabinet secretary oversees a particular area of government as the President's direct agent. Some Presidents have allowed their Cabinet members to argue public issues and

Theodore Roosevelt

Under TR, the presidency moved into the center spotlight of American life. By "carrying a big stick" and using executive powers fully, he helped create a sense of purpose and direction that added greatly to the institution of the presidency.

Woodrow Wilson

Under Wilson, the presidency came to dominate the legislative process. His programs came complete to the last comma, and he pushed them with all his power. He originated the press conference, demonstrating the appeal of forceful, eloquent presidential prose. And he took America into the world, for better or worse.

Franklin Roosevelt

Roosevelt's New Deal restored heart to America when it was needed most. Under his leadership, the country survived the Great Depression and passed safely through World War II—but also gained new insight into the social and economic needs that a compassionate government must meet.

Lyndon Johnson

Johnson's civil rights legislation did much to begin removal of generations of accumulated racial injustice. Because of high costs, however, many of Johnson's social programs have come under increasing attack in recent years.

Ronald Reagan

Reagan rebuilt America's military forces and used that renewed strength to negotiate nuclear disarmament with the Soviets. The Reagan policy of lowering taxes in hopes of increasing production led to huge budget deficits. Despite criticism of his work habits and intellect, he never lost his popularity.

to exert great influence. Other Presidents have turned their Cabinets into instruments whose main job was to carry out presidential policies.

Selection of the Cabinet. Presidents are free to select the members of their Cabinets. A complete changeover usually occurs when a new administration takes office, especially when the opposition party captures the White House. Presidents often appoint experienced national figures to serve in the Cabinet. Several Cabinet positions, however, are usually reserved for key political advisers.

Each nomination requires Senate approval before the new secretary can be sworn in. Almost all candidates are approved. If heavy opposition develops, the President is more likely to withdraw the nomination than to risk defeat on the Senate floor.

Duties of the Cabinet. Secretaries perform three main duties: (1) They manage the affairs of their departments. (2) They represent their departments in public and before Congress by giving speeches, writing legislation, and testifying before committees. (3) They advise the President on matters that concern their departments. Conflicts often arise between Cabinet departments when programs overlap. Who, for instance, should be responsible for the food stamp program—the Department of Agriculture or the Department of Health and Human Services? (The Department of Agriculture won that struggle.)

The Cabinet gathers only at the call of the chief executive. Some Presidents, like Dwight Eisenhower, have used Cabinet meetings to debate important policy decisions. Other Presidents prefer to make their decisions after conferring privately with the individual secretaries. With these Presidents, full-scale Cabinet meetings are largely ceremonial.

EXECUTIVE AUTHORITY

The laws passed by Congress often establish broad guidelines, leaving the President and the executive branch to work out the details. The complex regulations that make the laws more specific are called *executive orders*, and they have the force of law. Over 10,000 executive orders are now in effect. They regulate activities as diverse as aircraft flight patterns and the Peace Corps. The Supreme Court sometimes intervenes to strike down an executive order that the justices believe exceeds constitutional limits.

The President also exercises executive powers, as granted by the Constitution, to appoint federal officials. Under Civil Service laws this *patronage* power is limited to the highest ranking positions. These top executives, who include ambassadors to foreign countries, make up less than one percent of federal civil servants. As with Cabinet posts, most of these appointments require Senate approval.

The President's powers include *dismissal* of these same high officials. Exceptions to this rule include federal judges and officials of the regulatory agencies established by Congress. No constitutional basis for dismissal exists except through the use of impeachment. Nevertheless, tradition requires that officials who serve "at the President's pleasure" step aside when the President asks for their resignation.

Let's review for a moment

According to tradition, many parents look fondly at their newborn babies and say, "You can grow up to be President." That's not unreasonable because the Constitution says that almost all adult Americans are eligible. The President must be at least 35 years old, a natural-born citizen, and a 14-year resident of the United States. A look at history reveals many unwritten rules. Most Presidents have had experience gained in state or federal service along with a legal or military background.

Who elects America's Presidents? We all do—or do we? Read the fine print on a presidential ballot. People are really voting for electors, not a President. Designed to meet eighteenth-century needs, the *Electoral College* has at least one major flaw: the system can select a President who didn't win a majority of the popular votes.

The President wears many hats. As chief of state, the President is the living symbol of the nation. He shakes hands at White House receptions, welcomes foreign visitors, and speaks at the dedication of a new monument to the nation's war dead.

In the role of chief legislator, a President cannot pass a law, of course. The President, however, does influence Congress (1) by sending messages recommending new legislation, (2) by mobilizing public support for a bill, and (3) by using the veto power.

■ The U.S. President consults regularly with leaders of other countries. In July 1990, leaders of the seven major industrial democratic nations met in Houston, Texas, to discuss economic issues. From the left, European Community President Jacques Delors, Prime Minister Giulio Andreotti of Italy, Chancellor Helmut Kohl of then West Germany, President François Mitterand of France, President Bush, then Prime Minister Margaret Thatcher of Great Britain, Prime Minister Brian Mulroney of Canada, and Prime Minister Toshiki Kaifu of Japan.

As chief executive, the President administers the nation's laws. With the aid of the *Cabinet*, the President conducts the nation's business and determines the priorities of government. At the same time, the President oversees the day-to-day work of several million employees of the executive branch.

That sounds like a full-time job, doesn't it? Wait, there's more. Among many other duties, the President might be called on to update a nuclear arms treaty with the Soviet Union. Let's see how our chief diplomat handles this important task.

5. How does the President represent the United States as its chief diplomat?

When giving a luncheon for a visiting prime minister, the President is the nation's chief of state. Later that afternoon, when the two heads of government sit down to talk about a new trade treaty, the President acts as the country's chief diplomat. The President's powers in the conduct of foreign affairs include (1) the initiation of foreign policy, (2) the recognition of new foreign governments, and (3) the making of treaties.

INITIATING FOREIGN POLICY

The President's personal philosophy colors many aspects of U.S. relations with foreign countries. A number of important foreign policy decisions from our past retain the names of the Presidents who originated them. These "doctrines" represent broad policy guidelines or statements of the U.S. government's goals. The Monroe Doctrine of 1823 and the Truman Doctrine of 1947 are two examples. The Monroe Doctrine warned European powers not to interfere in Latin America. The Truman Doctrine dedicated the United States to the task of stopping the spread of communism.

Beginning with Woodrow Wilson, American Presidents have traveled abroad to meet with foreign heads of state. These *summit conferences* give leaders a chance to meet and to work out agreements regarding defense, trade, and other aspects of international relations. Technical advice on these trips comes from the Secretary of State and the State Department. The State Department also handles the day-to-day conduct of foreign affairs.

RECOGNIZING FOREIGN GOVERNMENTS

The President, on behalf of the United States, decides whether or not to accept the legal existence of another government. This is called the power of *diplomatic recognition*. Recognition does not mean that the United States supports the policies of the foreign government. Indeed, the United States has diplomatic relations with a number of countries whose governments pursue anti-American policies. If diplomatic relations worsen, the President has the power to withdraw all American diplomats from a country it once recognized.

Peaceful changes of government in foreign countries seldom disrupt diplomatic relations. If the change has been a violent one, the United States must decide whether or not to recognize the new government. Once diplomatic recognition is granted, formal relations between the two countries can be resumed. The power of diplomatic recognition gives the President a useful option. Only after a country has been recognized can it receive military or economic aid, take part in trade agreements, or have the right to set up an embassy and consulates in the United States.

MAKING TREATIES

In past centuries, the term *treaty* often referred to secret diplomatic agreements that bound nations to come to each other's aid in the event of war. This concept of "secret treaties" seldom applies today. The United States openly negotiates a great number of treaties with other countries. Some are military treaties, but most involve agreements on water rights, fishing grounds, international trade, economic aid, exchange of diplomats, and similar matters. As chief diplomat, the President takes final responsibility for all treaties. The signed documents are presented to the Senate for approval. Unless two-thirds of the senators present vote to ratify a treaty, it cannot take effect—even though the President has already signed it.

Emergencies sometimes force a President to negotiate a treaty quickly, without waiting for Senate approval. When this happens, the President issues an executive order, which carries the force of a formal treaty. President Franklin Roosevelt signed a famous agreement of that type in 1941. The "Lend-Lease" plan provided much-needed military aid to Great Britain for use in the war with Nazi Germany. Critics of presidential power have worried about this method of bypassing the Senate's control over treaties. Despite the criticism, all attempts to limit the President's treaty-making powers by means of a constitutional amendment have failed.

6. How does the President serve as chief politician?

Some Americans are surprised when the President takes an active role in national politics. If questioned, they'd say that the occupant of the White House should not become involved in the gritty details of political campaigning. In the real world, however, no President can afford to follow an "above-the-battle" policy. Presidents get involved in politics because they need legislators in Congress who will support the administration's programs. In addition, Presidents use political "muscle" to maintain party discipline in the face of challenges by the opposition party.

Even when the President's own party controls Congress, passage of an administration's legislative program requires great political skill on the part of the President. It's not unusual for small factions within the President's own party to band together for the purpose of driving a hard political bargain. "We'll vote for the budget decrease," the faction may tell the President, "if you'll drop your opposition to the program we favor." If the opposition party gains a majority in Congress, the President's job becomes even more difficult.

Presidents possess a useful arsenal of weapons with which to change the minds of reluctant members of Congress. These include: (1) Contacts with key legislators, either by phone

■ The wives of Presidents aid their husbands in many ways. Here, in 1979, Rosalyn Carter, wife of President Jimmy Carter, entertains Madam Cho Lin, wife of the head of China, at a time when the United States was re-establishing full diplomatic relations with China.

■ President George Bush at a news conference in the White House. Bush has held many meetings with the news media, often on short notice. Why are news conferences important?

■ Along with social duties, First Ladies are expected to devote themselves to worthwhile social causes. Barbara Bush, wife of President George Bush promotes the cause of literacy. She is shown reading to youngsters at a day-care center in Washington, D.C.

or in person. (2) Suggestions that the President might support or oppose "pet" bills or projects greatly desired by the members of Congress whose support the administration needs. (3) Withholding of federal spending for projects in the home districts of uncooperative legislators—or promises of increased spending for "friendly" lawmakers. (4) Requests for loyalty and cooperation "for the good of the party." (5) Direct appeals to the public. The President may go on television to ask the people to let Congress know that they approve of the administration's stand on an issue.

If the people like a President, they tend to vote for other members of the President's party. These national, state, and local politicians are said to "ride into office on the President's coattails." Some political analysts believe that the *"coattail effect"* no longer works its old magic. Even so, Presidents work hard at "grass roots" politics in order to win support for their policies.

The occupants of the White House have a built-in ability to make news. Whether Presidents are giving speeches, posing for pictures with local politicians, or handing out government jobs and money, the media flock to cover their activities. Newspaper reporters and television cameras follow every move. At election time, these activities pay off. Pollsters estimate that an incumbent President starts with an edge of five percentage points over any opponent. In this century, nine of the thirteen Presidents who ran for a second term were reelected.

7. Why does the President serve as commander-in-chief of the armed forces?

Imagine an Armed Forces Day review, with long lines of troops passing in front of the nation's top military commanders. Almost lost in the crowd of generals and admirals, one

FYI . . .
Practical Limitations on Presidential Power

Limitation	Discussion
Permissibility	No President may do anything that is not acceptable to the great body of public opinion, is illegal, unworkable, or unenforceable.
Available Resources	Since resources are always limited, the President must establish priorities for the best use of existing money, manpower, time, brains, and material.
Available Time	Deadlines and schedules exist for Presidents as well as everyone else. The budget is due by a certain date; military weapons take years to build; a term lasts only four years.
Previous Commitments	Presidents cannot escape the precedents set by former Presidents. Decisions made by Washington, Lincoln, and FDR still influence and bind them. Even their own actions become precedents. Once started, a course of action cannot easily be abandoned.
Available Information	Any presidential action is no better than the information on which it is based. How can a President know that a briefing is accurate? Is it complete, giving both sides of an issue?
Personality	Presidents bring their likes and dislikes, education, political philosophies, and life experiences to the conduct of the executive office. Their capacity for work and decision making also enter into the equation. Most of all, Presidents need the type of political genius that enables them to inspire and lead the American people.
Political Realities	Time and circumstances impose their own limits. FDR's New Deal would have died a quick death in the courts just a few years earlier. Johnson probably could not have recognized the People's Republic of China; Nixon could and did.

person in a business suit holds center stage. That civilian, the President of the United States, returns the soldiers' salutes as their commander-in-chief. The scene is a reminder that the Constitution puts ultimate control of the armed forces in civilian hands.

LESSONS OF HISTORY

History provides abundant reasons for placing the armed forces under the direction of a civilian government. The Declaration of Independence cites British attempts to "render the Military independent of, and superior to, the Civil power," as one of the causes of the Revolution. One need look no farther than this hemisphere, in fact, to draw an object lesson from Latin America's experience with military dictatorships. Many Latin American countries lack the firm tradition needed to keep their armed forces from overthrowing civilian rul-

■ President Harry Truman and General Douglas MacArthur on Wake Island in 1950. The following April (1951), the President relieved the general of his command on grounds of insubordination. Under what constitutional authority does the President exercise this power?

ers. As a result, government after government has fallen in and out of the hands of military dictators.

A dramatic test of civilian versus military control of the armed forces came during the Korean War in the early 1950s. General Douglas MacArthur, World War II hero and commander of the United Nations forces in Korea, wanted to expand the war into China. This policy brought MacArthur into direct conflict with his commander-in-chief, President Harry Truman. Truman believed that the political risks outweighed military concerns. He ordered the Air Force not to bomb the Chinese bases in Manchuria. When MacArthur criticized this decision in public, Truman fired him. The country gave the returning general a hero's welcome, but the armed forces remained loyal to their civilian commander-in-chief.

FINAL MILITARY AUTHORITY

As commander-in-chief, the President does much more than pin medals on military heroes. From the White House come far-reaching decisions that direct the American military in times of war and peace. In 1945, for example, Harry Truman made the decision to drop the atomic bomb on Japan. In a more recent example, George Bush sent U.S. forces into Saudi Arabia in 1990. Their mission was to help protect oil-rich Saudi Arabia from attack by Iraq, which had taken over neighboring Kuwait.

THE ROLE OF CONGRESS

The President does not have absolute control of the military. The Constitution gives Congress, not the President, the right to declare war. Franklin Roosevelt, for example, had to go before Congress to ask for a declaration of war the day after the Japanese attacked Pearl Harbor.

Nevertheless, many of our wars have not been formally declared. The Barbary War and the Civil War in the 1800s, Korea and Vietnam in this century, are examples of undeclared wars. In these cases, Presidents believed that political considerations made a formal declaration of war undesirable. Should the President have the power to order military action without the approval of Congress? The feeling that Presidents Johnson and Nixon abused this power in Vietnam led to the passage of the War Powers Resolution of 1973. This law states that the President must win congressional approval before committing troops for any lengthy period of time.

Congressional restrictions on the use of the armed forces have worried foreign policy experts in the White House, the Pentagon, and the State Department. They point to such successful examples of presidential freedom of action as Eisenhower's use of Marines in Lebanon in 1958 and Kennedy's dispatch of troops to Thailand in 1962. In both cases, prompt American responses prevented Communist takeovers in those countries. In 1983, the Supreme Court sharply limited the ability of Congress to interfere with the President's military actions. The ruling, which limited the use of the legislative veto in such laws as the War Powers Resolution, was considered a victory for the executive branch.

WARTIME POWERS

Along with directing battlefield strategy, the President holds extraordinary powers over domestic life during wartime emergencies. With congressional approval, the President may be empowered to (1) control all industrial efforts related to the war; (2) place ceilings on wages and prices; (3) regulate or ration food, clothing, and manufactured items; and (4) suspend some personal freedoms if such action becomes necessary to safeguard the war effort. The President must give up these near-dictatorial powers once the emergency has passed.

8. How does the President function as chief jurist?

Just as the Constitution gives the executive branch a voice in legislative matters, so does it give the President a direct hand in judicial matters. As provided by law, the President (1) appoints all judges of the federal judiciary, plus the marshals of the courts; (2) grants *pardons* to individuals accused or convicted of crimes; and (3) takes responsibility for carrying out court orders and decisions.

JUDICIAL APPOINTMENTS

Before the President fills a judicial post, most candidates must meet two tests: demonstrated competency in the law and solid credentials as a member of the President's own party. Republican Presidents usually pick Republi-

■ As the nation's chief jurist, Presidents select the judges who sit on the Supreme Court. When President Ronald Reagan chose a new associate justice in 1981, he made history by appointing Sandra Day O'Connor of Arizona the first woman justice. From the left: Nancy Reagan, President Reagan, Chief Justice Warren Burger, and the newly sworn in Justice O'Connor.

can judges; Democratic Presidents select from among qualified Democrats. White House staffers begin the selection process by preparing lists of qualified candidates. The lists are based on recommendations from bar associations, working judges, and party officials. As with most presidential appointments, the Senate must confirm the men and women selected to serve on the federal bench.

PARDON—THE FINAL APPEAL

President Ford made headlines and started a major controversy in 1974 by offering ex-President Nixon a "full, free, and absolute pardon . . . for all offenses against the United States." Once he was pardoned, Nixon could not be prosecuted for his part in the Watergate coverup. Many people objected to the pardon, but Ford's use of this constitutional privilege could not be challenged in Congress or in the courts. Most presidential pardons are issued after the courts have passed sentence. Ford's action, however, shows that a pardon can be given before a trial is held.

When considering a pardon, the nation's chief jurist has three choices: (1) The President may grant a full pardon, which restores civil rights, ends punishment or prevents it, and grants legal forgiveness for any criminal acts. (2) If the individual has already served time in prison, the President may *commute* the sentence. This either shortens the sentence or

Learning Skills

Interpreting Editorial Cartoons

Everyone who reads a newspaper is familiar with the cartoons that the editors use to brighten their pages. The day's news may be grim, but *Peanuts*, *Garfield*, and *The Far Side* almost always bring a smile to the reader's face. These cartoons sometimes make a social or political point, but their main purpose is to amuse.

The cartoons that appear on the editorial pages of a newspaper have a more serious purpose. An editorial cartoon may be funny, but its main purpose is to lead you to think seriously about an important issue. An editorial writer may use a thousand words to warn about the dangers of inflation, but a good cartoonist can present that very same message with a single drawing. The best editorial cartoons are built around easy-to-recognize figures and symbols. A single glance is enough to identify former President Reagan's familiar hairdo or Cuban President Fidel Castro's beard and cigar. Similarly, it's hard to misread the Statue of Liberty (freedom), an ICBM (the threat of nuclear war), and a fat, five-star general (Pentagon waste).

In simplifying their message, cartoonists tend to load the issue in favor of one side or the other. If you're not careful, you might "buy" the argument without thinking about it. For example, President Reagan inspired a number of editorial cartoons when he sent

cuts it off at the time served to date. (3) The President may grant a *reprieve*. This temporarily postpones execution of a sentence, whether it is payment of a fine, imprisonment, or death.

The President's power to pardon applies only to certain types of criminal cases. It extends to military as well as to civilian courts—but not to state courts. In addition, the President may not pardon a federal official who has been impeached and convicted.

CARRYING OUT COURT ORDERS

Presidents must carry out and enforce court decisions, even when they disagree with the rulings. In 1831, President Andrew Jackson directly challenged this constitutional requirement. When he received a Supreme Court decision involving Cherokee Indian lands, Jackson blustered, "John Marshall [the Chief Justice] has made his decision; now let him enforce it." Despite the President's duty under the Constitution to "take care that the laws be faithfully executed," Jackson defied the Supreme Court. The Indians lost their land and were forced to make a long march west to Oklahoma Territory.

Jackson's resistance did not set a precedent. In 1974, for example, President Nixon obeyed the Supreme Court, even though it was clear that the decision might cost him the presidency. Ordered to surrender the Watergate-

U.S. troops to the Caribbean island of Grenada in 1983. The President's critics accused him of using military force in the same way that the Soviets were using force in Afghanistan. Reagan's supporters were equally certain that the landings in Grenada prevented Communists from gaining access to a major airfield that Castro's workers were building on Grenada. The cartoons here represent these two points of view. What does Bob Englehart's cartoon (page 260) say about Grenada? What kind of response does John Deering's cartoon (page 261) make? Who makes the best argument?

As you can see, there's not much subtlety in an editorial cartoon. Flip through the pages of this book and find some additional examples. After looking at each one, write out your own analysis of the message. Does the cartoonist favor the Republican or Democratic side of political issues? Big business or consumers? Growth and development or environmental concerns? Compare your interpretations with those of your classmates.

Next, clip the editorial cartoons in a local newspaper for a week and interpret each one. Does the cartoonist's political philosophy support or conflict with the general editorial position of the newspaper? Watch for cartoons that take different sides of the same issue. In no time at all, you'll be an expert at interpreting these amusing, thought-provoking editorial statements.

JOHN DEERING
Courtesy Arkansas Democrat

■ Vice President Dan Quayle (right) in Venezuela in 1989 for the inauguration of the new Venezuelan president Carlos Andres Perez (left). Recent Vice Presidents have been given more to do than was once the case.

related tapes and records, Nixon bowed to the high court (and public opinion) and handed over the incriminating evidence.

9. What is the role of the Vice President?

The modern vice presidency was born in 1804, when the Twelfth Amendment was added to the Constitution. Previously, electors had voted for two people for President. The candidate who came in second became Vice President. Starting with the election of 1804, the electors have voted separately for President and Vice President. American voters do not have the same choice. They must cast their ballots for the presidential and vice presidential candidates of the same party.

Opponents of the Twelfth Amendment predicted that future Vice Presidents would be "carried into the market to be exchanged for the votes of some large states for President." As cynical as it sounds, that prediction has largely come true. Most vice presidential candidates know when they accept their nominations that they have been selected mainly to *"balance the ticket."* If the party nominates a southerner for President, it will almost certainly select someone from a different region for Vice President. A balanced ticket appeals to voters throughout the country and avoids bitter disputes within the party.

The practice of using the vice presidential nomination to attract votes led to a history-making change in American politics in 1984. The Democrats nominated Geraldine Ferraro, a member of Congress from New York, as their candidate for Vice President. By selecting a woman to run for the nation's second highest office, the Democrats were hoping that female voters would rally to the support of Walter Mondale, their presidential candidate. The Mondale-Ferraro ticket failed to develop a strong following, and the Democrats were buried by a Reagan landslide.

DUTIES OF THE VICE PRESIDENT

Given only a single constitutional duty—that of presiding over the Senate—Vice Presidents labor in a political vacuum. A Vice President's major responsibility is to be ready at any time to replace the President. The first holder of the job suggested that his title should be "His Superfluous Excellency." Thomas Marshall, Vice President under Woodrow Wilson, liked to tell this story:

"There were once two brothers. One ran away to sea. The other was elected Vice President and neither was heard of again."

In recent years, Presidents have made a serious effort to increase the importance of the Vice President's job. A 1949 law gave the "veep" a seat on the National Security Council. Vice Presidents have also been invited to

FYI . . .
Presidents Need to Laugh

The tensions and pressures of life in the White House can wear out a President who lacks a sense of humor. A good laugh restores balance and puts events into perspective. The following stories are good examples of this saving grace.

Abraham Lincoln: Lincoln often used humor to relieve tension or to make a point. As he was leaving for Gettysburg to dedicate the new national cemetery, his aides worried that he might miss the train.

"You fellows remind me of the day they were going to hang the horse thief," Lincoln said. "The road to the hanging place was so crowded with people going to the execution that the wagon taking the prisoner was delayed. As more and more people crowded ahead, the prisoner called out, 'What's your hurry? There ain't goin' to be any fun till I get there!' "

Theodore Roosevelt: Friends and foes both agreed that nothing could stop TR once he had made up his mind. Even so, the President apparently met his match in his young daughter, Alice. The President was trying to talk to a friend one day, but Alice kept running in and out of the office.

"Theodore," the man complained, "isn't there anything you can do to control Alice?"

"I can do one of two things," TR replied. "I can be President of the United States, or I can control Alice. I cannot possibly do both."

Calvin Coolidge: "Silent Cal" was a man of few words. The President didn't need words to exercise his sly sense of humor, however. At one breakfast meeting, Coolidge carefully poured his coffee and cream into a saucer. Anxious to be polite, some of his guests did the same. Then they waited for Coolidge to sip coffee from his own saucer. Instead, the President smiled, leaned down, and put the saucer on the floor for the cat.

Harry Truman: Truman was a down-to-earth Missourian who enjoyed a good joke. He pulled one of his best in 1945, when he took an old friend named Fred Canfil to an important meeting with Josef Stalin, leader of the Soviet Union. Knowing that Stalin liked to be called by his military title, Truman introduced Canfil to the Russian by saying, "Marshal Stalin, I want you to meet Marshal Canfil." Truman didn't tell Stalin that Canfil was really a federal marshal—a job that's roughly equal to that of a county sheriff. Thanks to the impressive title, Stalin and the other Soviets treated Canfil with all the courtesy due an official of highest rank.

Richard Nixon: Nixon's loss to John Kennedy in 1960 came in one of American history's closest elections. After hearing Kennedy's inaugural address, Nixon met one of the President's aides.

"I wish I had said some of those things," Nixon said.

"What part?" the aide wanted to know. "That part about 'Ask not what your country can do for you . . .'?"

"No," Nixon said. "The part that starts, 'I do solemnly swear.' "

Ronald Reagan: The good-natured Reagan often came up with a one-liner when things looked dark. He needed all of his famous sense of humor in 1981 after he was shot by a would-be assassin. Despite his serious chest wound, Reagan smiled at his doctors as he was wheeled into the operating room. "Please assure me that you are all Republicans," he said.

■ Vice Presidents don't have many official duties until that dramatic moment when they succeed to the presidency. Here, Lyndon Johnson takes the oath of office aboard an airplane following the assassination of John Kennedy in Dallas, Texas, in 1963. Jacqueline Kennedy (right), the slain President's widow, stands at the side of the new President. On Johnson's right is his wife, "Ladybird."

sit in on Cabinet meetings. Two recent Vice Presidents, Walter Mondale and George Bush, have chaired important presidential councils and handled overseas assignments. President Reagan, for example, sent Bush to Argentina, Austria, Italy, Morocco, Yugoslavia, and other countries as his personal representative.

ACCESSION TO THE PRESIDENCY

Despite these increased duties, the Vice President has little power and influence—until the death or disability of the President. When President Eisenhower was asked in 1960 to name one major decision that Vice President Nixon had influenced, he was unable to do so. That wasn't completely fair because Nixon had presided over Cabinet meetings as an unofficial acting President during Eisenhower's recovery from a heart attack. Eight of our Presidents have died in office and one has resigned. Each time, the Vice President has assumed the powers of the presidency.

Because of the increasing physical and mental strain that goes with being President, the casualty rate in the White House has been rising. Eight of the sixteen presidents between 1900 and 1988 have either died or spent time in the hospital while in office. Because of this uncertainty, today's Vice Presidents might disagree with John Garner, who was one of Franklin Roosevelt's Vice Presidents. The salty Texan once drawled, "Being Vice President of the United States ain't worth a bucket of warm spit."

THE TWENTY-FIFTH AMENDMENT

Serious constitutional questions regarding presidential disability and succession were answered by the Twenty-fifth Amendment (1967).

Presidential disability. Several times in our history, the President has been disabled for long periods. Garfield, Wilson, and Eisenhower were among them. With no machinery or precedents available, their Vice Presidents could not assume, even temporarily, the official duties of the presidency. Now, the Twenty-fifth Amendment specifies a procedure first worked out by Eisenhower and Nixon in 1958. The amendment provides that:

1. The Vice President can take over when the President notifies the President *pro tempore* of the Senate and the Speaker of the House in writing that "he is unable to discharge the powers and duties of his office."

2. Should the President be unable or unwilling to write this letter, the Vice President, with the approval of a majority of the Cabinet, may notify Congress of the President's disability. In this case, too, the Vice President serves as a temporary President. Should the President challenge the action of the Vice President and the Cabinet majority, Congress has the power to decide the question. A two-thirds vote of both houses is required to confirm the President's disability.

Presidential succession. The United States has never faced a situation in which both the President and Vice President died at the same time. If that should happen, the Presidential Succession Act of 1947 spells out the process for choosing a President. The Speaker of the House is first in the line of *succession,* followed by the President *pro tempore* of the Senate. If neither of these two officials can serve, the Secretary of State becomes President. After that, the succession passes down through a list of other Cabinet members.

If a Cabinet member should become President, it would not be the first time the United States was governed by a chief executive who was not an elected President or Vice President. The unusual chain of events started in 1973 when Vice President Agnew's resignation triggered the succession procedures spelled out in the Twenty-fifth Amendment. President Nixon nominated Gerald Ford, a Republican member of Congress, to replace Agnew. Congress quickly approved the choice. When Nixon resigned in 1974, Vice President Ford was elevated to the presidency. Ford, in turn, nominated Nelson Rockefeller, a former governor of New York, to take his place. Rockefeller became the nation's second nonelected Vice President. Thus, until Jimmy Carter was inaugurated in 1977, the two top jobs in the executive branch were held by men who had not been elected to their positions.

10. What is the job of the President's Executive Office?

One of the President's tasks is to direct the activities of all the departments, agencies, and commissions that make up the executive branch. To help the President manage this complex operation, the *Executive Office* coordinates the day-to-day flow of government business. It also advises the President on the most sensitive national and international matters. Established in 1939, the Executive Office actually consists of a number of separate offices and councils. All are directly responsible to the President.

THE JOBS OF THE EXECUTIVE OFFICE

The White House Staff. The White House Staff serves the President much as a military staff serves a general. The Chief of Staff heads up a team of special assistants, counselors, and secretaries who manage the President's daily affairs. Many staff members are long-term associates of the President. Others are recruited from universities or from the ranks of the President's political allies.

Although White House staff members stay in the background, Washington insiders know that they have political "clout." It is the Chief of Staff, for example, who arranges the President's schedule and controls access to the Oval Office. Presidential decisions are further influenced by the way in which the staff summarizes the arguments for and against each action. The staff also represents the President in meetings with Congress, the executive departments, the press, and the general public.

Office of Management and Budget. Managing the immense federal budget is the duty of the Office of Management and Budget.

■ President Bush and the White House staff share a lighthearted moment. Chief of Staff John Sununu is at the President's left. The staff tries to make sure that the President's workday goes smoothly. They draw up papers on policy matters, write speeches, set schedules, brief reporters, and keep the President informed about national and world events.

(For a summary of the OMB role in the budgetary process, see pages 231–232.) OMB economists and many other specialists advise the President on money matters, particularly in the areas of controlling the budget and evaluating the performance of federal programs. The importance of the OMB has increased greatly since the nation began struggling with serious budget deficits.

National Security Council. The National Security Council is one of the key policymaking bodies in the federal government. The National Security Adviser coordinates military activities with other agencies of government and advises the President on all aspects of national security. As a rule, the council meets weekly, but it may meet more often during emergencies. The other members of the NSC include the Vice President, the secretaries of State and Defense, the Chairman of the Joint Chiefs of Staff, and the Director of the Central Intelligence Agency. Research papers and plans prepared by the Department

of Defense, the Nuclear Regulatory Commission, the OMB, and other agencies supply the information the NSC needs for its decision making.

The NSC usually works quietly, but it drew national attention to the White House in 1987. The Reagan administration revealed that the NSC had been involved in a secret, possibly illegal plan to support the Nicaraguan Contras (forces opposed to the government in power in Nicaragua). The plan was funded with money diverted from the sale of arms to Iran. Members of Congress asked sharp questions about the President's apparent lack of control over the NSC. A Special Prosecutor was appointed and brought criminal charges against the members of the NSC who had taken part in the affair.

Office of Policy Development. The Office of Policy Development handles domestic problems, much as the NSC deals with foreign ones. The OPD helps the President assess national needs, recommends policies and pro-

FYI . . .
Fighting Drug Problems

Congress passed an omnibus drug bill in 1988 that committed more money and effort toward solving the nation's growing drug problem. The most widely publicized part of the bill was the creation of a cabinet-level position called the Director of the White House Office of National Drug Control Policy. When President Bush appointed William Bennett to the post, the former Secretary of Education was quickly dubbed the "drug czar." Although the director's job is to coordinate the government's drug-fighting programs, he can't force a department to follow his suggestions. As Bennett warmed to the task, the new czar proposed action on three fronts. First, he promised to beef up efforts to cut off the flow of drugs into the country. Second, he vowed that government would come down harder on both drug dealers and drug users. And third, he set himself the task of developing better drug education programs. In the long term, Bennett believes, there wouldn't be a problem if Americans refused to buy illegal drugs.

■ Drug czar William Bennett talking with young people about the evils of drug use and the need to stop the sale of drugs. What is the current status of the war on drugs?

grams, and oversees ongoing programs. Working through a series of project committees, the OPD may deal with broad program areas (national energy policy) or specific problems (cleaning up toxic wastes).

Council of Economic Advisers. Highly respected economists advise the President on all matters relating to the economic health of the country. The Council's members develop policies and programs that the President uses

PRESIDENTS OF THE UNITED STATES

Name	Party	Native state	Born–Died	Served
1. George Washington	Fed.	Va.	1732–1799	1789–1797
2. John Adams	Fed.	Mass.	1735–1826	1797–1801
3. Thomas Jefferson	Dem.-Rep.	Va.	1743–1826	1801–1809
4. James Madison	Dem.-Rep.	Va.	1751–1836	1809–1817
5. James Monroe	Dem.-Rep.	Va.	1758–1831	1817–1825
6. John Quincy Adams	Dem.-Rep.	Mass.	1767–1848	1825–1829
7. Andrew Jackson	Dem.	S.C.	1767–1845	1829–1837
8. Martin Van Buren	Dem.	N.Y.	1782–1862	1837–1841
9. William H. Harrison	Whig	Va.	1773–1841	1841
10. John Tyler	Whig	Va.	1790–1862	1841–1845
11. James K. Polk	Dem.	N.C.	1795–1849	1845–1849
12. Zachary Taylor	Whig	Va.	1784–1850	1849–1850
13. Millard Fillmore	Whig	N.Y.	1800–1874	1850–1853
14. Franklin Pierce	Dem.	N.H.	1804–1869	1853–1857
15. James Buchanan	Dem.	Pa.	1791–1868	1857–1861
16. Abraham Lincoln	Rep.	Ky.	1809–1865	1861–1865
17. Andrew Johnson	Nat. Union	N.C.	1808–1875	1865–1869
18. Ulysses S. Grant	Rep.	Ohio	1822–1885	1869–1877
19. Rutherford B. Hayes	Rep.	Ohio	1822–1893	1877–1881
20. James A. Garfield	Rep.	Ohio	1831–1881	1881
21. Chester A. Arthur	Rep.	Vt.	1830–1886	1881–1885
22. Grover Cleveland	Dem.	N.J.	1837–1908	1885–1889
23. Benjamin Harrison	Rep.	Ohio	1833–1901	1889–1893
24. Grover Cleveland	Dem.	N.J.	1837–1908	1893–1897
25. William McKinley	Rep.	Ohio	1843–1901	1897–1901
26. Theodore Roosevelt	Rep.	N.Y.	1858–1919	1901–1909
27. William H. Taft	Rep.	Ohio	1857–1930	1909–1913
28. Woodrow Wilson	Dem.	Va.	1856–1924	1913–1921
29. Warren G. Harding	Rep.	Ohio	1865–1923	1921–1923
30. Calvin Coolidge	Rep.	Vt.	1872–1933	1923–1929
31. Herbert C. Hoover	Rep.	Iowa	1874–1964	1929–1933
32. Franklin D. Roosevelt	Dem.	N.Y.	1882–1945	1933–1945
33. Harry S Truman	Dem.	Mo.	1884–1972	1945–1953
34. Dwight D. Eisenhower	Rep.	Texas	1890–1969	1953–1961
35. John F. Kennedy	Dem.	Mass.	1917–1963	1961–1963
36. Lyndon B. Johnson	Dem.	Texas	1908–1973	1963–1969
37. Richard M. Nixon	Rep.	Calif.	1913–	1969–1974
38. Gerald R. Ford	Rep.	Neb.	1913–	1974–1977
39. Jimmy Carter	Dem.	Ga.	1924–	1977–1981
40. Ronald W. Reagan	Rep.	Ill.	1911–	1981–1989
41. George H. W. Bush	Rep.	Conn.	1924–	1989–

to combat problems such as unemployment and the overseas trade deficit.

THE BURDEN OF THE PRESIDENCY

Even with the aid of the Executive Office, the President carries an enormous burden. Harry Truman liked to say, "The buck stops here." He meant that after all the staff work has been done, the responsibility for making decisions rests on the occupant of the Oval Office. Warren G. Harding, overwhelmed by the office, could only moan, "My God, this is a hell of a job!'' Many political scientists doubt that any one person can fulfill all the responsibilities and expectations that have been concentrated in this one office.

Even so, the voters turn out to elect a President every four years. Sometimes they reelect the incumbent and sometimes they choose a new and untested candidate. For the most part, the leaders elected to the office have responded to the trust placed in them. The feature on pages 250–251 reviews the contributions some outstanding Presidents have made to the office.

Reviewing
what you've learned

1. Out of millions of Americans, one emerges every four years to serve as President. The qualifications listed in the Constitution are few. A candidate must be age 35 or over, a natural-born citizen, and resident in this country for at least 14 years. In addition, Americans demand maturity, experience, leadership, and moral stature.

2. Presidents are not elected by the popular vote. It is the *Electoral College* that makes the final decision on who has won the presidency. Thus, it is possible that the candidate receiving the highest popular vote might not be elected President. Moreover, electors are not legally bound by the ballots cast by the voters in their states.

3. On any given day, the President may begin by acting as "chief of state," the ceremonial head of government. Later that same day, the President may serve as "chief legislator" in a meeting with congressional leaders to discuss an important bill. The President might then put on the hat of "chief executive" while conducting the daily business of government. This includes signing *executive orders*, meeting with the Cabinet, and overseeing the work of the federal bureaucracy.

4. As "chief diplomat," the President formulates and carries out the nation's foreign policy. The President exchanges visits with other heads of state, receives foreign diplomats, negotiates *treaties*, establishes trade relations, and extends *diplomatic recognition*. Many of these decisions require Senate approval. As "chief politician" and party leader, the President tries to "sell" the party's program and candidates to the public.

5. When military decisions must be made, the President becomes "commander-in-chief," ready to issue orders involving troop movements, strategic battlefield decisions, and wartime emergency measures on the home front. As commander-in-chief, the President maintains strict civilian control of the armed forces.

6. The President uses his authority as "chief jurist" to grant a *pardon* or a *reprieve* or to *commute* the sentence of an accused or convicted person. The President also appoints all members of the federal judiciary, including the members of the Supreme Court. Under the system of checks and balances, the President is also responsible for enforcing court decisions.

7. Aside from waiting to move into the White House in the event of the President's death or disability, the Vice President's only constitutional duty is to preside over the Senate. Recent Presidents have given their Vice Presidents added duties. These include attending *Cabinet* meetings, representing the administration overseas, and overseeing the work of government agencies.

8. The President relies on the *Executive Office* to provide the information, coordination, and counsel needed to run the government. The agencies of the Executive Office have a hand in almost all policy decisions made in the White House.

9. The presidency is more than the sum of its parts. It administers, legislates, makes policy, manages, and commands. At best, it offers the nation the closest thing Americans have to a symbol of their own identity. The nation looks to the White House for moral leadership, a sense of purpose, and a ready response to its needs.

Review questions and activities

"balance the ticket"	dismissal	patronage
Cabinet	Electoral College	reprieve
"coattail effect"	Executive Office	succession
commander-in-chief	executive order	summit conference
commuted sentence	pardon	treaty
diplomatic recognition		

REVIEW QUESTIONS

Select the response that best completes each statement or question.

1. Which of the following people would *not* be permitted to run for President under the Constitution? (*a*) A 37-year-old black woman. (*b*) The governor of Hawaii, born in Japan to American parents. (*c*) An 80-year-old man with only an elementary school education. (*d*) A well-known American diplomat who has spent the last six years outside the country. (*e*) All would be eligible.

2. Under the Twenty-second Amendment, the maximum time a President may serve is (*a*) four years. (*b*) eight years. (*c*) almost ten years. (*d*) almost twelve years. (*e*) no limit.

3. Which of the following would *not* be an example of the President's duties as chief of state? (*a*) Entertaining the British monarch. (*b*) Sending a message to Congress asking for money to build a space lab. (*c*) Signing an army officer's commission. (*d*) Awarding a medal for bravery to a Girl Scout. (*e*) Inviting a jazz musician to play at the White House.

4. When actually administering the federal government and its many programs and employees, the President is serving as (*a*) chief of state. (*b*) chief executive. (*c*) commander-in-chief. (*d*) chief politician. (*e*) none of these.

5. Which of the following officeholders could *not* be dismissed by a President? (*a*) A federal court of appeals judge. (*b*) The Secretary of State. (*c*) The Director of the Office of Management and Budget. (*d*) The Attorney General. (*e*) All can be dismissed as they all are appointed officials.

6. Rules and regulations written by the executive branch and signed by the President that carry out the wishes of Congress are known as (*a*) executive orders. (*b*) treaties. (*c*) checks and balances. (*d*) vetoes. (*e*) patronage.

7. A President might "persuade" Congress to pass a certain bill by   (a) threatening to veto other bills.   (b) withholding federal projects in the home districts of uncooperative legislators.   (c) appealing to the public for support.   (d) appealing for party unity.   (e) all of these.

8. When President Ford forgave President Nixon for any crimes he might have committed while in the White House, Ford was using the power to   (a) commute a sentence.   (b) grant a reprieve.   (c) overturn an impeachment conviction.   (d) grant a pardon.   (e) execute a court order.

9. Most presidential candidates choose vice-presidential running mates based on their   (a) stature as a possible President.   (b) ability to "balance the ticket" and carry a large number of regional or ethnic votes.   (c) contrast with the presidential candidate's political point of view.   (d) fund-raising abilities.   (e) political charisma.

10. Should a President and Vice President die in twin plane crashes, the next in line of presidential succession would be   (a) the Secretary of State.   (b) a newly elected Vice President, chosen in a special election.   (c) the Speaker of the House.   (d) the President *pro tempore* of the Senate.   (e) the Chief Justice of the United States.

CONCEPT DEVELOPMENT

1. Summarize the major responsibilities of the President of the United States by describing the various "hats" the chief executive wears.

2. Should another office be created to take over the ceremonial duties of the President? Summarize the arguments for and against this change. Explain how it could be accomplished.

3. What are the arguments for and against having a civilian President serve as commander-in-chief of the armed forces?

4. Argue the pros and cons of abolishing the Electoral College. Why have past attempts to do away with it failed?

5. Explain why you agree or disagree with the statement: "No one is capable of doing a good job in all of the roles demanded of the President."

HANDS-ON ACTIVITIES

1. Using available news sources, chart the President's activities for a two-week period. You might also write to the White House for a copy of the President's schedule. Identify which roles the President is fulfilling in each of the many daily activities. What conclusions can you draw about the pressures of the office?

2. Write a letter to the President at 1600 Pennsylvania Avenue NW, Washington, D.C. 20500. State your position on a current issue in clear, concise language. Share the response with the class.

3. Assign a different President to each member of your class. Ask each person to prepare a poster that illustrates that President's major accomplishments.

4. Set up a debate between two teams from your class on the topic: "Resolved, that the modern presidency has outgrown the checks and balances established by the Constitution." Many excellent articles that explore both sides of this question have appeared recently, some of them inspired by the Watergate and the Iran-Contra cases. Use the *Readers' Guide to Periodical Literature* to find your research materials.

12 Getting along with the world: The making of foreign policy

President George Bush ordered U.S. troops to invade Panama in 1989 to protect American interests there. This military action reminded the nation that three other American Presidents—Theodore Roosevelt, Lyndon Johnson, and Jimmy Carter—had already played major roles in the history of Panama and the Panama Canal. Roosevelt gained the land for the canal for the United States, Johnson helped keep the canal, and Carter agreed to hand it back to Panama.

U.S. interest in a canal across Central America revived during the Spanish-American War of 1898. In order to reach Cuban waters, warships from the U.S. Pacific fleet were forced to make a six-week voyage around the southern tip of South America. The answer to the problem of this long passage was clear: The United States must build a canal across Central America. The narrow isthmus of Panama was the most logical place for a canal, but Panama was a province of Colombia. In 1903, Secretary of State John Hay negotiated a treaty with a Colombian diplomat, Tomás Herrán. The treaty called for the United States to lease a six-mile-wide strip of land across Panama in return for $10 million in gold and a $250,000 annual rental. The U.S. government thought the terms were fair, but the government of Colombia refused the offer.

President Theodore Roosevelt didn't give up easily. He declared that the people of Panama, isolated by heavy jungle from the rest of Colombia, were ready to revolt. The Panamanians took TR's hint and launched a revolution in 1903. At Roosevelt's order, American naval forces took up stations off Panama to block the landing of Colombian reinforcements. Two days after the Panamanians won their victory, Roosevelt recognized the new country. The canal treaty was signed two weeks later. In return for $10 million and a $250,000 yearly rental payment, Panama gave control of a ten-mile-wide Canal Zone to the United States "in perpetuity." T.R.'s "big stick" diplomacy had opened the way for the successful construction of the Panama Canal.

After it was completed in 1914, the canal brought both prosperity and discontent to Panama. Over time, the rental was increased to almost $2 million annually, and jobs and U.S. dollars helped support the local economy. Still, the sight of 30,000 U.S. citizens, comfortable behind their Canal Zone fences, grated on Panamanian feelings. As a gesture, the United States agreed in 1960 to fly the Panamanian flag beside the American flag at specific places in the Canal Zone. The agreement was not always kept.

In 1964, a group of U.S. high school students raised the Stars and Stripes in the Canal Zone but refused to fly the flag of Panama. Their action touched off riots in the nearby cities. Before order could be restored, 25 people lay dead and 300 had been wounded. Some Americans thought the riots were the first step toward a Communist takeover of Panama.

President Lyndon Johnson was new to the White House when the news broke. Panama was Johnson's first foreign affairs test after he took the oath of office as President following the death of President Kennedy. President Johnson knew that people at home and abroad would judge him and his country by how well he handled the crisis. Acting with characteristic directness, Johnson phoned President Roberto F. Chiari of Panama and asked him to stop the violence. The uneasy truce that followed gave diplomats time to seek a peaceful solution. Johnson's quick action had saved important American foreign policy goals in the Caribbean.

The talks were still going on when President Jimmy Carter took office in 1977. In August of that year, two treaties were drawn up. In one, the United States agreed to return the Canal Zone to Panama, except for U.S. military and naval bases. The transfer was timed to take place six months after the treaty was approved by the U.S. Senate. The canal itself was scheduled to stay in U.S. hands until the end of 1999. The second treaty gave the United States the right to defend the canal against attack. Some Americans feared that if the United States failed to accept these terms, a Communist-inspired guerrilla war would break out in Panama.

At this time, the United States was smarting from its defeat in Vietnam. Public opinion polls showed that Americans wanted to hold on to Panama. After all, people argued, the canal had been built with American lives and dollars. Nevertheless, President Carter believed that the United States should return the canal to Panama. With Carter's strong support, the Senate approved the Panama treaties in April 1978.

Several conclusions may be drawn from these incidents: (1) The roots of many international problems reach deep into the past. (2) A President's foreign policy cannot ignore the needs of this country's national security. (3) In a complex world, disagreements between any two countries often involve other countries as well. (4) Diplomatic matters often drag on for many years before they are settled—and the settlement doesn't always make the United States happy.

■ President Jimmy Carter (left) signing a treaty in 1977 to return the Panama Canal to the people of Panama in 1999. Secretary General Alejandro Orfila of the Organization of American States looks on. At the right, President of Panama General Omar Torrijos Herrera also signs.

In the chapter, you will look at the major foreign policy functions of the United States—diplomacy, national defense, and intelligence-gathering. The questions to be answered include:

1. How has U.S. foreign policy developed over the years?

2. How does the government make foreign policy?

3. What is the role of the State Department?

4. What does the United States hope to accomplish with foreign aid?

5. What kind of role do international organizations play in U.S. foreign policy?

6. What is the United Nations accomplishing?

7. How does the Department of Defense protect national security?

8. How does the Central Intelligence Agency aid U.S. foreign policy?

9. What role do arms control and disarmament play in U.S. foreign policy?

1. How has U.S. foreign policy developed over the years?

The national interests of the United States spread out from the nation's borders like a worldwide network of nerve fibers. A copper miners' strike in Chile, a famine in the Sahara, an oil price increase in the Middle East—all can affect our national well-being. American economic, political, and military decisions cannot be made in a vacuum. The decision makers cannot ignore realities of international relationships.

Foreign policy may be defined as the principles that guide the United States as it tries to maintain satisfactory economic, political, and military relationships with both friendly and hostile countries. The "splendid isolation" that was once made possible by ocean barriers has vanished in an era of intercontinental missiles, international finance, and dependence on foreign trade. Few countries, how-

ever, agree on the policies for promoting mutual well-being. *Diplomacy*, therefore, is the art of establishing relationships that both sides can accept.

During the past 200 years, U.S. foreign policy has gone through a series of historic changes.

ISOLATIONISM

The first foreign policy principle of the United States was one of *isolationism*—the desire to remain separate from the rest of the world. The new nation needed time to work out the tangles in its new system of government and to tame the wilderness at its back door. In addition, Presidents Washington, Adams, and Jefferson believed that the infant republic had little to gain by taking part in the European conflicts of the late 1700s and early 1800s. When the Napoleonic wars swept across Europe, Jefferson set up an embargo that he hoped would keep the United States out of the conflict. The embargo failed. In 1812, the United States went to war with Great Britain in order to protect our freedom of trade on the high seas.

In the 1820s, the Monroe Doctrine signaled the end of America's isolationism. Issued by President James Monroe in 1823, the doctrine proclaimed that both North and South America were off-limits to further European colonization. The makers of U.S. foreign policy did not wish to see renewed Spanish or French domination of any part of the Western Hemisphere. Fortunately, the bold American statement paralleled Britain's own policy at the time. U.S. military power could not have enforced such a ban, but the British Navy could—and did.

IMPERIALISM

The second half of the 1800s found the United States edging toward the policy of *imperialism*. Under this policy, the United States took active steps to extend its influence over the other parts of the world that seemed vital for defense and trade.

Expansion in the Pacific. With the nation now stretching from shore to shore, Americans looked westward across the Pacific. In 1854, Commodore Matthew Perry ended Japan's own long period of isolation by negotiating a trade treaty with that country. A rich trade began moving across the Pacific to Japan and China. In 1867, the purchase of Alaska established American power in the northern Pacific.

Influence in the central Pacific was secured in 1898 by the annexation of Hawaii and the acquisition of the Philippines after the Spanish-American War. Secretary of State John Hay's Open Door policy helped save China from being carved up by European countries in 1900. This policy also insured that U.S. shipping would share equally in the rich China trade. By the time Teddy Roosevelt stepped in to serve as peacemaker in the Russo-Japanese War of 1904–1905, the United States seemed ready to take an active role in international politics.

Intervention in Latin America. The United States again turned its attention to Latin America in the period after the Civil War. Still citing the Monroe Doctrine, the federal government forced the French to abandon their foothold in Mexico in 1866–1867. U.S. diplomats mediated a dispute in 1902 over debts that Venezuela owed Great Britain and Germany. Imperialism also led to territorial expansion. The United States acquired Puerto Rico from Spain in 1898 and the Virgin Islands from Denmark in 1917.

The United States has, on many occasions, intervened directly in the political and economic affairs of its neighbors. American Presidents sent troops into Haiti, Nicaragua, Costa Rica, and Mexico in the early 1900s. In each case, the President decided that the Latin American country was acting against the best interests of the United States. Latin American protests finally led to Franklin Roosevelt's Good Neighbor policy of 1933, which promised that the United States would end its "gunboat diplomacy."

■ In 1904, President Theodore Roosevelt added a "corollary" to the Monroe Doctrine. The United States, he said, was prepared to act as the international police power in the Americas. This cartoon shows him protecting Santo Domingo from European claims.

FYI . . .
Major American Foreign Policy Goals From Independence to the 1990s

Over the past two centuries, American foreign policy has been governed by several key goals. Each goal has grown out of the special circumstances that surround it. Can you predict the foreign policy goals that will guide this country in the coming years?

Isolationism First spelled out in Washington's Farewell Address, 1796. Based on the desire to avoid alliances that would involve the U.S. in European wars. Contributed to the Monroe Doctrine in 1823. Gained strength in the 1930's as a reaction to World War I. Reborn again in the 1960's and 1970's after U.S. involvement in Vietnam.

Protection The willingness of the U.S. to protect its own interests and those of its allies. First used in the Monroe Doctrine, which guaranteed independence to the nations of Latin America. The Open Door Policy (1899–1900) carried a similar guarantee to the mainland of Asia. In recent times, the U.S. fought in two world wars to protect democracy and freedom throughout the world.

Intervention The use of U.S. military forces in foreign countries to further American political and economic goals. Used primarily in Latin America, a right reserved to the U.S. by the Roosevelt Corollary (1904–1905). Also used in the Middle East by Presidents Eisenhower (1958), Reagan (1982, 1987), and Bush (1990).

Imperialism The addition of territory to the United States by means of force, either political, military, or economic. Most historians include the following as examples of imperialism: the Mexican Cession, the gains from the Spanish-American War, the acquisition of the Panama Canal Zone, and the annexation of Hawaii.

Containment and Détente President Harry Truman proclaimed an American commitment to contain the spread of communism after World War II. The United States used economic, political, and military aid to help any country threatened by Communist aggression. The dangers of the Cold War and the arms race that followed led to a policy of détente between the United States and the Soviet Union. Under détente, each country accepts the other's legitimate interests. Better relations have led to treaties that reduce each nation's arsenal of nuclear missiles.

Alliances The U.S. continues to pursue military and economic partnerships with its friends and allies. This policy began with the Good Neighbor policy in Latin America. Today, it is based on regional alliances, such as NATO, and bilateral defense agreements with countries such as Japan and Israel.

The Good Neighbor policy did not put an end to U.S. interventions in Latin America. In the 1980s, for example, the United States responded to leftist movements in Central America by sending aid to the governments of El Salvador, Honduras, Guatemala, and Costa Rica. When the pro-Communist Sandinista government of Nicaragua threatened to upset the military balance in the region, President Reagan went even further. He sent military and economic aid to the anti-Communist forces (Contras) who were fighting to overthrow the Sandinistas. Reagan's policies helped lead to free elections in Nicaragua and the installation of a more democratic government.

American efforts to stamp out drug trafficking in Latin America have been less successful. President Bush did win a victory in the drug war when U.S. forces arrested Panama's General Manuel Noriega during the 1989 invasion. Noriega was flown to the United States to stand trial as a major figure in the drug trade.

INVOLVEMENT IN EUROPE

American foreign policy throughout the 1900s has been dominated by the question: To what degree should the United States involve itself in European affairs? The nation's efforts to steer clear of Europe's conflicts ended for a time with our entry into World War I (1917–1918). America's military and industrial might tipped the balance of the war in favor of the Allies. After Germany surrendered, France and Great Britain dominated the Versailles Peace Conference (1919). The two European powers rejected most of President Woodrow Wilson's plans for writing a just peace treaty. Wilson, in turn, compromised his beliefs in hopes that the League of Nations would be able to keep the peace. The Senate, however, refused to approve the treaty. The United States never joined the League.

The period of isolation that followed World War I ended in the flames of World War II (1939–1945). With the Japanese attack on Pearl Harbor and Germany's declaration of war in 1941, Americans could no longer stay out of the struggle against fascism. The United States quickly geared up for war and dedicated itself to the defeat of the Axis powers.

■ This 1919 cartoon shows the League of Nations as a policeman wooing Mother Earth while her "children," the nations of the world, look on. They wonder whether the League will "boss" them around. One reason the Senate gave for rejecting the League was fear of becoming involved in disputes that were not our concern.

WORLD LEADERSHIP

After the war, the United States abandoned isolationism and emerged as the leader of the Western democracies. This new policy developed (1) because our growing worldwide military and economic interests demanded it and (2) because Great Britain and France, the traditional world powers, had been greatly weakened by the war. American leaders helped design the United Nations as a peacekeeping agency for the postwar world. The Marshall Plan poured billions of U.S. dollars into the shattered nations of Europe. At the same time, the Truman Doctrine promised to help any nation that was threatened by Communist aggression. The idea of limiting communism to those countries where it already existed was called *containment*. Containment was a dominant force in American foreign policy discussions for the next 40 years.

The Truman decision to oppose Communist expansion led to a long cold war struggle between the Soviet Union and the United States. By virtue of their size, economic strength, and nuclear arsenals, the two super-powers dominated world affairs. The United States used its economic and political strength in an effort to contain communism within its pre-1946 boundaries. Economic and military aid flowed overseas to help our friends. U.S. dollars and know-how built bridges and roads, produced better crops, and constructed new industries. In 1949, President Truman made a long-range commitment to the defense of Europe. This country joined its western European allies in a military alliance known as the North Atlantic Treaty Organization (NATO).

A POLICY FOR THE FUTURE

The 1990s ushered in a new spirit of *détente* (peaceful competition) between the United States and the Communist bloc. The breakup of the Soviet Union's empire in Eastern Europe set the stage for fast-moving arms reduction talks and vastly improved trade relations. American foreign policy makers welcomed the end of the Cold War and moved quickly to encourage further political, social, and economic reforms by the democratic-style governments that replaced the iron rule of the Communist party.

A more realistic foreign policy has emerged from these events. The United States cannot turn its back on dangerous situations like the Arab-Israeli conflict or the spread of communism in Africa. The policymakers in Washington also realize that U.S. resources are limited. The nation now steers a course that falls somewhere between a retreat into isolationism and an acceptance of foreign commitments it can no longer afford.

2. How does the government make foreign policy?

In recent years, the challenge of managing U.S. relations with other countries has taken more and more of the President's time. Several reasons exist for this: (1) A growing interdependence among nations has increased the number and importance of U.S. contacts with other countries. (2) The executive branch possesses a near monopoly on sources of information about foreign affairs. (3) The public and Congress have increasingly accepted strong presidential leadership in foreign affairs. Disagreements with White House decision making in Vietnam and Central America may have reversed this last tendency to some degree.

Three major forces influence the making of foreign policy by the President and the White House staff: the Secretary of State and the State Department, Congress, and public opinion.

THE SECRETARY OF STATE

The Secretary of State ranks as the top presidential adviser on international affairs. How the President uses this advice depends on the personalities of the two involved. Some Presidents prefer to act on their own, leaving the Secretary of State to carry out policies formulated in the White House. By contrast, President Gerald Ford's experience was largely in domestic matters. Ford relied on Secretary of State Henry Kissinger when it came to foreign policy. Even so, Kissinger's policies were always subject to the President's approval.

A number of distinguished Americans have served as Secretary of State. The list includes Thomas Jefferson (the first to hold the post), James Madison, Henry Clay, William Jennings Bryan, and George C. Marshall. Along with

The Making of U.S. Foreign Policy

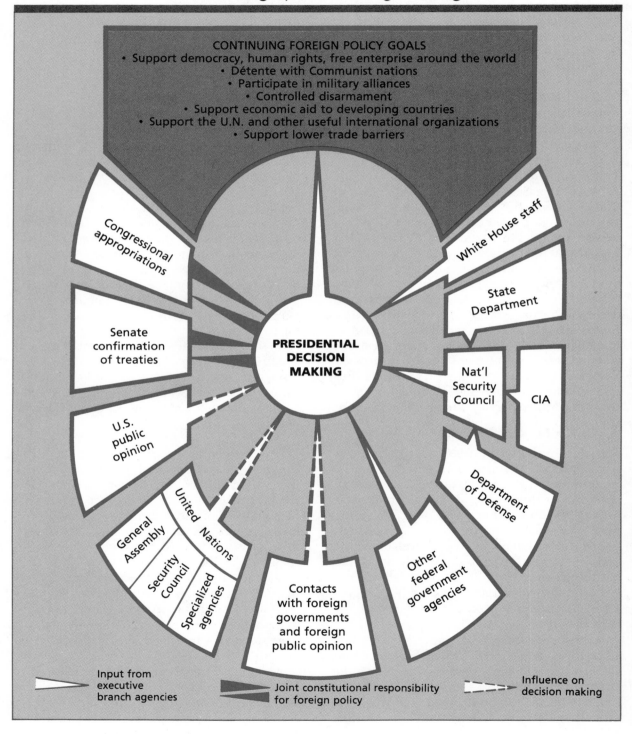

CONTINUING FOREIGN POLICY GOALS
• Support democracy, human rights, free enterprise around the world
• Détente with Communist nations
• Participate in military alliances
• Controlled disarmament
• Support economic aid to developing countries
• Support the U.N. and other useful international organizations
• Support lower trade barriers

Congressional appropriations

White House staff

Senate confirmation of treaties

State Department

U.S. public opinion

Nat'l Security Council

CIA

PRESIDENTIAL DECISION MAKING

Department of Defense

General Assembly

United Nations

Security Council

Specialized agencies

Contacts with foreign governments and foreign public opinion

Other federal government agencies

Input from executive branch agencies

Joint constitutional responsibility for foreign policy

Influence on decision making

the primary role of advising the President, the Secretary of State oversees the work of the State Department. The Secretary also takes care of certain types of official correspondence. It was to Secretary of State Kissinger, for example, that President Richard Nixon submitted his formal letter of resignation in 1974.

CONGRESS

Major foreign policy proposals often generate a lively controversy between Congress and the President. These battles usually end with the President winning most of what the administration wanted, but Congress isn't powerless. The Constitution gives Congress the power of the purse, and the Senate has the right to approve or reject treaties.

The power of the purse. Sooner or later, most foreign policy decisions call for the spending of money. If Congress does not approve of an increase in military aid to Central America, for example, it can refuse to appropriate the money. These debates usually end in a compromise, with the President receiving a large part of the original request.

The power to ratify treaties. Every treaty signed by the President must be ratified by a two-thirds vote of the Senate. Even though the President has signed the treaty, it cannot take effect until after the Senate acts. Recent Presidents have sometimes sidestepped this requirement through the use of executive agreements. These agreements have the force of law but do not require Senate approval. Despite occasional conflicts, Congress seldom challenges the executive branch's use of the treaty-making power. Four-fifths of all treaties submitted to the Senate have been ratified.

PUBLIC OPINION

Although Presidents make foreign policy, they cannot lead the nation where the people will not go. The occupant of the White House must be sensitive to public pressures. Opinion polls, pickets on Pennsylvania Avenue, newspaper editorials, personal conversations—all alert the President to the mood of the country. Woodrow Wilson's attempt to sell the League of Nations to the American people failed in a nation that was slipping back into isolationism. Likewise, widespread public protests forced the United States to withdraw from Vietnam despite the wishes of Presidents Johnson and Nixon.

3. What is the role of the State Department?

The President, with the help of the Secretary of State, decides the foreign policy of the United States. The State Department carries out that policy. Considered by many to be the elite branch of the federal civil service, the State Department employs more than 25,000 men and women. Many of these people work in a huge building located near the Potomac River in an area known in Washington as Foggy Bottom.

THE FOREIGN SERVICE

The Foreign Service represents the United States abroad. Two branches of the Foreign Service spread across the globe into every country with which the United States has diplomatic relations.

The diplomatic corps. The members of the diplomatic corps are the official contact points between the United States and other countries. The United States maintains an *embassy* (a diplomatic office) in the capital city of every country it recognizes. The embassy's chief diplomat is the *ambassador*, who is appointed by the President and confirmed by the Senate.

A U.S. ambassador transmits the official communications between the two nations, arranges treaties, and attends to other diplomatic matters. Ambassadors are constantly alert to events in the host country that may affect the United States. In addition, the embassy protects U.S. citizens and their interests. Another important duty is to explain U.S. laws, policies, and culture to the people of the host country. Large embassy staffs assist the ambassadors in the performance of their official duties.

■ Sometimes diplomatic work is dangerous. U.S. embassy personnel and their families in front of the embassy in Beijing, China, in the summer of 1989. They are waiting for transportation to the airport. During the harsh military crackdown on student demonstrations in Tiananmen Square in Beijing, the United States feared for the safety of U.S. citizens in China.

The consular service. The duty of protecting U.S. commercial interests falls to the second branch of the Foreign Service, the consular service. A *consul* works out of an American *consulate* in most major cities of the world. Consular officials must pass a civil service exam before they are appointed by the President and confirmed by the Senate. Their duties are to (1) promote U.S. trade and commerce, (2) aid American citizens with passport or other problems, (3) enforce U.S. customs regulations, and (4) assist people who wish to emigrate to this country.

STATE DEPARTMENT PERSONNEL

Most State Department jobs provide opportunities for travel, combined with interesting and useful work. Candidates must take competitive examinations to qualify for appointment. At one time, most ambassadors were political appointees who were better known for their party service than for their abilities as diplomats. This situation has improved in recent years. Many ambassadors now work their way up the Foreign Service career ladder.

STATE DEPARTMENT STRUCTURE

The State Department stands at the center of a vast information network. Radio, wire, and courier services link the department with its many embassies and consulates. Incoming reports go to the proper geographic bureau (the Bureau of Near Eastern or South Asian Affairs, for example) for study and action by experts on that region. Functional bureaus handle specific problems, such as arms control and relations with international organizations. The most important matters move upward to undersecretaries and to the Secretary of State.

OTHER FUNCTIONS

The State Department issues *passports* to Americans who wish to travel overseas. Passports extend the protection of international law to their holders and identify them as U.S. citizens. Before residents of some countries can visit the United States, they must obtain *visas* (permits to visit) from an American consulate. The government uses its control of visas as a means of screening out visitors whose presence in the United States would be undesirable.

State Department reports provide the government with information about events, conditions, and personalities in foreign countries. Without these insights, the making of foreign policy would be much more difficult.

4. What does the United States hope to accomplish with foreign aid?

Giving aid to other countries has been an important part of U.S. foreign policy since World War II. Foreign aid may take the form of *grants* (outright gifts) or long-term, low-interest loans. Aid may be given in dollars, but it usually takes the form of food, military equipment, technology, and the services of skilled technicians.

PROS AND CONS OF FOREIGN AID

Supporters of foreign aid believe that such programs are investments in national security. The United States, the defenders of foreign aid say, needs a world network of stable, non-Communist countries that are friendly to its political and economic goals. Many countries that need aid are poor and underdeveloped.

■ After World War II, the United States launched a generous and hugely successful aid program for war-torn Europe, known as the Marshall Plan. Here Marshall Plan grain from the United States is being unloaded for distribution in Athens, Greece.

Without U.S. aid, they might fall into Communist hands.

Opponents of foreign aid call it a "giveaway" that tries to buy friends—with little success. They cite cases of aid recipients who show little or no appreciation for American help. When the United States needs support in the United Nations, for example, the votes of these "friends" are often missing. Moreover, the critics add, the United States has many problems to be solved within its own borders. The nation cannot afford to feed and arm the rest of the world.

DEVELOPMENT OF AID PROGRAMS

Most of the loans that the United States made to its allies during World War I were never repaid. Even so, the United States funded a massive military assistance program during World War II. After the war, President Harry Truman and Secretary of State George Marshall convinced Congress that rebuilding the war-damaged countries of Europe would be in our best interests. Marshall argued that

foreign aid would help prevent Communist expansion, develop American markets in Europe, and strengthen the Western military alliance. Congress responded by voting billions of dollars for the Marshall Plan. With this aid, the people of western Europe were able to construct new factories, houses, rail lines, and other necessities. Additional aid helped to rebuild Japan.

In 1949, Truman extended foreign aid to Latin America, Africa, and Asia. He believed that the aid was needed to counter a growing Communist influence in these areas. In the early 1960s, President Kennedy increased the aid for Latin America in an ambitious program called the Alliance for Progress.

Unlike the Marshall Plan for Europe, the aid programs in the underdeveloped countries have not been totally successful. Many of these countries live under unstable governments and lack the industrial base needed to give their people an adequate standard of living. High birth rates also contribute to a slowing of economic growth. At times, poorly planned

■ In the summer and fall of 1990, President Bush sent U.S. troops to Saudi Arabia to help protect it from invasion by Iraq, which had seized neighboring Kuwait. U.S. naval forces in the Persian Gulf also contributed to the effort to stabilize the situation.

industrial growth has disrupted farm production and created food shortages. To make matters worse, newly established factories have sometimes been unable to find markets for their products. As a result, the return on aid given to developing countries has been disappointing to those who expected quick results.

U.S. FOREIGN AID TODAY

Since the end of World War II, American taxpayers have paid out hundreds of billions of dollars in foreign aid. In recent years, changes in foreign policy and increased congressional opposition have altered the amount and type of aid. Most foreign aid now takes the form of (1) military assistance to those countries most vulnerable to Communist takeover, (2) loans and credits made through international agencies, and (3) direct person-to-person aid of the type given by the Peace Corps.

1. *Military assistance.* United States money, equipment, and training help maintain strong military forces in friendly, non-Communist countries. In recent years, much of this aid has gone to South Korea, Turkey, Egypt, Israel, and El Salvador. Military assistance may also involve direct intervention by U.S. forces. In 1987, for example, Kuwaiti oil tankers were being blown up by Iranian mines and gunboats. The U.S. Navy took up the task of providing escort service through the Persian Gulf. This duty seemed to be ending when Iraq in 1990 invaded Kuwait. The United States quickly sent troops to Saudi Arabia as part of an international force to contain Iraq.

2. *Loans and credits.* Much of the economic aid given today flows through many international agencies. The World Bank, the Export-Import Bank, and the Inter-American Development Bank handle aid of this type. In cooperation with the State Department, the Agency for International Development (AID) administers foreign development loans. AID officials study requests for help with projects such as irrigation systems, electric power generation, highways, schools, and factories. The agency evaluates loans on the basis of their usefulness to the recipient as well as the possibilities of repayment. Because the United States requires that most AID money must be spent in this country, American factories benefit from increased orders.

3. *Person-to-person aid.* U.S. know-how has often helped work wonders abroad. Engineering, agricultural, and educational skills have become a major export to underdeveloped countries. Peace Corps volunteers live with their hosts and help build schools, improve crops, develop water systems, and teach basic education classes in dozens of underdeveloped nations.

■ A Peace Corps volunteer from Illinois (left) in Sierra Leone. He is acting as a technical adviser for a school construction project. The other worker is coating wooden beams with a preservative. Individuals of all ages participate in Peace Corps projects.

Let's review for a moment

Have you ever felt that life would be simpler if this country could ignore the rest of the world? The United States attempted to do just that in its early years by adopting a policy of *isolationism*. This was followed by decades of expansion and a more active interest in foreign affairs—the period of *imperialism*. Isolationist feelings grew strong again in the years after World War I, but World War II forced the United States into a position of world leadership. Since 1945, the nation has been committed to encouraging democracy and resisting the spread of communism throughout the world. That policy paid huge dividends in 1989–1990 when the citizens of Poland, Czechoslovakia, Hungary, and other East European countries replaced their Communist rulers with freely elected governments.

The President makes *foreign policy*, of course—but who helps in the process? The Secretary of State, for one, then Congress. Who else? All of us together, the American people! Presidents can't carry out a foreign policy that we don't want. If they try, the policy will collapse from lack of support—or the President's party will be voted out of office.

The President and Secretary of State rely on the State Department to carry out the nation's foreign policy. The department is made up of thousands of skilled professionals, many of whom are stationed in overseas *embassies* and *consulates*. These men and women practice the art of diplomacy as they protect and promote American interests around the world.

To promote our interests overseas, the United States gives billions of dollars to help friendly governments. The money helps develop their economies, improve education and health services, and maintain political stability.

5. What kind of role do international organizations play in U.S. foreign policy?

As leader of the Western democracies, the United States belongs to a number of international organizations. These bodies operate on either a regional or a worldwide basis. They have been created to pursue one or more goals: (1) to provide a place to discuss international problems, (2) to provide military security, and (3) to promote international commerce and raise living standards.

RESOLVING INTERNATIONAL PROBLEMS

The United Nations and the Organization of American States are examples of organizations that try to resolve problems in a peaceful manner.

The United Nations. The United Nations was formed to bring the countries of the world together in the cause of world peace. With the strong backing of President Franklin Roosevelt, the U.N. was established in San Francisco in 1945. Neither the earlier, unsuccessful League of Nations nor the U.N. was ever expected to serve as a world government. The U.N. was designed to settle international disputes in what everyone hoped would be a peaceful postwar world. The Cold War between the Western democracies and the Communist world, as well as the tendency for nations to divide into competing power blocs, have robbed the U.N. of much of its effectiveness. The sudden success of democratic movements within the Communist countries of Eastern Europe changed that gloomy picture in 1989, however. The new spirit of openness, known as *glasnost*, raised widespread hopes that the Cold War was finally over. With the danger of nuclear war greatly reduced, the U.N. seemed a proper forum in which old enemies could meet to resolve disputes and promote economic development.

The United Nations Charter created six main bodies:

■ U.S. Representative to the United Nations Thomas Pickering voting on a resolution in the Security Council. The Council cannot force a country to obey its rulings, but it can bring the weight of world opinion to bear on an aggressor, as it did with Iraq in 1990.

1. *General Assembly.* All member nations sit in the "town meeting of the world" known as the General Assembly. Every country, regardless of size, has one vote. The delegates debate matters relating to international politics, trade, and social welfare. General Assembly resolutions are not binding on the member nations, but they do carry the weight of world opinion.

2. *Security Council.* Fifteen nations make up the Security Council, which is responsible for preserving world peace. Each of the five permanent members (the United States, the Soviet Union, the United Kingdom, France, and the People's Republic of China) hold veto power over any Security Council action. Although the Security Council has the power to act against an aggressor nation for breaking the peace, the veto power has often blocked Council action. Threats to peace can be dealt with in the General Assembly when the Security Council cannot act.

3. *International Court of Justice.* Judges from 15 nations meet at The Hague in the Netherlands to resolve questions of international law. The court can hear a dispute only when both parties agree in advance to accept its jurisdiction.

4. *Trusteeship Council.* With colonialism out of favor after World War II, the Trusteeship Council was set up to protect the interests of "non-self-governing territories." The United States serves as the administrator for the Trust Territory of the Pacific, the last remaining trust territory.

5. *Economic and Social Council (ECOSOC).* This council was established to promote the health, working conditions, education, and cultural development of people everywhere. It coordinates the work of 13 specialized agencies, including the World Health Organization, the International Labor Organization, and the Food and Agriculture Organization.

6. *Secretariat.* Day-to-day administration is the task of the Secretariat, headed by the Secretary General. The second Secretary General, Dag Hammarskjold, expanded the role of the office by making it an instrument for settling international disputes.

The current Secretary General, Javier Pérez de Cuéllar, has been the most successful of the recent secretaries. Faced with a financial crisis in 1988, Pérez de Cuéllar pushed through a long-overdue restructuring of U.N. manage-

■ A member of the United Nations peacekeeping force bidding farewell to a former guerrilla in Namibia. The U.N. force monitored a cease-fire and supervised elections to set up an independent government in Namibia, which had won its freedom from South Africa after a long struggle.

ment and finances. The United States, which contributes more money to the U.N. than any other country, responded by paying $144 million in back dues. The Reagan administration had withheld the money as a protest against what it saw as the U.N.'s inefficiency and anti-American bias. At the same time, U.N. mediators were able to arrange cease-fire agreements in Afghanistan, the Persian Gulf, the Western Sahara, and Namibia. As a tribute to their efforts, the U.N.'s peacekeeping forces were awarded the 1988 Nobel Peace Prize.

The Organization of American States (OAS). The U.N. Charter allows its members to create their own regional organizations. A long series of inter-American agreements on economic and military cooperation led to the creation of the OAS in 1948. The OAS supports programs designed to bring about closer political, cultural, and social relations among its members. An older organization, the Pan American Union, now serves as its secretariat.

In practice, the United States has used the OAS chiefly to guard against further Communist penetration of the Western Hemisphere. Given the long history of U.S. involvement in Latin America, even the democratic Latin American states are suspicious of U.S. policies. U.S. intervention in the Dominican Republic (1965) and in Grenada (1983) gained only reluctant support from the OAS. That limited support changed to outright condemnation in December 1989 after the United States sent troops into Panama to depose the dictator of that Central American country. The OAS called for the withdrawal of U.S. troops by a vote of 20–1. The organization also asked the United States to guarantee the right of the people of Panama to choose their own form of government.

PROMOTING MILITARY SECURITY

No nation can stand alone in the event of war. The United States, therefore, has taken the lead in organizing a series of mutual defense alliances outside of the United Nations. Although the OAS Charter provides for military cooperation with Latin American nations, the main thrust of U.S. military pacts has been in Europe and Asia.

North Atlantic Treaty Organization (NATO). The North Atlantic Treaty Organization has long been the cornerstone of this country's military alliances. NATO's original purpose was to defend Western Europe against attack, particularly from the Communist bloc. The dramatic political changes that swept the Communist world in 1989 brought that phase of NATO's history to a close. Western leaders moved quickly to assure the East European countries that allowing a united Germany to join NATO would not threaten their security. NATO also took the lead in promising to use nuclear weapons only as a "last resort." The alliance then proposed a number of additional peacekeeping agreements, including deep cuts in the number of soldiers who face each other across Europe's national borders.

Sixteen countries belong to NATO: The United States, Canada, Iceland, Norway, Denmark, Great Britain, the Netherlands, Belgium, Luxembourg, Portugal, Germany, France, Italy, Greece, Turkey, and Spain. Political disputes have weakened the roles played by France, Greece, and Turkey in the alliance.

Other defense treaties. The United States has mutual defense treaties with over 40 countries, most of whom depend on the United States for military security. These treaties sometimes lead to domestic political disputes. One such argument arose when President Jimmy Carter canceled the treaty with Taiwan in favor of improved ties with mainland China. The Supreme Court affirmed in 1979 the President's right to end such treaties.

In the 1950s, the United States tried to form other alliances to help contain the spread of communism. These alliances weren't able to duplicate the success of NATO. The Southeast Asia Treaty Organization (SEATO) could not prevent Communist advances into Laos, Kampuchea (Cambodia), and Vietnam. Similarly, the Central Treaty Organization lost its effectiveness in the Middle East after the withdrawal of Iran, Iraq, and Pakistan.

PROMOTING ECONOMIC COOPERATION

The United States has long been a major force in world economic affairs. For many years, the United States dollar (backed by the nation's gold reserves and productive capacity) set the standard against which most of the world's currencies were measured. In recent years, the strength of the U.S. dollar has varied greatly. The dollar's value is influenced by such factors as the rate of inflation, the American trade imbalance, increases or decreases in interest rates, and the price of oil. The rise or fall of tensions between the Communist countries and the Western democracies is another major influence on the value of the dollar.

The United States is a member of several agencies that try to stabilize currency values and promote trade and development. The World Bank (International Bank for Reconstruction and Development), for example, was set up by the U.N. in 1945. The U.S. provided most of its $10 billion in initial capital. The bank provides large-scale loans to countries that lack the funds for major industrial and agricultural projects. Regional development agencies (the Inter-American Development Bank serves Latin America) provide similar assistance to the underdeveloped nations. These Third World countries have few resources with which to feed, clothe, and house their rapidly growing populations. In all of these organizations, the United States provides dollars and management skills to promote world economic stability.

6. What is the United Nations accomplishing?

The United Nations was designed to serve a world weary of war and anxious for peace. Although no major war has broken out since 1945, the U.N. has not been able to prevent a series of smaller wars. These failures tend to conceal the very real accomplishments of this international body.

FORCES THAT WORK AGAINST THE U.N.

Several factors have kept the U.N. from fulfilling the high hopes with which it was launched in 1945.

A new majority. The majority of the current membership (159) has joined since the U.N. was founded. Most of the original member countries belonged to the Western European bloc or to the Latin American bloc. Both of these groups were friendly to the United States and its interests. Many of the new members that joined in the 1960s and 1970s were emerging nations from Africa and Asia. With their entry, the comfortable U.S. voting majority vanished. A unified voting bloc of Third World countries, often joined by the Communist nations, began to pass resolutions that ran counter to American interests. In December 1988, for example, the General Assembly left New York and moved to Geneva, Switzerland, for three days. The action was taken to protest the U.S. refusal to grant a visa to Yasir Arafat, leader of the Palestinian Liberation Organization. After Arafat spoke in Geneva, the General Assembly voted 138–2 for a resolution (strongly opposed by the United States) that called on Israel to withdraw from the disputed territories and to meet with the PLO.

Security Council vetoes. Many of the conflicts brought to the Council have involved Communist aggression. As a result, the Soviet Union has used the veto over 100 times to deny the U.N. a role in restoring the peace. By contrast, the United States didn't use the veto during the U.N.'s first 25 years. After casting its first veto in 1970, the United States now uses it regularly to protect American interests.

Inadequate financial support. The U.N. has fallen deeply into debt in recent years. The Secretary General has cut expenses and laid off workers, but the budget is still underfunded. Many nations, including the United States, have not paid their full share of the costs. Others, including the Soviet Union, have refused to pay for peacekeeping activities of which they disapprove. The Third World majority in the General Assembly creates another financial problem. The U.N.'s critics point out that these countries pay less than two percent of the U.N. budget, but they often vote for expensive, wasteful projects.

The U.N.'S ACCOMPLISHMENTS

Even though the United Nations has not fulfilled the high hopes of its Charter, it should not be judged a failure. As long as delegates continue to meet and debate world issues, the risk of a third world war is lessened. In addition, the U.N.'s humanitarian agencies are making positive contributions to world health, education, and living conditions.

Food and Agriculture Organization (FAO). The FAO aims to raise levels of nutrition and food production. Its researchers helped develop the "miracle" strains of rice, wheat, and other staple foods that have increased world food supplies. FAO experts also teach farmers the new cultivation techniques required by the "green revolution."

World Health Organization (WHO). WHO specialists work to raise standards of health and sanitation in underdeveloped countries. The organization has led the fight against such deadly diseases as malaria, smallpox, and river blindness. WHO is also involved in the worldwide struggle against AIDS. One sign of WHO's good work is that Americans no longer need smallpox vaccinations before they visit foreign countries.

International Labor Organization (ILO). The ILO's goal is to raise the living standards and working conditions of workers throughout the world. The agency is unusual in that its councils are made up of employer and worker representatives along with the usual government bureaucrats.

Education, Scientific, and Cultural Organization (UNESCO). The specialists of UNESCO have done valuable service in improving international relations. The organization sponsors cultural exchanges, training programs, and exchanges of scientific information. The United States withdrew from the organization in 1984 because of anti-Western and anti-Israeli activities by its director, Amadou M'Bow of Senegal. Mr. M'Bow was defeated for reelection in 1987 by Frederico Mayor Zaragoza of Spain. Despite this change in leadership, the United States did not immediately rejoin UNESCO.

Other programs. Children, disaster vic-

■ The delegates to the United Nations often seem to do more talking than anything else. As this cartoon reminds us, however, it is better for people to talk about problems than to go to war over them. How effective has the United Nations been in keeping peace in the world?

tims, and refugees all receive attention from specialized U.N. agencies. UNICEF, for example, sends money and workers to the developing countries to help with mother and child care, nutrition, education, and social welfare. Sales of UNICEF greeting cards and folk art help support this work. Many refugees from wars and natural disasters owe their lives to United Nations programs for the care and resettlement of displaced peoples. Other U.N. agencies work on such problems as international communications, world weather forecasting, and the development of commercial air traffic.

7. How does the Department of Defense protect national security?

U.S. foreign policy tries to provide national security through peaceful, diplomatic means. When diplomacy fails, the nation may have to depend on its military strength. The Department of Defense (DOD) bears the primary responsibility for keeping the armed forces ready for any emergency.

The War Department was established in 1789 as one of the four original Cabinet offices. For many years, the department's authority was divided between rival departments of the Army and Navy. A 1947 reorganization created the Department of Defense, headed by the Secretary of Defense. Individual Army, Navy, and Air Force secretaries administer the individual services. The nerve center of the U.S. defense establishment is the Pentagon, a massive headquarters located just outside Washington, D.C.

DEFENSE DEPARTMENT STRUCTURE

Firm civilian control of military plans and operations begins with the commander-in-chief—the President. The line of command extends from the White House to the Secretary of Defense, the Deputy Secretary, the secretaries of the three armed services, and the undersecretaries and assistant secretaries of Defense. All are civilians, as are many of their assistants. As a group, these officials supervise all DOD activities, including finance, research and development, and public affairs.

Special DOD assistants meet with congressional committees to work out budgets and testify on legislative matters. Other specialists deal with complex problems that range from equipping foot soldiers to designing ICBMs. Modern weapons systems are expensive, and the DOD receives one of the largest appropriations in the federal budget. The Pentagon defends its budget requests as necessary to national security. Defense specialists warn that the current thaw in U.S.-Soviet relations has reduced—but not eliminated—the danger of nuclear war or small-scale regional conflicts.

■ Chairman of the U.S. Joint Chiefs of Staff Colin Powell (left) meeting with Egyptian Minister of Defense Sabri Abu-Taleb at the beginning of the Persian Gulf crisis in 1990.

THE JOINT CHIEFS OF STAFF

The Secretary of Defense's most important military advisers are the generals and admirals who work in the office of the Joint Chiefs of Staff. The President selects the Chairman of the Joint Chiefs, who thus becomes the nation's top military officer. The Chairman works closely with the Army Chief of Staff, the Chief of Naval Operations, the Air Force Chief of Staff, and the Marine Corps Commandant. Their tasks include (1) formulating military plans and operations; (2) solving problems of supply, training, and future needs; and (3) coordinating the activities of the various services. The Joint Chiefs also advise the National Security Council and sit in on meetings of the high-level Armed Forces Policy Council.

An appointment to the Joint Chiefs can create a conflict of interest for the nation's military leaders. Meetings often become quite heated, particularly when military judgments must give way to the President's political decisions. Interservice rivalries also hamper the work of the Joint Chiefs. The 1986 raid on Libya, for example, brought this problem into sharp focus. Unwilling to be left out, Air Force generals insisted on sending F-111 bombers to join the Navy's carrier-based planes. The Air Force won its role in the operation, even though the F-111s had to fly a long, roundabout route from bases in England.

THE DOD AS A CENTER OF CONTROVERSY

When he left the presidency in 1961, President Dwight D. Eisenhower issued a surprising warning. The former general used his farewell address to tell the nation that the military's "total influence—economic, political, even spiritual—is felt in every city, every statehouse, every office of the federal government." But in the late 1960s, as the war in Vietnam developed into a military and political disaster, the military lost much of its prestige and influence. The public and Congress became more willing to question the military's motives and requests. Today, many thoughtful citizens believe that the military and the defense industry exert too much influence on the federal government. Their criticisms can be summarized as follows:

1. The military-industrial complex. Eisenhower's speech took note of what has been called the *military-industrial complex.* This is the close relationship that has developed between Pentagon officials and defense industry leaders. Critics charge that the arms race with the Soviet Union has been used as an excuse to build an oversized army, navy, and air force. Big defense contracts have meant high profits for defense contractors, so they, naturally, want to keep on supplying as many goods as possible to the military. Former Senator William Proxmire, a frequent opponent of the defense establishment, described the "fast-moving, revolving door between the Pentagon and its big suppliers." In a recent year, defense contractors hired over 1,000 former Pentagon officials and retired military officers. According to some observers, having former **DOD** personnel on their payroll gives some industries an undue advantage when it comes to bidding on projects.

Americans of all political beliefs are divided over the possible dangers of the military-industrial complex. One side believes that the combination has been too successful in lobbying for ever higher military budgets and a military-oriented foreign policy. The military's defenders take the opposite view. They argue that increases in defense spending are necessary to keep the United States strong enough to withstand any possible military threat from a future enemy.

2. Waste and inefficiency. Wasteful spending has been the most obvious product of the military-industrial complex, its critics charge. Weapons systems are designed and put into production without apparent regard for how much they cost—or how well they work. The cost overruns charged against the B-1 bomber, Sheridan light tank, and MX missile are cited as examples of the inability of the military-industrial complex to stay within its budget. The addition of billions of dollars

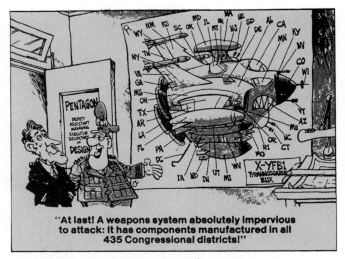

"At last! A weapons system absolutely impervious to attack: it has components manufactured in all 435 Congressional districts!"

■ In recent years, military spending has been reduced. What is the cartoonist saying about the military's efforts to influence congressional approval of weapons?

to military budgets in the early 1980s increased fears of further waste. President Reagan proposed and promoted the costly "Star Wars" anti-missile defense system, for example, even though many scientists warned that it would never work.

3. Civilian control of the military. Although the Constitution puts the military under civilian control, charges were made during the Vietnam War that military leaders sometimes acted without presidential approval. In 1972, for example, the Air Force carried out several bombing raids on North Vietnam in direct violation of orders then in effect. These incidents raised serious doubts about the willingness of the military to accept political decisions that go against strategic judgments.

4. Congressional supervision of military spending. Most members of Congress are reluctant to deny the funds that the military says are necessary for national security. Much of the waste in military spending, some observers contend, could be eliminated if Congress required stricter accounting for every dollar spent. In addition, if Congress would authorize long-term financing for some complex projects, contractors could carry on their research and development more efficiently. The military-industrial complex has many supporters in Congress who resist such reforms.

REFORM OF THE DOD

No major country can afford to do away with its armed forces. As a leader of the free world, the United States also carries the responsibility of providing security for its allies. Several reforms have been suggested that would not diminish military preparedness:

1. *Reduce the power of the military-industrial complex.* At the present time, many DOD military personnel move into the defense industry when they leave the armed forces. At the same time, defense industry officials are selected for sensitive posts at the Pentagon. As a result, a network of "contacts" creates favored treatment for those companies with the most influence. Rules to regulate this exchange of personnel between the military and defense industry have been established. New campaign financing laws have already cut back on the amount of money the defense industry can contribute to its political allies.

2. *Control Escalating Expenses.* Modern weapons will always be expensive. Even so, careful cost-accounting practices would provide an early warning when the costs of a weapon system rise far above the original estimates. The warning would give Congress a chance to re-examine the project and to kill it if necessary. Wider use of competitive bidding for new weapons will often cut costs in

Learning Skills

Comparing and Contrasting

When you study any of the social studies disciplines, you need "tools" to help make complex ideas easier to understand. In this text, you've learned skills such as how to interpret graphics and how to take notes and write summaries. An equally useful tool is the technique known as *comparing and contrasting.* When you compare, you're looking for similarities. When you contrast, you're looking for differences. Together, a comparing/contrasting list gives you a balanced picture of two related topics.

Suppose that your government teacher has asked you to report on the State Department and the Department of Defense. That is a rather complex assignment. A political scientist could write a book on the subject. What can you do? Attack the problem by comparing and contrasting. First, list all the ways in which the two departments are alike. Then, list the ways in which they're different. If the teacher will accept your answer in listing form, you're finished. If you are required to write an essay, you can use your listings as an outline.

What does a comparing/contrasting listing look like? Here's one for the State/Defense topic:

COMPARING

1. The Secretary of State and the Secretary of Defense are appointed to the Cabinet by the President.

2. Both secretaries are civilians; they must be confirmed by the Senate.

3. Both departments play an important role in advising the President on U.S. foreign policy.

4. Service in the upper levels of both departments is considered a high-prestige career.

5. Both departments carry on operations all over the globe.

half, according to a congressional staff study. In addition, the practice of developing duplicate weapons systems for each service should be stopped. During a period of tight budgets, the American people want the President and Congress to make sure that military appropriations are spent efficiently.

3. *Maintain civilian control.* Fortunately, the United States has never had to worry about a military takeover of the government. Presidents listen to the advice of their military advisers, but they insist on obedience to the civilian chain of command. When President Truman fired General MacArthur during the Korean War, he was upholding this principle. Today, both military and civilian leaders agree that Truman's decision was correct.

8. How does the Central Intelligence Agency aid U.S. foreign policy?

The art of gathering information about foreign governments has come a long way since 1929. That was when Secretary of State Henry L. Stimson said, "Gentlemen do not read each other's mail." He then ordered the government to stop spying on other countries. That directive probably did not last long because foreign policy cannot be made without accurate, up-to-date information. As former spymaster Allen Dulles wrote, "When the fate of a nation and the lives of its soldiers are at stake, gentlemen do read each other's mail—if they can get their hands on it."

CONTRASTING

1. Presidents depend on the State Department for diplomatic advice, but they turn to the Department of Defense when they need military advice. For example, if a President wants to write a new disarmament treaty with the Soviet Union, the State Department will carry on the negotiations and provide the diplomatic language. The DOD will advise the President on the military risks involved in taking weapons out of service.

2. Almost all members of the State Department are civilians. Except for the civilian secretaries and undersecretaries, the DOD is made up of the uniformed men and women of the armed forces.

3. The DOD consumes a large chunk of the federal budget and generates great controversy over the role of the military-industrial complex. The State Department is less controversial, and it costs much less to run.

4. Americans who travel abroad carry passports issued by the State Department, pass through State Department-operated customs points, and depend on U.S. embassies and consulates for advice and assistance. Unless war breaks out, travelers will seldom come in contact with the DOD's overseas military bases.

5. The Secretary of Defense is often called on to referee the long-standing, costly rivalry among the heads of the Army, Navy, and Air Force. The State Department's various offices operate with far less infighting.

You can probably think of additional comparisons and contrasts, but this gives you the basic idea. With this technique, you can handle general topics ("Discuss capitalism and communism") or more specific topics ("Discuss the SALT I and SALT II treaties").

"THINGS ARE QUIET, WHAT SAY WE GET UP A DOSSIER ON EACH OTHER?"

■ With concern about the evils of communism lessening, some people think that the power of the CIA is being weakened. "Dossier" means a file of information. The CIA keeps such files on individuals considered to be suspicious.

The President relies on the Central Intelligence Agency (CIA) for most of the nation's *foreign intelligence*. This is the data that the government gathers about the activities of other governments, terrorist groups, and the like. The CIA was established in 1947 to replace a hodgepodge of intelligence-gathering offices scattered throughout the military and civilian offices of the federal government. Even so, the CIA shares intelligence-gathering tasks with several lesser-known agencies. These include the Defense Intelligence Agency, the National Security Agency (both under the DOD), the State Department's Bureau of Intelligence and Research, and the Justice Department's Federal Bureau of Investigation.

THE CIA'S MISSION

The CIA charter makes the agency responsible for (1) gathering and evaluating foreign intelligence and (2) coordinating the other intelligence-gathering agencies of the United States. Until recently, CIA budgets were rarely questioned by Congress. Indeed, a sizable share of the millions needed to run the CIA each year is hidden in appropriations for other agencies.

CIA OPERATIONS

Most CIA operations never make the headlines. By their very nature, intelligence activities cannot survive the glare of publicity. Still, the agency has been credited with having had a hand in the overthrow of Communist-leaning governments from Iran and Indonesia to Guatemala and Chile. Thanks to the CIA, our foreign policy planners often know what a particular country will do when the United States proposes a certain course of action. Disarmament talks with the Soviet Union, for example, could not take place without hard information on the location, range, and accuracy of Soviet missiles.

For all its successes, the CIA's record also includes some failures. Faulty CIA execution of the Bay of Pigs invasion of Cuba in 1961 resulted in a shattering defeat. The agency also ran into difficulties in Vietnam, where its agents often misjudged the enemy's strength and misread its plans. In 1987, the CIA came under attack for helping arrange the sale of arms to Iran. This sale violated a strict policy against supplying arms to nations that sponsor international terrorism.

When CIA employees were found to be mixed up in the Watergate scandal, the agency drew a different type of protest. Critics feared that the use of the CIA in domestic spying (a violation of its legal authority, which is restricted to foreign intelligence gathering) was endangering First Amendment rights. The 1975 investigation of the agency also turned up other unsavory stories. Americans were shocked to learn, for example, that the CIA had thought about using the Mafia to assassinate Cuban Premier Fidel Castro.

REFORM OF THE CIA

Most critics of the CIA make two important points about the agency: (1) Congress should supervise its intelligence-gathering activities more carefully. (2) The CIA has too often become involved in domestic matters. Reforms have been suggested in each of these areas.

1. *Better supervision.* CIA officials have been accused of lying to Congress in their reports and testimony. The suggested reforms would involve Congress in deep and continuing supervision of all CIA activities, including full disclosure of CIA budgets. Sharing this information with Congress would carry with it the risk that sensitive materials would be made public. The CIA's supporters point out that some members of Congress "leak" secret documents. These leaks are a way of gaining publicity for the individual lawmakers or the causes they support.

2. *No domestic spying.* The CIA must stick to its legal task—the gathering of intelligence *outside* of the United States. The President, with the help of Congress, can oversee intelligence activities so as to ensure that "national security" does not extend to spying on Americans who hold unpopular views.

Two steps toward reforming the agency were taken in the spring of 1976. First, President Gerald Ford issued an executive order that reorganized the intelligence community. Ford placed overall supervision of intelligence policy in the hands of the National Security Council. Day-to-day management of all intelligence-gathering agencies was given to a three-member Committee on Foreign Intelligence, headed by the CIA director. Violations of the law, such as bugging the phones of U.S. citizens or plotting to assassinate foreign leaders during peacetime, were also forbidden.

Second, stung by accounts of past abuses, the Senate set up a new "watchdog" committee, the Senate Select Committee on Intelligence. The chairman of the committee, Senator Daniel Inouye of Hawaii, pledged that "the CIA and other intelligence agencies will not violate the civil rights of any American."

The success of these reforms rests largely on the strength and character of the President. The complex network of intelligence agencies adds greatly to the power of the Oval Office. A President who uses that power with restraint and with a sense of fair play is assuring the American people that the nation's intelligence-gathering operations will obey the rule of law.

9. What role do arms control and disarmament play in U.S. foreign policy?

From the 1790s onward, the United States has favored small peacetime armies. Beginning in the 1920s, the United States led the way toward general *disarmament*—a plan for all nations to reduce military forces to the minimum needed to maintain internal order. In 1921–1922, this country hosted the Washington Conference, which attempted to limit the size of world navies. American diplomats also signed the 1928 Kellogg-Briand Pact in which the major nations renounced war as a means of settling international disputes. Further efforts to bring about disarmament ended with the coming of World War II in 1939.

After a U.S. plane dropped the first atomic bomb on Hiroshima in 1945, American diplomats called for the international control of atomic weapons. Although the plan received United Nations approval, the Soviet Union rejected it. The reason became clear in 1949, when the Soviets exploded their own nuclear device. Each country went on to develop even more powerful warheads for their deadly intercontinental ballistic missiles (ICBMs). The arms competition between the United States and the Soviet Union became a "race with death" for the entire planet.

ATMOSPHERIC TEST BAN

In 1963, the United States and the Soviet Union took a small step toward nuclear arms control. The two nations signed a treaty banning nuclear testing in the atmosphere. World concern over the dangers of radioactive fallout was growing, and 90 other countries volunteered to abide by the pact. France, China, and India have not felt bound by the agreement. These nations have continued to test nuclear weapons in the open air. The other atomic powers confine their testing to underground explosions.

THE SALT TALKS

The United States first proposed a plan for *stategic arms limitation* in the 1950s. The plan called for a mutual reduction of key weapons such as missiles and warheads. The Soviets stalled the talks by refusing to allow inspection teams on their soil. Once American satellites began providing accurate data on the Soviet Union's military strength, the Strategic Arms Limitation Talks (SALT) began in the late 1960s.

SALT I. Years of hard bargaining ended in 1972 with the signing of an agreement called SALT I. The treaty limited development of costly antiballistic missile systems by both sides. It also froze for up to five years the existing number of offensive strategic missiles. This gave the United States over 1,700 ICBMs, while the Soviet Union was allowed 2,300. Although smaller in number, the American missiles were considered to be more accurate, and many carried multiple warheads. The Senate approved the treaty but added a resolution. The President was ordered not to make any agreement that would leave the Soviets with military superiority.

SALT II. Continuing talks, known as SALT II, aimed at achieving permanent limits on the number and destructiveness of strategic weapons. The treaty's critics pointed out that SALT II gave the Soviets superiority in some categories of weapons. After the Soviet Union invaded Afghanistan in 1979, President Carter abandoned efforts to have SALT II ratified. Despite this breakdown, both nations continued to observe the terms of SALT II. Further talks ended abruptly in 1983 when the United States began deploying cruise missiles in Europe. NATO planners believed that the missiles were needed to serve as a counterforce to a new generation of medium-range Soviet missiles.

AGREEMENT ON MISSILE REDUCTION

Talks between the United States and the Soviet Union were renewed in 1985. President Reagan announced that he would continue to respect the terms of SALT II, even though he believed that the Soviets were not complying fully with its terms. He also proposed a system for intercepting incoming missiles. Although the plan was officially known as the Strategic Defense Initiative (SDI), reporters soon nicknamed it "Star Wars."

In 1987, the United States and the Soviet Union sidestepped the SDI question. They agreed to eliminate an entire class of intermediate-range nuclear weapons. In a major

■ In 1987, Mikhail Gorbachev, head of the Soviet Union, and President Ronald Reagan signed a treaty to reduce each nation's arsenal of nuclear missiles. Here Gorbachev and Reagan exchange copies of the treaty.

breakthrough, the two countries agreed to allow the entry of inspection teams to verify that the missiles were being dismantled. That hopeful beginning led to Strategic Arms Reduction Talks (START) that bound the two nuclear powers to the elimination of some of the missiles already in service. Two parallel negotiations also made good progress toward reducing conventional arms and chemical weapons.

Reviewing
what you've learned

1. Over the years, U.S. foreign policy has shifted back and forth between *isolationism* and involvement with the rest of the world. Today, even though isolationism seems attractive to many people, no nation can endure without trade agreements and working political relations with other countries. As a leader of the Western democracies, the United States has developed a foreign policy that attempts to (1) contain communism, (2) promote democratic ideals, and (3) protect American interests.

2. The President must clear many foreign policy decisions with Congress. The Senate debates and approves (or rejects) treaties. Both houses appropriate the funds for foreign aid, the armed forces, the intelligence-gathering agencies, and the diplomatic corps. In the final analysis, the President cannot pursue policies that the American people will not accept.

3. The Secretary of State assists the President and also administers the State Department. Professional, highly trained experts staff the Foreign Service, which is made up of the diplomatic corps (the political side) and the consular service (aid to business and travelers). In many poorer countries, American foreign aid helps feed, educate, and train the people.

4. International aid programs provide friendly nations with military assistance and economic development loans. The economic loans and grants enable developing countries to build much needed highways, schools, and factories. Much of this economic aid flows through international agencies such as the World Bank and the Export-Import Bank.

5. The United Nations serves as an international forum for discussion and a channel for programs to improve public health, working conditions, and living standards. The technical agencies (WHO, FAO, and UNESCO, for example) have achieved greater success than the political bodies, whose main task is to keep the peace.

6. The United States belongs to NATO, a military alliance with Canada, Western European countries, Greece and Turkey. NATO members have pledged to support each other in event of an attack. Similar alliances elsewhere have collapsed. Troubles in Asia and the Middle East have forced the United States to seek new partners in those critical areas.

7. The Department of Defense does for military affairs what the State Department does for diplomatic matters. Civilian control of the armed forces is assured, for the Secretary of Defense and the leading DOD officials are all civilians. The highest-ranking military officers—the Joint Chiefs of Staff—advise the secretaries of the Army, Navy, and Air Force, the National Security Council, and the President.

8. Much of the background information necessary to make sound foreign policy comes from the Central Intelligence Agency. CIA agents gather information from many countries, using both modern and old-style espionage techniques. Complaints that CIA agents had spied on American citizens within the United States as well as the agency's involvement in plots against foreign governments have sparked attempts at reform. President Ford took the first step by clarifying the lines of authority over intelligence operations.

9. Efforts at *disarmament* have long occupied foreign policy planners. Progress has been made, particularly in ending nuclear testing in the atmosphere. With the threat of nuclear destruction hanging over everyone's head, the United States and the Soviet Union have also agreed to wide-ranging disarmament talks.

Review questions and activities

TERMS YOU SHOULD KNOW

ambassador	disarmament	isolationism
consul	embassy	military-industrial complex
consulate	foreign intelligence	passport
containment	foreign policy	strategic arms limitation
détente	grants	visa
diplomacy	imperialism	

REVIEW QUESTIONS

Select the response that best completes each statement or question.

1. The aspect of U.S. foreign policy represented by Teddy Roosevelt's acquisition of the Panama Canal is (*a*) isolationism. (*b*) imperialism. (*c*) world leadership. (*d*) containment of communism. (*e*) none of these.

2. The Monroe Doctrine attempted to (*a*) prevent further European interference in Western Hemisphere affairs. (*b*) involve the United States in the Napoleonic wars. (*c*) open China to foreign trade. (*d*) set up joint British–United States domination of Latin America. (*e*) open the territory west of the Mississippi.

3. The strongest voice in shaping foreign policy belongs to (*a*) Congress. (*b*) the State Department. (*c*) the CIA. (*d*) the President. (*e*) the Department of Defense.

4. The most effective way for both houses of Congress to join forces to prevent the President from following a particular foreign policy would be to (*a*) cut off budget support. (*b*) ask the courts for an injunction. (*c*) rally public opinion against that policy. (*d*) refuse to confirm a treaty. (*e*) pass a resolution against that policy.

5. The best argument for continuing foreign aid is that (*a*) giving away dollars buys good friends and allies. (*b*) the Soviet Union will take over any country we don't help. (*c*) the United States has more money than it knows what to do with. (*d*) economic and military aid helps the United States influence friendly governments. (*e*) it is good business; the loans bring in more money than the United States gives out.

6. Within the United Nations, the United States can always count on support from (*a*) the General Assembly. (*b*) the Security Council. (*c*) UNESCO. (*d*) the Secretariat. (*e*) none of these.

7. The most important American military alliance is (*a*) NATO. (*b*) SEATO. (*c*) OAS. (*d*) SALT II. (*e*) the Marshall plan.

8. The United Nations has more than lived up to the hopes of its founders. This statement is (*a*) true. (*b*) false. Nothing important has been accomplished by the U.N. (*c*) false. The U.N. has at times worked effectively to keep the peace and has done much humanitarian work, but it has been unable to solve many of the world's major problems.

9. The Department of Defense operates completely under civilian control, from the President on down to the various secretaries. This statement is (*a*) true. (*b*) false. In time of war, the military heads of the Joint Chiefs of Staff take control of the DOD. (*c*) false. Civilians control the DOD's relations with Congress and the civilian economy, but military leaders make all tactical and strategic decisions on use of the armed forces.

10. The CIA is forbidden to engage in spying on members of Congress because (*a*) the First Amendment prohibits it. (*b*) the CIA charter restricts the agency to investigations outside of the United States. (*c*) the separation of powers doctrine forbids it. (*d*) conflicts of interest might result when members of Congress must supervise the CIA. (*e*) all of these.

CONCEPT DEVELOPMENT

1. What are the general objectives of U.S. foreign policy? How would you modify these objectives over the next ten years?

2. Foreign aid has been a major part of U.S. foreign policy since World War II. What does the United States hope to accomplish by giving food and technical and military assistance to other countries?

3. What are the chief accomplishments of the United Nations? Why has the United States been critical of the U.N. in recent years?

4. Despite mistakes and misdeeds by the CIA and other intelligence agencies, no one seriously suggests doing away with these organizations. Why is it so important that the United States possess a strong intelligence capability?

5. What progress has been made in reaching international agreements on disarmament since World War II? Why has it been so difficult to move faster in this critical area?

HANDS-ON ACTIVITIES

1. Join four other students in staging a mock conference of foreign ministers from France, the Soviet Union, China, Saudi Arabia, and the United States. The conference has been called to deal with the question of sharing the world's dwindling oil reserves. What position would each country take? What conflicts can you foresee? Can the five of you arrive at a formula for compromise that all can support? If your conference is

presented before the class, allow the other students to ask questions of the "ministers," each of whom should answer in character.

2. Research the story of the Alliance for Progress. Try to discover what went wrong with this ambitious plan and what it did accomplish. Can you find any guidelines for future foreign aid programs in this experiment? Prepare a research paper or an oral report on the topic. Remember that it will be easy to favor one point of view or another. Try to present an objective viewpoint.

3. Prepare a poster illustrating the relative military strengths of the United States and the Soviet Union. Can you discover any indication that either country has gained superiority over the other?

4. Would you like to get paid for traveling in other countries? Investigate the possibility of a career in one of the government agencies that carries out U.S. foreign policy. Jobs range from clerk-typist to ambassador, from army private to U.N. translator. You can get help in your school's career center or guidance office, or from the public library. Look for information on job openings, pay scales, training requirements, living conditions, and other useful data.

13 Managing the nation's affairs: The Cabinet's role in domestic policy

▲ President George Washington and the first Cabinet. It consisted of the secretaries of State, Treasury, and War and the Attorney General.

Every President, from Washington onward, has seen the Cabinet in a different light. Some Presidents chose the most capable people they could find, even though it meant putting their rivals into positions of power. Washington, Jackson, and Lincoln followed this pattern. Other Presidents dismissed the Cabinet as having little importance. As William Howard Taft said, "The Cabinet is a mere creation of the President's will. It exists only by custom."

Harold Ickes, Secretary of the Interior under Franklin Roosevelt, agreed with Taft. "The President makes all of his own decisions and, so

303

far as the Cabinet is concerned, without taking counsel with a group of advisors," Ickes said. ". . . It is fair to say that the Cabinet is not a general council upon whose advice the President relies."

President Harry S Truman saw the Cabinet in a different light. "Cabinet positions are created by law at the request of the President to help him carry out his duties as chief executive under the Constitution," Truman wrote. "It is a very satisfactory arrangement if the President keeps his hands on the reins, and knows exactly what goes on in each department. When a Cabinet member speaks publicly, he usually speaks on authorization of the President, in which case he speaks for the President. If he takes it upon himself to announce a policy that is contrary to the policy the President wants carried out, he can cause a great deal of trouble." Any Cabinet member who violated this rule could expect to be chewed out by an angry Truman.

President Dwight Eisenhower used the Cabinet much as he had once used his military staff. He explained, "The Cabinet, from the beginning, met to consider together questions of general public concern, and to give me recommendations on new government-wide policies and instructions. In the first six months, for example, the Cabinet discussed such dissimilar questions as Spanish air bases and postal rates. While the Secretary of State and the Postmaster General made the basic presentations, all present were invited to participate in any ensuing argument. . . . I found its deliberations and debates enlightening as I faced important decisions."

By contrast, President Kennedy was almost openly scornful of the Cabinet. He held very few Cabinet meetings. In times of crisis he turned to other top-level groups, such as the National Security Council. When Lyndon Johnson took Kennedy's place, he tried hard to elevate the status of the Cabinet. Johnson held regular meetings, with everything planned out in advance. George Reedy, LBJ's press secretary, reported that the experience was like sitting with the preacher in the front parlor on Sunday. No one dared talk out of turn, and it was often a painful experience for everyone, he said. Cabinet members who wanted to influence the President had to wait until they could talk to him in private.

Historians have accused President Nixon of bypassing the Cabinet in order to concentrate power in the White House. The Presidents who followed Nixon have tended to follow that pattern. Historian Arthur M. Schlesinger, Jr. calls this trend the creation of an Imperial Presidency. Schlesinger writes, "As for the Cabinet, . . . it has served Presidents best when it has contained men strong and independent in their own right, strong enough to make the permanent government responsive to government policy and independent enough to carry honest dissents into the Oval Office, even on questions apart from their departmental jurisdiction."

In the preceding chapter, you studied the headline-making tasks of the departments of State and Defense. These departments deal primarily with foreign affairs. In this chapter you will learn about the 12 other Cabinet departments that help the President administer the domestic affairs of the United States. As Daniel Webster said in 1824, "The country is increasing. There is a great deal more work to be done."

1. How does the Treasury Department manage the nation's financial affairs?

2. How does the Justice Department administer the nation's legal system?

3. How does the Commerce Department aid businesses and consumers?

4. What is the role of the Department of Energy?

5. What is the role of the Department of Health and Human Services?

6. How does the Department of Education influence U.S. schools?

7. What does the Department of Labor do for American workers?

8. How does the Department of Agriculture assist U.S. farmers?

9. How does the Department of the Interior manage natural resources?

10. How does the Department of Transportation oversee systems of transportation?

11. What is the role of the Department of Housing and Urban Development?

12. How does the Department of Veterans Affairs serve former military personnel?

1. How does the Treasury Department manage the nation's financial affairs?

Most people know that the Treasury Department produces the money they use every day. But printing dollar bills and minting new quarters is only a small part of the Treasury's tasks.

As with all Cabinet posts, the President appoints the Secretary of the Treasury, subject to confirmation by the Senate. Alexander Hamilton served as the first in a long line of able Americans who have held the job. Among many other duties, the Treasury Department advises the President on all matters of domestic and foreign economic policy; performs a variety of fiscal services, such as collecting taxes, coining and printing money, and issuing payment checks. Treasury also provides certain law enforcement services. The secretary

Expenditures by Cabinet Departments, 1990

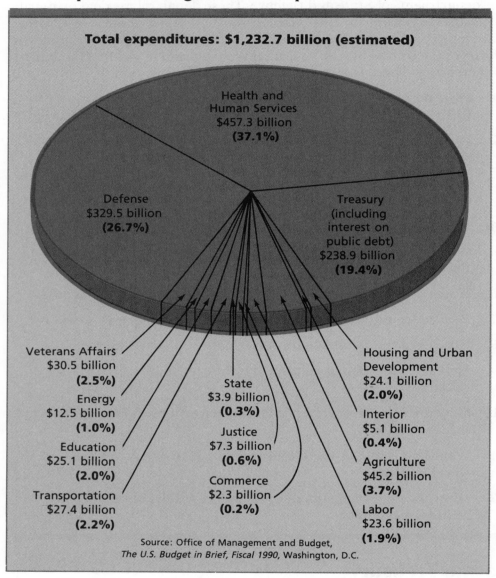

Total expenditures: $1,232.7 billion (estimated)

Health and Human Services $457.3 billion (37.1%)

Defense $329.5 billion (26.7%)

Treasury (including interest on public debt) $238.9 billion (19.4%)

Veterans Affairs $30.5 billion (2.5%)

Energy $12.5 billion (1.0%)

Education $25.1 billion (2.0%)

Transportation $27.4 billion (2.2%)

State $3.9 billion (0.3%)

Justice $7.3 billion (0.6%)

Commerce $2.3 billion (0.2%)

Housing and Urban Development $24.1 billion (2.0%)

Interior $5.1 billion (0.4%)

Agriculture $45.2 billion (3.7%)

Labor $23.6 billion (1.9%)

Source: Office of Management and Budget, *The U.S. Budget in Brief, Fiscal 1990*, Washington, D.C.

coordinates the Treasury's work on economic problems with other agencies. For example, the programs to combat inflation and trade deficits also involve the Office of Management and Budget.

A number of important government agencies make up the Treasury Department. Some, such as the Internal Revenue Service, are familiar to every American. Others, such as the Comptroller of the Currency, seldom appear in the headlines despite the importance of their work.

INTERNAL REVENUE SERVICE (IRS)

The Internal Revenue Service can never be accused of being the public's favorite federal agency. But someone must collect the billions

■ A U.S. Customs inspector has discovered illegal drugs in a shipment of roses from Colombia. Screening imports for illegal goods, particularly drugs, is a major responsibility of Customs.

of tax dollars that fund government operations each year, and the IRS has been given that job. In addition, the IRS works hard to make sure that all Americans pay their fair share of taxes. Seven regional offices oversee more than 60 IRS districts, one or more in each state.

Congress has authorized the IRS to collect revenue from a number of sources other than personal and corporate income taxes. Three of these are (1) excise taxes (so-called luxury taxes on items such as playing cards, liquor, cigarettes, gasoline, and airline tickets), (2) estate taxes (taxes on the value of property and money people leave when they die), and (3) gift taxes (taxes on gifts and donations that exceed a minimum amount).

CUSTOMS SERVICE

The members of the Customs Service are among the first officials travelers see when they enter the United States. Customs officers collect duties and taxes on imported merchandise and control the movement of goods in and out of the country. Once a major source of government income, customs duties now provide less than two percent of the annual federal budget. Customs inspectors work at all major harbors, airports, and border crossing points (about 300 in all). Catching drug smugglers has become one of their most important (and difficult) responsibilities.

Customs duties are set by Congress and fall into three categories: (1) specific duties, a fixed amount per item imported; (2) ad valorem duties, a percentage of an item's value; and (3) mixed rates, a combination of the first two. Customs rates run from zero to as high as 100 percent or more of an item's value. Congress often raises duties to protect U.S. industries that are being hurt by low-priced imports.

TREASURER OF THE UNITED STATES

Many people confuse the Treasurer of the United States with the head of the department, the Secretary of the Treasury. The Treasurer of the United States receives, holds, and pays out the public's money for the federal government. This official's signature appears on every piece of currency and every government check—around a billion checks per year! The Treasurer's office also supervises the U.S. Savings Bond Division, the U.S. Mint, and the Bureau of Engraving and Printing.

UNITED STATES MINT

The coins that jingle in our pockets pour out of three mints, located in Philadelphia, Denver, and San Francisco. The United States Mint also has depositories for gold (Fort Knox, Kentucky) and silver (West Point, New York). The first mints were founded in 1792. From that year until the country dropped the gold standard in 1933, the government produced gold, silver, and copper coins. The production of silver coins ended in 1964, when the silver in a coin became worth more than the coin's face value. Today's "silver coins" are made from an alloy of copper and nickel bonded to a core of copper and zinc. U.S. mints produce about 15 billion coins a year. Three out of four of these coins are pennies.

BUREAU OF ENGRAVING AND PRINTING

The Bureau of Engraving and Printing designs and prints all U.S. paper money, postage stamps, Treasury bonds, revenue stamps, and other documents. Paper money is printed in seven denominations from $1 to $100. The older, higher value bills ($500, $1,000, $5,000, and $10,000) are removed from circulation whenever they show up in the Federal Reserve System. The bureau is also experimenting with new forms of currency that will be harder to counterfeit. Its currency printing operation has long been a favorite tourist attraction in Washington, D.C.

SECRET SERVICE

Two very different tasks keep the Secret Service busy. One job involves the prevention of counterfeiting. Treasury agents, generally known as "T-men," take pride in their record. They seize almost 90 percent of all counterfeit money before it reaches the public.

The Director of the Secret Service also supervises a corps of agents who provide protection for leading government figures. The President and Vice President and their families, presidential candidates, former Presidents, and visiting heads of state all receive Secret Service protection. Agents do not hesitate to risk their own lives when an assassin threatens the President. One agent died while defending President Truman in 1950. Another was wounded in the 1981 attempt on President Reagan's life.

OTHER DIVISIONS

The Treasury Department also includes a number of lesser-known agencies. Four are particularly important. The *Bureau of the Public Debt* supervises public borrowing. The *Bureau of Alcohol, Tobacco and Firearms* administers federal law as it affects those products. The *Financial Management Service* keeps the government's accounts. The *Office of the Comptroller of the Currency* administers banking law and supervises national banks.

GENERAL ACCOUNTING OFFICE

The General Accounting Office (GAO) is known as "the watchdog of the Treasury," but it's not a part of the Treasury Department. Congress established the GAO as an independent agency in 1921 to make sure that public money is spent in the way the legislators intended. Headed by the Comptroller General, GAO accountants report back to Congress on management and efficiency in the Treasury Department and elsewhere in the executive branch. The Comptroller General is appointed by the President and confirmed by the Senate for a 15-year term.

2. How does the Justice Department administer the nation's legal system?

The Attorney General, as head of the Department of Justice, is the nation's top law enforcement officer. The only Cabinet member not given the title of secretary, the Attorney

General (AG) has a number of important jobs. The AG serves as the chief legal adviser to the federal government, investigates and prosecutes offenses against federal law, and represents the United States in cases before the Supreme Court. The AG also supervises the federal prison system and administers immigration and naturalization laws.

The various divisions of the Justice Department back up the Attorney General with the skilled lawyers and bureaucrats needed to enforce federal law. The Solicitor General (SG), for example, represents the federal government when it takes cases to the Supreme Court. As the government's "chief lawyer," the Solicitor General has a major voice in deciding what cases the high court will be asked to review. The SG also supervises the preparation of the Justice Department's briefs and legal arguments.

BUREAU OF PRISONS

The Bureau of Prisons operates the federal government's large system of penitentiaries, correctional institutions, and prison camps. Prisoners are assigned to maximum- or minimum-security prisons according to the severity of their offenses. All prisoners are given opportunities to take part in counseling, training, work experience, education, and recreation. A little-known corporation, *Federal Prison Industries, Inc.*, manages prison workshops and sells goods and services to federal agencies. The bureau's halfway houses and community programs help released prisoners while they're readjusting to life on the "outside."

FEDERAL BUREAU OF INVESTIGATION (FBI)

The FBI investigates any violation of federal law not assigned to another agency. Over 180 federal crimes fall under FBI jurisdiction. These crimes include espionage, treason, kidnapping, bank robbery, many violations involving interstate transport of stolen goods, violations of the election laws, and assaulting or killing the President. The bureau's director assigns priorities to areas that most affect society—organized crime, drug trafficking,

■ Police forces around the nation rely on FBI fingerprint files to help identify suspects. The files contain some 169 million prints. The FBI also has a highly respected crime laboratory in which scientists analyze evidence.

terrorism, and white collar crime. FBI agents cooperate with state and local police forces, maintain extensive fingerprint files, develop new crime-fighting technologies, and run training courses for state and local police officers.

J. Edgar Hoover took over the FBI in 1924 and developed it into one of the world's most efficient police forces. Hoover's death in 1972, after 48 years on the job, came at a time when Congress was taking a critical interest in the bureau's methods. Of particular concern to civil rights activists were illegal FBI wiretaps, secret information files, and break-ins. In recent years, the FBI has regained some of its

■ Resident illegal aliens in Florida lining up to apply for legal status under the Immigration Reform and Control Act of 1986. The Immigration and Naturalization Service maintains offices throughout the United States and in Thailand, Mexico, and Italy.

lost respect. FBI agents, for example, have become skillful at setting up undercover "sting" operations. In one well-publicized case, agents exposed a group of government officials who accepted favors from foreign business interests. In another case, they cracked down on Department of Defense officials who were releasing secret information to defense industry consultants.

IMMIGRATION AND NATURALIZATION SERVICE (INS)

Hundreds of thousands of foreigners enter the United States each year to live, work, and prepare themselves for citizenship. The INS has a twofold job: (1) to aid immigrants who legally enter and apply for naturalization and (2) to prevent the illegal entry of aliens and to deport those who enter without proper permits.

Until the early part of this century, the government actively encouraged immigration. An average of over one million people a year flocked to the United States to help build the new nation. After World War I, Congress cut back on immigration by setting up quotas based on the immigrants' countries of origin. These quotas reduced the number of entries to around 150,000 immigrants a year from countries outside the Western Hemisphere. The number of immigrants allowed into the country varied with each change in the immigration laws. Congress set the current limit of 270,000 in 1980. No more than 20,000 immigrants from any one country are allowed to enter each year.

The law also lists several classes of immigrants who do not count against the total. These include the immediate relatives of U.S. citizens, members of the professions, workers whose skills are needed in this country, and refugees from Communist countries. Congress has also lowered the barriers for special groups, such as Cubans who fled from their country's Communist dictatorship and refugees from Vietnam and Cambodia. When all of these exceptions are added in, the United States now opens its borders to about 600,000 immigrants a year.

The nation's biggest immigration problem lies in the millions of aliens who enter the United States illegally. After years of debate, Congress passed the Immigration Reform and Control Act of 1986. The law allowed illegal aliens who lived continuously in the United States between January 1, 1982, and May 1988 to apply for legal immigration status. About 2 million aliens filed their papers during the program's first phase, which ended in mid-1988. In order to block the entry of new illegals, the INS was given the power to levy fines from $250 to $10,000 against employers who hire them. Congress reasoned that if they knew they couldn't find jobs, illegals would be less likely to come to this country.

ANTITRUST DIVISION

The Antitrust Division spearheads efforts to prevent large corporations from forming monopolies. Monopolies work against the public interest because they allow companies to control all or most of the market in their particular products. Action against companies that use illegal means to destroy competition dates back to the early 1900s. After World War II, a wave of mergers among giant corporations seemed likely to create a new series of monopolies. Government antitrust lawyers took action to keep this from happening.

When it can, the Antitrust Division acts before the monopoly or near-monopoly can be formed. A notice to the companies that it will oppose a proposed merger may be enough to keep the monopoly from taking shape. If necessary, Justice Department lawyers file a law-suit against a company they feel is breaking the antitrust laws. If the Justice Department wins the case, the federal courts will order the breakup of the monopolistic company into smaller, competing companies. One of the most famous antitrust cases forced John D. Rockefeller's Standard Oil Company to split up in 1911. A similar victory broke up the giant American Telephone and Telegraph Company (AT&T) in the early 1980s.

DRUG ENFORCEMENT ADMINISTRATION (DEA)

The nation's war against drugs has turned the spotlight on the Drug Enforcement Administration. The DEA enforces federal laws dealing with the illegal use of narcotics and other dangerous drugs. It regulates the legal manufacture of these controlled substances and works with the Public Health Service to supervise their use in medical research.

The DEA's administrator reports to the director of the FBI, and its agents work side by side with FBI agents on major drug cases. In order to combat drug smuggling, the agency also cooperates with foreign governments, state law enforcement agencies, and the Coast Guard. On the prevention side, the agency sponsors a national drug abuse education program. The DEA has won many small victories, but drug dealers are still winning the war. Until the public learns to say "NO!" to drugs, large quantities of cocaine, heroin, and marijuana will continue to flow into the country.

OTHER DIVISIONS

As one of the government's busiest departments, Justice runs a number of other important divisions. One of these is the *Civil Rights Division*, which enforces federal laws that protect individual Americans from racial or other forms of discrimination. The *Civil Division* handles most of the cases to which the U.S. government is a party, and the *Tax Division* deals with civil and criminal cases that originate in tax law. Finally, the *Land and Natural Resources Division* handles civil cases that involve government land and real property, Indian affairs, and environmental laws.

3. How does the Commerce Department aid businesses and consumers?

The Department of Commerce promotes the development of the U.S. economy. Commerce officials assist the mining, manufacturing, retail, shipping, and fishing industries, both at home and overseas. The department began its existence as the Department of Commerce and Labor in 1903. Labor became a separate agency in 1913. Along with its business interests, the Commerce Department serves the average American through its weather, weights and measures, and statistical services.

CENSUS BUREAU

Every ten years (1980, 1990, 2000, and so on) the Bureau of the Census sends its census takers out to check on the growth of the American population. The census supplies the important data used for apportioning the House of Representatives' 435 seats among the states (see pages 177–178). The census also provides valuable information on changing patterns in American housing, recreation, and family life. Special censuses at shorter intervals gather additional data on agriculture, industrial and business growth, transportation, and construction.

NATIONAL BUREAU OF STANDARDS

The goal of the National Bureau of Standards is to strengthen and advance the nation's science and technology. In pursuit of this goal, the NBS develops and safeguards the nation's standards of physical measurement. The original weights and measures, which were calibrated with extreme accuracy, provide the standard against which all others are measured and corrected. They are kept in the bureau's laboratories in Washington, D.C. The NBS also operates a testing and scientific research center.

Anyone who has tried (and failed) to remem-

■ A census taker in the Chinatown section of New York City in 1990. She is recording information in households that did not receive forms to fill out. Many large cities complained that their populations were undercounted. Why would this concern the places affected?

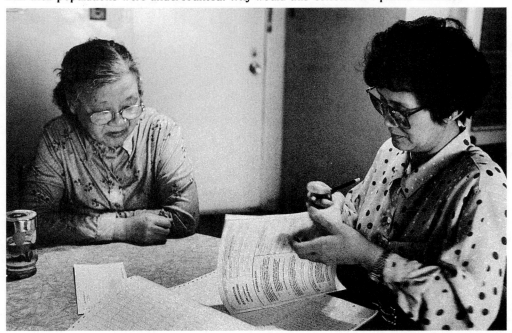

ber the number of fluid ounces in a quart has reason to wonder why the United States chose the British system of measurement. The process began when Congress officially adopted British measures in 1836. Most of the world adopted the metric system, but the United States didn't change. Using a different system makes it harder to sell goods overseas, however. As a result, the government has spent millions of dollars in an effort to convert the nation to metrics. Despite these efforts, Americans tend to reject kilograms, meters, and Celsius temperatures. So far, they prefer their familiar pounds, yards, and degrees Fahrenheit.

PATENT AND TRADEMARK OFFICE

The Patent and Trademark Office administers the laws that give individuals or corporations the exclusive right to make, use, or sell their inventions and designs. The office grants patents for a period of 17 years and rarely renews them. The office also registers trademarks, drawings, and slogans. These rights last for 20 years and are easily renewed. Copyrights, which protect authors' rights to the books, essays, and music they create are handled by the Library of Congress.

NATIONAL OCEANIC AND ATMOSPHERIC ADMINISTRATION (NOAA)

The NOAA concerns itself with the oceans, the weather, and the environment. The agency issues warnings when natural disasters such as tornados, hurricanes, earthquakes, and volcanic eruptions threaten life and property. In addition, the NOAA tries to protect marine animals, particularly endangered species such as whales. Along with predicting tides and currents, the agency's scientists study the ocean as a source of minerals and energy.

People make a lot of jokes about weather forecasters. Nevertheless, farmers, pilots, sailors, and the general public depend on the NOAA's *National Weather Service*. Weather Service technicians keep track of weather conditions around the globe. Weather stations, planes, ships, and a network of satellites gather the data about winds, clouds, and temperatures from which an accurate forecast can be made. The aviation industry, in particular, could not operate without the Weather Service.

OTHER AGENCIES

The widespread interests of the Department of Commerce involve a number of important agencies. The *International Trade Administra-*

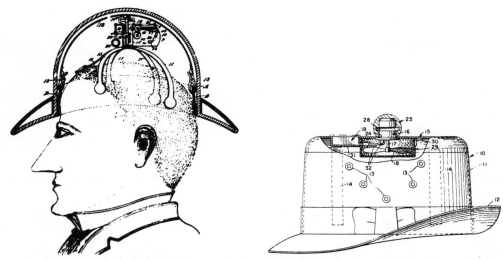

■ The Patent Office helps protect the ingenuity of America's inventors. The diagram on the left shows a self-tipping hat for a man with his arms full. Invented by James C. Boyle in 1896, it is patent number 556,248. On the right is a diagram for a hat cooled by a fan driven by a solar-powered motor. Patent number 3,353,191, it was invented by Harold W. Dahly in 1967.

tion, for example, helps promote foreign trade. It holds trade fairs overseas, reports on opportunities for increasing exports, and operates trade centers in key foreign cities. The *Bureau of Economic Analysis* is the fact-finding agency of the department. This bureau publishes statistics on the state of the economy, the growth of the gross national product, and other important business conditions.

The *Minority Business Development Agency* coordinates federal and private efforts to help businesses owned by minorities. The agency furnishes management and technical assistance through a network of regional and district offices. Similarly, the *Economic Development Administration* helps areas suffering from poverty and high unemployment. The agency brings government and private employers together to create new jobs.

The *National Technical Information Service* gathers and publishes information on American and foreign technology. It stocks nearly 2 million titles for sale to interested customers. Finally, the *U.S. Travel and Tourism Administration* works to bring more foreign visitors to this country. USTTA overseas field offices make sure that the world's tourists hear about Disneyland, the Grand Canyon, and other American showplaces.

Let's review for a moment

Under the overall direction of the President, the 14 Cabinet departments oversee the daily operations of government. All departments but one operate under the direction of a secretary; the *Justice Department* is led by the *Attorney General*. Each department head is appointed by the President and confirmed by the Senate.

Treasury Department officials collect the government's taxes, pay its bills, and keep track of its bookkeeping. Major divisions include the *Internal Revenue Service* (tax collection), the *Customs Service* (duty collection), the *United States Mint* (coinage), the *Bureau of Engraving and Printing* (paper money and stamps), and the *Secret Service* (tracking down counterfeiters and guarding the President).

The *Justice Department* supervises the enforcement of federal law. As the nation's top law officer, the Attorney General provides legal advice to the President along with running the department. The *Federal Bureau of Investigation* is probably the best-known division in Justice. Other divisions include the *Bureau of Prisons*, which runs the federal prison system, and the *Drug Enforcement Administration*, which helps to send drug dealers to those prisons. The *Immigration and Naturalization Service* administers the immigration laws and helps legal immigrants meet U.S. citizenship requirements. If you think General Conglomerates has an unfair stranglehold on widgets, tell the *Antitrust Division*. The division's lawyers will investigate the case and use the courts to break up the monopoly, if necessary.

The *Department of Commerce* promotes the full development of the nation's economic resources. In practice, it can also tell you how many people live in your community (*Census Bureau*), if your yardstick is accurate (*National Bureau of Standards*), how to protect the rights to your antigravity machine (*Patent and Trademark Office*), and if it will rain on graduation day (*National Weather Service*).

4. What is the role of the Department of Energy?

In the early 1970s, the United States stumbled into an energy crisis. Gas shortages developed when Arab suppliers raised prices and reduced shipments of the imported oil that fueled American factories and automobiles. As long lines formed at gas stations, people looked to Washington for help, but the federal government was poorly equipped to deal with the crisis. In addition, the country faced shortages of natural gas, the need to improve conservation practices, and a thousand related problems. In 1977, Congress tried to untangle the mess by forming a new Cabinet department made up of some 50 federal energy agencies—the Department of Energy (DOE).

Once started, DOE found that its efforts to coordinate federal energy policies were hampered by a lack of agreement on what that policy should be. In the early 1980s, the Reagan administration wanted to eliminate the department, but Congress disagreed. Now well into its second decade, DOE is still struggling to design an overall energy program that the White House, Congress, consumers, energy suppliers, business, and industry will accept.

KEY ENERGY AGENCIES

The *Federal Energy Regulatory Commission* (FERC) operates within the DOE as an independent agency. FERC has the important job of setting rates for the transmission and sale of natural gas and the transmission and sale of electricity. FERC also licenses hydroelectric power projects and establishes rates for shipping oil by pipelines.

The DOE has a number of other important agencies under its control. For example, the *Economic Regulatory Administration* (ERA) controls the pricing, importing, and transporting of crude oil. The *Energy Information Administration* gathers and publishes data on energy technology, production, demand, use, and distribution. The *Office of Civilian Radioactive Waste Management* is concerned with storing nuclear fuel and the even more difficult problem of getting rid of radioactive waste. Finally, five power administrations market the electric power generated by federally constructed dams throughout the nation.

RESEARCH AND DEVELOPMENT

One of DOE's most important jobs is to coordinate all federal activities relating to energy research and development. DOE's staff supervises federal energy research programs in fossil fuel research, underground energy transmission, solar heating and cooling, geothermal power, and alternative automobile power systems. In the critical field of nuclear research and development, DOE works closely

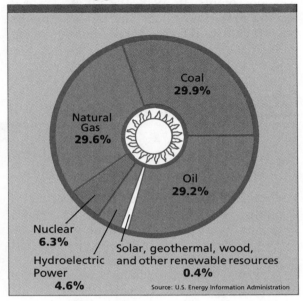

Where Does the Energy Come From?

Coal 29.9%

Natural Gas 29.6%

Oil 29.2%

Nuclear 6.3%

Hydroelectric Power 4.6%

Solar, geothermal, wood, and other renewable resources 0.4%

Source: U.S. Energy Information Administration

with the Department of Defense to provide the nation with its powerful nuclear arsenal.

Thus far, nuclear power has not delivered on its promise of providing an unlimited supply of cheap energy. As a result, the United States still depends on fossil fuels—oil, natural gas, and coal. Because fossil fuels will run out someday and because these fuels pollute the air, the DOE promotes research into the use of wind, sun, tides, and geothermal power as energy sources for the future.

THE DOE HAS MANY CRITICS

The DOE's critics charge that it has lost sight of its primary goals. Instead of practicing conservation and serving as a watchdog for nuclear safety, they say, the department has become too friendly with the defense and nuclear weapons industries. Sixty percent of the department's budget now goes to military programs such as the Strategic Defense Initiative (Star Wars), for example. With more money being spent on nuclear warhead research, less is available for civilian energy programs.

The second major criticism points to the DOE's lax supervision of the nation's nuclear weapons plants. In 1988, the public learned for the first time that some of these plants have regularly released large amounts of radioactive particles into the air. The plants have also dumped radioactive waste into rivers and allowed it to seep into underground water supplies. How many people, the critics ask, will die of cancer because of this criminal

Learning Skills

Analyzing Photos

An old bit of folk wisdom tells us that "a picture is worth a thousand words." There is some truth in that statement, isn't there? A photograph freezes a moment in time and saves it for us to study at our leisure.

By that logic, the photos that appear in a textbook should be just as important as the words that make up the text. If you're a typical student, however, you probably skip right over the photos. This attitude can be summed up as "I'm not going to be tested on this, am I?" A picture may be worth a thousand words, but it doesn't have any value if you don't "listen" to what it's saying.

Think back to the picture of the young woman with the roses on page 307. Who is she? Where was she when the picture was taken? What is she doing? What else is shown in the picture? Write down whatever you can remember. Afterward, look at the picture. Did you get anything right? If you're like most people, you probably failed this little test.

How can you do a better job of getting information from photos? Here are some suggestions that will help.

1. Give the pictures in your text just as much attention as you give the words on each page.

2. Ask yourself: "Why did the authors choose this picture? What are they trying to tell me?"

3. Look for clues that tell you when the picture was taken. Clothing and hairstyles, for example, are almost as good as a newspaper headline when you're trying to date a photograph.

4. After you've looked carefully at the picture, read the caption. A properly written caption helps you understand how the picture relates to a specific section of the chapter. Do you see things now that you didn't see before?

5. Ask yourself what probably happened just before the picture was taken and what may happen next. Did the subjects pose for the shot or is it a "stop-action" shot?

6. Does the picture tell the whole truth? Analyze the photo from a technical standpoint. Perhaps the photographer cut someone or something out of the picture. Perhaps the timing of the shot or the lighting portrays only one side of the story.

Now, follow these rules when you look back at the picture on page 312. What does the photo tell you about census takers and how they work? Do you see things in the picture that you missed when you saw it for the first time? Maybe that picture isn't worth a *thousand* words, but it's certainly worth a couple of hundred. And it's a lot easier to remember than the rest of the words on that page!

carelessness? The DOE admits that safety was ignored in the past, but it vows to fix the problem. Experts believe that rebuilding unsafe facilities and cleaning up the environment will take at least 20 years and will cost at least $100 billion.

5. What is the role of the Department of Health and Human Services?

The Department of Health and Human Services (HHS) was created in 1979 to replace the old Department of Health, Education, and Welfare. This huge department receives about two-fifths of all federal appropriations. These dollars enable the federal government to play a major role in promoting the health, education, and social welfare of every American. Dozens of agencies administer HHS's widespread activities.

SOCIAL SECURITY ADMINISTRATION

The Social Security Administration was created as part of the New Deal legislation of the 1930s. The agency (see also pages 223–224) provides retirement, survivors, disability, and health insurance programs for many elderly or otherwise needy people. When new workers apply for their Social Security numbers, accounts are set up in their names. The workers and their employers pay matching contributions into the fund. The amount they pay is calculated as a percentage of wages up to a federally established ceiling. Since 1966, most Americans over 65 have also been eligible for a hospital insurance program known as Medicare. The federal Social Security system also works with state governments to provide unemployment payments, aid to dependent children, and training programs that teach job skills to the unemployed.

PUBLIC HEALTH SERVICE (PHS)

The Public Health Service, under the leadership of the Surgeon General, has the task of promoting the nation's physical and mental

■ **U.S. Surgeon General C. Everett Koop publicizing scientific information about the addictive effects of nicotine. Koop, who served between 1981 and 1989, was the best-known public health spokesperson of recent times.**

health. The PHS aids the development of health services for all Americans, and conducts research in public health problems, enforces quarantines, and examines immigrants. The Surgeon General has worked hard in recent years to alert the nation to health hazards stemming from the use of tobacco, alcohol, and other harmful substances. The warnings printed on packages and posted in stores are the direct result of the Surgeon General's efforts. Dr. C. Everett Koop, President Reagan's Surgeon General, was particularly active in this area. Dr. Koop went so far as to urge a ban on cigarette advertising and on smoking in the workplace.

Some of the nation's most important research and treatment facilities are administered by the PHS. Two national institutes—the *National Institute on Alcohol Abuse and Alcoholism* and the *National Institute on Drug Abuse*—are working to find ways of helping people cope with the mental and physical problems caused by addictive behaviors. At the same time, disease control remains a primary task of the PHS. The *Centers for Disease Control* conduct research and respond to public health emergencies. Similarly, the *National Institutes of Health* are research centers where scientists seek cures for cancer, AIDS, heart disease, arthritis, and other diseases. In addition, the PHS administers programs of health care grants to state and local governments, primarily for hospital construction or support of medical schools.

FOOD AND DRUG ADMINISTRATION (FDA)

Early in this century, a group of muckraking journalists exposed the unhealthy conditions that were common in food-processing plants. One of the most notable muckrakers was Upton Sinclair, who took on the meatpacking industry in *The Jungle*. Congress responded by creating the Food and Drug Administration to guard the quality, purity, and safety of products purchased by the American consumer. The scientists and inspectors of the agency enforce truthfulness in advertising, standards of quality and cleanliness for foods, adequate proof of the safety and effectiveness of medicines, and proper labeling. It was the FDA, for example, that forced food processors to list the nutritional values of their products on package labels.

Now part of the Public Health Service, the FDA has been accused of moving too slowly in taking dangerous products off the market. Fast action is especially needed, consumer advocates say, when suspected cancer-causing substances are found in food. These critics also point to what they regard as a too-friendly relationship between FDA officials and the drug industry. Even so, the agency has prevented a number of health disasters through its testing and screening of new drugs and food additives. (See pages 472–474 for a dramatic example of FDA's scientists at work.)

HEALTH CARE FINANCING ADMINISTRATION

The Health Care Financing Administration (HCFA) administers two giant health insurance programs. Medicare is HCFA's best-known program. Under Medicare, the federal government provides basic health benefits for people who are receiving Social Security. The second program is Medicaid, which helps the states pay for medical services for the poor and medically needy. HCFA is also responsible for maintaining the quality of medical care paid for by Medicare and Medicaid.

6. How does the Department of Education influence U.S. schools?

Before 1979, 170 federal education programs were scattered throughout the federal government. Congress established the Department of Education in 1979 to coordinate these programs. Although President Reagan said in 1980 (and again in 1984) that he would like to abolish the department, the threat has not been carried out. Indeed, President George Bush, who wants to be known as the "education President," has given the department the task of improving America's schools. Reagan and Bush both called for a new emphasis on discipline and academic achievement.

The Department of Education's opponents worry that it will gradually take control of the nation's public schools. To prevent this, Congress wrote a series of restrictions into law. As additional security, an Intergovernmental Advisory Council on Education was created, with membership drawn from state and local governments. The council's job is to evaluate the department's impact on education at the state and local levels. Congress also put strict limits on staff growth within the department.

■ I. King Jordan at a news conference after being named the first deaf president of Gallaudet University. Students at Gallaudet boycotted classes and staged demonstrations in 1988 to protest the hiring of a hearing president. This person resigned, and Jordan was chosen.

The Department of Education administers federal scholarships, loans, grants, and direct aid to state departments of education. Special funds aid gifted students, the mentally and physically handicapped, library development, and vocational education. Two of the notable institutions funded by the department are Gallaudet University and Howard University. Both campuses are in Washington, D.C. Gallaudet provides a liberal arts education for the hearing impaired, and Howard accepts a special responsibility for educating African Americans.

In addition, the department supports educational research, compiles statistics on education, and plans international teacher exchanges. It also runs schools for overseas dependents and migrant workers and administers science education and college housing loan programs.

7. What does the Department of Labor do for American workers?

Despite the large number of Americans who work for a living, the Department of Labor is one of the Cabinet's smallest departments. The department promotes the well-being of workers by improving working conditions, providing better job opportunities, and administering protective legislation. The President often selects a well-known labor leader to serve as Secretary of Labor.

EMPLOYMENT STANDARDS ADMINISTRATION (ESA)

Any employer who engages in interstate commerce must obey the Fair Labor Standards Act of 1938. The Employment Standards

■ Elizabeth Dole, Secretary of Labor 1989—1990, with United Mine Workers' union head Rich Trumpke and special mediator W. J. Usery. They were celebrating the end of a long, bitter coal miners' strike in 1989. One of but a handful of women who have held Cabinet posts, Dole served in a variety of government positions over a period of 25 years.

Administration enforces the parts of the act that relate to minimum wages, overtime pay, equal pay, and child labor. The administration also supervises working conditions on projects carried on under federal contracts. New laws that protect the rights of minorities and women have left the ESA with additional tasks. ESA personnel, for example, promote affirmative action programs. Under these agreements, contractors who work for the government agree to hire minorities, women, veterans, and the handicapped.

BUREAU OF LABOR STATISTICS

The Bureau of Labor Statistics is a statistical and fact-finding agency. It provides businesses and unions with information on employment, productivity, wages, prices, and hours of work. Its publications are often used as the basis for settling wage disputes, calculating cost-of-living raises, and negotiating new contracts.

OTHER DEPARTMENT AGENCIES

Other agencies within the Department of Labor also touch the lives of millions of American workers. One of the most important is the *Occupational Safety and Health Administration* (OSHA), which enforces codes that protect the safety of workers in factories and offices. The *Mine Safety and Health Administration* oversees safety and health rules wherever miners work. The *Employment and Training Administration* checks up on the operation of unemployment services by the states. The agency also supports job-training and apprenticeship programs.

8. How does the Department of Agriculture assist U.S. farmers?

A long time ago, the Department of Agriculture represented the largest single group of workers in America. Now, improved technology has reduced the number of Americans working in agriculture from one in two in 1900 to one in fifty today. At the same time, rising food costs have cut deeply into everyone's budget. Farmers often get the blame even though they receive only about a third of each dollar consumers spend on food.

AGRICULTURAL RESEARCH

The Department of Agriculture sponsors the world's largest agricultural research program. Employees of the *Agricultural Research Service* study soil chemistry, animal diseases, soil erosion, pest control, and antipollution techniques. The service maintains experiment stations throughout the country. Each station tries out new seeds, cultivation methods, fertilizers, and other techniques in order to improve production in its own region.

MARKETING HELP AND CREDIT

The days when farmers ate most of their produce and sold the rest in local markets are long gone. Today, farming is a complex business. Department of Agriculture consultants advise farmers, packers, and processors on the demand for their products, commodity prices, transportation conditions, and preservation of foods. Other experts help farmers sell their wheat, corn, soybeans, and other products to overseas customers. In the drive to increase the nation's sales to foreign customers, food has become this country's leading export. Because food also plays a key part in foreign aid programs, Agriculture coordinates its work with the State Department.

Through the *Farmers Home Administration*, farmers can borrow money to buy land, equipment, and livestock and to build irrigation systems. Farmers who borrow money from their farm cooperatives to bring electricity to their farms and ranches can have their loans guaranteed by the *Rural Electrification Agency*. Even with these services, some farmers need more financial help than the government can provide. Small farmers have been pinched by drought, low crop prices, and high interest rates on their loans. As a result, many farm families have lost their land and equipment.

PRICE SUPPORTS

Since the 1930s, the federal government has followed a double policy of (1) supporting minimum prices for farm products and (2) limiting the acreage planted to specific crops. If the price of wheat, for example, falls so low as to threaten wheat farmers with ruin, the government buys huge quantities of the grain at a price set by Congress. With less wheat on the market, prices tend to increase. The government also supports prices by limiting the number of acres planted, thus keeping overproduction to a minimum. Farmers who reduce their corn acreage, for example, receive cash payments to make up for lost income.

The *Commodity Credit Corporation's* job is to administer price support and allotment payments. The *Agricultural Stabilization and Conservation Service* decides on the actual number of acres to be held out of production. As a further service, farmers may purchase insurance against crop failures from the *Federal Crop Insurance Corporation*.

CONSERVATION PROGRAMS

Programs to preserve our national forests and to prevent soil erosion are managed by the Department of Agriculture. The *Forest Service* manages more than 150 national forests and conducts extensive reforestation programs. The *Soil Conservation Service* administers thousands of soil conservation districts, covering over 90 percent of the nation's farmlands. The service gives away millions of seedlings and helps farmers bring eroded land back into production.

OTHER AGENCIES

Among the department's smaller agencies is the *Extension Service*, through which county agents provide educational programs. In addition to teaching about new farming techniques, the agents offer marketing assistance, 4-H programs for young people, and information on nutrition and home economics. The *Food and Nutrition Service* administers the food stamp program for the nation's needy. Health standards are protected by the *Food Safety and Inspection Service*, which grades food and inspects plants, and the *Animal and Plant Health Inspection Service*, which checks for diseases and plant pests.

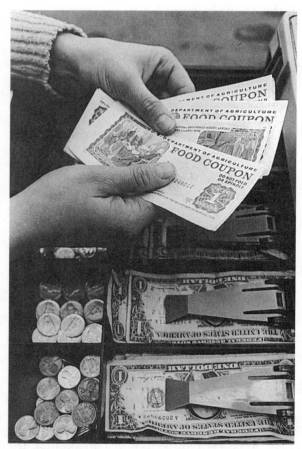

■ Along with its services to American farmers, the Department of Agriculture provides food coupons to low-income families and low-cost lunches to schoolchildren.

9. How does the Department of the Interior manage natural resources?

Officials of the Department of the Interior have the task of managing, conserving, and developing America's natural resources. The department watches over millions of acres of federal land, promotes mine safety, protects fish and wildlife, and manages federal hydroelectric systems. In addition, Interior oversees the affairs of more than half a million people who live on Indian lands and in overseas territories.

BUREAU OF LAND MANAGEMENT

The Bureau of Land Management acts as landlord for hundreds of millions of acres of government real estate. The size of the task can be measured by the fact that the federal government owns well over half of Alaska and Nevada. Six other states have over 40 percent of their acreage tied up in the same way. Like any good landlord, the bureau tries to make a profit from the land it manages. It develops grazing lands and grants leases for the mining of minerals. Oil companies interested in offshore exploration and drilling must also lease their sites from the bureau.

BUREAU OF RECLAMATION

Engineers of the Bureau of Reclamation work to turn arid western lands into productive recreational or agricultural areas. Irrigation and hydroelectric power projects such as those at Grand Coulee and Hoover dams illustrate the size and complexity of this job. The bureau also has the important task of developing water resources to meet the nation's increasing needs.

NATIONAL PARK SERVICE

Rangers and naturalists of the National Park Service manage more than 340 national parks, recreation areas, and monuments. They also guard many historic or archeologically im-

■ Backpackers in the Grand Teton National Park in Wyoming. The growing number of visitors and the increased encroachment of commercial interests threaten the future of our parks and wilderness areas. The work of the National Park Service is hampered by a small budget.

portant sites. Some 60 million visitors a year enjoy the natural beauty of such national parks as Yellowstone, Grand Canyon, and Crater Lake. Not all the nation's parks are in wilderness areas. The *Urban Park and Recreation Program* has helped cities set up nature study parks, playgrounds, and paths for hiking and bicycling.

GEOLOGICAL SURVEY

Engineers and surveyors of the Geological Survey map the geographic and geologic face of the United States. Geological Survey maps show the location of mineral deposits, the height of mountains, and the flow of water in rivers. Private industry uses these charts to locate sites for mineral exploration or routes for roads and rail lines. Backpackers also depend on the maps to guide them safely across wilderness areas.

BUREAU OF MINES

The Bureau of Mines is primarily a research agency. The bureau's experts are assigned to look for better and safer methods of developing the nation's mineral resources. One of the bureau's most important projects is that of finding ways to use low-grade domestic ores as replacements for imported minerals. The bureau also studies solid waste recycling and the reclamation of land damaged by mining operations. Because it's a research agency, the Bureau of Mines does not enforce health and safety rules. That task belongs to the *Mine Safety and Health Administration*, which is part of the Department of Labor.

FISH AND WILDLIFE SERVICE

Conservationists from the Fish and Wildlife Service protect wild animals in America. The service conducts hunting and trapping campaigns against predators that threaten endangered species, manages wildlife refuges, and works with foreign governments to conserve migratory wild fowl. The service's hatcheries stock the nation's streams and lakes with millions of fish each year for the enjoyment of sport fishers.

BUREAU OF INDIAN AFFAIRS (BIA)

The Bureau of Indian Affairs tries to help Native Americans, particularly those living on reservations, maintain their own customs and culture. The BIA's main tasks are to assist Native Americans in the wise use of their land and resources and to provide health, education, and welfare services to the tribes.

The size of the BIA's task can be seen in these grim statistics: Native Americans are the nation's poorest, worst educated, and least employed minority group. Native American babies are 70 percent more likely than white babies to die before their first birthdays. At the same time, Native American leaders complain that the BIA treats their people like "retarded children." Native Americans are demanding a greater voice in their own affairs, more jobs, improved schooling, and better health care.

OFFICE FOR TERRITORIAL AND INTERNATIONAL AFFAIRS

Guiding the economic and political development of the U.S. overseas territories is the job of the Office for Territorial and International Affairs. U.S. territories include the Trust Territory of the Pacific Islands, Guam, American Samoa, and the Virgin Islands. Assistance is offered to each territory's government.

OFFICE OF SURFACE MINING RECLAMATION AND ENFORCEMENT

This branch of the Interior Department enforces federal laws that protect the environment from the destructive aftereffects of strip mining. The damage results when mining companies cut away hills and fields to reach the underlying coal seams. The agency works with the mining companies and the states to restore these blighted sites to their original state.

10. How does the Department of Transportation oversee systems of transportation?

The Department of Transportation took its place in the Cabinet in 1967. Congress created the DOT to ensure the effective administration of federal transportation programs and the development of fast, safe, efficient, and low-cost transportation systems.

FEDERAL AVIATION ADMINISTRATION (FAA)

All air travel in the United States falls under the jurisdiction of the FAA. The agency writes and enforces safety rules, promotes civil aviation, and operates a nationwide system of air traffic control and navigation. FAA inspectors also certify aircraft and their pilots as part of the agency's air safety program. Safety inspections and maintenance programs were strengthened in 1988–1989 after a series of accidents and structural failures focused public attention on the country's aging fleet of passenger aircraft.

FEDERAL HIGHWAY ADMINISTRATION

Officials of the Federal Highway Administration oversee the construction and safe use of the nation's highways. The agency administers the federal highway grants that helped build the 44,000-mile Interstate Highway System. Other duties include assisting the states in developing programs to make highways safe and beautiful, setting up training programs for major transport companies and government agencies, and regulating commercial carriers in interstate and foreign commerce. The agency also enforces federal safety laws that regulate the movement of explosives and hazardous wastes.

NATIONAL HIGHWAY TRAFFIC SAFETY ADMINISTRATION (NHTSA)

NHTSA experts carry out programs aimed at improving the safety of motor vehicles and their drivers. Research sponsored by the NHTSA aims at developing crash-resistant cars that can protect their occupants and reduce repair costs. Educational programs, some of which emphasize pedestrian safety and control of drunk driving, are part of NHTSA's efforts. The highway death rate is another priority target. The 55-mph speed limit has saved many lives, but Congress was pressured into approving a 65-mph speed limit on some interstate highways in 1987.

FEDERAL RAILROAD ADMINISTRATION

Although a government-controlled corporation called Amtrak carries many of the nation's train passengers, privately owned railroads still transport much of the freight. In support of the railroads, the Federal Railroad Administration coordinates all federal programs that affect rail transport. The agency also enforces safety regulations, administers financial aid for troubled railroads, and conducts development and research in support of improved intercity ground transportation. In 1988, concern over suspected drug use by railroad employees led to tougher licensing requirements for locomotive engineers and more consistent enforcement of railroad safety laws.

URBAN MASS TRANSPORTATION ADMINISTRATION (UMTA)

The urgent need for improved mass transit facilities led to the creation of this agency in 1968. UMTA assists the states and cities in developing improved mass transportation facilities, equipment, and routes. The agency encourages the integrated use of existing regional facilities, but it also looks ahead to the building of subways, monorail lines, and special bus lanes on freeways. Once a project is approved, UMTA helps pay the costs with federal funds voted by Congress.

MARITIME ADMINISTRATION

The Maritime Administration works to maintain a strong and up-to-date merchant marine. Because the United States needs a large number of cargo ships during both peace and war, the government pays a subsidy for building and operating the ships. This support enables U.S. merchant ships to compete with the vessels of other nations, which operate with lower crew salaries and weaker safety standards. The Maritime Administration operates a Merchant Marine Academy at Kings Point, New York. The academy trains the young men and women who will someday captain the nation's merchant ships.

ST. LAWRENCE SEAWAY DEVELOPMENT CORPORATION

The St. Lawrence Seaway Development Corporation, a government-owned company, operates the U.S. portion of the seaway between Montreal and Lake Erie. Thanks to the seaway, Great Lakes cities such as Chicago, Detroit, and Milwaukee are now international ports. Heavily traveled and self-supporting, the St.

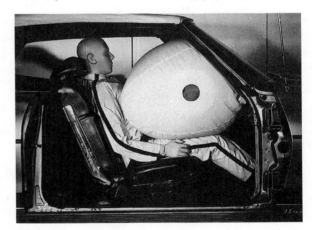

■ The NHTSA has been involved in testing the effectiveness of air bags in motor vehicles to protect the driver and passengers from injuries during crashes.

Lawrence Seaway provides a safe and efficient water route from the upper Midwest to the Atlantic Ocean.

COAST GUARD

During peacetime, the Coast Guard serves under the Department of Transportation. In time of war, it becomes part of the Navy. The Coast Guard's primary job is to enforce maritime rules and rescue sailors whose ships are in trouble. In keeping the seaways safe, the Guard maintains lighthouses, watches for icebergs, conducts boating safety classes, and conducts safety inspections of commercial and pleasure boats. The Coast Guard also plays a vital role in the war against drugs. Its patrol boats are constantly on the lookout for the criminals who try to smuggle cocaine, heroin, and marijuana into the United States. The Coast Guard trains its officers at its own academy in New London, Connecticut.

11. What is the role of the Department of Housing and Urban Development?

The Department of Housing and Urban Development (HUD) was added to the Cabinet in 1965. Congress had set up so many programs to help the cities with their housing problems that it became necessary to bring them together in one department. Robert C. Weaver, the first Secretary of Housing and Urban Development, was also the first black to hold Cabinet rank.

HUD's primary job is to administer programs that help urban communities with their housing needs. For example, HUD provides mortgage insurance that helps families buy their own homes, and it oversees rent subsidies for low-income families. In addition, HUD promotes programs to combat discrimination in housing, to aid in the rebuilding of older neighborhoods, and to preserve city centers from decay. Finally, when natural disasters strike, HUD moves in to furnish financial help in the form of grants and low-interest loans.

HUD, after many years of quiet and mostly constructive work, made the wrong kind of headlines in 1989 and 1990. The nation was shocked by revelations that HUD had been victimized by poor management, waste, and corruption during the years of the Reagan presidency. A congressional investigation revealed that former government officials were paid huge commissions for helping wealthy developers win HUD contracts. At the same time, crooked real estate agents pocketed millions of dollars from the sale of foreclosed properties—money that rightfully should have gone to HUD. Jack Kemp, who took over as HUD secretary in 1989, was given the difficult task of cleaning up the mess and pointing HUD back toward its original purpose.

FEDERAL HOUSING COMMISSIONER (FHC)

A significant number of the new houses being built in the United States carry HUD-guaranteed mortgages, which banks write at attractive interest rates. If the Federal Housing Commissioner's office hadn't put up these guarantees, many homeowners wouldn't have been able to buy their houses. In another program, the FHC furnishes the financing for housing projects designed for the elderly, the handicapped, and the poor. The office also pays part of the rent for many low-income families.

COMMUNITY DEVELOPMENT BLOCK GRANTS

Heavily populated cities and counties can apply for Community Development Block Grants. These grants give local governments the cash they need to carry out a wide range of community development projects. Many cities are now moving ahead with such tasks as rebuilding decaying housing, attracting new business and industry, and building recreational facilities.

URBAN DEVELOPMENT ACTION GRANTS

The Action Grant program encourages private investment in depressed urban areas. The investments generated by the grants bring

■ Jack Kemp (center with vest), HUD secretary under Bush, walking with a tenant leader in a public housing complex in Philadelphia. After taking office, Kemp toured many such projects to see which ones worked the best. Why is it necessary for the government to develop low-cost housing?

new jobs and increased tax revenues into distressed cities and counties. Once new economic life has started, the local government is expected to continue the recovery on its own.

URBAN HOMESTEADS

When HUD gains title to empty, run-down houses, the department turns them over to state or city governments. Local officials then make the properties available to urban "homesteaders." The new owners must agree to repair, maintain, and live in the houses for five years. If they keep their end of the bargain, the homesteaders receive title to the properties. The program is modeled after the homestead laws that helped settle the West during the last century. Congress pays the costs with an annual appropriation.

12. How does the Department of Veterans Affairs serve former military personnel?

Until 1989, America's veterans were served by an independent agency called the Veterans Administration. With one out of every three Americans a potential beneficiary of its services, the VA was already one of the government's largest agencies in terms of budget and number of employees. Veterans and their supporters in Congress believed that they would have even more access to the President and more influence on budget decisions if the head of the VA belonged to the Cabinet. The long battle ended in 1988 when President Reagan signed a bill making the Department of Veterans Affairs the fourteenth Cabinet department. The legislation became effective in March 1989.

THE LARGEST HEALTH CARE SYSTEM

Everything about the VA is large. The department has 245,000 employees (the federal government's second largest civilian work force, behind the U.S. Postal Service) to serve a population of over 27 million veterans and their 53 million dependents. Those numbers will increase, the VA estimates, until by the year 2000, 2 of every 3 men over 65 will be veterans. Services to these individuals, particularly medical benefits, are costly. Benefits paid to World War II veterans, for example, now total over $500 billion.

Many of the VA's workers staff the nation's largest medical system. The VA manages over 172 hospitals, 260 outpatient clinics, 122 nursing homes, and almost 198 outreach centers for Vietnam vets. Eligible veterans receive general medical and dental services, hospital treatment, home nursing, physical therapy, and counseling for emotional problems.

BENEFITS AND GENERAL ASSISTANCE

A national network of VA service centers provides information and assistance to veterans, their dependents, and their survivors. In addition to medical care, services of the VA include vocational rehabilitation, pension

■ Veterans from World Wars I and II in a nursing home in New York City run by the Department of Veterans Affairs. The men are getting ready for a 4th of July picnic. Taking care of the health needs of veterans is a growing expense for the VA.

payments, and compensation for disabled and retired veterans. The VA guarantees over 12 million home loans and operates the nation's fifth largest life insurance program. Since 1944, more than 20 million veterans and members of the armed forces have received educational benefits under the VA-administered GI Bill. In addition, the VA provides educational aid for spouses and children of veterans killed or disabled while on active service. When a veteran dies, he or she is entitled to free burial in one of 111 VA cemeteries.

Reviewing
what you've learned

1. Twelve Cabinet departments manage the nation's domestic affairs. Cabinet appointments are made by the President but require Senate confirmation. In searching for Cabinet members, Presidents look for talented men and women who can administer large, complex operations.

2. The *Treasury Department* collects the government's taxes, pays its bills, keeps its books, and prints its money. Major divisions include the *Internal Revenue Service*, the *Customs Service*, the *United States Mint*, the *Bureau of Engraving and Printing*, and the *Secret Service*.

3. The Attorney General ranks as the President's top legal adviser. The *Justice Department* also enforces federal law through a variety of divisions. A few of them are the *Bureau of Prisons*, the *Federal Bureau of Investigation*, the *Immigration and Naturalization Service*, the *Antitrust Division*, and the *Drug Enforcement Administration*.

4. Commercial activities of all kinds, from mining and manufacturing to shipping and fishing, receive assistance from the *Department of Commerce*. The *Census Bureau* keeps track of the nation's population patterns, and the *National Oceanic and Atmospheric Administration* predicts changing climatic conditions and protects endangered marine animals. The department promotes foreign trade and encourages foreign visitors to come to the United States. It also aids minority-owned businesses and low-income areas suffering from high unemployment.

5. Problems that arose during the 1970s led to the creation of two Cabinet departments to handle programs related to energy and to education. The *Department of Energy* was established in 1977. Its task is to coordinate the government's efforts to safeguard existing energy supplies and find new sources of power. An independent agency, the *Federal Energy Regulatory Commission*, sets rates for transporting and selling natural gas, electricity, and oil in pipelines. The *Economic Regulatory Administration* controls the importing and pricing of crude oil.

The *Department of Education* was formed in 1979 to coordinate a number of widely scattered federal education programs. The department's budget finances a variety of programs designed to improve education without imposing federal control. Recent Presidents have used the department to promote their goal of improving the quality of American education.

6. The *Department of Health and Human Services* spends more than any other department. The *Social Security Administration* helps the retired, disabled, and sick. The *Public Health Service* and the *Food and Drug Administration* help HHS guard the nation's health.

7. American workers look to the *Department of Labor* to enforce federal laws governing working conditions, wage rates, and safety standards. The *Employment Standards Administration* makes sure that employers observe minimum wage and child labor laws. The Department of Labor also gathers information about workers and enforces laws dealing with the health and safety of factory, office, and mine workers.

8. The *Department of Agriculture* helps farmers through its programs of research, marketing, credit assistance, price supports, and conservation. Important agencies include the *Agricultural Research Service* (improved plant yields), the *Farmers Home Administration* (loans), the *Commodity Credit Corporation* (price supports), the *Forest Service* and *Soil Conservation Service* (reforestation and soil reclamation), and the *Extension Service* (educational and youth programs).

9. Management, conservation, and development of America's natural resources are the responsibility of the *Department of the Interior*. The *Bureau of Land Management* watches over millions of acres of federal land. The *Bureau of Reclamation* irrigates and develops arid western land. The *National Park Service* oversees the national park system. The *Fish and Wildlife Service* protects the nation's wild animals, birds, and fish. The *Bureau of Indian Affairs* tries to help Native Americans improve their economic and social position in American society. The *Office for Territorial and International Affairs* aids the development of American overseas possessions.

10. The *Department of Transportation* wrestles with the nation's complex transportation problems. Air traffic moves under the supervision of the *Federal Aviation Administration*. Similar agencies, the *Federal Highway Administration* and the *Federal Railroad Administration*, supervise the highways and railroads. The *National Highway Traffic Safety Administration* has helped cut down the death toll on our roads. The *Urban Mass Transportation Administration* encourages cities to develop better ways of moving large numbers of people. The *Coast Guard* rescues capsized sailors, patrols for icebergs, and intercepts smugglers.

11. The nation's housing problems, mostly concentrated in large metropolitan areas, led to the creation of the *Department of Housing and Urban Development*. *Community Development Block Grants* and *Urban Development Action Grants* help cities rebuild decaying sections of downtown areas. The *Federal Housing Commissioner* guarantees low-cost mortgages as a way of encouraging home ownership. HUD also sponsors an urban homestead plan that gives homes to low-income families that move in and fix them up. Other HUD agencies provide rent subsidies, fight discrimination in housing, and provide assistance after natural disasters.

12. The nation's veterans received their own voice in the Cabinet when the *Department of Veterans Affairs* was created in 1989. The VA, formerly an independent agency, spends its $30 billion budget on medical care and financial services for veterans, their dependents, and their survivors. It provides hospital care, insurance, loan guarantees, educational benefits, counseling, and other benefits.

Review
questions and activities

AGENCIES YOU SHOULD KNOW

Antitrust Division (Justice)
Bureau of Engraving and Printing
Bureau of Indian Affairs
Bureau of Land Management
Bureau of Prisons
Census Bureau
Coast Guard
Drug Enforcement Administration
Federal Aviation Administration
Federal Bureau of Investigation
Federal Highway Administration
Fish and Wildlife Service
Food and Drug Administration
Forest Service
Immigration and Naturalization Service

Internal Revenue Service
Maritime Administration
National Highway Traffic Safety
   Administration
National Park Service
Occupational Safety and Health
   Administration
Patent and Trademark Office
Public Health Service
Secret Service
Social Security Administration
Surgeon General
United States Mint
Urban Mass Transportation
   Administration

REVIEW QUESTIONS

Select the response that best completes each statement or question.

1. On which of the following consumer items is an excise tax *not* levied? (*a*) playing cards. (*b*) cigarettes. (*c*) automobile tires. (*d*) gasoline. (*e*) children's clothing.

2. The only pure, 100 percent silver coin still produced by the United States Mint is (*a*) the nickel. (*b*) the dime. (*c*) the quarter. (*d*) the half-dollar. (*e*) no pure silver coins are minted for everyday circulation.

3. The agency that guards Presidents and their families is the (*a*) FBI. (*b*) Border Patrol. (*c*) Secret Service. (*d*) Coast Guard. (*e*) Internal Security Division of the Justice Department.

4. The approximate number of immigrants from all countries now allowed to enter the United States each year is (*a*) less than a thousand. (*b*) 20,000. (*c*) 270,000. (*d*) about 600,000. (*e*) about a million.

5. Which of the following is no longer a Cabinet department? (*a*) Housing and Urban Development. (*b*) Commerce. (*c*) Agriculture. (*d*) Postal Service. (*e*) Labor.

6. Maintaining the quality and purity of the American diet is the responsibility of the (*a*) Food and Drug Administration. (*b*) Public Health Service. (*c*) Social Security Administration. (*d*) Fish and Wildlife Service. (*e*) Drug Enforcement Administration.

7. The practice of paying farmers *not* to grow a certain crop developed as a means of (*a*) rewarding political supporters in the farm states. (*b*) building up surpluses for foreign sales. (*c*) maintaining farm prices at reasonably profitable levels. (*d*) using up surplus federal funds. (*e*) none of these.

8. Which of the following is *not* a job of the Department of Transportation? (*a*)

Developing mass transit. (*b*) Regulating airline fares. (*c*) Maintaining railroad safety. (*d*) Reducing the highway death rate. (*e*) Enforcing maritime rules.

9. Programs aimed at rebuilding the old, run-down sections of our cities fall under the jurisdiction of the Department of (*a*) the Interior. (*b*) Housing and Urban Development. (*c*) Commerce. (*d*) Energy. (*e*) Health and Human Services.

10. Which of the following departments is the newest member of the Cabinet? (*a*) Energy. (*b*) Transportation. (*c*) Veterans Affairs. (*d*) Housing and Urban Development. (*e*) Education.

CONCEPT DEVELOPMENT

1. Why does the President need the advice and administrative services of the Cabinet? Would it be better if the secretaries and the attorney general were elected rather than appointed?

2. Name the 12 domestic Cabinet departments that provide services to the American people. Briefly describe the important activities of each department.

3. Federal departments have been created to aid labor, business, and industry, but no Cabinet department has been established to protect consumer interests. List some arguments in favor of a Department of Consumer Affairs.

4. What factors in the changing American society have led to the rapid growth of the federal bureaucracy? What are some of the positive and some of the negative results when government expands in this way?

5. How does the role of a typical department—such as Agriculture—change as the nation's population moves to the cities and the economy becomes more industrialized?

HANDS-ON ACTIVITIES

1. Consult the *United States Government Manual* in your library for organization charts of the various departments. Select one department and transfer its structure to a poster. Use the poster as a visual aid while you describe to the class the activities of the many bureaus and offices that make up the department. Point out specific bureaus that may have offices in your own community.

2. Ask an official from one of the many federal agencies described in this chapter to visit your class to talk about the work carried on by that organization. Let the speaker know that your classmates will want to ask some questions of their own. Direct the questions to agency policies, projects, and career possibilities.

3. Divide the class into small groups, each assigned to write on a particular agency. Have each group report on a specific question or problem they have uncovered in their reading. For example, what is the current FBI position on wiretaps? Will the Mint ever again produce silver coins for everyday use? What degree of accuracy can be expected from the Weather Service? Report to the class on (a) the general work of the agency and (b) the answers to the particular questions the group investigated.

4. Welfare programs often arouse strong feelings in a community. Locate the office or offices in your community that administer federal and state welfare programs. Interview officials there to determine the nature and extent of the payments and services they provide. What is being done to help people get off the welfare rolls? Talk to some of the welfare recipients waiting in line at the office. Finally, write a paper that describes your research and observations. Be sure that your paper answers these important questions: Is the welfare system being abused by the recipients and officials who administer it? What can be done to improve the welfare system?

14 The "fourth branch" of government: The independent agencies

Consider these situations for a moment:

▲ Regulating broadcasting rights and information on food labels are two functions of independent agencies.

- Your favorite radio station fades out as soon as you've driven more than five miles away from your town. Other stations can be heard for hundreds of miles. Who told WROK it couldn't have a stronger broadcasting signal?
- The new and improved miracle soap you bought turns out to be the same old product in a more colorful box. Only the higher price is new. Shouldn't something be done about consumer rip-offs like that?

333

- You're fed up with paying high long-distance charges when you telephone out of state. You ask around and discover that you can save money by switching to another long-distance phone service. What happened to the days when there was only one long-distance company?

- Your little cousin complains that breakfast isn't much fun anymore. She says her parents stopped buying her favorite cereal when they checked the package and found out that it was mostly sugar. Who's forcing the food processors to list the nutritional value of their products?

- Try setting up a bus line to take people to the beach or lake during the summer. Sounds like a simple exercise in free enterprise, doesn't it? Wait until you start trying to cut through all the red tape. You'll find that free enterprise is anything but "free."

- You want to fly to your brother's wedding on the other side of the country. Money's tight, so you look for the airline with the cheapest fare. Eight phone calls later, you're totally confused. Each airline has a different "deal," depending on when you fly, how long you stay, and whether you want "frills" like lunch and dinner. What's going on?

By now, you've probably guessed that a common theme ties all of these everyday situations together: The federal government is at work. Each of these cases can be traced back to one of the government's *independent agencies*. Congress created most of these agencies to regulate the actions of companies engaged in interstate commerce (telephone companies and television stations). Other independent agencies administer important federal programs (environmental protection or the supervision of atomic energy).

The power of the independent agencies to affect the nation's economic life grew rapidly for most of this century. The agencies wrote and enforced regulations that affected everything from oil prices and airline schedules to automobile bumpers and the safety of prescription drugs. In the mid-1970s, a backlash developed. Politicians of both parties began chipping away at the power of the independent agencies. Recent administrations have reduced the power of some agencies and abolished others.

In this chapter, you will learn how the independent agencies came into being and how some of them work. Along with learning the names of the agencies that are responsible for the cases cited above, you'll find answers to the following questions:

1. **Why were the independent agencies established?**

2. **How do the independent agencies operate?**

3. **What is the role of the Interstate Commerce Commission?**

4. What is the role of the Federal Communications Commission?

5. How did deregulation affect the Civil Aeronautics Board and the airlines?

6. How does the Federal Trade Commission protect consumers?

7. How do the independent agencies protect American workers?

8. How does the Securities and Exchange Commission protect investors?

9. Why were the independent administrative agencies established?

10. What do some of the other independent agencies accomplish for the public?

11. Who regulates the regulators?

1. Why were the independent agencies established?

President Woodrow Wilson asked Congress to create the Federal Trade Commission in 1914. Wilson believed the new agency was needed to "make men in a small way of business as free to succeed as men in a big way."

Wilson knew that the Constitution has little to say about the specifics of organizing the executive branch. Instead, the Framers wisely left the creation of administrative agencies for later Congresses and Presidents. Over the years, a workable system of administration emerged, centered around the departments that make up the Cabinet.

In time, Congress decided that the Cabinet could no longer administer every aspect of the country's mushrooming economy. The Department of Agriculture, for example, carried out policies relating to wheat production, but it had no authority to regulate the transport of that wheat to market. Congress, therefore, delegated part of its constitutional power over interstate commerce to independent, specialized agencies. Each agency was given *regulatory authority* in its special field. As a result, political scientists say that these agencies now operate as a *"fourth branch"* of the federal government. Each agency combines some of the legislative, executive, and judicial powers that normally belong to Congress, the White House, and the federal court system.

EMPHASIS ON INDEPENDENCE

The independence of the regulatory agencies has always been carefully protected. Some of the reasons:

Protection from pressure. The agency must be guarded from undue pressures brought by the business or industry it regulates. Farmers, for instance, lobbied the Interstate Commerce Commission into existence in 1887. They wanted the government to regulate the fees charged by railroads for the transport of farm products. It soon became obvious that the new agency could not set railroad rates unless it was protected from the influence of the powerful railroad owners.

Similarly, an agency must be shielded from political pressure. The Federal Communications Commission, for example, has the job of evaluating applications for broadcasting licenses. The agency can't do its job fairly if members of Congress can command favorable treatment for their friends.

National security concerns. Some agencies deal with highly sensitive matters, and

■ The early 1900s was an era of "let the buyer beware." The makers of patent medicines often added forms of opium to products. The promotion of such products led to the creation of the independent regulatory agencies.

violations of their independence could damage national security. The Central Intelligence Agency, which gathers and evaluates information collected by a worldwide data gathering network, clearly fits this category.

A WORKABLE COMPROMISE

Originally, the independent agencies were a response to the excesses of the commercial and industrial revolution that began in the 1800s. The era was ruled by a philosophy of "let the buyer beware." Strong businesses strangled the weak. Inferior, overpriced food and merchandise flooded the market. Alarmed and angry, the American people called on Congress for protection.

The agencies that developed out of that call for regulation are uniquely American institutions. Socialists and Communists claim that only government ownership can control big business. The United States, by contrast, chose government regulation instead of government ownership. The American theory states that rates, prices, operating procedures, and profits of certain industries should be set by a regulatory authority.

Today's independent agencies are surrounded by controversy. Critics claim that they are either too powerful or too weak. Their defenders say they serve a vital economic and social need. Both sides, however, accept the need for regulation. Only the amount of regulation is in dispute.

2. How do the independent agencies operate?

As noted earlier, the independent agencies combine the functions of the three major branches of government. They serve as *legislative bodies* when they write regulations on their own (the Federal Communications Commission sets the maximum broadcasting power for radio stations). They assume *executive powers* when they enforce their own regulations (the Interstate Commerce Commission checks to be sure that trucks have proper safety features). They act as a *judicial body* when they hold hearings for accused violators and hand out fines or suspensions (the Securities and Exchange Commission can suspend sales in a company's stock). These powers are sometimes called "quasi-legislative" or "quasi-judicial." (*Quasi* is a Latin word meaning "to some degree.")

ORGANIZATION

Congress writes the laws that create the independent agencies. An agency may be formed in response to a request from the President or because Congress sees the need. Their names vary, but most are known as boards, commissions, or administrations. All are funded by yearly appropriations from Congress.

Learning Skills

Researching Information About Government

Imagine for a moment that you've been fired from your job, and that you think it's because of your age, or sex, or race. You know vaguely that you should contact someone, somewhere, to file a complaint. Where do you go? How do you file the complaint? Many injustices go unreported because people don't know what to do. At another time, you want to find a simple but elusive fact: How many Americans voted in the last general election?

If you know where to go to research information about government, you won't be stumped by problems like these. The secret is in knowing the right reference books for each type of question. The following list will get you started. Even small libraries will have most of these titles:

The phone book. Most phone books have listings for local, state, and federal government offices. If you can't find the number of the Equal Employment Opportunities Commission, look for the phone number of the field office for your district's member of Congress. A staffer will tell you what you want to know.

Almanacs. Almanacs have several things going for them. First, they're printed every year, so their facts are up-to-date. Second, they're easy to use. An extensive index helps you find just about anything from the population of London to your governor's salary.

U.S. Government Manual. This yearly publication lists a wealth of information about the organization of the federal government. The manual contains descriptions (including addresses and phone numbers) of the divisions of all three branches of government, plus the independent agencies. If you want to write directly to the head of the EEOC, the name and address are printed in this book.

The Statistical Abstract of the United States. This book is like an almanac that's primarily devoted to information about the United States. It does include some statistics about other countries. The *Abstract* compares current statistics with similar data from past years, and it breaks the numbers down on a state-by-state basis. How did your state vote in the last ten presidential elections? This useful book can tell you.

United States Statutes at Large and *United States Code.* If you want to know the exact wording of a law that was passed by a particular Congress, turn to *U.S. Statutes.* This weighty volume contains all public and private laws and resolutions enacted during a session of Congress. If you want to search out the entire body of U.S. labor law, turn to the *U.S. Code* and its annual supplements. Here, the nation's permanent laws have been codified (arranged according to subject).

Monthly catalog of government publications. The U.S. government publishes many useful books and pamphlets throughout the year. If you want to know what's available, take a look at this monthly catalog. In addition to listing the titles, the catalog tells you how to order copies of anything that looks interesting.

In addition to the basic sources described here, your state puts out its own reference materials. If knowledge really is power, there's an abundance of power waiting for you on your library shelves. All you have to do is put it to use.

Most independent agencies are headed by a board of commissioners. Members are appointed by the President subject to confirmation by the Senate. Unlike members of the Cabinet who serve at the pleasure of the President, commissioners serve long terms (usually seven years). They may be removed only "for cause." This job security helps protect the commissioners from congressional and White House influence, but they are never totally free of such pressures.

The five to eleven commissioners who run each agency establish policy, hold hearings, and make major decisions. A professional staff of economists, lawyers, investigators, accountants, clerks, and secretaries handles the day-to-day paperwork. The staff enforces agency regulations and gathers data for the use of the commissioners. Since these bureaucrats tend to stay on the job from one administration to another, they greatly influence the work of the agency.

CONTROVERSY OVER POLICY

Because they operate with so much freedom and authority, the independent agencies sometimes come into conflict with the administration or Congress. Serious disagreements are likely to arise when a new President wins the White House. The incoming administration may find its policies blocked by agencies still committed to opposing ideas. The President's frustration is increased by the fact that commissioners serve staggered terms. Only a few members can be replaced in any given year.

Arguments over the government's economic policies are typical. The Federal Reserve System may begin by restricting the money supply as part of its fight against inflation. The Secretary of the Treasury, on the other hand, may wish to stimulate business by increasing the flow of money into the economy. Secure in its power to control the money supply, the Federal Reserve usually wins a battle of this type. Not even the President can order its governors to change their policy.

Despite this independence, commissioners do respond to the wishes of Congress, the President, and the public. In fact, an agency's relationship with the industry it regulates sometimes becomes so close as to raise questions regarding conflict of interest (see Section 11—pages 352–354—for a discussion of this issue). Companies that object to an agency decision have the option of taking the case to a U.S. court of appeals. The courts, however, have usually supported the regulatory authority of the agencies.

3. What is the role of today's Interstate Commerce Commission?

A long-simmering feud between farmers and the railroads grew into a hot national issue after the Civil War. Farmers claimed that the railroads charged exorbitant freight rates, discriminated against particular towns and shippers, cheated on billings, and conspired to eliminate competition. Some states attempted to regulate interstate rail commerce by passing what were known as Granger laws. When the railroads took their case to court, the laws were overturned by the Supreme Court. The Court ruled that only the federal government can regulate interstate commerce.

DEVELOPMENT OF THE ICC

The Interstate Commerce Act of 1887 grew out of this battle. The act set up the first regulatory agency, the *Interstate Commerce Commission (ICC)*. Although adverse court decisions weakened the ICC during its early years, the Hepburn Act of 1906 greatly strengthened the agency's regulatory power. Originally limited to supervision of the railroads, the ICC's charter was expanded to include the trucking industry in 1935. Today, the ICC regulates all overland interstate commerce that moves by bus, truck, train, pipeline, and inland waterway (but not private automobiles). ICC regulations cover the transport of people as well as freight. All transportation facilities, including waiting rooms, warehouses, and the vehicles themselves, come under agency jurisdiction.

When the federal government adopted pol-

■ The trucking industry was chosen for one of the first experiments in deregulation. With the ICC no longer allowed to set freight rates, truckers cut costs, some by putting worn-out trucks on the road. Complaints were also made about the growing number of double-trailer trucks. Truck accidents increased by more than 25 percent at a time when truck mileage was up less than 20 percent.

icies aimed at reducing its control of business, the ICC began to deregulate the trucking industry. Decontrol, which Congress approved in 1980, has not made everyone happy. Independent truckers, for example, claim that large trucking companies are cutting rates and driving smaller firms out of business.

ICC ORGANIZATION

ICC activities are directed by five commissioners. As with all independent agencies, the President nominates the commissioners and their chairman for confirmation by the Senate. Commissioners serve staggered seven-year terms, so that no more than two terms can expire in any given year. No more than three commissioners may be of the same political party. Widespread ICC functions are administered through regional and area offices.

REGULATING OVERLAND TRANSPORT

ICC regulators identify three classes of shippers: (1) common carriers with fixed routes and schedules of pickups and deliveries, (2) common carriers operating under contract with shipping companies, and (3) private carriers owned by shipping companies. The ICC influences the operation of both common and private carriers in several ways:

Setting rates. The trend toward *deregulation* has not ended the importance of the ICC's rate hearings. Rates set too low can ruin a carrier; those set too high can be a hardship for the public. To insure compliance with its rulings, the ICC requires that rate schedules be published. It also forbids the practice of rebating a percentage of the established rate to favored customers. ICC commissioners hold public hearings when they are reviewing rates and schedules. If either the carriers or their customers disagree with an ICC decision, they may take their case to the federal courts.

Guaranteeing service. Deregulation has eroded the ICC's power to control the routes serviced by transport companies. In the past, ICC examiners often refused to allow a railroad or bus line to drop a money-losing route if doing so would harm a community. Today, many companies compete for business on the most heavily traveled routes. This competion keeps freight rates low, but small, out-of-the-way towns may find themselves left with little or no service.

Setting safety standards. Both equipment and operators must meet ICC safety standards. These complex regulations establish maintenance procedures, safety equipment, and load limits. Drivers must satisfy rules that cover their physical condition, training, and age. In addition, owners and operators must buy insurance for the protection of passengers, drivers, freight, and property.

Regulating business procedures. Deregulation reduced the ICC's power to control the way transport companies do business. Formerly, ICC rules required the use of standard accounting procedures and the filing of regular reports. Companies also had to gain ICC approval before they could issue stocks or bonds. The ICC's critics claim that the easing of these rules has saved millions of dollars in paperwork. Despite deregulation, the ICC still has plenty of work to do. The ICC commissioners rule on applications for mergers, administer railroad bankruptcy laws, and settle disputes over rates among competing modes of transportation.

4. What is the role of the Federal Communications Commission?

The concept of independent regulatory agencies gave the federal government a way to deal with new technologies. After all, the telegraph didn't exist when the Constitution was written. The rapid spread of the telegraph, followed by the telephone and radio, made regulation of the communications industry a necessity. Congress finally passed legislation in 1934 that established the *Federal Communications Commission (FCC)*. As the television industry developed, it also came under FCC regulation.

FCC ORGANIZATION

Five commissioners set FCC policy under guidelines established by Congress. FCC employees staff dozens of field offices, monitoring stations, and a mobile network. All of these facilities have the job of watching for violations of federal broadcasting standards.

REGULATING THE AIRWAVES

The airwaves are public property, and the FCC regulates their use "in the public interest." The agency's regulations cover key areas:

Broadcasting licenses. The right to operate a radio or television station can mean big profits for the successful bidder. Radio and television channels are limited in number, however, and broadcasters must compete for FCC licenses. Once awarded, licenses must be renewed every three years. A station that can't prove that it has performed a satisfactory amount of public service may lose its license. The FCC also sets limits on a station's broadcasting power and hours of operation.

Influence on program content. The FCC may not act as a censor (broadcasters are expected to practice self-censorship), but the agency does affect program content through its licensing power. Limits have been set on the minutes of commercials allowed per hour, and a certain number of public service broadcasts are required. Despite these rules, the public often criticizes the quality of the programs that come into the nation's living rooms. The FCC responds by investigating such matters as the effect of broadcast violence on children and the slanting of political news.

Equal time requirement. For almost 40 years, FCC rules required that broadcasters take a nonpartisan position on controversial matters. If a station gave free airtime to one candidate or one political viewpoint, it had to give equal time to opposing candidates or points of view. Similarly, if a station took an editorial position on an issue, it had to make time available to speakers who held opposing views.

Always controversial, the equal time requirement vanished in 1987. First, President Reagan vetoed a bill that would have turned the FCC ruling into law. Next, the FCC's commissioners voted to do away with the requirement completely. Congressional supporters fought back by trying to attach the equal time requirement to an important budget bill. The rider was thrown out at the last minute by the conference committee.

Other areas of broadcasting. In addition to regulating radio (AM and FM) and television (VHF and UHF), the FCC supervises three other areas of broadcasting. (1) Cable television now serves an increasing number of communities. The FCC awards franchises and regulates the material sent out over the cable. (2) FCC examiners monitor and license marine, amateur, police, fire, industrial, and citizen's band radio frequencies to prevent misuse. The increasing popularity of cellular car phones, cordless phones, and paging "beepers" has made this task much more complex. (3) Microwave and satellite transmission facilities also fall under FCC jurisdiction.

Long-distance telephone service deregulated. The FCC still regulates local telephone companies, which have a monopoly within their franchise areas. An antitrust suit against American Telephone and Telegraph Company led to deregulation of long-distance service in 1984. Other companies immediately began cutting their rates to compete with AT&T for long-distance customers. Deregulation also means that customers can buy their own phones and plug them into company lines. Under the old FCC rules, this was not allowed.

5. How did deregulation affect the Civil Aeronautics Board and the airlines?

The *Civil Aeronautics Board (CAB)* was established in 1938. For 40 years, the CAB regulated air travel in the same way that the ICC controlled overland transport. The agency was responsible for regulating the civil air transport industry and for promoting air travel and commerce. It also supervised the airlines that carried the mail and coordinated the civil air industry with national defense needs.

Deregulation caught up with the CAB in 1978. Congress passed the Airline Deregulation Act, which greatly reduced the CAB's powers. Then in January 1985, the CAB was abolished. Its remaining jobs were transferred to other agencies. The critical job of keeping the air lanes safe was left to the Federal Aviation Administration (FAA). From a financial standpoint, deregulation turned the airlines loose to compete for passengers and profits in a free market.

■ The words the man is speaking refer to the first known telephone message. Alexander Graham Bell, inventor of the telephone, shouted through the instrument to his assistant, Watson. The breakup of AT&T and the deregulation of long-distance service has made the phone business much more complicated. Customers are now responsible for many services that once were free.

"MR WATSON, OR SOMEBODY—COME HERE, I WANT YOU"

■ The fierce competition unleashed by deregulation, some critics think, may lead cost-conscious airlines to cut corners when it comes to keeping their planes safe to fly. Although fares may have come down, some passengers think it has been done at the expense of service. What does the cartoonist seem to be saying about deregulation?

EFFECTS OF DEREGULATION

The most immediate effect of deregulation was to increase the number of airlines. In 1978, 38 airlines in the United States offered passenger service to air travelers. Within five years, that number had doubled and doubled again to 154. Many of these were small airlines that began flying into remote areas not served by major carriers.

Deregulation also meant financial hardships for some airlines. Without the CAB to control fares, price wars broke out. Several major carriers, plus some of the smaller airlines, were unable to compete and went into bankruptcy. It was common in the 1980s for airlines to buy one another out or to merge their operations. Others stayed in business by asking their workers to accept pay cuts. Rather than see their jobs disappear, pilots and other employees sometimes agreed to work for less money.

For airline passengers, deregulation brought both good news and bad news. The accident rate did not increase despite predictions that the airlines would neglect aircraft maintenance and other safety precautions. Fare wars lowered ticket costs on most major routes for those travelers who could fly during off-peak hours and seasons. All in all, more people flew more miles in more planes than ever before. The bad news came as the air control system staggered under the increased traffic. Many flights were delayed as planes waited for take-off or landing clearances. Several accidents blamed on aging planes increased the public's worries about safety. Customers also had trouble figuring out the complex fare system.

HAS DEREGULATION BEEN HELPFUL?

For now, the future of deregulation is clouded. Cutthroat competition has left many airlines in financial trouble. When an airline goes bankrupt, its workers lose their jobs and the public loses the advantage of competition. Opponents of deregulation also fear that continued fare wars will wipe out all but the strongest carriers. If that happens, the survivors may feel free to boost fares sky-high. Airline deregulation, on the other hand, represents a success story for those who want government to get out of the marketplace. If all goes well, the deregulators argue, the death of the CAB may lead to better, cheaper service and a more efficient industry.

Let's review for a moment

Are you still wondering why your hometown radio station fades out so quickly? It's not that the owners can't afford a stronger transmitter. It's because the FCC restricts good ol' WROK to only 500 watts. On the other hand, if you've been confused by all those supersaver air fares, that's because the CAB no longer regulates the cost of an airline ticket. No one tells the airlines what they have to charge to fly you across the United States these days.

The *independent agencies* have earned their informal title of "the *fourth branch* of government." Given their authority by Congress, they have a hand in almost every commercial enterprise in the United States. Wouldn't it be easier for the government to take over the railroads and the television stations? Not if you believe in free enterprise. The regulatory agencies represent a compromise between absolute government control and all-powerful corporations.

Deregulation has cut back some of the *Interstate Commerce Commission's* power. But the ICC still controls freight rates and enforces safety standards. Traditionally, the agency regulated service by railroads, trucks, buses, pipelines, and inland waterways. Still thinking about starting your own bus line? The red tape will come mostly from state and local governments—unless you're planning to cross a state line. Then the ICC will join in to tell you what you can and can't do.

The *Federal Communications Commission* regulates radio and television broadcasting, along with local telephone service. Long-distance phone service has been deregulated. Did your local radio station broadcast an editorial that made you angry? You can ask for a chance to reply, but the FCC no longer guarantees your right to free air time.

The most obvious example of deregulation at work is found in the airline industry. Congress put the *Civil Aeronautics Board* out of business. A confusing tangle of air fares and schedules has resulted, thanks to free-market forces. Deregulation has brought lower fares and increased competition. It has also driven some airlines into bankruptcy.

Now, where will you go to complain about that box of deceptively packaged soap? If you know your regulatory agencies, you'll try the Federal Trade Commission.

6. How does the Federal Trade Commission protect American consumers?

Congress established the Federal Trade Commission in 1914. The agency's first task was to enforce the Clayton Antitrust Act, which was passed later the same year. The FTC was given two objectives: (1) to maintain the free enterprise system by helping business and industry comply with the antitrust laws and (2) to protect consumers from unfair trade practices.

FTC ORGANIZATION

Five FTC commissioners serve overlapping seven-year terms. As with most other agencies, an executive director supervises the staff. This leaves the commissioners free to concentrate on writing policy and hearing important cases. The agency divides its work among three bureaus: Competition, Consumer Protection, and Economics.

■ Many FTC regulations protect consumers. Labels on clothing give information about fabric content, place of manufacture, and care required. The FTC helps credit card users by requiring the issuing company to spell out true interest charges on the unpaid balance.

FTC JURISDICTION

The Federal Trade Commission aids consumers in three areas:

Antitrust regulation. The FTC promotes free and fair competition in interstate commerce by preventing companies from acting in *restraint of trade*. FTC examiners watch for illegal pricing, such as price-fixing, price discrimination, and rebates or discounts that are given to large buyers but not to smaller retailers. In addition, the FTC tries to prevent illegal agreements (such as arrangements that join companies that otherwise would be competitors). Chrysler's 1987 purchase of American Motors could not go forward, for example, until the FTC approved the merger of the two automakers.

Consumer protection. The FTC's best-known efforts have come in the field of consumer protection. The agency requires honest packaging (no deceptive sizes and shapes) and proper labeling of textile and fur products (rabbit fur was once sold under 20 or more

different names). When complaints piled up against the nation's funeral homes, the FTC wrote new rules that helped reduce shady business practices in that industry. The FTC also safeguards registered trademarks, so competitors can't steal the names a company creates for its products.

A recent FTC consumer protection effort has been focused on "truth in lending." The agency's rulings have helped everyone who borrows money or uses a credit card. Appliance stores and other lenders must clearly state the true interest rates and total interest costs of installment loans at the time of purchase. Similarly, credit card billings must state the true interest rates charged to a cardholder on the unpaid balance. Finally, the Fair Credit Reporting Act gives consumers the right to examine their credit files and to remove inaccurate information.

Economic reports. FTC statistics provide information on changes in the economy that affect business competition. Detailed, quarterly summaries of business activities help policymakers choose programs that will keep the economy healthy.

ENFORCEMENT

The FTC is one of the most active of all agencies when it comes to enforcing its decisions. Most companies will agree to stop a particular practice when FTC personnel ask them to do so. Consumers can trigger this process by making a complaint to the FTC. If the case goes to court, the FTC may ask for a court order telling the company to "cease and desist." If the company continues to violate the ruling, the FTC may bring suit in federal district court. A ruling against the company carries possible fines of up to $10,000 per day for continued violations.

7. How do the independent agencies protect the nation's workers?

By its very nature, the Department of Labor cannot meet all of the needs of American workers. Because of its position in the Cabinet, the department's leadership reflects the labor policies of the current administration. To help resolve this problem, Congress has created independent agencies to deal with some of the problems that arise in the field of labor relations.

THE NATIONAL LABOR RELATIONS BOARD (NLRB)

The National Labor Relations Board was set up in 1935 by the Wagner Act. It was later strengthened by the Taft-Hartley Act (1947) and the Landrum-Griffin Act (1959). Congress designed the agency to step in when one side to a labor dispute claims that the other is using an unfair labor practice.

Employers hated the NLRB at first. They thought the agency would always support the unions. The NLRB, however, was so successful at defusing explosive labor conflicts that it became a permanent part of the labor scene. Today, the NLRB maintains field offices throughout the United States. The agency's mediators enter a labor dispute only when an employer, a union, or a third party asks for help.

The NLRB has the power to issue complaints, petition the courts for injunctions, obtain settlements, and insure compliance with court orders. The NLRB also conducts secret ballot elections when a union is trying to organize a group of workers. This allows workers to vote for or against the union without being unfairly pressured by either side. NLRB representatives conduct other types of elections as well. Two unions, for example, may be claiming the right to speak for the same workers, or a company's workers may be voting to end a union-shop agreement.

THE FEDERAL LABOR RELATIONS AUTHORITY (FLRA)

The Federal Labor Relations Authority was established in 1978 to mediate labor disputes that involve federal employees. The FLRA administers the laws that guarantee government workers the right to bargain collectively and to join labor organizations of their own choosing. Federal workers also have the right to take part in decisions about salaries and working conditions.

The FLRA supervises union elections, investigates charges of unfair labor practices, makes arbitration awards, and handles jurisdictional disputes. Most important, FLRA mediators help to settle disputes between federal agencies and their workers. If talks break down, the FLRA holds fact-finding hearings in which both sides have a chance to be heard.

THE OFFICE OF PERSONNEL MANAGEMENT (OPM)

The Office of Personnel Management was created in 1978 to take over many tasks of the old U.S. Civil Service Commission. The OPM's primary task is to administer a merit system for federal employment. This means that government workers must be recruited, examined, trained, and promoted solely on the basis of their skills and performance. Race, religion, sex, political beliefs, and other nonmerit factors are not supposed to influence personnel decisions.

FYI...
How to Make a Complaint to a Federal Regulatory Agency

The National Consumer Law Center at Boston University Law School has listed five points that should be covered in a well-drawn application for complaint:

1. Include the name and address of the company you are complaining about. This should be accompanied by an explanation that the company is engaged in a significant amount of interstate commerce.

2. Attach copies of any documentary evidence involved, such as advertisements or letters.

3. Describe the facts as clearly and completely as you possibly can. This is the information that probably will be most important in the staff's deciding whether to investigate further or to send you a polite brush-off.

4. As much evidence as possible that other consumers have been victims of the same deceptive practice should be included. The greater the number of consumers victimized, the more likely it is that the commission will take some action. If other consumers are willing to sign affidavits [notarized statements], the application will have even more impact. There is little likelihood that they will actually be called as witnesses in formal hearings, but it is possible that they will be interviewed if the agency decides to conduct an investigation.

5. The application for complaint must be signed by the consumer or the consumer's attorney, with a return address provided.

Making an application for a complaint is the simplest means of gaining access to the regulatory process. Consumers who wish to become more deeply involved are invited to consult the source from which this advice was taken: *Working on the System: A Comprehensive Manual for Citizen Access to Federal Agencies*, edited by James R. Michael with Ruth C. Fort.

The OPM's regional offices and its many employment centers actively promote affirmative action programs. These programs are designed to find jobs in and out of government for women, minorities, veterans, and the handicapped. Typical of the OPM's affirmative action efforts are the Federal Equal Opportunity Recruitment Program, the Federal Women's Program, the Hispanic Employment Program, and the Veterans Employment Program. These programs affect three million federal government workers, as well as many workers in the private sector.

8. How does the Securities and Exchange Commission protect investors?

The great stock market crash of 1929 wiped out the savings of thousands of Americans. In the years leading up to the crash, the stock market became a dangerous place for unwary investors. They were at the mercy of financial sharks who promised quick profits. State legislatures tried to control the fast-talking stock promoters but with little success. The public's faith in the honesty of the stock market was in jeopardy. Congress responded by creating the Securities and Exchange Commission (SEC) in 1934.

SEC ORGANIZATION

The SEC operates under the direction of five members who are appointed to staggered five-year terms. The commissioners oversee the work of lawyers, economists, analysts, and other employees who work out of SEC regional offices.

SAFEGUARDS FOR INVESTORS

The SEC's commissioners cannot guarantee the safety of an investment. Honest companies sometimes go bankrupt, leaving stockholders with suddenly worthless securities. The SEC does provide safeguards in two areas:

1. *Full disclosure.* SEC regulations require that companies make full disclosure of all financial information relating to new offerings of their stocks and bonds. Any sale of securities not registered with the SEC is illegal. Registration of the stock with the SEC does not signify government approval of the issue. The best an investor can be certain of is that the information contained in the stock description (called a prospectus) is accurate under penalty of law.

2. *Market regulation.* SEC officials follow up on the disclosure rules by regulating the way in which stocks and bonds are traded after they are first offered. Elaborate rules govern the operation of stock exchanges and brokerage houses and the conditions under which sales are made. Agency inspectors investigate and prosecute illegal stock trades made by speculators who have access to "inside" information. Violations of this rule led to a major stock market scandal in 1987–1988. Speculators who made huge profits through the use of information not available to the general public were exposed and sent to prison.

Sales on margin (stock sold on credit) and in futures (a commodity purchased now to be delivered later) are strictly regulated. The percentage of the stock's price that must be paid in cash varies according to the SEC's judgment of market conditions and the general national economy.

OTHER SEC CONCERNS

The SEC takes an interest any time a corporation's securities show a sudden change in value. The agency sits in on bankruptcy hearings in order to represent the interests of the investors who bought the corporation's securities. SEC studies also look into market conditions and recommend new regulations to protect investors. After the market crashed in October 1987, for example, the SEC took a hard look at the use of computer programs that automatically trigger massive sales of stocks by wealthy corporate and institutional investors. "Circuit breakers" were added to the system so that computer-generated sales can be cut off when the market falls too far

■ A scene on the floor of the New York Stock Exchange. The professionals who buy and sell stocks are strictly regulated by the Securities and Exchange Commission.

INDEPENDENT AGENCIES OF THE FEDERAL GOVERNMENT, 1991

The federal government's wide-ranging role as guardian, regulator, and promoter of the American way of life shows clearly in this list of independent agencies.

ACTION
Administrative Conference of the U.S.
African Development Foundation
Central Intelligence Agency
Commission of Fine Arts
Commission on Civil Rights
Commodity Futures Trading
    Commission
Consumer Product Safety Commission
Defense Nuclear Facilities Safety Board
Environmental Protection Agency
Equal Employment Opportunity
    Commission
Export-Import Bank of the U.S.
Farm Credit Administration
Federal Communications Commission
Federal Deposit Insurance Corporation
Federal Election Commission
Federal Emergency Management
    Agency
Federal Housing Finance Board
Federal Labor Relations Authority
Federal Maritime Commission
Federal Mediation and Conciliation
    Service
Federal Reserve System
Federal Trade Commission
General Services Administration
Inter-American Foundation
Interstate Commerce Commission
Merit Systems Protection Board
National Aeronautics and Space
    Administration

National Archives and Records
    Administration
National Credit Union Administration
National Foundation on the Arts and
    Humanities
National Labor Relations Board
National Mediation Board
National Railroad Passenger
    Corporation (AMTRAK)
National Science Foundation
National Transportation Safety Board
Nuclear Regulatory Commission
Occupational Safety and Health
    Review Commission
Office of Government Ethics
Office of Personnel Management
Panama Canal Commission
Peace Corps
Pension Benefit Guaranty Corporation
Postal Rate Commission
Railroad Retirement Board
Resolution Trust Corporation
Securities and Exchange Commission
Selective Service System
Small Business Administration
Tennessee Valley Authority
U.S. Arms Control and Disarmament
    Agency
U.S. Information Agency
U.S. International Development
    Cooperation Agency
U.S. International Trade Commission
U.S. Postal Service

too quickly. Two other areas that have attracted particular attention have been holding companies and mutual funds.

Holding companies. A *holding company* exists to own other companies. If a holding company is suspected of violating antitrust laws, the Federal Trade Commission moves in to investigate. The SEC's regulation of holding companies requires full disclosure of their finances and elimination or reorganization of poorly managed companies. The SEC also supervises holding companies in the electrical and natural gas industries.

Mutual funds. Investors buy stock in mutual funds so that the fund can invest the money in the stocks and bonds of many other companies. Mutual fund buyers are trying to minimize their risks by relying on the investment judgment of expert fund managers. Mutual funds make their profits by charging an annual fee for their services. The SEC does not meddle with the investment decisions made by the fund. Instead, the agency protects investors by controlling management fees, mergers, "inside" deals, and other practices that might affect a fund's operations.

9. Why were the independent administrative agencies established?

In addition to the regulatory agencies, Congress has created a second type of independent agency, the *administrative agency*. Many similar activities are carried out by the various Cabinet departments. A number of politically sensitive duties, however, have been assigned to agencies in the "fourth branch" of government. These administrative agencies normally carry on their work outside the direct control of the legislative or executive branches.

TENNESSEE VALLEY AUTHORITY

Socialists believe that government should own and manage a nation's major industrial complexes. In the Tennessee Valley Authority (TVA), the U.S. federal government created a unique independent agency that does exactly that. Congress started the TVA in the depression year of 1933 for the "orderly and proper physical, economic and social development" of an entire region—the 41,000 square miles of the Tennessee River Valley. Today, the seven-state system of dams, power stations, research labs, and recreational areas serves a population of more than four million. A three-member board of directors (appointed by the President to nine-year terms) sets policy for the massive TVA operation.

TVA's responsibilities. Two primary tasks occupy most of the TVA's attention: flood control and development of hydroelectric power. Other TVA programs include maintenance of a 650-mile channel for navigation, reforestation and soil conservation programs, agricultural research, particularly in fertilizers, and development of recreational areas.

Controversy. Controversy has swirled around the TVA since its birth. The issue was taken to court, but the Supreme Court ruled

■ The Chickamauga Dam on the Tennessee River near Chattanooga, Tennessee, one of the flood control and power-producing structures in the Tennessee Valley Authority. Critics wonder whether it is fair for the government to provide cheap power in competition with private utilities.

in 1936 that the project was constitutional. Critics still urge the government to sell its facilities to private enterprise. Tax-exempt government power stations, they claim, should not compete with taxpaying utility companies. TVA has also come under attack by its own customers. Residents in the region have seen their electric bills go up steeply in recent years, and industrial rates have doubled.

The TVA's supporters answer these criticisms by listing the agency's successes. They point out that the formerly depressed region has gained greatly in per capita income, and yearly floods no longer wreck the valley's farms and towns. In addition, most farms in the region now have electricity, and large areas have been reforested. Finally, the abundant power has attracted many new industries to the valley. Without this progress, the region might have cost the government many more dollars for social welfare programs.

THE UNITED STATES POSTAL SERVICE

One of the nation's oldest public services, the Post Office Department was founded by the

■ The Post Office is counting on technology, such as automatic mail sorting equipment, to cut costs and improve service. Raising postal fees alone will not lower the large deficit the Postal Service runs each year. Is providing daily mail service to homes and offices a vital government function?

Second Continental Congress in 1775. From the start, the department lost money. The government accepted the yearly deficits because it believed that a low-cost postal system helped to tie the country together.

In the Postal Reorganization Act of 1970, Congress removed the Post Office Department from the Cabinet and turned it into the U.S. Postal Service. As head of an independent federal agency, the Postmaster General no longer holds a Cabinet seat. The sponsors of the changeover hoped that the Postal Service would become more efficient as well as self-supporting. Today, despite greatly increased postal rates, the nation's post offices still run in the red.

The service. The United States Postal Service employs hundreds of thousands of workers. Only the Department of Defense has more federal employees. Over 150 billion pieces of mail pass through the system every year. The Postal Service provides other services in addition to selling stamps and delivering mail. Employees take applications for passports, sell money orders, and distribute the stamps that allow hunters to kill certain migratory birds.

Controversies and complaints. The Postal Service has had its share of controversy. In the 1800s, for example, bitter political battles raged over the question of patronage. The party in power enjoyed the privilege of rewarding its supporters with appointments to post office jobs. As a result of widespread abuses, the department was placed under civil service late in the century. That didn't stop Presidents from continuing to name leading political supporters as Postmasters General well into the mid-1900s.

Of more recent concern are rising complaints about high postage rates and slow mail service. In 1958, the stamp that sent a one-ounce letter to any address in the United States cost only three cents. That same stamp in 1991 cost 29 cents, with further increases on the horizon. The Postal Service has tried to improve matters by investing in costly equipment intended to automate mail sorting and handling. Even so, Americans complain that mail carriers are making fewer deliveries and mail takes longer to reach its destination. One newspaper article charged that a colonial horse and rider could beat today's delivery time for a letter traveling from Philadelphia to New York.

Diminishing the deficit. Postal Service deficits run into hundreds of millions of dollars a year. A major reason for the losses lies in the rate schedule. Mail is divided into various classes, depending on content and the level of service. Personal and business letters are known as first class and cost the most. Books, newspapers, magazines, and other printed materials can be mailed at lower rates. Clearly, the cost of handling these bulky materials is greater than the cost of delivering a first-class letter.

Congress, however, insists on using the mails to encourage the free flow of printed information. Postal Service officials say that the nation can have one or the other: a profitmaking system in which everyone pays what the service costs or a deficit-ridden system that provides low-cost mail service.

The Postal Service also points out that its new technology is beginning to pay off. Zip-tronic machines take advantage of ZIP Codes to sort letters at a rate of one every second. Automated bulk mail plants near big cities speed up handling of parcel post and magazine shipments. Also, guaranteed overnight mail delivery to major cities is now available.

10. What do some of the other independent agencies accomplish for the public?

So far, this chapter has discussed only a few of over 50 independent federal agencies. The list changes frequently because Congress often creates new agencies or combines existing ones.

What do the other agencies do? Here's a sampling:

Environmental Protection Agency. The EPA was established by President Nixon in 1970. The agency spends its $5.5 billion budget in an attempt to control pollution at its source, clean up existing conditions, and find better ways to protect the environment. Major EPA programs are presently trying to solve the problems of air and water pollution, acid rain, and toxic waste disposal. The agency is also involved in removing cancer-causing asbestos fibers from older buildings and in protecting the ozone layer by controlling emissions of ozone-destroying chlorine compounds.

Equal Employment Opportunity Commission. The EEOC works to end job discrimination based on race, religion, sex, age, or national origin. The commission's *affirmative action program* requires that companies doing business with the federal government hire minority, female, and handicapped employees. People who believe that they have been discriminated against at work can file a complaint with the EEOC. The agency's critics charged in 1988 that slow staff work caused the loss of some complaints that weren't acted on by the legal deadline. As a result of the

criticism, the EEOC took steps to catch up on its backlog.

Federal Deposit Insurance Corporation. The FDIC protects bank depositors by insuring individual savings accounts in banks that belong to the Federal Reserve System. When bad loans and poor management combined to cause a number of banks to fail in the late 1980s, FDIC insurance paid off depositors up to a maximum of $100,000 for each account. A more serious epidemic of failures hit the savings and loan industry at the same time. Bailing out the ailing S&Ls soon exhausted a similar insurance fund, the Federal Savings and Loan Insurance Corporation (FSLIC). When Congress was forced to approve a costly rescue operation, the lawmakers also reorganized the banking regulatory system. A new Office of Thrift Supervision (replacing the old Federal Home Loan Bank Board) was given the giant task of nursing the S&L industry back to health. At the same time, the FDIC was made responsible for administering deposit insurance for both banks and S&Ls.

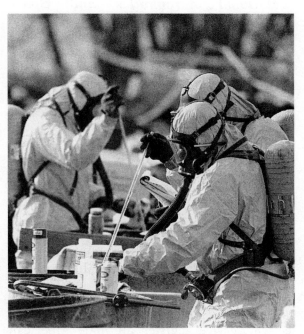

■ EPA workers taking test samples from storage drums at a paint manufacturing plant. Cleaning up hazardous wastes is a major task facing the government and private industry. No one yet knows the best way to do it.

Federal Reserve System. The Federal Reserve plays a major role in keeping the U.S. economy on an even keel. It controls the nation's credit, regulates the amount of money in circulation, and supervises the work of the 12 Federal Reserve Banks. Federal Reserve Banks issue the bulk of the nation's paper currency and serve as banker for the federal government. They also advance funds to member banks that need ready cash.

In the late 1970s, the FRS Board of Governors took a drastic step in the fight against inflation. The rediscount rate (the interest rate charged banks that borrow from the FRS) was raised to an all-time high. Economic theory said that high interest rates would reduce the money supply and discourage unnecessary borrowing. The strong medicine did reduce inflation to a manageable level, but a slowdown in business activity plunged the country into a recession. Despite serious deficits in the federal budget and in the balance of trade, the economy made a strong recovery during the 1980s.

National Aeronautics and Space Administration. NASA plans, coordinates, and controls the national space program. Its successes include the manned moon landing (1969), a soft landing on Mars (1976), and the first flight of the space shuttle (1981). The agency suffered a severe setback when the space shuttle *Challenger* exploded shortly after liftoff in January 1986. The tragedy left the nation in mourning and led to a major reorganization of NASA. The shuttle program was suspended until 1988 while NASA's engineers designed a safer space shuttle. In 1990, President George Bush called on NASA to move ahead with plans to land astronauts on Mars.

Selective Service System. The Selective Service administers the military conscription system, better known as the draft. With voluntary enlistments holding up, no one has been drafted into the armed forces since July 1973. Even so, the law requires that the Selective Service register all male American citizens and resident aliens when they reach the age of 18.

Smithsonian Institution. The Smithsonian manages a number of national museums that preserve the nation's historical and cultural heritage. The Smithsonian also carries on important scientific research. Its museums include the National Museum of American History, the National Portrait Gallery, and the National Air and Space Museum.

United States Information Agency. The USIA promotes better understanding of this country around the world. The agency's specialists use radio, television, films, books, newspapers, exhibitions, and cultural exchanges to publicize the culture, politics, and foreign policy of the United States. The head of USIA also advises the President and Secretary of State on changes in world public opinion.

11. Who regulates the nation's regulators?

Richard Olney, chief legal counsel for several eastern railroads, once wrote a reassuring letter to a railroad company president. The railroad man was worried that the newly formed Interstate Commerce Commission would interfere in his business. Olney told him that the ICC "can be made of great use to the railroads. ... The older such a commission gets to be, the more inclined it will be found to take the business and railway view of things."

Olney wrote his letter in 1887. Critics of the ICC and other regulatory agencies believe that little has happened since then to prove him wrong. The President's own economic advisers have pointed out that ICC-controlled freight rates cost consumers hundreds of millions of dollars a year in overcharges. Similarly, the Hoover Commission blasted the Federal Trade Commission. The commission's report called the FTC's operation, programs, and administrative methods inadequate and its procedures cumbersome. These criticisms leave many Americans doubtful as to the ability of the federal "watchdogs" to guard the public interest.

CRITICISM OF REGULATORY AGENCIES

The charges against the independent regulatory agencies vary according to the nature of the agency's activities. Some criticisms are common to many agencies, however.

Regulators who don't regulate. Despite efforts to provide commissioners with immunity to pressure, the agencies cannot escape outside influence. Much of that influence comes from the very industries they regulate. Because agency heads should be "experts," Presidents often reach into corporate offices for their appointees. Low budgets, small staffs, and natural sympathies all tend to tie the agency to the corporations it supposedly controls. At the other end of the cycle, agency personnel often leave their jobs for better-paying positions with the firms they formerly regulated. When they need a favor, it's natural for them to contact their friends within the regulatory body.

Pressure from Congress and the White House also complicates the regulatory process. One legislator may help a home-state television station sail through its FCC license hearings. Another may help automakers evade a new safety regulation. Congressional influence comes from its control of the agency's budget, but the President holds the power of political life and death. Bureaucrats, anxious to protect their jobs and chances of advancement, ignore the administration's wishes at their own peril.

Indifference to the public interest. Regulatory agencies hold regular hearings, but many public groups (consumers, poor people, minorities) are seldom heard. Consumer advocates such as Ralph Nader believe that in a misguided effort to protect business interests, the antitrust laws have been almost forgotten. The result, Nader charges, is that "bigness" now equals "goodness" in the eyes of the regulatory agencies.

Overregulation. Well-meaning bureaucrats, armed with governmental red tape, sometimes create high costs and inefficiency in the industries they regulate. Rate schedules may remain unchanged despite changing market conditions. New technology can't be used because of outmoded work rules. Excessive paperwork keeps office workers from performing more productive tasks. Critics point out that government regulation has created a large bureaucracy with a mighty appetite for re-

"Something went wrong here"

■ Critics of the regulatory agencies charge that the federal "watchdogs" have lost sight of their primary job: protecting the public.

ports that no one reads. Needless regulation, they claim, adds over $100 billion a year to the costs of goods and services in the United States.

Regulation by compromise. Regulatory agencies move slowly and cautiously. Fearful of upsetting company presidents, bank directors, and congressional committee members, agency officials "study" issues to death. Court challenges can delay a proposed regulation for years. When the agency finally does write a new rule, it's usually one that business "can live with." The textile industry and the FTC, for example, spent years debating the need to make all children's sleepwear flame-retardant. While they argued, a number of toddlers burned to death.

PROPOSED REFORMS

Reform attempts have come and gone since the 1946 Administrative Procedure Act tried to move the regulatory agencies toward "fair and uniform procedures." As consumer groups work to open the agencies to public supervision, recommendations for reform are still coming in from all sides.

Abolish the regulators. The most dramatic proposal urges that all regulatory agencies be disbanded. Where still needed, their functions could be given to appropriate Cabinet departments.

Regulate the regulators. An independent agency already exists—the Administrative Conference of the United States—that could serve as general supervisor of the regulatory agencies. At present, the Administrative Conference can only study regulatory problems and suggest reforms. In order to "regulate the regulators," the ACUS would need greater authority over the independent agencies, a larger budget, and a bigger staff.

Accelerate antitrust prosecution. The Justice Department should greatly speed up its prosecution of antitrust cases. General Motors and IBM, one argument claims, should long ago have been split into smaller companies. Antitrust laws do have teeth, however, as AT&T found out. After years of courtroom battles, the threat of further antitrust action forced the giant telephone company to split up into smaller, regional systems.

Increase congressional supervision. A number of critics contend that Congress should spend more time supervising the regulatory agencies. When necessary, budget controls can be used to keep the agencies tuned in on their primary job—that of protecting consumers. Finally, senators and representatives must stop using the agencies for selfish political and economic purposes.

Protect whistle-blowers. The results generated by the 1986 amendments to the False Claims Act show what happens when Congress does act to protect the public interest. The law dates back to 1863, when Civil War soldiers found that profit-hungry contractors were mixing sawdust into the gunpowder supply. Congress gave citizens the right to file lawsuits against dishonest companies. Along with performing a civic duty, the "whistle-blower" can receive up to 30 percent of any damages levied by the courts. Since the 1986 amendment provided improved job protection for whistle-blowers, over 140 lawsuits have been filed under the act. Typical is the $69.5 million in damages awarded to two former Ashland Oil Company executives. The jury made the award because Ashland fired the two men after they "blew the whistle" on the company for paying bribes.

Establish a consumer agency. Many consumer advocates insist that creation of a Consumer Protection Agency is long overdue. Even though the government does provide a wide range of consumer services, the proposed agency would give consumers a more powerful voice. The CPA would represent the public before other federal agencies and in the courts. In addition, the agency would collect and publish consumer information from the government's busy research facilities.

Reviewing
what you've learned

1. *Independent agencies* are called the *"fourth branch"* of the federal government. Possessed of their own legislative, judicial, and executive powers, they operate independently of Congress and the White House. The regulatory agencies represent a compromise between total government ownership of industry and the opposite extreme of all-powerful private corporations. Where once the regulatory agencies were constantly growing in power, the current trend is toward *deregulation*. This has meant a return to free markets and less government control of business and industry.

2. The *Interstate Commerce Commission* is the oldest of the independent agencies. The ICC regulates all overland and inland waterway transport in the United States, except for automobiles. Agency examiners set rates and safety standards, regulate securities, and guarantee service at "reasonable rates." The ICC hopes that competition will be increased and shipping rates lowered by the deregulation of the trucking industry.

3. Radio and television broadcasting, along with telegraph and local telephone services, is controlled by the *Federal Communications Commission*. The FCC licenses the use of the public airways, sets broadcast standards, and holds hearings on telephone rates. Long-distance telephone service has been deregulated.

4. The *Civil Aeronautics Board* was abolished in 1985. With regulation ended, the government no longer sets airline fares nor does it limit the number of airlines flying into each city. Increased competition has reduced fares but has forced some airlines into bankruptcy. Other airlines have reduced the salaries of their workers in order to stay in business.

5. The *Federal Trade Commission* tries to maintain the free enterprise system and eliminate unfair trade practices. Although some consumer activists argue that the FTC hasn't moved fast enough, the agency has made some progress. "Truth in lending" laws grew out of FTC efforts as did the ruling that people have the right to inspect their own credit files.

6. Three regulatory agencies serve the needs of American workers. The *National Labor Relations Board* prevents unfair labor practices and supervises union elections. The *Federal Labor Relations Authority* performs the same services for federal employees. The *Office of Personnel Management* makes sure that government workers are hired and paid according to merit.

7. The *Securities and Exchange Commission* cannot guarantee that investors will make money. It does require full disclosure of all investment information by a company that is selling stocks and bonds. In addition, investors are protected by controls on margin buying, the futures market, *holding companies*, mutual funds, and the stock market itself.

8. The independent agencies often serve a particular group of people. Americans who deposit money in a commercial bank or a savings and loan, for example, know that the *Federal Deposit Insurance Corporation* (FDIC) guarantees their accounts up to $100,000. Another independent agency, the *Tennessee Valley Authority,* has raised the living standards of the inhabitants of a seven-state region. Along with building flood control dams and generating hydroelectric power, the TVA provides camping and fishing facilities for over 4 million people.

9. The *United States Postal Service* keeps the nation's mail moving—too slowly, some critics charge. Faced with annual deficits, Congress removed the old Post Office Department from the Cabinet in 1970. Heavy labor costs, combined with congressional insistence on keeping rates low, account for most of the Postal Service's budget deficits. The Postal Service has invested heavily in automated equipment in hopes of improving service and bringing the deficit under control.

10. Some business leaders believe that the economy has been overregulated by the independent agencies. They cite complex, time-wasting regulations and the high cost of government-required paperwork as two examples. Consumer advocates have their own complaints. They charge that regulators sometimes ignore the public interest, allowing discussions of serious problems to drag on for years. In addition, agency heads sometimes cave in to outside pressures, either from Congress or from the industry they regulate. Reform proposals range from abolishing all regulatory agencies to creating a consumer "super agency."

Review questions and activities

TERMS AND AGENCIES YOU SHOULD KNOW

administrative agency
affirmative action program
Civil Aeronautics Board (CAB)
deregulation
Environmental Protection Agency (EPA)
Equal Employment Opportunity Commission (EEOC)
Federal Communications Commission (FCC)
Federal Deposit Insurance Corporation (FDIC)
Federal Labor Relations Authority (FLRA)
Federal Reserve System
Federal Trade Commission (FTC)
"fourth branch"
holding company

independent agencies
Interstate Commerce Commission (ICC)
National Aeronautics and Space Administration (NASA)
National Labor Relations Board (NLRB)
Office of Personnel Management (OPM)
regulatory authority
restraint of trade
Securities and Exchange Commission (SEC)
Selective Service System
Smithsonian Institution
Tennessee Valley Authority (TVA)
U.S. Information Agency (USIA)
U.S. Postal Service

REVIEW QUESTIONS

Select the response that best completes each statement or question.

1. The independent agencies are sometimes spoken of as the "fourth branch" of government service because (*a*) the Constitution created the first agencies to regulate the other three branches. (*b*) they combine legislative, executive, and judicial powers. (*c*) most of them have their own police forces. (*d*) politicians cannot be elected without their assistance. (*e*) they all regulate interstate commerce.

2. In creating the regulatory agencies, Congress delegated to them part of its power over (*a*) the executive branch. (*b*) the judicial branch. (*c*) interstate commerce. (*d*) administration of the civil service. (*e*) the general welfare.

3. The method of overland transport that is *not* regulated by the Interstate Commerce Commission is (*a*) railroads. (*b*) trucks. (*c*) pipelines. (*d*) inland waterway craft. (*e*) private automobiles.

4. Despite the regulatory authority of the Interstate Commerce Commission, a railroad or bus line may discontinue any route that loses money. This statement is (*a*) true. (*b*) false, because the agency requires that routes be continued even if the routes are losing money. (*c*) false, because the growing population of the United States and its need for public transportation makes it impossible for any routes to lose money.

5. The power that the Federal Communication Commission does *not* exercise is that of (*a*) censorship of program content. (*b*) regulation of broadcasting transmitter power. (*c*) reviewing a station's efforts to provide public service programs. (*d*) supervision of citizen's band radio broadcasting. (*e*) regulation of programs transmitted over cable television.

6. The independent agency most directly involved in consumer protection is the (*a*) Interstate Commerce Commission. (*b*) Office of Personnel Management. (*c*) Federal Communications Commission. (*d*) Federal Trade Commission. (*e*) Securities and Exchange Commission.

7. The Securities and Exchange Commission protects investors by (*a*) keeping the mechanisms of the securities market honest. (*b*) denying companies that might lose money the right to sell stock. (*c*) taking over all aspects of the issuing and marketing of securities. (*d*) controlling stock prices so that they cannot fall. (*e*) keeping its hands off the stock market and letting free enterprise take its course.

8. A major criticism of the Tennessee Valley Authority has been that (*a*) the TVA has not been successful in its development work. (*b*) the government should not compete with private power companies. (*c*) flood control projects ruined the natural beauty of the area. (*d*) only the wealthy have profited from the agency's work. (*e*) other depressed regions have not copied the idea.

9. The independent agencies often find their independence threatened by pressure from Congress, the White House, and the industries they regulate. This statement is (*a*) true. (*b*) false, the agencies are immune to outside pressures. (*c*) false, the public would never permit the agencies to be pressured by outside interests.

10. Which of the following is *not* suggested as a reform of the regulatory agencies? (*a*) Set up an agency to speak for consumers. (*b*) Cut back the power of the agencies. (*c*) Increase antitrust prosecutions. (*d*) Do not appoint agency heads who come from the same industries they are supposed to regulate. (*e*) Double the number of agencies so as to spread out the work load.

CONCEPT DEVELOPMENT

1. What conditions led to independent agencies being established in the late 1800s?

2. Explain several important ways the independent agencies regulate the economic life of the United States.

3. What factors have led to the current trend toward deregulation? Discuss the effect of deregulation on the airline industry and the trucking industry.

4. Select one of the federal regulatory agencies described in this chapter and evaluate its performance in detail.

5. What complaints are most often brought against the independent regulatory agencies? Suggest the reforms that you feel would be most effective in solving these problems.

HANDS-ON ACTIVITIES

1. Use your library's copy of the current *United States Government Manual* to look up the major independent agencies described in this chapter. For each agency, prepare an information sheet that lists (a) name of the director, (b) agency name and address (including local offices), and (c) a brief summary of the agency's responsibilities. Distribute the information around your school (and in the community, if you wish) as

a means of encouraging people to write to the appropriate agencies with complaints or suggestions about problems that need attention. Other useful sources for this project are Dana Shilling's *Fighting Back: A Consumer's Guide for Getting Satisfaction* (New York: Quill, 1982) and Arthur Best's *When Consumers Complain* (New York: Columbia University Press, 1981).

2. You don't have to be a lawyer to stand up for consumers' rights. Ask a local supermarket manager for permission to survey the store's customers. Over a period of several days, ask the people shopping there to list their complaints about such practices as deceptive packaging, unfair pricing, misleading advertising, and other improper practices. Compile your results, make recommendations for correcting the problems, and send them to:

> Director, Office of Public Affairs
> Federal Trade Commission
> Washington, D.C. 20580

Your letter, along with other complaints from the public, will help FTC examiners gather the data they need to improve trade standards.

3. Arrange a debate between two teams of students who will take the role of (a) the directors of a heavily regulated company (a major railroad, perhaps) and (b) the head of the appropriate regulating agency (the ICC in this case). Let each side state its case for and against regulation. Your debaters will have to do some research, including interviews with people who work for the business, the regulating agency, and consumers' groups. Let the class vote on whether regulation should be continued, lessened, or increased for this industry.

4. Organize your class to conduct a careful survey of environmental pollution in your community. Check on all types of pollution—air, water, noise, and waste disposal. Make accurate observations of your own but also talk to local and county officials about what they are doing to solve these problems. If the study generates enough interest, you can start an environmental protection club to assist in gathering information and lobbying for changes. The Environmental Protection Agency will send information on projects and procedures that have worked in other towns and cities.

5. One of the complaints people have about modern life is that individual citizens are helpless against the power of corporations and governments. Test that assumption by making a survey of people's attitudes. Ask at least 20 people this question: Assume that you are angry about the lack of good children's programs on television. You decide to take the matter to the Federal Communications Commission. Which of the following do you think would be the most likely result?

(*a*) The bureaucrats at the FCC won't bother to answer my letter.

(*b*) The agency will send me a form letter. The letter will tell me very politely not to bother them.

(*c*) Someone from the FCC will contact me to ask for further information. There's not much chance, though, that the agency will follow up by taking any effective action.

(*d*) I'm confident the FCC will take my complaint seriously. Government agencies move so slowly, however, that I'll be old and gray before I get satisfaction.

(*e*) The FCC will move promptly and efficiently to correct the problem.

What conclusions about people's attitudes toward government can you draw from the data? Report back to your class on the results of your survey.

Unit Five

The Judicial Branch of American Government

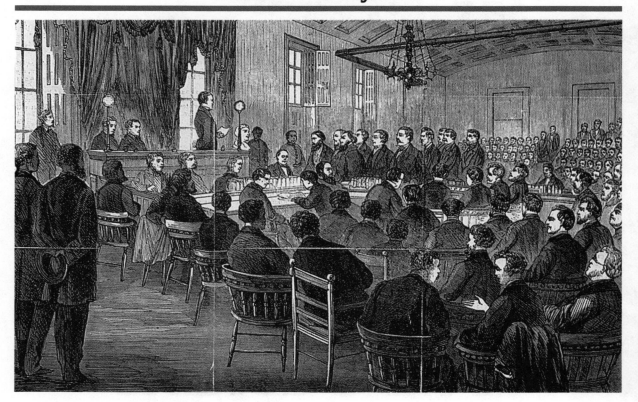

15 The U.S. court system

Outsiders sometimes see America and its people more clearly than those who live here. Alexis de Tocqueville was one of the keenest of all such observers. This young French nobleman visited the United States in the early 1830s. His goal, he said, was to find out why democracy was succeeding here while, at the same time, it was failing in his own country.

The French overthrew their king in 1789, the same year that George Washington was sworn in as President of the United States. The revolution brought democracy to France, but popular rule soon gave way to the Reign of Terror, the dictatorship of Napoleon Bonaparte, and the restoration of the monarchy. In 1830, democracy suffered further blows as the government censored the press, dissolved the elected Chamber of Deputies, and tried to influence the upcoming election. By

▲ The judge delivering the charge to the jury in a murder trial in 1868.

360

contrast, the United States was thriving under the democratic leadership of President Andrew Jackson.

In the United States, de Tocqueville discovered, majority rule did not confer absolute power upon the winners. He marveled at the way the three branches of government interacted to guard the nation's freedoms. One of the most important democratic forces, he concluded, was the court system.

In his book *Democracy in America*, de Tocqueville wrote, ". . . I am not aware that any nation of the globe has hitherto organized a judicial power in the same manner as the Americans. The judicial organization of the United States is the institution which a stranger has the greatest difficulty in understanding. He hears the authority of a judge invoked in the political occurrences of every day. . ."

De Tocqueville then asked himself a question. How, he wondered, in a court system that seems much like any other, do judges wield such authority?

The explanation, the Frenchman decided, lay in three special characteristics of American judicial power. A judge, he wrote, "can only pronounce a decision when litigation has arisen. He is conversant only with special cases, and he cannot act until the cause has been duly brought before the court. . . . the Americans have acknowledged the right of judges to found their decision on the *Constitution* rather than on the *laws*."

The American jury system also earned de Tocqueville's admiration. "The institution of a jury invests the people with the direction of society," he wrote. "The jury cannot fail to exercise a powerful influence on the national character. . . . It imbues all classes with respect for the thing judged, with the notion of right. If these two things be removed, the love of independence becomes a mere destructive passion."

Finally, the visitor was impressed with U.S. lawyers. "In America, there are no nobles . . . and the people are apt to mistrust the wealthy; lawyers consequently form the highest political class . . . The courts of justice are the visible organs by which the legal profession is enabled to control the democracy. The judge is a lawyer. . . . His legal attainments have raised him to a distinguished rank among his fellows. . . . Armed with the power of declaring the laws to be unconstitutional, the American magistrate perpetually interferes in political affairs."

In the 1990s, as in the 1830s, visitors are still impressed by the role played by the courts in protecting American freedoms. This chapter will explore this universally respected system of justice and the state and federal courts that administer it.

1. **How were the federal courts established?**

2. **How does the system of state courts operate?**

3. **When does a court have the right to hear a case?**

4. How are judges selected, and what do they do?

5. What happens when a case goes to trial?

6. How well does the U.S. jury system work?

7. What powers do the courts exercise?

1. How were the federal courts established?

When the Constitutional Convention met in 1787, the delegates knew that the nation's court system did not work well. Each state interpreted the laws of the United States as it saw fit. As a result, no court had the power to resolve conflicts among the states. In addition, court decisions made in one state had no legal force in any other state.

This judicial anarchy led to the creation of the federal court system. Article III of the Constitution states:

The judicial power of the United States shall be vested in one Supreme Court, and in such inferior courts as the Congress may from time to time ordain and establish.

Congress received the expressed power to establish these courts in Article I, Section 8, Clause 9 (see page 522). Out of that congressional mandate emerged a three-level federal court system—district courts, the courts of appeals, and the Supreme Court.

DISTRICT COURTS

The first level of federal courts—the district courts—were set up in 1789, the first year of Washington's administration. The district courts exercise *original jurisdiction* in federal matters. That is, they serve as trial courts for all cases arising under the laws of the United States. The only exceptions are the few instances in which the Supreme Court retains original jurisdiction and in cases heard by special federal courts (see page 365).

COURTS OF APPEALS

The courts of appeals were created by Congress in 1891 to ease the Supreme Court's work load. The nation's highest court was being buried under a flood of appeals from the district courts. Courts of appeals stand midway between the district courts and the Supreme Court. Only when a lower court has declared an act of Congress unconstitutional may a case be appealed directly to the Supreme Court.

Eleven judicial circuits serve the 50 states. A twelfth court hears cases on appeal for the District of Columbia. One justice of the Supreme Court is also assigned in an advisory role to each circuit. Most cases are heard by a three-judge "bench." Either the defense or the prosecution may appeal a case to the courts of appeals, as long as federal jurisdiction is involved.

Appeals are normally accepted only on the basis of (1) an improper courtroom procedure or (2) an incorrect application of the law. If a lower court judge improperly excludes testimony or gives incorrect instructions to the jury, for example, the defense attorney has grounds for filing an appeal. Appeals may not be made on the basis of evidence presented at the original trial. Because the Supreme Court reviews only about four percent of the cases it is asked to consider, decisions made by the courts of appeals are usually the final word on most district court decisions.

SUPREME COURT

The judiciary is equal in power and status to the legislative and executive branches of the federal government. Under the American system of checks and balances, the Supreme Court often plays a crucial role in charting

The Path to the Supreme Court

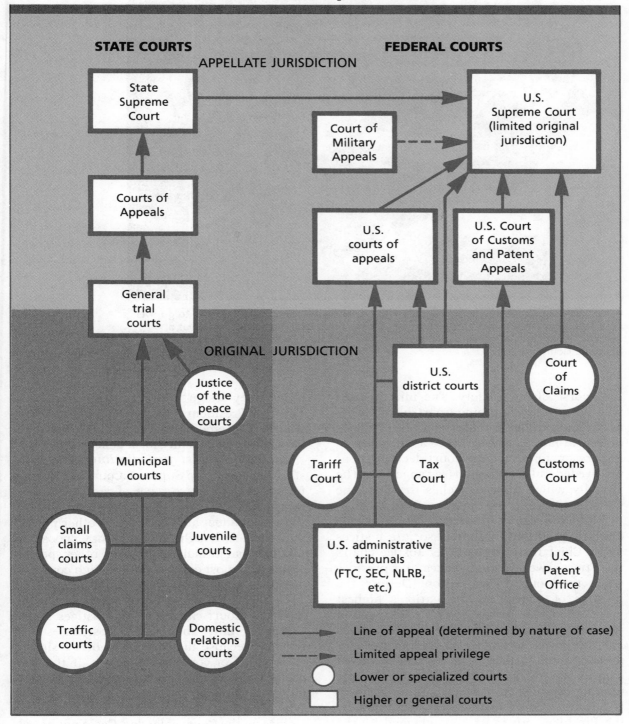

STATE COURTS FEDERAL COURTS

APPELLATE JURISDICTION

State Supreme Court

U.S. Supreme Court (limited original jurisdiction)

Court of Military Appeals

Courts of Appeals

U.S. courts of appeals

U.S. Court of Customs and Patent Appeals

General trial courts

ORIGINAL JURISDICTION

Justice of the peace courts

U.S. district courts

Court of Claims

Municipal courts

Tariff Court

Tax Court

Customs Court

Small claims courts

Juvenile courts

U.S. administrative tribunals (FTC, SEC, NLRB, etc.)

U.S. Patent Office

Traffic courts

Domestic relations courts

Line of appeal (determined by nature of case)

Limited appeal privilege

Lower or specialized courts

Higher or general courts

■ Associate Justice Anthony M. Kennedy with two of his law clerks. Justices like to go over legal arguments with clerks before meeting with the other eight justices to work out a decision. What types of cases do the justices consider? How do these cases reach the Supreme Court?

the course of our society. The nine justices who occupy the Supreme Court bench serve as the final decision makers on all questions of federal law. They also serve as the court of final resort for any lower court decisions that involve federal jurisdiction (see page 362). The path by which a case reaches the Supreme Court is shown in the diagram on page 363.

Supreme Court justices. The Supreme Court is made up of eight associate justices and a Chief Justice. The Chief Justice chairs the Court's weekly conferences and presides when the Court is in session. Despite the prestige of serving as the nation's highest judge, the Chief Justice's vote is only one of nine when a case is being decided. Congress has the power to change the number of Supreme Court justices. The total has varied from a low of five to the present nine, the number established in 1869.

Supreme Court justices are appointed by the President but must be confirmed by the Senate. The justices hold their seats for life unless they resign, retire, or are impeached. Thus, a President fortunate enough to fill several Supreme Court vacancies can change the Court's philosophy for a generation.

Supreme Court jurisdiction. The Constitution limits the Supreme Court to original jurisdiction over two types of cases: (1) those that involve two or more of the states and (2) those that affect ambassadors or other public ministers. Although the Court may choose to take original jurisdiction in a few other special situations, most cases reach the high court on an appeal called a *writ of certiorari*.

Of the 5,000 or so cases appealed to the Supreme Court each year, the justices agree to review only about 200. Most cases are rejected because they do not involve a significant point of constitutional law. If the Supreme Court refuses to hear a case, the decision of the lower court is automatically upheld. When the Court does accept a case, it is given a place on the Court calendar. Cases not heard during one session are carried over to the next.

The Supreme Court at work. The nine justices hear arguments during a term that begins in October and generally runs through June. The time set aside for arguments in each case is limited, usually one hour per side. Extensive *briefs* (written summaries of legal precedents and other information) are filed to support the oral arguments. The justices then take the case under advisement. This begins a period of study and discussion that is held in strict privacy.

The justices vote on each case during their Friday conferences. At least six justices must be present, and at least four must agree before a decision can be made. The voting majority that decides a case usually presents a written explanation called a "majority opinion." Any justice who disagrees with the majority view may write a "minority opinion." In a 5–4 decision, the dissenting justices sometimes file as many as four minority opinions. In many cases, the Court simply announces its decision, without presenting written opinions. Because of the complex and controversial nature of the cases heard by the Court, close votes are common.

OTHER FEDERAL COURTS

A number of special courts established by Congress complete the federal court system. These lower-level courts include:

Territorial courts. U.S. overseas possessions (Guam and the Virgin Islands), the Commonwealth of Puerto Rico, and the trust territory of the Northern Mariana islands use territorial courts. They replace district courts for matters involving federal law.

Courts of the District of Columbia. Because of its unique legal position, the District of Columbia has its own district-level federal courts.

Court of Military Appeals. Armed forces personnel who violate military law must be tried by a military court. Court-martial convictions involving imprisonment or other severe penalties are reviewed by the civilian judges of the Court of Military Appeals. The court may confirm the punishment given by the lower court, or it may decide to reduce the sentence.

Tax Court. A panel of 19 judges, appointed by the President, serves as a court of last appeal in tax cases. Tax Court judges hear civil cases appealed by citizens who disagree with decisions made by the Internal Revenue Service. The court's jurisdiction does not extend to criminal cases.

Claims Court. Although the United States cannot be sued without its consent, Congress has determined that certain types of suits are permissible. The U.S. Claims Court was established in 1982 to hear these claims. Typical of the claims heard by the court are suits filed by plaintiffs who claim they were not fairly compensated when the government acquired their property for public use. Other cases heard by the court involve claims for the refund of federal income and excise taxes.

2. How does the system of state courts operate?

Even more clearly than in the federal courts, state courts exist to settle disputes between individuals or between private citizens and government. Criminal cases dominate the newspaper headlines, but the state courts hear many civil cases as well.

COMMON LAW AND EQUITY

The state courts base many of their decisions on *statutory laws* (laws written by the various levels of government). At other times, they turn to two additional kinds of law as a basis for their judgments: common law and equity.

The United States operates under many laws that were not written by our lawmakers. Dating back to early Anglo-Saxon Britain, a body of unwritten law has developed that is called *common law.* Customs, usage, and previous decisions made by judges when applying the common law make up this important segment of our legal heritage. Even though statutory law may override common law in specific cases, judges often use common law *precedents* (decisions reached in similar cases)

■ In addition to handling more and more cases, judges in New York City have to cope with tiny courtrooms. Budget problems have kept the city from building needed new courthouses. Here a Bronx Housing Court judge presides over a room one-sixth the size it should be.

in making their decisions. Only in Louisiana, with its French heritage, are judges restricted to enforcing statutory laws. Judges in Louisiana must base both civil and criminal rulings on specific laws rather than on precedent and common law.

The laws of *equity* provide fairness and justice when neither statutory nor common law can protect a citizen's rights. In practice, statutory and common law provide the means for resolving a matter after the event. Equity attempts to prevent an injury from happening, as when citizens petition the courts to stop the construction of a dump site near their homes. In this case, as in most cases in equity, the court issues an *injunction*. An injunction is a legal document that can either prohibit or require a certain action.

MINOR STATE COURTS

Most states have four types of minor courts to handle less serious problems. Many cases heard in these lowest-level courts do not require a jury trial. Even though the legal problem

involved may be relatively simple, most people take their appearance in one of these courtrooms very seriously.

Justice of the peace courts. In some states, the judicial system begins with the justice of the peace courts (also known as magistrates' courts or police courts). JPs are officials elected by the community to resolve minor legal problems. They hear cases involving traffic violations, for example, except in cities that have special traffic courts. The JP court often hears cases involving family and neighborhood disputes, "drunk and disorderly" charges, or other minor violations. In some cities and towns, the JP's salary is paid out of the costs and fines charged to those who use the court.

Small claims courts. What happens when your neighbor's dog digs up your garden but the owner refuses to pay for the damages? What can you do if a department store refuses to refund the $42.45 it owes you? When relatively small amounts of money are involved, you can take your case to small claims court.

These courts provide a fast, low-cost means of resolving civil conflicts. They also leave the higher courts free to consider more serious matters.

Juvenile courts. The law provides special courts for juveniles (young people under 16 or 18 years of age, depending on the state). Generally, the juvenile court's task is to correct the young person's behavior before more serious offenses occur. The juvenile court judge, sometimes aided by court-appointed experts in psychology and child welfare, makes decisions without the help of a jury. The judge has the power to (1) dismiss charges, (2) suspend sentences, (3) place the offender on probation, (4) assess fines, or (5) sentence the individual to a reform school or work camp. Because of the court's power, recent court rulings have provided juveniles with more protection, including the right to an attorney.

Domestic relations courts. Because the community has a stake in keeping families together, domestic relations courts (called family courts in some states) are provided to settle family disputes. Trained counselors work with the judges, who use their experience and authority to help families cope with problems of desertion, abuse, and other domestic traumas.

MUNICIPAL COURTS

The municipal courts rank a step above the minor courts. Many municipal courts consist of divisions that handle specific types of cases, such as (1) *probate* (the hearings that settle questions involved in a dead person's estate); (2) civil suits (disputes between two or more parties over legal rights and duties); and (3) minor criminal offenses (misdemeanor violations). The municipal courts have replaced the older police and magistrates' courts in many larger communities.

GENERAL TRIAL COURTS

The first state court that has the power to hear all types of cases is the general trial court. Different states give different names to these courts: circuit courts, superior courts, district courts, courts of common pleas, and county courts. General trial courts have wide jurisdiction, including both original and appellate jurisdiction (see pages 367–369). Individuals bringing a case to this court may either request a jury trial or waive the right to a jury. In a case heard without a jury, the presiding judge hears the evidence and makes the decision.

STATE APPEALS COURTS

The state appeals courts exist to lighten the load of the state supreme courts. More than one-half of the states have these appeals courts, which are known by a variety of names. Except in the rare cases over which they possess original jurisdiction, the appeals courts do not hear witnesses or judge evidence. The judges, who are elected in most states, review the fine points of law that were raised in the trials that come to them on appeal. They make their decisions on such narrow legal grounds as whether or not the trial judge gave proper instructions to the jury.

STATE SUPREME COURTS

Standing atop the pyramid of state courts is the state supreme court. This court serves as (1) the final interpreter of a state's laws and constitution and (2) a final court of appeal for lower court decisions. In most cases, the supreme court's decisions are final. Parties to a legal matter may appeal the decision of the state supreme court to the U.S. Supreme Court only when a federal question is involved. The most common cases appealed to the Supreme Court involve interpretations of the Constitution or the application of federal laws.

3. When does a court have the right to hear a case?

As you learned in the previous section, courts are often limited in their *jurisdiction*. That means they may try only certain types of cases. The legislation that establishes each court normally spells out its jurisdiction.

TYPES OF JURISDICTION

The four types of jurisdiction are as follows:

1. *Exclusive jurisdiction.* Exclusive jurisdiction applies when a case may be heard only in a certain court. The federal Tax Court, for example, holds exclusive jurisdiction over appeals from decisions of Internal Revenue tax referees.

2. *Concurrent jurisdiction.* Some cases involve matters within the jurisdiction of both federal and state courts. This is known as concurrent jurisdiction. When concurrent jurisdiction applies, the *plaintiff* (the person bringing the suit) usually has the right to choose between the two court systems. In some cases of concurrent jurisdiction, the *defendant* (the person accused and summoned into court) is allowed to make this choice.

3. *Original jurisdiction.* When a court has the right to hear a case *de novo* (for the first time), that court has original jurisdiction. Municipal and general trial courts hold orig-inal jurisdiction over the great majority of civil and criminal actions tried in the United States.

4. *Appellate jurisdiction.* A court holds *appellate jurisdiction* when it receives cases on appeal from a lower court. As the name implies, appeals courts exist in order to exercise this type of jurisdiction.

STATE AND FEDERAL JURISDICTIONS

State and federal courts divide their jurisdictions according to the contents of the case. Most of the cases heard by the courts fall under the jurisdiction of the state courts. Most legal matters, after all, involve either violations of state or local laws or conflicts between citizens living in the same state.

Federal courts exercise jurisdiction when the case involves any of the following:

1. All cases in law and equity arising under the Constitution.

■ Many civil suits begin with an accident. This is the tail section of a United Airlines plane that crashed while attempting an emergency landing in Sioux City, Iowa, in 1989. Undoubtedly, many involved in the crash filed civil suits against United in the hope of collecting damages. Court calendars are clogged with such cases, which may take years to resolve.

2. All cases in law and equity arising under the laws of the government of the United States.

3. All cases in law and equity arising under treaties made under the authority of the United States.

4. All cases of admiralty and maritime jurisdiction.

5. Controversies to which the United States is a party.

6. Controversies between two or more states.

7. Controversies between a state and citizens of another state.

8. Controversies between citizens of different states.

9. Controversies between a state (or its citizens) and a foreign country (or its citizens).

10. All cases affecting ambassadors, other public ministers, and consuls.

CIVIL AND CRIMINAL JURISDICTIONS

A court's jurisdiction may also depend on whether the case falls under the civil or criminal law codes.

Civil cases. A case heard under *civil procedure* usually involves a dispute between two or more people. Most civil cases center on property and personal rights. Typical civil suits include divorce cases, arguments over property lines, disputes over debts, bankruptcy, and personal injury cases. The state doesn't takes sides in civil cases. Instead, it provides the legal setting—the courtroom and court officials—in which the conflict can be settled. The private parties (which may be companies as well as individuals) hire attorneys to represent them. Civil cases are usually heard before a judge and jury. If both parties agree, the judge may hear the case without a jury.

Criminal cases. A *criminal procedure* must be brought when an individual stands accused of committing an act prohibited by law. Criminal codes put crimes into two categories: (1) *Misdemeanors* are minor offenses punishable by a small fine or imprisonment of less than a year. (2) *Felonies* are offenses serious enough

to warrant heavy fines, long prison terms, or even the death penalty. Felonies usually involve crimes against people and property, such as grand theft, aggravated assault, arson, kidnapping, rape, and murder. Petty theft, drunkenness, cruelty to animals, gambling, and reckless driving are common misdemeanors.

4. How are judges selected, and what do they do?

Black-robed judges, whether they sit on the Supreme Court bench or in a small-town courtroom, represent all of the impressive dignity of the law. Given their prestige and power, you might think that society would select the men and women who fill these positions with great care. This is not always the case.

ELECTION VERSUS APPOINTMENT

Judges who serve in the state courts gain their offices either by election or by appointment, depending on the state. If the judges are chosen by appointment, they are nominated by either the governor or the state legislature. Until the 1860s, almost all judges were selected in this way. After that time, many states began to elect judges directly. They believed that democracy was better served when the people voted for their officials. In about three-fourths of the states, for example, trial court judges are elected by their community or district.

Neither direct election nor appointment is a fully satisfactory process for choosing judges. When it comes to selecting judges, everyone agrees that the candidates should possess such virtues as proper legal training, experience in courtroom procedures and law enforcement, an even temperament, and total honesty. Unfortunately, an election campaign seldom gives voters an accurate picture of a candidate's qualifications. Not only do voters have little access to the judge's judicial record, but judges themselves have little time or money to devote to campaigning.

To some degree, the appointment process

■ A federal judge presides over a drug smuggling case. The Justice Department lawyer (center) is addressing the jury. The defendants are at right. The media uses sketches like these because of restrictions on cameras in courtrooms.

provides a better way of choosing candidates for the bench. The governor's staff, or the legislature, can question each candidate. If the hearings are thorough, a prospective judge's record and qualifications can be evaluated and made public. Both supporters and opponents have a chance to speak for or against the candidate. On the negative side, the appointment process sometimes leads to the selection of judges whose qualifications are political, not judicial.

All federal court judges owe their appointments to the President. The Constitution did not include qualifications for service in the federal judiciary. Nor has Congress established any. As a result, Presidents are free to select almost any reasonably qualified candidate. Most federal judges are drawn from the state courts, the law profession, and the faculties of leading law schools. In making their choices, Presidents tend to select judges who share their own political views, but they must also choose individuals who can win confirmation in the Senate.

TERM OF OFFICE

Long terms in office protect many judges from the need to worry about popularity or running for reelection. Federal appointments carry a life term for the period of the judge's "good behavior." If federal judges commit crimes or fail to perform their duties, they may be impeached by the House of Representatives. Over the years, only a handful of federal judges have been removed from office by impeachment. In 1986, a federal judge was convicted of a crime and sentenced to prison for the first time in the nation's history. Most vacancies on the federal bench occur because of resignations, retirements, or deaths. By contrast with the federal judiciary, six years is the most common term in the state courts. Some states appoint judges to eight- or twelve-year terms. A very few grant life terms.

SALARIES

Judicial salaries must be kept high enough to attract trained and talented people to the profession. Many men and women who become judges could earn greater incomes in private law practice. When asked why they chose to be judges, they list a sense of public service and freedom from the pressures of practicing law among their reasons. Generous pension plans also make service on the bench a desirable career. Federal judges, for example, may retire at age 65 with a full salary after only 15 years on the bench.

THE JUDGE'S JOB

Anyone who watches a judge at work would agree that the job is a demanding one. Yet, as the cartoon on page 371 points out, even the wisest interpretation of the law does not make everyone happy. Although they're often burdened by heavy caseloads, judges must not rush the business of the court. To do so might harm the very citizens who depend on the courts for justice.

Judges take on many specific duties when they put on the robes of office. Some of these duties are: (1) ruling on points of law, (2) determining whether evidence should be admitted, (3) conducting the complex mechanism of a trial, (4) studying legal briefs, (5) balancing the rights and needs of society against those of a defendant, (6) setting a reasonable sentence, (7) choosing between conflicting precedents, (8) giving clear and proper instructions to the jury, and (9) maintaining a calm and dignified manner no matter what happens in the courtroom.

Let's review for a moment

Suppose you want to attack a ruling that prevents your group from passing out leaflets at a local shopping mall. Where in the U.S. court system would you begin your fight? Since your constitutional rights are involved, you should start with the federal district court. If you lose there, the court of appeals may rule on the questions of law or

"How Are We Going To Stop Lawlessness If You Fellows Insist On Observing The Laws?"

■ The courts engage in a perpetual balancing act, applying the law so as to protect society without taking away individual rights guaranteed by the constitution.

procedure (but not evidence) that arose at your hearing. What are your chances of carrying your case to the Supreme Court? Not very good. The high court hears only about four percent of the cases that come to it.

Most Americans gain their first courtroom experience (as *defendant, plaintiff,* or juror) in a state court. Your state's court system begins with a cluster of minor courts—small claims, traffic, juvenile, domestic relations. More serious cases move upward into the municipal and general trial courts. Appeals from these courts are heard by the state appeals court or the state supreme court.

The law defines the role of each court in hearing cases. *Original jurisdiction* authorizes a court to be the first to hear a case. *Appellate jurisdiction* allows a higher court to hear the same case on appeal. Exclusive jurisdiction limits a case to one specific court, while concurrent jurisdiction means that the parties involved have a choice of state or federal courts. The courts further divide their time between civil and criminal cases. *Civil* suits involve disputes between two or more parties. *Criminal* cases try a defendant for breaking the law.

Ever think it might be fun to be a judge? The pay and prestige are high, and federal judges hold their jobs for life. On the negative side, judges have heavy work loads, and they must make life-and-death decisions. Many judges, including the entire federal judiciary, are appointed to the bench. The states usually require their judges to run for office.

---

5. What happens when a case goes to trial?

As you know from watching television, most courtrooms look much the same. But the courtroom is only a stage. The true drama is played out by the "actors" in the courtroom—and every trial is different. To begin with, civil cases are not like criminal cases. While not all of the steps outlined below occur in every case, the general process applies to most courts.

TRYING A CIVIL SUIT

A civil suit begins when the plaintiff files suit with the help of a lawyer. Court officials notify the defendants in the suit so that they may prepare a defense. From that point on, a time-honored sequence of events takes place.

1. *Summoning witnesses.* Each party to the suit has the right to ask the court to require the appearance of its own witnesses at the trial. The judge can force reluctant witnesses to appear by using legal orders called *subpoenas*. A witness who refuses to obey a subpoena may be held in *contempt of court*. This is a serious matter, for contempt of court is a criminal offense.

2. *Setting a trial date.* With the first steps out of the way, the suit takes its place on the court calendar, or *docket*. Heavy caseloads may delay the actual trial dates by as long as two years or more. Because of this frustrating wait, as well as the costs of a court trial, many cases are settled out of court. (Lawyers' fees are expensive. Some people cannot afford to take time away from their jobs or family responsibilities. Thus, it may be to everyone's advantage to settle quickly before the case goes to trial.)

3. *Selecting a jury.* When the trial date finally arrives, either side has the right to demand a jury trial. Court officials select citizens for jury duty from lists of registered voters, licensed drivers, and state taxpayers. The attorneys choose the petit jury members (see page 379) from a panel chosen at random by court clerks. Careful questioning eliminates jurors whose biases might affect their judgments about the case. The attorneys have the right to dismiss a limited number of prospective jurors without stating a reason.

4. *Conducting the trial.* Once the jury has been chosen, the attorneys make their opening statements. For the first time, the jury hears an account of what each side will try to prove. Witnesses are then called to testify under oath. The plaintiff's attorney tries to establish the facts of the case by asking the witnesses questions. A moment of drama sometimes arises when attorneys begin their cross-examination of the witnesses who are testifying for the other side. The lawyers probe for weaknesses, hoping to discredit the accuracy of a witness's testimony.

Before a civil trial begins, the attorneys sometimes present briefs to the judge. The briefs summarize court decisions handed down in similar cases. This process of citing precedents is called *stare decisis*, a Latin phrase meaning, "it stands decided." Since both sides will usually be able to find precedents that support their arguments, the briefs do not always simplify a case. Despite this fact, judges find that the briefs are helpful in raising the points of law that will come up during the trial.

During the trial, a court reporter takes down all of the testimony, word for word. This

■ A lawyer questioning a witness while the judge and jury look on. Lawyers have to learn how to ask the sort of questions that will get the answers they want from witnesses. What does the prosecuting attorney try to do? What does the defendant expect of a lawyer?

record, which also includes the lawyers' final pleas, is known as the *transcript*. The transcript provides a permanent record of the trial and serves as the basis for a possible appeal.

5. *Reaching a verdict.* When all the arguments have been completed, the case is ready for the jury. The judge gives the jury a set of instructions called a *charge*. A typical charge summarizes the points of law raised by the case and lists the questions of fact to be decided. If the evidence appears to be overwhelmingly in favor of one side, the judge may order the jury to bring in a directed verdict. This means the judge believes that no other decision could reasonably be reached.

After the charge, the jury retires to the jury room. No one is allowed to violate the jury's privacy. While the jury is attempting to reach a *verdict*, it remains in the custody of the court. If the judge fears that the jury's decision might be influenced by the media or by contacts with other people, the jury may be *sequestered.*

The members of a sequestered jury are kept in hotel rooms when they're not in court.

Some juries reach a verdict quickly, but others take several days to arrive at a decision. An elected foreman presides over the meetings, but every juror's vote counts equally. Two-thirds of the states require a unanimous verdict in civil cases (a 12–0 vote), while the others accept 8–4 or 10–2 majorities. If the jury cannot reach agreement, it is known as a "hung jury." The judge will ask the jurors to try again. If the jury is still "hung," a *mistrial* must be declared. A mistrial leaves the case right where it started. If the plaintiff wishes to pursue the matter, a new trial must be held.

In most trials, the jury does reach a verdict. The judge tells the foreman to read the jury's findings in open court. At that point, the judge usually approves the verdict and announces the terms of its execution. If the jury has found the defendant guilty of negligence, for exam-

STAGES IN A CRIMINAL TRIAL FOLLOWING COMMISSION OF A FELONY

Stage	Agencies involved	Action taken	Other possible actions
1. Apprehension	Police Court may furnish warrants	Investigation Apprehension Arrest Booking	Case dropped for insufficient evidence
2. Indictment	Magistrate Court Prosecuting attorney Grand jury	Preliminary hearing Setting of bail Evidence considered by grand jury Indictment handed down Case placed on docket	Charges reduced Case dismissed
3. Trial	General trial court	Arraignment Plea Jury selection Witnesses testify Prosecution and defense argue the case Jury returns a verdict	Court accepts a lesser plea Mistrial declared Defendant acquitted Appeal to higher court
4. Sentencing	General trial court State penal system	Judge and/or jury pronounce sentence: fine, imprisonment, or both Sentence begins	Suspended sentence Probation Pardon Parole

ple, it may also establish the money damages to be paid to the plaintiff.

6. *Establishing judgment.* The judge often has the final word. If a jury has given the plaintiff an excessive award for damages, the judge may reduce the figure to a smaller amount. In cases where plaintiff and defendant waived a jury trial, the judge studies the evidence and precedents before reaching a verdict. At the end of the trial, the judge sets time limits for the payment of damages and court costs. If necessary, the judge also issues court orders to ensure that the parties in the case obey the court's decision.

TRYING A CRIMINAL CASE

A trial in a criminal court differs in many ways from a trial in a civil court. Although individual cases sometimes require special treatment, almost all criminal cases follow a pattern that begins with apprehension and continues through indictment, trial, and sentencing (see the table on page 374).

1. *Apprehending the suspect.* Unless someone is caught while committing a crime or arrested in suspicious circumstances, the police need an *arrest warrant* to take a suspect into custody. This legal document describes the suspected criminal, the nature of the offense, and the magistrate (or judge) before whom the suspect is to be brought. Any trial judge may issue a warrant. Law enforcement officers normally make all arrests, but everyone has the right to make a *citizen's arrest*. This is not always a wise course of action. Aside from the danger of personal injury, the person making a citizen's arrest may be sued if the arrest is made without just cause.

2. *Indicting the accused.* After the arrest, police or court officials bring the accused before a magistrate or judge. If the crime is a misdemeanor (a traffic violation, for example), the accused may be tried at once or released to return later for trial. In felony cases, the court holds a preliminary hearing to see if the evidence is strong enough to establish a reasonable probability of guilt. If so, the judge orders the accused to stand trial.

A judge has three ways of making sure that the accused returns for the trial. (a) The accused may be released on his or her promise to return on the trial date. (b) The accused may be required to post *bail* as a condition of release from jail. Bail is usually set as a sum of money ranging from less than $100 to a million dollars or more. The money may be posted by the accused, by family or friends, or by a licensed bail bondsman. The accused forfeits the bail money if he or she fails to return on the proper date. (c) The accused may be held without bail. These are usually cases involving murder or other serious crimes, or ones in which the judge thinks that the accused might "jump bail" and disappear.

At this point, the prosecuting attorney examines the testimony given at the preliminary hearing. A prosecuting attorney is a law enforcement official found in both the federal and state court systems. If the evidence of guilt seems great enough, he or she prepares a *bill of indictment* that summarizes the state's case. A grand jury (see page 379) hears the bill of indictment and studies the evidence. If the members of the grand jury agree with the prosecuting attorney, the foreman writes "a true bill" across the face of the indictment. Court officials then place the case on the docket

of the appropriate trial court. On the other hand, the grand jury may decide that there isn't enough evidence to support the indictment. When that happens, the case is dismissed and the accused is discharged.

3. *Conducting the trial.* When the court date arrives, the defendant makes a *plea* before the court. This process is called *arraignment*. If the accused enters a guilty plea, the court normally takes quick action. The judge hands down a sentence that may include imprisonment, fine, or probation. If the defendant pleads not guilty, the trial judge sets a date for the trial.

All defendants have the right to be represented by an attorney. For those who cannot afford to hire one, the court provides a public defender. Because of crowded courts and high court costs, defense attorneys often engage in a process called *plea bargaining*. In a typical plea bargain, the defendant agrees to plead guilty to a lesser charge. If the court accepts the plea, the defendant accepts the penalty for the less serious crime and escapes trial on the more serious charge.

A criminal trial begins with the selection of a jury, much as in a civil trial. Once the jury has been seated, the defense and prosecuting attorneys make their opening statements. Afterward, the state presents its case. The prosecutor uses physical evidence and witnesses to establish the proof required under the law. If the case seems weak, the defense may move for a directed verdict of not guilty. Failing in this, the defense then offers its case. Prosecution and defense witnesses are both subject to cross-examination. Any witness who commits *perjury* (lying under oath) risks a fine or imprisonment. Defendants may testify in their own defense, but they cannot be forced to take the stand. The jury is told that a defendant's failure to testify cannot be thought of as evidence of guilt.

After both sides have presented their cases, each attorney makes a final speech to the jury called a *summation*. A good summation reviews the arguments in the case and tries to convince the jury of the defendant's guilt or innocence. The judge then instructs the members of the jury. When they leave the courtroom, they understand the laws that apply to the case, and they know what verdicts they can return.

4. *Sentencing the criminal.* The members of the jury debate the evidence and the testimony of the witnesses. In a criminal trial, the jury's verdict must be unanimous (12–0). If only one juror holds out for a not-guilty verdict, the defendant cannot be convicted. If the jury doesn't settle its differences, the judge declares a mistrial. When the verdict is "guilty as charged," the trial enters its penalty phase. In some states, a separate hearing is held to determine the fine or prison sentence. In others, the jury is asked to recommend the punishment. In a third group of states, the judge decides the penalty.

Learning Skills

Recognizing Bias

Would you make a good juror? Much would depend on how good you are at recognizing bias—your own and that of others.

Imagine that you're trying to convince a friend that the Red Sox is the best team in the American League. If you're like most sports fans, you start by describing each player's strong points. Then you demolish the Yankees, Blue Jays, and the other teams in the league. When you're finished, it sounds as though the Red Sox will never lose another game!

Now, think about that argument or others like it. When you feel strongly about an issue, don't you tend to emphasize the positive and eliminate the negative or vice versa? After all, the statistics may show that the Red Sox isn't the best team in the league. A simple word for one-sided views is *bias*. Bias is any belief or preference that interferes with impartial judgment.

If you're biased in favor of the Red Sox, that doesn't hurt anything. But bias also creeps into attitudes that involve more important issues. If you're on a jury, would you let a bias against people of a different skin color affect your judgment? Would you tend to believe people of your own religion and disbelieve those who follow a different faith? You're the only one who can answer these questions.

Along with admitting to their own biases, good citizens check for bias in the media and in our politicians. Here are some rules that will help you spot biased points of view:

1. Everyone has biases. Some hide them better than others.

2. Be wary of someone who works too hard at "selling" you an idea or a product. When our own self-interest is involved, we're more likely to show our biases.

3. Look at all sides of an issue. One politician may tell you that the jury system has failed, and another may say that juries are better than ever. Whom can you believe? Before you vote, you'll have to extract what's true from the obvious biases each person brings to the debate.

4. Do your own research and your own thinking. If you read only one newspaper, for example, you'll probably absorb its biases without realizing it.

Finally, catalog your own biases. That's a tough job, but now's a good time to start. Divide a sheet of paper into two columns. Label one side, "What I believe in," and label the other, "What I'm against." Over the next several days, write down everything that comes to mind, from favorite foods to government policies. When you know your own biases, you'll be better at spotting the biases of others.

FYI . . .
How to Choose the Right Lawyer

Most Americans come into contact with the courts at some time or another. Their visit may be as simple as paying a traffic ticket or as complicated as filing for an injunction against the operators of a toxic waste dump. In all but the simplest cases, anyone who appears in court should be represented by a lawyer. A single mistake in completing the paperwork, or in questioning a witness, can result in the loss of a case. That's why it makes sense to have the best lawyer available to represent you. Legal experts give the following advice about choosing a lawyer:

1. Ask your friends for recommendations. If you don't find someone in this way, contact your local bar association. Most bar associations will refer you to lawyers who do the type of work you need, but they won't make recommendations.

2. For most routine legal work, such as drawing up a will, a low-cost legal clinic may be all you need. Check the phone book for the name of a clinic in your area.

3. When you locate a lawyer, make an appointment to talk about the case. If you don't feel comfortable with the person, try someone else. Ask about the lawyer's training and experience. You want someone who has a good track record with cases like yours.

4. Put all agreements in writing, particularly those listing fees and costs. You may be asked to pay a fee, known as a retainer, in advance. If you're filing a civil damage suit, find out whether the lawyer charges an hourly rate or a percentage of the amount you win.

■ A lawyer talking with clients. What legal requirements does a lawyer have to fulfill before being allowed to represent clients in court?

A verdict of not guilty frees the defendant from custody at once. A defendant who has been found guilty may appeal the verdict to a higher court. Appeals are allowed when defendants and their attorneys can show that grounds exist for a successful appeal. During the appeal process, the defendant may remain free on bail.

6. How well does the U.S. jury system work?

The Framers of the Constitution believed that the right to a fair trial by a jury of one's peers is a keystone of American civil rights. The Fifth, Sixth, and Seventh amendments to the Constitution all touch on this guarantee. De-

From Crime to Punishment

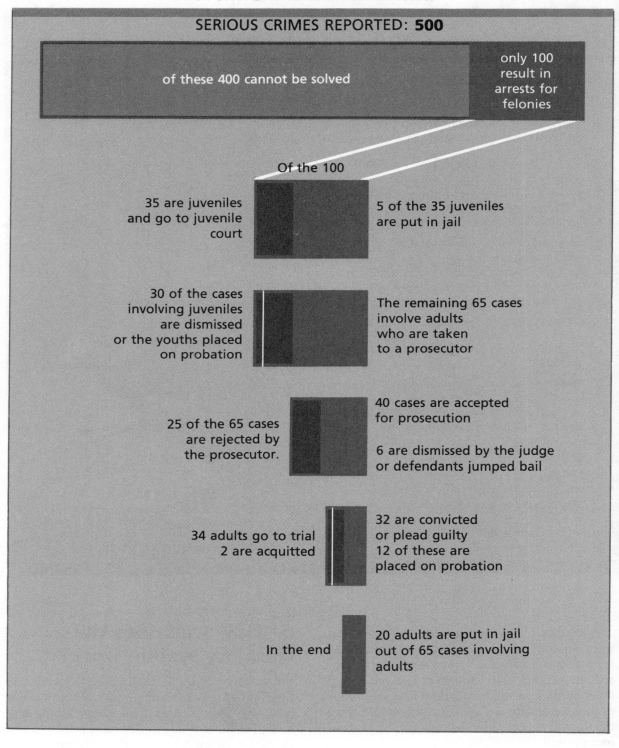

SERIOUS CRIMES REPORTED: **500**

of these 400 cannot be solved

only 100 result in arrests for felonies

Of the 100

35 are juveniles and go to juvenile court

5 of the 35 juveniles are put in jail

30 of the cases involving juveniles are dismissed or the youths placed on probation

The remaining 65 cases involve adults who are taken to a prosecutor

25 of the 65 cases are rejected by the prosecutor.

40 cases are accepted for prosecution

6 are dismissed by the judge or defendants jumped bail

34 adults go to trial
2 are acquitted

32 are convicted or plead guilty
12 of these are placed on probation

In the end

20 adults are put in jail out of 65 cases involving adults

■ The process of jury selection begins when a citizen receives a summons to appear for jury duty. Once a jury is selected, the 12 jurors (plus an alternate) are sworn in. Most courts ask jurors to serve for two weeks or until a case is finished.

spite this background, criticism of the jury system has grown in recent years.

TYPES OF JURIES

Juries are of two types: the *grand jury* and the *petit jury*. Each plays an important role in the American court system.

Grand jury. Before the petit jury can try a case, the grand jury must decide whether or not the accused should be brought to trial. The grand jury studies the evidence, hears witnesses, questions law enforcement officials, and finally approves or disapproves the bill of indictment. The grand jury also has the right to investigate suspicions of wrongdoing. A vigorous probe by a grand jury may expose corrupt practices in a city's purchasing office, for example.

The size of a grand jury may range from six to twenty-three, depending on the state. Members of a grand jury are drawn from the regular pool of jurors and serve for a month at a time. During its existence, a grand jury meets daily and usually hears many cases. The members of a petit jury are dismissed after hearing a single case.

Critics charge that grand juries are slow and expensive. To solve this problem, many states now allow a prosecuting attorney to file with the court an accusation known as an "information." If the judge approves the information, the accused is held over for trial. Informations are used to speed up the trial process in most minor crimes, and they are being used in felony cases, too.

Petit jury. The petit jury is sometimes called a trial jury. There are usually twelve jurors, but as few as six may hear a case. Jury members listen to the evidence presented during the course of a trial. Then they retire to deliberate and arrive at a verdict. Jury members are expected to set aside their biases and to forget everything they may have heard or read about the case. Serving on a petit jury can be a difficult task. Some trials drag on for many weeks. During this time, the jury must remain alert to all the twists and turns of the testimony.

No one ever grew rich serving on a jury. A typical juror receives only a small *per diem* payment to cover expenses. Most employers, however, pay their workers' regular salaries

The Rocky Path to the Jury Box

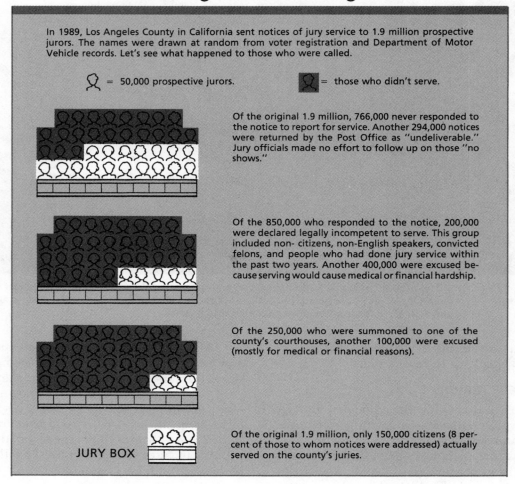

In 1989, Los Angeles County in California sent notices of jury service to 1.9 million prospective jurors. The names were drawn at random from voter registration and Department of Motor Vehicle records. Let's see what happened to those who were called.

= 50,000 prospective jurors.   = those who didn't serve.

Of the original 1.9 million, 766,000 never responded to the notice to report for service. Another 294,000 notices were returned by the Post Office as "undeliverable." Jury officials made no effort to follow up on those "no shows."

Of the 850,000 who responded to the notice, 200,000 were declared legally incompetent to serve. This group included non-citizens, non-English speakers, convicted felons, and people who had done jury service within the past two years. Another 400,000 were excused because serving would cause medical or financial hardship.

Of the 250,000 who were summoned to one of the county's courthouses, another 100,000 were excused (mostly for medical or financial reasons).

JURY BOX

Of the original 1.9 million, only 150,000 citizens (8 percent of those to whom notices were addressed) actually served on the county's juries.

while they're on jury duty. If the jury is sequestered, the court pays the cost of the hotel rooms. Some states also pay for meals.

CRITICISMS OF THE JURY SYSTEM

Many critics attack the day-to-day operation of American juries rather than the jury system itself. Most of the criticism falls under one of two headings:

1. *Faulty jury selection procedures.* The jury system is supposed to ensure that defendants will be fairly tried by their peers. A defendant's peers are people much like him or her. They are people who understand the community's values and who can relate to the defendant's motives while they're reaching a verdict. Today, the jury selection process sometimes seems to work against the goal of finding a jury of one's peers.

Each state chooses jurors in its own way, but these are some typical problems: (a) Where jury lists are taken from voter rolls, people who don't register are never called. (b) The courts exempt specific groups such as lawyers, the self-employed, and mothers with small children from jury duty. (c) Attorneys tend to dismiss qualified jurors whose only fault is that they have strong opinions about community problems. (d) Juries in many towns and cities are overloaded with older people, housewives, and ethnic majorities. Minority defendants seldom see anyone of their own ethnic group on these juries. (e) Many people evade jury duty. They don't want to be bothered, or they worry that they'll be tied up on a case that may last a long time.

2. *Compromised verdicts.* No matter how carefully a judge prepares a jury, human nature always influences the verdict. After a long trial, full of pauses and recesses, the jury settles into its final task with relief. Immediately, differences of opinion develop. Conflicts arise over what the evidence and testimony really mean. Each juror brings a different set of values, biases, and experiences to the jury room. Finally, with one eye on the clock, the jury moves toward a compromise. To report a "hung jury" is an admission that the trial has been in vain. Thus, the final verdict sometimes has more to do with fatigue and emotion than with reason and justice.

PROPOSALS FOR JURY REFORM

Many proposals for reforming the jury system have been advanced, but few have been accepted. The most successful change has come in the addition of ethnic minorities to juries. Many cities now make a serious effort to provide a true cross section of the community on the jury selection lists. Other reforms that have been discussed include (1) reducing jury size, (2) relaxing the requirement for unanimous verdicts, and (3) replacing juries with panels of judges. Despite its weaknesses, the jury trial is still considered by most Americans to be their best protection against the awesome power of the government and its courts.

7. What powers do the nation's courts exercise?

The main task of the courts is to hand down decisions in cases of civil or criminal law. Custom and statutes, however, ask the courts to do other jobs that go beyond deciding an individual's guilt, innocence, or liability.

OTHER COURT POWERS

1. *Judicial review.* Federal courts, as well as the higher state courts, are often called on to review actions taken by the executive and legislative branches of government. Does a new city law regulating "adult" movie houses violate the state constitution? Did the police exceed their powers in conducting drug busts on a high school campus? Any citizen may petition the courts to conduct a judicial review of the actions of a local, state, or federal agency. Furthermore, the decision of the courts in these matters must be accepted as final.

2. *Habeas corpus.* A basic right carefully protected by the courts is that of *habeas corpus.* Under this legal doctrine, an imprisoned person has the constitutional right to know why he or she was jailed and to have a speedy trial. *Habeas corpus* forces police officials to show cause before a judge as to why a person being held in custody should not be freed. If they fail to do so, the prisoner must be released.

3. *Injunctions.* Most often used in civil cases, an injunction is a legal order that either (a) forbids a certain action or (b) orders that a particular action be taken. For example, an injunction might order a factory to stop polluting a river, or it might demand that a school allow suspended students to return to class.

4. *Writs of mandamus.* A court order that forces government officials to fulfill their public duty is called a *writ of mandamus.* An example of this writ would be an order that requires a police department to protect a minority group during a tense conflict over school desegregation.

5. *Warrants.* Many law enforcement procedures require court permission before police officers can act. *Arrest warrants* and *search warrants*, for example, have a dual purpose. They permit the actions described in their titles, but they also set limits on the conditions under which these actions may be carried out.

6. *Contempt of court.* Courts possess an enforcement power that allows them to make sure a judge's orders will be obeyed. A contempt of court citation may be issued against a witness who refuses to testify, a lawyer who violates court procedures, or a company that ignores an injunction. Contempt citations carry the threat of fine or imprisonment.

LIMITATIONS ON ADVISORY OPINIONS

When the executive branch asked the Supreme Court to rule on pending legislation during George Washington's first administration, the Court refused. This tradition, based on the belief that the Court could only rule on cases that had actually been brought to trial, holds firm to this day. Congress cannot know in advance whether a given law, especially one that raises a constitutional question, will be accepted or struck down by the judiciary.

By contrast, many states allow the legislature or the governor to ask the state supreme court about the legality of a bill before it is passed. That advisory opinion is not binding on the court if someone challenges the law at a later time. Political scientists say that this prevents the passage of unconstitutional laws.

Reviewing what you've learned

1. The federal court system begins at the district court level where cases involving federal jurisdiction are tried. Appeals move upward to the courts of appeals and from there to the Supreme Court. The Supreme Court seldom overturns decisions issued by the courts of appeals. The Supreme Court's right of judicial review stands as the ultimate check on the other two branches.

2. The minor courts in each state handle traffic, juvenile, domestic relations, and small claims cases. Municipal and general trial courts hear more serious cases. The state appeals courts and the state supreme courts accept cases on appeal and interpret state and local laws.

3. Along with statutory law, the courts are guided by common law and equity. Legal and social traditions, plus the precedents established by earlier decisions, make up the *common law*. *Equity* provides a means of protecting a citizen's rights even though those rights have not yet been violated.

4. *Jurisdiction* refers to the right of a particular court to hear a case. The most important kinds of jurisdiction are (1) *original jurisdiction*, which means that the court has the right to hear the case for the first time, and (2) *appellate jurisdiction*, which means that a court receives a case on appeal from a lower court. Other kinds of jurisdiction are exclusive and concurrent. Appeals normally may be made only on the basis of points of law.

5. *Civil cases* generally involve disputes between two parties. *Criminal cases* begin when someone is charged with breaking the law. *Misdemeanors* are minor offenses that carry short prison terms or light fines. *Felonies* are crimes serious enough to be punished by long prison terms or heavy fines.

6. The nation's judges are expected to be honest and wise in the ways of the law. Some state court judges are elected to the bench. Many others, including all federal judges, gain their jobs by appointment.

7. Before a case comes to trial in a civil court, the plaintiff must first file suit. Next, *subpoenas* are issued to witnesses, and the trial date is set. The trial begins with the selection of a jury, unless the judge is going to hear the case without a jury. After attorneys for the two sides present their cases, the jury deliberates and returns a *verdict*. If the jurors cannot agree, a new trial may

be scheduled. Either the judge or the jury sets the amount of damages to be paid if the *plaintiff* wins the case.

8. Criminal cases begin with the arrest of a suspect. A *bill of indictment* must be obtained before the accused may be tried. After the preliminary hearing, *bail* may be allowed if the judge believes it is safe to release the *defendant*. The trial begins with jury selection, then moves on to hear the testimony given by prosecution and defense witnesses. After the jury returns a verdict of guilty or not guilty, the defendant is either sentenced or freed.

9. *Grand juries* hand down indictments stating that a crime may have been committed. *Petit juries* render verdicts of guilt or innocence. Critics complain that jury selection procedures lead to juries that do not truly represent the community.

10. Courts possess a number of powers beyond that of trying cases. Judges may issue a *writ of habeas corpus* or a *writ of mandamus*. They must sign *arrest warrants* and *search warrants* before police officers can take action. They issue *injunctions* to protect the public welfare. *Contempt of court* citations allow courts to enforce their orders with threats of fines or imprisonment. *Judicial review* provides the courts with a powerful check on the other branches of government. No law may remain in force after the courts have struck it down.

Review questions and activities

TERMS YOU SHOULD KNOW

appellate jurisdiction	docket	plea
arraignment	equity	plea bargaining
arrest warrant	felony	precedents
bail	grand jury	probate
bill of indictment	*habeas corpus*	search warrant
brief	injunction	sequestered
charge to a jury	judicial review	statutory law
citizen's arrest	jurisdiction	subpoena
civil procedures	misdemeanor	summation
common law	mistrial	transcript
contempt of court	original jurisdiction	verdict
court of appeals	perjury	writ of *certiorari*
criminal procedure	petit jury	writ of *mandamus*
defendant	plaintiff	

REVIEW QUESTIONS

Select the response that best completes each statement or question.

1. The Constitution provides full and complete details on how the federal court system should be organized and administered. This statement is   (*a*) true.   (*b*) false; no mention is made in the Constitution of a federal court system.   (*c*) false; the Constitution states that a federal court system shall be established but leaves it up to Congress to fill in the details.

2. The proper path for a typical case through the federal courts would be from (*a*) court of appeals to district court to Supreme Court. (*b*) district court to court of appeals to Supreme Court. (*c*) Supreme Court to district court to court of appeals. (*d*) plaintiffs may begin at any level they can afford. (*e*) none of these.

3. Final authority for deciding on the constitutionality of a federal law lies with the (*a*) Supreme Court. (*b*) court of appeals. (*c*) U.S. district courts. (*d*) state supreme courts. (*e*) Congress of the United States.

4. As in many civil and criminal courts, the decisions of the Supreme Court judges must be unanimous (9–0). This statement is (*a*) true. (*b*) false; only a 7–2 majority is required. (*c*) false; a 5–4 majority is enough to establish a Supreme Court decision.

5. A typical case heard in a civil suit would be: (*a*) two neighbors argue about the exact dividing line between their properties. (*b*) a pedestrian is arrested for public drunkenness. (*c*) a driver is arrested for felony hit-and-run. (*d*) a politician violates a law limiting campaign contributions. (*e*) all of these.

6. The police in your town are threatening to go on strike, and there's no state law to stop them. In order to prevent the strike, you can file suit under (*a*) the common law. (*b*) equity. (*c*) criminal law codes. (*d*) appellate jurisdiction. (*e*) none of these; everyone has the right to strike for better wages.

7. The local dry cleaner ruined your best outfit but has refused to replace it. The best place for you to file suit would be in (*a*) domestic relations court. (*b*) justice of the peace court. (*c*) general trial court. (*d*) small claims court. (*e*) municipal court.

8. Along with a knowledge of the law, a good judge should have (*a*) strong political connections. (*b*) an independent income, because judges' salaries are low. (*c*) absolute personal honesty and an understanding of human nature. (*d*) a happy-go-lucky personality. (*e*) all of these.

9. In order to control unruly behavior in the courtroom, a judge would probably issue (*a*) a writ of *habeas corpus*. (*b*) an injunction. (*c*) a writ of *certiorari*. (*d*) a contempt of court citation. (*e*) a writ of *mandamus*.

10. The foreman of the grand jury reads the verdict: "Guilty as charged, your honor." This situation can't happen, because (*a*) a grand jury hands down an indictment, not a verdict. (*b*) the verdict should be announced by the judge. (*c*) a grand jury sits only for civil cases in which no guilt is in question. (*d*) grand juries hear only appeals in which interpretations of the law are in question. (*e*) a grand jury doesn't have a foreman.

CONCEPT DEVELOPMENT

1. What qualifications should a federal judge bring to the bench?

2. Discuss the various types of jurisdictions: (a) state v. federal, (b) civil v. criminal, (c) original v. appellate.

3. Imagine that a local bank has been robbed. Trace the case through the court system, from arrest through final sentencing. Point out how the defendant's rights are protected at every step of the process.

4. Summarize the strengths and weaknesses of the jury system. Suggest at least two reforms that might improve it.

5. Describe two cases that would be heard in each of these courts: (a) traffic, (b) juvenile, (c) domestic relations, (d) small claims, (e) municipal, (f) state appeals, (g) state supreme.

HANDS-ON ACTIVITIES

1. How fair are the jury selection procedures in your community? Who is called for jury duty, and what procedures are followed in selecting jurors to hear a case? Begin by researching the actual procedures. Then interview several lawyers, a judge, and several people who have served on juries. Report to your class on the results of your study. Is the system equitable? Are all racial, ethnic, and social groups fairly represented? What could be done to improve the process?

2. Help your teacher arrange a class field trip to a local courtroom. If the entire class can't go, make the visit yourself. Study the courtroom procedures, the types of cases being tried, and the behavior of the people in the courtroom. Do you sense the power and dignity of the law? Imagine yourself in the role of the judge. Would you have done anything differently? Write a report on your experience.

3. Stage a mock trial in your classroom. Select a civil or criminal case related to your own community. Appoint a judge, attorneys, plaintiff and defendant, a jury, and other court officials. Structure the trial by writing out a scenario that describes the situation in some detail. This will keep your classmates from turning the trial into a comedy. Witnesses can be subpoenaed (teachers make good witnesses). The attorneys should conduct stiff cross-examinations. After the jury has given its verdict, lead a discussion to find out what your class learned about trials.

4. Do some extra reading on the Supreme Court and its role in our governmental system. Check out some of its recent decisions. What types of cases has it been working on? Can you divide the justices into blocs of moderates, liberals, and conservatives? Report back to the class on your research.

5. Invite a local judge and a trial lawyer to speak to your class. Ask them to cover such subjects as (a) the law as a profession, (b) the citizen's role in law enforcement, and (c) life in the courtroom.

16 The courts speak: Landmark cases that have altered the course of American life

▲ Mary Beth and John Tinker displaying the armbands they wore to protest the war in Vietnam. The symbol on the bands stands for peace.

Landmark cases do not always involve major historic events. Many times, these cases reach the courts because average citizens believe their rights have been violated.

One such case began in 1965. At that time, the United States was committed to defending South Vietnam against Communist aggression. Hundreds of thousands of American soldiers were fighting a long, bloody war in the rice paddies and jungles of our Vietnamese ally. Many

Americans supported the war effort. Others joined an antiwar movement. These protesters insisted that the United States withdraw its forces from South Vietnam.

In Des Moines, Iowa, a group of junior and senior high school students staged their own protest against the war. Three of the students were Mary Beth Tinker, 13, her brother John, 15, and Christopher Eckhardt, 16. Along with some other students, the trio agreed to wear black armbands to school. They decorated the armbands with peace symbols. As part of their protest, the students also planned to fast for two days.

When word of the protest leaked out, the school board ruled that wearing armbands would disrupt the learning process. School administrators followed up with a policy that banned armbands on campus. Mary Beth, John, and Christopher defied the policy and wore their armbands to school. School officials promptly suspended them.

The parents of Mary Beth and John took the suspension to court. The students were represented by the American Civil Liberties Union (ACLU). The ACLU lawyers argued that the ban on armbands violated the First Amendment right to free speech. The U.S. District Court and the U.S. Circuit Court of Appeals ruled against the Tinkers. Instead of giving up, the family appealed the case to the Supreme Court.

The justices of the Supreme Court do not accept every case brought before them. They accepted the case of *Tinker* v. *Des Moines Independent Community School District* because they felt that two important issues were involved. Was wearing an armband really a form of free speech? Did the students' rights conflict with the school's obligation to maintain order? The Court finally issued its ruling in February 1969.

On the key issue, the Court ruled in favor of Mary Beth, John, and Christopher. The justices stated that wearing an armband was, indeed, symbolic "speech." Thus, the First Amendment protections applied to the armbands. The justices pointed out that the school already permitted the wearing of buttons that supported political candidates. Justice Abe Fortas summed up for the majority. He wrote that the students "are entitled to freedom of expression of their views."

Two justices issued strong minority opinions in the case. Justice Hugo Black said that the ruling could lead to disorder in the schools. The armbands, he felt, distracted other students from their studies. Black wrote: ". . . after the Court's holding today, some students in the Iowa schools and, indeed, in all schools will be ready, able, and willing to defy their teachers on practically all orders."

The majority opinion did make it clear that "freedom of expression" has limits. Justice Fortas said that the students may not "interfere with appropriate discipline in the operation of the school." A protest rally that blocked the entrance to the school, for example, would not be protected under the ruling. In brief, the Court declared that students do have freedom of speech—but that freedom cannot be allowed to override the rights of others.

In deciding this and other landmark cases, the Supreme Court is acting like the baseball umpire who said, "No pitch is a ball or a strike until I call it." In that sense, the Court's task is to remind the American people that no law or regulation can be considered final until it is judged against the "strike zone" defined by the Constitution.

This chapter will introduce you to nine more landmark cases that have had a lasting impact on the nation's history. In one way or another, all of them have affected your life. These cases and the questions they answered are:

1. **How did the courts gain the power of judicial review?** (*Marbury* v. *Madison*)

2. **Are there any limits on the implied powers granted to Congress?** (*McCulloch* v. *Maryland*)

3. **How far may Congress go in regulating interstate commerce?** (*Gibbons* v. *Ogden*)

4. **How did a case involving slavery help lead to the Civil War?** (*Dred Scott* v. *Sandford*)

5. **How far may state laws go in limiting a corporation's business activities?** (*Munn* v. *Illinois*)

6. **Which is stronger—business monopolies or the federal government?** (*Northern Securities Company* et al. v. *United States*)

7. **Do the war powers include the right to lock up citizens who haven't committed a crime?** (*Korematsu* v. *United States*)

8. **Are segregated schools automatically unequal?** (*Brown* v. *Board of Education of Topeka*)

9. **Should any restrictions be placed on police when making arrests?** (*Miranda* v. *Arizona*)

1. How did the courts gain the power of judicial review?

(*Marbury* v. *Madison*)

The Supreme Court has not always been the respected third branch of government that Americans know today. One man—the fourth Chief Justice, John Marshall—had as much to do with the creation of the modern Supreme Court as did the Constitution. The case that Marshall used to establish the strength of the Court grew out of what seemed to be a trivial matter.

FACTS OF THE CASE

In the election of 1800, President John Adams, the Federalist candidate, lost his bid for re-election to Thomas Jefferson, a Democratic-Republican. On the evening of March 3, 1801 (his last day in office under the old inauguration schedule), President Adams was still making appointments. He was awarding loyal Federalists with appointments as federal judges.

Finally, Adams worked his way down to the least important of the federal judicial posts. These were the 42 justices of the peace for the District of Columbia. The President signed the commissions, and Secretary of State John Marshall affixed the Great Seal of the United States to the documents. At least four of the completed commissions, including one made out to William Marbury, were never delivered.

After he took office, an angry President Jefferson realized that Adams had taken the appointment of a large number of federal judges out of his hands. He ordered his Secretary of State not to deliver the four remaining commissions. Deprived of his position, Federalist William Marbury brought suit in the Supreme Court. He was joined by the three other men who believed that they had been similarly "robbed" of their offices. The suit asked for a writ of *mandamus* that would order James Madison, the new Secretary of State, to deliver the commissions. The suit reached the Supreme Court in December 1801. Marshall, the recently appointed Chief Justice, eagerly accepted jurisdiction over the case.

LEGAL STEPS IN THE CASE

As the case developed, it became apparent that it involved far more than Marbury and his place on the federal bench.

1. *Jurisdiction.* Marbury asked the Supreme Court to take original jurisdiction under a provision of the Judiciary Act of 1789. Section 13 of this law stated that the Supreme Court could issue writs of *mandamus* in cases involving "persons holding office under the authority of the United States."

2. *Marshall's dilemma.* Marshall knew that if he issued the writ, Madison would ignore it. Jefferson would then back up his Secretary of State. Public opinion was sure to side with the popular President. The Court would be left with no means of enforcing its decision.

3. *The solution.* Marshall's solution was a masterpiece of judicial logic. First, he pointed

■ Under the leadership of John Marshall, Chief Justice from 1801 to 1835, the Supreme Court gained equal status with the executive and legislative branches of the federal government.

out the obvious fact that the original jurisdiction of the Supreme Court was limited by the Constitution to two types of cases: (a) those involving foreign diplomats and (b) those involving the states. When the Judiciary Act added another original jurisdiction to the Court's powers, Congress had, in effect, amended the Constitution.

4. *Marbury's case thrown out of court.* The Constitution, Marshall pointed out, cannot be changed by an act of Congress. Therefore, he concluded, the Judiciary Act of 1789 must be declared unconstitutional. The case was thrown out of court. If Marbury wished to pursue his suit, he would have to begin again in a lower court.

RESULTS OF THE CASE

Marbury never did receive his commission. His unsuccessful lawsuit, however, ranks as the most important case in American legal history. In declaring an act of Congress unconstitutional, Marshall claimed for the Court a power not given (nor denied, for that matter) in the Constitution. Thus emerged the doctrine of *judicial review:* any act of Congress, as well as any act of the President or officials of the executive branch, can be tested by the courts to see if the acts are legal under the Constitution. Judicial review gave the courts the power that allowed them to emerge as a co-equal branch of government.

2. Are there any limits on the implied powers granted to Congress?
(*McCulloch* v. *Maryland*)

The case of *McCulloch* v. *Maryland* centered on the leading financial institution of a young and growing country—the Bank of the United States. Something far more important than the bank's future was at stake, however. At its heart, the case dealt with the liberal interpretation of the implied powers clause of the Constitution. How far could Congress go in carrying out its expressed powers? In the early 1800s, the Supreme Court resolved this thorny issue.

FACTS OF THE CASE

In 1791, Alexander Hamilton, a Federalist and the first Secretary of the Treasury, helped create the Bank of the United States. He designed the bank as the agency through which federal funds would be spent and tax collections would be made. The government owned only a part of the bank; control was placed in private hands. The Jeffersonians opposed Hamilton's Federalist project. They said it violated *states' rights* guaranteed by the Ninth and Tenth Amendments. In this case, the right was that of a state to charter its own banks.

The charter of the first Bank of the United States was allowed to lapse in 1811 at the end of its 20-year term. Five years later, a second national bank was given a similar charter. As before, the new bank was a private institution.

With headquarters in Philadelphia, the bank's 18 branch offices spread from Portsmouth and Boston in the north to Savannah and New Orleans in the south.

LEGAL STEPS IN THE CASE

The renewal of the bank's charter added fuel to the growing political debate over states' rights. The battle moved to the Supreme Court after the state of Maryland brought suit against the Bank of the United States.

1. *Maryland passes a law.* In February 1818, the state of Maryland passed a law that placed the Baltimore branch of the Bank of the United States in a difficult position. Under the law, the bank was ordered to buy stamped paper (paper that carried an expensive tax stamp) on which to issue its bank notes. The bank was also ordered to pay a franchise fee of $15,000 a year to the state. If the bank paid these fees, it wouldn't be able to make a profit.

2. *The bank ignores the law.* The new law went into effect on May 1, 1818. The date passed without any sign that the Baltimore branch intended to obey the regulations. As a result, the state brought suit against James W. McCulloch, the bank's Baltimore cashier.

3. *Appeal to the Supreme Court.* The Baltimore County Court passed judgment in favor of the state. The Maryland Court of Appeals confirmed the lower court's findings. The bank then appealed to the United States Supreme Court. Attorneys argued the case in February 1819.

4. *Arguments.* Maryland's lawyers argued that as a sovereign state, Maryland had the right to tax any bank doing business within its borders. Moreover, they added, Congress had created the bank without proper constitutional authority. The federal lawyers replied that the Constitution gave Congress the authority to carry out its expressed powers. Since one of these expressed powers was the right to regulate money, Congress could use any reasonable means of doing so. Therefore, the lawyers concluded, chartering a bank fell within the reasonable exercise of the implied powers granted by the Constitution.

■ The Bank of the United States was the focus of a stormy political battle during the early 1800s. A conflict between the bank and the state of Maryland led to the landmark *McCulloch* v. *Maryland* decision. The ruling upheld Congress's use of the "necessary and proper" clause.

5. *Decision.* The Court handed down a unanimous decision in favor of the bank. The ruling caused great bitterness among the Jeffersonians. Of the seven judges, they had expected to lose only the votes of the two Federalists.

RESULTS OF THE CASE

Two important constitutional traditions emerged from *McCulloch* v. *Maryland*. First, the decision confirmed the power of Congress to make its own decisions about what actions are reasonable in carrying out its constitutional duties. As a result, few real limits exist on what Congress may do as long as the legislation falls under the "necessary and proper clause." This power is not absolute, for laws must be able to survive judicial review by the courts.

Second, the Court rejected the idea that one level of government has the right to tax any other level of government or any of its agencies. As Marshall put it, "The power to tax involves the power to destroy." The federal government may not tax the income of the states, nor may the states tax the income of their cities, schools, counties, or other governmental bodies.

3. How far may Congress go in regulating interstate commerce?

(*Gibbons* v. *Ogden*)

By 1824, the new nation was expanding rapidly westward. Quarrels between the states and the federal government over the extent of federal powers still hampered development. *Gibbons* v. *Ogden* settled the conflict once and for all. In addition, the case gave John Marshall the chance to make one of the few popular decisions of his many years on the bench.

FACTS OF THE CASE

In 1789, John Fitch lost his monopoly for running steamboats on the waters of New York State. Even though Fitch was the inventor of the steamboat, New York transferred the monopoly to the wealthy chancellor of the state, Robert Livingston. By 1807, Livingston had joined forces with inventor Robert Fulton. The two men launched a service that carried passengers up the Hudson from New York City to Albany.

After Livingston and Fulton died, the monopoly passed to Livingston's brother, John. Competition developed in 1819, when Aaron Ogden and Thomas Gibbons of New Jersey began a passenger service across the Hudson River from New York City to Elizabethtown, New Jersey. This created a conflict, because the Livingston monopoly claimed control of steamboats traveling across the Hudson as well as up the river. The partners soon split up over the issue of cooperating with Livingston. Ogden invested most of his wealth with the New York company, hoping to control traffic across the river.

Ogden's action kept Gibbons from operating a competing ferry service in New York waters. Aided by financier Cornelius Vanderbilt, Gibbons filed suit against the restrictive state laws of New York. In support of his right to run a passenger service, Gibbons pointed to his coasting license. This license granted him the privilege of operating a ship off the coast of the United States. He had obtained the license from the federal government under a U.S. statute passed in 1793.

LEGAL STEPS IN THE CASE

The issues in the case involved far more than the question of Gibbons and his steamboats. The future of the federal government's power

■ View of the upper New York Harbor in the 1830s. New Jersey would be to the right. The ferry route disputed in *Gibbons* v. *Ogden* was in this general area. The Supreme Court's ruling in the case confirmed the federal government's right to regulate interstate commerce. John Marshall's opinion in this case gave a very broad definition of commerce. Which section of the Constitution gives Congress authority over commerce?

to regulate interstate commerce lay in the hands of the courts. The arguments developed in this fashion:

1. States' rights upheld. In October 1819, the New York Court of Chancery ruled that the federal law did not authorize interstate commerce. It merely gave an American identity to licensed vessels, the court said. Did the federal license grant ships the right to travel from port to port within a state as well as from port to port between different states? The court said it did not.

2. Appeal denied. New York's Court of Errors upheld the lower court. The decision said that Gibbons' federal coasting license did not override the New York laws that had granted the steamboat monopoly now held by Ogden. Gibbons' lawyers tried to show that the coasting license had been issued under the power of Congress to regulate interstate commerce, but the appeals court rejected their argument. Gibbons then took his case to the Supreme Court.

3. Webster argues for federal control. After several delays, the Supreme Court heard the case in February 1824. Daniel Webster, a well-known orator and constitutional lawyer, and U.S. Attorney General William Wirt represented Gibbons. The two men argued that New York's monopoly laws conflicted with federal law and must, therefore, be struck down. Webster's logic went to the heart of the matter. The power of Congress to regulate interstate commerce, he said, permitted the federal government to regulate commerce of any kind on any waters involved in the passage of goods or people between the states.

4. Decision. Chief Justice John Marshall wrote the Court's unanimous opinion. He said that interstate commerce referred to any and all trade between the states, not just to mere buying and selling. Since the passage of Gibbons' steamboat between New York and New Jersey obviously met this definition, the Coasting Licensing Act of 1793 was held to be superior to the statutes of the state of New York. Marshall thus freed the steamboat from state laws that granted monopolies to a favored few.

RESULTS OF THE CASE

Gibbons died a millionaire, Ogden a bankrupt. Beyond personal gain or loss, however, the decision foreshadowed federal regulation over all types of interstate traffic. Steamboats, trains, buses, and airplanes would operate under federal rules. In addition, telecommunications, pipelines, and private cars would also be subject to federal regulation. Marshall's ruling has been called the "emancipation of American commerce." *Gibbons* v. *Ogden* gave interstate commerce a mighty boost by taking it out of the hands of state legislatures and the special interest groups that often dominate them.

4. How did a case involving slavery help lead to the Civil War?

(*Dred Scott* v. *Sandford*)

The pages of judicial history are filled with cases that were apparently filed to bring justice to an individual. In reality, many of these cases were meant to settle a point of law. The famous Dred Scott decision illustrates this practice. By the time the courts finally decided his case, Scott was a frail old man, destined to die within the year. For the divided nation, the Court's decision that slavery could not be contained by compromise and federal law led to secession and civil war.

FACTS OF THE CASE

Dred Scott was born into slavery in Virginia sometime around 1795. After his owner took him to Missouri in 1827, Scott was bought and sold by several other slaveholders. He lived with John Emerson, an army surgeon, in the territories of Illinois and Wisconsin for almost five years. Under the Missouri Compromise of 1820, slavery was prohibited in these territories.

Scott was returned to Missouri in 1838. There he became the property of Dr. Emerson's widow, Mrs. Irene Emerson. When Mrs. Emerson moved to New York, she left her slave in

Missouri. Scott came to the attention of an abolitionist named Henry Blow, who filed a lawsuit in the Missouri courts in 1846. Because of Scott's years in free territory, the suit asked the court to declare him a free man.

The lower court found for Scott, but the Missouri Supreme Court reversed the decision in 1852. Dred Scott remained a slave. In time, he became the property of Mrs. Emerson's brother, John Sanford of New York.

Learning Skills

Telling Fact From Opinion

An old television program featured a police officer who was famous for saying, "Just give me the facts, ma'am." Sgt. Friday wasn't interested in people's opinions. He knew that catching and convicting criminals required careful attention to the facts.

What, exactly, was Sgt. Friday looking for? A *fact* is a bit of information that can be proven to be true. An *opinion* is what someone thinks is true. That doesn't mean that all opinions are untrue; it does mean that opinions are difficult to verify. Read the statements that follow and separate the facts from the opinions:

1. Washington, D.C., is the capital of the United States.
2. The federal employees who live and work in Washington, D.C., are overpaid for the amount of work they do.
3. The President appoints the justices of the Supreme Court with the advice and consent of the Senate.
4. Far too many Supreme Court decisions violate the principle of judicial restraint.
5. The case of *Dred Scott* v. *Sandford* helped the Republican party win the election of 1860.
6. The abolitionists who filed the *Dred Scott* case didn't care about Scott; they were only interested in attacking slavery.

If you picked items 1, 3, and 5 as statements of fact, you scored 100 percent. Items 2, 4, and 6 may be true, at least in part, but they cannot be verified as facts. If someone wanted to argue about these choices, you could prove the facts with the help of a reference book. You couldn't do that with the opinions.

In real life, telling facts from opinions is equally tricky. The article that follows describes the 1987 nomination of Robert Bork to the Supreme Court. Which of the numbered sentences are facts and which are opinions?

(*1*) The U.S. Senate will meet next week to begin hearings on President Reagan's nomination of Robert Bork to the Supreme Court. (*2*) Liberal and conservative groups have already spent $20 million to attack and defend the nomination. (*3*) The battle over Bork will be the biggest and nastiest the Senate has seen in this century. One opponent pointed out that (*4*) in eight cases in which corporations challenged the federal government over regulatory issues, Bork sided with business interests every time. The President came to Bork's defense by saying, (*5*) "Robert Bork won't put his opinions ahead of the law."

You probably had to read this article several times before making your decisions. That's a good reminder that facts and opinions don't always stand out clearly. You have to read carefully and thoughtfully. Practice this skill when you read a newspaper or watch a television news program. Even the best reporters sometimes mix in a few opinions with their facts. (The facts are items 1, 2 and 4; 3 and 5 are opinions.)

A PUBLIC MEETING

WILL BE HELD ON

THURSDAY EVENING, 2D INSTANT,

at 7½ o'clock, in ISRAEL CHURCH, to consider the atrocious decision of the Supreme Court in the

DRED SCOTT CASE,

and other outrages to which the colored people are subject under the Constitution of the United States.

C. L. REMOND,
ROBERT PURVIS,

and others will be speakers on the occasion. Mrs. MOTT. Mr. M'KIM and B. S. JONES of Ohio. have also accepted invitations to be present.
All persons are invited to attend. Admittance free.

■ The Supreme Court's decision in the case of Dred Scott (b. 1795?–d. 1858) permitted slavery to expand into free territory and led indirectly to the Civil War. The Court's ruling brought a quick and angry reaction from the North, as the public meeting poster demonstrates.

In 1854, the national argument over slavery was revived by the passage of the Kansas-Nebraska Bill. This law gave the two territories the right to decide for themselves whether to be free or slave. Abolitionists revived the Scott suit, charging Sanford with "assault and battery" in carrying Scott off to his new home. The case was heard in a federal court in Missouri as *Dred Scott* v. *Sandford* (a misspelling, one of many errors in the case).

LEGAL STEPS IN THE CASE

After a federal circuit court decided against Scott, the U.S. Supreme Court agreed to hear an appeal in 1856. The case was packed with political dynamite. A new antislavery group, the Republican party, had run its first national campaign that same year. It lost the presidency to Democrat James Buchanan. In a move of doubtful political ethics, the President-elect wrote to the Court in February 1857. Buchanan asked the justices to decide the

question of the spread of slavery one way or the other.

1. *Legal questions.* The case hinged on three legal issues:

a. Was Scott legally a citizen of Missouri and therefore entitled to sue Sanford (a New York resident) in a federal court?

b. Did Scott's years of residence in free territory entitle him to his freedom?

c. Was the Missouri Compromise of 1820 constitutional? If not, "free territories" (where slavery was illegal) could no longer exist.

2. Decision. The Supreme Court announced its decision on March 6, 1857. The majority ruled that Scott was a slave and, therefore, not qualified to bring suit. Had the Court stopped there, the case might have done little serious harm to the national political scene. Instead, the Court responded to the new President's urging and went much further. In his opinion, Chief Justice Roger Taney pointed out that slaveholding was legal under the Constitution. The compromises of 1820 and 1850 had attempted to make slavery illegal in certain states and territories. That meant that these acts of Congress were, in effect, amendments to the Constitution. Therefore, the ruling went on to say, the compromises were unconstitutional. Slavery could legally exist in any state.

RESULTS OF THE CASE

The Court's action further split the already divided nation. The South rejoiced, but the North was bitterly disappointed. Many voters turned to the Republicans and supported the total abolition of slavery. The Democrats worried that the growing abolitionist feeling could cost them the White House. The Republicans proved them right by electing Abraham Lincoln in 1860, and the southern states seceded. The nation stood on the edge of a bloody civil war.

Let's review for a moment

Do the courts play an important role in shaping the course of American history? These four cases answer that question with an emphatic "Yes!" Did you see the common thread that tied the first three cases together? Under John Marshall, the Supreme Court established itself as an equal partner with the legislative and executive branches in a strong central government.

Marbury v. *Madison* began with the plea of an unhappy man who felt that his federal judgeship had been unfairly denied. Out of this case came the concept of *judicial review.* This important principle gives the federal courts the power to decide the constitutionality of congressional and presidential actions.

McCulloch v. *Maryland* approved the creation of a national bank. More to the point, the case established the right of Congress to exercise its implied powers. It also limited the ability of any one level of government to tax another.

Gibbons v. *Ogden* gave Marshall the opportunity to free interstate commerce from state interference. Without his broad definition of interstate commerce, every state border today might stand as a barrier to the free passage of people and goods.

The final case, *Dred Scott* v. *Sandford,* helped lead the nation into the Civil War. The Supreme Court's decision ended the effort to reach a political compromise over slavery. These efforts stretched from the writing of the Constitution through the Compromise of 1850.

After the Civil War, huge corporations created new problems for a rapidly industrializing country. Could the courts take effective action against these giants? Let's find out.

5. How far may states go in limiting a corporation's business activities?

(*Munn* v. *Illinois*)

Within 20 years after the first train chugged slowly out of Chicago, Illinois, in 1848, the city grew tenfold. As the city grew, so did the grain shipping and storage businesses based there. These giant concerns operated in ways that seemed to defy the laws of the state.

FACTS OF THE CASE

Midwestern railroads carried millions of bushels of grain into Chicago each year. Midwestern farmers had no choice but to market their grain through Chicago, and they found them-

■ Grain elevators similar to those in the upper right of this engraving of Chicago from the Michigan Central Railway played a key role in the case of *Munn* v. *Illinois*. The Supreme Court's decision gave each state the right to regulate commerce within its borders.

selves at the mercy of the railroads and warehouse owners. Some of these profit-hungry wholesalers cheated their customers. Their underhanded practices included (1) delivering grain to warehouses other than those specified by the farmer; (2) grading high-quality grain as low; (3) charging excessively high storage fees; (4) spreading rumors that the grain was spoiling, thus forcing distress sales of quality wheat to speculators; (5) mixing poor grain with good and selling the mixture as premium; and (6) signing false receipts claiming storage for grain that didn't exist.

Among the worst of the companies was Munn & Scott. When the company's dishonest practices couldn't be ignored any longer, an investigation into its activities began. Munn & Scott's managers tried to cover up the fact that they were charging farmers for storing grain they had already sold by building false bottoms in their silos. Then they covered the boards with a few feet of grain and claimed that the silos were full. The trick was discovered when an employee told authorities the truth.

LEGAL STEPS IN THE CASE

Despite strict laws, similar illegal practices still take place. Not long ago, for example, investigators discovered that a baby food producer was selling apple juice that was mostly sugar water. In the 1870s, however, the right of government to "interfere" with business by forbidding such acts was very much in question. The legal process developed like this:

1. Farmers rebel. In 1870, a new farmers' organization, the National Grange of the Patrons of Husbandry, spoke out for its members. The Grange supported Illinois warehouse owners who refused to follow the dishonest practices of companies such as Munn & Scott. The political pressure generated by the Grange led to passage of amendments to the Illinois state constitution. These amendments authorized the regulation of warehouses and railroads.

2. New laws. In 1871, the same farmers' group secured passage of Illinois laws that forbade railroad rate discrimination, set maximum freight and passenger rates, banned certain shady warehouse practices, and set a limit on storage rates. A state Railroad and Warehouse Commission was set up to enforce the regulations.

3. *The state of Illinois brings suit.* Munn & Scott refused to take out a state-required license or to admit state officials to their grain elevators. The company claimed that the state laws were unconstitutional. The state brought suit and won a judgment in a lower court. In 1872, the Illinois Supreme Court accepted the case on appeal. In the meantime, Munn & Scott went bankrupt in a grain speculation deal. George Armour & Company absorbed the smaller business, but the case went on.

4. *The court finds for the public welfare.* Arguments in the state supreme court centered on the constitutional issue. Munn & Scott lost. The court ruled that a state clearly has the right to regulate all activities that affect the *public welfare.*

5. *The railroads' appeal.* The spread of state regulation alarmed the powerful railroad interests. The rail companies appealed the Munn & Scott case (along with a number of similar cases from other states) to the United States Supreme Court. Now known as *Munn* v. *Illinois*, the suit reached the Court in 1876.

6. *State laws upheld.* By a 7–2 vote in 1877, the high court upheld the Grange-inspired laws. Munn & Scott's business did not involve interstate commerce, the Court pointed out. This meant that they could not claim that federal jurisdiction overrode the power of the state to regulate them. The state legislature clearly possessed the power to regulate state commerce, the majority opinion continued. If the people do not like a state law, they should go to the polls, not to the courts.

RESULTS OF THE CASE

The Supreme Court's refusal to examine the content of the Illinois regulations is an excellent example of *judicial restraint.* The courts, the decision says, are not interested in taking over the rightful powers of the legislative branch.

Munn v. *Illinois* has never been overruled. During one period in history (1895–1937),

justices who believed more strongly in industrial capitalism did invalidate some state regulatory laws. They ruled that these laws were violations of the *due process clauses* of the Fifth and Fourteenth amendments. These amendments state that no one shall be deprived of life, liberty, or property without due process of law. Today, as in 1877, the courts approve legislation that regulates commerce so as to "promote the greatest good for the greatest number."

6. Which is stronger—business monopolies or the federal government?
(*Northern Securities Company* et al. v. *United States*)

The Northern Securities trial of 1903 attracted more public attention than any case since the Dred Scott decision. The ingredients were surefire box office. There was the glamour of big names, including J.P. Morgan, the nation's top financier; James Hill, western railroad tycoon; and E.H. Harriman, a rival railroader. Further, the issue was one most people could understand: Does government have the power to regulate the growth of huge interstate trusts? In addition, this case involved millions of dollars—always an attention getter.

FACTS OF THE CASE

Cutthroat business practices were common in 1900. The great corporations and their colorful owners competed for the tremendous profits generated by the rich and growing country. The railroads stood in the front ranks of these enterprises.

Two railroads—the Northern Pacific, owned by Morgan, and the Great Northern, owned by Hill—ran parallel from Minnesota to the Pacific. Harriman's Union Pacific followed the same route farther south. All three lines linked up with the Chicago, Burlington & Quincy Railroad, which led to the rich Chicago market. The three railroad men knew that whoever gained control of the Burlington would have a clear advantage over the competition. In 1900, Hill tried for a takeover but failed. The next year, Morgan succeeded in buying a majority interest in the smaller line.

Harriman struck back with a plot designed to gain control of Morgan's Northern Pacific. He waited until Morgan and Hill (who ran their railroads in close cooperation) were both away from New York. Then Harriman bought 370,000 of the 800,000 shares of Northern Pacific's common stock plus a majority of the preferred stock. Both stocks carried voting rights. The Morgan forces discovered the danger and prevented a complete takeover. The two sides broke the stalemate with a compromise that elected Harriman and several supporters to the Northern Pacific's governing board.

Morgan decided to protect himself against further raids. A few months later, he announced the creation of a corporation too large to be taken over by anyone. His new *holding company* (a corporation that exists only to own stock in other companies) was called the Northern Securities Company. Capitalized at $400 million, the new company controlled the three Morgan and Hill railroads—the Northern Pacific, the Great Northern, and the Burlington.

This concentration of power did not escape notice in Washington. There, a new and untested President occupied the White House. Theodore Roosevelt had gained the presidency in 1901 after William McKinley, "the businessman's friend," had fallen victim to an assassin's bullet. Early in 1902, Roosevelt ordered an investigation of the Northern Securities Company. In March, the government filed a federal suit in St. Paul, Minnesota. The suit charged the company with violation of the Sherman Antitrust Act of 1890.

LEGAL STEPS IN THE CASE

The vaguely worded Sherman Antitrust Act had seen little use in the dozen years of its existence. The law's main intent was to forbid illegal combinations of businesses that acted in *restraint of trade*. In other words, the Sherman Act gave the government authority to

■ Financial wizard J. P. Morgan. His railroad holding company was declared illegal by the Supreme Court in 1904. President Theodore Roosevelt applauded the decision.

prevent monopolies from restricting the free flow of interstate commerce by reducing or eliminating competition. Was the Northern Securities Company such a monopoly within the meaning of the law? The courts would have to decide.

1. Sherman Act upheld in lower court. A four-judge federal circuit court found against Northern Securities in April 1903. The judges ruled that the railroads were, in fact, competing companies. To place them under one management would have the effect of reducing competition. This ruling meant that the provisions of the antitrust law applied to the case.

2. Appeal to the Supreme Court. Morgan and his lawyers carried their appeal to the Supreme Court. The defense argued that the merger had not restrained trade. It only had the potential to do so, they said. Should a company be penalized for size alone? The government's attorneys replied that by combining the rail lines, Northern Securities effectively controlled transportation across a major segment of the country.

3. *Decision.* In 1904, the Supreme Court reported a 5–4 decision against the Northern Securities Company. Justice John Marshall Harlan wrote that no scheme or device could more clearly come within the meaning of the Sherman Act. On this close vote, the Sherman Antitrust Act survived as a means of limiting "unreasonable" restraints of trade.

RESULTS OF THE CASE

The long-range importance of the case had little to do with the railroads themselves. Hill and Morgan continued to run their parallel lines as a team. The government, however, had established its right to regulate business for the common good. Teddy Roosevelt now had the "big stick" he needed to maintain stricter control over other big corporations.

■ This 1906 cartoon shows President Theodore Roosevelt swinging his "big stick" at all types of trusts. He was known as a "trust-buster."

7. Do the war powers include the right to lock up citizens who haven't committed a crime?
(*Korematsu* v. *United States*)

Most Americans view their government and its law enforcement officers as friends and protectors. People know that they won't be arrested and imprisoned unless they break the law. Everyone is protected by civil rights even when the national origins of some residents identify them with a wartime enemy. During World War I, for instance, national feelings ran high against Germany, but German-Americans were neither arrested nor interned. That tradition broke down in the early days of World War II. Backed by orders from Washington, army troops rounded up Japanese-Americans and locked them in relocation camps.

FACTS OF THE CASE

World War II began for the United States with the Japanese bombing of Pearl Harbor, Hawaii, on December 7, 1941. Almost overnight, anti-Japanese feelings on the West Coast of the United States reached a state of near hysteria. People feared that their Japanese-American neighbors would become spies and saboteurs if Japanese forces invaded the mainland. In February 1942, President Franklin Roosevelt issued an executive order that authorized the creation of military areas. Defense authorities were given the power to exclude from those areas any and all persons who might endanger the national security.

A month later, Lt. Gen. John DeWitt named the entire West Coast to a depth of about 40 miles as Military Area No. 1. The general's next step was to establish a curfew. All people of Japanese origin were ordered to stay in their homes between 8 P.M. and 6 A.M. each day. Next, in May 1942, Gen. DeWitt ordered the removal from the district of all Japanese-Americans. Men, women, and children were collected and taken to "war relocation centers." This was a polite name for what Euro-

■ Japanese-Americans in 1942 having their luggage examined before being taken to an evacuation center in southern California. From there they were sent to relocation camps. In 1990, the U.S. government began to send each survivor of the camps a letter of apology and a check for $20,000.

peans had learned to call "concentration camps." Congress backed up the military by making it a crime to violate the removal orders.

In all, about 112,000 people were moved to ten relocation centers. The camps were located in isolated areas of six western states and Arkansas. Many families had only 48 hours to pack and to dispose of their property. Bargain hunters moved in and bought up farms, businesses, and homes for a few cents on the dollar. All but two of the hastily constructed camps were set up in barren desert areas. Each family who arrived at Topaz, Utah, for example, was assigned to one dusty 20-by-25-foot room in a tarpaper-covered barracks.

About 70,000 of the Japanese-Americans who were sent to the relocation camps were native-born citizens. Even though they had been imprisoned by their own country, most of the internees began each day by reciting the Pledge of Allegiance. No Japanese-American was ever found guilty of committing sabotage or espionage against the United States.

LEGAL STEPS IN THE CASE

Three cases questioning the legality of the Japanese removal were taken to the Supreme Court. In *Hirabayashi* v. *United States* (1943), the Court upheld the curfew. The ruling stated that the order was a valid measure intended to prevent acts damaging to the war effort. In *Ex parte Endo* (1944) the Court examined the removal order. The resulting decision stated that an American citizen of Japanese ancestry whose loyalty had been established could not be held in a War Relocation Center. The most important of the three cases was *Korematsu* v. *United States* (1944). This case dealt with the government's right to remove citizens of Japanese origin from the West Coast.

1. *Lower court conviction.* Fred Korematsu was tried and convicted in a federal district court. His crime was that of remaining in San Leandro, California, in spite of the Civilian Expulsion Order. The Circuit Court of Appeals confirmed the conviction. Korematsu's lawyers appealed to the Supreme Court, which agreed to review the decision.

2. *Legal basis of exclusion questioned.* Korematsu's lawyer argued that the 1942 act that allowed the military to evacuate civilians was unconstitutional. Congress exceeded its war powers by delegating this authority. In addition, the lawyer said, all danger of a Japanese invasion of the West Coast had vanished by the time the exclusion order was issued. Finally, the issue of prejudice was raised. Were Korematsu and his fellow Japanese-Americans removed because of their race?

3. *Decision.* The Court upheld the lower court decision by ruling that the removal was necessary. It was impossible, the justices said, to separate quickly any disloyal Japanese-Americans from the loyal majority. Thus, the exclusion was a burden that citizens had to bear when the nation's shores were threatened. Further, the Court stated, the exclusion was a response to a military danger and was not based on racial prejudice. Congress had acted within constitutional limits.

RESULTS OF THE CASE

The Supreme Court decided the Korematsu case on December 18, 1944. By that time, more than 33,000 of the evacuees had been resettled in 47 states and the District of Columbia. In addition, 2,500 young Japanese-Americans had volunteered for military service directly from the relocation centers. Many others were drafted. Sent to Europe to fight, these men quickly earned a reputation as some of the Army's bravest soldiers.

After the war, Japanese-Americans refused to accept the Korematsu decision as final.

Slowly, public sentiment shifted in their favor. In 1982, a congressional committee revealed that naval intelligence had reported in 1942 that there was no threat of a Japanese invasion. Therefore, the relocation was unnecessary. In 1983, the Congressional Commission on Wartime Relocation and Internment of Civilians urged Congress to make a national apology. The National Council for Japanese-American Redress brought a damage suit (*United States* v. *Horhi* et al.) on behalf of the surviving evacuees. The U.S. Court of Appeals for the District of Columbia found that the claims for compensation were justified. The case went to the Supreme Court on appeal in 1987. The high court overruled the appeals court and rejected the claims.

The quest for compensation then turned to Congress. In 1988, Congress passed a law that offered the nation's apologies for the "grave injustice" done to the wartime evacuees. In addition, the bill awarded tax-free payments of $20,000 to each of the 60,000 evacuees who were still alive. During the signing ceremony, President Ronald Reagan said, "It's not for us today to pass judgment upon those who may have made mistakes while engaged in that great struggle [World War II]. Yet we must recognize that the internment of Japanese-Americans was just that, a mistake."

8. Are segregated schools automatically unequal?

(*Brown* v. *Board of Education of Topeka*)

In the 1950s, many Americans joined in an attack on school segregation. They believed that segregation shackled the minds of black people as surely as chains had once imprisoned their bodies. The decision of the Supreme Court in *Brown* v. *Board of Education of Topeka* grew out of that concern. The result still affects classrooms across the country.

FACTS OF THE CASE

The case of *Brown* v. *Board of Education* was the final step in a long string of segregation cases. In May 1896, the United States Supreme Court announced a decision in a Louisiana railroad suit, *Plessy* v. *Ferguson.* The ruling supported the *Jim Crow laws* used by some 30 states to segregate public facilities (schools, beaches, restaurants, and railroad cars, for example) under the *"separate but equal"* doctrine. This meant that separation by race was legal as long as the public facilities for blacks and whites were of equal quality. *Plessy* did not mention schools, but they were covered in a 1927 decision, *Gong Lum* v. *Lee.*

The changing social climate in the late 1940s and the 1950s brought the "separate but equal" doctrine under attack. Led by the National Association for the Advancement of Colored People (NAACP), blacks filed several suits that struck successfully at Jim Crow laws. The attack on segregated schools was part of that effort.

LEGAL STEPS IN THE CASE

The case called *Brown* v. *Board of Education* combined several suits that questioned the legality of segregated schools. Four states and the District of Columbia were represented. Although local conditions differed slightly from suit to suit, the basic arguments were similar.

1. *"Separate but equal" doctrine upheld.* In Topeka, Kansas, where the *Brown* case began, a three-judge federal panel ruled that *Plessy* v. *Ferguson* and its "separate but equal" doctrine was still the law of the land.

2. *Appeal to the Supreme Court.* In December 1952, the Supreme Court agreed to review all five school segregation cases. Thurgood Marshall, an eminent black attorney, argued the plaintiff's case. (In 1967, Marshall was appointed by President Lyndon Johnson to the high court as an associate justice.)

3. *Basic questions.* In June 1953, the Court broke a six-month silence to ask both sides to answer four questions:

a. Did the Fourteenth Amendment, as passed by Congress and ratified by the states, intend to abolish school segregation? As written, the amendment appears to guarantee equal protection under the law.

b. If no such intent existed, did those who

■ Black Americans won a long-sought victory over segregated schools in the Supreme Court's *Brown* v. *Board of Education of Topeka* ruling in 1954. A mother and her daughter on the steps of the Supreme Court building looking at a newspaper announcing the decision.

wrote the amendment think that it entitled Congress or the Supreme Court to act on school segregation?

c. If the intent of the amendment was unclear, did the Court itself have the power to abolish segregated schools?

d. If the Court did declare an end to segregation, would such a declaration take immediate effect or could integration proceed on a gradual basis?

The NAACP lawyers consulted with legal scholars, sociologists, and educators from every section of the country. They filed their response in November 1953, and the Court heard the oral arguments a month later.

4. *Decision.* In May 1954, Chief Justice Earl Warren read a unanimous decision that declared racially separate schools to be "inherently unequal." Citing sociological evidence, the Court stated that separate schools automatically gave black children a "feeling

■ Earl Warren was Chief Justice of the United States from 1953 to 1969. During the Warren years, the Supreme Court made the landmark decisions that gave new meaning to the civil rights amendments to the Constitution.

of inferiority as to their status in the community that may affect their hearts and minds in a way unlikely ever to be undone." With these words, the Supreme Court formally overturned *Plessy* v. *Ferguson.*

RESULTS OF THE CASE

Political scientists consider *Brown* v. *Board of Education* a landmark in the history of American justice. The Warren Court acted decisively in what it considered to be the public interest. Opponents of the Court replied that the decision was "political." Indeed it was, because court decisions always carry political implications. Judges must always be aware of the changing needs of the society they serve.

Enforcement of the desegregation decision began in the South but later spread to other sections of the country. Correcting racial segregation in the schools has created a long series of controversies over busing and community control of schools. Whatever social turmoil it created, however, the *Brown* decision shows that the Constitution is still capable of growth and evolution.

9. Should any restrictions be placed on the police when making arrests?
(*Miranda* v. *Arizona*)

Rising crime rates in the 1960s focused attention on two opposing viewpoints regarding law enforcement. On one hand, the public demanded that the police take vigorous action to protect their communities. On the other hand, concern was growing that heavy-handed police activities could damage the nation's cherished constitutional rights. The conflict reached the Supreme Court in the case of *Miranda* v. *Arizona.*

FACTS OF THE CASE

In March 1963, an 18-year-old girl was kidnapped and physically abused near Phoenix, Arizona. Ten days later, the police arrested Ernesto Miranda, age 23, for the crime. Taken to the police station, he was questioned without being told that he had the right to remain silent and to have a lawyer present. The victim picked him out of a police lineup. After two hours of further questioning, Miranda made an oral confession.

Despite his attorney's objection, Miranda's confession was admitted as evidence at his trial. Found guilty, Miranda received a long prison term. The verdict was upheld on appeal to the Arizona Supreme Court. The court ruled that the defendant's constitutional rights had not been violated because Miranda did not specifically request a lawyer. Miranda and his attorney then asked the United States Supreme Court to review the case.

LEGAL STEPS IN THE CASE

In 1964, the Supreme Court had already begun to concern itself with the extension of Bill of Rights guarantees to state court trials. The well-publicized Miranda case continued this movement.

1. *Right to counsel.* In the 1964 case of *Escobedo* v. *Illinois,* the Court ruled in a 5–4 vote that the defendant had been denied his constitutional rights. In this case, the police

■ Suspect in a Maine county sheriff's office being read his Fifth Amendment rights. These "Miranda" rights must be read to suspects when apprehended. Each police officer carries a card with the rights listed on it. Basically, the suspect has a right to remain silent and to have a lawyer.

would not let Escobedo see a lawyer until after he confessed.

2. Negative precedents. *Escobedo* and *Miranda* both raised the same question. Did the Fourteenth Amendment (through either the due process clause or the privileges and immunities clause) extend Bill of Rights protections to cases tried under state laws? Until the 1960s, the amendment had always been limited to federal court cases. After the question was first asked in 1873, a total of 53 justices ruled against extending Fourteenth Amendment protections to the state court cases. Only one justice had ever ruled in favor of it.

3. Changing Supreme Court rulings. Beginning in the early 1960s, the Court began to decide appeals on the basis of *selective incorporation*. This meant that the Court picked individual guarantees from the Bill of Rights and applied them to state cases. Previous decisions had already been made involving (a) protection against self-incrimination (*Malloy* v. *Hogan*, 1964); (b) the right of the poor to free legal counsel (*Gideon* v. *Wainwright*, 1963);

and (c) protection against unreasonable search and seizure (*Mapp* v. *Ohio*, 1961).

4. Decision. Chief Justice Warren delivered the majority opinion in the Miranda case in 1966. Three justices dissented. Warren took note of the stresses that arrest and questioning place on a suspect. Under these conditions, he wrote, suspects held in custody must be informed in clear terms that (a) they have the right to remain silent and (b) they have the right to consult with an attorney. Thus, the *Miranda* decision says that all of us, innocent or guilty, are shielded by the Constitution from the misuse of power by law enforcement agencies.

RESULTS OF THE CASE

As with every major Supreme Court decision, *Miranda* left a legacy of change. Police officers, for example, had to learn new methods of questioning suspects. In the beginning, critics claimed that many suspects escaped trial because of technical flaws in their arrest and booking that had nothing to do with their guilt or innocence. Over the years, however, the chorus of complaints has decreased. For one thing, statistics show that suspects confess in about the same numbers as before.

The police still win convictions when they follow the rules and use proper investigative techniques. In addition, the Supreme Court has gradually given law enforcement agencies more tools for doing their job. In 1984, the Court ruled for the first time in *United States* v. *Leon* and *Massachusetts* v. *Sheppard* that illegally obtained evidence can be used in criminal trials. As long as the police obtain the evidence "in good faith," it can be presented to the jury.

The debate over *Miranda* involves a question that goes to the heart of a free society. Have citizens lost the right to be protected from criminals in the rush to safeguard the rights of the lawbreakers? Whatever the answer turns out to be, the results of *Miranda* can be seen on every television crime show. As soon as the police make an arrest, the suspects are informed of their rights according to the *Miranda* formula. Even *Miranda*'s strongest critics admit that rising crime rates can't be blamed solely on a ruling that protects a suspect's right to legal counsel.

Reviewing what you've learned

1. The courts of the United States have remained responsive to the nation's social, political, and economic problems. The early decisions discussed in this chapter were concerned with the exercise of federal power. The later cases gave the Supreme Court the chance to protect the individual.

2. *Marbury* v. *Madison* established the principle of *judicial review*, which forever confirmed the federal courts as a co-equal branch of government. Congressional power under the concept of implied powers was secured in *McCulloch* v. *Maryland*, while *Gibbons* v. *Ogden* released interstate commerce from the control of individual state legislatures.

3. A debate over individual rights began to surface when the slavery question split the country. *Dred Scott* v. *Sandford*, by striking down the compromise legislation of 1820 and 1850, led directly to the Civil War. Still, despite the Union victory, segregation laws haunted the nation's sense of justice. Not until 1954 did the Supreme Court, in *Brown* v. *Board of Education of Topeka*, end the "separate but equal" doctrine that had been used to justify school segregation.

4. The Supreme Court also moved against the big corporations. In *Munn* v. *Illinois*, the states gained the right to regulate corporations for the public benefit even though private companies lose some freedom as a result. The Sherman Antitrust Act became an effective government weapon against monopoly combinations after *Northern Securities Company et al.* v. *United States* confirmed its usefulness.

5. In *Korematsu* v. *United States*, the Supreme Court upheld the 1942 relocation and detention of American citizens of Japanese ancestry. The Court ruled that individual liberties could be overturned in the interests of national defense during wartime.

6. In *Miranda* v. *Arizona*, the Supreme Court in 1966 brought state courts into line with federal guarantees of the right to counsel and against self-incrimination. Faced with a choice between police power and individual rights, the Court came down on the side of the individual.

Review questions and activities

TERMS YOU SHOULD KNOW

due process clause
holding company
Jim Crow laws
judicial restraint
judicial review

public welfare
restraint of trade
selective incorporation
"separate but equal" doctrine
states' rights

MATCHING QUESTIONS

For each legal principle described, choose from the list the case that best illustrates the principle.

a. *Marbury* v. *Madison*

b. *McCulloch* v. *Maryland*

c. *Gibbons* v. *Ogden*

d. *Dred Scott* v. *Sandford*

e. *Munn* v. *Illinois*

f. *Northern Securities* et al. v. *United States*

g. *Korematsu* v. *United States*

h. *Brown* v. *Board of Education of Topeka*

i. *Miranda* v. *Arizona*

1. A federal judge orders the city of Boston to bus students between neighborhood schools in order to obtain racial balance.

2. A large computer manufacturing company is taken to court and charged with monopolizing the sale of computers to business and industry.

3. During a repeat of the Cuban Missile Crisis, the federal government proclaims a national emergency. The Army moves in and relocates Cuban-Americans from their homes along the Gulf Coast. Civil rights groups file suit to prevent the evacuation.

4. The state of Arkansas passes a law taxing the income of the cities and counties within the state.

5. The district attorney in Reno loses a murder conviction when the court discovers that the defendant did not know he was entitled to counsel despite his inability to pay legal fees.

6. The Supreme Court upholds an Iowa law that places a ceiling on the rates a firm can charge doctors for malpractice insurance.

7. The Supreme Court refuses to hear an appeal from a company that was challenging a state law prohibiting greyhound racing in the state.

8. Arizona attempts to enforce a law banning the import of California oranges as a way of helping Arizona citrus growers.

9. The Justice Department takes action when the three largest oil companies agree to set uniform prices for gasoline.

10. A federal court rules that the President must spend funds voted by Congress for low-income housing units even though he opposes the policy.

CONCEPT DEVELOPMENT

1. Explain the role taken by the Supreme Court in opposing the executive branch in *Marbury* v. *Madison*.

2. Evaluate the contributions of Chief Justice John Marshall to the development of the federal court system.

3. Discuss the concept of implied powers as interpreted by the courts. Are there any areas left in which government cannot act?

4. List the current members of the Supreme Court, along with their political philosophy—liberal, moderate, or conservative. Where does the balance of power appear to lie? How will the Court's makeup affect decisions in the fields of racial justice, law enforcement, and other social issues during the next few years?

5. What do critics mean when they charge that the Supreme Court is "making law, not interpreting it"?

HANDS-ON ACTIVITIES

1. This chapter discussed only ten out of thousands of Supreme Court decisions. Use library reference sources to locate some additional important decisions. Select one or two to describe in an oral class presentation or a written report. A few cases that relate to the First Amendment are *Near* v. *Minnesota*, 1931 (censorship); *Sheppard* v. *Maxwell*, 1966 (unfair publicity in a court trial); *New York Times* v. *Sullivan*, 1964 (newspaper libel); and *Pierce* v. *Society of Sisters*, 1925 (religious education); *Texas* v. *Johnson*, 1989 (flag burning, free speech). The list goes on and on. Can you find cases of even greater interest?

2. Select one of the chapter's cases to dramatize for your class. An effective technique is to do it in the form of a reading, with well-rehearsed actors reading their parts from a script. A narrator can fill in background and provide transition from one event to the next. Individual voices portray the plaintiff, judges, defendants, and other participants. A possible variation is to record the scene on tape, with music and sound effects like a 1940s radio show. College textbooks on constitutional law make excellent sourcebooks for this project.

3. Set up a debate on the topic, "*Resolved*, That the Supreme Court of the United States should confine itself to its constitutionally defined tasks and should leave legislation to Congress and its enforcement to the executive branch." The debate teams will need to research this controversial topic.

4. Conduct a survey among members of your community to discover how many people can (a) name any or all members of the Supreme Court and (b) name or describe any recent Court rulings. If you find that many of your subjects "strike out" on these questions, you may want to discuss in class why there is such ignorance of our most important court. Is there any danger in this? Is there any way that voters can influence the Supreme Court?

Unit Six

State and Local Government in the American System

17 Government in the fifty states

Can you imagine yourself as the governor of California? If the state's voters elected you, you'd be following in the footsteps of some well-known Americans. Earl Warren went on to become Chief Justice of the Supreme Court. A few years after Ronald Reagan left the governor's office, he was elected to the White House.

▲ The California State Capitol in Sacramento. It is modeled after the nation's capitol in Washington.

As governor, you won't have much time to think about your future. You'll be busy every minute. You and your staff will have to answer the 1,500 or more letters that arrive in your office every day. Your phone will ring every four seconds. There's even a touch of danger in all of this. Security officers must inspect every package and screen every

410

visitor. Before you pose for a picture with a group of voters, you have to be sure none of them is there to shoot you.

Your office is in the capitol building in Sacramento. If you enter through the door used by the public, you'll cross a dark green rug to the receptionist's desk. On the desk lies a list of your appointments for today. As you pick up the list, the receptionist pushes a buzzer that unlocks the door leading to your office. You walk down a corridor lined with the offices of your various secretaries—Legislative, Executive, Legal, Press, Appointments, Cabinet, and Schedule. You stop for a moment to admire the Frederic Remington painting of forty-niners panning for gold that hangs on the white wall.

You pass through a set of double doors and enter your red-carpeted office. You've heard the joke a thousand times: "The carpet's red so you can't see the blood." No one has ever died here, but political blood is shed every time you veto a bill passed by the legislature. You take your seat behind a large, U-shaped desk that was built by prisoners at San Quentin. A stack of papers catches your eye. Your private secretary has laid out the letters and documents that need your immediate attention.

As you start work, you're feeling a little discouraged. You feel better after you pause to read the framed quotation from Abraham Lincoln:

> If I were to try to read, much less answer, all the attacks made on me, this shop might as well be closed for any other purpose. I do the very best I can, and I mean to keep on doing so until the end. If the end brings me out all right, what is said against me won't amount to anything. If the end brings me out wrong, ten angels swearing I was right would make no difference.

A look at the schedule tells you that your first appointment is in the Governor's Conference Room next door. You're a little early, so you circle the room, admiring the wooden Mexican tables and the 12 matching leather chairs. The clock dates back to 1849, but it still keeps good time. The capitol building manager winds it every two days. From the bank of windows, you look out over the well-kept capitol grounds.

A sudden thought takes you down the hallway to your private study. This is a less formal, smaller office. The shelves are lined with mementos from your political campaigns. Beside the small desk is a wooden cabinet with an intercom. Inside is a special red telephone, your direct line to the White House. If that phone ever rings, you know it will be for an emergency of some sort. You turn in your swivel chair and study the family photos that line the table behind your desk. Being governor doesn't leave much time for family get-togethers.

Some of your favorite mottos hang on the wall. You look at one of them and smile. It says, "There's no limit to what people can do or where they can go if they don't mind who gets the credit." You wouldn't be a successful politician if you didn't have a sense of humor.

You still have ten minutes before your meeting, so you pick up a pad of yellow paper. The minutes from the last meeting on the state budget are lying on the desk. You study them for a minute and then you jot down some notes for the speech you'll deliver on Saturday. You usually turn this job over to your speechwriters, but this talk will be covered by network television. You want to be at your best when you talk directly to your bosses—the state's millions of voters. As often happens, you're just getting started when your secretary comes in to tell you that the meeting is ready to start. Your workday has begun.

The governor of California, along with the other 49 state governors, plays a major role in the political life of the American people. In this chapter, you'll read about the responsibilities and problems of state government. The questions that will be explored include:

1. What does a typical state constitution contain?

2. What are the powers exercised by the states?

3. How do governors administer their states?

4. What role does the legislature play in state government?

5. How do states use their powers to protect the public safety?

6. How do states pay the costs of government?

7. How do states regulate corporations?

8. What is the role of a state in educating its citizens?

9. How does the federal government cooperate with state governments?

1. What does a typical state constitution contain?

A state constitution is the supreme law of the state. No act of the state, its counties, and its cities is legal if it violates the state constitution. At the same time, a state constitution must conform to the U.S. Constitution. Following the federal model, the states wrote constitutions that established governments based on the principles of separation of powers and popular sovereignty. All the states have an executive (governor), a legislature, and a judicial system. Forty-nine states set up two-house (bicameral) legislatures. Only Nebraska has a unicameral legislature, although other states have studied the possibility of changing to a one-house system.

ORGANIZATION

Most state constitutions divide into seven basic sections:

1. A preamble, or general statement of the powers and purposes of state government.

2. A bill of rights.

3. Provisions for the executive, legislative, and judicial branches of state government, describing terms in office, powers, and duties.

4. A description of the political subdivi-

How the Constitution Divides Power Between the Federal Government and the States

POWERS OF THE FEDERAL GOVERNMENT	SHARED POWERS	POWERS OF STATE GOVERNMENTS
1. To conduct foreign relations	1. To levy and collect taxes	1. To regulate trade within the state
2. To declare war	2. To borrow money	2. To establish local governments
3. To regulate interstate and foreign commerce	3. To establish superior and inferior courts	3. To protect the public health, safety, and morals
4. To regulate immigration and establish laws permitting naturalization	4. To enforce laws	4. To ratify constitutional amendments
5. To raise and maintain armed forces	5. To apprehend and punish lawbreakers	5. To determine qualifications of voters
6. To govern territories and admit new states	6. To charter banks and other corporations	6. To conduct elections
7. To print and coin money	7. To take land for public use	7. To change state constitutions and the form of state and local governments
8. To establish post offices and post roads	8. To provide for the general welfare	8. To establish and support public schools
9. To grant patents and copyrights		9. To license various occupational specialties
10. To make all laws "necessary and proper" to carry out its constitutional responsibilities		10. To exercise the "reserved powers" not granted to the federal government nor prohibited to the states

sions of the state, including the powers held by local government.

5. General provisions regarding voting, taxes, elections, the budget, schools, and other aspects of state business.

6. Provisions for amending the constitution.

7. The amendments themselves.

By the time these seven areas are covered, most state constitutions take up dozens of pages. One of the longest—Alabama's 129,000-word constitution—is over 18 times longer than the U.S. Constitution and its amendments.

REASONS FOR LENGTH AND SPECIFIC CONTENT

Several factors combine to make state constitutions both longer and more specific than the national Constitution.

Ease of amendment. Most state constitutions can be amended by a relatively simple process. Once the legislature or the people of the state propose an amendment, it can be ratified by a majority vote in the next general election. Special-interest groups have found that amending a state constitution is sometimes easier than pushing a new law through the legislature. Supporters of a new law also know that it is very difficult to repeal a law that has been ratified as a constitutional amendment.

Distrust of state government. Rightly or wrongly, many people distrust their state governments. Fearful that their basic rights might be abused by the legislature or the governor, they insist that specific rules for business and personal conduct be written into the constitution. A civil rights proposal that Congress would pass as statute law would be proposed as a constitutional amendment in many states.

Outmaneuvering the courts. State supreme courts often find state laws unconstitutional. In response, legislatures may rewrite a law and ask the voters to incorporate it into the constitution. Once that is done, the matter is out of the hands of the courts. Many of the hundreds of amendments found in the constitutions of Alabama, California, South Carolina, and Texas were added in order to bypass the courts.

2. What are the powers exercised by the states?

All powers not granted to the federal government by the U.S. Constitution are reserved to the states by the Ninth Amendment. That fact leaves the states, both large and small, with a major responsibility for the well-being of the people who live within their borders. In a century marked by political, social, and economic change, state governments have been forced to demonstrate their own flexibility. California and New York, for example, raise and spend more money than do many large nations.

BASIC STATE AUTHORITY

The basic authority of an individual state lies in three areas:

Public safety. A state needs the authority to ensure the public safety. It may make and enforce laws affecting the health, safety, morals, welfare, and education of all who live within its boundaries.

Regulation of business. All states regulate the conduct of business within their borders. Chartering corporations, licensing and regulating business operations, and collecting sales and income taxes are accepted as part of a state's responsibility to promote the general welfare.

Regulation of political subdivisions. The states regulate many aspects of the economic and political life of their counties, cities, and towns. A state government, for example, may revise county lines, raise taxes, or force school districts to unify.

■ A Florida Department of Agriculture technician spraying yards in a section of Miami to control the Mediterranean fruit fly. This insect threatened the citrus industry.

SPECIFIC STATE RESPONSIBILITIES

The specific responsibilities of state government have developed out of the three basic powers described above. The following list will give you an idea of a typical state's impact on the lives of all of its residents:

Agriculture. The state works with farmers to improve crops, control pests, and promote conservation. State experts generally coordinate their programs with those of the U.S. Department of Agriculture.

Banking. The state issues charters to state banks, maintains a system of bank examiners, and writes banking regulations.

Civil defense. The state coordinates with the appropriate federal agencies its programs for handling the needs of citizens affected by the ravages of war and natural disasters.

Commerce. The state grants charters to corporations and regulates their activities. State agencies aid business and industry, issue licenses, and regulate utilities.

Conservation. The state preserves natural resources and wildlife, and cooperates with federal conservation agencies.

Education. The state finances and oversees a system of state colleges and universities. It works with local school boards in financing the public schools and setting standards for the courses they teach.

Elections. The state establishes boundaries for federal and state legislative districts. It regulates local, state, and national elections.

Family relations. The state makes laws that regulate marriage, divorce, child support, and abortion.

Food and drugs. The state licenses pharmacists and monitors the sale of controlled substances. Its agencies set standards for the sale of raw and processed food. County inspectors make on-the-spot inspections of sanitary conditions in restaurants and retail stores as well as checks to make sure that consumers receive honest weights and measures.

Health care. The state licenses doctors, nurses, and other health-care workers. With federal help, it maintains hospitals and pays

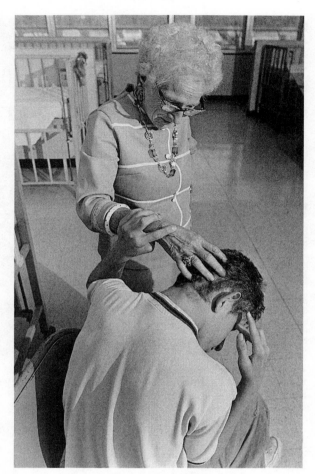

■ A volunteer foster grandmother gives comfort to a mentally handicapped teenager in a state facility in Rhode Island in the late 1980s.

for the care of people who cannot afford private doctors.

Highways. The state builds and maintains bridges, tunnels, and the state highway system. It oversees the design and construction of federally financed interstate highways.

Insurance. The state regulates the operations of the insurance industry in the state by setting standards of disclosure, coverage, and payment.

Labor. The state maintains an employment service and sets standards for working conditions and the employment of minors. It

■ One of the standards states set for automobiles is the amount and type of noxious fumes that vehicles are permitted to emit. Many states require yearly auto safety inspections, and a few pay particular attention to smog control equipment.

provides a mediation service for labor disputes.

Law enforcement and public safety. The state polices its highways, aids local law enforcement agencies, and trains National Guard units. It also runs its own court and prison systems.

Local government. The state approves boundaries for new towns and subdivisions. It helps finance local governments by refunding a share of the state sales tax.

Motor vehicles. The state licenses drivers and vehicles. It also sets standards for the operation of commercial and private cars, trucks, and buses.

Welfare. The state oversees many welfare programs that aid the needy. Its agencies funnel state and federal money to the counties and cities and help them obey the guidelines for spending the funds.

3. How do governors administer their states?

Because they carried out the king's policies, colonial governors were often hated by the American colonists. Today, attitudes have changed. State governors have earned the right to be called the "presidents" of their states. In fact, a number of governors have used their state *gubernatorial* (from the Latin word for governor) experiences as a base for moving on to the White House.

QUALIFICATIONS

Minimum age requirements for a governor range from 21 to 34. About three-quarters of the states set a minimum age of 30. Candidates must be United States citizens, qualified voters, and residents of the state (five years is the typical requirement). Membership in a political party is not required. Political common sense, however, tells candidates that it's almost impossible to win a race for governor without party backing.

TERMS OF OFFICE

All states elect their governors by the direct vote of the people. Governors were originally elected for one-year terms, but since 1920 all governors have been given terms of at least two years. Most states now allow a full four-year term. Elections are held in "off years," when a presidential election isn't competing for the attention of the voters. About half the states limit their governors to two consecutive terms; four states restrict them to a single term. Several governors have evaded these rules and kept the job "in the family" by running their spouses for the office.

RESPONSIBILITIES

The governor's job closely resembles that of the President, minus the responsibilities of foreign affairs and national security. Generally, governors have five major tasks: (1) They command the state's law enforcement, National Guard, and emergency forces. (2) They play a key role in moving new laws through their legislatures. (3) As ceremonial heads of state, they represent the political, social, and moral beliefs of their people. (4) They are the chief administrative officers of their states, and people look to them for civic leadership. (5) They serve as leaders of their political parties at both the state and national levels.

Two of these jobs call for further discussion. A governor's success depends largely on his or her legislative and administrative abilities.

Legislative leadership. Like the Presi-

■ L. Douglas Wilder being sworn in as governor of Virginia in January 1990. He is the first elected black governor in the United States. Wilder's children look on as retired Supreme Court Justice Lewis Powell administers the oath of office outside the state capitol in Richmond.

State governments: terms, salaries, and memberships of the executive, legislative, and judicial branches

| | GOVERNOR | | LEGISLATURE | | | | | HIGHEST COURT | | |
| | | | Membership | | Term, years | | | | | |
STATE	Term, years	Annual salary	Upper house	Lower house	Upper house	Lower house	Salaries of members	Members	Term, years	Annual salary
Alabama	4(c)	$ 70,223	35	105	4	4	$ 45/day	9	6	$83,880
Alaska	4	81,648	20	40	4	2	22,140/yr.	5	3/10	85,278
Arizona	4	75,000	30	60	2	2	15,000/yr.	5	6	75,000
Arkansas	2	35,000	35	100	4	2	7,500/yr	7	8	67,660
California	4	85,000	40	80	4	2	40,816/yr.	7	12	103,469
Colorado	4	70,000	35	65	4	2	17,500/yr.	7	10	72,000
Connecticut	4	78,000	36	151	2	2	30,400/2 yrs.	7	8	86,835
Delaware	4(b)	80,000	21	41	4	2	22,173/yr.	5	12	97,300
Florida	4(c)	98,904	40	120	4	2	20,748/yr.	7	6	92,882
Georgia	4(b)	86,706	56	180	2	2	10,251/yr.	7	6	80,514
Hawaii	4	80,000	25	51	4	2	27,000/yr.	5	10	78,500
Idaho	4	55,000	42	84	2	2	8,000/yr.	5	6	62,737
Illinois	4	93,266	59	118	4–2	2	35,661/yr.	7	10	93,266
Indiana	4(c)	77,200	50	100	4	2	11,600/yr.	5	2/10	66,000
Iowa	4	70,000	50	100	4	2	14,600/yr.	9	8	65,200
Kansas	4	65,000	40	125	4	2	120/day	7	6	59,143
Kentucky	4(a)	69,731	38	100	4	2	100/day	7	8	72,358
Louisiana	4	73,440	39	105	4	4	16,800/yr.	7	10	66,566
Maine	4	70,000	33	151	2	2	16,500/2 yrs.	7	7	77,300
Maryland	4(c)	85,000	47	141	4	4	24,000/yr.	7	10	86,900
Massachusetts	4	85,000	40	160	2	2	39,040/yr.	7	Life	65,000
Michigan	4	106,690	38	110	4	2	45,450/yr.	7	8	106,610
Minnesota	4	91,460	67	134	4	2	22,244/yr.	9	6	73,981
Mississippi	4(a)	63,000	52	122	4	4	10,000/sess.	9	8	59,000
Missouri	4(c)	83,790	34	163	4	2	21,211/yr.	7	12	81,009
Montana	4	50,452	50	100	4	2	59.12/day	6	8	50,452
Nebraska	4(c)	58,000	49	—	4	—	4,800/yr.	7	6	49,764
Nevada	4	77,500	21	42	4	2	7,800/2 yrs.	5	6	73,500
New Hampshire	2	72,146	24	375-400	2	2	200/2 yrs.	5	to age 70	70,102
New Jersey	4(c)	85,000	40	80	4	2	35,000/yr.	7	7	93,000
New Mexico	4(a)	63,000	42	70	4	2	75/day	5	8	60,375
New York	4	130,000	61	150	2	2	57,500/yr.	7	14	115,000
North Carolina	4(b)	109,728	50	120	2	2	11,124/yr.	7	8	81,348
North Dakota	4	60,862	53	106	4	2	90/day	5	10	59,140
Ohio	4	65,000	33	99	4	2	36,500/yr.	7	6	83,250
Oklahoma	4	70,000	48	101	4	2	32,000/yr.	9	6	71,406
Oregon	4(c)	75,000	30	60	4	2	9,300/yr.	7	6	74,172
Pennsylvania	4(c)	105,000	50	203	4	2	47,000/yr.	7	10	91,500
Rhode Island	2	49,900	50	100	2	2	5/day	5	(d)	90,697
South Carolina	4(a)	84,897	46	124	4	2	10,000/yr.	5	10	83,883
South Dakota	4(c)	60,816	35	70	2	2	8,000/2 yrs.	5	8	58,684
Tennessee	4	85,000	33	99	4	2	16,500/yr.	5	8	60,000
Texas	4	91,600	31	150	4	2	7,220/yr.	9	9	79,310
Utah	4	60,000	29	75	4	2	65/day	5	10	64,000
Vermont	2	71,200	30	150	2	2	340/week	5	6	63,900
Virginia	4(a)	108,000	40	100	4	2	18,000/yr.	7	12	94,907
Washington	4	93,900	49	98	4	2	15,000/yr.	9	6	82,700
West Virginia	4	72,000	34	100	4	2	7,200/yr.	5	12	55,000
Wisconsin	4	86,149	33	99	4	2	31,236/yr.	7	10	76,859
Wyoming	4	70,000	30	62	4	2	60/day	5	8	63,500

(a) Cannot succeed self in office.
(b) May serve only two terms, consecutive or otherwise.
(c) May not serve third consecutive term.
(d) Term of good behavior.
Source: Adapted from *Information Please Almanac*.

dent, governors propose legislative programs and work for their passage. They "rally the troops" to defeat bills they dislike and veto those that pass over their objections. Governors support their programs with speeches and interviews that receive widespread attention in the media. If public pressure does not produce results, governors turn to the standard techniques of political persuasion. They call up supporters and opponents to promise rewards and threaten reprisals. Plenty of useful politicking gets done during meetings at the governor's mansion.

Governors also serve on influential state boards. These seldom-seen but important bodies regulate higher education, the penal system, corporations, state hospitals, and other state agencies. In an emergency, all governors can call their legislatures into special sessions to deal with pressing public issues.

The yearly state budget is a key part of every governor's program. When governors set spending goals, they also are setting state priorities. All but three states give the governor the right to prepare the state budget before it is sent to the legislature. In 43 states the governors possess a power denied to the President—the *item veto*. This means that they may strike out individual items from the budget without rejecting the whole budget. A few states allow the governor to reduce amounts as well as to eliminate specific appropriations.

Administrative responsibilities. No governor possesses the total executive authority given to the President. Most governors share their administrative tasks with other state officials. Governors must work closely with their state attorney generals when it comes to law enforcement, for example. Even so, governors have the power to pardon or reprieve convicted criminals and to commute sentences. State laws on *extradition* (returning fugitives or suspected lawbreakers to other states) require the governor's approval before the transfer can be made.

Another source of gubernatorial strength lies in the power of appointment. Because many judges, members of state boards and commissions, and high-level administrators

■ A governor spends time promoting the positive features of a state. Governor John Ashcroft of Missouri has the happy task of rooting for two major league baseball teams in his state—the St. Louis Cardinals and the Kansas City Royals.

owe their jobs to the governor, they tend to follow the boss's lead. The states differ in the ways the governor's appointments are confirmed. Some states require legislative approval, others do not. Once appointed, officials can usually be removed only after legislative or judicial hearings.

REMOVAL FROM OFFICE

All of the states except Oregon have constitutional provisions for removing a governor from office by impeachment. In this century, a handful of governors have lost their jobs through this procedure. One recent example is Governor Evan Mecham of Arizona, who was impeached, convicted, and removed from office in 1988. A little over a fourth of the states allow voters to remove a governor by the recall, but only one governor has lost a recall election. As with Presidents, the wrath of the voters is usually withheld until election time.

OTHER STATE EXECUTIVES

Governors receive administrative assistance from a number of state officials. Some are elected and some are appointed, as spelled out in the state constitution. The trend has been toward a unified executive branch with fewer elected officials.

Lieutenant governor. All but a few states elect a lieutenant governor. This second-in-command official is elected at the same time as the governor and for the same term of office. Because people vote separately for each state office, they sometimes elect a lieutenant governor who is of a different political party from that of the governor. Indeed, it is not unusual for many of the top state offices to be divided between Democrats and Republicans. Most lieutenant governors preside over the state senate and serve as acting governor when the governor is out of the state. As acting governors, they may veto or sign bills, make appointments, and perform other official duties. If the lieutenant governor is from the opposing party, a governor often passes up out-of-state trips that would give the lieutenant governor a chance to make important decisions. The lieutenant governor succeeds to the state's highest office upon the death, resignation, or impeachment of the governor.

Attorney general. The majority of the states elect their chief law enforcement officers. Some political scientists say that the attorney general's office is the second most important in the state. The attorney general has three main duties: (1) to see that state laws are enforced, (2) to represent the state in court either as chief prosecutor or as defense attorney, and (3) to serve as legal adviser to state government. These high-visibility duties give attorney generals a lot of political clout.

Secretary of state. As chief clerk and recording officer, the secretary of state handles much of the detail work that is part of a state's official business. Most secretaries of state supervise elections, certify their results, and safeguard the state's official papers. They also issue certificates of incorporation, register trademarks, and place the state seal on official documents.

State treasurer. The state treasurer collects state tax revenues and pays bills that have been approved by the state auditor. The treasurer also banks excess state funds and supervises the sale of state bonds.

State auditor. States differ in the way they organize the office of auditor (or comptroller, as the office is sometimes called). Basically, an auditor examines the accounts of state agencies and authorizes the spending of state funds for legal purposes. The auditor also determines in advance whether the spending by state agencies is authorized by law. In about a quarter of the states, the jobs are divided between two separate offices. The official examining the accounts is appointed by the legislature; the official determining the legality of the expenditures is appointed by the governor.

Superintendent of public instruction. The superintendent of public instruction oversees the public schools and enforces the laws relating to education. Through their influence on curriculum, textbook adoptions, and teacher licensing, superintendents affect the instructional program in every school district. The states are divided when it comes to selecting their top state school officials. In about one-third of the states, the superintendent is elected. In others, the superintendent is appointed by the governor or the state board of education.

Let's review for a moment

Day by day, federal government officials grab most of the headlines. Many Americans take notice of their state government only when the governor or legislature does something they don't like. It takes an increase in the sales tax or a cut in school funding to arouse strong emotions.

Do you disagree with that view? Okay, name your state's top officials. Let's see, there's Governor So-and-so. And Lieutenant Governor What's-her-name. Oh yes, what about Attorney General Whozit? . . . Well, you get the idea.

You're also well informed on the latest changes in your state constitution, aren't you? If not, you're not alone. That's too bad though, because the state constitution is the blueprint for your state government. A typical state constitution contains many of the provisions found in the U.S. Constitution: separation of powers, checks and balances, a bill of rights, and a plan for organizing the executive, legislative, and judicial branches. The difference is that the state constitution is longer and has been amended more often than the federal constitution.

State authority touches your life in three major areas. The citizens of your state have given the government the right to (1) enforce the law and protect public safety, (2) regulate business and commerce, and (3) supervise the state's political subdivisions. Talk to a member of your city council, and it won't take long to discover that the state has its hand in many local activities. Your community's street maintenance, public health services, law enforcement, and tax collection are only a few examples.

The governor and other state administrative officials possess the executive authority. Lawmaking duties, of course, belong to the state legislatures. Let's see how they work.

4. What role does the legislature play in state government?

For most Americans, their state legislator is the closest contact they have with state government. State legislators must live in the districts they serve, and many manage businesses, practice law, or raise families there, too. Despite the importance of the position, many states pay their legislators poorly. Service in the legislature is considered a part-time job, and lawmakers are paid only for the days that the legislature is in session. Other states recognize the importance of attracting highly

qualified legislators and pay higher salaries. Most states also provide additional funds for office expenses and for travel and mailing costs. (The table on page 418 compares the salaries, length of terms, and other data for the top officials in all 50 state governments.)

ORGANIZATION

In a bicameral legislature, the upper house is known as the senate and the lower house is often called the house of representatives. A

■ Activity on the floor of the New York State Assembly, the lower house of the legislature, late in a legislative session. Sessions generally end with a flurry of activity as many bills are brought to the floor for a vote.

handful of states have named their lower house the assembly; a few others call it the house of delegates. Thirty-eight states summon their legislatures into session every year (including California, which holds two-year sessions). The 12 others meet every other year unless the governor calls a special session. Beginning in the 1960s, the Supreme Court issued a series of "one-man, one-vote" rulings—*Baker* v. *Carr* (1962), *Wesberry* v. *Sanders* (1964), and *Reynolds* v. *Sims* (1964). These rulings required that states be divided into legislative districts with nearly equal numbers of voters.

Leadership. The organization of a state legislature resembles that of the United States Congress. A speaker elected by the majority party usually presides over the lower house. The lieutenant governor presides over the senate. Both houses assign their members to a number of standing committees. Committee members write the bills that regulate everything from agriculture to taxes and from education to wildlife conservation.

State legislative committees play an important role in the lawmaking process. Most of the legislation passed each session is hammered out in meetings between the governor, powerful committee heads, and party leaders. In this system, with its emphasis on party discipline, the average legislator has little influence. Newly elected members soon learn the first rule of legislative life: If you don't cooperate with the party leadership, your own bills will never be reported out of committee.

Legislative councils. In the states that require legislatures to meet only once in two years, *legislative councils* (sometimes called interim committees) keep the work moving. Members chosen from both houses meet several times during the period between sessions

Learning Skills

Writing to Your Legislator

To many Americans, politicians are remote figures who might as well be living on another planet. Actually, politicians are approachable, and they want to know what their constituents are thinking. You can prove it by writing letters to the men and women who represent you on your city council, in your state legislature, or in Congress. Legislators welcome your letters, and they'll make sure you receive an answer.

Writing to a legislator isn't a difficult skill to master. Just follow these rules:

1. *Know why you're writing.* Outline your thoughts and arguments before you begin to write the letter. Do you need information? Are you upset about the potholes in the street that runs by your house? Do you want the legislator to vote for a particular bill? A good outline is the first step toward writing a clear, concise, and well-argued letter.

2. *Use your own words.* Legislators tend to ignore mass mailings of preprinted cards and letters. A personal letter, written from the heart, will receive more attention than a thousand photocopied letters from a special-interest group.

3. *Choose the proper legislator.* Write to the legislator who is most likely to be able to take action. Writing to your representative in Washington about potholes in a city street won't get the action you want. That same representative, however, would be a good person to answer your questions about a new child care bill.

4. *Be specific and be positive.* If you're writing about a bill, describe it by its proper name and number. If you want

to prepare legislation. A professional staff supports the legislators by supplying research data, writing bills, and scheduling hearings.

Direct democracy. More than 20 states allow voters to write and pass their own legislation via the initiative. A slightly larger number of states allow the popular referendum, which gives citizens the right to approve or disapprove a bill passed by the legislature. These forms of direct democracy (see pages 161–163) bypass or overrule the state legislature. People are most likely to turn to referendums and initiatives when the legislature has failed to solve a pressing state need.

PROBLEMS WITH STATE LEGISLATURES

Despite their power and influence, state legislatures are seldom held in high esteem by the citizens they serve. Some of the reasons are as follows:

Political games. Politics is the "name of the game" in most state legislatures just as it is in Congress. Members may speak their convictions on a particular bill, but party discipline almost always rules when the votes are counted. Stalemates often develop when the governor is of one party and the opposition party controls the legislature. If a compromise cannot be worked out, the legislation dies or emerges in a weakened form.

Nonparty splits. Legislatures frequently are split by north vs. south, liberal vs. conservative, or rural vs. urban conflicts. The differences may also split both political parties and lead to a stalemate in the legislative process. For example, urban lawmakers may refuse to support farm programs, and rural lawmakers may retaliate by refusing to support needed metropolitan-area waste disposal projects.

---

information, ask specific questions. Present your arguments as logically as you can. If you're asking the legislator to vote against a new bill, point out the faults in the bill in an objective manner. Always ask for a response.

5. *Edit your first draft.*
draft quickly, following your original outline. Then read it over, slowly and carefully. Does it say what you want to say? Correct your grammar and spelling. You're not working for a grade, but a thoughtful, well-written letter gets more attention.

6. *Prepare your final copy.* Write your final copy in ink, or type it if you can. This is a business letter, so you'll want to include the date, an inside address, a proper salutation, and your own address following your signature. You can probably find the addresses of your elected officials in the phone book under "City, County, State, and Federal Government Offices." (Or call the League of Women Voters in your area.) Address your legislator by title or with the phrase, "The Honorable." A typical inside address and salutation would look like this:

The Honorable Pat Reynolds
House of Representatives
Washington, DC 20515

Dear Mr. [or Ms.] Reynolds:

Writing to your representatives doesn't mean that they'll always vote your way. Your letters will give you the feeling that you're taking an active role in the decision-making process. Isn't that what democracy is all about?

FYI . . .
A Year's Crop of New Laws

In a recent year, the California legislature harvested a crop of 1,504 bills that were signed into law by the governor. Some of the new laws were important, others affected only a few people. Useful or not, the laws reflect the interests, needs, and problems of the state. Here's a sampling of the new laws:

Anti-gridlock law. Drivers who block traffic by allowing themselves to be trapped in an intersection by a red light are liable to fines of $50 to $500. [AB 667]

High-speed trains. A commission will be set up to study the building of 300-mph magnetic-levitation trains to carry gamblers between Los Angeles and Las Vegas. [AB 1839]

Teenage drunk drivers. Judges can order convicted teenage drunk drivers to visit emergency rooms, morgues, and alcoholic treatment centers. The visits would show the young drivers the results of driving under the influence. [AB 1400]

Adult felonies. Any adult who induces children to commit a felony can be sentenced to seven years in prison. [SB 1053]

Foster grandparent law. Teenagers who commit misdemeanors will be assigned to a foster grandparent program. The foster grandparents will provide counseling and friendship. [AB 211]

Overdue child support. Single parents are allowed to collect overdue child support payments for five years after the dependent child reaches the age of eighteen. [SB 1380]

Slumlord law. If landlords refuse to make needed repairs and are convicted of building code violations, the courts may order them to live in their own run-down apartment buildings.

Freedom for water beds. Landlords may not refuse to rent to tenants who sleep on water beds. The tenants must provide proof of insurance against possible water damage. [SB 1645]

Animals in pickup trucks. Drivers of pickup trucks may no longer carry animals in the open bed of their trucks unless the animals are safely leashed. Working farm dogs are exempted from the law. [AB 128]

Help for business. A state hotline will be set up to help small business owners obtain advice on how to cut through state red tape. [AB 864]

■ Is it legal in California for this dog to ride in the back of a truck?

Lobbyists. Lobbyists and special-interest groups have won spectacular successes at the state level. Unethical lobbyists find it easy to "wheel and deal" when working with poorly paid, inexperienced legislators. The lobbyists offer special favors, investment information, campaign contributions, and even cash in return for votes. In addition, a state that receives much of its money from a particular industry (agriculture, oil, or aerospace, for example) is likely to enact laws favorable to that enterprise. Those states that have attempted to regulate lobbying have met with little success.

Last-minute laws. In many states, the end of a legislative session brings on a rush of last-minute bills. The lawmaking process, normally slow and orderly, moves faster and faster. Bills receive quick hearings and debate is held to a minimum. One study showed that the California legislature, racing the clock at the end of a session, passed laws at a rate of one every three minutes! Fair, well-thought out laws seldom come out of this chaos. Many of the last-minute bills benefit only special-interest groups.

REFORM PROPOSALS

Suggestions for improving the state legislatures have always been easy to find. The problem lies in putting reforms into effect. Here are some of the most common proposals:

1. Remove limits on the length of the sessions. A legislature can't do its best work when sessions are both short and infrequent.

2. Attract better-qualified legislators by raising salaries and benefits.

3. Enlarge professional staffs. Overworked legislators tend to rely on lobbyists because they don't have sufficient staff of their own.

4. Put an early cut-off date on the introduction of new bills. This will ease the logjam at the end of the session.

5. Enact tough conflict-of-interest laws. This will prevent lawmakers from introducing or supporting bills in which they have a personal financial interest.

6. Pass strict campaign reform laws. With a state senate campaign costing up to a million

dollars, many state legislatures have become "the best that money can buy." Candidates who accept large donations find that lobbyists expect legislative favors in return. Most reform proposals copy the federal model and call for public funding of campaigns. They also ask for limits on how much money a candidate can accept from special-interest groups.

5. How do the states use their powers to protect the public safety?

Protecting the public safety is one of the most basic responsibilities of government. Citizens expect to be guarded from the dangers of natural disaster, fire, and crime. In the United States, the law enforcement and court systems are usually run by city and county authorities. The federal courts take over when a federal law has been violated. In a number of areas, the state does play a direct public safety role.

STATE POLICE

The development of the automobile created a serious problem for local police. Small-town officers couldn't cope with the problems generated by heavy traffic and fast-moving criminals. An organization with a broader range of authority was needed. Using the famous Texas Rangers as a model, the states developed their own state police forces. Most state police are organized into two divisions: (1) A highway patrol enforces traffic safety on the state's highways. (2) An administrative authority coordinates law enforcement activities among local police forces across the state.

SPECIALIZED ENFORCEMENT OFFICIALS

Most states also support a number of specialized enforcement officials. These include fish and game wardens, fire wardens, weights and measures inspectors, and liquor control officers. Until recently, most of these officials went about their duties without wearing guns. As urban problems moved out of the cities, some forestry officials began carrying weapons and making arrests.

PENAL INSTITUTIONS

Managing the nation's prison systems is one of law enforcement's most costly and difficult jobs. Federal, state, and local agencies share the responsibility. Minor offenders against state laws are held in city jails, while those serving a year or less usually stay in county jails. Criminals convicted of serious offenses against state laws are housed in state-run prisons. Federal penitentiaries hold prisoners convicted of crimes by the federal courts.

Federal and state prisons hold over 600,000 inmates, and the number is growing every week. At a cost of up to $30,000 a year per prisoner, the total prison bill runs into the billions of dollars. More than nine out of ten prisoners are held in state prisons. As the number of inmates increases, prisons have become severely overcrowded. Packed into tiny cells and lacking adequate recreational facilities, the inmates often vent their frustration by starting riots.

Schwadron in *The Wall Street Journal*

"I sentence you to be put on a waiting list for a prison cell."

■ What to do about overcrowded prisons during a budget crisis and calls for tougher jail sentences is a major problem in many states.

Failure of rehabilitation. Until recently, the major trend in prison management was to replace punishment with *rehabilitation*. A successful rehabilitation program helps prisoners recover their self-esteem, learn new skills, and return to society as productive, law-abiding citizens.

Today, almost everyone connected with the criminal justice system agrees that current methods of rehabilitation aren't working very well. As former Governor Edmund G. Brown of California said, "[Prisons] don't rehabilitate, they don't deter, they don't punish, and they don't protect." For every 1,000 prisoners released from prison, statistics show, over 500 of them will end up behind bars again.

Some penologists (experts on prisons) urge that only the most violent criminals should be sent to prison. All other offenders, they suggest, should be kept within the community. They can be housed in halfway houses, social welfare facilities, drug treatment centers, and mental health institutions. Experiments that allow nonviolent prisoners to work at their regular jobs during the day and return to prison each night have been successful on a small scale. In a high-tech variation of this policy, prisoners go to work during the day but are confined to their homes at night. Instead of human guards, they are monitored by small radio transmitters that are securely strapped to their ankles. If a prisoner strays from home during the evening, the device alerts the local police.

Prison as punishment. Many Americans believe that prisons exist only to punish the guilty. Those who hold this hard-line view believe that public safety must be the first priority of law enforcement. They demand tough action to solve the problems of rising crime rates, soaring prison costs, and failed rehabilitation programs.

Conviction for violent crimes, the hardliners say, should carry an automatic prison sentence. The offenses most often mentioned in this regard are murder, rape, robbery, burglary, arson, and drug dealing. Since the parole system hasn't prevented repeat offenses, the argument continues, convicts should serve

■ National Guardsman directing traffic in downtown Charleston, South Carolina, after Hurricane Hugo struck in September 1989. In the background, crews clear downed trees from the street. The Guard patrolled the streets and enforced a curfew to prevent looting.

their full sentences. The hard-liners also believe that automatic sentences will keep the potential criminals from committing crimes. Released convicts, moreover, would stay "straight" in order to avoid a second, longer term in prison.

An equal body of research has been collected to support either side of this argument. As with many other social problems, no final answer has been found.

NATIONAL GUARD

Each state maintains its own National Guard. The members of the Guard train one weekend a month and two weeks during the summer so that they'll be ready for service in an emergency. Until activated for federal service by the President, each state's National Guard remains under the control of the governor. Although Guard units can be called to active duty at any time, state officials prefer to use regular law enforcement personnel whenever possible.

Critics point to inadequate leadership and training as reasons for not using the Guard during civil disturbances. A tragic example of the Guard's poor preparation was seen at Kent State University (Ohio) in 1970. Called in to control campus demonstrations against the war in Vietnam, inexperienced National Guard troops opened fire and killed four students. By contrast, many Guard units have performed well in wartime and during natural disasters. Governors often call on the National Guard to patrol streets to prevent looting after a city has been struck by a tornado, flood, or earthquake. During the summer of 1988, some National Guard units were called out to help fight raging forest fires in several western states.

6. How do states pay the costs of government?

State governments are no strangers to the rise in the cost of living. Increased costs for everything from salaries to paper clips have led to state and local tax bills that total hundreds of billions of dollars every year. Despite the need for more and more money, both the federal Constitution and the individual state constitutions limit the states' ability to raise tax revenues. States cannot tax imports, for example, nor can they borrow from foreign governments.

WHERE THE MONEY COMES FROM

States once counted on the property tax for most of their tax revenues. Today most of the money collected from property taxes goes to support counties, cities, and towns. The states now depend on other sources of income:

■ When states can't increase revenues by raising taxes, they turn to non-tax sources of money. State-run lotteries bring in millions, often to aid education.

State income taxes. Forty-three states—all but Alaska, Florida, Nevada, South Dakota, Texas, Washington, and Wyoming—collect income taxes from individual taxpayers. Forty-five states—all but Nevada, South Dakota, Texas, Washington, and Wyoming—require corporations to pay a tax on their profits. Income and corporation taxes make up almost 40 percent of the revenues collected by the states. Like the federal income tax, state income taxes are usually progressive—the rates increase as the taxpayer's net income increases. Unlike federal taxes, the rates vary widely from state to state. Pennsylvania charges a flat rate of 2.35 percent on all taxable income, for example, while New York collects a maximum rate of 13.75 percent.

State sales tax. The single most important source of tax revenue for the states is the *general sales tax.* Forty-five states collect this tax, which levies a fixed percentage on most retail sales. Some consumer items are usually exempted from the tax—food and medicine, for example. All states also levy *selective sales taxes* on items such as gasoline, tobacco products, and alcoholic beverages. Because everyone pays the same percentage, economists call the sales tax a regressive tax. The lower-income family pays the same tax on a new television set as does the wealthy family.

Sales taxes are popular with state officials for two reasons. First, they're easy to collect. Second, the state can accurately predict the amount of money the tax will produce. Such knowledge helps state officials plan their budgets more realistically.

Other state revenues. The states have been quite successful in finding additional ways to balance their budgets. Some of the other sources of revenue include vehicle registration and license fees, inheritance and estate taxes, business license fees, and tolls on bridges and roads. Most states also take in revenue from state-operated industries (liquor stores, bus lines, harbor facilities, and the like) and gambling (casinos, pari-mutuel betting, and lotteries). More than half of the states have gone into the lottery business.

Federal contributions. The federal government supports state budgets with tens of billions of dollars annually. Federal money is often earmarked for particular projects. The most common federal grants are for freeways, urban renewal, housing projects, hospital construction, improvement of law enforcement, education, and social welfare programs.

State borrowing. A number of states sell bonds as a means of raising the money needed to build schools, highways, and other major construction projects. Other states must operate on a "pay-as-you-go" basis because their constitutions prohibit borrowing.

WHERE THE MONEY GOES

More than half of every state tax dollar returns to the cities and counties. This money supports essential services such as courts, schools, health clinics and hospitals, social welfare, housing, recreation, and public roads. The largest category in the budget is for education, although the amount spent on welfare programs is the fastest growing part of the budget.

About a third of each state tax dollar pays for programs that are administered directly by the state. These include the costs of governing the state plus the maintenance of state hospitals, colleges and universities, parks, prisons, and other institutions. The remainder of the state budget is spent on construction of public facilities and paying the interest on state debts. A few fortunate states have enough revenue to set up "rainy day" reserve funds.

7. How do the states regulate corporations?

Like friendly enemies, the states and the corporations that do business within their borders play a constant game of tug-of-war. The states must collect corporate income taxes and protect their citizens from economic and environmental abuse by the powerful corporations. The size and economic strength of today's giant corporations make this a difficult task. Because they are so important to the financial health of the state—in terms of jobs as well as revenues—politicians can't ignore the big companies. Corporation executives can bring heavy pressure to bear on any legislature that attempts to raise taxes or increase controls over business operations. Despite the public's belief that most corporations are giant, multimillion-dollar businesses, the opposite is closer to the truth. Many corporations are quite small. These small enterprises are often formed by doctors and other professionals who incorporate themselves to gain tax benefits.

THE CORPORATION'S "MAGNA CARTA"

In 1819, Chief Justice John Marshall issued a landmark ruling in the case of *Dartmouth College* v. *Woodward.* Marshall's decision was later called "the Magna Carta of the corporation." The case began when New Hampshire passed a law that changed the private college's charter and brought it under state control. After listening to Daniel Webster's strong defense of his alma mater's independence, Marshall issued his ruling. He said that once a state gave a charter to a corporation (whether a college or a business), that agreement was protected by the U.S. Constitution. He reminded New Hampshire that no state may enact a "law impairing the obligation of contracts."

The meaning of Marshall's decision is clear: once a charter had been issued, the state's power to regulate a corporation's activities is limited. Court cases interpreting the Fourteenth Amendment expanded this protection by including corporations in the definition of the word "persons." Corporations have all the legal rights (except for political rights such as voting) that a state's citizens have.

HOW TO FORM A CORPORATION

Individuals who wish to form a corporation must obtain a certificate of incorporation from the state. This *corporate charter* is usually issued by the secretary of state. The charter describes the type of business in which the corporation may engage. The rules and regulations that govern a corporation's business activities are also listed.

Three general requirements must normally be met before the state will issue a charter:

Comparison of Corporation Revenues With Those of Five Large State Governments (1987)

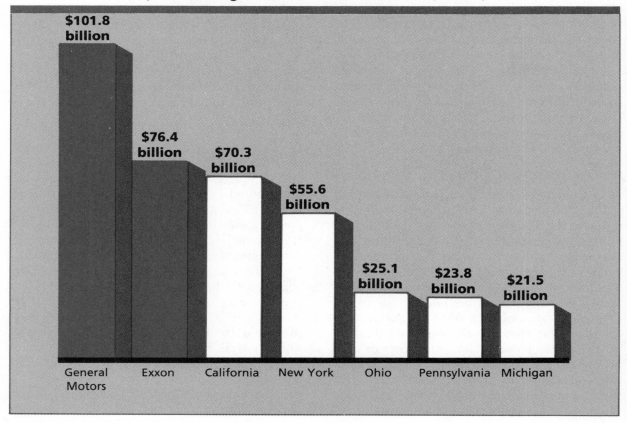

General Motors: $101.8 billion
Exxon: $76.4 billion
California: $70.3 billion
New York: $55.6 billion
Ohio: $25.1 billion
Pennsylvania: $23.8 billion
Michigan: $21.5 billion

(1) The corporation must have a legitimate and reasonable purpose. (2) The corporation must possess measurable assets, such as capital, a patent, land, or technical know-how. (3) Most states also specify the minimum number of people who may participate in ownership. Only after it has been incorporated does the business have the right to raise money by selling stocks and bonds.

Rules and standards for corporate behavior vary widely from state to state. A corporation with headquarters in one state may take out its charter in another state in order to benefit from the second state's more liberal laws. Once incorporated in one state, a corporation may operate in all states under the protection of Article IV of the Constitution.

ADVANTAGES OF INCORPORATION

Incorporation has a number of advantages. Most important, the ownership of stock in a corporation carries *limited liability*. If the business fails, the stockholders cannot lose any more money than they have invested. In addition, the corporation has a life of its own. Even after the founders die, the business continues. Finally, by issuing stocks and bonds, the corporation can raise the huge sums needed to build plants, develop products, and open new markets.

BENEFITS AND PROBLEMS

When a large corporation enters a state, it brings jobs, tax revenues, and the development of natural resources. These benefits must be balanced against the problems created by business and industry, such as traffic jams, pollution, and overloaded city services.

8. What is the role of a state in educating its citizens?

Every state constitution requires that the state pay for a system of free public education. Today, almost 50 million students attend public schools from kindergarten to university. The total bill for educating them (federal, state, and local expenditures) is approaching $300 billion dollars a year—the largest single item in state budgets. Education is a big business.

ORGANIZATION

Each state legislature enacts laws that govern the public schools of the state. These *education codes* pass on the day-to-day operation of the schools to various levels of local government.

Local school districts. In over one-half of the states, local school districts are the basic unit of school administration. A district usually serves an entire town or city, or it may spread across several neighboring towns. In some southeastern and western states, the counties are responsible for local education. Similarly, the northeastern states often give control of the schools to the townships. Only in Hawaii are there no local school districts. The state's Department of Education administers all of Hawaii's public schools.

Consolidation of school districts. As a rule, states encourage their smaller districts to consolidate into larger, more economical units. Because this trend has been strongest in rural areas, the little red schoolhouse has almost disappeared. Students ride buses to distant, more efficient unified schools.

Line of authority. Most states entrust the overall supervision of the public schools to a policy-making body called the state board of education. The board members are assisted by the superintendent of public instruction.

Their job is to make sure that local districts obey state rules on graduation requirements, compulsory attendance, textbook adoption, the licensing of teachers, and other matters. Even while the states are gradually assuming more control over the schools, local boards of education cling to a philosophy of *local control*. As a result, courses of study, discipline, and teacher salaries often differ greatly from one district to another.

FINANCING THE SCHOOLS

Schools receive financial support from three main sources: local property taxes, state appropriations, and federal funding. The amount of state aid to districts varies widely from state to state but averages about 60 percent of a district's budget. Federal assistance gen-

■ During the 1980s, federal support of education decreased by about $12 billion a year. States also have not had the funds to add to their education budgets. How do the consequences of underfunding affect our country?

erally funds specific programs, such as language courses for students who don't speak English.

The schools' critics have long complained that an accident of geography may determine the quality of a child's education. The revenue that school districts receive from local taxes varies with the value of the land, housing, and businesses in the community. Thus, a well-to-do district may be able to spend $4,000 a year per pupil, while a poorer district a few miles away may only have $3,000 to spend. Recent court decisions have ordered the states to equalize funding so that all of their students have equal educational opportunities.

HIGHER EDUCATION

In addition to its public elementary and secondary schools, each state supports a system of higher education. Out of over 12 million students enrolled in colleges and universities, four out of five attend state-supported schools.

Many states have established a system of two-year colleges (called junior or community colleges) as a means of reaching more post-secondary students of all ages. Junior colleges also lift some of the financial burden from the colleges by operating cost-effective programs for freshmen and sophomores. Students who transfer to a four-year college after spending two years in a junior college are less likely to drop out before they graduate.

Colleges of any type are expensive to run. State tax dollars must make up the difference between low tuition charges and the actual costs of a higher education.

ISSUES IN PUBLIC EDUCATION

No area in American life is free from problems. Public education, however, seems to attract an overload of critics and self-proclaimed experts.

■ A biology teacher demonstrating a scientific principle to students in a lab. School districts have to find funds to equip science labs, pay teachers' salaries, and finance all of the other expenses of providing young people with an education. Where do such funds come from?

Federal aid. The federal government has reduced its support of public education since 1980, but cutbacks have not ended the debate over this form of aid. Those people who oppose federal aid believe the money will lead to federal control of what the schools teach and how they teach it. These critics believe strongly in local control of their schools. They rally behind the battle cry: "We won't let Washington tell us how to educate our children!"

Supporters of federal aid argue that it will take federal money to give students in every state an equal education. Their argument makes more sense when the differences in state spending are compared. In a year when Utah was spending $2,455 per student, New York was spending $6,299. People who support federal aid also believe that Washington should pay for specific programs (computer education, for example) that the poorer school districts cannot afford.

Aid to church-supported schools. State legislatures regularly pass bills that authorize aid to church-supported schools. Typically, the bills are meant to help parents pay for tuition, transportation, textbooks, and other expenses. Just as regularly, the courts strike down the laws as violations of the constitutional separation of church and state. In a major exception to this pattern, the Supreme Court ruled in *Mueller* v. *Allen* (1983) that a Minnesota law was constitutional. The law allows parents to take a state income tax deduction for the costs of sending their children to any school—public, private, or church sponsored.

Religious groups make two practical points in support of state aid. First, they say, parents who send their children to church-supported schools also pay taxes for the support of public schools. Second, if all of the students currently enrolled in church-supported schools were to switch to the public schools, the system would be overloaded. Across the country, for example, almost 3 million students attend Catholic elementary and secondary schools.

Upgrading education. Recent books and government reports have blasted the public schools as a "national disaster." This concern about the quality of public education has triggered a long-running national debate. Supporters of the system admit that the schools are not perfect. They blame most of the problems on crowded classrooms, low budgets, and a society more tuned in to television than to the great books. Opponents blame the schools for low test scores, increased truancy, violence on campus, and other signs of unrest.

The problem began in the 1960s when many students rebelled against traditional school programs and discipline. The schools responded with the "new math" and experimented with more relaxed teaching methods. At the same time, the curriculum was broadened to offer a "cafeteria" of high-interest elective courses. Some of the courses were worthwhile, but many had little academic content. Today, discipline is tighter and the schools have increased their math, science, and English requirements. Test scores are rising again, and grade-conscious students are taking their schooling more seriously.

9. How does the federal government cooperate with state governments?

When the Founders of our country chose a federal system, they guaranteed that the national government and the states would be forced to work together. As the nullification and secession disputes of the mid-1800s show, federalism has not always been a peaceful process. In this century, the conflicts have been both general and specific. One major argument is over the federal government's use of *mandates*. The states complain that Congress never gives money without tying "strings" to the package. One common mandate, for example, spells out detailed rules for preventing discrimination in the operation of federally funded programs. Other disagreements have arisen over the ownership of offshore oil deposits and the division of tax revenues. In addition, the states have argued that federal antipollution rules are often unrealistic.

■ State and federal agencies worked together to direct the clean up of the oil spill in Prince William Sound in Alaska in 1989 and 1990. The incident pointed up the problem some states have with what they term as federal interference in the use of resources.

AREAS OF COOPERATION

Despite these and other disputes, federal-state cooperation has been achieved in two important areas.

Technical agreements. State and federal officials have worked out agreements on matters such as the regulation of interstate commerce and the sharing of research data. State and federal agencies work together on flood control, hydroelectric and nuclear power, sewage treatment projects, and joint law enforcement programs. Regular conferences bring state and federal officials together to share views and problems.

Financial assistance. Ever since the federal government began making land grants to the states in the late 1700s, federal money has been finding its way back to the states. Today, this aid falls into two categories: shared revenue arrangements and grants-in-aid.

1. *Shared revenue arrangements.* State and local governments cannot tax federal lands and programs. To help make up for this lost income, Washington shares its revenues for the sale or lease of its lands with the states, counties, and cities.

2. *Grants-in-aid. Grants-in-aid* are given for specific purposes—highway construction, unemployment and welfare benefits, and dozens of other programs. The states welcome the money, except for the mandates that Congress ties to the grants. These "strings" include limitations on how and where the money is spent, plus a requirement that the state put up a share of the costs.

Another type of federal aid known as *block grants* carries fewer strings than do grants-in-aid. Block grants provide money for a specific group (or block) of activities. Within that block, state and local governments can choose the activities on which they wish to spend their grant money. In the 11 years that Urban Development Action Grants (UDAGs) were available, for example, $4.6 billion in federal money helped create 550,000 jobs. The grants also attracted $27 billion in private investment to hard-pressed cities. UDAGs, along with sewage treatment grants and housing grants, fell victim to congressional budget cutting in 1988. Those cuts left Community Development Block Grants as the only program of this type left intact. The program was worth $3 billion in 1989 to cities overwhelmed by housing, waste disposal, transportation, and other problems.

TOWARD GREATER FEDERAL CONTROL

The long-term trend in federalism has been toward increased federal control. The two main reasons for this have been (1) the growth of the federal budget and the taxing power that goes with it and (2) court rulings that have consistently added to federal power. During the 1980s, President Reagan tried to "streamline" federal grants in order to reduce the number of mandates tied to them. For the most part, lawmakers resisted Reagan's efforts and added even more mandates to the grants they approved. In turn, the states have increased their own control of local government. Thus, political power in the United States has grown more and more centralized.

Should the nation attempt to reverse this trend? That's a question that American voters will have to answer.

Reviewing
what you've learned

1. The nature and powers of a state's government is defined by its constitution. All state constitutions contain the same separation of powers and system of checks and balances found in the U.S. Constitution. Most contain many provisions that the federal government would pass as statute laws. This situation reflects the people's distrust of state legislatures as well as the ease with which special-interest groups in a state can put constitutional amendments on the ballot.

2. State government touches the lives of its people in three major areas: (1) enforcement of laws regarding public safety, (2) regulation of business and industry, and (3) supervision of county and city government. From agriculture to welfare, the state administers and regulates the affairs of private citizens and corporations.

3. State governors perform many of the same jobs as the President. Elected for a four-year term in most states, they act as the state's chief executive officer, supervise law enforcement, promote legislation, take part in public ceremonies, and provide political leadership. Other important members of the state administration include the lieutenant governor, the attorney general, and the secretary of state.

4. The state legislatures, 49 of which are bicameral, are organized much like the U.S. Congress. A speaker elected by the majority party presides over the lower house, and the lieutenant governor presides over the senate. The committee system has grown in importance as legislation has become more complex. Some state legislatures meet only once during their two-year terms. *Legislative councils* carry on business when the full membership isn't in session.

5. Protection of the public safety is divided between state and local authorities. State government must (1) maintain a state police force and other specialized law enforcement agencies, (2) run a state penal system, and (3) maintain National Guard units for use in emergencies. As city jails and state prisons overflow with prisoners, critics charge that the penal system has failed to deter crime and *rehabilitate* criminals. They call for reforms that include speedier trials, longer jail terms, and an end to parole.

6. State tax revenues are drawn from a variety of sources. The most important are (1) state income taxes levied on individuals and corporations; (2) *general* and *selective sales taxes;* (3) miscellaneous sources, including license fees and state-operated businesses; (4) federal sources; and (5) state borrowing. Most state revenues go to support local government, particularly education, social welfare, the courts, and highways.

7. Once a *corporate charter* has been granted to a corporation, the state's ability to regulate the business is limited by the terms of the charter. Incorporation limits the liability of the investors in a business and enables the company to raise capital by selling shares of stock. States vary in their treatment of corporations. Large corporations bring more jobs and tax revenues to a state, but they may require increased public services.

8. Each state assumes responsibility for the free public education of its citizens. A state board of education oversees the curriculum and sets graduation requirements. Within the framework of a state's *education code*, each local school board runs its own elementary and secondary schools. State colleges and universities complete the system of public education. The business of education is complicated by disagreements over federal aid (and the loss of local control), state aid to religious schools (largely denied by the courts), and the need to improve education (lots of theories but no hard answers).

9. Under the federal system, the states work closely with the national government. Federal money helps the states finance many projects and services through shared revenue arrangements, *grants-in-aid*, and *block grants*. It also brings with it federal influence over decisions that many people believe should be made by state and local governments.

Review questions and activities

TERMS YOU SHOULD KNOW

block grants
corporate charter
education code
extradition
general sales tax
grants-in-aid
gubernatorial
item veto

legislative council
limited liability
local control
mandate
nullification
rehabilitation
selective sales tax

REVIEW QUESTIONS

Select the response that best completes each statement or question.

1. Most state constitutions (*a*) are shorter than the federal Constitution. (*b*) do not contain a bill of rights. (*c*) cannot be easily amended. (*d*) provide for three separate branches of state government. (*e*) do not mention schools, elections, or taxes.

2. The activities of state government have an effect on almost everything an individual does in daily life. This statement is (a) true. (b) false; state governments have little impact on individual citizens. (c) false; state governments affect only an individual's education, taxes, and safety.

3. To influence the legislature's action on an important bill, a governor could *not* (a) use the item veto. (b) hold press conferences and make speeches. (c) engage in political arm-twisting. (d) hold private meetings with key lawmakers. (e) issue a declaration that the law is unconstitutional.

4. Next to the governor, the most important state official is probably the (a) lieutenant governor. (b) attorney general. (c) treasurer. (d) secretary of state. (e) superintendent of public instruction.

5. The only way to remove incompetent or dishonest governors from office is to impeach them. This statement is (a) true. (b) false; the federal government can remove governors from office if the federal courts issue injunctions against them. (c) false; in some states a governor may be removed by a recall election.

6. You've decided to incorporate your computer business. Which requirement can you safely ignore? (a) You must have a good reason for incorporation. (b) You must have assets such as capital and equipment. (c) You must be doing business in at least three states. (d) You must apply to the state for your charter. (e) You must meet state requirements as to the number of owners the corporation will have.

7. The largest single source of income for the state is (a) the property tax. (b) the sales tax. (c) the individual and corporate income tax. (d) federal grants-in-aid. (e) state-operated lotteries.

8. The biggest single item in the budget of state and local governments is for (a) welfare. (b) public roads and highways. (c) the operating expenses of state government. (d) prisons and other law enforcement agencies. (e) public schools and state-supported colleges.

9. The advantage of incorporating a business is that no one can lose more than the amount invested. This concept is known as (a) securing a corporate charter. (b) limited liability. (c) issuing securities. (d) having the legal status of a "person." (e) corporate tax exemption.

10. Federal aid to schools is welcomed by many educators. Others object because they fear that federal money also means that the government will (a) take away their jobs. (b) force the schools to teach religious subjects. (c) gain greater control of school curriculum and policy. (d) impose higher property taxes. (e) all of these are possible outcomes.

CONCEPT DEVELOPMENT

1. Describe the organization of your state government. What are its strengths and weaknesses?

2. Why have Americans increasingly looked to Washington rather than to their state capitals for solutions to individual and community problems? Why do many people feel this is a trend that should be reversed?

3. Under the American federal system, divorce laws, voting procedures, regulation of business, and similar legal questions differ from state to state. Is this desirable? Why or why not?

4. From what sources does your state government draw its income? What are the major services it provides with these funds?

5. Most public schools are regulated by local, county, state, and federal government agencies. Which governing body holds the balance of power in your school district? If you had the authority, what would you change in your school?

HANDS-ON ACTIVITIES

1. Invite your local representative to the state legislature (or a staff member) to speak to your class the next time he or she is in town. Ask your speaker to describe a typical day in a state legislator's life. Some additional questions: What are the "hot" issues that face the current legislature? How does one run for office? What are the rewards of serving? What careers are available in state government?

2. Make a poster that compares your state with three or four states from different regions of the country. Make the comparison on the basis of (a) population, (b) per capita income, (c) amount spent per student in public schools, (d) governor's salary, (e) legislative salaries, and (f) any other factors that you consider important or interesting. Use illustrations with your figures to make the poster more attractive. An almanac is a handy source for this type of research (but be sure it's a current edition).

3. You may remember that this chapter describes the sales tax as a regressive form of taxation. In other words, rich and poor alike must pay the same amount of tax on most of the products they buy. Find out how many dollars your state collects in sales taxes each year. Now think of ways that this amount of money might be raised without using the sales tax. You might want to involve the class in the search. What about going in the opposite direction and cutting down on the state budget? What would you take out of the budget in order to eliminate the sales tax?

4. Discuss with your principal or superintendent the question of federal and state control of the schools. You might ask: How much money does your district receive from these two sources? How much control do the federal and state governments actually exercise? What future trends do the local officials foresee? Do they believe strongly enough in local control to pass up federal money? Report the results to your classmates.

18 Governing America's counties and cities

County (koun´tee), noun.   1. Obsolete except historically: an earldom.   2. In Great Britain and Northern Ireland, one of the territorial divisions constituting the chief units for administrative, judicial, and political purposes.   3. In the United States, the largest division of local government.

City (sit´ee), noun.   1. An inhabited place of greater size, population, or importance than a town or village.   2. In Britain, an incorporated town of major size having the status of an episcopal see.   3. In the United States, usually a large or important municipality governed under a charter granted by the state.

These definitions describe counties and cities without giving a sense of what they really are. Clearly, they're not just points on a map. These units of local government are real places where real people live and work and play. How well do they work? A modern Rip Van Winkle, waking from his long sleep, would find that technology has changed the way people live. Rip might feel at home in a rural community, once he learned to cope with today's machines. But a visit to a modern urban area—with its crime, pollution, and traffic—would likely frighten him out of his wits.

Are America's cities dying? It's true that they're in trouble, but the rumors of their collapse have been greatly overstated. Most people still enjoy the excitement, vitality, and opportunities of city life. But lack of money has caused many city governments to cut back on services.

> Kevin Roberts handed in his badge today. He's been a county deputy sheriff for only six months and now he's being laid off. His face shows a mixture of anger and bewilderment. "This is a rich county," he says. "How come it can't afford enough police officers?" The county's busy life pulses all around him, but Kevin doesn't feel it. "They can't do this!" he rages. "I'm a good cop. They need me!"

Kevin's right. The community does need him. Crime has become a major threat to the quality of life in many cities and counties. Along with countless muggings, burglaries, rapes, and assaults, Americans murder 20,000 of their fellow citizens every year. A climate of senseless violence leads people to lock themselves in their homes, afraid to go out at night.

Within sight of shining glass-walled skyscrapers, decaying slums fester in the humid summer nights. Well-meaning politicians talk about urban blight, but talk doesn't feed babies or mend broken toilets. The reality of the cities lies in the long blocks of grimy apartments where mothers keep a vigil for rats.

> Dora Jimenez knows a lot about rats. "I saw one the other day while I was cooking supper," she says. "At night, we hear them scratching in the walls. My little Gloria was bitten, and now she screams and screams whenever we put her to bed. My husband put out a trap, but it didn't work so good. The rat pulled it away with him and he died inside the walls. The smell made us sick. If we had enough money we'd move out of here tomorrow."

Dora's city and county don't want her to move. If cities and counties lose their inhabitants, they die. In order to keep their residents they're working hard to bring in the business and industry that create jobs and taxes. At the same time, they're beginning the expensive job of repairing and replacing the aging infrastructure—the roads, bridges, sewers, and other systems that make city life possible.

Their families think Carl and Teri Vitelli are crazy. After ten years of commuting from the suburbs, they've moved back into the inner city. "It wasn't just the lost hours on the expressway," Carl says. "I missed the excitement of the busy, lively streets I knew when I was growing up." Teri grew up in the suburbs, and the city used to scare her. Now, she says, she wouldn't dream of leaving the city. She and Carl have restored an old town house and have gotten involved in city politics. "We couldn't afford a house like this where we lived before," they say, "and everything's within walking distance. We feel more alive than we have in years!"

People like the Vitellis are proving the experts wrong. It wasn't too long ago that political scientists were predicting the end of county and city governments. Because the problems are too big for local agencies to solve, they said, state and federal governments will be forced to take control of local affairs. But county and city governments, large and small, have survived. In order to understand their problems and how they govern themselves, this chapter explores the following questions:

1. **What is the relationship of the county to the state?**

2. **How are the nation's counties governed?**

3. **What are the jobs of county government?**

4. **How do counties fund the yearly budget?**

5. **What problems face county governments—and how can they be solved?**

6. **What is the legal basis for city government?**

7. **What are the different forms of city government?**

8. **How are smaller towns and villages governed?**

9. **How do cities pay the costs of government and public services?**

10. **What are the goals of city planning and zoning?**

11. **How does the growth of suburbs create problems for the cities?**

12. **How do cities deal with the most critical problems?**

1. What is the relationship of the county to the state?

A state cannot possibly conduct all the business of government from offices in its capital. To solve this problem, the 50 states have been divided into a variety of smaller divisions to administer state laws, serve the public welfare, and guard public safety. The states have generally done this in two ways: (1) Permanent geographic subdivisions have been created to administer the law and provide public services. (2) State agencies have set up branches

Counties Vary Greatly in Geographic Size and Population

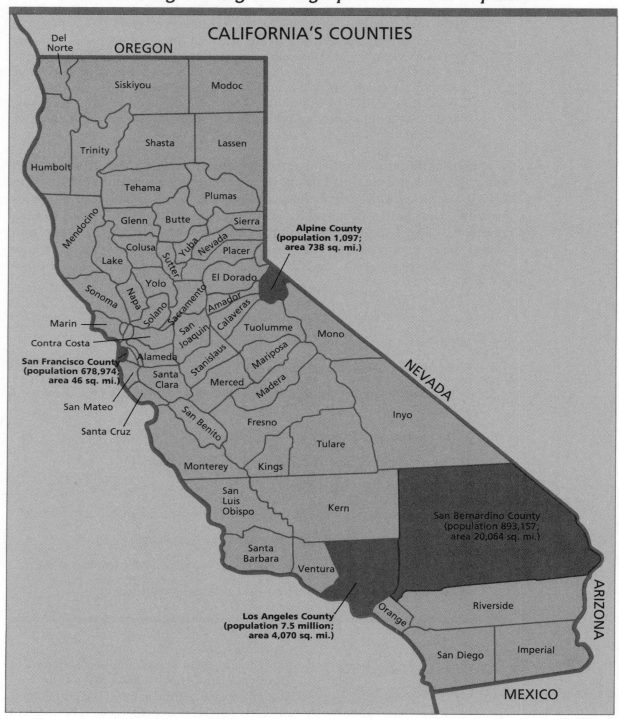

CALIFORNIA'S COUNTIES

Alpine County
(population 1,097;
area 738 sq. mi.)

San Francisco County
(population 678,974;
area 46 sq. mi.)

San Bernardino County
(population 893,157;
area 20,064 sq. mi.)

Los Angeles County
(population 7.5 million;
area 4,070 sq. mi.)

in the local communities. The Department of Motor Vehicles, for example, operates offices throughout the state.

These subdivisions are called *counties* in every state but two. Alaska is divided into *boroughs*, and Louisiana is made up of *parishes*. Connecticut and Rhode Island have counties but no county governments. The role of the county as a creation of the state was spelled out by Judge John F. Dillon of the Iowa Supreme Court in the case *City of Clinton v. Cedar Rapids and Missouri Railroad Company* (1868). "Dillon's Rule," as the decision is known, states that "Municipal corporations [counties] owe their origins to and derive their powers from the [state] Legislature. It breathes into them the breath of life, without which they cannot exist. As it created, so it may destroy. If it may destroy, it may abridge the control. . . . [counties] are, so to phrase it, the mere tenants at will of the Legislature."

Because their governments were created by the state, counties can exercise only the authority given them by state legislatures. That authority varies greatly from state to state. Earlier in this century, the states tended to ignore county governments while they transferred power to the cities. Today, many states are attempting to streamline and strengthen county governments—not always successfully.

HISTORICAL BACKGROUND

By the time the first colonists left Great Britain for the New World, British counties (or shires) had been established for centuries. Each shire was an administrative department under the national government. The title of county sheriff, for example, can be traced back to the medieval English "shire-reeve." Then as now, the sheriff enforced the law, guarded prisoners, and carried out the orders of the courts.

In the last century, many American political leaders began their careers in county government. New York's Tammany Hall, the nation's oldest political machine, rose to power by capturing control of the county courthouse. Later, when the cities increased in wealth and population, ambitious politicians shifted their attention to city hall.

NUMBER AND SIZE OF COUNTIES

The 50 states contain 3,041 counties. The number of counties per state ranges from 254 in Texas to three in Delaware and Hawaii. In geographical size, counties range from California's San Bernardino County (20,064 square miles) to New York County (22 square miles).

County population figures show similar contrasts. In the last census, Los Angeles County counted over 8 million residents in its 4,070 square miles. Cook County (Chicago), Illinois, bulged at the seams with over 6 million in only 958 square miles. At the other end of the scale, Alpine County in California's mountainous north has just over 1,000 people. That's less than two residents for each of the county's 738 square miles.

COUNTIES VARY GREATLY

Most counties are divided into cities, towns and unincorporated areas. People who live in the unincorporated areas look to the counties for services such as law enforcement, fire protection, and schools. When a city or town incorporates, it usually takes over the services formerly handled by the county. Small towns that can't afford their own fire or police departments often contract with the county for these services.

Some counties do not fit that pattern. A few counties, for example, consist only of a single city. The city of San Francisco and the county of San Francisco share the same boundaries. New York City, on the other hand, is divided into five boroughs, each of which is actually a county. The five are Manhattan (New York County), Brooklyn (Kings County), the Bronx (Bronx County), Queens (Queens County), and Richmond, or Staten Island, (Richmond County). In New England, each county is divided into townships, leaving no unincorporated areas within the county.

COUNTIES HAVE OUTGROWN THE HORSE AND BUGGY

Originally, state legislatures drew many county lines with the horse and buggy in mind. Lawmakers believed that county residents should be able to travel to the county seat, conduct their business, and return home the same day. Automobiles have replaced the horse and buggy, but counties have stayed in business to administer state-supported programs of education, welfare, recreation, library services, and many others.

Each county has a *county seat*, a town or city in which county government offices are located. In rural areas, the county seat still serves as the center of regional government. Historically, towns competed vigorously to be named the county seat. The town that was selected could count on more business as well as a measure of increased prestige.

A Typical County Government

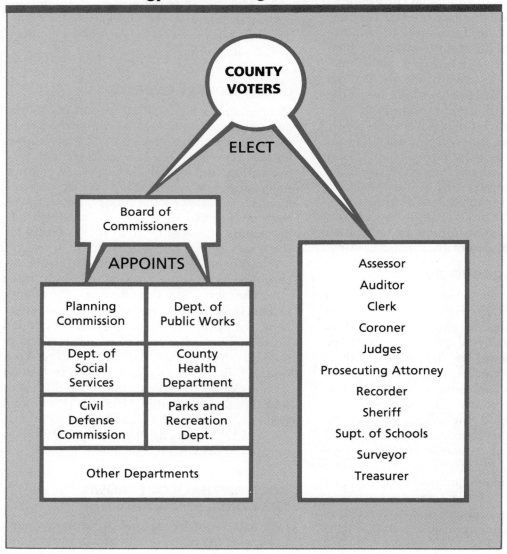

COUNTY VOTERS

ELECT

Board of Commissioners

APPOINTS

Planning Commission	Dept. of Public Works
Dept. of Social Services	County Health Department
Civil Defense Commission	Parks and Recreation Dept.
Other Departments	

Assessor
Auditor
Clerk
Coroner
Judges
Prosecuting Attorney
Recorder
Sheriff
Supt. of Schools
Surveyor
Treasurer

County Manager Form of County Government

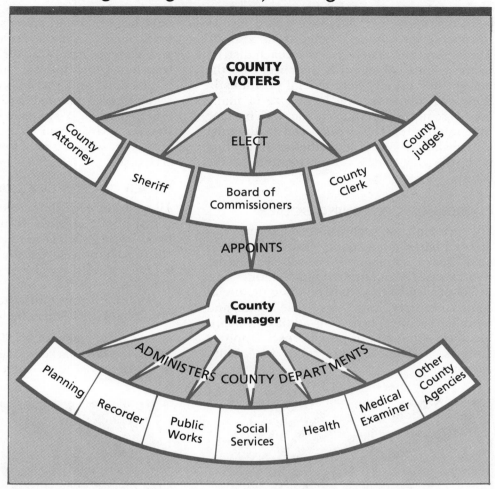

2. How are the nation's counties governed?

Unlike state governments, which tend to follow the federal model, county governments vary widely. Generally, they are administered by elected boards. Board members share the executive authority. Very few counties have a chief executive officer.

COUNTY GOVERNING BODIES

Most county governing bodies are organized as either a board of commissioners or a board of supervisors. In some counties, these boards are called by different names, such as levy courts or fiscal courts.

Board of commissioners. Over two-thirds of the nation's counties are governed by a *board of commissioners*. These boards are most common in the smaller counties of the South and West. Voters usually elect three to seven commissioners to terms of four years. In some states, each commissioner represents a specific district within the county. In others, the commissioners are elected at large by all the county's voters.

Board of supervisors. In about a third of the states, the counties are governed by a *board of supervisors.* A typical board has 15 members, but numbers range from 5 to 80. The supervisors are elected from each district in the county. Along with their work on the board, they usually hold official positions in their own districts. The large size of many boards requires that much of the work be done by committees. This works well in drawing up legislation, but is less efficient in dealing with the day-to-day administration of the county.

POWERS OF GOVERNING BODIES

The principle of separation of powers was ignored when most county boards were created. Board members often exercise legislative, executive, and limited judicial functions. As county legislators, they regulate the use of county property, levy taxes, issue bonds, and establish zoning laws. In addition, board members regulate business licenses, approve budgets, and appropriate funds for county operations.

County boards use their executive authority to administer the county's welfare programs, jails, hospitals, and schools. They also collect taxes, maintain roads, build county facilities, and keep records of births, deaths, and land transfers. Other duties include the supervision of elections and the enforcement of county regulations. A county board takes on a judicial function when it sits as a tax review board. Review boards hear complaints from local taxpayers who are unhappy with their property taxes.

OTHER COUNTY OFFICIALS

All counties need the services of a large number of public officials. In many counties, the majority of officials are elected in a general election. In others, just the county board and a few key officials are elected; the rest are appointed.

Some of the most important county officials (in alphabetical order) include:

1. ***County assessor.*** The assessor determines the fair market value for each property in the county. The property taxes that pay for

■ Storage rooms for records of deeds, usually related to the transfer of property. What county official keeps track of this information? Why are such records important?

■ A Dade County, Florida, sheriff's patrol boat. Why would such a craft be useful in southeastern Florida? What responsibilities does a sheriff's office have?

local schools, sewage systems, and other county services are based on this assessment.

2. County auditor. The county auditor (or comptroller or controller) oversees the county's financial affairs, issues warrants to pay its bills, and keeps its accounts in balance.

3. County clerk. This important officer serves as secretary to the county board and supervises local and general elections. As custodian of county records, the clerk issues marriage and hunting licenses, keeps trial records, and records divorces. Some clerks double as county business managers.

4. County coroner. The coroner conducts autopsies to determine the cause of death of anyone who dies under unusual circumstances. If evidence of a crime is found, a coroner may issue warrants for the arrest of suspects.

5. Prosecuting attorney. This important law enforcement official is often called a district attorney. The prosecuting attorney carries out criminal investigations, submits evidence to grand juries, and directs the prosecution of indicted suspects.

6. County recorder. Also called the registrar of deeds, the county recorder maintains property records and issues deeds.

7. County sheriff. Since most cities and villages have their own police forces, the county sheriff enforces the law in the county's unincorporated areas. The sheriff's office runs the county jail, carries out court orders, controls traffic, investigates crimes, and makes arrests.

8. County superintendent of schools. This official oversees the administration of the county's elementary and secondary schools. Unless a local school board is violating the education code, the county superintendent cannot order the board to follow any particular policy.

9. Other officials. Counties create other offices as needed. A typical county might also have a *county treasurer* to receive and collect county funds and a *county surveyor* to survey and record property boundaries. *Public health officers* conduct clinics, give inoculations, and keep health records. *County agricultural agents* spend most of their time aiding farmers, but they also give assistance to home gardeners.

3. What are the jobs of county government?

County government operates within strict limits set by the state constitution and state law. Even so, the county has been given a number of important jobs to do.

WELFARE

The people of the United States have always given the county the task of caring for the poor and needy. County officials coordinate their own welfare programs with those funded by the state and federal governments. Today, the county poor farm and workhouse have been replaced by Social Security, aid for dependent children, food stamps. rent subsidies, and other welfare measures. The escalating scope of these services has become the fastest growing and most costly of county services.

Neglected and delinquent children receive shelter in county juvenile halls or county-supervised foster homes. Most larger counties maintain hospitals for the mentally ill, the elderly, and the handicapped. Finding decent housing for senior citizens, low-income families, and the homeless is the newest problem facing the counties.

HEALTH

County health officers are concerned with disease control, clean air and water, and proper medical care. This burden may rest on a single doctor in a county with a small population. Larger counties usually fund a variety of programs, including free medical care for the needy, medical and dental education programs, public health nurses, and supervision of waste disposal.

EDUCATION

Programs for exceptional children (the physically handicapped, for example) often come under county control. The county's other educational services are usually restricted to advisory and teacher-training services for local school districts. The county office also distributes state aid and supervises each school district's financial business.

HIGHWAYS

Road construction and maintenance ranks second (after welfare) as the county's biggest expense. This is true even though the federal and state highway systems carry much of the traffic load. Counties often lack the money to improve their own roads. When this happens, the county board must ask the voters to approve road-construction bonds. County board members sometimes serve as road supervisors for their own districts.

ADMINISTRATION OF JUSTICE

The county is the basic unit within the state's justice system. Municipal and superior court

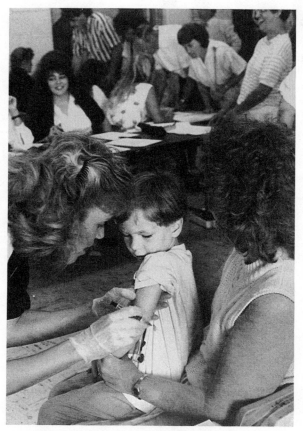

■ A public health nurse in Onondaga County in central New York State in 1990 giving an injection of gamma globulin to a child. The county held inoculation clinics to curb the spread of a hepatitis epidemic.

■ An annual event in late summer in many rural counties is the county fair. A popular attraction at the fair is the horse pull. This one is taking place in Wisconsin.

trials are held in county courthouses. The courthouse also provides other facilities, from juvenile hearing rooms to the county jail. Because crime does not recognize geographic boundaries, the sheriff coordinates county law-enforcement activities with state and city authorities.

ELECTIONS

The county plays a major role in state elections. It sets up precincts and wards, prints ballots, chooses election judges, and hires workers. After the election, county officials often collect and count the ballots.

TAXATION

Typically, counties are both tax collectors and paymasters. Many counties, for example, collect auto licensing fees with one hand and distribute state school funds with the other. Counties also collect property taxes, business and building permit fees, and sales taxes. Setting the rate at which property will be taxed is a difficult decision. The rate must be high enough to fund county operations and services, but it must be fair to the county's property owners.

OTHER COUNTY FUNCTIONS

Growing populations demand more and more county services. As a result, many counties now operate parks and recreation programs, airports, paramedic units, water and sewage systems, and public housing projects. The best-managed counties include all of these programs in their master plans for future development.

4. How do counties fund the yearly budget?

With annual budgets in the most heavily populated counties running $5 billion or more, finances have become a major concern. To manage this large-scale operation, a typical county government must make many tough financial choices. The board members levy and collect taxes and place bond issues before the voters. In addition, they equalize taxes throughout the county, negotiate salaries and benefits for county employees, and wrestle with budget problems. In order to balance the budget, the board may be forced to cut services, ask employees to do without a raise, or delay construction projects.

SOURCES OF COUNTY INCOME

The major source of county income (over 50 percent in most counties) is the *property tax.* Governing boards may not set tax rates as high as they might wish. Public pressure, especially during an election year, tends to keep tax increases under control. In addition, many states forbid the raising of property taxes above a legal maximum. Some states even divide the property tax into the maximum amounts that can be assessed for specific purposes. A typical tax bill lists these services, which include the general fund, roads and bridges, fire protection, libraries, schools, and payments on county bonds.

Counties also receive state and federal funds that support welfare, education, and other specific programs. Additional money comes from revenues shared with the state, such as sales taxes, auto license fees, business license fees, and fines collected for traffic violations and other court-ordered penalties. Some counties also operate toll bridges, harbors, and office buildings that bring in extra funds.

5. What problems face county government—and how can they be solved?

Many political scientists, economists, and urban planners believe that county governments are costly and inefficient. These critics charge that the counties are trying to govern a modern, urban society with horse-and-buggy methods.

Consider Los Angeles County: The five-member Board of Supervisors administers the nation's largest county government—300 spe-

THE PROPERTY TAX: WHERE DOES THE MONEY GO?

(A SAMPLE COUNTY TAX BILL)

County agency from which homeowner receives services	Percent of total tax paid for service	Average home-owner's yearly tax bill
County	48.49	$1,212.25
Schools	19.45	486.25
Fire protection	16.75	418.75
Public library	4.29	107.25
Community college	2.88	72.00
Local city services	2.07	51.75
Sanitation district	1.73	43.25
Flood control district	1.45	36.25
Lighting maintenance	1.28	32.00
Water district, road district, and sewer maintenance	1.61	40.25
TOTAL	100.00	$2,500.00

cial districts, 80 boards and commissions, and 53 departments. It takes over 70,000 county workers to keep this huge system running. Eighty-one cities and two islands lie within the county's boundaries. The cities range in size from Vernon (less than 100 people) to Los Angeles (over 3.4 million people).

Of the 8 million people who live in Los Angeles County, only 1 million look directly to the county for services. The taxpayers who live in each city within the county pay both city and county taxes. Because of this double payment, the taxpayers of the city of Los Angeles pay about 40 percent of the county's taxes. Despite the millions of dollars they pay to the county each year, these taxpayers receive few county services in return.

Similar county-city overlaps exist across the United States. These unfair situations aren't the only difficulties facing the counties. Some of the other problems are as follows.

UNDERPOPULATED COUNTIES

As population has shifted away from rural areas, many counties have been left with few people to serve. Counties with less than 50,000 inhabitants usually lack the tax resources to support adequate county services. As long as they exist, however, state constitutions force them to provide most of the services offered by wealthier counties. In order to provide police and fire protection, small counties have closed libraries, cut health programs, and laid off maintenance workers.

LIMITED AUTHORITY

Some state constitutions give the county governing boards too little power. These boards lack the authority to raise much-needed taxes, supervise elected officials, and enact the ordinances (laws) needed to govern the county.

LACK OF A CHIEF EXECUTIVE

Almost all county governments operate without a chief executive. This means that each member of the governing board has an equal voice in every decision. Government-by-committee often results in inefficiency, vote trading, and a general lack of coordination. A

■ A patron returning books to a library closed for lack of county funds. Because of an increasing budget deficit and lack of new tax revenues, Butte county in northern California cut back services in late 1990.

handful of counties have solved this problem by hiring a trained administrator to serve as *county manager.* These officials handle the daily affairs of the county under the guidance of the governing board. A larger number use a county administrator. These officials have only a limited executive authority, but they do improve administrative efficiency.

TOO MANY ELECTED OFFICIALS

When officials must run for election, they are less likely to accept discipline from the governing board. In addition, the long list of candidates typical of many counties is confusing to voters. Political scientists believe that abolishing or combining some offices would increase efficiency without harming representative government. They also support the county manager plan, which works best when most of the elected officials are replaced with appointed department heads.

DUPLICATION OF SERVICES

As the Los Angeles example illustrates, city taxpayers often pay double for police, fire protection, and other services. Attempts to consolidate services usually bog down in political power struggles between city and county officials. When there is an overlap, city and county governments should be merged. When that isn't possible, either the county or the city should cut back its activities in order to eliminate duplication.

NEED FOR NEW REVENUE

Rising property taxes have triggered a number of taxpayer revolts. The rebellion began in 1978 when California voters passed Proposition 13. Prop 13 limited property taxes to one percent of the 1975 assessed value. As a result, schools, libraries, cities, counties, and other government agencies lost up to 60 percent of their income. Contributions from the state made up some of the lost revenue, but many services (such as street repair and recreation programs) had to be trimmed. Similar tax revolts have taken place in Michigan, Connecticut, and other states.

Faced with limits on the amount they can raise from property taxes, counties need new sources of revenue. When they turn to the voters to ask for tax increases, however, they're usually turned down. People won't approve higher taxes until they're convinced that counties are spending their present tax dollars wisely. On another level, the counties want the states to end the practice of mandating programs that must be paid for out of county budgets. California counties, for example, spend 50 percent of the revenue they raise locally on mental health services, public defenders, and other programs required by federal and state governments.

HIGH ADMINISTRATIVE COSTS

A common complaint about counties is that their administrative expenses are too high.

Money that should go to welfare programs, the critics say, go instead to pay the salaries of a bloated county bureaucracy. In their own defense, county officials say they need the staff to produce the mountain of paperwork required by federal and state agencies. Experts who have studied the problem agree with this defense. In its effort to make sure its money is well spent, Congress often makes federal programs difficult and costly to administer.

Better coordination of all programs would reduce administrative costs even further. As things now stand, staff work is duplicated at many levels. A single national policy on medical assistance for the poor and elderly, for example, would clear out the present jungle of federal, state, and county programs. Everyone would benefit—including the taxpayers who foot the bills.

Let's review for a moment

Most people are much more aware of their city's history and government than they are of their county's. You never heard a song about Harris County, Texas, did you? Many of the people who live in Houston may not even know that it is Harris County that provides some of their civic services.

County governments were created by state legislatures to handle law enforcement, tax collection, and the like. Today's counties also provide welfare, public health, education, fire protection, and highway services. Who governs your county? Most likely, it's a *board of supervisors* or a *board of commissioners*. Both types of boards exercise legislative, executive, and limited judicial powers. Few counties elect or appoint a chief executive. The long list of officials who head the county's departments includes the assessor, auditor, clerk, coroner, prosecuting attorney, recorder, sheriff, superintendent of schools, and surveyor.

The *property tax* is the main source of income for counties. Other revenue comes from state and federal funding, vehicle and license fees, the sales tax, and court fines.

The counties are having trouble balancing their budgets, but state laws and voter resistance restrict their ability to raise taxes.

Critics say that many county governments are wasteful and inefficient. All too often, counties duplicate the programs being paid for by the cities that lie within the county. Counties also need relief from mandated state and federal programs that use up much of their tax revenues.

Now, where do the cities fit into the pattern of local government? Let's find out.

6. What is the legal basis for city government?

For most Americans, rural life exists only on the television screen. The great majority of people in the United States live and work in urban areas. City life provides jobs, shopping, entertainment, freedom, and privacy. Statistics show clearly that most of us will spend our lives in or near a big city.

Like counties, cities are established by the states. Mayors and city councils owe their power to govern to their state constitutions and their state legislatures. Despite this close legal relationship, cities do not always live at peace with state government. New York City officials, for example, have long argued that the state legislature favors upstate, rural areas when it makes out the state budget.

SCOPE OF CITY CHARTERS

A city holds the status of a legal corporation within the state. It has the right to acquire, hold, and dispose of property; enact ordinances; raise money by taxation; sue and be sued (under certain circumstances); and exercise the right of eminent domain. The source of this authority lies in the *city charter*, which defines the city's powers, its method of government, and the duties of city officials. In effect, a charter serves as a city's constitution.

All state legislatures have the right to issue city charters. At the present time, the United States has over 35,000 incorporated (char-tered) cities. Many of them are very small. Illinois has over 1,200 *municipalities* (towns or cities having the right of self-government), Iowa almost 1,000. Because state legislatures are protective of state powers, they have limited the rights given to the cities. By the same token, state courts generally interpret city charters very narrowly. Even so, the charters contain many of the same express and implied powers that are found in state constitutions and in the federal Constitution.

TYPES OF CHARTERS

City charters can be divided into five types:

General charter. Originally, states issued the same general charter to all cities within their borders. The needs of small mountain towns, however, are very different from those of large manufacturing centers. As a consequence, no state today issues general charters to all of its cities.

Classified charter. Some states group cities by population and issue classified charters to all cities within a particular category. Although it is an improvement over the general charter, the classified charter may cause problems for two cities of similar size but different economies. A St. Louis suburb, for example, faces urban problems far removed from those of a southern Missouri farming community.

Special charter. In a few states, the legislature issues an individual charter to every city that meets the legal requirements for incorporation. The special charter allows the lawmakers to design charters that meet the special conditions found in each community. On the other hand, it encourages the state to interfere in purely local affairs.

Optional charter. Some states write a series of optional charters that are geared to specific city needs. This type of charter gives a city the freedom to match a charter to its individual circumstances. Massachusetts offers its cities a choice of 5 optional charters. New York has 6 and New Jersey offers 14. City residents in these states are given the chance to vote for the charter that they think best fits their needs.

The Three Basic Forms of City Government

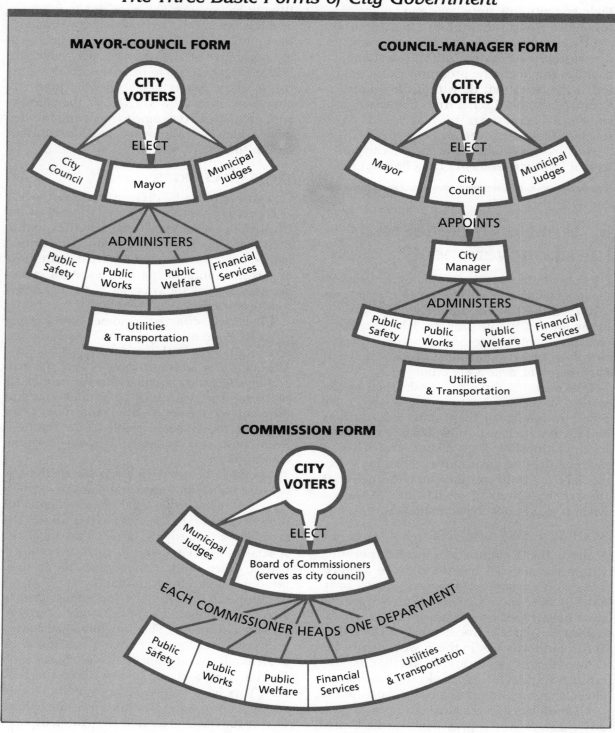

MAYOR-COUNCIL FORM

CITY VOTERS

ELECT

City Council — Mayor — Municipal Judges

ADMINISTERS

Public Safety — Public Works — Public Welfare — Financial Services

Utilities & Transportation

COUNCIL-MANAGER FORM

CITY VOTERS

ELECT

Mayor — City Council — Municipal Judges

APPOINTS

City Manager

ADMINISTERS

Public Safety — Public Works — Public Welfare — Financial Services

Utilities & Transportation

COMMISSION FORM

CITY VOTERS

ELECT

Municipal Judges — Board of Commissioners (serves as city council)

EACH COMMISSIONER HEADS ONE DEPARTMENT

Public Safety — Public Works — Public Welfare — Financial Services — Utilities & Transportation

Home rule charter. Three-fourths of the states now give each qualified city the chance to write, adopt, and amend its own charter. The home rule charter allows the people of a community to create a form of city government best suited to local conditions. In some of these states, a city must have a minimum population to qualify for *home rule*. California, for instance, requires a population of at least 3,500.

7. What are the different forms of city government?

Most of the large cities in the United States have a system of government that falls into one of three general categories:

MAYOR-COUNCIL FORM

The *mayor-council system* is the oldest form of city government and the most widely used. It provides a separation of powers similar to the system found in the federal model. The mayor administers the daily affairs of city government and enforces the *ordinances* (city laws) passed by the council. As the city's legislators, the council members hold hearings, write and pass ordinances, and establish city policy. The mayor and the council are popularly elected. The voters in each of the city's council districts select their own representative for a term that runs from two to four years. The mayor runs for election "at large" (as a representative of the entire city).

This form of city government permits wide variations in the power given to the mayor. Although they're not members of the city council, some mayors preside over council meetings and vote in case of a tie. Two variations on the mayor-council system affect the mayor's executive powers:

Strong-mayor system. Cities that use the strong-mayor plan allow the city's chief executive to veto ordinances, appoint department heads, and prepare the budget. Most big cities in the United States, including Chicago and New York, use this form of government.

Weak-mayor system. The weak-mayor form of city government concentrates power

■ Austin, Texas, City Manager Dr. Camille Barnett (left) conferring with Mayor Lee Cooke at a council meeting in late 1990. What do city managers do?

in the hands of the council. Weak mayors must share their power with the council and other elected officials. They can propose ordinances and lobby the council, but they serve mainly as ceremonial figures. Political scientists believe that this plan spreads decision making too widely. If something goes wrong, it's hard to know who made the mistake. Good government can still result, as the city of Los Angeles has shown.

COMMISSION FORM

In 1901, a terrible flood nearly destroyed Galveston, Texas. Afterward, the residents wanted to reform their government so that it could take prompt, efficient action during an emergency. They also wanted a simple system that would place administrative authority in the hands of elected officials. The result was the *commission form* of city government. Under

■ David Dinkins (standing, in light suit, at right), the first black mayor of New York City, receiving union proposals from the director of the municipal union at the start of labor contract negotiations in the summer of 1990.

this system, voters elect commissioners (five is the usual number) who have both executive and legislative powers. As executives, each commissioner manages a major city department. As legislators, they each have an equal vote on the city council.

Responsibilities.   The council decides on the department that each member will administer. The five most common city departments are public safety (police and fire), public works, public welfare and health, financial services, and utilities and transportation. Some cities allow one of the commissioners to be named as mayor, but the office does not carry any extra authority. All decisions must be made by majority vote.

Pros and cons.   The commission form has three advantages: (1) the number of elected officials is kept to a minimum; (2) the commissioners have the power to act promptly; and (3) the voters know who is responsible for running each of the city's departments. The

disadvantages grow out of the fact that commissioners combine legislative and executive authority. If the members can't agree on an issue, no one has the power to make a final decision. In addition, like county supervisors, the commissioners sometimes rule their departments like medieval barons. Because they appoint many city officials, they sometimes profit from their own spoils system.

COUNCIL-MANAGER FORM

As urban problems grew and budgets soared, the need for trained, nonpolitical city managers became apparent. The *council-manager form* of government began in the South and is really a variation on the mayor-council system. A city that uses this method is governed by a strong council, a weak mayor, and a city manager appointed by the council. The city manager, who is often college trained in municipal affairs, replaces the mayor as the administrator of the city's departments.

Advantages. Thousands of cities, including half of those with populations over 250,000, employ city managers. The council-manager plan's chief advantage lies in the ease with which responsibilities can be fixed. The council sets policy, and the manager carries it out. Politics and administration are kept separate. In smaller cities, the reduced work load makes it easier for busy citizens to find the time to serve on the council.

Disadvantages. City managers often find themselves caught between opposing factions in the community. Political infighting on the council may paralyze decision making. Another problem develops when council members expect miracles from the professional they've hired to save their city. No matter how skilled, a city manager can't balance a budget when there's not enough money.

8. How are smaller towns and villages governed?

Many smaller communities govern themselves under the *township* form of government. This system started in New England during the colonial period. As small congregations moved out from Boston and other ports, they set up town governments that combined church and community influences. The people called their settlements "towns," after the English tradition. The term "township" became common outside of New England. People used it to refer to both the central cluster of buildings and to the surrounding territory. Early townships were irregular in shape and averaged about 20 square miles in size.

The township concept moved west with the

■ Direct democracy is alive and well in Massachusetts town meetings. These meetings give every voter a chance to vote on important issues. Once their populations rise above a few thousand, however, most communities are forced to give up this old and honored custom.

settlers, extending in a broad belt from the Atlantic Coast to Nebraska. Townships never took root in the South and West. Smaller communities in these regions usually remain under county control until they incorporate themselves as cities.

POWERS OF THE TOWNSHIP

The original townships had little contact with central government—the monarch and the royal agents. When the Revolution started, townships showed their independence by sending money to help the war effort. As the nation developed, townships became part of the governing system established under each state's constitution.

As a result of this development, townships exercise only those powers provided by the state constitution and by state legislators. The township's voters and their elected officials deal largely with local matters—roads, schools, welfare, and property taxes. In some townships, officials also administer public works and enforce local ordinances.

ADMINISTRATION OF THE TOWNSHIP

Where it still exists, the most noteworthy feature of town government is the *town meeting*. These assemblies, open to all of the township's voters, are one of the few surviving examples of direct democracy. Citizens are encouraged to attend an annual meeting, where they debate important local matters before voting on them. If the local Democrats or Republicans want to present a unified position at the town meeting, they hold a party caucus ahead of time.

The day-to-day government of a township rests in the hands of elected *selectmen*, or a board of trustees. This small group of officials does much the same job as commissioners or city council members. The usual term of office is three years. A town clerk often acts as combined city manager, recorder, secretary, and license clerk. Police authority is vested in the town constables, and a school committee oversees the schools. Many townships also employ a treasurer, justices of the peace, and road commissioners.

9. How do cities pay the costs of government and public services?

In the early 1980s, cities saw their budgets grow by leaps and bounds. After spending $838 for each of its more than seven million people in 1970, for example, New York City's budget more than tripled to over $4,000 per capita 20 years later for a slightly smaller population. City after city has come close to bankruptcy as expenses run ahead of revenues.

SOURCES OF REVENUE

Hard-pressed city councils make use of a variety of revenue sources. Like the counties, cities depend heavily on property taxes. The city council sets the rates, although its ability to raise revenue may be restricted by state-mandated ceilings. In addition, almost all cities collect a sales tax, and many levy a one or two percent city income tax. State and federal grants provide another important source of money, but the funds are usually earmarked for specific projects or services. Other revenue sources include taxes on public service corporations, city license fees, and income from municipal enterprises (water and power companies, bus lines, and the like), endowments, and trust funds. When it builds parks, storm drains, and other projects, the city bills local property owners for these improvements. A typical special assessment district adds $20 to $50 to an annual tax bill.

When state law permits, cities sell municipal bonds to finance expensive projects. Voters must approve the bonds before they can be issued. American cities have sold enough bonds to build up a total debt of over 100 billion dollars. Much of the debt is in long-term securities, which future residents will be paying off 10 and 20 years from now.

WHERE THE MONEY GOES

The services offered by city government differ little from those provided by the states or counties. Beginning with the largest expenditures, cities must budget for education, police and fire protection, sewage and garbage disposal, public welfare, and health services. Another important city responsibility is to build and maintain what economists call infrastructure: highways and roads, water and power systems (when not provided by private utilities), parks, and housing.

WHO SPENDS THE MONEY

The city budget cycle begins when the department heads submit estimates of their needs for the coming year. The city council must then perform a difficult juggling act. First, revenues must be estimated as accurately as possible. Second, spending priorities must be established so that the tax rates can be determined. These numbers are published in a

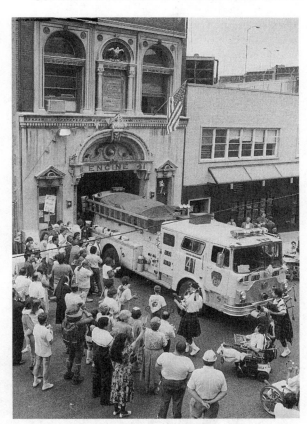

■ A city's efforts to trim the budget by closing underused facilities may be undermined by citizen opposition. Residents of the South Bronx in New York City reversed an order to close a firehouse.

■ Finding adequate funding for maintaining aging streets, sewer systems, bridges—the infrastructure— is difficult for cities. Here workers repair a broken 30-inch water main under a city street.

proposed budget for everyone to see. At this point, the city's special interest groups attend the council meetings to argue for their favorite projects and programs. Finally, the budget must be adopted. Ideally, the spending plan should provide the necessary city services and fair wages for city employees—all at a minimum cost in taxes.

10. What are the goals of city planning and zoning?

Life in American cities is a trade-off. On the positive side, cities offer convenience, cultural attractions, jobs, and choices. On the negative side, many cities have grown too fast, without plan or form. Too many people, too many cars, too much pollution—indeed, too much of everything except revenues—have overwhelmed the schools, sewage systems, roads, and other services. The job of city planners is to solve these problems before they destroy the attractions of city life.

ROLE OF CITY PLANNING

To combat overcrowding and unplanned growth, most large cities have set up permanent *city planning commissions*. The idea of planning the orderly growth of a community isn't new. Washington, D.C., for example, still follows the master plan designed by Pierre-Charles L'Enfant in 1791. Most city planning

■ A major challenge facing city planners today is bringing decaying central cities back to life. As part of that process, a planner shows off a model of a rebuilt downtown area to a city official.

commissions are small, with three to five members appointed by the city council or mayor. Many colleges offer special courses in this important field.

CONCERNS OF THE CITY PLANNER

City planners work in three broad areas: physical layout and resources, city zoning, and urban renewal.

Physical layout and resources. Planning for the future must take a number of factors into account. These include population growth, water and power needs, revenue sources, housing, and incentives for attracting business and industry. The problems of pollution, waste disposal, crime, and decaying inner cities also present planners with serious problems.

Zoning decisions. City planners rely on *zoning* as a primary tool in their day-to-day work. Zoning is the practice of dividing the city into residential, commercial, industrial, and other special districts. Every city in the United States of over 100,000 population (except Houston, where residents reject the idea) has adopted a zoning plan. Only specified types of buildings are permitted in a particular zone. In an R-1 zone, for example, property owners are restricted to construction of single-family dwellings. Restrictions on building heights, lot sizes, and other matters may also be included in the zoning plan.

Zoning hearings often spark vigorous public arguments. Any property owner has the right to apply for a variance to the local zoning ordinance. Zoning commissions hesitate to grant such requests because too many exceptions can destroy the entire plan. Political pressures increase when a zoning change would increase the value of a piece of land. The rezoning of farmland for manufacturing, for example, can make its owners wealthy overnight.

Urban renewal. Inner cities decay when businesses move out of the downtown area. The loss of tenants in the commercial buildings makes it impossible for owners to earn enough income from their properties to pay for taxes and upkeep. Decay in residential areas happens when once-handsome houses are subdivided into crowded, poorly maintained apartments. Other buildings are abandoned. Vacant lots fill with debris, and the streets fall into disrepair. The problem becomes a vicious cycle. Middle class residents move out, property values fall still lower, and the decay moves faster and faster.

To reverse this trend, *urban renewal* projects have become a common sight in many downtown areas. The rebuilding is financed by federal money, which Congress first made available in the late 1940s. Well-planned renewal projects fit in with the city's master plan, and private developers earn tax incentives for taking part. A typical renewal project rebuilds the central shopping area, preserves historic landmarks, restores decaying housing, and replaces the old structures that cannot be saved. The return of commercial life brings jobs, theaters, and high-rise apartments. The city profits from increased tax revenues and a new sense of vitality.

11. How does the growth of the suburbs create problems for the cities?

The map of a typical *metropolitan area* shows a central city surrounded by a jigsaw puzzle of incorporated suburbs. The metropolitan area of New York City, for example, has well over a thousand different political bodies. Each one has its own power to tax and spend. These smaller, suburban municipalities have grown more by chance than by design. They prize their independence and only rarely cooperate with nearby cities, large or small.

SUBURBS SHARE PROBLEMS WITH NEARBY CITIES

The suburban cities share at least three major problems with the central cities:

Urban problems cross city lines. Major problems (air pollution, traffic congestion, and unemployment, for example) don't stop at city boundaries. It does little good for a city to

■ This cartoon was created years ago. How many of the problems do cities still face? What does the cartoonist seem to be saying about the future of cities?

clean up the smoke from its factories if the oil refinery in a neighboring suburb doesn't take similar action.

Services are duplicated. Even though most suburban cities are relatively small and close to the central city, many maintain their own fire, police, water, and other departments. A single metropolitan-area fire department, for example, would eliminate one costly duplication.

Services are unequal. Metropolitan areas are often split into "have" and "have not" communities. These social and economic differences usually mean that the "haves" receive better city services than do the "have nots." Modern, well-equipped schools frequently exist within a few miles of run-down, grafitti-covered campuses in the central city.

Central cities are caught in a tax bind. Many people who work in the central cities live and pay their property taxes in the suburbs. While they're in the city, however, they demand a full range of city services, such as police and fire protection. The businesses and residents of the central city are forced to carry a heavier tax burden in order to provide services for commuters. Faced with escalating taxes plus a rising crime rate, traffic congestion, and other problems, more urban inhabitants flee to the suburbs. Some cities have partly solved this tax bind by enacting laws that tax the income nonresident commuters earn within the city. These taxes are often called nonresident taxes or commuter taxes.

PROPOSED SOLUTIONS

Five main solutions have been proposed for dealing with these problems. All involve far-reaching changes in the present structure of city and county government.

Annexation of suburbs. A number of cities have reached out to annex the surrounding communities. Jacksonville, Florida, has grown to a sprawling 760 square miles. Juneau, Alaska, the nation's largest city in land area, is bigger than Rhode Island (3,108 square miles to 1,212 square miles). Los Angeles covers 465 square miles but still takes in only about 30 percent of the population of Los Angeles County. By annexing suburbs, a city gains tax revenues from residents for whom it has already been providing services.

Annexation is a complex legal process, and the steps differ in each state. As might be expected, the residents of the suburb usually refuse to accept annexation by their giant neighbor. They may have problems of their own, but they generally feel a sense of having control of their affairs that big-city residents do not.

Consolidation of city and county. Where city and county have nearly identical boundaries, consolidation can end duplicate services and provide a better tax base. These neat accidents of geography seldom happen, however. Most metropolitan areas spread across several county lines. Voters, moreover, usually resist city-county consolidation as vigorously as they resist city-suburb annexation.

Forming special districts. Cities and suburbs have learned to join together in *special districts* in order to tackle area-wide problems. These special districts usually deal with a single public need—water supply, mass transit, hospitals, or a similar service. Each city and suburb in the district sends an elected or appointed representative to the governing board of the special district. A well-managed special district combines two vital ingredients for solving big-city problems: area-wide planning and a broad tax base. Once they're set up, these boards often conduct their business with little public attention. Unless they're caught in a headline-making scandal, board members may feel free to grant favors to special-interest groups.

Intercity cooperation. Some communities have combined to form metropolitan councils. The job of these councils is to combat common problems, such as traffic congestion, pollution, and crime. The federal government also requires intercity cooperation before it sends many types of aid to the cities. Through the intercity council, individual cities contract with their counties to provide services at a specified fee. This avoids costly duplication of services. Intercity cooperation breaks down when one of the member cities refuses to accept the result of a vote taken by the council. Since the organization has no legal power of its own, members cannot be forced to accept its decisions.

Metropolitan government. Some heavily populated areas have created a new level of government. Known as a *metropolitan system*, the new government takes over departments and services that are of concern to an entire region—transportation, sewage, traffic flow, and planning. City governments retain control over purely local affairs. Toronto, Canada, pioneered this ambitious concept, but it has not been widely adopted. Residents apparently fear that these "super-governments" will become too powerful for local voters to control.

12. How do cities deal with the most critical problems?

Ask urban Americans to name the six biggest problems faced by their city. They'll probably list crime and narcotics, traffic congestion, pollution, the homeless, breakdowns in public utilities and services, and uncontrolled growth. These are problems that threaten everyone's quality of life, and none of them will be easy to fix.

CONTROLLED GROWTH

Communities all across the United States are taking a hard look at the problems created by rapid growth. Builders are putting up too many office buildings and apartments, some community leaders say. They charge that no one seems to worry about the impact the new tenants will have on traffic, schools, and other essential services.

The *slow-growth movement* is a response to this problem. Typically, slow-growth supporters try to pass ordinances that put limits on new construction. In Lodi, California, for example, voters created a "green belt" around their community. No one may build on this land unless the project is approved by a public vote. Since 1981, only one project in five has been approved.

For their part, builders say that growth and development are natural forces that cannot be resisted. They believe that the slow-growth movement will smother economic development and lead to higher taxes. Opponents also claim that well-to-do communities are using slow-growth ordinances as a way of keeping out the poor and ethnic minorities.

TRAFFIC PROBLEMS

Most American city centers were laid out before the development of the automobile. Narrow streets and inefficient traffic control systems have not been able to handle the increasing number of motor vehicles that crowd

■ Traffic-choked streets cause great problems for cities. In an effort to unclog its roadways, Los Angeles, California, has opened the first portion of a 150-mile commuter rail line. The Blue Line runs between downtown Los Angeles and Long Beach.

into our cities. The resulting traffic jams cost more than lost time and strained nerves. The inability to move people and goods drives business out of a city. Freeways were once thought to be the solution, but they failed to solve inner-city congestion. Instead, they dumped more cars and trucks onto downtown streets that were already overcrowded. The resulting traffic jams cause delays, frayed tempers, and increased air pollution.

Traffic engineers now suggest a number of other solutions. First, they try to improve traffic flow by banning parking on major streets and by using more one-way streets. When money is available, they install computer-controlled signals and widen existing streets. Finally, they tempt motorists out of their cars with low-cost bus service. Computerized signals improved the traffic flow in downtown Los Angeles by 15 percent, for example, but most great cities still suffer from hardened traffic arteries.

Now, city planners are turning to *rapid transit* as the answer to the traffic nightmare. They are hopeful that monorails, subways, and other people movers will untangle the near gridlock by taking thousands of cars off the roads. New rapid transit systems have been built in Washington, D.C., San Francisco, and Atlanta, but dozens of others remain in the talking stage.

Rapid transit has been stalled by two major roadblocks. First, voters are reluctant to pass the huge bond issues required to build rapid transit systems. Because metropolitan areas sprawl over many square miles, a subway system can easily cost billions of dollars to build. Second, Americans don't want to give up the comfort and convenience of driving their own cars. Despite these obstacles, the federal government has promised to aid cities that want to build rapid transit systems. When federal budget cutbacks are made, however, rapid transit programs are among the first to feel the ax.

POLLUTION

Americans finally awoke to the problems of environmental pollution during the 1960s. Air, water, and noise pollution have all become national headaches, with no easy remedies in sight.

Air pollution. Breathing smoggy, polluted air has become a health hazard in many cities. Cities aren't the only places at risk, however. The New England countryside may look clean and peaceful, but millions of pounds of chemicals drift down on towns, fields, and woods every year. To make it worse, sulphur dioxide and nitrogen oxides from factory emissions combine with moisture in the air to create acid rain. The deadly rain kills trees, wildlife, and farm crops.

Water pollution. Industrial waste, sewage, and runoffs of pesticides and fertilizers are poisoning our waters. Lakes and rivers "die," choked with pollutants and unable to support life. Urban wastes wash onto the beaches and threaten the health of anyone who swims in the polluted water. Cities are limited in their ability to fight back. As with acid rain, the pollution often comes from far outside their boundaries.

Noise pollution. Cities are noisy places, and they're getting noisier. Jet airplanes shatter the peace of neighborhoods that lie under their flight paths. Jackhammers chatter during the day, and the roar of traffic is constant. The result is not merely a nuisance. Exposure to high noise levels can lead to increased stress, damaged hearing, and lower productivity.

Counterattack on pollution. Cities have won a few victories over air pollution by banning backyard incinerators, controlling factory emissions, and putting smog controls on autos. Other antipollution measures include the setting of stricter controls on waste disposal, the use of monitoring systems to enforce antinoise laws, and using the federal "super fund" to clean up toxic waste sites. Help has come from state and federal governments in the form of national auto emission standards and strict controls on the dumping of chemicals into drains and waterways. Regional agencies have been formed to combat air and water pollution that affect neighboring cities, counties, and states. The hard truth, however, is that many cities are running out of places to dump their household garbage, industrial trash, and toxic waste.

■ Cities have to monitor the bodies of water within their boundaries and those from which their drinking supplies come to make sure the water is safe to use. Stricter controls, education, and concerned citizens are weapons cities are using against pollution.

REGULATION OF PUBLIC UTILITIES

Public utilities (gas, water, electricity, and transportation) are a city's lifeblood. An electrical blackout or a cutoff in water service disrupts urban life as surely as would an epidemic. Some cities own their own utilities, but most Americans are served by privately owned utility companies. Cities allow these companies to act as *natural monopolies* (industries that do not lend themselves to normal competition). Letting two electric companies compete for business in the same town, for example, would only create higher costs. As monopolies, however, utility companies must accept government regulation.

A few large cities have local public utility commissions, but most utility rates and conditions of service are set by state regulatory agencies. Because the utility companies usually serve many cities, state agencies can do a more effective job of regulating them. Utility companies are less likely to exert improper influence on a state board than on a city board.

Most of the cities that operate public utilities also own water systems and bus lines. The record of these departments proves that city ownership does not guarantee efficient management or low costs. Well-governed cities tend to have well-run utilities. Poorly governed cities are more likely to find that their utilities produce more bureaucratic bumbling than they do kilowatts of power.

BIG-CITY CRIME

In the past two decades, the rate of violent crime has more than tripled. A typical year's crime report shows over 3 million burglaries, 7 million larceny-thefts, over a million stolen motor vehicles, about 20,000 murders, and countless drug offenses. It's easy to understand why many Americans are afraid to go out alone at night.

Why is crime increasing so quickly? No one knows all the answers, but social scientists point to a number of factors that contribute to America's crime rate. First, the

Learning Skills

Conducting a Survey

After you've been in school for 12 years, you know how to dig out information, don't you? If the assignment tells you to find the latest statistics on crime in the United States, you pull out an almanac or the *Statistical Abstract*. You know that the answers to most questions can be found in a reference book.

Here's another question: How do the citizens of your town or city feel about their local government? You won't find the answers in the library. This time, you'll have to go out and ask people for their opinions. By conducting your own opinion survey, you can do for your community what the Gallup Poll does for the nation. Here's how to get started:

Decide on the topic of the survey. Good surveys focus on a single topic. Let's imagine that you want the city council to spend more money on a summer recreation program. You know that recreation is important, but the council won't increase the budget. If you can prove that the residents support a better recreation program, the council members might change their minds.

Choose your subjects. If you're surveying recreation needs, you'll probably want to survey a cross section of all age groups. This means that you should choose subjects in direct ratio to the percentage they represent in the city's population. If one out of five persons is a senior citizen, then you should make sure that 20 percent of your subjects are older people. Age is only one factor to consider. Making sure you have a fair sampling from each neighborhood is another. You can add other factors that apply to your own community.

Write the survey. A well-written survey should meet the tests of clarity, fairness, and ease of scoring.

1. Clarity means that your subjects can read and understand the questions. Use short sentences written in simple, clear language. Test your questions before starting the survey.

2. Fairness means that the questions aren't "loaded" so as to obtain the answers you want. Here's an example: "The city council's neglect of the recreation program must

twin problems of poverty and unemployment are a major cause of crime. Teenage unemployment reaches close to 80 percent in some communities. When people are hungry and desperate, they may see crime as the only way out of their misery. Second, the nation's epidemic of drug abuse is another factor. Selling and using illegal drugs create a climate of lawlessness that spreads through all levels of society.

Third, the breakdown of family life and a general loss of respect for authority add to the problem. In an era marked by high divorce rates, political corruption, and ultra violent films, America seems to have lost some of its traditional values. Fourth, easy access to guns makes it more likely that criminal behavior will be violent behavior. Some teenage street gangs now carry more firepower than do the police. Finally, the chances of being caught and convicted of a crime are relatively small. Police officers complain that lenient judges return criminals to the streets faster than they can be arrested.

Coping with crime. Some crime statistics have fallen in recent years, but the criminal justice systems remains under attack. The federal government tried to help by pouring large sums of money into local law enforcement. The states built new prisons, and the stop. (a) Yes. (b) No." Most people, reading that statement, would assume that the council is neglecting recreation, whether it is or not. To "unload" the question, rewrite it to read "What areas of city life, if any, do you feel the city council is neglecting?"

3. Ease of scoring means that the results can be compiled quickly and accurately. Questions such as "What do you think of the city's present recreation program?" are easy to write, but hard to score. Every subject will write something different, and some will write several paragraphs. Multiple-choice questions are better. Write such a question in this way: "The city's present recreation program (a) is excellent, (b) is satisfactory, (c) needs improvement, (d) is terrible, (e) no opinion." With questions like that, you can compile the results from hundreds of surveys in a few minutes.

Administer the survey. After you've duplicated the survey, go out and administer it. Stopping people on the street is a hard way to go, and mailing your surveys is expensive. The rule is: go where the people are. If you know that you need a hundred children, go to an elementary school and ask for their help in filling out the survey. If you need 50 older people, try the local senior citizens' center. Be ready to furnish your subjects with a pen or pencil. Most people will be cooperative, but there will always be a few who won't take the time to help.

Compile and interpret the results. When you compile the finished surveys, you may have to throw out a few that are incomplete or that were treated as a joke. Once you've counted up the numbers, you have to decide what they mean. Perhaps you'll find that the only age groups that support a better recreation program are children and teenagers. Surveys, you'll find, don't always prove what you want them to prove. On the other hand, the survey may give you exactly the ammunition you need to sell the city council on that new summer softball league. With your numbers in hand, you won't be guessing when you go before the council to make your presentation.

cities used the funds for training, computer networks, and improved equipment. But arresting suspects is only part of the problem. Critics point out that it often takes as long as a year to bring an indicted criminal to trial. In addition, they object to the frequent use of plea bargaining by overworked prosecutors and judges. Plea bargaining allows the accused to plead guilty to a lesser crime if the judge will dismiss a more serious charge. Finally, convicted criminals are sometimes released early because of overcrowded prisons.

Reviewing
what you've learned

1. County governments were created by the states to handle law enforcement and local matters. Most counties administer a wide range of welfare, health, education, highway, law enforcement, and financial services. In recent years, the states have hampered county operations by mandating many special programs and by taking over some traditional county functions.

2. County governments vary according to a county's size and the laws of its state. The most common types are *boards of supervisors* and *boards of commissioners*. Both exercise legislative, executive, and limited judicial powers. Elected county officials usually include the assessor, auditor, clerk, coroner, prosecuting attorney, recorder, sheriff, superintendent of schools, and surveyor.

3. The *property tax* is the county's main financial support. Other revenue comes from sales taxes, state and federal funds, vehicle and other license fees, and court fines. Many counties are short of funds, but they cannot raise taxes because of voter resistance and statutory limits imposed by the states. Other problems facing counties are the lack of a chief executive, duplication of services already provided by the cities, and the existence of too many elected officials.

4. The rights and duties of city government are spelled out in state-issued charters. The *mayor-council* system, with its division of executive and legislative functions, is the most common. The *commission form* elects a board of commissioners who combine executive and legislative functions. In the *council-manager form*, a council and a mayor make policy, but administrative authority is placed in the hands of a trained manager appointed by the council. Many smaller communities have kept the *township* form of government. Its most notable feature is the *town meeting*, which brings citizens together to vote on community affairs.

5. The most important sources of city revenue are property taxes, sales taxes, license fees, and state and federal grants. The bulk of city expenditures go to pay for public safety services, welfare, street maintenance, and recreation.

6. Most large cities now rely on *planning commissions* to develop master plans for future expansion and an orderly development of services. *Zoning* regulations limit land use and keep residential, business, and manufacturing areas separate. With financial help from the federal government, *urban renewal* projects have rebuilt decaying inner cities.

7. The flight to the suburbs has left the cities with fewer taxpayers. To add to the difficulty, cities still must provide services for suburban commuters. To solve these problems, some cities have annexed nearby suburbs or have consolidated city and county governments. Others have created *special districts* that cross city lines to work on common problems.

8. The problems of rapid growth, the homeless, traffic congestion, pollution, regulation of utilities, and crime also trouble city government. Some cities are fighting the stresses that come with rapid growth by passing *slow-growth* ordinances. With traffic congestion increasing, planners are turning to *rapid transit* systems as one way to get cars off the road. Environmental controls are starting to make inroads on air, water, and noise pollution. Most cities allow private utilities to furnish water, gas, electricity, telephone, and transportation services. Because these companies operate as *natural monopolies*, they must accept city (or state) regulation of their rates and policies.

9. The increase in big city crime can be traced to causes such as unemployment, poverty, drug abuse, family breakdown, and ineffective courts. More police have been hired, and officials are using new law-enforcement techniques. Even so, the social and economic costs of crime are a heavy burden on the cities.

Review questions and activities

TERMS YOU SHOULD KNOW

board of commissioners
board of supervisors
borough
city charter
city manager
city planning commission
commission form
council-manager form
county

county seat
home rule
mayor-council system
metropolitan area
metropolitan system
municipality
natural monopoly
ordinances
parish

property tax
rapid transit
selectmen
slow-growth movement
special district
town meeting
township
urban renewal
zoning

REVIEW QUESTIONS

Select the response that best completes each statement or question.

1. The most common kind of county governing body is the (*a*) board of commissioners. (*b*) board of supervisors. (*c*) county manager. (*d*) county administrator. (*e*) levy court.

2. The county official who is responsible for establishing the value of homes and businesses for tax purposes is the county (*a*) clerk. (*b*) recorder. (*c*) sheriff. (*d*) auditor. (*e*) assessor.

3. A couple applying for a marriage license should go to the office of the county (*a*) clerk. (*b*) recorder. (*c*) coroner. (*d*) auditor. (*e*) assessor.

4. The fastest growing and most costly of county services is (*a*) education. (*b*) maintenance of roads. (*c*) welfare. (*d*) administration of justice. (*e*) recreation.

5. The main source of county revenues is (*a*) auto and business licenses. (*b*) state grants. (*c*) sales taxes. (*d*) property taxes. (*e*) court fines.

6. The type of city charter that permits a city's voters to write, adopt, and amend their own charter is the (*a*) special charter. (*b*) general charter. (*c*) classified charter. (*d*) optional charter. (*e*) home rule charter.

7. The form of city government that combines executive and legislative power in a single body is the (*a*) mayor-council form. (*b*) commission form. (*c*) council-manager form. (*d*) strong-mayor system. (*e*) weak-mayor system.

8. To get permission to build an apartment building in a single-family residential area of a city, a property owner would first go to the (*a*) city council. (*b*) mayor. (*c*) state senator or representative. (*d*) zoning commission. (*e*) police department.

9. Voters frequently turn down plans for consolidation of city and county services and governments because (*a*) they don't want to give up local control to regional governments. (*b*) these plans cost more. (*c*) regional governments may be unconstitutional. (*d*) no regional government has ever worked successfully. (*e*) none of these.

10. Rising crime rates can be traced to   (*a*) widespread abuse of drugs.   (*b*) a loss of respect for authority.   (*c*) unemployment and poverty.   (*d*) breakdown of the traditional family.   (*e*) all of these.

CONCEPT DEVELOPMENT

1. Describe the forms of government that exist in your city and county. How well do the systems work?

2. How does the system of property assessment work? What abuses are sometimes found in the assessment of private property?

3. What steps can cities take to cope with the problems caused by the flight of middle-class residents to the suburbs?

4. Why have communities adopted zoning ordinances? How has zoning sometimes failed? Find out about the zoning regulations in your community and make a report to the class on the major rules.

5. What forces have contributed to the dramatic increase in big-city crime? What should cities do to increase safety?

HANDS-ON ACTIVITIES

1. Do a little checking to find out if there is any duplication of services between your county and the cities within its borders. The most visible overlaps are usually in public services—law enforcement, fire protection, lifeguards, and the like. How much coordination and consolidation has taken place? Find out the full story by talking to city and county officials and then report to the class.

2. Attend a meeting of the governing body of your county or local community. At this meeting you will quickly learn a great deal about how government works in your particular area. Pay particular attention to the issues discussed and voted on, the roles taken by various officials, the amount of public participation, and the personalities of the board members. Write about your experience for the school newspaper.

3. The gap that often exists between young people and the police can be narrowed. One of the best programs is the "ride-along" plan operated by some police departments. A "ride-along" gives local citizens an opportunity to observe police officers at work by going on patrol with them. Call your local police to find out if they have this program. If they do, make an appointment to take advantage of it. If they don't, talk to the chief of police about starting one.

4. Make a poster showing the organization of your community's government. Show which officials are elected and which are appointed. Label each position with the name of the present incumbent. How efficient is this form of government? How could it be improved?

5. Many local governments allow 18-year-olds to run for public office. People just like you are serving on city councils, planning commissions, and school boards. Would you be interested? Even if you don't want to run for office, getting involved in a local election can be both exciting and educational. Watch for a chance to take part in your community's next election campaign. Local campaign workers will welcome you with open arms.

Unit Seven

Looking Ahead

Dr. Frances Kelsey probably did not think that she would be doing anything heroic . . .

19 Career opportunities in public service

▲ Dr. Frances
Kelsey receiving
an award for
keeping a danger-
ous drug from
being sold in the
United States.

For most Americans, heroism is something we hear about on the ten o'clock news. Very few of us ever have an opportunity to save lives or prevent disaster. Dr. Frances Kelsey probably did not think that she would be doing anything heroic on the day in 1960 when the application for a new drug arrived on her desk. Dr. Kelsey, a scientist employed by the Food and Drug Administration, picked up the papers and began her routine review.

The application came from the William S. Merrill Company of Cincinnati, Ohio. It asked the FDA to approve the marketing of a tranquilizer with the trade name of Kevadon. Following 20 months of testing, Merrill felt confident in describing Kevadon as "a very safe and effective new drug for the symptomatic treatment of nervous tension and insomnia."

Kevadon (better known by the generic name thalidomide) was first used in Europe in 1957. It was the latest in a series of tranquilizing drugs that were proving to be invaluable in quieting out-of-control mental patients. In addition, many otherwise healthy people had become dependent on tranquilizers as a safe way to ease the tensions of modern life. The drug companies' profits from the pills were huge and still growing. Eager to cash in on the bonanza, the companies pressed the FDA for quick approval of their new products.

No one expected the FDA to delay the issuance of a certificate for thalidomide. At that time, the agency had a reputation for close and friendly cooperation with the drug industry. Dr. Kelsey, however, refused to be hurried. After studying the test data submitted by Merrill scientists, she recommended that certification be delayed. Further studies were needed, she said.

Her decision rocked the agency. The drug company filed an appeal. For the next 14 months, the argument dragged on. Dr. Kelsey was bombarded by constant political and professional criticism, but she held fast to her decision. At the same time, a number of American doctors were receiving samples of thalidomide for testing on their patients. Of the nearly 16,000 Americans who eventually used the drug, about 200 were pregnant women. This was a fact the nation would soon regret.

Part of Dr. Kelsey's hesitation was based on a tragedy that had begun in West Germany in 1958. Hundreds of babies were born with their arms and legs shortened, misshapen, or missing. Deformed infants began to appear in other countries as well. A Hamburg University pediatrician, Dr. Widukind Lenz, finally solved the mystery in 1961. When taken by pregnant women, thalidomide caused "seal limb" deformities in their unborn children. Estimates place the final total of crippled infants at well over 7,000. Almost all lived in Western Europe.

Thanks to Dr. Kelsey's brave, stubborn stand, thalidomide was not released for general use in the United States. Some deformed babies were born here, but the numbers were few. In 1962, President Kennedy called attention to Dr. Kelsey's work. He awarded her the nation's highest award for government workers—the gold medal for public service. Later that year, Congress tightened controls on the experimental use of new drugs on humans. The 1962 amendment to the Food, Drug, and Cosmetic Act of 1938 stands as another of Dr. Kelsey's honors.

It's rare that a government worker has the chance to save us from a dangerous drug. But there are millions of unseen workers who safeguard our daily well-being. Among them are the flight controllers who guide giant airliners to safe landings and the meat inspectors whose USDA stamps tell us that our meat is safe to eat. Less dramatically, other workers process the paperwork that keeps the vast machinery of government moving. Whatever the specific job, public employment offers well-paid, interesting work that serves the general public.

Surprisingly, many job seekers turn to government employment only as a last resort. That's unfortunate, because your local, state, and federal governments offer a wealth of challenging jobs. To help you think about this possible career choice, this chapter will examine the opportunities, requirements, and rewards of government service. The following questions will be examined:

1. **What opportunities exist in government careers?**

2. **How does civil service work at each level of American government?**

3. **How does the system of competitive exams work?**

4. **How do colleges and other educational institutions train people for government service?**

5. **What are the advantages and disadvantages of working for government?**

6. **What are the pay scales and advancement chances in government service?**

7. **How do you apply for a government job?**

1. What opportunities exist in government careers?

If you're sitting in a typical class of 35 students, look around you. The odds are that five of you will become full-time government employees. Put another way, in the 1980s one out of seven civilian workers received their paychecks from a government agency of some type. Even though the rate of growth in government jobs has leveled off, public sector jobs will continue to provide a major source of employment.

GOVERNMENT EMPLOYEES ARE FOUND EVERYWHERE

Government service extends far beyond Washington, D.C. Not counting members of the armed forces, the federal government employs about three million people. The remainder of the nation's public employees work for the 50 state governments or one of the 83,000-plus state and local governing bodies. These in-

clude over 3,000 county governing boards, about 36,000 municipalities and townships, and over 44,000 school and special districts. Each hires an average of 160 employees.

You don't have to move away from home, therefore, to work for the government. California, for example, has about 1.77 million federal, state, and local government employees. By contrast, the nation's capital employs about 258,000 federal and District of Columbia workers. Think about the people you pass every day—letter carriers, police officers, fire fighters, sanitation workers, recreation workers, the secretaries at city hall. Each one of them is a government employee. So is your teacher, if you're attending a public school.

GOVERNMENT REQUIRES MANY SKILLS

Government requires the skills of many types of workers (see page 475). Over 15,000 occupational specialties have been defined at the various levels of American government. About

LOCAL, STATE, AND FEDERAL GOVERNMENTS HAVE OPENINGS FOR ALL KINDS OF WORKERS

The 60 jobs listed below are a sampling of the hundreds of openings you can expect to find posted at a government employment office on any given day.

City/County	*State*	*Federal*
Airport Operations Manager	Armory Custodian	Accounting Technician
Animal Control Officer	Agricultural Program Specialist	Aircraft Mechanic
Asphalt Worker	Automotive Equipment Standards	Clerk Typist
Assistant Librarian	Engineer	Contract Administrator
Clerk Typist	Baker	Correctional Officer
Crane Operator	Carpenter	Electronics Worker
Custodian	Chief Dentist	Family Advocacy Specialist
Electrician's Helper	Clinical Dietician	Film Processing Technician
Employment Counselor	Dental Assistant	Fire Protection Inspector
Floor Finisher	Duplicator Operator	Information Assistant
Laboratory Helper	Electrician	Management Analyst
Licensed Vocational Nurse	Groundskeeper	Mathematical Statistician
Maintenance Mechanic	Health Education Consultant	Meatcutting Worker
Pipefitter	Labor Relations Manager	Offset Press Operator
Plan Check Engineer	Mailing Machine Operator	Police Officer
Research/Lab Assistant	Nurse Consultant	Purchasing Agent
Sandblaster	Pharmacy Assistant	Secretary (Typing)
Senior Accountant	Programmer	Supervisory Engineering
Staff Research Associate	Psychiatric Technician	Technician
Welder	Senior Structural Engineer	Supply Clerk
	Toxicologist	Warehouse Worker

the same number of workers hold blue-collar jobs as fill white-collar positions. Along with the mechanics, the equipment operators, and the forest rangers that it hires, the federal government also needs engineers, computer operators, and lawyers.

The greatest increase in government employment came in the late 1940s, after the end of World War II. The population was growing rapidly, and the American people wanted more services from government. Federal employment kept pace with the demand. At the same time, state and local governments were also expanding. The increased hiring was partly financed by federal grants-in-aid and revenue-sharing programs. The days of rapid growth are now over, but that one-in-seven figure still makes government a major employer.

2. How does civil service work at each level of American government?

Hiring government employees was a simple matter in this country's early years. Presidents filled their administrations with loyal supporters. When the federal government was limited in size and authority (George Washington ran the United States with only a thousand federal workers), political patronage seemed to cause little harm.

By the mid-1800s, this "spoils system" had mushroomed into a national scandal. Corrupt political "machines" dominated the major cities. Government payrolls at every level were padded with political appointees. Many of them knew little more about their jobs than how to collect their salaries. By the late 1800s, as government grew in size, the dangers of the spoils system had become clear. Even then, it took a tragedy to convince the nation's political leaders that the hiring of government employees had to be regulated.

GROWTH OF CIVIL SERVICE

In 1881, a disappointed office seeker assassinated President James A. Garfield. The shock led to the passage of a federal civil service law, the Pendleton Act of 1883. From the beginning, the *civil service system* established two basic principles for federal employment: (1) job selection on the basis of merit (as determined by competitive exams) and (2) protection from political pressure.

When first enacted, the law applied to only 10 percent of the nation's federal employees. Major extensions of the coverage were added under Grover Cleveland and Theodore Roosevelt. By 1953, when the Pendleton Act was 75 years old, about 90 percent of federal jobs fell under civil service.

STATE AND LOCAL GOVERNMENTS ARE CATCHING UP

Caught up in their own politics, state and local governments were slow to follow the federal example. Today, almost all of them use some type of merit system as a basis for hiring employees. This development was speeded up by the federal government. Congress told the states to hire their employees on merit if they wanted to receive federal grants-in-aid.

All major cities and most smaller municipalities have full or partial merit systems. School districts, townships, and counties also have followed the trend toward hiring under a merit system. Fewer and fewer employees each year hold their jobs as payoffs for a political debt. By adopting merit systems, local governments also avoid the federal lawsuits that were common when they allowed discrimination to influence their hiring practices.

CONDITIONS OF EMPLOYMENT

The states and local governing bodies that operate civil service systems usually follow the federal example. Typical criteria for employment include open competition, equal opportunity without reference to race, sex, or age, and freedom from political interference. Some agencies have special rules, such as the requirement that employees must live in or near the city that employs them. Other typical regulations prohibit moonlighting on a second job and forbid the hiring of a relative in the same department. Miscellaneous rules regarding clothing, hairstyles, beards, or other personal matters may also exist.

3. How does the system of competitive exams work?

A person who wants to apply for a federal, state, or local job will normally be required to take a *competitive examination*. The process begins when the opening is announced through public notices. In cities and towns, the printed announcements appear on town hall, courthouse, and post office bulletin boards. Newspapers, radio and television stations, schools, employment offices, placement bureaus, and federal job information centers also publicize the date and location of the exams. Announcements can generally be found for both local positions and for state and federal jobs. Some of the state and federal jobs may require a move to another city.

READING THE JOB ANNOUNCEMENT

A typical job announcement provides important information about the job and the exam. If you read it carefully, you'll learn the job title and description, the agency that's seeking applicants, and the location of the position. You'll also discover the filing deadline and exam dates, the eligibility requirements, and a description of the exam.

Anyone interested in applying for the job should read the announcement with great care. Applicants who do not meet the job requirements cannot take the exam. Work experience and education are the two most common requirements, either separately or in combination. Specific skills, such as the ability to drive a truck or to type a minimum number of words per minute, are mandatory for many positions. Hiring agents are sometimes allowed to give credit for experience in unrelated fields. A background that includes service in the armed forces or volunteer work in the community would be helpful to an applicant.

BASIC REQUIREMENTS FOR APPLICANTS

According to federal regulations, applicants for most public service jobs must be at least 18 years old. All applicants must be American citizens. A physical handicap does not normally bar people from applying, provided they can meet the job's physical requirements. The government, in fact, is the country's largest employer of the handicapped.

Young people who leave school at age 16 or 17 can be hired only if they have been out of school for three months and have completed a specific training program. Some special programs provide summer work for students who are 16 or older. Part-time employment is available for a few high school students but only if they stay in school. The school must certify that they're keeping up with their studies and that they're attending regularly.

TAKING THE EXAM

If the job announcement states that a written test is required, the applicants fill out employment request forms. Civil service officials check the forms to make sure that the applicants meet the basic requirements for the job. The office then advises them as to the times and places where the exam will be held.

The most successful applicants are those who study for the exam. If you can't find a class at a local adult night school or community college, you can work from specially prepared guides. These guides review important information and provide sample questions similar to those that appear on the exam. You can borrow study guides from a public library or buy them at a bookstore. Those who fail the exam may retake it as long as the position remains open. Other applicants who pass may be disappointed in their scores. They may retake the test as long as applications for the job are still being accepted.

LIST OF ELIGIBLES

The civil service office tells the applicants whether or not they passed the test and what score they earned. Those who meet the minimum requirements are placed on a *list of*

(*Text continues on page 480.*)

CITY OF TORRANCE

TORRANCE, CALIFORNIA 90503

INVITES APPLICATIONS FOR

LIBRARY ASSISTANT
O P E N

FINAL FILING: Thursday, October 4, 1990 by 5:00 p.m.

SALARY RANGE: $2117 to $2706 per month.

BENEFITS: 100% City paid retirement (PERS) ● Family Health and Dental plans ● Flexible Benefit program provides tax free options for medical, dental and child care expenses ● $10,000 Life insurance policy ● 10 paid Holidays annually ● 60 hours Vacation the first year (vacation accrual rate increases with service) ● Employee Assistance Plan

POSITION: A Library Assistant performs paraprofessional and clerical library work; assists with children's programs, book reviews, audiovisual and cataloguing. This position also supervises subordinate staff and does related work as required.

REQUIREMENTS: Three years of full-time public library experience. College credit in the areas of English, history, general reference, introduction to children's literature, books for young people, storytelling, basic principles of cataloguing, or audiovisual may be substituted for the experience on the basis of 30 semester units OR three quarters for each year of the required experience to a maximum of two years.

EXAMINATION: The examination consists of a written test (weighted 60%) and an interview (weighted 40%). Factors tested in the examination process may include the following:

Knowledge of: Practices and procedures of modern library operations, including filing and indexing; the Dewey Decimal System; general information sources such as almanacs, atlases and encyclopedias.

Ability to: Read, write and comprehend library material at high school graduate level; follow oral and written instructions; establish and maintain effective working relationships with the public and follow employees; keep records and prepare reports.

TEST DATES: The written test is tentatively scheduled for Monday, October 15, 1990 with interviews tentatively set for Tuesday, October 30, 1990. Testing will take place at the Personnel Services Building, 3231 Torrance Boulevard, Torrance, CA.

SPECIAL NOTES: (1) Current permanent and temporary employees of the City may be given preference in certification from the eligible list resulting from this examination. (2) The City of Torrance Conflict of Interest Code requires that employees in this classification file an annual financial disclosure statement. (3) Handicapped applicants who require special testing arrangements must contact the Civil Service Department prior to the Final Filing Date.

9/12/90-59CG

CIVIL SERVICE DEPARTMENT, 3231 TORRANCE BOULEVARD, 90503 · (213) 618-2969
SEE APPLICANT INFORMATION ON REVERSE SIDE
EQUAL OPPORTUNITY/AFFIRMATIVE ACTION EMPLOYER

■ An announcement for a city government job

Federal Civil Service Announcements

A listing of competitive examination announcements which cover jobs throughout the United States unless otherwise noted.

Information about other Federal jobs not included in this listing or for which examining has been decentralized is available at local Federal Job Information Centers (FJIC's). Employment opportunities vary by occupation and geographic area. For full information on opportunities, salaries, application procedures, and **open periods for receipt of applications,** contact an FJIC. FJIC's are listed in major metropolitan telephone directories under "U.S. Government." Federal employment opportunities also are posted in State Job Service (State Employment Security) offices.

In most occupations there are few GS-14 and GS-15 level jobs. When vacancies occur at these levels they are published in Senior Level Recruiting Bulletins or agency vacancy announcements.

All qualified applicants receive consideration for Federal jobs without regard to race, creed, color, political affiliation, sex, or national origin.

Administration, Finance and Accounting

Accountant/Auditor, GS-510-5/9, competition notice CN-510, open until further notice.

IRS Agent, GS-512-5/11. Announcement IRS-01.

Farm Credit Administration Positions: Credit Examiner (Agricultural) and **Operations Specialist** (Agricultural), GS-1101-9/14, and **Association Auditor** and **Bank Auditor,** GS-510-5/12. Announcement 435.

Commissary Store Management Positions, GS-5/12, with the Air Force, Navy, and Marine Corps worldwide. Announcement AFCOM-2-01. **Commissary Store Manager,** GS-11/12, open entire quarter. **Commissary Officer,** GS-11/12, open entire quarter. **Commissary Management Specialist,** GS-11/12, open entire quarter.

International Radio Broadcaster, GS-1001-5/14. **Radio Broadcast Technician,** WB-3940-2. International Communications Agency, Room 1158, 1776 Pennsylvania Ave. N.W., Washington, D.C. 20547. Continuously open nationwide.

Medical and Health-Related Positions

Audiologist/Speech Pathologist, GS-556-9/12, competition notice VA-0665. Most positions are with the Veterans Administration. Open entire quarter.

Dietitian, GS-630-7/11, competition notice VA-0630. Most positions are with the Veterans Administration. Open entire quarter.

Pharmacist, GS-660-9/11, competition notice VA-0660. Most positions are with the Veterans Administration.

Engineering, Physical Sciences, and Mathematics

Professional Engineering Positions, GS-5 thru GS-15. See competition notice CN-800.

Aerospace Technologist (AST) Positions, GS-7 through GS-15, with NASA. Apply to NASA Headquarters, Personnel Policy and Program Management, NPM-28, Washington, D.C. 20546.

Physical Sciences Positions, GS-5 thru GS-15. See competition notice CN-1300.

Mathematics and Related Positions, GS-5 thru GS-15. See competition notice CN-1500.

Visual Arts, GS-5/7. Announcement 448. Slide portfolio and applications must be submitted. See announcement for details.

Social Science and Related Positions

Professional Librarian Positions, GS-7 to GS-12. See competition notice CN-1410.

Social Worker, GS-185-9/11. Competition notice VA-0185. Positions are with the Veterans Administration, Department of Medicine and Surgery only. Requires Master's degree in social work. Applicants should call before applying. Call: 1-800-368-6008. (Virginia residents call: 1-800-552-3045.) Or write: Veterans Administration, Special Examining Unit for OPM, P.O. Box 24269, Richmond, VA 23224-0269.

Professional Educator Positions, GS-5 thru GS-9. Competition Notice CN-1710. May open during the quarter. See CN-1710 for details and application procedures.

■ An announcement for federal government jobs

eligibles. The applicants with the highest scores are placed at the top of the list. Making the list doesn't guarantee a position, however. The job seekers' chances depend on their position on the list and how well they meet the requirements for a specific job. The call to start work also depends on an agency's budget and how fast it can fill the jobs that are open.

4. How do colleges and other educational institutions train people for government service?

The government hires people for an amazingly wide range of jobs. Almost any type of training will prepare people for one or more civil service positions. A researcher proved that by looking through a dictionary of occupations, trying to find vocational skills that wouldn't be of use to the government. After a long search, only one job title turned up—that of "stripteaser."

Anyone who wants to prepare for a public service job can gain the necessary training at a vocational school, community college, or four-year college. Some of the courses are practical, while others prepare students for graduate-level training. Typical of the practical courses are training programs in police and fire science, computer programming, and public health nursing. Courses leading to degrees in the professions include engineering, law, medicine, and social work. Political science, which deals with the theory and structure of government, is a major department at most colleges.

SPECIAL FEDERAL PROGRAMS

The federal government has developed two programs that reward the person who goes on to college after high school.

Two-year college graduates. Graduates who have taken the proper courses at a two-year college (or who have completed two years at a four-year college) can qualify for many worthwhile jobs. Positions on this list include accounting assistants, personnel technicians, purchasing and supply assistants, statistical assistants, tax examiners, and law enforcement technicians. Two years of experience in related administrative or technical work may be accepted in place of college training. Successful applicants start with a rating of GS–4 on a scale that runs from GS–1 to GS–18. (GS stands for the "general schedule" on which federal salaries are based.)

Four-year college graduates. The federal government also needs well-educated, talented people for upper-level administrative and professional positions. Trainees do not need specialized training or job experience. They do need a college degree plus a passing grade of 70 percent on a four-hour written exam. Here, too, work experience can be substituted for all or part of the college training. Applicants who qualify receive a GS–5 rating. Those who have a year of graduate work, a law degree, or who score 90 or above on the test (and have earned a B– average) begin at the GS–7 level. The public tends to think that almost all of these people work in Washington, D.C., but that's not the case. An IRS attorney is as likely to work in Ogden, Utah, as in the nation's capital.

Let's review for a moment

The law of averages tells us that you or one of your close friends will choose a career in government service. How can we be so sure? Well, one out of seven Americans already works for a local, state, or federal government agency.

The expanding role of government requires qualified workers of almost every imaginable skill. All but the highest level federal positions are filled by the *civil service system,* which rewards merit rather than political connections. States and cities also have switched to the use of competitive exams based on the federal model.

Let's assume that you're interested in a government job. Perhaps you'd like to work as a flight controller for the Federal Aviation Administration. How do you get started?

A Typical Worker's Lifetime Earnings Prove That It Pays to Stay in School

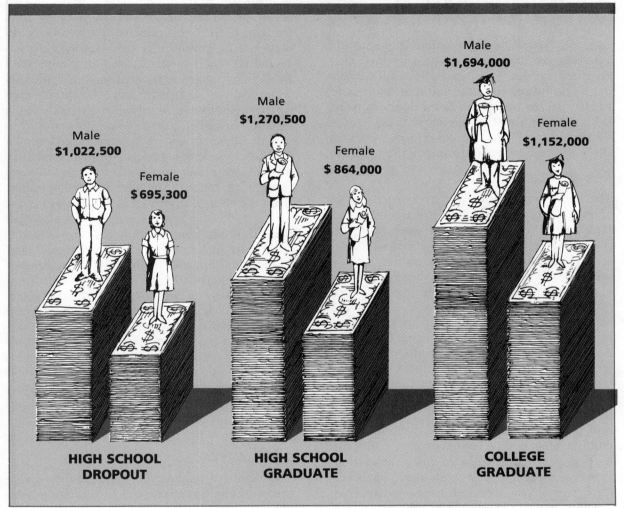

Male
$1,022,500

Female
$695,300

Male
$1,270,500

Female
$ 864,000

Male
$1,694,000

Female
$1,152,000

HIGH SCHOOL DROPOUT

HIGH SCHOOL GRADUATE

COLLEGE GRADUATE

■ Parents and teachers have always told young people that "education pays." The statistics on lifetime earnings for typical workers verify this idea. College graduates earn in excess of a million dollars more than high school dropouts. The numbers also testify to an injustice in American economic life: For every dollar a man makes, a woman makes about 68 cents.

First, check the qualifications for the position. You may need additional schooling before you qualify. Next, watch for announcement bulletins that tell you about the available jobs, the requirements for the position, and the procedure for filing your papers. If the agency accepts your application, you will be notified when and where to show up for the test. Congratulations! You passed with a score of 92. Your name has been placed on the *list of eligibles*. As soon as a position opens up, you'll be told to report for work.

5. What are the advantages and disadvantages of working for government?

The job hasn't been invented that's totally satisfying to those who do it every day. Government service is no exception. All government employees, from the youngest secretaries in city hall to the presidential advisers in the White House, must weigh advantages against disadvantages. For most government workers, the positive benefits outnumber the negative.

ADVANTAGES

The days when government service meant starvation wages and low prestige vanished long ago. The advantages of working for almost any governing body now include:

Good salaries. Typically, people think in terms of one simple question when considering a new job: "How much does it pay?" Most government agencies now pay salaries that are comparable to those paid by private enterprise for work of a similar type. Legislators and administrators review salary schedules frequently and make adjustments as needed. Observers note that government pay at the lower GS levels is somewhat higher than in private industry. Upper-level administrators and professionals, however, fall behind their counterparts outside of government. Because of this difference, a large number of high-ranking government officials leave each year for better-paying jobs in business or industry.

Civil service workers earn salary increases in several ways. Federal employees who begin at a particular GS grade, for example, receive annual raises for the first three years. After that, their raises come less often, stopping when they reach the top of their grade. Most workers will earn promotion to a higher GS rank long before they reach the top pay category in the lower grade. Each higher grade carries with it a larger paycheck and increased responsibility.

Job security. In the years when government salaries trailed behind those of private industry, job security stood out as the main attraction of public service. Once they've been hired, workers must earn satisfactory ratings during a probationary period. After passing that hurdle, most government employees can count on having their jobs as long as they want to keep them. Supervisors regularly review their employees' work, however, to ensure that each person remains productive. Examiners award ratings of outstanding, satisfactory, or unsatisfactory. Unsatisfactory ratings usually result in nothing more serious than a transfer to a less demanding job.

Job satisfaction. For people who want to do useful work that benefits their community or society, government service can be very rewarding. Much of the job satisfaction comes from the chance to provide assistance to those in need. Public service employees also feel good about making decisions that can improve the quality of life for other Americans.

Fringe benefits. Most civil service jobs provide generous fringe benefits. In addition to their salaries, workers receive sick leave, paid holidays and vacations, group life and medical insurance, pension plans, and unemployment compensation. Some jobs also include travel opportunities and contact with important politicians. At the very highest levels of government service, administrators qualify for chauffeur-driven limousines and other special benefits.

DISADVANTAGES

The negative aspects of government service are not always apparent, but anyone who applies for a civil service position should be aware of them.

Lack of recognition. One major disadvantage is that most civil servants are part of a large, nearly invisible work force. As tiny cogs in a huge, impersonal machine, they feel faceless and powerless. When people complain about rude, inefficient bureaucrats, they're probably talking about civil service workers who don't feel good about themselves or their jobs.

Restrictions on political activities. The Hatch Act of 1939 prevents federal employees from taking part in certain political activities. They're not allowed to campaign for a candidate, collect campaign contributions, or serve as a delegate to a political convention. Most state and local government employees work under similar limitations. The right to vote is not restricted, of course, nor is the basic right to speak out on public issues.

Restrictions on bargaining rights. Unions of government employees occupy a gray area in American labor relations. Laws and court decisions have sometimes denied these groups the right to strike. All new federal employees are required to sign a pledge that they will not strike against the government. This rule was written into the Taft-Hartley Act in 1947.

Nevertheless, as unions of public workers have grown more militant, "job actions" have increased in frequency. It's not unusual for a city's police officers to call in sick with the "blue flu" when bargaining for a pay raise breaks down. Instead of striking, customs officers may "work to rule" by checking each traveler's luggage with excessive care. By cre-

ating long delays at airports and border crossings, this job action puts pressure on the government to settle the dispute. Strikes by fire fighters and hospital workers have become almost routine, even though such actions defy both the spirit and the letter of the law.

Cutbacks and layoffs. During periods of inflation and tight budgets, reductions in government work forces have become common. Cutbacks have forced many cities to lay off such vital workers as police officers, public health workers, and fire fighters. When layoffs occur, the employees who lose their jobs are those who lack seniority, have low performance ratings, hold a temporary appointment, or lack previous government service (in the armed forces, for instance). Women and members of ethnic minorities are often hit hardest by these layoffs. Because they are usually the last to be hired, few of them have the seniority they need to protect their jobs.

Other limitations. Some federal agen-

■ An urban park ranger helping children create sand castles on a New York City beach. Such government jobs can bring a lot of satisfaction. But these jobs are often the first to be cut back in a budget crunch because they are not considered to be essential.

cies, such as the FBI, move their employees around. Restrictions exist at other agencies on hiring members of the same family. A more unusual problem occurs when employees go to the media or to the legislature to complain that their agencies are wasting the public's money. Instead of fixing the problem, embarrassed administrators sometimes pressure the "whistle blowers" to transfer, take demotions, or quit their jobs.

6. What are the pay scales and advancement chances in government service?

Public servants are no longer forced to sacrifice their well-being in order to work for the government. That philosophy died in 1923, when the federal government ended a salary and classification schedule that had remained unchanged for 70 years. The Federal Salary Reform Act of 1962 went even further. In that legislation, Congress set up an ongoing policy of defining and adjusting federal salaries.

Most federal, state, and local officials accept the fact that they must pay competitive salaries. Even when they don't, government employees are organized to bargain for better salaries and benefits. Workers who compare entry-level government salary scales with those of private industry find little difference between the two.

FEDERAL PAY SCALES

A single salary schedule now governs civil service compensation. Every effort has been made to reward equal work with equal pay, regardless of the job or agency. In 1990, the average starting salaries of each of the 15 main federal pay grades ranged from $10,213 at GS–1 to $57,158 at GS–15. One out of four federal employees was rated as GS–4 or GS–5, with an average starting salary of almost $15,000. One out of five was paid as GS–11 or GS–12. At these levels the average starting salary jumps to almost $32,000. GS–4's and 5's generally work at clerical jobs, while GS–11's and 12's occupy managerial and administrative positions.

FEDERAL STARTING SALARIES, 1990

Grade	Number of federal workers in grade (out of 1,000)	Annual salary
GS-1	2	$10,213
GS-2	21	11,484
GS-3	79	12,532
GS-4	129	14,067
GS-5	135	15,738
GS-6	61	17,542
GS-7	96	19,494
GS-8	20	21,589
GS-9	99	23,846
GS-10	15	26,260
GS-11	105	28,852
GS-12	100	34,580
GS-13	78	41,121
GS-14	38	48,593
GS-15	18	57,158
GS-16	3	} *
GS-17	1	
GS-18	[rare]	

* These positions are filled by presidential appointment only.

Salary figures do not include fringe benefits such as vacation time, medical care, and sick leave. The federal retirement program predated Social Security by 15 years. Employees who entered federal service after 1983 are covered under the Federal Employees Retirement System, which is part of the Social Security System and pays the same benefits.

CHANCES FOR PROMOTION

Government service offers excellent advancement opportunities. Many of the men and women now serving at GS–11 and above began at the bottom of the ladder. Because most agencies fill vacancies by promoting their own employees, workers with high efficiency ratings and proper training can move upward. In keeping with civil service policy, promotion is based on merit—the worker's demonstrated ability to perform. Well-trained, experienced employees who take the exams for *merit promotions* start with a big advantage over outsiders.

Speed of promotion depends primarily on the employee's ability and energy. Advancement also depends on the size of the agency or department and the openings that occur because of retirements, resignations, or promotions. Ambitious workers look for openings at other agencies when their way is blocked in their own office. In addition, employees who learn new skills usually receive prompt recognition. Many agencies provide on-the-job training that can lead to promotions and salary increases. Other chances for advanced training can be found at nearby colleges and vocational schools or in home study.

7. How do you apply for a government job?

Looking for the right job requires organization, patience, and determination. The following steps will help you discover the position that's right for you.

FIND OUT WHAT JOBS ARE AVAILABLE

Begin your job search by locating the hiring centers that are close to you. Logical places

The Path to a Job With Uncle Sam

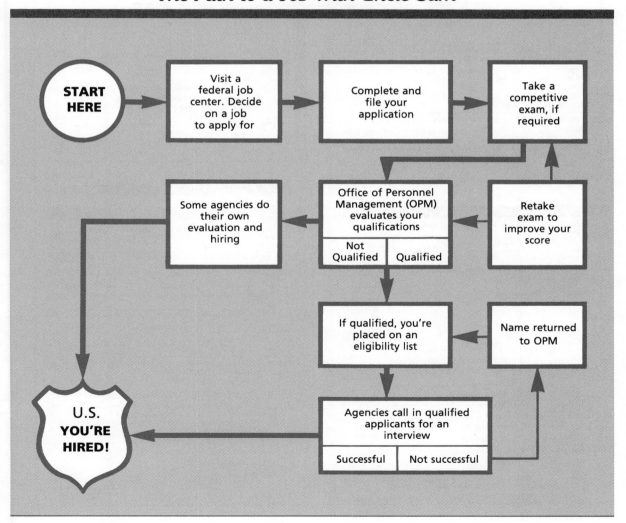

(*Text continues on page 488.*)

Application for Federal Employment—SF 171

Read the instructions before you complete this application. *Type or print clearly in dark ink.*

Form Approved:
OMB No. 3206-0012

GENERAL INFORMATION

1 What kind of job are you applying for? *Give title and announcement number (if any)*

2 If the announcement lists several job titles, which jobs are you applying for?

3 Social Security Number

4 Birth date *(Month, Day, Year)*

5 Name *(Last, First, Middle)*

Street address or RFD number *(include apartment number, if any)*

City   State   ZIP Code

6 Other names ever used

7 Sex *(for statistical use)*
☐ Male   ☐ Female

8 Home Phone
Area Code   Number

9 Work Phone
Area Code   Number   Ext.

10 Were you ever employed as a civilian by the Federal Government? If "NO", go to 11. If "YES", mark each type of job you held with an "X".
☐ Temporary   ☐ Career-Conditional   ☐ Career   ☐ Excepted
What is your highest grade, classification series and job title?

Dates at highest grade: FROM   TO

11 Do you have any applications for Federal employment on file with the U.S. Office of Personnel Management? If "NO", mark here ☐ and go to 12. If "YES", write below and continue in 47 the information for each application: (a) the name of the office that has your application; (b) the title of the job; (c) the date of your Notice of Results; and (d) your rating.

FOR USE OF EXAMINING OFFICE ONLY

Material
☐ Submitted
☐ Returned

Entered register:

Notations:

Form reviewed:
Form approved:

Option	Grade	Earned Rating	Preference	Aug. Rating
			☐ 5 Points (Tent.)	
			☐ 10 Pts. (30%) Or More Comp. Dis.	
			☐ 10 Pts. Less Than 30% Comp. Dis.	
			☐ Other 10 Points	
			☐ Disallowed	

Initials and Date

☐ Being Investigated

ANNOUNCEMENT NO.

APPLICATION NO.

FOR USE OF APPOINTING OFFICER ONLY

Preference has been verified through proof that the separation was under honorable conditions, and other proof as required.

☐ 5-Point   ☐ 10-Point—30% or More Compensable Disability   ☐ 10-Point—Less Than 30% Compensable Disability   ☐ 10-Point—Other

Signature and Title

Agency   Date

AVAILABILITY

12 When can you start work? *(Month and Year)*

13 What is the **lowest** pay you will accept?
Pay $ per   OR Grade

14 Are you willing to work:	YES	NO
A. In the Washington, D.C., metropolitan area?		
B. Outside the 50 United States?		
C. Any place in the United States?		
D. Only in *(list the location[s])*		

15 Are you willing to work:		
A. 40 hours per week (full-time)?		
B. 25-32 hours per week (part-time?)		
C. 17-24 hours per week (part-time)?		
D. 16 or fewer hours per week (part-time)?		
E. In an intermittent job (on-call/seasonal)?		
F. Weekends, shifts, or rotating shifts?		

16 Are you willing to take a temporary job lasting:		
A. 5 to 12 months (sometimes longer)?		
B. 1 to 4 months?		
C. Less than 1 month?		

17 Are you willing to travel away from home for:		
A. 1 to 5 nights each month?		
B. 6 to 10 nights each month?		
C. 11 or more nights each month?		

MILITARY SERVICE AND VETERAN PREFERENCE

	YES	NO
18 Have you served on active duty in the United States Military Service? If your only active duty was training in the Reserves or National Guard, answer "NO". If "NO", go to 22.		
19 Were you honorably discharged from the military service? If your discharge was changed to "honorable" or "general" by a Discharge Review Board, answer "YES". If you received a clemency discharge, answer "NO". If "NO", explain in 47.		
20 Did you or will you retire at or above the rank of major or lieutenant commander?		

21 List the dates, branch, and serial number for all active duty service.

FROM	TO	BRANCH OF SERVICE	SERIAL NUMBER

22 Place an "X" in the box next to your Veteran Preference claim. Mark only **one** box. See the instructions for eligibility information.

☐ **1** NO PREFERENCE

☐ **2** 5-POINT PREFERENCE—You must show proof when you are hired.

10-POINT PREFERENCE—If you claim 10-point preference, you must complete a Standard Form 15, which is available at any Federal Job Information Center. ATTACH THE COMPLETED SF 15 TO THIS APPLICATION, TOGETHER WITH THE PROOF REQUESTED IN THE SF 15.

☐ **3** Non-compensably disabled or Purple Heart recipient.

☐ **4** Compensably disabled (less than 30%).

☐ **5** Spouse, widow(er), or mother.

☐ **6** Compensably disabled (30% or more).

THE FEDERAL GOVERNMENT IS AN EQUAL OPPORTUNITY EMPLOYER

Page **1**   PREVIOUS EDITION USABLE   NSN 7540-00-935-7150   171-106

Standard Form 171 (Rev. 2-84)
Office of Personnel Management
FPM Chapter 295

■ **A typical federal job application form**

◄───── ATTACH ANY ADDITIONAL FORMS AND SHEETS HERE ─────►

EDUCATION

25 Did you graduate from high school? *If you have a GED high school equivalency or will graduate within the next nine months, answer "YES"*

26 Write the name and location *(city and state)* of the last high school you attended

YES ☐ If "YES", give month and year of graduation.

NO ☐ If "NO", give the highest grade you completed.

27 Have you ever attended college or graduate school? YES ☐ If "YES", continue with 28
NO ☐ If "NO", go to 31

28 NAME AND LOCATION *(city, state and ZIP code)* OF COLLEGE OR UNIVERSITY *If you expect to graduate within nine months, give the month and year you expect to receive your degree.*

	MONTH AND YEAR ATTENDED		NO. OF CREDITS COMPLETED	TYPE OF DEGREE (e.g. BA, MA)	YEAR OF DEGREE
	From	To	Semester Hours OR Quarter Hours		
1)					
2)					
3)					

29 CHIEF UNDERGRADUATE SUBJECTS
Show major on the first line

	NO. OF CREDITS COMPLETED
	Semester Hours OR Quarter Hours
1)	
2)	
3)	

30 CHIEF GRADUATE SUBJECTS
Show major on the first line

	NO. OF CREDITS COMPLETED
	Semester Hours OR Quarter Hours
1)	
2)	
3)	

31 Have you completed any other courses or training related to the kind of jobs you are applying for *(for example, trade, vocational, Armed Forces, or business)*? YES ☐ If "YES", give the information requested below. *(More courses?—Use a sheet of paper)*
NO ☐ If "NO", go to 32.

	MONTH AND YEAR TRAINING COMPLETED	TOTAL CLASSROOM HOURS	SUBJECT(S)	NAME AND LOCATION OF SCHOOL *(City, state, and ZIP code, if known)*	CERTIFICATE, DIPLOMA, etc. *(if any)*
1)					
2)					
3)					

SPECIAL SKILLS, ACCOMPLISHMENTS AND AWARDS

32 List your special qualifications, skills or accomplishments that may help you get a job. *Some examples are: skills with machines; most important publications (do not submit copies); public speaking and writing experience; membership in professional or scientific societies; patents or inventions; etc.*

33 How many words per minute can you:

TYPE? TAKE DICTATION?

Agencies may test your skills before hiring you.

34 List job-related licenses or certificates that you have, such as: *registered nurse; lawyer; radio operator; driver's; pilot's; etc.*

LICENSE OR CERTIFICATE	DATE OF LATEST LICENSE OR CERTIFICATE	STATE OR OTHER LICENSING AGENCY
1)		
2)		

35 Do you speak or read a language other than English *(include sign language)*? YES ☐ If "YES", list each language and place an "X" in each column that applies to you.
Applicants for jobs that require a language other than English may be given an interview conducted solely in that language. NO ☐ If "NO", go to 36.

LANGUAGE(S)	CAN PREPARE AND GIVE LECTURES		CAN SPEAK AND UNDERSTAND		CAN TRANSLATE ARTICLES		CAN READ ARTICLES FOR OWN USE	
	Fluently	With Difficulty	Fluently	Passably	Into English	From English	Easily	With Difficulty
1)								
2)								

36 List any honors, awards, or fellowships you have received. For each, give the year it was received.

REFERENCES

37 List three people who are **not related** to you and who know your qualifications and fitness for the kind of job(s) for which you are applying. Do not list supervisors you listed under 24

FULL NAME OF REFERENCE	PRESENT BUSINESS OR HOME ADDRESS *(Number, street, city, state, and ZIP code)*	TELEPHONE NUMBER(S) *(Include area code)*	BUSINESS OR OCCUPATION
1)			
2)			
3)			

Page 3

■ **Note:** Supplemental information may be required when filling out the application. The complete form covers four full pages.

to look include city hall, the county courthouse, the state employment office, or a federal job information center. Many phone directories list local, state, and federal offices in a special section. If none are listed, you can ask your school counselor, a librarian, or a telephone information operator for the phone number of the nearest branch of the Federal Office of Personnel Management. State employment offices also maintain full listings of current job notices. Visit one of these offices to see what kinds of jobs are open. You'll meet counselors there who will help you with aptitude testing and career guidance.

CONSIDER YOUR QUALIFICATIONS

Once you know what jobs are available, match the job descriptions to your own abilities, training, and interests. It makes sense to sit down and write out a summary of your personal background, education, and work experience. This is called a *résumé*. Writing a

Learning Skills

Interviewing for a Job

Do you remember how nervous you were when you applied for your first job? Your hands were probably sweaty, and your stomach was doing flip-flops. Now, think of how you'll feel when you apply for a full-time job. Whether it's in government service or in private industry, you'll want to put your best foot forward.

Applying for any job involves several steps. As you've learned in this chapter, you have to survey the job market, evaluate your own interests and skills, prepare a résumé, and fill out application forms. If it's a civil service job, you'll have to take a competitive exam. Then comes the interview. You'll have to talk to someone who can either give you the job or say, "Thanks, but no thanks."

It's possible to overcome the nervousness that all applicants feel when they walk into the personnel office. Here are some important rules of the interview game:

Rule 1: Do your homework. Going to an interview without preparing for it is like starting off on a trip without planning your route. In either case, you're likely to get lost. *First*, know yourself and what you can bring to the job. Review your own résumé and make a mental list of your strengths. If you believe in yourself, it's easier to make others believe in you, too. *Second*, find out as much as you can about the agency (or company) for which you might be working. Interviewers are impressed by applicants who can talk about the agency's work or the company's products. A little library research may do the job, but it also helps to talk to other employees. *Third*, know what you're willing to accept in terms of salary, location, and job title. Interviewers respect applicants who speak frankly about their wishes, but they expect them to be realistic.

Rule 2: Dress for the interview. Many young job applicants forget that the adult world may not share their ideas of proper dress. You're selling yourself in an interview, so make the best sales pitch you can. Whether you're applying for a job as a mechanic or an accountant, it's best to dress in a fairly conservative outfit. For men, that means a jacket and tie. For women, it means a businesslike dress or suit. Good grooming also counts. The attention you pay to your hair and hands tells the interviewer that you care about your public image.

Rule 3: Rehearse the interview ahead of time. Rehearsal is the process of going résumé helps you to evaluate your own job prospects. Later, placement officers will use it to compare your qualifications with those of other applicants.

FILL OUT THE APPLICATION

Think of the application as your personal letter to a possible employer. Since the personnel officer won't talk to you in person at this time, your application must speak for you. Answer all the questions fully and honestly. Type the application if possible. If you don't type, use a pen and write legibly. Pick up two application forms if you can—one for practice, the second for the final "perfect" copy.

Put your experience in the best possible light. A job selling brushes door-to-door sounds more impressive if described as "direct sales representative"! Similarly, don't hesitate to apply for more than one position if you're qualified. Competition for government jobs is intense, and it's increasing.

through every step of the interview in your mind—before it happens. Think of all the questions that might be asked and practice your responses. After you've done some mental rehearsal, ask a friend or family member to play the role of the interviewer. An hour or two of rehearsal will leave you feeling more relaxed and better prepared for the real thing.

Rule 4: Be on time and be prepared. Anyone who's late to an interview has already flunked the first test. Leave yourself enough time to account for traffic jams or crowded elevators. Make it a rule to travel with at least two pens, your Social Security card, letters of reference, and a fresh copy of your résumé.

Rule 5: Relax and enjoy the interview. When the time comes, smile and shake hands with your interviewer. You know you'll be good at this job, and you want to project that impression. Good interviewers know how to put you at ease, but you can help yourself by taking some deep breaths just before you walk into the office. Sit up in your chair, keep your hands quiet, and focus your attention on the interviewer. This is your big opportunity!

Think of each interview as a learning experience, even if you don't get the job. After it's over, review everything that happened. Find ways to improve your weak areas and to build on your strengths. Did tough questions such as "Tell me something about yourself" or "What salary do you expect?" give you trouble? Write out good answers and rehearse them so you can cope more smoothly with unexpected questions during your next interview.

Rule 6: Follow up with a brief thank-you note. While you're waiting for a decision, write to the interviewer to say "thanks." Say that you appreciated the chance to apply for the job and that you're more interested than ever in working for the company. Interviewers don't receive many letters of this type, and they'll be much more likely to remember you. You will stand out in a positive way.

Will these six rules guarantee you a good job? No, there's nothing certain when it comes to job interviews. Someone else may have more experience or better skills. But if you follow the advice given here, you will know, win or lose, that you gave the interview your best shot.

PREPARE FOR THE EXAM

Competitive exams require careful preparation. The fact that you have worked at a similar job is not a guarantee of success. Visit the public library or a local bookstore to pick up a study guide that will help you prepare for the exam. The guide will review the material you need to know, and you can test yourself on sample exam questions. It also helps to talk to people who hold similar jobs. Ask them for advice on taking the exam

Many adult night schools, vocational schools, and community colleges offer courses that prepare people to take civil service tests. Although this preparation is useful, the government does not require it. More important, watch out for schools that "guarantee" that their students will be offered jobs. No one can guarantee you a job offer. Even if you pass the test, you may be low on the eligibility list, or there may not be any openings.

Regardless of how you prepare yourself, give the exam your best effort. Use it to show your future employer that you have the skills that will make you a success on the job.

BE TESTWISE

You'll be notified of the time and place of the exam by mail. Take this "ticket" with you to the test site—and be on time! Take several pens and pencils and anything else that the exam instructions call for. It's best to be overprepared—pencils do break and pens do run dry. When the test starts, follow the proctor's directions exactly. Answer truthfully if you're asked to state the minimum salary you'll accept and whether you would accept a job in another city.

If you're testwise, you will begin with an advantage over the other applicants. Keep these simple guidelines in mind:

1. Plan your work carefully. You may not finish the exam if you don't budget your time. On a one-hour, 100-question exam, you should aim at completing 25 items every 15 minutes.

2. Most examinations are written to be graded by electronic scoring machines. Essay questions are seldom used today. Mark your answers in the proper column, and erase thoroughly if you want to change an answer.

3. Answer the easy questions first. Go back to the harder ones if time permits. If you finish early, recheck your answers.

4. Wrong answers are seldom subtracted from your score. It pays to make your best guess rather than leave a question blank.

Civil service exams are meant to answer two questions: Does the applicant have the skills and information required by the job? If not, does the applicant have the aptitude for learning how to do the job? Some applicants will be asked to take a performance test in addition to the pencil-and-paper exam. Depending on the job, a performance test might ask the job seeker to use a word processor, operate a forklift, or program a computer.

UNCLE SAM WANTS YOU

The door to government employment is open. Pick the right job, prepare carefully, and relax while you're taking the exam. If you do so, the chances are good that you'll make the list of eligibles. Uncle Sam needs qualified, hardworking people. Why shouldn't you be one of them?

Reviewing
what you've learned

1. Vocational counselors list a career in public service as a good possibility for anyone who is looking for a life's work. Government jobs call for almost every possible skill, and about one in seven American workers now earns a government paycheck. Most government agencies, whether at the local, state, or federal level, offer attractive salaries. The opportunities for promotion and job satisfaction are good.

2. Most federal and many state and city positions are earned by merit under a *civil service system*. Jobs under civil service are announced through bulletins, which describe the work to be done, the agency seeking employees, and the dates for the *competitive exams*. Applicants for these positions should be sure that they are properly qualified before submitting an application. After the exam, civil service officials notify the successful applicants of their scores and place their names on a *list of eligibles*. The eligible applicants are ranked according to their score on the exam and how well their backgrounds and experience meet the requirements of the job.

3. Government pay scales compare favorably with the salaries paid for similar jobs in private industry. Employees are placed on a salary schedule according to the job they do, their education, and time spent in government service. Fringe benefits often surpass those of private industry, and job security is greater. Openings exist in public service for employees with little or no schooling. The better-paid positions are reserved for people with college degrees or special skills. The major disadvantages of government employment are twofold. First, the public often fails to appreciate the work done by its own employees. Second, public employees must accept restrictions on their political activities.

4. Job announcement bulletins and government hiring offices let people know what jobs are available. Applicants should match their qualifications to the positions listed. After submitting their applications, qualified job seekers are notified as to the dates of their competitive exams. Most exams are objective, written tests. Some jobs also require that applicants take a performance test. Tests can be taken several times, either to erase a failing score or to improve a passing one. Home study, a school training course, and taking practice tests can pay off in a greatly improved score

Review questions and activities

TERMS YOU SHOULD KNOW

civil service system
competitive examination
list of eligibles

merit promotion
résumé

REVIEW QUESTIONS

Select the response that best completes each statement or question.

1. The example of Dr. Frances Kelsey and her brave stand during the thalidomide controversy shows that public employees (*a*) completely control the free enterprise system in the United States. (*b*) are never subject to political or professional pressure. (*c*) sometimes have a chance to perform services that involve questions of life and death. (*d*) are concerned mostly with their paychecks and the right to strike. (*e*) are better and more efficient than workers in private industry.

2. Out of 100 American workers, the number who might be expected to be employed by some level of government is about (a) 6. (b) 10. (c) 14. (d) 25. (e) 32.

3. Government employees do *not* receive higher pay for (a) college training. (b) service in the armed forces. (c) time spent on the job. (d) supporting the President's political party. (e) promotions from a lower GS grade to a higher one.

4. The goal of the civil service system is to (a) protect public employees from political pressure. (b) ensure that properly qualified people are hired for government jobs. (c) provide job security for competent workers. (d) establish a system of merit promotions. (e) all of these.

5. Announcement of government job openings would *not* be likely to appear (a) on a city hall bulletin board. (b) in a government mailing addressed to "Occupant." (c) in the newspaper. (d) at a state employment office. (e) at a school counseling office.

6. Passing the competitive exam for a government job guarantees that the applicant will be hired. This statement is (a) true. (b) false; the applicant must still be approved by the political party in power. (c) false; applicants are placed on a list of eligibles from which they are hired as jobs open up.

7. When compared with jobs in private industry, government service provides (a) higher salaries at all levels of employment. (b) greater freedom to engage in political campaigns. (c) greater job security. (d) little or no supervision. (e) more frequent transfers from job to job and place to place.

8. Promotion in government jobs usually depends on (a) knowing the right people. (b) playing office politics. (c) competitive exams. (d) making political contributions. (e) no real factor; promotions are so rare as to be almost nonexistent.

9. Which of the following is *not* good advice for someone who is taking a competitive exam? (a) Learn everything you can about the position before you take the test. (b) Follow the examiner's instructions exactly. (c) Make yourself known to the examiner by asking to borrow a pencil. (d) Keep an eye on the clock so you will know how long you have to finish the test. (e) Do the easy questions first, then go back to the hard ones.

10. Starting salaries for the entry-level federal government jobs are generally lower than salaries paid for similar jobs in private industry. This statement is (a) true. (b) false; even though the law requires that government salaries be less, fringe benefits make up the difference. (c) false; starting salaries in the lower-level GS positions are generally higher than for similar positions in private industry.

CONCEPT DEVELOPMENT

1. What would you include in a checklist of the advantages and disadvantages of working for a government agency?

2. How would you go about applying for a government job? List all the necessary steps leading to your first day on the job.

3. How do extra years of schooling pay off for anyone planning a career in government work?

4. Why does the government fill job openings through competitive exams? List some of the rules applicants should follow when they're preparing to take one of these exams.

5. Why do many people have a negative image of government employees? What can be done to change this feeling?

HANDS-ON ACTIVITIES

1. Organize your class to check out the sources of information about government jobs in your community. Have each student bring in whatever information he or she can find—job titles, pay scales, educational requirements, and the like. Make comparisons of the salaries and benefits with similar jobs in private industry. Post the results on your bulletin board. By the time you're finished, you'll probably discover some rewarding jobs that you didn't know existed.

2. Invite a school counselor or a career guidance officer to talk to your class about public service opportunities in your area. Your speaker will have firsthand information on current openings and can advise you on educational requirements, chances for travel, and other specific aspects of careers in government.

3. This chapter has been mostly concerned with civil service jobs, but careers in politics are attractive, too. What does politics have to offer? Do some research on your own, and share the results with the class. Start with library research so you can compile a list of questions on what it means to be a successful politician. Next, send your questions to your representatives at the state capital and in Washington, D.C. In order to gain a local viewpoint, use the same questions to interview a member of the village, city, town, or county government. Look for the rewards and satisfactions of service in elective office—but don't ignore the negative side.

4. Visit some government offices and pick up job application forms. Ask your teacher to duplicate them so that the class can have the experience of filling out these lengthy papers. Ask someone in your counseling office or career center to evaluate the completed applications. Your "score" will be a measure of your ability to follow directions and present yourself in the best possible light.

5. Organize a class debate on the topic, "*Resolved*, Government employees should be denied the right to strike against the public interest under penalty of fines, loss of their jobs, or imprisonment." The debate teams will find ample background material in the library, but they can also contact government and union officials for additional materials. After the debate, ask class members to discuss their own feelings about this issue.

20 Where do we go from here? The future of American government

A high school student (right) sits on a local school board.

Psychics and fortune-tellers make their living trying to predict the future. Some of them may be sincere, but scientists know there's nothing scientific about their guesses. For a more realistic picture of what the future holds, thoughtful people turn to the social sciences. A group of sociologists known as "futurists" are the specialists in this field of determining the possibilities that lie ahead. Instead of auras and Tarot cards, futurists base their predictions on the forces—past and present—that are shaping today's world.

Alvin Toffler, an American futurist, sees history as a series of great "waves" that crash upon human society from time to time. Like tidal waves, these changes in technology sweep away everything in their path. Toffler says that the "First Wave" was the development of agriculture. With a reliable food supply in hand, people began to build the first civilizations about 8,000 years ago. The "Second Wave" didn't arrive until the 1600s. This was the age of the industrial revolution, when machines changed the way people lived and worked. Industrialization brought the abundance of material goods we enjoy today as well as a population explosion.

A "Third Wave," Toffler reports, is now beginning. This new wave is the electronic revolution—the age of computers. With their speed and accuracy, computers generate immense amounts of information. The role of government is sure to change during this Third Wave, Toffler tells us. During the Second Wave, government wrote the rules that enabled people to live together in large social groups. These rules governed every aspect of daily life, from marriage and divorce to labor, religion, business, and education. As society became more complex, government became larger and more expensive. Governing bodies collected more and more taxes and regulated more and more aspects of our lives.

All that is going to change, Toffler predicts. As he sees it, Third Wave governments will be more responsive to the needs of their people:

> Today, as the Third Wave of change begins to batter at this fortress of [government's] managerial system, the first fleeting cracks are appearing in the power system. Demands for . . . shared decision-making, for worker, consumer, and citizen control, and for participatory democracy are welling up in nation after nation. New ways of organizing along less . . . [formal] lines are springing up in the most advanced industries. Pressures for decentralization of power intensify. And managers become more and more dependent upon information from below. Elites themselves, therefore, are becoming less permanent and secure. All these are merely early warnings— indicators of the coming upheaval in the political system.
>
> The Third Wave, already beginning to batter at these industrial structures, opens fantastic opportunities for social and political renovation. In the years just ahead, startling new institutions will replace our unworkable, oppressive, and obsolete . . . structures.

Toffler goes on to say that, compared with those of today, governments of the future will be hard to recognize.

> In all likelihood, it will require a protracted battle to radically overhaul—or even scrap—the United States Congress, the Central Committees and Politburos of the Communist industrial states, . . . the giant ministries and entrenched civil services of many nations, the constitutions and court systems—in short, much of the unwieldy and increasingly unworkable apparatus of supposedly representational governments.

In addition to his Third Wave concept, Toffler also gave us the idea of *future shock*. Future shock strikes a society when too much change takes place too quickly. Toffler believes that people who are battered by rapid change suffer from stress and become disoriented. Will humans be able to adjust to the future shock created by the Third Wave? No one really knows.

Scientists do know that Spaceship Earth carries a limited cargo of resources for its ever-growing passenger list. As proof of this threat to our future, computers have been programmed with data on diminishing resources, population growth, pollution, and other political and economic factors. A growing number of the computer readouts flatly predict worldwide disaster during the next century.

Toffler argues that we can prevent calamities such as famine, fuel shortages, the greenhouse effect, and nuclear war. First, he cautions, we must regulate the rate of change that the Third Wave is bringing with it. People must have roots. They must have a feeling of security and a belief that the future is worth working for. Until governments lay down their nuclear weapons, people will never feel comfortable with what lies ahead.

The future is too important to be left entirely in the hands of the politicians. Even though no final answers can be found for the serious challenges we face, futurists believe that there is hope. This final chapter, therefore, will examine the following questions:

1. What positive changes does the future hold?

2. What negative changes await us in the future?

3. What will the future hold for the federal government?

4. What does the future hold for state and local government bodies?

5. What does the American trend toward polyculturalism mean?

6. What role will future citizens play in shaping governmental decisions?

7. How will tomorrow's citizens react to change?

1. What positive changes does the future hold?

Many modern writers are pessimistic about the future. Their novels and films foresee a world dominated by totalitarian states in which people are reduced to a robotlike existence. In Ray Bradbury's *Fahrenheit 451*, Anthony Bur- gess's *A Clockwork Orange*, George Orwell's *1984*, and Aldous Huxley's *Brave New World*, dictatorial governments crush all opposition.

In the face of this pessimism, other thoughtful writers have taken an opposite position. Confident that the human race has always managed to avoid impending destruction, the optimists base their predictions on trends they believe are already visible. Their views suggest that:

1. People will use technology to develop a humane and prosperous society. In this less competitive world, the industrial nations will share their wealth with the underdeveloped countries. All of humanity will share in the benefits of proper diet, medical care, and housing.

2. The rate of change will be brought under control. People will be free to choose whatever life-style makes them comfortable.

3. Increasing hours of leisure will give individuals the chance to develop their recreational and artistic interests.

4. Population will continue to grow but at a slower rate. Improved crops and a more efficient use of our resources will allow society to keep pace with the increased demand.

5. People will live and work in supercities, but these great urban centers will grow upward rather than outward. Clusters of hundred-story skyscrapers will be surrounded by "green belts" of parks and farmlands.

6. Backbreaking manual labor will disap-

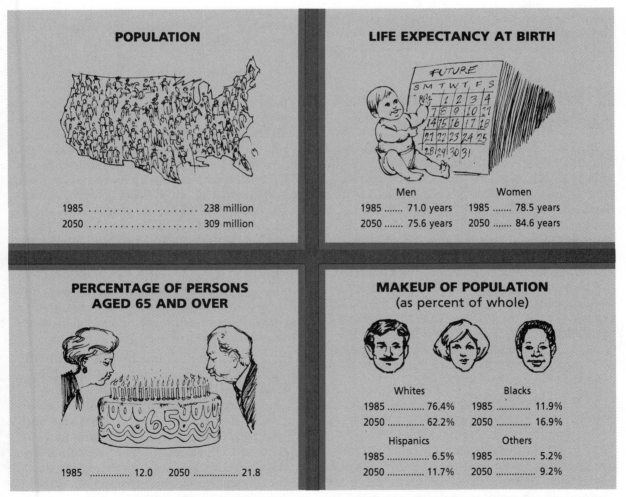

POPULATION				**LIFE EXPECTANCY AT BIRTH**		
				Men		Women
1985	238 million			1985 .... 71.0 years		1985 .... 78.5 years
2050	309 million			2050 .... 75.6 years		2050 .... 84.6 years

PERCENTAGE OF PERSONS AGED 65 AND OVER				**MAKEUP OF POPULATION** (as percent of whole)		
				Whites		Blacks
				1985 .... 76.4%		1985 .... 11.9%
				2050 .... 62.2%		2050 .... 16.9%
				Hispanics		Others
1985 .... 12.0		2050 .... 21.8		1985 .... 6.5%		1985 .... 5.2%
				2050 .... 11.7%		2050 .... 9.2%

■ Census Bureau projections for the future predict population trends that will create an older more ethnically diverse culture. The chart shows some of the changes you can expect to see in the United States during your lifetime.

pear as computer-controlled machines come on line. Workers will have a greater voice in the way they do their jobs.

7. Education will become a lifelong process. People will be encouraged to enroll in school at any stage of life.

8. People will accept each other as valuable partners in building a better society. National and racial differences will become less important.

9. Life expectancy will continue to increase. Researchers will conquer cancer, heart disease, AIDS, and other diseases that afflict humanity.

None of these dreams are beyond us. To make them come true will require sacrifice and hard work on the part of both governments and individuals.

2. What negative changes await us in the future?

If the pessimists are correct, future governments will face hard decisions unknown to today's public officials. Population pressures, for instance, may force governments to adopt the Chinese policy of limiting couples to a single child. A world that's running out of oil and gas will have to ration its resources carefully. The genie's bottle of scientific research also may create unexpected problems. Breakthroughs in gene-splicing techniques and the development of new mind-altering drugs, for example, may require increased government regulation.

As these examples suggest, the governments of the future may be forced to cope with a number of negative possibilities:

1. The need for stricter law enforcement and increased taxation will allow government to put greater limits on individual freedoms.

2. In a crowded, resource-poor society, organized minorities will demand a greater voice in decision making. If government does not respond, the have-nots may feel the need to use terrorist tactics to achieve their goals.

3. Consumer products will become scarce

as resources are diverted to higher priority uses. As happens in wartime, governments will ration food, clothing, fuel, and the other necessities of life.

4. Mental illness and random violence will increase. People will feel lost and alienated in a society that no longer seems to care for the individual.

5. People will find it more difficult to make positive contributions to society. Rioting at sports events, gambling, drug use, and other antisocial behaviors will increase.

6. Inflation will start a new upward spiral. Living standards will fall as prices soar to levels almost impossible to imagine today.

7. Present-day values will become outmoded as social institutions crumble. The family, the church, and moral codes will either disappear or take on radical new forms.

8. Continued destruction of the environment will make the planet almost unlivable. The greenhouse effect will raise temperatures, smog will sear people's lungs, and the oceans will be choked with waste.

9. Giant international corporations will make huge profits by controlling world trade. Business leaders will work hand-in-glove with government leaders to protect their interests.

10. A Third World country will use a nuclear weapon against one of its neighbors. The regional conflict will escalate into World War III.

None of these negative predictions is inevitable. Both pessimists and optimists, however, agree that the time for shaping the future is now. Indira Gandhi, the former prime minister of India, put it this way:

The future is as much with us as is the past and present. So far, comfort, speed, and efficiency have been offset by the degradation of the environment, increasing disparities between . . . countries and the race in the manufacture and acquisition of sophisticated arms. . . . The future is a question mark. . . . Tension grows, but at the same time, there is a parallel peace movement. Either nuclear war will annihilate the human race and destroy the earth, . . . or men and women all over

■ The contrasts between the lives of America's "haves" and "have nots" worry futurists. Will such differences bring about social unrest? What can be done to narrow the gap?

must raise their voices for peace and for an urgent attempt to combine the insights of different civilizations with contemporary knowledge. We can survive in peace and good will only by viewing the human race as one, and by looking at human problems in their totality. . . .

As individuals, most of us are powerless to make the decisions called for in Mrs. Gandhi's speech. Only through the mechanism of government can a people focus their nation's strength and determination on meeting these challenges.

3. What will the future hold for the federal government?

Tomorrow's federal government will continue to face four major challenges: (1) to protect civil liberties and encourage individuals to develop themselves to their full potential, (2) to preserve the quality of the environment, (3) to maintain civil order and political unity,

■ Can our society help the needy find jobs and homes without taxing the middle and upper classes out of their comfortable standard of living?

and (4) to keep the peace. Accomplishing these goals will require careful planning and coordination. The executive, legislative, and judicial branches will undoubtedly be forced to modify their structure and procedures.

EXECUTIVE BRANCH

Most political scientists expect the presidency to grow in strength and influence. Congress is divided politically and handicapped by lack of staff. Only the President has the ability to move quickly and decisively when fast-moving events demand immediate action. Several changes would better equip the executive branch to handle its foreign and domestic tasks:

Superdepartments. Proposals have already been made which would combine the functions of related executive departments into *superdepartments.* Bringing all related agencies and bureaus together under a single administrator would eliminate overlapping programs and make those that are left more efficient.

The power entrusted to these superdepartments would turn their directors into something close to assistant presidents. In dealing with other countries, for example, a Superdepartment of Foreign Affairs would formulate policy, develop programs, and oversee all U.S. relations with foreign countries. This superdepartment would combine the work now done by the Department of State, National Security Council, international banking agencies, and various agricultural and information agencies. In a similar way, a number of domestic agencies would consolidate their operations. Regional headquarters in major cities would bring federal decision making closer to the people.

Reorganization of independent agencies. The independent administrative agencies would be reorganized and overlapping jurisdictions would be eliminated. Much of the power to make policy now given to the independent agencies would be returned to the President and Congress. The newly streamlined agencies would concentrate on enforcing the law.

New chief of state. Many political scientists agree that the President has too much to do. The work load could be reduced by handing over purely ceremonial tasks, such as greeting important visitors, to an elected chief of state. Respected ex-Presidents would be logical candidates for this job. Precedents for this change already exist in France, Germany, and other countries. While the office would not have any real authority, the chief of state would be in an excellent position to speak as the nation's conscience.

Balanced budgets. With superdeficits threatening the nation's economic stability, the President and Congress will be forced to ask the American people to make some sacrifices. The spending plans for the decade of the 1990s will be balanced by increasing government revenues and cutting some defense and social programs.

LEGISLATIVE BRANCH

When the 116th Congress meets in the year 2020, Americans will expect to see a truly representative government at work. Futurists believe that the following changes will take place:

Increased citizen involvement in lawmaking. Communications between people and their elected representatives will be improved at every level. Two-way television links will allow instant electronic surveys of how the people want Congress to vote on major issues. Neighborhood advisory councils will revive the spirit of the traditional New England town meeting. On a national level, political action groups will send spokespersons to Washington from every segment of society. No longer will lobbyists speak only for powerful unions, corporations, and other special-interest groups.

Establishment of national goals. Congress will work harder to develop a consensus of national goals. Three-year and five-year plans will ensure that progress is made in major target areas. President Kennedy showed the value of such planning in the early 1960s when he committed the United States to landing an astronaut on the moon by 1970. Efforts

Technology Will Improve Life in the Future

Replacement body parts will become common. Cures for cancer, arthritis, and the common cold will be found.

Domed cities will be built on floating platforms at sea. Metals that "remember" their original shape will make auto repairs cheaper.

A permanent space station will provide a jumping-off point for colonization of the moon and Mars.

Voters will use a two-way telecom system to let the President and Congress know how they feel about important national issues.

at reaching a consensus will grow increasingly important as the nation becomes more diverse. Americans will be reminded that their similarities far outweigh their differences.

Increased efforts to check the executive branch. Congress will find it more and more difficult to oversee the actions of the executive branch. The legislature will have to work overtime to match the growing strength of the presidency. One critical task for Congress is to act as the people's protector against big government's lack of sensitivity to the needs of the individual citizen. The executive branch's computers, for example, already are capable

of gathering and storing a complete life history on every citizen. A government with the ability to pry into every citizen's life is no longer just science fiction.

Increased congressional strength will come from three sources:

1. *Changes in the political environment.* Reflecting a continuing population shift, more members of Congress will come from the cities and suburbs. The new legislators will take the place of members who now give rural areas a stronger voice in Congress than their populations warrant. In addition, growing numbers

"SEE, WITHOUT ME YOU'RE NOTHING!"

ROSS   R-51373

ROTHCO ORIGINAL

■ Computers sometimes seem as if they have minds of their own, but we must remember that they are tools. How can we keep computer networks from invading our privacy?

New courts. The federal court system is collapsing under the weight of its caseload. Specialized federal courts will be set up to hear cases growing out of the enforcement of government regulations and cases involving individual and corporate rights.

Restriction of the Court's power. With the lower courts handling a greater load, the Supreme Court will be free to hear more cases that raise the most important constitutional questions. The Court will, however, lose the power to issue broad directives that override the authority of the other two branches. In addition, some critics suggest that the Court's decisions should be tested against the Constitution every 20 years. This process would further reduce the high court's tendency toward judicial activism.

of minority citizens will turn out on election day to elect a Congress that more truly represents every American.

2. *Internal reform.* A younger, more representative Congress will put an end to the seniority system and reduce the power of the House Rules Committee. Congress will further strengthen the rules that govern the ethical behavior of its members. In a Congress more responsive to new ideas, more young people will be attracted to political careers.

3. *Greater access to information.* Congress will expand its use of electronics. Even today, committee hearings and floor debates are reaching many homes via television. In the future, Congress will be able to poll the voters by means of two-way television. Citizens will press "yes" or "no" buttons on their sets to let their representatives know how they feel about important national issues. In addition, Congress will expand its own computer data banks in order to reduce its reliance on the executive branch for information.

JUDICIAL BRANCH

Changes and reforms in the judicial branch will center on the work of the Supreme Court.

4. What does the future hold for state and local government bodies?

The creaky mechanism of federal-state-local relations will need major reforms if the American federal system is to regain its vitality. A combination of state constitutional amendments and passage of a national Modernization of State and Local Governments Act could bring about a number of changes:

REGIONAL GOVERNING BODIES

Regional governing bodies that cross state lines would be created to deal with common problems of health, education, welfare, and the environment. Candidates for some form of regional government include such closely related states as the Dakotas, the Carolinas, Arizona/New Mexico, Vermont/New Hampshire, and Montana/Wyoming/Idaho. These interstate plans are not expected to lead to the consolidation of existing states into "superstates," however. Along with losing some of the pride that attaches to a state's individual identity, each state would lose some of its representation in the Senate if it became part of a superstate.

Learning Skills

Keeping Up With the News

Citizen activists keep up with the news. If they don't, they can't make informed judgments about the issues. How can you comment intelligently about the federal budget if you don't know that Congress just passed a bill that cuts the deficit by $30 billion? The secret to keeping up with events is to make the news a part of your daily routine.

Good news watchers don't have to spend every waking moment watching, listening, or reading. The secret to being well informed is to follow some simple rules.

Rule 1: Concentrate. You have to pay careful attention to what the reporter is saying or writing. News events can be complicated and there may be more than one side to a story. It won't do much good to hear that an airliner went down in Colorado without learning that the crash was caused by a freak wind shear. Without that extra information, you might be left with the feeling that air travel is more dangerous than it really is.

Rule 2: Get your news from more than one source. It's almost impossible for a broadcaster or reporter to be completely objective. To prove this, read the account of a major political event in a Republican newspaper and then read the same story in a Democratic paper. You may like the Channel 4 news, but switch over to Channel 7 once in a while. Similarly, if *Time* is your favorite newsmagazine, pick up *Newsweek* every now and then.

Rule 3: Learn to separate fact from opinion. Most newspapers and news broadcasters do a good job of separating their news stories from their editorial opinions. In a newspaper, the stories that appear on page one usually give you the straight

who, what, where, when, why, and how of the event. On the editorial pages, you'll find clearly labeled opinion pieces. Even though the newspaper's editors disapprove of the new welfare reform bill, for example, they'll report the facts of the story on page one. You'll have to turn to the editorial page to learn that they fear the bill will bankrupt the federal treasury.

Rule 4: Turn to a newsmagazine for depth of coverage. Because newspaper reporters and newscasters work on tight deadlines, they usually don't explore a story in depth. The weekly newsmagazines have the time and resources to dig more deeply. If you want to learn more about welfare reform than your local media can provide, turn to publications such as *Time, Newsweek,* or *U.S. News & World Report.* Along with current news, these magazines will keep you informed about current events in the arts, medicine, technology, sports, and religion. You'll have to turn to local sources, however, if you're going to keep up with hometown news.

Rule 5: Beware of news that's too good to be true. There are newspapers that feature headlines such as, "Ancient mummy gives birth to healthy three-headed alien." These publications are good for a laugh, but don't put much faith in their accuracy. They'll print almost anything that will sell a few more copies.

Believe it or not, you're already keeping up with the news. You probably know every song on the latest recording put out by your favorite group, and you likely know who won last year's Super Bowl. Turn that same kind of interest to keeping up with the political news, and you'll soon be an expert on both local and national issues. That's how active, involved citizens are made!

REFORM OF STATE GOVERNMENT

Reforming and modernizing state governments will provide improved services at lower cost. One useful reform would be to provide longer terms for a smaller number of elected officials. Giving the states increased borrowing power, streamlining state boards and commissions, and increasing state aid to local governments also would help.

Legislatures would be improved by scheduling annual sessions, paying legislators an adequate salary, and limiting the amount of money spent on election campaigns. Stronger legislatures would be more likely to write the laws that the public wants and needs. This would eliminate the confusion that arises when frustrated citizens put too many initiatives and referendums on the ballot.

IMPROVEMENT OF LOCAL SERVICES

Counties, cities, and special districts will join together to form regional governments. This would end the costly duplication of services that is so common today. The trend toward increasing state control of local affairs will be reversed so as to keep government closer to the people it serves. Where the state can't loosen its grip, it can set up neighborhood service centers. These centers will allow people to meet face-to-face with state officials who can answer their questions and help solve their problems.

■ The first high school graduating class of the next century was born in 1982. Of every 1,000 babies born in the United States that year, 10.6 died before their first birthday. Seventeen other nations had better infant mortality rates, including Japan (6.0), Sweden (6.4), and Canada (8.5). When these children entered the first grade in 1988, one in four came from a poor family. Before they finish school, one in seven is likely to drop out. Along with rebuilding our cities and reforming our government, better ways of caring for children must be found.

EQUALIZATION OF THE TAX BASE

Urban problems can be attacked through large grants-in-aid drawn from state funds. If the funds are given out according to need, the gulf that now exists between have and have-not communities will soon narrow. All states will rely more on personal and corporate income taxes and less on property and sales taxes.

RESTRICTION OF ZONING POWER

City zoning boards would be forced to allow the construction of low-cost housing. At the same time, cities would be encouraged to draw up rational, comprehensive growth plans as a way of eliminating the eyesores created by "urban sprawl." Well-designed master plans will put a stop to the current battle between developers and the slow-growth movement.

THE NEED FOR FEDERAL FUNDING

Economists have estimated that reforming our political system will cost $50 billion a year. At a time when money is badly needed for rebuilding America's aging roads, sewers, schools, and other structures, that money will be hard to find. Logically, the cost should be divided among the federal government, the states, and local governments. Voting for higher taxes to pay for these reforms will be a true test of the nation's will.

Let's review for a moment

The future contains the promise of greatness—or disaster. People working through responsive government bodies have the opportunity to improve the quality of life for everyone. Cities can be rebuilt as places of beauty and centers of culture and commerce. Science and technology can give us the time and tools with which to build a better, more peaceful world.

At the same time, we cannot ignore the pessimists. In our own century, we have seen the growth of the drug culture, a polluted environment, the collapse of social institutions, and international conflict. Whatever happens, government will be at the forefront of the change that is certain to come.

What can government do to prove the pessimists wrong? Individual rights must be protected, the quality of life must be improved, civil order must be maintained, and war must be prevented. Further, the three branches of the federal system can reorganize themselves to become more responsive to the needs of the people.

State, county, and municipal governments will join regional governing bodies as a way of eliminating duplication and providing better service. At the same time, individual citizens will be given a bigger role in decision making. Neighborhood offices will be established so that each of us can deal directly with our state and federal governments.

---

5. What does the American trend toward polyculturalism mean?

A long-held myth was challenged in the 1960s. The old idea of the United States as a *melting pot* gave way to an acceptance of the concept of *polyculturalism*. This change forced the American people to rethink a number of widely accepted beliefs.

THEORY OF THE MELTING POT

The concept of the United States as a cultural melting pot dominated social thinking for a hundred years. Supporters of the theory believed that a distinct American culture existed, one with a set of values that everyone accepted. Immigrants were expected to discard their own cultures and adopt American ways. The myth was often backed up by reality. Even when the older immigrants held tightly to their cultures, their children quickly discarded the ways of the old countries. Only a few second-generation immigrants bothered to learn the languages their parents spoke. Schools

■ In many big cities, a variety of cultures and ethnic groups may share an area or they may live in different neighborhoods—all within a few blocks of each other. How can people of widely differing life-styles be unified without destroying what is unique about each group?

taught people to be Americans, and non-Western cultures were largely ignored.

POLYCULTURALISM REVIVED

In the 1960s, many Americans rejected the melting pot theory in favor of a polycultural approach. This belief accepts all cultural backgrounds as valid and valuable. Black groups proclaimed that "black is beautiful." The Hispanic community promoted its Spanish and Latin American heritage. The diverse cultures of the American Indians and Asian Americans also gained a new respect. The schools joined in and began to offer courses in ethnic studies.

STANDARD VALUES QUESTIONED

Polyculturalism is not limited to ethnic and racial minorities. In the early 1960s, the hippie movement challenged the politics, life-style, and legal system of the majority. The punk rockers of the 1980s were the direct descendants of the hippies. Each generation feels the need to shock the "old folks" and to find new ways of self-expression. Futurist Alvin Toffler thinks this process has been speeded up by

the age of electronics. As each new fad and style emerge, the media spread the word to every city and town and farm in the nation.

Alternative life-styles embrace a wide diversity of values. A few of them reject the Puritan work ethic that is so much a part of traditional American culture. Some surfers and skiers, for example, commit themselves to a life defined by the pursuit of pleasure. By contrast, the "yuppies" of the 1980s actively embraced the work ethic and the material success that went with it. These "young, urban professionals" pursued success and Aspen condos as eagerly as another group pursued New Age enlightenment.

Futurists who predict a state-imposed uniformity have not given full weight to the growth of polyculturalism. Toffler knows that poverty and despair have locked many people into an almost choiceless existence. He believes, however, that economic opportunities will move sharply upward by the early 2000s. Better schools, good-paying jobs, and improved public services will give people the freedom to select their life-styles from many socially acceptable alternatives.

ROLE OF GOVERNMENT

The problem for society will be to find a social consensus that is wide enough to accept the new ways of thinking. Some of these alternative life-styles will come into conflict with majority concepts of morality, property rights, and social justice. Government, for its part, must design new educational programs, political systems, and a unifying culture. If it is successful, our polycultural society will be well and truly integrated. If it is not, the nation may turn to a totalitarian system of government. Whatever name it goes by, such a government would destroy personal freedom in the name of national security, discipline, and morality.

6. What role will future citizens play in shaping governmental decisions?

Graduation speakers have long called on their audiences to go out and improve the world. Today, young people take that charge literally. They are troubled by the problems of pollution, civil rights, poverty, crime, and other social issues. Moreover, they are insisting on doing something about such problems. Many young Americans feel that unless they do, tomorrow's world may not be worth living in.

Unfortunately, a generation gap often divides the young and the old. Idealistic young people tend to focus on what is bad in the current system. Older people, who have a greater stake in the existing society, are more anxious to preserve what is worthwhile from the past. Those who expect government to resolve this conflict without assistance will be disappointed. Americans must submerge their differences and work together to build a political and economic system capable of solving our problems.

INCREASED CITIZEN PARTICIPATION

The role of tomorrow's citizens will not change dramatically. As always, democracy provides two political opportunities: the right to vote and the right to play a direct role in making political decisions. There are several ways in which people can become more involved in the nation's decision making:

Ombudsman. A few governmental units in the United States have already adopted the Swedish concept of the *ombudsman*. This official's only job is to help the individual citizen obtain fair treatment from government. Overlapping bureaucracies have become so complex that the individual needs the help of this "friend at court" when dealing with the many levels of government.

Neighborhood government. As mentioned earlier, many government agencies will open branches at the community level. People will join together in *neighborhood councils*, whose leaders will carry their decisions to local agencies and governing bodies. When citizens know that their voices are heard by those in power, the current feelings of alienation will lessen.

■ Futurists think local governments will gain more prominence in the 21st century because local officials are close at hand and better understand local problems.

National plebiscites. A polycultural society cannot rely on today's inefficient and sometimes unresponsive legislative process. To set future goals, the *plebiscite* (a nationwide direct ballot on a political issue) will offer a way for all subgroups to be heard. People will have a yes-or-no vote on important public decisions. After everyone joins in a country-wide debate, Americans will vote to accept or reject each proposal.

Return to direct democracy. Another solution would be to establish *social future assemblies* all over the United States. These large-scale "town meetings" would represent every economic, political, and social group in the United States—labor, business, education, religious organizations, women, ethnic groups, the poor, young people, and so on. The assemblies would have the power to make decisions in local matters, and state and federal officials will listen carefully when they speak out on larger issues.

Serving on an assembly would be a little like doing jury duty, but with one exception: *everyone* would serve when called upon. By returning to this grass roots concept of direct democracy, all Americans would be stimulated to take active roles in government.

AMERICANS AS WORLD CITIZENS

Tomorrow's citizens will be even more involved in international affairs. In a world in which nations depend on each other to an ever greater degree, a number of truths will make themselves felt:

1. Industrial technology requires access to raw materials from all over the globe. Many industries already operate on a worldwide scale.

2. Depletion of resources and environmental pollution affect all nations.

3. Modern communications make an international exchange of cultural influences inevitable.

4. World regulatory agencies, perhaps based

■ High divorce rates sometimes make it seem as though the traditional nuclear family has disappeared. Actually, the basic unit of mother, father, and children is still alive and well. When they can, Americans preserve and protect the nuclear family because they know that stable homes are more likely to produce good citizens.

on the United Nations model, will take on greater importance.

5. A war anywhere on the globe affects people everywhere.

The citizens of the future cannot escape the fact that they will be living in a world community. Friendly relations will depend on more than cultural exchange and competition in the Olympics. As consumers of a large share of the world's resources, Americans may have to sacrifice some of their luxuries in order to share the planet's food, minerals, and oil with all peoples.

7. How will tomorrow's citizens react to change?

The only thing that's certain about the future is that humans will have to cope with change. If we're to meet that challenge, we'll have to depend on our problem-solving ability. You don't have to be a scientist to understand that on any scale of physical development, the human animal ranks far down the list. Our bodies lack such useful adaptations as the tiger's strong jaws, the porcupine's sharp quills, or the elephant's thick hide. The dolphin outswims us, the antelope outruns us, and the baboon outclimbs us.

Only a single physiological feature raises human beings above our fellow creatures. *Homo sapiens* has the largest and most complex brain (in relation to body size) in the animal kingdom. Even so, scientists tell us that we use only a fraction of the brain's potential. Perhaps untapped powers to resist physical illness or to communicate by mental telepathy lie waiting to be developed.

Like our species, American social institutions have also been evolving. The first chapter of this text traced the development of government, which began as an outgrowth of family and tribal organization. Today, it is obvious that the basic social unit of the family is also in transition. Social critics worry that more and more children are growing up in a society that does not meet their basic needs for love and security. Whether that trend continues or not, tomorrow's children will certainly inherit a far different world.

EFFECTS OF CHANGE

Those who understand the concept of future shock know that many people react negatively to change. Their behavior is marked by anxiety, hostility to authority, senseless violence, physical illness, and depression. Victims of too much rapid change feel that their lives are out of control. They want desperately to reduce the number of decisions that they're forced to make.

Psychologists have developed a rating system that assigns point values to the life changes that cause stress. The death of a spouse rates a maximum of 100 points, for example, while moving to a new home counts 20. Doctors can now predict that anyone with a high score on the life-change scale—anyone who undergoes a great deal of stress—will almost certainly come down with a serious illness. The more radical the change, the more severe will be its effect on the human body.

Stress caused by rapid change also occurs in the life of a nation. The many demands that face tomorrow's politicians make it clear that change—even radical change—will occur in government, too. Governmental change carries its own price tag. The American people will have to pay their share of the bill by taking a more active role in decision making and by enduring the physical stress caused by change.

Change should not be thought of only in negative terms. To eliminate change would be to stop growth and progress. The old saying, "A change is as good as a vacation," has much to recommend it. The worry is that the *rate* of change will leave people unable to adjust to new life situations.

AN APPEAL FROM THE AUTHORS

A notorious criminal was once asked to name one contribution he had made to society. His response: "I paid my taxes." The judge was not impressed, and rightly so. If your future role as an American citizen consists only of

■ Every individual can make a difference in improving one's community and government. Learn what it means to be an activist—a concerned, involved participant in public affairs.

paying taxes and griping about things you don't like, someone else will make tomorrow's decisions. As things now stand, that "someone else" will probably be speaking for an organized pressure group. As you know, pressure groups often pursue narrow, selfish goals and ignore the real needs of our society.

It seems fitting, therefore, to conclude this text with an urgent appeal. *We ask that you make a commitment to participate in government decision making.* As you read this, very few teenagers would describe their future goals with the statement, "I want to become a politician." That's too bad, because the nation needs citizens who will devote themselves to building new and better political institutions.

Where do you start? Young adults in many states are already running for school boards, city councils, and city commissions. What's more, they're winning a fair share of those elections. You can begin by matching your own values against the way things are being done by your local school board, city or town council, or county board. Next, study the politics of your community. Locate the governing body that has the power to bring about the change you think is needed.

Once you know how the system works, speak up. You can write letters or ask for a place on the agenda when public hearings are being held. If you find that you enjoy politics, take a role in the next election. You might even think about running for office. In short, learn what it means to be an *activist*—a concerned, involved participant in public affairs.

The opposite of active is passive. Passive people wait for others to make decisions. Instead of making things happen, passive people let things happen to them. The future of the United States—your future—demands improvement in the quality of life. Without more involvement and more activism, this great country could someday join the other cultures that have failed the test of history.

Reviewing
what you've learned

1. Futurists base their predictions about the future on social trends and changes in technology. The optimists point out that humanity has always risen to the challenge of the future. Improved technology and greater understanding of human psychology, optimists say, will enable us to improve the quality of life. Pessimists forecast a future disrupted by alienated minorities, authoritarian government, the collapse of social institutions, and the destruction of the environment.

2. In the future, the federal government will continue to commit national resources to four great goals: protection of individual rights, improvement of the quality of life, maintenance of civil order, and the keeping of the peace. Many executive departments may be consolidated into *superdepartments*. The independent agencies are likely to be reorganized to increase their effectiveness. A new, ceremonial position of Head of State may be created. Congress may encourage citizens to take a more active part in proposing legislation. The legislature should establish national goals and improve its oversight of the executive branch. New federal courts may be created to relieve the logjam of cases that now clog the court system. Such a development would give the Supreme Court more time to decide constitutional issues. But the Court is likely to lose the power to issue broad rulings that are better left to the legislative process.

3. State and local governments are also likely to undergo major reforms. These might include the creation of *regional governing bodies* to deal with problems shared by several states. If the reforms come about, people will benefit from a streamlined state government, improved local services, and the equalization of the tax base.

4. American society has begun to reject the idea of the *melting pot*, in which everyone must conform to a single, dominant culture. There is now an increased acceptance of *polyculturalism* with its growing number of subcultures. These are based on race or nationality, moral values, and economic interests. Although polyculturalism brings a new richness to American life, it is breaking up the traditional social order.

5. The citizens of the future will probably be more willing to reform society and less interested in preserving old institutions. The cost of government, measured in dollars and in the stress caused by change, will undoubtedly increase. Americans will continue to register their political will by voting. In addition, their voices will become more powerful as *ombudsmen, neighborhood councils, plebiscites,* and *social future assemblies* emerge as channels for a national dialogue on goals and priorities. International affairs will increasingly affect each person's life.

6. Change is more likely to occur in a beneficial way when citizens become social and political *activists*. Only when a large percentage of the American people are fully involved in political life can the United States fulfill the promise of its founding.

Review questions and activities

TERMS YOU SHOULD KNOW

activist
future shock
melting pot
neighborhood councils
ombudsman

plebiscite
polyculturalism
regional governing bodies
social future assemblies
superdepartments

REVIEW QUESTIONS

Select the response that best completes each statement or question.

1. "Future shock" refers most specifically to (*a*) the development of electronic technology. (*b*) the accelerating rate of change and the stress it causes in society. (*c*) the possibility of future nuclear wars. (*d*) the rise of totalitarian systems of government. (*e*) the failure of government to solve the problems of urban life.

2. An *optimistic* view of the future would suggest that (*a*) population growth will outstrip the world food supply. (*b*) governments will become more authoritarian. (*c*) nations will be unable to settle their disputes peacefully. (*d*) increased leisure time will turn most people into television addicts and violence freaks. (*e*) science will find cures for diseases such as cancer and heart disease.

3. The United States government of the future will probably *not* have as a goal (*a*) the expansion of American control over underdeveloped nations. (*b*) the protection of American civil rights. (*c*) the preservation of environmental quality. (*d*) the maintenance of civil order. (*e*) the greater involvement of citizens in political decision making.

4. The creation of the office of Chief of State would (*a*) increase the overall effectiveness of the President. (*b*) permit the officeholder to serve as the conscience of the American people. (*c*) relieve the President of purely ceremonial duties. (*d*) provide a suitable position for an older, widely respected national leader. (*e*) accomplish all of these goals.

5. The purpose of a plebiscite on national goals would be to (*a*) reach unanimous public agreement on a particular issue. (*b*) give the President a chance to bypass Congress in obtaining new legislation. (*c*) offer citizens a chance to vote on issues facing the country. (*d*) bypass the Supreme Court's power of judicial review. (*e*) enable Congress to reduce the executive branch's authority over the federal bureaucracy.

6. One important advantage of consolidating county or state governments would lie in the possibility of (*a*) levying new taxes on interstate commerce. (*b*) eliminating duplicated services and handling more efficiently problems that cross political boundaries. (*c*) bringing government closer to the people. (*d*) ending regional traditions and cultural patterns. (*e*) none of these is an advantage.

7. The rise of polyculturalism in American society means the end of democratic institutions. This statement is (*a*) true. (*b*) false; polyculturalism has had little impact on American society and will soon die out. (*c*) false; a culturally diverse

society can retain democratic institutions as long as all subcultures have a voice in the decision-making process and accept the decisions of the majority.

8. A public official whose only job is to help individuals cope with problems involving government agencies is the (*a*) bureaucrat. (*b*) plebiscite. (*c*) inspector general. (*d*) delegate to the neighborhood council. (*e*) ombudsman.

9. Each of the following is a possible result of rapid changes in a person's life situation *except* (*a*) depression. (*b*) physical illness. (*c*) senseless violence. (*d*) inability to make decisions. (*e*) reduction of decisions to be made.

10. The future of a free society depends largely on the willingness of all American citizens to take an active role in local, state, and national governments. This statement is (*a*) true. (*b*) false; the Constitution will protect American citizens, no matter what governments do. (*c*) false; the opportunity to influence political decisions is already closed off at most levels of government.

CONCEPT DEVELOPMENT

1. What is meant by the term "Third Wave"? Can you find any examples of Third-Wave changes that are taking place in your own community?

2. Pick out a major problem faced by the American government today. What do you think will have been done about this problem in ten years? In the year 2035?

3. Trace the history of polyculturalism in the United States. How will we resolve this tendency of society to split into competing subcultures?

4. Explain how you would develop strategies for involving people more directly in government affairs at local, state, and national levels.

5. Will citizens of the next century look on this decade as a "golden age"? Why or why not?

HANDS-ON ACTIVITIES

1. Throughout history, thoughtful writers have explored the possibility of building a perfect society. In 1516, Sir Thomas More created the name "Utopia" for such a place. Suppose you had the power to construct your own utopia. What would it be like? How would you balance the desire to safeguard personal freedoms with the need to keep individuals from harming one another? Would your government be democratic? Would your economy be capitalistic? Remember, anyone can imagine a lovely world of sweetness and light. Once you take into account the realities of human nature, limited resources, and international rivalries, can you still devise a utopia? Once you've put your imagination to work, share the results with your classmates.

2. If you're 18, you're probably eligible to run for several local civic offices. You may not feel ready for that sort of challenge, but it would be interesting to see what other young people across the country are doing. Research the question in your library (try the *Readers' Guide to Periodical Literature* for sources) and share the information with your classmates. If any young people in your community are serving on a governing board, invite them to talk to your class about their experiences.

3. If you've never read any of the futuristic novels mentioned earlier (*Fahrenheit 451*, *A Clockwork Orange*, *1984*, or *Brave New World*), give one or more of them a try. Along with being enjoyable reading, they all project existing social trends into a terrifying future.

4. An interesting class project would be for each of you to write to a different public figure. Choose state and federal politicians, high-ranking bureaucrats, military leaders, and the like. You can find names and addresses in the *United States Government Manual*, available at the reference desk of most libraries. Ask each official the same question: "What changes do you think will take place in American government and society during the next 20 years?" Compile the results in a booklet so you can distribute it in your school and community. Not everyone you write to will respond, of course, but you should receive enough answers to stimulate some interesting discussion.

5. How do you feel about this book? The authors welcome your comments. Write to us in care of the publisher: Amsco School Publications, 315 Hudson Street, New York, NY 10013. We'd be pleased to hear that you loved the book, but we also want to know what you found difficult, boring, or useless. Tell us how you feel about the writing style, the vocabulary, the visuals, the organization—in short, anything that either interested or annoyed you. We promise that when the book is revised, your suggestions will guide our decisions about what to change, what to delete, and what to add.

Appendix

The Declaration of Independence

(Adopted in Congress July 4, 1776)

The Unanimous Declaration of the Thirteen United States of America

When, in the course of human events, it becomes necessary for one people to dissolve the political bands which have connected them with another, and to assume among the powers of the earth, the separate and equal station to which the laws of nature and of nature's God entitle them, a decent respect to the opinions of mankind requires that they should declare the causes which impel them to the separation.

We hold these truths to be self-evident, that all men are created equal, that they are endowed by their Creator with certain unalienable rights, that among these are life, liberty and the pursuit of happiness. That to secure these rights, governments are instituted among men, deriving their just powers from the consent of the governed. That whenever any form of government becomes destructive of these ends, it is the right of the people to alter or to abolish it, and to institute new government, laying its foundation on such principles and organizing its powers in such form, as to them shall seem most likely to effect their safety and happiness. Prudence, indeed, will dictate that governments long established should not be changed for light and transient causes; and accordingly all experience hath shown that mankind are more disposed to suffer, while evils are sufferable, than to right themselves by abolishing the forms to which they are accustomed. But when a long train of abuses and usurpations, pursuing invariably the same object evinces a design to reduce them under absolute despotism, it is their right, it is their duty, to throw off such government, and to provide new guards for their future security.— Such has been the patient sufferance of these colonies; and such is now the necessity which constrains them to alter their former systems of government. The history of the present King of Great Britain is a history of repeated injuries and usurpations, all having in direct object the establishment of an absolute tyranny over these states. To prove this, let facts be submitted to a candid world.

He has refused his assent to laws, the most wholesome and necessary for the public good.

He has forbidden his governors to pass laws of immediate and pressing importance, unless suspended in their operation till his assent should be obtained; and when so suspended, he has utterly neglected to attend to them.

He has refused to pass other laws for the accommodation of large districts of people, unless those people would relinquish the right of representation in the legislature, a right inestimable to them and formidable to tyrants only.

He has called together legislative bodies at places unusual, uncomfortable, and distant from the depository of their public records, for the sole purpose of fatiguing them into compliance with his measures.

He has dissolved representative houses and repeatedly, for opposing with manly firmness his invasions on the rights of the people.

He has refused for a long time, after such dissolutions, to cause others to be elected; whereby the legislative powers, incapable of annihilation, have returned to the people at large for their exercise; the state remaining in the meantime exposed to all the dangers of invasion from without, and convulsions within.

He has endeavored to prevent the population of these states; for that purpose obstructing the laws for naturalization of foreigners, refusing to pass others to encourage their migration hither, and raising the conditions of new appropriations of lands.

He has obstructed the administration of justice, by refusing his assent to laws for establishing judiciary powers.

He has made judges dependent on his will alone, for the tenure of their offices, and the amount and payment of their salaries.

He has erected a multitude of new offices, and sent hither swarms of officers to harass our people, and eat out their substance.

He has kept among us, in times of peace, standing armies without the consent of our legislature.

He has affected to render the military independent of and superior to the civil power.

He has combined with others to subject us to a jurisdiction foreign to our constitution, and unacknowledged by our laws; giving his assent to their acts of pretended legislation:

For quartering large bodies of armed troops among us;

For protecting them, by a mock trial, from punishment for any murders which they should commit on the inhabitants of these states;

For cutting off our trade with all parts of the world;

For imposing taxes on us without our consent;

For depriving us in many cases, of the benefits of trial by jury;

For transporting us beyond seas to be tried for pretended offenses;

For abolishing the free system of English laws in a neighboring province, establishing therein an arbitrary government, and enlarging its boundaries so as to render it at once an example and fit instrument for introducing the same absolute rule into these colonies;

For taking away our charters, abolishing our most valuable laws, and altering fundamentally the forms of our governments;

For suspending our own legislatures, and declaring themselves invested with power to legislate for us in all cases whatsoever.

He has abdicated government here, by declaring us out of his protection and waging war against us.

He has plundered our seas, ravaged our coasts, burned our towns, and destroyed the lives of our people.

He is at this time transporting large armies of foreign mercenaries to complete the works of death, desolation and tyranny, already begun with circumstances of cruelty and perfidy scarcely paralleled in the most barbarous ages, and totally unworthy the head of a civilized nation.

He has constrained our fellow citizens taken captive on the high seas to bear arms against their country, to become the executioners of their friends and brethren, or to fall themselves by their hands.

He has excited domestic insurrections amongst us, and has endeavored to bring on the inhabitants of our frontiers, the merciless Indian savages, whose known rule of warfare, is an undistinguished destruction of all ages, sexes and conditions.

In every stage of these oppressions we have petitioned for redress in the most humble terms: our repeated petitions have been answered only by repeated injury. A prince whose character is thus marked by every act which may define a tyrant is unfit to be the ruler of a free people.

Nor have we been wanting in attention to our British brethren. We have warned them from time to time of attempts by their legislature to extend an unwarrantable jurisdiction over us. We have reminded them of the circumstances of our emigration and settlement here. We have appealed to their native justice and magnanimity, and we have conjured them by the ties of our common kindred to disavow these usurpations, which would inevitably interrupt our connections and correspondence. They too have been deaf to the voice of justice and of consanguinity. We must, therefore, acquiesce in the necessity, which denounces our separation, and hold them, as we hold the rest of mankind, enemies in war, in peace friends.

We, therefore, the representatives of the United States of America, in General Congress, assembled, appealing to the Supreme Judge of the world for the rectitude of our intentions, do, in the name, and by the authority of the good people of these colonies, solemnly publish and declare, that these united colonies are, and of right ought to be free and independent states; that they are absolved from all allegiance to the British Crown, and that all political connection between them and the state of Great Britain, is and ought to be totally dissolved; and that as free and independent states, they have full power to levy war, conclude peace, contract alliances, establish commerce, and to do all other acts and things which independent states may of right do. And for the support of this declaration, with a firm reliance on the protection of Divine Providence, we mutually pledge to each other our lives, our fortunes and our sacred honor.

Signed by John Hancock of Massachusetts as President of the Congress and by the fifty-five other Representatives of the thirteen United States of America.

The Constitution of the United States of America

Note: Footnotes, headings, and explanations have been added to aid the reader. The explanations within the body of the text are enclosed in brackets [ ]. The parts of the Constitution that are no longer in effect are printed in *italic* type. Capitalization, spelling, and punctuation have been modernized.

PREAMBLE

We the people of the United States, in order to form a more perfect Union, establish justice, insure domestic tranquility,[1] provide for the common defense, promote the general welfare, and secure the blessings of liberty to ourselves and our posterity [descendants], do ordain [issue] and establish this Constitution for the United States of America.

ARTICLE I. CONGRESS

Section 1. Legislative Power All legislative powers herein granted shall be vested in a Congress of the United States, which shall consist of a Senate and House of Representatives.

Section 2. House of Representatives [1] The House of Representatives shall be composed of members chosen every second year by the people of the several states, and the electors [voters] in each state shall have the qualifications requisite [required] for electors of the most numerous branch of the state legislature.

[2] No person shall be a representative who shall not have attained to the age of twenty-five years and been seven years a citizen of the United States, and who shall not, when elected, be an inhabitant of that state in which he shall be chosen.

[3] Representatives and direct taxes[2] shall be apportioned among the several states which may be included within this Union according to their respective numbers [population], *which shall be determined by adding to the whole number of free persons, including those bound to service for a term of years* [indentured servants], *and excluding Indians not taxed, three-fifths of all other persons.*[3] The actual enumeration [census] shall be made within three years after the first meeting of the Congress of the United States, and within every subsequent term of ten years, in such manner as they shall by law direct. The number of representatives shall not exceed one for every thirty thousand, but each state shall have at least one representative; *and until such enumeration shall be made, the State of New Hampshire shall be entitled to choose three, Massachusetts eight,*

---

[1] "Insure domestic tranquility" means *assure peace within the nation.*

[2] Modified by Amendment XVI, which granted Congress the power to levy a direct tax on individual incomes rather than on the basis of state populations.

[3] "Other persons" refers to slaves. Amendment XIII abolished slavery; Amendment XIV specifically eliminated the three-fifths formula.

Rhode Island and Providence Plantations one, Connecticut five, New York six, New Jersey four, Pennsylvania eight, Delaware one, Maryland six, Virginia ten, North Carolina five, South Carolina five, and Georgia three.[1]

[4] When vacancies happen in the representation from any state, the executive authority [governor] thereof shall issue writs of election[2] to fill such vacancies.

[5] The House of Representatives shall choose their Speaker and other officers; and shall have the sole power of impeachment.[3]

Section 3. Senate [1] The Senate of the United States shall be composed of two senators from each state, *chosen by the legislature thereof,*[4] for six years; and each senator shall have one vote.

[2] *Immediately after they shall be assembled in consequence of the first election, they shall be divided as equally as may be into three classes. The seats of the senators of the first class shall be vacated at the expiration of the second year, of the second class at the expiration of the fourth year, and of the third class at the expiration of the sixth year,*[5] so that one-third may be chosen every second year; *and if vacancies happen by resignation, or otherwise, during the recess of the legislature of any state, the executive [governor] thereof may make temporary appointments until the next meeting of the legislature, which shall then fill such vacancies.*[6]

[3] No person shall be a senator who shall not have attained to the age of thirty years and been nine years a citizen of the United States, and who shall not, when elected, be an inhabitant of that state for which he shall be chosen.

---

[1]Temporary provision.

[2]"Issue writs of election" means *call a special election.*

[3]"Power of impeachment" means *right to charge federal officials with misconduct.*

[4]Replaced by Amendment XVII, which provided for popular election of senators.

[5]Temporary provision, designed to organize the first Senate in such a way that, thereafter, only one-third of its members would be subject to replacement at each successive election.

[6]Modified by Amendment XVII, which permits a governor to select a temporary replacement to fill the vacancy until the next election.

[4] The vice president of the United States shall be president of the Senate, but shall have no vote, unless they be equally divided [tied].

[5] The Senate shall choose their other officers, and also a president pro tempore [temporary presiding officer], in the absence of the vice president, or when he shall exercise the office of president of the United States.

[6] The Senate shall have sole power to try all impeachments.[7] When sitting for that purpose, they shall be on oath or affirmation.[8] When the president of the United States is tried, the chief justice [of the United States] shall preside; and no person shall be convicted without the concurrence of two-thirds of the members present.

[7] Judgment in cases of impeachment shall not extend further than to removal from office, and disqualification to hold and enjoy any office of honor, trust, or profit under the United States; but the party convicted shall nevertheless be liable and subject to indictment, trial, judgment, and punishment, according to law.

Section 4. Elections and Meetings of Congress [1] The times, places, and manner of holding elections for senators and representatives shall be prescribed [designated] in each state by the legislature thereof; but the Congress may at any time by law make or alter such regulations, except as to the places of choosing senators.

[2] The Congress shall assemble at least once in every year, *and such meeting shall be on the first Monday in December,*[9] unless they shall by law appoint a different day.

Section 5. Rules and Procedures of the Two Houses [1] Each house shall be the judge of the elections, returns, and qualifications of its own members,[10] and a majority of each shall

---

[7]"To try all impeachments" means *to conduct the trials of officials impeached by the House of Representatives.* When trying such cases, the Senate serves as a court.

[8]If taking an oath violates a member's religious principles, that person may "affirm" rather than "swear."

[9]Amendment XX changed this date to January 3.

[10]This provision empowers either house, by a majority vote, to refuse to seat a newly elected member.

constitute a quorum[1] to do business; but a smaller number may adjourn from day to day, and may be authorized to compel the attendance of absent members, in such manner, and under such penalties, as each house may provide.

[2] Each house may determine the rules of its proceedings, punish its members for disorderly behavior, and with the concurrence of two-thirds, expel a member.

[3] Each house shall keep a journal[2] of its proceedings, and from time to time publish the same, excepting such parts as may in their judgment require secrecy; and the yeas [affirmative votes] and nays [negative votes] of the members of either house on any question shall, at the desire of one-fifth of those present, be entered on the journal.

[4] Neither house, during the session of Congress, shall, without the consent of the other, adjourn for more than three days, nor to any other place than that in which the two houses shall be sitting.

Section 6. Members' Privileges and Restrictions [1] The senators and representatives shall receive a compensation for their services, to be ascertained [fixed] by law and paid out of the treasury of the United States. They shall in all cases except treason, felony [serious crime], and breach of the peace [disorderly conduct], be privileged [immune] from arrest during their attendance at the session of their respective houses, and in going to and returning from the same; and for any speech or debate in either house, they shall not be questioned in any other place.[3]

[2] No senator or representative shall, during the time for which he was elected, be appointed to any civil office under the authority of the United States, which shall have been created, or the emoluments [salary] whereof shall have been increased, during

such time; and no person holding any office under the United States shall be a member of either house during his continuance in office.

Section 7. Lawmaking Procedures [1] All bills for raising revenue shall originate in the House of Representatives; but the Senate may propose or concur with amendments as on other bills.

[2] Every bill which shall have passed the House of Representatives and the Senate shall, before it becomes a law, be presented to the president of the United States; if he approve, he shall sign it, but if not, he shall return it, with his objections, to that house in which it shall have originated, who shall enter the objections at large on their journal, and proceed to reconsider it. If after such reconsideration two-thirds of that house shall agree to pass the bill, it shall be sent, together with the objections, to the other house, by which it shall likewise be reconsidered, and, if approved by two-thirds of that house, it shall become a law. But in all such cases the votes of both houses shall be determined by yeas and nays, and the names of the persons voting for and against the bill shall be entered on the journal of each house respectively. If any bill shall not be returned by the president within ten days (Sundays excepted) after it shall have been presented to him, the same shall be a law, in like manner as if he had signed it, unless the Congress by their adjournment prevent its return, in which case it shall not be a law.[4]

[3] Every order, resolution, or vote to which the concurrence of the Senate and House of Representatives may be necessary (except on a question of adjournment) shall be presented to the president of the United States; and before the same shall take effect, shall be approved by him, or, being disapproved by him, shall be repassed by two-thirds of the Senate and House of Representatives, according to the rules and limitations prescribed in the case of a bill.

Section 8. Powers of Congress The Congress shall have power:

[1] To lay and collect taxes, duties, imposts,

---

[1]A "quorum" is the *number of members that must be present in order to conduct business.*

[2]This journal is published as the *Congressional Record.*

[3]"They shall not be questioned in any other place" means that *they may not be sued for slander or libel.* Freedom from arrest during congressional sessions and freedom of speech within the halls of Congress—two privileges granted to members of Congress—are known as *congressional immunity.*

---

[4]If Congress adjourns before the ten-day period is up, the president can kill a bill by ignoring it ("putting it in his pocket"). Therefore, this type of presidential rejection is called a *pocket veto.*

and excises,[1] to pay the debts and provide for the common defense and general welfare of the United States; but all duties, imposts, and excises shall be uniform [the same] throughout the United States;

[2] To borrow money on the credit of the United States;

[3] To regulate commerce with foreign nations, and among the several states, and with the Indian tribes;

[4] To establish a uniform rule of naturalization [admitting to citizenship], and uniform laws on the subject of bankruptcies throughout the United States;

[5] To coin money, regulate the value thereof, and of foreign coin, and fix [set] the standard of weights and measures;

[6] To provide for the punishment of counterfeiting[2] the securities and current coin of the United States;

[7] To establish post offices and post roads;

[8] To promote the progress of science and useful arts by securing for limited times to authors and inventors the exclusive right to their respective writings and discoveries;[3]

[9] To constitute tribunals [establish courts] inferior to [lower than] the Supreme Court;

[10] To define and punish piracies and felonies committed on the high seas[4] and offenses against the law of nations [international law];

[11] To declare war, grant letters of marque and reprisal,[5] and make rules concerning captures on land and water;

[12] To raise and support armies, but no appropriation of money to that use shall be for a longer term than two years;

[13] To provide and maintain a navy;

[14] To make rules for the government and regulation of the land and naval forces;

[15] To provide for calling forth the militia[6] to execute [carry out] the laws of the Union, suppress insurrections [rebellions], and repel invasions;

[16] To provide for organizing, arming, and disciplining [training] the militia, and for governing such part of them as may be employed in the service of the United States, reserving to the states respectively the appointment of the officers, and the authority of training the militia according to the discipline [regulations] prescribed by Congress;

[17] To exercise exclusive legislation[7] in all cases whatsoever, over such district (not exceeding ten miles square) as may, by cession of particular states, and the acceptance of Congress, become the seat of government of the United States, and to exercise like authority over all places purchased by the consent of the legislature of the state in which the same shall be, for the erection of forts, magazines [warehouses for explosives], arsenals, dockyards, and other needful buildings; and

[18] To make all laws which shall be necessary and proper for carrying into execution the foregoing powers and all other powers vested by this Constitution in the government of the United States, or in any department or officer thereof.[8]

Section 9. Powers Denied to the Federal Government [1] *The migration or importation of such persons as any of the states now existing shall think proper to admit shall not be prohibited by the Congress prior to the year 1808; but a tax or duty may be imposed on such importation, not exceeding ten dollars for each person.[9]*

---

[1]"Duties, imposts, and excises" are forms of taxation. Duties and imposts are taxes on imports. Excises are taxes on goods produced or services performed within a country.

[2]Making an imitation with the intent of passing it as the genuine article.

[3]Copyright and patent laws, passed by Congress on the basis of this clause, protect the rights of authors and inventors.

[4]Open ocean; waters outside the territorial limits of a country.

[5]Letters of marque and reprisal are government licenses issued to private citizens in time of war authorizing them to fit out armed vessels (called

privateers) for the purpose of capturing or destroying enemy ships.

[6]Citizen soldiers who are not in the regular armed forces but are subject to military duty in times of emergency; for example, the National Guard.

[7]"To exercise exclusive legislation ... over such district" means *to be solely responsible for making the laws for a designated area.*

[8]This is the so-called "elastic clause" of the Constitution, which allows Congress to carry out many actions not specifically listed.

[9]This temporary provision prohibited Congress from interfering with the importation of slaves ("such persons") before 1808.

[2] The privilege of the writ of habeas corpus[1] shall not be suspended, unless when in cases of rebellion or invasion the public safety may require it.

[3] No bill of attainder[2] or ex post facto law[3] shall be passed.

[4] No capitation [head] or other direct tax shall be laid, unless in proportion to the census or enumeration herein before directed to be taken.[4]

[5] No tax or duty shall be laid on articles exported from any state.

[6] No preference shall be given by any regulation of commerce or revenue to the ports of one state over those of another; nor shall vessels bound to, or from, one state be obliged to enter, clear, or pay duties in another.

[7] No money shall be drawn from the treasury, but in consequence of appropriations made by law; and a regular statement and account of the receipts and expenditures of all public money shall be published from time to time.

[8] No title of nobility shall be granted by the United States; and no person holding any office of profit or trust under them shall, without the consent of the Congress, accept of any present, emolument, office, or title, of any kind whatever, from any king, prince, or foreign state.

Section 10. Powers Denied to the States
[1] No state shall enter into any treaty, alliance, or confederation; grant letters of marque and reprisal; coin money; emit bills of credit;[5] make anything but gold and silver coin a tender [legal money] in payment of debts; pass any bill of attainder, ex post facto law, or law impairing the obligation of contracts,[6] or grant any title of nobility.

[2] No state shall, without the consent of the Congress, lay any imposts or duties on imports or exports, except what may be absolutely necessary for executing its inspection laws; and the net produce [income] of all duties and imposts, laid by any state on imports or exports, shall be for the use of the treasury of the United States; and all such laws shall be subject to the revision and control of the Congress.

[3] No state shall, without the consent of Congress, lay any duty of tonnage,[7] keep troops[8] or ships of war in time of peace, enter into any agreement or compact with another state or with a foreign power, or engage in war unless actually invaded or in such imminent [threatening] danger as will not admit of delay.

ARTICLE II. THE PRESIDENCY
Section 1. Executive Power [1] The executive power shall be vested in a president of the United States of America. He shall hold his office during the term of four years,[9] and, together with the vice president, chosen for the same term, be elected as follows:

[2] Each state shall appoint, in such manner as the legislature thereof may direct, a number of electors, equal to the whole number of senators and representatives to which the state may be entitled in the Congress; but no senator or representative, or person holding an office of trust or profit under the United States, shall be appointed an elector.

[3] *The electors shall meet in their respective states, and vote by ballot for two persons, of whom one at least shall not be an inhabitant of the same state with themselves. And they shall make a list of all the persons voted for, and of the number of votes for each; which list they shall sign and certify, and transmit sealed to the seat of the government of the United States, directed to the president of the Senate. The president of the Senate shall, in the presence of the Senate and House of Representatives, open all the certificates, and the votes shall then be*

---

[1] A "writ of habeas corpus" is a court order obtained by a person taken into custody, demanding to know the reasons for imprisonment. If the court rules that the reasons are insufficient, the prisoner is released.

[2] A law that deprives a person of civil rights without a trial.

[3] A law that punishes a person for a past action that was not unlawful at the time it was committed.

[4] Modified by Amendment XVI.

[5] "Emit bills of credit" means *issue paper money.*

[6] "Impairing the obligation of contracts" means

weakening the obligations persons assume when they enter into legal agreements.

[7] "Duty of tonnage" means a *tax based upon a vessel's cargo-carrying capacity.*

[8] Other than militia.

[9] Amendment XXII limits a president to two terms.

counted. The person having the greatest number of votes shall be the president, if such number be a majority of the whole number of electors appointed; and if there be more than one who have such majority, and have an equal number of votes, then the House of Representatives shall immediately choose by ballot one of them for president; and if no person have a majority, then from the five highest on the list the said House shall in like manner choose the president. But in choosing the president, the votes shall be taken by states, the representation from each state having one vote; a quorum for this purpose shall consist of a member or members from two-thirds of the states, and a majority of all the states shall be necessary to a choice. In every case, after the choice of the president, the person having the greatest number of votes of the electors shall be the vice president. But if there should remain two or more who have equal votes, the Senate shall choose from them by ballot the vice president.[1]

[4] The Congress may determine the time of choosing the electors, and the day on which they shall give their votes; which day shall be the same throughout the United States.

[5] No person except a natural-born citizen, *or a citizen of the United States at the time of the adoption of this Constitution*,[2] shall be eligible to the office of president; neither shall any person be eligible to that office who shall not have attained to the age of thirty-five years and been fourteen years a resident within the United States.

[6] In case of the removal of the president from office, or of his death, resignation, or inability to discharge the powers and duties of the said office, the same shall devolve on the vice president, and the Congress may by law provide for the case of removal, death, resignation, or inability, both of the president and vice president, declaring what officer shall

---

[1]Replaced by Amendment XII.

[2]Temporary provision.

[3]Modified by Amendments XX and XXV. Also, *United States Code Annotated, Title 3, Sec. 19*, provides as follows:

(a) (1) If, by reason of death, resignation, removal from office, inability, or failure to qualify, there is neither a President nor Vice President to discharge the powers and duties of the office of President, then the Speaker of the House of Representatives

then act as president, and such officer shall act accordingly, until the disability be removed, or a president shall be elected.[3]

[7] The president shall, at stated times, receive for his services a compensation, which shall neither be increased nor diminished during the period for which he shall have been elected, and he shall not receive within that period any other emolument from the United States, or any of them.

[8] Before he enter on the execution of his office, he shall take the following oath or affirmation:

"I do solemnly swear (or affirm) that I will faithfully execute the office of President of the United States, and will, to the best of my ability, preserve, protect, and defend the Constitution of the United States."

Section 2. Powers of the President [1] The president shall be commander in chief of the army and navy [all the armed forces] of the United States, and of the militia of the several states, when called into the actual service of the United States; he may require the opinion in writing of the principal officer in each of

---

shall, upon his resignation as Speaker and as Representative in Congress, act as President.

(2) The same rule shall apply in the case of the death, resignation, removal from office, or inability of an individual acting as President under this subsection.

(b) If, at the time when under subsection (a) of this section a Speaker is to begin the discharge of the powers and duties of the office of President, there is no Speaker, or the Speaker fails to qualify as Acting President, then the President *pro tempore* of the Senate shall, upon his resignation as President *pro tempore* and as Senator, act as President.

. . .

(d) (1) If, by reason of death, resignation, removal from office, inability, or failure to qualify, there is no President *pro tempore* to act as President under subsection (b) of this section, then the officer of the United States who is highest on the following list, and who is not under disability to discharge the powers and duties of the office of President, shall act as President: Secretary of State, Secretary of the Treasury, Secretary of Defense, Attorney General, Postmaster General, Secretary of the Interior, Secretary of Agriculture, Secretary of Commerce, Secretary of Labor, Secretary of Health, Education, and Welfare, Secretary of Housing and Urban Development. [Note: some department names have changed and other departments have been added.]

the executive departments upon any subject relating to the duties of their respective offices; and he shall have power to grant reprieves[1] and pardons[2] for offenses against the United States except in cases of impeachment.

[2] He shall have power, by and with the advice and consent of the Senate, to make treaties, provided two-thirds of the senators present concur; and he shall nominate, and, by and with the advice and consent of the Senate, shall appoint ambassadors, other public ministers and consuls, judges of the Supreme Court, and all other officers of the United States whose appointments are not herein otherwise provided for and which shall be established by law; but the Congress may by law vest the appointment of such inferior officers as they think proper in the president alone, in the courts of law, or in the heads of departments.

[3] The president shall have power to fill up all vacancies that may happen during the recess of the Senate, by granting commissions which shall expire at the end of their next session.

Section 3. Duties and Responsibilities of the President He shall, from time to time, give to the Congress information of the state of the Union, and recommend to their consideration such measures as he shall judge necessary and expedient [advisable]; he may, on extraordinary [special] occasions, convene both houses, or either of them, and in case of disagreement between them with respect to the time of adjournment, he may adjourn them to such time as he shall think proper; he shall receive ambassadors and other public ministers; he shall take care that the laws be faithfully executed, and shall commission [appoint] all the officers of the United States.

Section 4. Impeachment The president, vice president, and all civil officers[3] of the United States, shall be removed from office on impeachment for, and conviction of, treason, bribery, or other high crimes and misdemeanors [offenses].

---

[1]A "reprieve" is a postponement of the execution of a sentence.

[2]A "pardon" is a release from penalty.

[3]"Civil officers" include executive and judicial officials, but not members of Congress or officers in the armed forces.

ARTICLE III. THE SUPREME COURT AND OTHER COURTS

Section 1. Federal Courts The judicial power of the United States shall be vested in one Supreme Court, and in such inferior [lower] courts as the Congress may from time to time ordain and establish. The judges, both of the Supreme and inferior courts, shall hold their offices during good behavior, and shall, at stated times, receive for their services a compensation, which shall not be diminished during their continuance in office.

Section 2. Jurisdiction of Federal Courts [1] The judicial power shall extend to all cases in law and equity[4] arising under this Constitution, the laws of the United States, and treaties made, or which shall be made, under their authority; to all cases affecting ambassadors, other public ministers, and consuls; to all cases of admiralty and maritime jurisdiction;[5] to controversies to which the United States shall be a party; to controversies between two or more states, between a state and citizens of another state,[6] between citizens of different states, between citizens of the same state claiming lands under grants of different states, and between a state, or the citizens thereof, and foreign states, citizens, or subjects.[7]

[2] In all cases affecting ambassadors, other public ministers, and consuls, and those in which a state shall be a party, the Supreme Court shall have original jurisdiction.[8] In all the other cases before mentioned, the Supreme

---

[4]"Cases in law" refers mainly to disputes that arise from the violation of, or the interpretation of, federal laws, treaties, or the Constitution. "Equity" is a branch of the law that deals more generally with the prevention of injustice.

[5]Legal disputes involving ships and shipping on the high seas, in territorial waters, and on the navigable waterways within the country.

[6]Modified by Amendment XI, which provides that a state may not be sued in the federal courts by a citizen of another state (or by a citizen of a foreign country). A state, however, retains the right to sue a citizen of another state (or a citizen of a foreign country) in the federal courts.

[7]Modified by Amendment XI.

[8]"Original jurisdiction" means the authority of a court to hear cases that have not previously been tried by lower courts.

Court shall have appellate jurisdiction,[1] both as to law and fact, with such exceptions and under such regulations as the Congress shall make.

[3] The trial of all crimes, except in cases of impeachment, shall be by jury; and such trial shall be held in the state where the said crimes shall have been committed; but when not committed within any state, the trial shall be at such place or places as the Congress may by law have directed.

Section 3. Treason [1] Treason against the United States shall consist only in levying [carrying on] war against them, or in adhering to [assisting] their enemies, giving them aid and comfort. No person shall be convicted of treason unless on the testimony of two witnesses to the same overt [open; public] act, or on confession in open court.

[2] The Congress shall have power to declare the punishment of treason, but no attainder of treason shall work corruption of blood or forfeiture except during the life of the person attainted.[2]

ARTICLE IV. INTERSTATE RELATIONS

Section 1. Official Acts and Records Full faith and credit shall be given in each state to the public acts, records, and judicial proceedings of every other state.[3] And the Congress may, by general laws, prescribe the manner in which such acts, records, and proceedings shall be proved, and the effect thereof.

Section 2. Mutual Obligations of States
[1] The citizens of each state shall be entitled to all privileges and immunities of citizens in the several states.

[2] A person charged in any state with treason, felony, or other crime, who shall flee from justice and be found in another state, shall, on demand of the executive authority of the state from which he fled, be delivered up, to be removed to the state having jurisdiction of the crime.[4]

[3] *No person held to service or labor in one state, under the laws thereof, escaping into another, shall, in consequence of any law or regulation therein, be discharged from such service or labor, but shall be delivered up on claim of the party to whom such service or labor may be due.*[5]

Section 3. New States and Territories
[1] New states may be admitted by the Congress into this Union; but no new state shall be formed or erected within the jurisdiction of any other state; nor any state be formed by the junction [joining] of two or more states, or parts of states, without the consent of the legislatures of the states concerned as well as of the Congress.

[2] The Congress shall have power to dispose of and make all needful rules and regulations respecting the territory or other property belonging to the United States; and nothing in this Constitution shall be so construed [interpreted] as to prejudice [damage] any claims of the United States, or of any particular state.

Section 4. Federal Guarantees to the States
The United States shall guarantee to every state in this Union a republican form of government, and shall protect each of them against invasion; and on application of the legislature, or of the executive (when the legislature cannot be convened), against domestic violence [riots].

ARTICLE V. AMENDING THE CONSTITUTION

The Congress, whenever two-thirds of both houses shall deem [think] it necessary, shall propose amendments to this Constitution, or, on the application of the legislatures of two-thirds of the several states, shall call a convention for proposing amendments, which, in either case, shall be valid, to all intents and purposes, as part of this Constitution when ratified by the legislatures of three-fourths of the several states, or by conventions in three-fourths thereof, as the one or the other mode

---

[1] "Appellate jurisdiction" means the authority of a court to review cases that have previously been tried by lower courts.

[2] Punishment imposed on someone for treason may not be extended to that person's children or heirs.

[3] The official acts of each state must be accepted by the other states. The "full faith and credit" clause applies to court judgments, contracts, marriages, corporation charters, etc.

[4] The delivery by one state or government to another of fugitives from justice is called *extradition*.

[5] Since the phrase "person held to service or labor" refers to a slave, this clause was nullified by Amendment XIII.

[method] of ratification may be proposed by the Congress; provided *that no amendment which may be made prior to the year 1808 shall in any manner affect the first and fourth clauses in the ninth section of the first article; and*[1] that no state, without its consent, shall be deprived of its equal suffrage in the Senate.

ARTICLE VI. MISCELLANEOUS PROVISIONS

Section 1. Public Debts All debts contracted and engagements [agreements] entered into before the adoption of this Constitution shall be as valid [binding] against the United States under this Constitution as under the Confederation.

Section 2. Federal Supremacy This Constitution, and the laws of the United States which shall be made in pursuance thereof, and all treaties made, or which shall be made, under the authority of the United States, shall be the supreme law of the land; and the judges in every state shall be bound thereby, anything in the constitution or laws of any state to the contrary notwithstanding.[2]

Section 3. Oaths of Office The senators and representatives before mentioned, and the members of the several state legislatures, and all executive and judicial officers, both of the United States and of the several states, shall be bound by oath or affirmation to support this Constitution; but no religious test shall ever be required as a qualification to any office or public trust under the United States.

ARTICLE VII. RATIFICATION

The ratification of the conventions of nine states shall be sufficient for the establishment of this Constitution between the states so ratifying the same.

Done in convention, by the unanimous consent of the states present, the 17th day of September, in the year of our Lord 1787, and of the independence of the United States of America the twelfth. In witness whereof we have hereunto subscribed our names.

Signed by   George Washington [President and Deputy from Virginia] and 38 other delegates

Amendments to the Constitution

Note: The first ten amendments to the Constitution, adopted in 1791, make up the Bill of Rights. The year of adoption of later amendments (11 to 26) is given in parenthesis.

AMENDMENT I. FREEDOM OF RELIGION, SPEECH, PRESS, ASSEMBLY, AND PETITION

Congress shall make no law respecting an establishment of religion, or prohibiting the free exercise thereof;[3] or abridging [reducing] the freedom of speech or of the press; or the right of the people peaceably to assemble, and to petition the government for a redress [correction] of grievances.

AMENDMENT II. RIGHT TO BEAR ARMS

A well-regulated militia being necessary to the security of a free state, the right of the people to keep and bear arms shall not be infringed [weakened].

AMENDMENT III. QUARTERING OF TROOPS

No soldier shall, in time of peace, be quartered [assigned to live] in any house without the consent of the owner, nor in time of war, but in a manner to be prescribed by law.

AMENDMENT IV. SEARCHES AND SEIZURES

The right of the people to be secure [safe] in their persons, houses, papers, and effects [be-

---

[1] Temporary provision.

[2] This "supremacy clause" means that federal laws always override state legislation in cases of conflict.

[3] "The free exercise thereof" refers to freedom of worship.

longings] against unreasonable searches and seizures shall not be violated; and no [search] warrants shall issue but upon probable cause,[1] supported by oath or affirmation, and particularly describing the place to be searched, and the persons or things to be seized.

AMENDMENT V. RIGHTS OF THE ACCUSED; PROPERTY RIGHTS

No person shall be held to answer for a capital or otherwise infamous crime unless on a presentment or indictment of a grand jury,[2] except in cases arising in the land or naval forces, or in the militia, when in actual service in time of war or public danger; nor shall any person be subject for the same offense to be twice put in jeopardy of life or limb;[3] nor shall be compelled in any criminal case to be a witness against himself; nor be deprived of life, liberty, or property without due process of law;[4] nor shall private property be taken for public use without just compensation.[5]

AMENDMENT VI. ADDITIONAL RIGHTS OF THE ACCUSED

In all criminal prosecutions [trials], the accused shall enjoy the right to a speedy and public trial by an impartial [fair] jury of the state and district wherein the crime shall have been committed, which district shall have been previously ascertained by law; and to be informed of the nature and cause of the accusation; to be confronted with the witnesses against him; to have compulsory process for obtaining witnesses in his favor;[6] and to have the assistance of counsel for his defense.

---

[1]"Probable cause" means *a reasonable ground of suspicion.*

[2]"A capital or otherwise infamous crime" refers to serious offenses punishable by death or by imprisonment. Before someone may be tried for such a crime, a grand jury must decide that sufficient evidence exists to bring that person to trial.

[3]A person may not be tried twice for the same offense (double jeopardy).

[4]"Due process of law" means *proper legal procedure.*

[5]The government has the power of *eminent domain,* or the right to take private property for public use. This provision requires the government to pay the owner a fair price for such property.

[6]The accused person has the right to request the

AMENDMENT VII. CIVIL SUITS

In suits at common law[7] where the value in controversy shall exceed twenty dollars, the right of trial by jury shall be preserved, and no fact tried by a jury shall be otherwise reexamined in any court of the United States, than according to the rules of the common law.

AMENDMENT VIII. BAILS, FINES, AND PUNISHMENTS

Excessive bail shall not be required, nor excessive fines imposed, nor cruel and unusual punishments inflicted.

AMENDMENT IX. RIGHTS NOT LISTED

The enumeration [listing] in the Constitution of certain rights shall not be construed to deny or disparage [weaken] others retained by the people.

AMENDMENT X. POWERS RESERVED TO THE STATES AND PEOPLE

The powers not delegated to the United States by the Constitution, nor prohibited by it to the states, are reserved to the states respectively, or to the people.

AMENDMENT XI. SUITS AGAINST STATES (1798)

The judicial power of the United States shall not be construed to extend to any suit in law or equity, commenced or prosecuted against one of the United States by citizens of another state, or by citizens or subjects of any foreign state.

AMENDMENT XII. ELECTION OF PRESIDENT AND VICE PRESIDENT (1804)

[1] The electors shall meet in their respective states, and vote by ballot for president

---

court to issue an order, or subpoena, compelling a witness to appear in court.

[7]"Common law" is law based on custom and precedent (past decisions made in similar cases). Originating in England, it was brought to the English colonies by the early settlers and became the foundation of the American legal system.

and vice president, one of whom at least shall not be an inhabitant of the same state with themselves; they shall name in their ballots the person voted for as president, and in distinct [separate] ballots the person voted for as vice president; and they shall make distinct lists of all persons voted for as president, and of all persons voted for as vice president, and of the number of votes for each, which lists they shall sign and certify, and transmit sealed to the seat of the government of the United States, directed to the president of the Senate.

[2] The president of the Senate shall, in the presence of the Senate and House of Representatives, open all the certificates, and the votes shall then be counted; the person having the greatest number of votes for president shall be the president, if such number be a majority of the whole number of electors appointed; and if no person have such majority, then from the persons having the highest numbers not exceeding three on the list of those voted for as president, the House of Representatives shall choose immediately, by ballot, the president.[1] But in choosing the president, the votes shall be taken by states, the representation from each state having one vote; a quorum for this purpose shall consist of a member or members from two-thirds of the states, and a majority of all the states shall be necessary to a choice. And if the House of Representatives shall not choose a president whenever the right of choice shall devolve upon them, *before the fourth day of March next following*,[2] then the vice president shall act as president, as in the case of the death or other constitutional disability of the president.

[3] The person having the greatest number of votes as vice president shall be the vice president, if such number be a majority of the whole number of electors appointed; and if no person have a majority, then, from the two highest numbers on the list, the Senate shall choose the vice president; a quorum for the purpose shall consist of two-thirds of the whole number of senators, and a majority of the whole number shall be necessary to a choice. But no person constitutionally ineligible to the office of president shall be eligible to that of vice president of the United States.

AMENDMENT XIII. ABOLITION OF SLAVERY (1865)

Section 1. Slavery Forbidden Neither slavery nor involuntary servitude [compulsory service], except as a punishment for crime whereof the party shall have been duly convicted, shall exist within the United States, or any place subject to their jurisdiction.

Section 2. Enforcement Power Congress shall have power to enforce this article [amendment] by appropriate [suitable] legislation.

AMENDMENT XIV. CITIZENSHIP AND CIVIL RIGHTS (1868)

Section 1. Rights of Citizens All persons born or naturalized in the United States, and subject to the jurisdiction thereof, are citizens of the United States and of the state wherein they reside.[3] No state shall make or enforce any law which shall abridge the privileges or immunities of citizens of the United States; nor shall any state deprive any person of life, liberty, or property, without due process of law;[4] nor deny to any person within its jurisdiction the equal protection of the laws.[5]

Section 2. Apportionment of Representatives in Congress Representatives shall be apportioned among the several states according to their respective numbers, counting the whole number of persons in each state, excluding Indians not taxed.[6] But when the right to vote at any election for the choice of electors for president and vice president of the United States, representatives in Congress, the executive and judicial officers of a state, or the members of the legislature thereof, is denied to any of the *male* inhabitants of such state,

---

[1] Only twice has the House of Representatives chosen the President: Thomas Jefferson in 1801 and John Quincy Adams in 1825.

[2] Changed to January 20 by Amendment XX.

[3] This clause made the former slaves citizens.

[4] The primary purpose of this clause was to protect the civil rights of the former slaves. However, after the Supreme Court broadened the meaning of the word "person" to include "corporation," the clause began to be used to protect business interests as well.

[5] The "equal protection" clause has served as the legal basis for many civil rights cases.

[6] This clause nullifies the three-fifths formula of Article I, Section 2.

being *twenty-one* years of age and citizens of the United States, or in any way abridged, except for participation in rebellion or other crime, the basis of representation therein shall be reduced in the proportion which the number of such *male* citizens shall bear to the whole number of *male* citizens *twenty-one* years of age in such state.[1]

Section 3. Persons Disqualified From Public Office No person shall be a senator or representative in Congress, or elector of president and vice president, or hold any office, civil or military, under the United States, or under any state, who, having previously taken an oath, as a member of Congress, or as an officer of the United States, or as a member of any state legislature, or as an executive or judicial officer of any state, to support the Constitution of the United States, shall have engaged in insurrection or rebellion against the same, or given aid or comfort to the enemies thereof. But Congress may, by a vote of two-thirds of each house, remove such disability.

Section 4. Valid Public Debt Defined The validity [legality] of the public debt of the United States, authorized by law, including debts incurred for payment of pensions and bounties [extra allowances] for services in suppressing insurrection or rebellion, shall not be questioned. But neither the United States nor any state shall assume or pay any debt or obligation incurred in aid of insurrection or rebellion against the United States, or any claim for the loss or emancipation [liberation] of any slave; but all such debts, obligations, and claims shall be held illegal and void.

Section 5. Enforcement Power The Congress shall have power to enforce, by appropriate legislation, the provisions of this article.

AMENDMENT XV. RIGHT OF SUFFRAGE (1870)

Section 1. African Americans Guaranteed the Vote The right of citizens of the United States to vote shall not be denied or abridged by the United States or by any state on account of race, color, or previous condition of servitude [slavery].

Section 2. Enforcement Power The Congress shall have power to enforce this article by appropriate legislation.

---

[1]Italicized words in this section were invalidated by Amendments XIX and XXVI.

AMENDMENT XVI. INCOME TAXES (1913)

The Congress shall have power to lay and collect taxes on incomes, from whatever source derived, without apportionment among the several states, and without regard to any census or enumeration.

AMENDMENT XVII. POPULAR ELECTION OF SENATORS (1913)

[1] The Senate of the United States shall be composed of two senators from each state, elected by the people thereof, for six years; and each senator shall have one vote. The electors [voters] in each state shall have the qualifications requisite for electors of the most numerous branch of the state legislatures.[2]

[2] When vacancies happen in the representation of any state in the Senate, the executive authority of such state shall issue writs of election to fill such vacancies: Provided, that the legislature of any state may empower [authorize] the executive thereof to make temporary appointments until the people fill the vacancies by election as the legislature may direct.

[3] *This amendment shall not be so construed as to affect the election or term of any senator chosen before it becomes valid as part of the Constitution.*[3]

AMENDMENT XVIII. PROHIBITION (1919)[4]

Section 1. Intoxicating Liquors Prohibited
After one year from the ratification of this article, the manufacture, sale, or transportation of intoxicating liquors within, the importation thereof into, or the exportation thereof from the United States and all territory subject to the jurisdiction thereof, for beverage purposes, is hereby prohibited.

Section 2. Enforcement Power *The Congress and the several states shall have concurrent power to enforce this article by appropriate legislation.*

---

[2]This amendment changed the method of electing senators as given in Article I, Section 3.

[3]Temporary provision designed to protect those elected under the system previously in effect.

[4]This entire amendment was repealed in 1933 by Amendment XXI.

Section 3. Conditions of Ratification *This article shall be inoperative unless it shall have been ratified as an amendment to the Constitution by the legislatures of the several states, as provided in the Constitution, within seven years from the date of the submission hereof to the states by the Congress.*

AMENDMENT XIX. WOMEN'S SUFFRAGE (1920)

[1] The right of citizens of the United States to vote shall not be denied or abridged by the United States or by any state on account of sex.

[2] Congress shall have power to enforce this article by appropriate legislation.

AMENDMENT XX. PRESIDENTIAL AND CONGRESSIONAL TERMS[1] (1933)

Section 1. Terms of Office The terms of the president and vice president shall end at noon on the 20th day of January, and the terms of senators and representatives at noon on the 3d day of January, of the years in which such terms would have ended if this article had not been ratified; and the terms of their successors[2] shall then begin.

Section 2. Convening Congress The Congress shall assemble at least once in every year, and such meeting shall begin at noon on the 3d day of January, unless they shall by law appoint a different day.[3]

Section 3. Presidential Succession If, at the time fixed for the beginning of the term of the president, the president-elect[4] shall have died, the vice president-elect shall become president. If a president shall not have been chosen

---

[1]This amendment is often called the "Lame Duck" Amendment because it shortened the period (from four months to two) between the elections in November and the time when defeated officeholders or officeholders who do not run again (known as "lame ducks") leave office.

[2]A "successor" is a person who is elected or appointed to replace another in a public office.

[3]This section changed the date given in Article I, Section 4.

[4]A "president-elect" is a person who has been elected to the presidency but has not yet assumed office.

---

before the time fixed for the beginning of his term, or if the president-elect shall have failed to qualify, then the vice president-elect shall act as president until a president shall have qualified; and the Congresss may by law provide for the case wherein neither a president-elect nor a vice president-elect shall have qualified, declaring who shall then act as president, or the manner in which one who is to act shall be selected, and such person shall act accordingly until a president or vice president shall have qualified.

Section 4. Selection of President and Vice President The Congress may by law provide for the case of the death of any of the persons from whom the House of Representatives may choose a president whenever the right of choice shall have devolved upon them, and for the case of the death of any of the persons from whom the Senate may choose a vice president whenever the right of choice shall have devolved upon them.

Section 5. Effective Date *Sections 1 and 2 shall take effect on the 15th day of October following the ratification of this article.*[5]

Section 6. Conditions of Ratification *This article shall be inoperative unless it shall have been ratified as an amendment to the Constitution by the legislatures of three-fourths of the several states within seven years from the date of its submission.*[6]

AMENDMENT XXI. REPEAL OF PROHIBITION (1933)

Section 1. Amendment XVIII Repealed The Eighteenth Article of amendment to the Constitution of the United States is hereby repealed.

Section 2. Shipment of Liquor Into "Dry" Areas The transportation or importation into any state, territory, or possession of the United States for delivery or use therein of intoxicating liquors in violation of the laws thereof is hereby prohibited.[7]

Section 3. Conditions of Ratification *article shall be inoperative unless it shall have been ratified as an amendment to the Constitu-*

---

[5]Temporary provision.

[6]Temporary provision.

[7]This section allowed individual states to prohibit the use of intoxicating liquors if they wished to.

tion by conventions in the several states,[1] *as provided in the Constitution, within seven years from the date of the submission hereof to the states by the Congress.*[2]

AMENDMENT XXII. LIMITING PRESIDENTIAL TERMS (1951)

Section 1. Limit Placed on Tenure No person shall be elected to the office of the president more than twice, and no person who has held the office of president, or acted as president, for more than two years of a term to which some other person was elected president shall be elected to the office of the president more than once. *But this article shall not apply to any person holding the office of president when this article was proposed by the Congress, and shall not prevent any person who may be holding the office of president, or acting as president, during the term within which this article becomes operative from holding the office of president or acting as president during the remainder of such term.*[3]

Section 2. Conditions of Ratification *This article shall be inoperative unless it shall have been ratified as an amendment to the Constitution by the legislatures of three-fourths of the several states within seven years from the date of its submission to the states by the Congress.*[4]

AMENDMENT XXIII. SUFFRAGE FOR WASHINGTON, D.C. (1961)

Section 1. D.C. Presidential Electors The district constituting [making up] the seat of government of the United States shall appoint in such manner as the Congress may direct:

A number of electors of president and vice president equal to the whole number of senators and representatives in Congress to which the district would be entitled if it were a state, but in no event more than the least populous state;[5] they shall be in addition to those appointed by the states, but they shall be con-

sidered, for the purposes of the election of president and vice president, to be electors appointed by a state; and they shall meet in the district and perform such duties as provided by the Twelfth Article of amendment.[6]

Section 2. Enforcement Power The Congress shall have power to enforce this article by appropriate legislation.

AMENDMENT XXIV. POLL TAXES (1964)

Section 1. Poll Tax Barred The right of citizens of the United States to vote in any primary or other election for president or vice president, for electors for president or vice president, or for senator or representative in Congress, shall not be denied or abridged by the United States or any state by reason of failure to pay any poll tax or other tax.

Section 2. Enforcement Power The Congress shall have the power to enforce this article by appropriate legislation.

AMENDMENT XXV. PRESIDENTIAL SUCCESSION AND DISABILITY (1967)

Section 1. Elevation of Vice President In case of the removal of the president from office or his death or resignation, the vice president shall become president.

Section 2. Vice Presidential Vacancy Whenever there is a vacancy in the office of the vice president, the president shall nominate a vice president who shall take the office upon confirmation by a majority vote of both houses of Congress.

Section 3. Temporary Disability Whenever the president transmits to the president pro tempore of the Senate and the Speaker of the House of Representatives his written declaration that he is unable to discharge the powers and duties of his office, and until he transmits to them a written declaration to the contrary, such powers and duties shall be discharged by the vice president as acting president.

Section 4. Other Provisions for Presidential Disability [1] Whenever the vice president and a majority of either the principal officers of the executive departments, or of such other body as Congress may by law provide, trans-

---

[1]This was the first amendment to be submitted by Congress for ratification by state conventions rather than state legislatures.

[2]Temporary provision.

[3]Temporary provision.

[4]Temporary provision.

[5]At the present time, the District of Columbia is entitled to three electors.

---

[6]By providing for electors, this amendment gave residents of Washington, D.C., the right to vote for president and vice president.

mit to the president pro tempore of the Senate and the Speaker of the House of Representatives their written declaration that the president is unable to discharge the powers and duties of his office, the vice president shall immediately assume the powers and duties of the office as acting president.

[2] Thereafter, when the president transmits to the president pro tempore of the Senate and the Speaker of the House of Representatives his written declaration that no inability exists, he shall resume the powers and duties of his office unless the vice president and a majority of either the principal officers of the executive department, or of such other body as Congress may by law provide, transmit within four days to the president pro tempore of the Senate and the Speaker of the House of Representatives their written declaration that the president is unable to discharge the powers and duties of his office. Thereupon Congress shall decide the issue, assembling within 48 hours for that purpose if not in session. If the Congress, within 21 days after receipt of the latter written declaration, or, if Congress is not in session, within 21 days after Congress is required to assemble, determines by two-thirds vote of both houses that the president is unable to discharge the powers and duties of his office, the vice president shall continue to discharge the same as acting president; otherwise, the president shall resume the powers and duties of his office.

AMENDMENT XXVI. VOTE FOR 18-YEAR-OLDS (1971)

Section 1. Lowering the Voting Age The right of citizens of the United States, who are 18 years of age or older, to vote shall not be denied or abridged by the United States or by any state on account of age.

Section 2. Enforcement Power The Congress shall have power to enforce this article by appropriate legislation.

Books of Interest to Students

(The chapter each book is most closely related to is indicated in parenthesis.)

Unit One   The Principles Behind American Government

Bowen, Catherine Drinker. *Miracle at Philadelphia*. Little, Brown, 1966. Classic account of the Constitutional Convention, the discussions, struggles, compromises, and the leading figures who took part. (2)

Corwin, Edward S. *The Constitution and What It Means Today*. Princeton Univ. Press, 1980. A section by section analysis of the document, mainly through a discussion of Supreme Court cases since the 1790s. (3)

Faber, Doris, and Harold Faber. *We the People: The Story of the United States Constitution Since 1787*. Charles Scribner's Sons, 1987. Written in a lively style, the book presents an interpretation of the document and its evolution over the years. (3)

Gerberg, Mort. *The U.S. Constitution for Everyone: A Guide to the Most Important Document Written by and for the People of the United States*. Perigee, 1987. An introduction to the document; written in an easily understood style. (3)

Morris, Richard B. *The Constitution*. Lerner Publ., 1985. A short, easily understood history of the creation of the Constitution from the Articles of the Confederation to the adoption of the final document in 1789. It also includes a simplified outline of the Constitution. (2)

Morris, Richard B. *Witness at the Creation*. Holt, Rinehart, 1985. Account of the people who wrote the Constitution. Centers on Alexander Hamilton, John Jay, and James Madison and their part in creating and ratifying the document. (2)

Perry, Richard L., editor. *Sources of Our Liberties*. American Bar Assoc., 1987. Thirty-two documents, from the Magna Carta to the Bill of Rights, with annotations and comments. (2)

Raynor, Thomas. *Politics, Power, and People: Four Governments in Action*. Franklin Watts, 1983. A comparison of the political systems of two democracies (the United States and Great Britain) and two authoritarian systems (the Soviet Union and Argentina). (1)

Suter, Coral, and Marshall Croddy. *American Album: 200 Years of Constitutional Democracy*. Constitutional Rights Foundation, 1986. Chronological account of people, events, and issues related to the Constitution and its impact on American life. (3)

Unit Two   The American Political Process

Archdeacon, Thomas J. *Becoming American: An Ethnic History*. The Free Press, 1983. Detailed survey of the role of immigration in shaping the U.S. national character. (4)

Bach, Julie, editor, and others. *Civil Liberties: Opposing Viewpoints*. Greenhaven Press, 1988. Discussion of topics such as separation of church and state, free speech, right to privacy, government protection of the rights of minorities. (4)

Broder, David S. *Behind the Front Page*. Simon & Schuster, 1987. A reporter describes how the press handled the selection of political stories in the 1970s. He also discusses the ethical issues faced by journalists. (7)

Corbin, Carole Lynn. *The Right to Vote*. Franklin Watts, 1985. Straightforward history of the efforts of minorities and women to win the right to vote. Discusses the impact of voters on U.S. politics. (6)

Frank, Beryl. *The Pictorial History of the Republican Party. The Pictorial History of the Democratic Party*. Castle Books, 1980. These two books present, by election years, the issues, slogans, and publicity items of the various campaigns. (5)

Grant, Joanne, editor. *Black Protest: History, Documents, and Analyses, 1619-Present*. Fawcett Premier Book. Well-done documentary history of protest. (4)

Green, Mark. *Who Owns Congress?* Dell, 1982. Thought-provoking account of the influence of PACs and other sources of money on legislators. Also contains suggestions for reform. (7)

Hentoff, Nat. *The First Freedom: The Tumultuous History of Free Speech in America*. Delacorte Press, 1980. Presents details of famous incidents involving the right of free speech. (4)

Hyman, Sidney. *Youth in Politics*. Basic Books, 1972. Still-relevant account that highlights the role young people play in the electoral process. The book focuses on the 1960s. (5)

Kalven, Harry, Jr. *A Worthy Tradition: Freedom of Speech in America*. Harper, 1988. Critical but positive examination of the American view of freedom of speech. (4)

Maddox, Robert L. *Separation of Church and State; guarantor of religious freedom*. Crossroad, 1987. Includes discussion of issues of school prayer, tax support for religious schools, and political lobbying by religious groups. (4)

Mayer, Martin. *Making News*. Doubleday, 1987. Describes how newspapers handled particular stories and how media control public's view of world. (7)

Modl, Thomas, editor. *America's Elections: Opposing Viewpoints*. Greenhaven Press, 1988. Presents views on who should vote, financing elections, the role of political parties, and how to reform presidential elections. (6)

National Party Conventions, 1931–1984. Congressional Quarterly, 1987. Comprehensive accounts of happenings at the various conventions. (5)

Ornstein, Norman, Andrew Rohut, and Larry McCarthy. *The People, the Press and Politics: The Times Mirror Study of the American Electorate*. Addison-Wesley, 1988. An analysis of the "beliefs" of each of 11 sociopolitical groups that the study divided the U.S. population into. (7)

Reinsch, J. Leonard. *Getting Elected: From Radio and Roosevelt to Television and Reagan*. Hippocrene Books, 1988. Description of the impact of media on elections by a media adviser to several Presidents. (5)

Samuels, Cynthia K. *It's a Free Country! A young person's guide to politics and elections*. Atheneum, 1988. Easy to comprehend account of the way people get elected and the nature of politics in the United States. Gives case histories of elected officials and tips on how to participate in campaigns. (5)

Sexton, John, and Nat Brandt. *How Free Are We? What the Constitution Says We Can and Cannot Do*. M. Evans & Co., 1986. In question-and-answer format, the authors present in a lively way the history of the Constitution, individual liberties, court decisions, and how the Constitution affects our daily lives. (4)

Taylor, C. L. *Censorship*. Franklin Watts, 1986. A short but comprehensive analysis of the issue of censorship. Focuses on the application of the First Amendment. Easy to follow. (4)

Whitney, Sharon, and Thomas Raynor. *Women in Politics*. Franklin Watts, 1986. History of women's participation in American political life. Includes interviews with current political figures. (5)

Wilson, Reginald. *Think About Our Rights; civil liberties and the United States*. Walker, 1988. Easily understood account of the rights and responsibilities shared by U.S. citizens and discussion of how civil rights issues affect young people. (4)

Unit Three   The Legislative Branch of American Government

Baker, Ross K. *House and Senate*. W.W. Norton, 1989. Insider's view of Congress. Interviews with lawmakers, staff members, journalists, lobbyists. (8)

Coy, Harold (revised by Barbara Dammann). *Congress*. Franklin Watts, 1981. Short, easy to understand account of the workings of Congress, its relationship with the other two branches, and the influence of pressure groups. (8)

Davis, Bertha. *The National Debt.* Franklin Watts, 1987. Easy to comprehend analysis of the debt crisis, the economic implications, the federal budget-making process, and the impact of government borrowing and spending. (10)

Drury, Allen. *Advise and Consent.* Doubleday, 1959. Novel about the workings of Congress by a person who knows government well. Still relevant. (8)

Reid, T. R. *Congressional Odyssey: The Saga of a Senate Bill.* W. H. Freeman, 1980. Case study of the passage of a bill. Details the legislative process that the Waterways Act of 1979 went through. (9)

Unit Four   The Executive Branch of American Government

Boller, Paul F., Jr. *Presidential Campaigns.* Oxford, 1984. History of campaigns. Background on candidates, the times. Includes anecdotes. (11)

Cooney, James A. *Think About Foreign Policy: The U.S. and World.* Walker, 1988. Easy to comprehend account of the structure and historical development of foreign policy and the impact of the policies on U.S. citizens. (12)

Every Four Years: The American Presidency. W.W. Norton, 1984 (Smithsonian Books). Well-illustrated, colorful account of the evolution of the presidency from George Washington to Ronald Reagan. (11)

Ferrara, Peter J. *NATO, An Entangled Alliance.* Franklin Watts, 1984. Discusses development of NATO and issues relating to the alliance. (12)

Kronenwetter, Michael. *The Military Power of the President.* Franklin Watts, 1988. Easy to understand analysis of the President's role in directing military affairs. Discusses the President's constitutional powers and declared and undeclared wars. (12)

Nincic, Miroslav. *United States Foreign Policy: Choices and Tradeoffs.* Congressional Quarterly, 1988. An in-depth and comprehensive look at the making of U.S. foreign policy and the issues facing the nation. (12)

Provensen, Alice. *The Buck Stops Here; The Presidents of the United States.* Harper-Collins, 1990. Informal, illustrated history of the American presidency. Anecdotal information about the men who have held the office. (11)

Smith, Elizabeth Simpson. *Five First Ladies: A Look into the Lives of Nancy Reagan, Rosalynn Carter, Betty Ford, Pat Nixon, and Ladybird Johnson.* Walker and Co., 1986. Discusses the duties and privileges of the wife of a President and how each woman coped with and was challenged by the role. (11)

Smith, Hedrick. *The Power Game: How Washington Works.* Random House, 1988. Comprehensive analysis of how government officials, politicians, and bureaucrats maneuver to gain influence. (13)

Wall, Peter. *American Bureaucracy.* W.W. Norton, 1977. Still valid description and critique of the role of government agencies and how they operate.

White, Theodore. *The Making of the President, 1960.* Atheneum, 1962. The first and the best of a series of books, through the 1960s and 1970s, on presidential campaigns by a journalist. Detailed account on each candidate and the process of getting nominated and elected. (11)

Unit Five   The Judicial Branch of American Government

Baum, Lawrence. *The Supreme Court.* Congressional Quarterly, 1985. A straightforward explanation of how the Court works, using charts, diagrams, historic cases. (15)

Cox, Archibald. *The Court and the Constitution.* Houghton Mifflin, 1987. Description of how the Court has "kept the Constitution a vital, creative instrument." (16)

Cox, Archibald. *Freedom of Expression.* Harvard Univ. Press, 1981. Very short examination of the Warren Court and its decisions on freedom of expression. Emphasizes the effect these decisions have had on personal privacy, fair trials, and national security. (16)

David, Andrew. *Famous Supreme Court Cases.* Lerner Publications, 1980. Landmark cases in the 20th century. Focuses on civil rights. (16)

Davis, Daniel S. *Behind Barbed Wire: The Imprisonment of Japanese Americans During World War II.* E. P. Dutton, 1982. Background of the injustices committed against the Japanese Americans. (16)

Fincher, E. B. *The American Legal System.* Franklin Watts, 1980. Short, easy to comprehend account of how civil and criminal courts at the state and federal levels operate. (15)

Friend, Fred W., and Martha J. H. Ellis. *The Constitution: That Delicate Balance.* Random House, 1984. Entertaining insight into the judicial system. (15)

Guinther, John. *The Jury in America.* Facts on File, 1988. (Research project by the Roscoe Pound Foundation.) Traces the evolution of the jury. Clears up some misconceptions about civil juries. (15)

Hyde, Margaret O. *The Rights of the Victim.* Franklin Watts, 1983. Analysis of what it means to be a crime victim and how victims are treated in the justice system. Also sets forth victims' legal rights, help that may be required, and steps to take to avoid being the victim of crime. (15)

Joseph, Joel D. *Black Mondays: Worst Decisions of the Supreme Court.* National Press, 1987. Decisions considered to be major blunders.

Kolanda, Jo, and Patricia Curley. *Trial By Jury.* Franklin Watts, 1988. In-depth, easy to understand study of jury trials—the procedures, the jargon, testifying by witnesses, presentation of evidence. (15)

Lehman, Godfrey. *What You Need to Know for Jury Duty.* Cowles Education Corp., 1968. Still-valid description of what to expect when one serves on a jury. Lively, interesting. (15)

Lewis, Anthony. *Gideon's Trumpet.* Vintage Books, 1986. Story of James Earl Gideon's fight for the right of a poor person to be represented by a lawyer in court. Supreme Court took up the case and made a decision that became famous. (16)

Olney, Ross R., and Patricia J. Olney. *Up Against the Law: Your Legal Rights as a Minor.* Lodestar Books, 1984. Written for young people who may have legal problems. Defines rights and tells how the legal system works. (15)

Rehnquist, William H. *The Supreme Court: How It Was, How It Is.* William Morrow, 1987. Supreme Court Chief Justice traces the development of the Court through a few key cases. Good on legal insight and commentary.

Unit Six   State and Local Government in the American System

Beyle, Thad L., editor. *State Government.* Congressional Quarterly, 1987. Essays on current issues, activities, politics, and bureaucracy in state government. (17)

Goode, Stephen. *New Federalism: State's Rights in American History.* Franklin Watts, 1983. Easy to understand discussion of state and federal views of the question of state's rights from 1789 to the 1980s. (17)

Jackson, Kenneth T. *Crabgrass Frontier: The Suburbanization of the United States.* Oxford Univ. Press, 1985. History of suburbs in America. Includes social issues, economic analysis, and architectural commentary. (18)

Judd, Dennis R. *The Politics of American Cities; Private Power and Public Policy.* Little, Brown, 1984. Thorough survey of urban government. Includes problems and relations with state and federal agencies. (18)

Mowry, George E. (revised edition by G.E.M. and Blaine A. Brownell). *The Urban Nation, 1920–1980.* Hill and Wang, 1981. Account of the transformation of American life during this 60-year period—the growth of cities, of mass production, and of the mass consumption economy. (18)

Unit Seven   Looking Ahead

Baxter, Neale. *Opportunities in Federal Government Careers.* VGM Career Horizons, 1985. Describes the variety of jobs available, requirements, opportunities for promotion, and how to get more information. (19)

Bramley, Franklyn M. *Space Colony: Frontier of the 21st Century.* Lodestar Books, 1983. Describes what life in a space colony might be like. Photographs and diagrams. (20)

Federal Careers Directory. U.S. Government Printing Office, 1990. Information about government jobs. (19)

Fogel, Barbara R. *Energy: Choices for the Future.* Franklin Watts (Impact Books), 1985. Short, easy to understand discussion of the problems each American must face to solve the limitations on energy sources. Presents alternative solutions. (20)

Gallup, George, Jr. *Forecast 2000: George Gallup, Jr., Predicts the Future of America.* William Morrow, 1984. Gallup polled people listed in "Who's Who in America" about what they considered the five most serious problems in the United States to be in the 1980s and in 2000. He discusses each problem. (20)

Heppelheimer, T. A. *The Real Future.* Doubleday, 1983. Of 12 chapters, 10 are on specific problems such as oil, war, electronics. The last two on the future are the most interesting. (20)

Orwell, George. *1984.* Harcourt, 1949. Classic novel on futuristic super-government. (20)

Pagels, Heinz R. *The Dreams of Reason.* Simon & Schuster, 1988. Describes the ability of computers to simulate complex systems and predicts the future influence of computers. (20)

Toffler, Alvin. *The Third Wave.* William Morrow, 1980. Analyzes the three massive changes ("waves") that have altered civilization since its beginning. The last two chapters discuss the future of government. (20)

Glossary

Absentee Ballot paper ballot requested by a voter who cannot physically go to the polls to vote.

Activist person who joins in actions to promote a political cause.

Affirmative Action policies adopted by governments and businesses to insure job rights to minority groups.

Alien person born in one country who lives in a different country without changing his or her citizenship.

Ambassador the top diplomat sent by one country to represent its interests in another country.

Amendment a proposal by a legislative body to change a bill or law or a formal change in a constitution.

Appellate Jurisdiction the right of a court to hear a case on appeal from a lower court.

Appropriation Bill a legislative proposal to spend money for a particular purpose.

Arraignment a courtroom hearing in which a suspect is formally charged with a crime.

Arrest Warrant a legal form issued by a court that allows a law enforcement officer to take a suspected criminal into custody.

Bail money or securities posted to guarantee that a person charged with a crime will appear for trial.

Balance of Payments Deficit the amount by which a nation's imports exceeds its exports.

Bicameral Legislature a lawmaking body made up of two houses.

Bill a proposed law that will be debated and voted on by a legislative body.

Bill of Attainder a law that permits law enforcement officials to find a person guilty without going through a trial. Bills of attainder are forbidden by the Constitution.

Bloc a group of lawmakers who act together for a common purpose.

Boondoggles wasteful projects passed by Congress for the benefit of special interest groups.

Budget a spending plan prepared for any governmental body for a particular period of time.

Bureaucracy, Bureaucrats the nonelected officials who work for a government and carry out its policies.

Cabinet the heads of the 14 executive branch departments who advise the President on domestic and foreign policy.

Capitalism an economic system based on private ownership of property and the means of production and on the right to invest one's capital to make a profit.

Caucus a closed meeting held by political party members or legislators for the purpose of deciding policy or selecting candidates.

Checks and Balances the ways in which one branch of government influences and limits the actions of the other branches.

Citizenship the rights and responsibilities of a country's citizens and the protection given to them. Citizenship is gained by being born in a country or by being born to citizen-parents abroad or by going through the naturalization process.

City Charter a grant issued by a state that gives a city permission to organize its own government. The charter also lists the city's rights and obligations under the laws of the state.

Civil Procedure a case heard by a court that concerns a dispute between two opposing parties. Civil procedures usually involve controversies over property or personal relationships.

Civil Service System a process of hiring government employees based on a combination of competitive tests and a check of an applicant's educational and personal qualifications.

Closed Primary an election in which registered members of a political party vote for candidates who will represent their party in a later general election.

Closure (Cloture) a procedure by which legislators can stop unlimited debate (a filibuster) on a bill.

Coattail Effect the positive influence a popular or strong party candidate has on the support given by voters to a weaker party candidate. For example, a senatorial candidate can be swept into office on the "coattails" of a popular presidential candidate.

Commission Form a system of city government in which each elected official (commissioner) is responsible for a different department of the city's administration. Together the commissioners act as a legislature on the order of a city council.

Common Law the body of written and unwritten rights and legal practices inherited from Great Britain that form the basis of the American system of justice.

Communism a system of economics and government based on state ownership of all resources and property and state control of the means of production. It is generally a totalitarian system of government.

Commute a Sentence the power of a chief executive to reduce the prison time served by a convicted criminal.

Concurrent Resolution identical bills passed by both houses of a legislature that state their views or opinions on an issue.

Confederate Government a system of government in which most of the power is held by the member states, leaving the central government relatively weak.

Conference Committee a committee made up of members from both houses of a legislature. Conference committees usually meet to compromise the differences in bills passed by each house.

Confirmation Process the process by which a legislative body holds hearings and then votes approval or disapproval of the personnel appointments made by the chief executive.

Conservative a political viewpoint that believes in limiting the role of government in people's lives.

Constitution the basic set of laws governing the actions of a political body. The U.S. Constitution defines this country's basic system of government and safeguards the rights of the people.

Constitutional Convention a meeting of delegates whose job is to agree on changes in an old constitution or on the writing of a new one.

Constitutional Monarchy a system of government in which a constitution limits the monarch mainly to ceremonial duties and gives political power to the country's elected officials.

Consulate the office from which consuls to a foreign country represent their country's interests. Consulates are found in most large cities.

Consuls officials sent to foreign countries to represent their country's business interests and to assist its citizens.

Contempt of Court a legal citation against a person who violates a court order.

Corporate Charter the legal document issued by a state that gives a corporation the right to do business and to sell securities.

Council-Manager Form a system of city government in which an elected lawmaking council sets policy and appoints a city manager to administer city departments.

County a political subdivision of a state.

Criminal Procedure the steps in a criminal trial, beginning with the apprehension of the suspect and proceeding through indictment, trial, conviction, and sentencing.

Crossover Voting when members of one party vote for candidates of another party in an open primary. Crossover voting is legal in only a few states.

Cross Sample a method of accurately measuring public opinion by questioning a carefully selected segment of each major group in the total population.

Debt Ceiling a figure approved by a legislative body that establishes the maximum amount the government is permitted to owe.

Defendant the person accused and summoned into court.

Deficit Spending when a governmental body spends more in a given period than it receives in revenues.

Delegated Powers expressed powers granted to a government by its constitution.

Democracy a system of government in which all power remains in the hands of the people.

Depression a period of low economic activity characterized by increasing unemployment levels.

Détente a period of reduced tensions between two countries that previously have had serious disagreements.

Dictatorship a system of government in which one person or party holds absolute power.

Diplomacy the process of carrying on beneficial relations with the governments of foreign countries.

Diplomatic Corps the government officials who carry on relations with foreign countries.

Diplomatic Recognition the establishment of normal relations by one country with the government of another country.

Direct Democracy form of government in which all citizens participate in the political decision making.

Disarmament the process of reducing or eliminating a country's military forces.

Discharge Procedure the process by which legislators take a bill away from a committee so that the bill can be debated by all members of the legislative body.

Disfranchisement the process of denying the right to vote to an individual or to a group of people.

District Courts the lowest level of federal courts. The district courts serve as trial courts for cases arising under the laws of the United States.

Docket a calendar of the cases to be heard by a court.

Double Jeopardy trying a person a second time for a crime the person has already been acquitted of. This practice is prohibited by the Fifth Amendment to the U.S. Constitution.

Due Process the obligation of the state to observe the laws protecting individual rights before it inflicts punishment of any kind.

Elastic Clause the section of a constitution that gives the government the power to do whatever is necessary and proper to carry out its other responsibilities.

Electoral College group of people chosen by the voters in each state to elect the President and Vice President. This method of indirect election is provided for in the Constitution.

Embassy the building in a foreign capital city that houses a country's diplomatic staff; the office of the ambassador.

Eminent Domain the power of a state to take private property for public use. The state must pay a fair price for property taken under the right of eminent domain.

Enumerated Powers also known as expressed powers, these are the specific powers granted to Congress by Article I, Section 8, of the Constitution.

Equal Protection of the Laws the obligation of the state to treat all of its people alike.

Equity laws that provide fairness and justice when neither statutory law nor common law can protect a person's rights.

Excise Tax a tax placed on the manufacture, sale, or use of a product.

Executive Branch the division of a government that enforces the law and administers its daily activities.

Executive Order a directive issued by a chief executive that has the force of law.

Executive Session a meeting held by a government body that is not open to the public.

Export Tax a tax levied by a government on products leaving the country. Export taxes are forbidden by the U.S. Constitution.

Ex Post Facto *Law* a law that makes illegal an action that was legal at the time the law was passed. Such laws are forbidden by the Constitution.

Expressed Powers the powers granted to a government that are specifically spelled out by its constitution.

Extradition the right of one government to ask for the return of a suspected criminal from within the borders of a second government.

Fascism a totalitarian system of government under which a dictator maintains rigid control over all aspects of the people's lives.

Federal Government a system of government that divides the power between the central government and its member states.

Felony a criminal offense serious enough to be penalized by a heavy fine or a long prison term. (Murder and kidnapping are felonies.)

Feudalism a political-economic system in the Middle Ages, based on a series of reciprocal relations between lords and vassals.

Filibuster a legislative tactic in which the opponents of a bill speak at length in order to prevent or delay its passage.

Fiscal Year a twelve-month budgeting period established by a governing body. Fiscal years can begin at any time during the calendar year.

Forbidden Powers those powers specifically denied to a government by its constitution.

Foreign Policy the guiding principles that influence a country's diplomatic relations with other countries.

Fourth Branch a name given to the federal government's independent agencies in recognition of their great influence on national affairs.

Franchise the right to vote.

Free Enterprise the economic system that allows people who live in a capitalistic country the freedom to choose the way they make their living.

General Election an election in which registered voters cast ballots for candidates running for local, state, and national offices.

Gerrymandering the practice of dividing a state into voting districts, often oddly shaped, that favor the political party in power.

Government a system for making and enforcing rules; the organization that carries out public policy decisions.

Grand Jury a group of people selected to hear evidence relating to a crime in order to decide whether or not to return an indictment against a suspect to bring the person to trial.

Gross National Product (GNP) the total value of all goods and services produced by a country during a given year.

Habeas Corpus a writ, or court order, that requires law enforcement officials to bring accused persons before a court and give reasons why they should be imprisoned. If the reasons are weak, the accused must be set free. This protection against unlawful arrest is guaranteed by the Constitution.

Hearing a meeting held by a legislative committee for the purpose of gathering information about a specific public issue.

Home Rule the power of a local government body to create its own charter and choose its own form of government.

Immunity From Prosecution a promise that someone facing possible criminal charges will not be tried for the crime. In exchange for immunity, the individual usually agrees to cooperate fully with the authorities who are investigating the crime.

Impeachment the legal process by which an elected official accused of wrongdoing can be removed from office.

Imperialism a policy designed to extend a nation's power and influence over territory that lies outside its boundaries.

Implied Powers powers not specifically granted in a constitution but which can be justified as necessary if the government is to carry out its duties.

Inauguration the ceremony marking the swearing in of elected officials to their offices.

Independent Agencies administrative bodies established by Congress to regulate specific aspects of the national economy and to administer a wide variety of governmental programs.

Independent Voters people who vote for the candidates they believe will do the best job, regardless of party label.

Indictment a summary of the prosecution's case against a suspect presented to a grand jury, which decides whether the evidence is strong enough to warrant indicting the suspect, or bringing the person to trial.

Indirect Democracy a democratic system of government in which the people elect representatives to make political decisions for them. An indirect democracy can also be called a representative democracy or a republic.

Indirect Tax tax placed on manufacturers and other primary producers that is eventually passed on to consumers in the form of higher prices.

Inflation a sharp and continuing increase in prices.

Informal Amendment changes in the interpretation of the Constitution brought about by court decisions and new legislation.

Initiative the right of the citizens of a state to petition their legislature for a new law. If enough registered voters sign the petitions, the measure is put before all the voters at the next general election.

Injunction a court order that forbids or requires a specific action.

Intelligence information about the world situation gathered in public and in secret by government agencies.

Interstate involving two or more states.

Isolationism the belief that a country should not become involved in international affairs; in particular, the desire to avoid "entangling alliances."

Item Veto the power of chief executives to strike out those portions of a newly passed bill that they find objectionable before signing the bill into law.

Joint Resolution an expression of opinion on a matter of public concern adopted by both houses of a legislative body.

Judicial Branch the division of government that includes the courts and justice system. The judicial branch has the duty of interpreting the law.

Judicial Review the power of the courts to examine the actions of the executive and legislative branches of government and the nation's laws and to declare them void if they do not conform to the Constitution.

Judicial Restraint a judicial philosophy under which the courts limit themselves to interpreting the law and do not intrude on the powers of the legislative and executive branches of government.

Jury see grand jury and petit jury.

Left Wing a strongly liberal political viewpoint. Extreme left-wing views are often referred to as socialistic or communistic.

Legislative Branch the lawmaking body of a government, such as a congress or a parliament.

Libel the publication of false statements that damage someone's reputation.

Liberal a political viewpoint that supports the greater use of government as a means of achieving social progress.

Lobbyist a person or group of people who try to influence legislators on behalf of special-interest groups.

Logrolling the process by which legislators support someone else's bill in hopes of gaining support for their own bills.

Loopholes provisions in state or federal legislation that allow some individuals and businesses to avoid full compliance.

Loose Construction the belief that the federal government should make generous use of the implied powers granted by the Constitution.

Majority Leader the floor manager of the majority political party in a legislature. The majority leader's job is to supervise the party's handling of legislative business.

Majority Opinion the verdict that decides a court case. The opinion must be supported by more than half of the judges hearing the case.

Majority Party the political party that receives more than half the votes in an election.

Majority Vote the support of an issue or candidate by at least one more than half of the voters casting ballots.

Martial Law a situation in which constitutional law is suspended and the government is put under military rule.

Mass Media the film, broadcast, and print media that help shape public opinion.

Mayor-Council System a city government in which power is divided between an elected council, which makes policy, and an elected mayor, who administers the city's day-to-day business.

Mercantilism an economic theory popular in the 1600s that stated that the role of colonies was to enrich the home country.

Metropolitan Area a central city and its surrounding suburbs.

Minority Leader the floor manager of the minority political party in a legislature. The minority leader's job is to supervise the party's handling of legislative business.

Minority Opinion an opinion issued by one or more of the judges who disagree with the majority opinion in a court case.

Minority Party the political party that receives less than half the votes in an election.

Misdemeanor a minor criminal offense, less serious than a felony. Misdemeanors are usually punished by a fine or a brief jail sentence. (A traffic violation is a misdemeanor.)

Mistrial a trial that ends without a verdict. Most mistrials occur because a jury cannot reach a verdict or because the judge has made an error in the conduct of the trial.

Moderate a middle-of-the-road viewpoint held by people who generally support the present political system and who oppose extreme political measures.

Monarchy a totalitarian system of government in which all power is held by a hereditary ruler, usually a king or queen.

Municipality a city or town incorporated for the purpose of local self-government.

Nation a geographic area with clearly defined boundaries whose people are united under an independent government.

National Debt the total amount of money owed by a nation's government to its creditors.

Natural Monopoly a type of business or industry that would not be improved by allowing competition, such as public utilities.

Naturalization the process by which aliens become citizens of a country.

Nominating Convention a meeting of delegates whose job is to select the party's candidates for an upcoming election.

Off-Year Election a congressional election held in years when there is no presidential election.

Oligarchy a system of government in which decisions are made by a small, privileged group.

Ombudsman an official who investigates people's complaints against their local or state governments and who helps them solve their problems.

Open Primary an election held to select candidates for a later general election that is open to all voters, regardless of their party membership.

Ordinance a law passed by the governing body of a city or town.

Original Jurisdiction the power of a court to hear a case when it is first brought into the judicial system.

Override the passage of a law by a legislative body over the veto of the chief executive.

Pardon the freeing of a suspected or convicted criminal from any further trial or punishment by the President or the governor of a state.

Parliamentary System a form of government in which the people elect representatives to a lawmaking body that combines legislative and executive duties. The chief executive,

known as the prime minister, must be an elected member of the legislature.

Party Whips legislators who try to line up support from other members of their party for or against a particular bill.

Patronage a public official's power to hand out jobs, building contracts, and other favors to party supporters.

Perjury the crime of lying while under oath.

Petit Jury a chosen panel of twelve people who determine the innocence or guilt of a person in a trial.

Petition to ask a government official for support of a cause or a redress of grievances. Petitions can be verbal or in writing and can be submitted by an individual or a group.

Plaintiff person who files a lawsuit in an attempt to seek redress for a violation of rights.

Platform a political party's listing of what it stands for and what it will attempt to do if its candidates are elected.

Plea in a court case, the response of defendants regarding their guilt or innocence.

Plebescite a national election in which all the people have the right to express their opinion on an important issue.

Pocket Veto action whereby a chief executive kills a bill by refusing to accept or reject it by the time the legislature adjourns. The bill cannot become law without the executive's signature, and the veto cannot be overridden because the legislature is not in session.

Police Powers the powers given to a government to protect the public safety. Typical police powers are arrest, search and seizure, and imprisonment.

Political Action Committee (PAC) section of a special interest group created to give campaign funds to favored candidates.

Political Machine a group of people who control a city or state government as a means of serving their own self interests.

Political Party an organization of people who join together to achieve their common political goals by electing candidates who share their views.

Poll Tax a tax that had to be paid before a person could vote. In 1964, poll taxes were made unconstitutional for national elections.

Popular Sovereignty the right of a people to

make their own laws. In American history, popular sovereignty also refers to the argument over a territory's right to decide the issue of slavery for itself when it became a state.

Pork Barrel appropriations for questionable projects to benefit a legislator's home district.

Precedents decisions reached in earlier court cases that can be applied to a case presently being tried.

Precinct a political subdivision of a town or city, set up primarily for election purposes.

President Pro Tempore the member of a legislature who takes over when the presiding officer is absent or unable to serve.

Presidential Preference Primary an election in which each party's voters select the presidential candidate their state delegates will support at the national nominating convention.

Pressure Group a group organized to lobby for the passage of legislation favorable to its members.

Primary an election in which members of a political party choose their party's candidates for the coming general election.

Private Bill a proposed law that would primarily benefit one particular individual or group.

Progressive Tax a tax with rates that increase as income increases, such as the income tax.

Propaganda information slanted to persuade people to think a certain way or to believe the truth or falsity of a point of view.

Property Tax a tax collected on the value of real estate and personal property.

Proposition a public issue submitted to the voters for passage or rejection.

Public Bill a proposed law that would benefit the entire population served by a legislature.

Public Opinion the attitudes of the people on issues that affect the general welfare, particularly those that involve the government.

Quorum Call a roll call to see if the required number of members are present for a legislature to conduct its business legally.

Radical a political viewpoint that supports extreme or revolutionary changes in the existing system of government.

Reactionary a right-wing political viewpoint that rejects most forms of government interference in the lives of its people.

Reapportionment the periodic redrawing of a state's electoral districts so that all districts will be reasonably equal in population.

Recall the legal process that gives voters a chance to remove elected officials from office before the end of their term.

Recession a time in the business cycle marked by declining business activity and increased unemployment.

Recount an official second counting of election ballots, triggered by a legal challenge of the first count.

Referendum the legal process that gives the voters a chance to express their approval or rejection of a particular issue or proposed law.

Registration the legal process by which a citizen signs up to vote.

Regressive Tax a single-rate tax that weighs more heavily on low income people than on the wealthy, such as a sales tax.

Reprieve an official order by a chief executive to delay temporarily the carrying out of an execution or prison sentence.

Representative Democracy a form of government in which the people elect representatives to make political decisions for them.

Republic an indirect, or representative, form of democracy.

Reserve Clause a clause in a constitution stating that all powers not specifically given to the central government are retained by the member states or by the people.

Reserved Powers all powers that are not granted to the federal government and that belong to the states and to the people, according to the Tenth Amendment.

Resolution a statement passed by a legislative body that expresses the majority's view on a current issue.

Restraint of Trade anything a corporation, union, or other organization does that limits free competition.

Rider an amendment that deals with a different subject from the main topic of the bill to which the rider is attached.

Right Wing a strongly conservative political viewpoint. Extreme right-wing views are often referred to as reactionary or fascist.

Sales Tax tax based on a percentage of the

selling price of goods people buy; a general tax is one placed on most goods—food and medicine are generally excepted; a selected tax is one placed on specific goods, often tobacco products and alcoholic beverages.

Search Warrant a legal order, issued by a court, that allows law enforcement officers to look for evidence in a specific place.

Secret Ballot a system of voting that allows voters to keep their choices secret. The government provides uniform numbered ballots that list all candidates. A ballot is given to each voter at the polling place and is marked in private. First developed in Australia, the system is sometimes called the Australian ballot.

Separation of Powers the division of the government into legislative, executive, and judicial branches. The theory is that separation of powers provides a system of checks and balances.

Slander saying something untrue that harms another person's reputation.

Socialism a political system in which the government owns all major industries, utilities, and other services.

Sovereignty freedom from control; power of a nation to make its own laws, carry on relations with other countries, and set economic goals.

Speaker the presiding officer of the lower house of a legislative body, often the leader of the majority party in the legislature.

Special Election an election held between general elections for a specific purpose, such as a recall.

Split-Ticket Voting when voters support some of their own party's candidates while also voting for candidates from other parties.

Standing Committee a permanent legislative committee that deals with a particular area of legislation, such as agriculture or the budget.

Stare Decisis the use of precedents to help judges make proper decisions in their handling of civil trials.

State sovereign nation; self-governing subdivision of a national government.

States' Rights the authority and privileges reserved to the states as opposed to those granted to the federal government in the Constitution.

Statutory Law the written law, passed by a legislature.

Straw Poll an informal poll of people's opinions.

Strict Construction the belief that the federal government is limited to the express powers granted by the Constitution.

Subpoena a court document that orders an individual to appear before the court or to produce evidence needed by law enforcement officials.

Summit Conference a meeting of the heads of state from two or more major countries.

Tariff a tax on imports, also called a customs tax or duty.

Third Party in American politics, any political party other than the two major parties.

Totalitarianism a system of government in which power is concentrated in the hands of a single person or party and in which political opposition is not permitted.

Township a unit of local government, usually a subdivision of a county, found in many Northeastern and Midwestern states.

Treason betrayal of one's country; an action that gives aid and comfort to the enemies of one's country.

Treaty a written agreement between the governments of two or more nations.

Unanimous Consent a practice in legislatures under which business can be conducted speedily as long as no member disagrees.

Unicameral Legislature a lawmaking body made up of only one house.

Unitary Government a system of government in which power is concentrated in the central government, with member states serving as administrative arms of the central authority.

Unwritten Constitution customs and traditions that influence governmental procedures and practices but are not part of the formal constitution.

Urban Area any place where many thousands of people live close together, as in a city and its suburbs.

Veto the power of a chief executive to reject any law passed by a legislative body.

Voice Vote a method of voting in legislative bodies in which the presiding officer listens to the "ayes" and "nays" and decides which side has the majority. No record is kept of an individual's vote.

Ward a political subdivision found in some cities, set up primarily for election purposes.

War Powers expressed power granted to Congress; the legal authority that allows a chief executive to use military force to defend the country

Writ of Certiorari a legal order from a higher court to a lower court asking for records on a case that the higher court is to review.

Writ of Mandamus a court order that requires public officials to do their duty according to the law.

Write-in Vote when a voter adds the name of a candidate not printed on the ballot originally.

Writs of assistance general search warrants, used by the British during the colonial period, that did not put any limits on the extent of the search.

Zoning regulations passed by local governments to limit the uses of private property.

INDEX

ACKNOWLEDGMENTS

Page
1 Billy E. Barnes
3 Ulrike Welsch
4 Renee Lynn/Photo Researchers
5 Frederick D. Bodin/Stock, Boston
6 Spencer Grant/Photo Researchers
8 Bettmann Archive
11 Bettmann Archive
12 Bettmann Archive
13 (right) N.Y. Public Library Picture Collection
15 Bettmann Archive
17 AP/Wide World
21 UPI/Bettmann
23 UPI/Bettmann
29 Dick Adair, Honolulu Advertiser/Rothco
33 Bettmann Archive
34 UPI/Bettmann
36 Bettmann Archive
42 (bottom) Library of Congress
45 Bettmann Archive
47 Bettmann Archive
50 Bettmann Archive
51 Bettmann Archive
59 Library of Congress
62 Bettmann Archive
64 Andrea Mohin/NYT Pictures
66 Bob Riha/Gamma-Liaison
67 (all) Bettmann Archive
84 AP/Wide World
87 AP/Wide World
88 David Jennings/NYT Pictures
90 (top) Wicks, The Newhall Signal, 1989/Rothco (bottom) Bill Mauldin, Chicago Sun Times/King Features
94 Jeff MacNelly, The Richmond News Leader/ Reprinted by permission: Tribune Media Services
95 UPI/Bettmann

Page
99 Bettmann Archive
101 AP/Wide World
103 UPI/Bettmann
108 AP/Wide World
111 (top) UPI/Bettmann (bottom) AP/Wide World
114 Bettmann Archive
115 Bettmann Archive
116 Bettmann Archive
121 AP/Wide World
123 UPI/Bettmann
124 UPI/Bettmann
125 UPI/Bettmann
126 UPI/Bettmann
131 From The Austin Statesman, courtesy of the Lyndon Baines Johnson Library
133 Bettmann Archive
135 Calvin & Hobbes by Bill Watterson/Universal Press Syndicate
137 AP/Wide World
141 Bob Daemmrich/Stock, Boston
142 Mike Luckovich, New Orleans Times-Picayune
146 Chris Bennion/NYT Pictures
148 Paul Conrad. Copyright, 1980, Los Angeles Times. Reprinted by permission.
152 UPI/Bettmann
155 Ellis Herwig/Stock, Boston
157 David Wells/The Image Works
159 From THE HERBLOCK GALLERY (Simon & Schuster, 1968)
162 Donald Dietz/Stock, Boston
164 Calvin & Hobbes by Bill Watterson/Universal Press Syndicate
166 AP/Wide World
172 The Granger Collection
175 Peter Souza/Woodfin Camp
179 Bettmann Archive
183 U.S. House of Representatives Photography Collection

Page
189 Copyright 1979 by HERBLOCK in The Washington Post
190 Al Liederman/Rothco
191 Alexandra Avakian/Woodfin Camp
197 UPI/Bettmann
200 U.S. House of Representatives Photography Collection
201 AP/Wide World
206 U.S. House of Representatives Photography Collection
207 The Washington Post
208 From THE HERBLOCK BOOK (Beacon Press, 1952)
211 (top) Paul Hosefros/NYT Pictures (bottom) U.S. House of Representatives Photography Collection
212 Bettmann Archive
219 Bill Graham/Rothco
224 Peter Menzel/Stock, Boston
225 (top) Ellis Herwig/Stock, Boston (bottom) AP/Wide World
226 Dick Wright, The San Diego Union
231 Al Liederman/Rothco
235 AP/Wide World
240 UPI/Bettmann
244 NYT Pictures
246 AP/Wide World
247 AP/Wide World
249 AP/Wide World
253 AP/Wide World
255 (top) UPI/Bettmann (bottom) AP/Wide World
256 AP/Wide World
258 UPI/Bettmann
259 AP/Wide World
260 Bob Englehart, Hartford Courant/Copley News Service
261 John Deering, Arkansas Democrat

565